LADYBIRD, LADYBIRD

Eric W. Pasold

LADYBIRD LADYBIRD

A STORY OF PRIVATE ENTERPRISE

MANCHESTER
UNIVERSITY PRESS

Published by
MANCHESTER UNIVERSITY PRESS
Oxford Road, Manchester M13 9PL

ISBN 0 7190 0682 1

Printed in Great Britain
by W & J Mackay Limited, Chatham

Contents

List of plates

COLOUR PLATES

MAPS

Acknowledgements

Plates

For permission to reproduce illustrations the author and publishers are indebted to Con. H. Lomax, frontispiece, and the Ladybird pictures facing page 650; Deutsches-Museum, Munich, 4, 5; Bildarchiv der Oesterreichischen Nationalbibliothek, Vienna, 14, 15, 17; Bildarchiv der Wiener Verkehrsbetriebe, Vienna, by special permission of the Direktion, 16; Archiv Fischer Novak, 21, 23, 24, 25, 26, 28, 37, 50, 51; R. Marterer, 27; Verlagsarchiv (Stoja), 31, 32, 33; Schmidt-Glassner, 48, 49; *The Observer*, London, 57; Clayton Evans, London, 58, 59, 61, 73, 77, 78, 79, 94, 96, 105, 113; Guildhall Library, London, 66, 86, 87; British Airways, London, 68; *The Aeroplane*, London, 69; Associated Press, London, 74; Keystone Press Agency, London, 75, 84; *Daily Mirror*, London, 85; *The Draper's Record*, London, 91; Illustrated Newspapers Ltd, London, 92; *The Daily Graphic*, London, 100, 101, 102; Czechopress, Prague, 103; Ronald A. Chapman, London, 106, 107, 108, 109, 110, 111.

Text illustrations

Franz Gruss, Graslitz page 4; Amarotico Fleissen and Munich page 255; *The Sun*, London, 637.

Foreword

IT IS NOT often that a businessman writes his autobiography, and I did not intend to write mine when I started on this book some twenty years ago. It was to be purely the history of our family enterprise, but it became difficult to keep the two apart. I was born in the factory, played among cases of cotton yarn and knitting machines before I could read, attended textile college, came into the firm as a matter of course, and so, in the process of penning the business saga, I have written the story of my life. Perhaps I have revealed more of myself than I should have done, but does it matter, now that I am retired and in the happy position of not having to sell anything to anybody?

Father died young, leaving the family firm to his three sons, of whom I was the eldest. It fell to me, at the age of twenty-three, to pilot the enterprise through the economic crisis of the early 1930s. Rolf and Ingo, eight and ten years younger than I, were still schoolboys but became partners as soon as they were old enough to have their names entered in the trade register, and the success of the enterprise was largely due to our lifelong close and harmonious co-operation. To some of the people we had to deal with it seemed *too* close. Three brothers who owned everything jointly, whose worldly possessions were all in a common pool, and who kept no records of funds paid in by one and withdrawn by another, were a phenomenon neither the auditors nor the various tax inspectors had ever met before. It was at the insistence of the Inland Revenue that the auditors eventually split the joint account into three separate ones, but we never took the division seriously.

It seems incredible that I should remember the days before the first world war as well as I do. Emperor Franz Josef sat on the throne of the Austro–Hungarian Monarchy, Tsar Nicholas II reigned at St Petersburg (now Leningrad), King Edward VII regularly spent a summer holiday at Marienbad (now Mariánské Laznè), and the British Empire was the greatest power in the world. A few years later, when I was a schoolboy, came the war and the Bolshevik revolution. Russia was taken over by the Soviets, the map of Europe was redrawn beyond recognition and the new State of Czechoslovakia emerged. Barely twenty years afterwards the borders were redrawn again, this time by Hitler. And look at the atlas now: Central and Eastern Europe have once again been carved up in different pieces, the British Empire has disappeared, to be replaced by a rapidly disintegrating Commonwealth of Nations, and the Middle East, not so long ago among the poorest areas of the world, is becoming one of its most influential. All this has happened in the short span of fifty years. In the same time equally dramatic changes have transformed trade and industry. I can still see Grandfather's clerks standing at tall pedestal desks, entering figures into ledgers and writing letters in copperplate longhand with pen and inkpot. And now we have computers, electronically controlled knitting machines, atomic power and aeroplanes flying at supersonic speeds. Labour-saving machinery and mass-production techniques have raised the living standard of the masses to levels undreamed of a generation or two ago, their bicycles have been replaced by motor cars, their houses are equipped with television sets, washing machines and fitted carpets. It sounds like a fairy tale. I hope it will be as interesting for the reader to pursue the progress of the Pasold enterprise during this period of unprecedented change as it is for me to relate it.

For whom have I written this book? Primarily for myself. It has been a fascinating exercise, and I hope I have succeeded in some small measure not only in describing the activities of our two firms but also in conveying something of the industrial and commercial life of the period and how it was affected by world events and politics. It would be too much to expect that my many friends on both sides of the Channel, Conservative and socialist, English, Scots, German, Czech, Austrian and the expelled Sudetenlanders, our old employees in Britain and abroad and everyone else who may read these pages will agree with everything I say, for they all have points of view of their own. I can only claim that I have done my best to be fair and, according to my lights, to draw an objective picture.

I have tried to be completely honest. Memory can play tricks, even eye-witness accounts are not always identical, and I am only human; what is truth to me may be biased opinion to someone else. But fortunately I have not had to rely very much on memory. There are few periods in my life which are not documented by diaries, notes, letters, log books, minutes, business memoranda, balance sheets, title deeds, newspaper cuttings, hotel bills, old passports and a wealth of other things, evidence that has prevented flights of fancy and kept my feet firmly on the ground. I have always been a hoarder, and my collection of private and business records is, I feel, unique. I started keeping diaries at school and, with the exception of a few years in the 1920s, have the complete set up to the present day. But perhaps the most illuminating information comes from my voluminous correspondence with Rolf and Ingo, my brothers. Sharing the management of our English and Czechoslovak factories, Rolf and I alternated between the two countries, writing to each other almost daily. Ingo, who looked after the firm's interests for about thirty years in South Africa and Canada, was a less prolific writer, but we were nevertheless in continuous touch, and I have thousands of confidential letters exchanged between the three of us, all neatly filed and indexed. Purists among historians may object to my use from time to time of direct speech, but I feel that I can in this way convey the atmosphere of some scenes better than by indirect and usually much longer descriptions, even if I have not a verbatim record of every conversation. My problem has not been to find material, but to decide how much of it to ignore, and if the book has grown to such a tome it is because I have not the heart to leave out more.

The continuous decline in the value of money during the period I am describing makes it very difficult to compare the ever-shifting cost of production, prices and incomes. Decimalisation, the conversion from 240 to 100 pence in the pound, has added to the problem, and the fact that the relative rates of exchange between the currencies of various countries have also continued to change has complicated matters still more. In 1926 the pound was worth $5 or 25 Swiss francs, by 1946 it had fallen to $4·30 or 17·35 Swiss francs and by 1976 to $1·85 or 4·60 Swiss francs. Before the war a newspaper cost a penny, which means that a pound bought 240 newspapers. If, in 1976, a newspaper costs 10 new pence, the price has risen twenty-fourfold. Similar comparisons of the price of food, textiles, motor cars or real estate would each show different increases and the table at the end of this book is therefore inevitably of limited use. The dramatic fall in the value of sterling, once the world's leading currency, compared with the value of the money of other countries, reflects the steep decline of the British economy which successive governments have failed to arrest. This is not the place to examine the causes of the 'English disease', as it is called abroad, but I am convinced that sterling would not be at the bottom of the league if the whole of British industry had worked as hard and well as we and our workpeople did at Langley and at our branch factories. Speaking as an entrepreneur and employer with half a century's practical experience in several countries, I claim that, given the right lead and incentive, there is no better management and labour anywhere than British, or should I perhaps specifically say English in this context?

This is not only my story. The ups and downs of Pasolds Ltd were shared by our old employees and friends, by Mr Hurst and Mr Colmer, Jock Watson, Winnie Pohl, Adolf Köhler, Bernard Walker, Gustav Passler, Mrs Martin and many, many others. And it is also the story of our colleagues and employees at Adolf Pasold & Sohn, of Johann Feiler, our works engineer, Albert Schreiner, the chief accountant, Georg Hoyer, Adolf Geipel, Emilie Böhm, Eva Zapf, Franz Bergmann and hundreds more. I can see them now as they were forty years ago, decent, loyal, hard-working men and women, at Fleissen and Leibitschgrund just as at Langley. It was a tragedy that by an accident of geography our two firms were in opposite camps during the war, each doing what was expected of it, a situation that called for diplomacy and caused us much anxiety and heart searching.

Fate has been kind to me. I have been fortunate in meeting a large number of interesting people and have made good friends in many different walks of life. I have learned that most businessmen are frustrated, that politicians seem to be a necessary evil and that trade union militants dictate to both without assuming the responsibilities of either. I know civil servants who write poetry, there are members of Parliament who sing and commissars who believe in God, although the reverse is more often true. If I have failed to do justice to everyone, owing to the inadequacy of my perception or limits of expression, I hope I shall be forgiven, and if now and again I laugh a little at some of my friends they may like to know that I laugh much more at myself, albeit with a straight face. I do not take myself nearly as seriously as this book may imply.

I am frequently asked whether I would still be a textile manufacturer if I had my life all over again. Why not, within the limits set by modern conditions? The Pasolds were weavers and knitters for ten generations, and in one form or another textiles will be wanted as long as mankind survives. To build another textile empire would be an exciting challenge. I believe the qualifications needed for success are the same today as they were fifty years ago: integrity, drive, common sense, imagination, know-how, endurance—in addition to which an ambitious young man should now develop a good television personality; the age of television, I imagine, has only just begun. Not wanting to be held to ransom by politicians and militants, I would not attempt to finance factories and plant with my own capital. The days of owner-managers are disappearing: someone else must now provide the money. Apart from the sociological changes that are taking place, manufacturing is becoming more mechanised, production units are getting larger, machines more complicated and expensive. Unless an industrial concern is allowed to generate sufficient capital to replace old methods and plant continually with new it does not remain competitive, and this, unfortunately, is the position in which British private enterprise is left by confiscatory taxation combined with governmental and trade union interference. If it is the nation's wish that an ever larger part of the economy should be run on these lines, then it is the taxpayer who must finance it instead of the entrepreneur.

Modern young men may accept these conditions as natural and cope with them, but at my age and with my background I find it difficult to imagine that directing such a business would be as rewarding as it was to direct Pasolds Ltd. A State-owned enterprise has feet of clay and stands little chance of being as efficient as one that is privately owned and managed. Less efficiency means more waste, be it of manpower, time, raw material, electricity, water, paper or many other things and so the cost of manufacture rises. The consumer has to pay for the satisfaction of knowing that, in the words of Karl Marx, he now owns the means of production and that no one makes a profit. Ignorance, jealousy or spite? There is no competition, no reward for special effort and no profit in the socialist millenium. Why is our society determined to go bankrupt rather than let the businessman earn a profit by making the wheels of industry hum? Are hundreds of thousands to be kept out of work because taxation is so high, interference so great that it does not pay him to use his energy and ingenuity to provide employment? It could be otherwise if the nation so decided. I refuse to believe that the talent for discovery and invention, the spirit of enterprise and adventure which made Britain the greatest industrial and trading nation of the world and created the Empire can have died. The pioneers, entrepreneurs, founders and organisers of new industries are still among us, but the vital role they play in every economy is no longer recognised. Frustrated, abused and deprived of the fruit of their labours, they have little incentive to burn the midnight oil. If the army of pygmies in the Cabinet, at Whitehall, Westminster and Transport House got off their backs I feel sure they would set the leaderless country on the course to prosperity. Britain could become great again!

It remains for me to thank Mr Negley Harte, whose enthusiasm convinced me that my story was worth publishing, my friend Kenneth Ponting, the research director of the Pasold Research Fund, and Miss Ruby Way, my faithful secretary, for the help they have given me with the preparation of the manuscript, Mr Frank Guest, managing director of Pasold Ltd for letting me use the Ladybird publicity material, and the publishers, especially Mr J. M. N. Spencer, Mr R. H. Offord and Mr E. M. Nettleton, for their patience in dealing with a sometimes rather difficult author.

1976   E.W.P.

Overleaf

Genealogy of the Pasold family. Spelling, especially of names, was not consistent centuries ago, and that of our family appears in old records as Pesolt, Pesold, Bezold, Päsold, Paesold or Pasold. Even in one and the same document it is sometimes spelt in different ways. This chart shows how it is entered in the church registers. I use 'Pasold' throughout the book

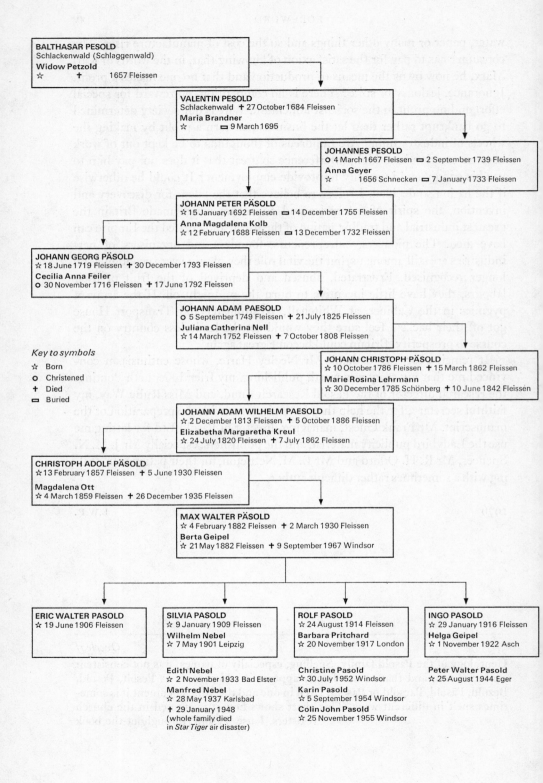

BALTHASAR PESOLD
Schlackenwald (Schlaggenwald)
Widow Petzold
☆   ✝   1657 Fleissen

VALENTIN PESOLD
Schlackenwald   ✝ 27 October 1684 Fleissen
Maria Brandner
☆   ⌐ 9 March 1695

JOHANNES PESOLD
O 4 March 1667 Fleissen   ⌐ 2 September 1739 Fleissen
Anna Geyer
☆   1656 Schnecken   ⌐ 7 January 1733 Fleissen

JOHANN PETER PÄSOLD
☆ 15 January 1692 Fleissen   ⌐ 14 December 1755 Fleissen
Anna Magdalena Kolb
☆ 12 February 1688 Fleissen   ⌐ 13 December 1732 Fleissen

JOHANN GEORG PÄSOLD
☆ 18 June 1719 Fleissen   ✝ 30 December 1793 Fleissen
Cecilia Anna Feiler
O 30 November 1716 Fleissen   ✝ 17 June 1792 Fleissen

JOHANN ADAM PAESOLD
O 5 September 1749 Fleissen   ✝ 21 July 1825 Fleissen
Juliana Catherina Nell
☆ 14 March 1752 Fleissen   ✝ 7 October 1808 Fleissen

Key to symbols

☆   Born
O   Christened
✝   Died
⌐   Buried

JOHANN CHRISTOPH PÄSOLD
☆ 10 October 1786 Fleissen   ✝ 15 March 1862 Fleissen
Marie Rosina Lehrmann
☆ 30 December 1785 Schönberg   ✝ 10 June 1842 Fleissen

JOHANN ADAM WILHELM PAESOLD
☆ 2 December 1813 Fleissen   ✝ 5 October 1886 Fleissen
Elizabetha Margaretha Kreul
☆ 24 July 1820 Fleissen   ✝ 7 July 1862 Fleissen

CHRISTOPH ADOLF PÄSOLD
☆ 13 February 1857 Fleissen   ✝ 5 June 1930 Fleissen
Magdalena Ott
☆ 4 March 1859 Fleissen   ✝ 26 December 1935 Fleissen

MAX WALTER PÄSOLD
☆ 4 February 1882 Fleissen   ✝ 2 March 1930 Fleissen
Berta Geipel
☆ 21 May 1882 Fleissen   ✝ 9 September 1967 Windsor

ERIC WALTER PASOLD
☆ 19 June 1906 Fleissen

SILVIA PASOLD
☆ 9 January 1909 Fleissen
Wilhelm Nebel
☆ 7 May 1901 Leipzig

Edith Nebel
☆ 2 November 1933 Bad Elster
Manfred Nebel
☆ 28 May 1937 Karlsbad
✝ 29 January 1948
(whole family died
in *Star Tiger* air disaster)

ROLF PASOLD
☆ 24 August 1914 Fleissen
Barbara Pritchard
☆ 20 November 1917 London

Christine Pasold
☆ 30 July 1952 Windsor
Karin Pasold
☆ 5 September 1954 Windsor
Colin John Pasold
☆ 25 November 1955 Windsor

INGO PASOLD
☆ 29 January 1916 Fleissen
Helga Geipel
☆ 1 November 1922 Asch

Peter Walter Pasold
☆ 25 August 1944 Eger

I

BACKGROUND
1300–1910

The city of Eger, which, together with the Egerland, was pawned in 1322 by Ludwig of Bavaria to the king of Bohemia as security for a debt of 20,000 silver marks. The debt was never repaid, and so the Egerlanders became subjects of the Bohemian Crown

THE EARLIEST RECORDS of our family lie buried in the archives of the ancient city of Eger in the western corner of the old kingdom of Bohemia, which is now behind the Iron Curtain. In 1312 and 1320 they describe the Pasolds as farmers and modest landowners. One was Prior of the Dominican monastery there in 1345. From the court books we know that in 1370 and 1376 they were engaged in bloody feuds in which one was killed and another outlawed, but Eckhart Pasold survived.

Burgrave Johannes of Nuremberg coveted the Pasolds' land, and in 1417 the city fathers sent a letter of protest to King Wenceslas at Prague complaining that the burgrave had cheated Pasold of his farm. It was of no avail; the farm was lost. But fortunes change, and Paul Pasold was mayor of the city of Eger from 1496 to 1502. Jacob Pasold, a member of the Furriers' Guild, travelled regularly from 1513 to 1532 to the Leipzig Fair and sat on Eger's city council for twenty-five years.

In 1517 Martin Luther nailed his ninety-five theses to the door of the castle church at Wittemberg and found ready response across the border in Bohemia. The Hussites translated his sermons into Czech and accepted him as their spiritual leader. About 1550 the Pasolds became Protestants, and lived in peace and prosperity until the Thirty Years War ravaged the country with fire, sword and plague. Bohemia's population was reduced from three million to 780,000, and the work of a century was destroyed. The Counter-reformation that followed drove more than a hundred thousand staunch Bohemian Protestants into exile. The early emigrants were allowed to sell their houses and take part of their belongings with them. Those who delayed were lucky if later they escaped with their lives.

Faced with the cruel alternative of returning to the fold of the Roman Catholic Church or leaving his homeland, Balthasar Pasold held out with characteristic stubbornness in the wealthy tin and silver mining town of Schlaggenwald in the west of the kingdom. At last he could stand the persecutions no longer. Abandoning his worldly possessions, he fled, but without leaving the country. We do not know the circumstances of his death, nor what led his widow and children to Fleissen, the remote farming community close to the Saxon border. Was it perspicuity or luck—if one can call it that—that led the family to find refuge there? The climate was rough, the soil stony and the people poor, but the hamlet enjoyed a unique privilege. Although on Bohemian territory it had, by a quirk of history, been granted religious freedom under the terms of the peace treaty of Westphalia in 1648.

Arriving with empty pockets, they could barely afford a tiny cottage and a weaving loom. For three generations they kept alive first by working for, then by competing against, two dozen other hungry linen weavers. Only the fourth generation, Johann Georg Pasold, who was born in 1719, could lay claim to success. He became a respected member and master of the Weavers' Guild of Fleissen.

Towards the end of the eighteenth century the stocking frame, an incredibly complex machine made of iron, reached the village. Invented in England in 1589 by William Lee, it revolutionised the knitting trade. In the middle of the seventeenth century one of Colbert's spies brought the knowledge of it to France, where a flourishing stocking industry developed. Fleeing Huguenots escaping from the terror of religious fanaticism smuggled their knitting frames across the border to Switzerland and central Europe. Legend has it that Johann Adam Pasold, the young son of the master weaver, had a dream in which a ladybird appeared and revealed to him the secret of frame knitting.

And this, so the legend says, was how the Pasolds became knitters. Be that as it may, more dependable sources of information, the old church registers and other documents, merely describe Johann Adam as Master of the Stockingers' Guild of Fleissen and official spokesman for the community.

Johann Christoph followed in his footsteps. The iron stocking frame had meanwhile been redesigned in the near-by Erzgebirge, and many of its moving parts were now made of wood. This reduced the very high price and made the machine far less formidable. Surrounded by forest, the people of Fleissen were skilled wood carvers and able to carry out quite intricate repairs provided they could be done with a carving knife. The number of knitters grew. Many of the weavers now broke up their looms and bought stocking frames.

In 1847 Fleissen consisted of 150 households. The cottages of the weavers resounded with the bangs and clatter of flying shuttles, those of the stockingers with the throb of wooden cogs and the metallic screeches of descending sinkers, and in all of them whirled spinning and winding wheels. There were no fewer that fifty-one stockingers and twenty-four weavers in the village. In addition a Viennese financier had established a cotton spinning and weaving mill there employing forty hands, but, unable to hold his own against the cunning cottagers, he operated at a loss and eventually went bankrupt. Most of the twenty-seven farms also had weaving looms. For eight months of the year they were stored in the loft, but when the harvest was over the farmers erected them in their living rooms, and while the fields lay under two feet of snow they and their families spun and wove their own linen. There were six bakers, four millers, shoemakers and bricklayers, three tanners, tailors, carpenters and stonemasons, two innkeepers, potters, smiths and butchers, one soapmaker, dyer, cooper, wheelwright, merchant, clergyman and labourer. The village was largely self-supporting. In addition it sold most of its textiles outside, and so, in modern terms, had a very active balance of trade.

Technical progress continued. A French watchmaker named Fouquet invented a circular machine on which one could knit much faster than on the stocking frame. It was made of cast iron, steel and brass and hung from a beam below the ceiling. The workman no longer sat on a bench in his frame carrying out the sequence of knitting motions manually, which was a highly skilled operation and took five years of apprenticeship to master. He now stood upright and merely turned a handle which made the circular machine revolve, and as it went round it knitted. He still required much skill, for there was a good deal that could go wrong with the delicate mechanism, but four years sufficed to learn it. And while the price of such a circular machine was much higher than that of a wooden stocking frame, it produced a very much greater yardage of fabric and soon began to make the stocking frame obsolete.

In the '70s weaving came to an end in the village, and in the '80s the stockingers, with their old hand frames, could no longer earn a living. One after another they gave up the struggle, and their sons found employment as knitters, mechanics or foremen in the expanding workshops or factories equipped with circular machines. But there too the pace quickened and technological progress continued. Fouquet, that inventive Frenchman, designed the large loopwheel which made circulars with small loopwheels obsolete. Mechanically operated wire cards replaced the large wooden pull-off discs which had to be raised by hand and retied whenever a yard of fabric had been knitted. Chaineuses, stop motions and pattern wheels appeared. Manufacturers who lacked the resources or courage to acquire the new machines were squeezed out of business by the more enterprising ones. Those who held their own in this process of elimination became industrialists and ever larger employers. The majority became employees.

The arrival of a knitting machine in the village was a major event. Most 'circulars' were too large to be taken up the stairs and had to be hoisted through an enlarged window opening

Johann Adam Wilhelm Pasold failed to maintain the lead his grandfather had established. He let himself be overtaken by Josef Friedl, an enterprising competitor, who brought the first circular knitting machine to Fleissen in 1858 and the second a year later—one with two, the other with four loopwheels. Now Johann Adam Wilhelm scraped all his capital together and also bought two circulars, larger ones than Friedl's, with four and eight loopwheels respectively. The business prospered, and by 1884 it had six circular machines—one of 24 in. diameter with four loopwheels, one of 36 in. diameter with eight loopwheels, one of 42 in. diameter with ten loopwheels, two of 54 in. diameter with twelve, and one of 92 in. diameter with twenty loopwheels—and employed some twenty hands. Meanwhile his son, Christoph Adolf Pasold—Adolf for short—had taken it over. He bought out his brother in 1891 and added three more circulars, two of 24 in. diameter with four loopwheels and one of 38 in. diameter with eight loopwheels. And if the reader should feel bored with such technical deatails, let me explain that they were of the greatest interest to the people of Fleissen. Diameter, gauges, the number of loopwheels and the relative performance of every knitter's machines provided a never-ending topic for the local inns and every supper table.

Adolf enlarged his premises. The workshop became a factory, but however hard Adolf and his wife worked, the Friedls grew faster. In 1885 they bought the spinning and weaving mill of the Viennese financier, which they converted into a knitting plant, and in 1889 they made the village gasp by installing a steam engine. The extent of their trade could be gauged by the fact that they had a *Schreibstube*, a separate room for the sole purpose of writing letters, keeping books and making out invoices. Today we call it an office and take it for granted, but in those days it was something sensational at Fleissen. Not even the Geipels, the wealthy leather manufacturers, had an office. It seemed impossible to keep pace with the Friedls.

Nor were they the only serious rivals. By now Stübiger, Lehrmann, Reichel and Braun each had a number of circular machines and were forging ahead. Business was booming. In the past the knitters and weavers of Asch and Fleissen took their merchandise by road to Pilsen market, the most important fair in the kingdom, where traders from all over Bohemia foregathered four times a year to buy and sell. Then in 1870 the railways came and made the whole vast Austro-Hungarian Monarchy accessible to them. It was not actually as simple as that: opposition from the short-sighted farming community prevented Fleissen from getting a station, and manufacturers had to cart their merchandise to the one at Eger, 25 km away, but the door was open. Selling agents were engaged in Prague, Vienna, Budapest, Tarnopol, Innsbruck, Triest and other distant cities, and there was no shortage of orders.

To begin with, the knitters of Fleissen had made little else than stockings, mostly fleece-lined ones. The fleece was produced not by laying-in a soft backing thread and brushing it, as people learned to do later and still do today, but by taking small tufts of wool or cotton between thumb and forefinger and hooking them, one by one, over the individual needles. This was done not only on the wooden stocking frames but also on the circulars, an incredibly slow process.

Through the contact with so many new buyers in different parts of the Monarchy the demand widened, fresh ideas came, and Fleissen began to manufacture other garments, mainly underwear, in addition to stockings, which were no longer fashioned but cut and sewn out of the fabric knitted on circular machines.

Max Pasold was born in 1882, went to the village school at Fleissen, the *Realschule* at Eger and finally the commercial college at Pilsen, from where he bombarded his father with letters requesting him to install a steam engine. At last the tired parent replied, 'If you want steam, come home and make it!' That brought Max back to Fleissen at the age of seventeen.

It was the second battle he won. The first had been for a bicycle his father bought him a few years earlier, a 'penny-farthing', as they were called in England, which was then still the only one in the village. Max already knew a great deal about piston engines and now asked Skoda of Pilsen and Ringhofer of Prague for advice and quotations, but his final choice fell on a second-hand boiler of 6 a.t.ü. (88 lb per sq. in.) pressure and a 20 h.p. steam engine which drove, with a broad leather belt, a 120 volt dynamo. The Skoda works designed the power transmission and offered to provide several experienced mechanics to help with the installation. Max figured out that the plant was just the right size and ideally suited to supply the necessary power for the knitting machines and electricity for the lighting, but his father found it hard to understand that the tremendous force of twenty horses should be needed to drive machinery which half as many men could turn by hand. However, after some hesitation he sanctioned the expenditure and the contracts were placed. No attempt was made to estimate the saving in the cost of production which, it was hoped, would result from power drive. Too many imponderables made such calculations illusory. Steam stood for progress, and that was sufficient reason for adopting it.

Max proceeded with the conversion, enthusiastically supported by Johann Feiler, the firm's able young technician, engineer and foreman. Between them they decided on the position and height of the chimney, argued about the location of the boiler and agreed on the foundations for the steam engine with its large flywheel. They rearranged the knitting machines and fitted them with pulleys to be driven by flat leather belts from the line shafts, which were supported by friction bearings bolted to the ceiling. The old wooden hand winding wheels were discarded to make room for a sixteen-spindle winding machine bought second-hand from Asch. Electric wiring was laid throughout the premises and a board fixed in each workroom on which the porcelain switches and fuses were mounted. Young Max was in his element and so busy with tape measure, sketchbook and screwdriver that he hardly found time to prove to his father how well the college had taught him the art of double entry book-keeping. He had an excellent head for figures and his handwriting was copper-plate.

The conversion caused great upheaval in 1899 and much apprehension, but on the whole the workpeople welcomed the change to power drive. There was great excitement when the steam engine started up for the first time, when one row of machines after another began to turn and finally the wheels in the whole factory rotated in unison. With broad grins on their faces the knitters watched their circulars revolving as if by magic. Each of them could now operate two machines, and the electric light made shift work easy. Production rose dramatically, but no one was afraid of losing his job. Business was brisk and demand grew fast.

The sewing had in the past been done by out-workers, women who fetched the cut pieces of material from the factory in large baskets, which they carried on their backs, and joined them together at home on their footpedal chain-stitch machines. But now, with steam power available, sewing benches were erected and more and more of the sewing was done in the factory. The same applied to the knitting machines which hung in the cottages of out-workers. Most of them were moved to the factory to be driven by power.

The little steam engine soon had to drive so many wheels that it wheezed and panted under the heavy load. On winter mornings, when the oil in all the friction bearings was cold and stiff and the wax on the leather belts stuck to the pulleys, it did not want to start at all. Weller, the stoker, shovelled coal into the furnace and weighted down the safety valve to raise the pressure until the boiler trembled and hissed and steam blew from every joint.

Once again the premises became too small, and in 1905 a large four-storey factory was built. It even had a goods lift and room for an office. Max's dream of a typewriter, which his father had rejected for so long as frivolous, now came true. In addition a larger power plant was installed with a boiler three times the size of the old one and a brand new Skoda steam engine of 70 h.p. which had a Radowanowitsch regulator.

Adolf was proud of his growing business and, secretly, of his clever son, but there was one weakness in the enterprise they could not overcome—the shortage of water. Water was a scarce and valuable commodity at Fleissen, a source of continuous conflict and lawsuits. Adolf had a well dug on his site at great expense in 1882. It was 32 m deep and the yield had been adequate for his modest needs, but now the boiler needed water. Could the stream be tapped which was only a few hundred metres away? Unfortunately the Friedls sat in between. They would never permit a competitor to lay a pipe across their property, nor would it be prudent to locate this lifeline in such a vulnerable position. There was no alternative but to make do with the existing well and use the precious liquid with stringent economy. The exhaust steam from the engine, for instance, was used for the central heating, but the condensate was too oily to be fed into the boiler. What a pity that this valuable hot water had to run away unused! Shortage of water was to worry the Pasolds for half a century to come.

In addition to technical matters the never-ending chain of commercial problems which are part of every business, and the contact with customers, widened Max's experience. He came to Vienna with his father for the first time at the age of fifteen during the school holidays. It was a business trip, of course, for Adolf Pasold did not spend time and money travelling for pleasure. They arrived on Sunday evening and spent the week visiting customers. Weary from climbing stairs and standing about warehouses all day, they were on their feet again after supper to see the smart shops on the Graben and Kärntner Strasse, the mighty St Stephen's Cathedral and the Hofburg from which their kind emperor Franz Josef reigned so wisely over the great Austro-Hungarian Monarchy. His portrait hung in every schoolroom, and young Max was devoted to him. On Friday evening they ate a *Backhendel*, a roast chicken, in the Prater, the huge amusement park, and took a ride on the *Riesenrad*, the giant wheel built by an Englishman, a marvel of modern engineering. On Saturday they travelled home.

That first visit set the pattern which Max followed with only minor variations when later he came to Vienna on his own. He discovered, for instance, that for little money he could go to the Opera, and it cost nothing at all to stand outside the Hotel Sacher to watch Austrian archdukes, Bohemian princes, Polish noblemen and Honved officers in their resplendent uniforms stroll through its portals. If one was fortunate one might even see the emperor. The Monarchy had many wonderful cities. One after another he made business journeys to most of them and got to know the habits and peculiarities of their people. This knowledge was necessary for a successful trader. The century began in prosperity, stability and confidence. Austria's money, like that of most European States, was backed by ample gold reserves, taxes were low and one krone bought a three-course meal in a restaurant. Everyone worked and saved.

It was on a Friday morning late in August 1905 that a telegram arrived from Pressburg:

DELIVERY NOT UP TO SAMPLE REFUSING ACCEPTANCE
HOLDING CONSIGNMENT YOUR DISPOSAL
SIGNED KANNENGIESSER AND STIEGLITZ

Adolf Pasold read the message three times and then called his wife Magdalena, a good-looking woman who supervised the cutting and sewing departments. He showed her the telegram.

'It's a whole railway truck, the one we loaded at Eger on Monday. What do you make of it, Lena?'

'It's a try-on. They want a price concession,' she replied. 'There's nothing wrong with the goods. I checked every dozen myself. They don't need them yet, the season hasn't started!'

A good deal of money was at stake, and Adolf was worried. He drafted a telegram to Sandor Szente, the agent in Budapest, but then had second thoughts.

'Max, if you hurry you can catch the afternoon train to Vienna, and in the morning you'll be at Pressburg. Demand to see what is wrong with the merchandise, and don't come back until you've settled the dispute. Refuse to let them return the goods, but don't fall out with K. & S. We can't afford to lose them as customers. Let's see how good a negotiator you are!'

Stiff after spending the night on the hard wooden seat in the train, Max Pasold walked from the station towards the Danube. He looked up at the burnt-out castle on the Schlossberg which dominated the old town of Pressburg, studied the street names and read the varying German, Hungarian and Slovak name plates over the shops, until he came to the premises of Kannengiesser & Stieglitz. The front door was locked, but he found the side entrance open. Hearing voices in a back room, he knocked and entered. The lively Yiddish-German conversation came to an abrupt end. Herr Stieglitz, his sons Itzig and Moritz, the old Momma and the two Kannengiesser brothers stared at him. It was an unnerving moment.

Salomon Stieglitz, a tall, dark man-about-town, greeted him with ill concealed surprise.

'What are you doing here on the Sabbath, Herr Pasold?'

Max summoned his courage. 'I've come in answer to your telegram to see the merchandise which you say is not up to standard!'

'What, already?' asked Stieglitz. 'Give us a chance, the goods are not unpacked yet!'

The conversation in the background started again, a little more subdued than before, and in Hungarian, which Max could not follow.

'I don't understand,' he said. 'How can you say the merchandise is not up to sample if you haven't seen it? Let's look at it together, Herr Stieglitz.'

Stieglitz was taken aback. 'What, today—on the Sabbath? I can see you do not understand. The truck is still at the station!'

'But I am here to inspect the goods,' Max insisted. 'That is why Father sent me!'

'A very respectable and wise gentleman, your father,' said Stieglitz. 'I always point him out to Itzig and Moritz as an example!'

'I am not going back to him without having this matter settled, Herr Stieglitz, even if I have to sit in your office until Monday!' Max replied firmly.

'You are still very young, Herr Pasold,' said Stieglitz. 'But you are keen, and I like to help keen young men. Tell your father to give me 5 per cent discount and we need not look at the merchandise!'

'But, Herr Stieglitz, Father would never agree. There is nothing wrong with the goods, I assure you.'

'Your father is a very intelligent man. He knows that business is business. We cannot open the truck on Monday, or Tuesday or Wednesday, in fact we are all away travelling for the next two weeks—it's the beginning of the season. If you can't wait it will be best to return it.'

'You are making things very difficult for me, Herr Stieglitz. Shall we say one per cent discount? Or shall we ask the Chamber of Commerce to arbitrate?'

'Who is talking of the Chamber of Commerce?' demanded Stieglitz, throwing up his hands. 'Are we not old friends? I am always willing to do a deal. Let's make it 4 per cent!'

'Father will disown me if I give more than one per cent,' Max replied haltingly, 'but would you be satisfied if I asked him to agree to 2 per cent?'

'Done, young man!' agreed Stieglitz with a triumphant smile. 'I am no match for you!' And, turning to his sons, 'Look at young Herr Pasold, he's a chip off the old block! He's got the better of your own father. I've only made 2 per cent, he has made 3 per cent out of the bargain!'

The dispute settled, although not quite to his liking, Max Pasold interrupted his return journey at Vienna and booked into a small commercial hotel in the textile quarter. Most of the wholesale merchants were Jews, and officially their warehouses were closed, but the district along the Franz Josefs Quai was the only part of the capital really familiar to him and so he gravitated there automatically.

But this was Saturday afternoon, and he felt a little lost. He walked through the newly planted park by the side of the Danube canal, watched the rowing for a while and wondered whether some of the striped vests worn by the men in the boats were made in his father's factory. Then he walked to the Schottentor and the Börse. Strolling back along Börse Gasse to Concordia Platz, Salzgries and Rudolfs Platz, he read the familiar names of Leopold Rosenzweig & Söhne, who were such price cutters, Füchsel & Merkel, the largest buyers of striped vests or *Ruderleibchen* as they were called, Emanuel Sinai, who invariably found fault with the merchandise to have an excuse for delaying payment, and many other old customers. The premises of David Grün-

stein, the volatile little Galician who came to Fleissen twice a year to buy
seconds, were firmly locked. So was the door of Nohel & Co., who were so
upset by the late delivery of their spring order that Herr Nohel had sworn to
place all future business with Friedl. A good firm, Nohel's! Inevitably some
day Friedl would deliver late, young Max reflected, and then Nohel would
again buy from Adolf Pasold. At least he hoped he would.

In between the warehouses of the merchants were those of textile manufacturers who held stocks in Vienna, such famous firms at Mauthner, Schroll
and Hämmerle. It seemed natural enough for leading wholesalers to have
their businesses in Vienna, but for knitwear and hosiery manufacturers in the
provinces to maintain permanent staff and stock rooms in the capital was a
very different matter. Almost reverently Max contemplated the nameplates
of Wilhelm Benger Söhne of Bregenz, Anton Klinger & Co. of Zeidler,
Christ. Fischers Söhne of Asch and Wolf Blumberg Söhne of Auperschin.
What giants they were in comparison with the manufacturers at Fleissen, not
one of whom had even a small office in Vienna. And he promised himself that
some day he would put the nameplate of Adolf Pasold over the entrance of
one of these buildings.

Even though their owners refused to receive callers, most of the business
houses were at work and Max guessed at the activities inside. Wooden cases
from Teplitz were being opened. Presumably they contained knitted goods.
A carrier unloaded bales of woollen cloth from Reichenberg and linen from
Silesia. In an open doorway round the corner men were unpacking a consignment of shawls with large jacquard designs richly interwoven with gold
and silver threads. They came from Rossbach and were for resale to the
Orient. Others handled silk bought from dealers at Bozen. And there were
stacks of red fezs made at Strakonitz for the Balkans, Turkey and Egypt.
Vienna was the busy trade centre not only for the vast Austrian Empire but
the whole of south-eastern Europe and even Asia Minor.

Sauntering down Gonzaga Gasse and turning into Morzin Platz, he came
upon a small crowd surrounding a bright red automobile which stood in front
of No. 5, the office and warehouse of the world-famous weavers Christian
Geipel & Sohn of Asch. It caused open-mouthed admiration, and the chauffeur was busy keeping the inquisitive urchins from fingering it. Every kind
of machinery always fascinated Max, but nothing was quite as exciting as
mechanical carriages, and this one was a beauty. Craning his neck to study
the levers, pedals and knobs, he failed to notice the figure of Herr Geipel
emerging from the building. Gustav Geipel of Asch was even then almost a
legend, a millionaire bachelor who had retired from the management of his
firm at the early age of forty-four and devoted his time and money to the
betterment of his fellow men. Yet the more he gave away the wealthier he

seemed to grow. By the time he died in 1914 he had, much to the resentment of his relatives, given away the best part of ten million kronen to his home town—a huge fortune.

And now a miracle happened to young Max. Herr Geipel recognised him in the crowd and invited him for a ride round the Ring. A few sharp turns with the starting handle, a bang or two, and the engine sprang to life. To the cheers of the onlookers, and accompanied by a dozen boys who had no difficulty in keeping up with the vehicle, they travelled down the Quai and then, dodging an electric tram, swung into the Stuben Ring. It was an eerie and somewhat alarming sensation to be propelled through the traffic without horses, independent of rails or a network of overhead wires. The chauffeur was obviously a highly competent man. He seemed to know precisely when to manipulate the controls, shifting his lever without the slightest sign of hesitation. The engine, he explained, had the fantastic power of sixteen horses and could propel the vehicle at twice the speed, but in the city he was not allowed to go faster than a trotting horse.

They drove past the Post Office Giro Bank, with its unusual front of screwed-on marble slabs, past the Art Museum built in Italian Renaissance style, alongside the beautiful Stadtpark and past the marble statue of Schubert, to the Opera. After safely negotiating the busy Opera Square they passed between the imperial palace on the right, the two enormous museums and the Maria Theresia memorial on the left, towards the dazzling white parliament building in its breathtaking Greek style. Everywhere people stopped, stared and waved. Herr Geipel waved back at the men on the sidewalks and in the passing landaus and chaises, and raised his hat to the ladies who caught his eye. There were a few tense moments when horses shied or pedestrians got in the way, but there was no accident. The chauffeur always gave ample warning by hooting his horn, a brass trumpet with a rubber ball.

Construction work on the Ring was going on apace. The sun shone and the Viennese were out in their thousands looking at the magnificent new buildings which were rising everywhere. Workmen hammered the last paving stones, rows of trees were being planted and parks with flower beds and fountains laid out. No other city would be able to boast of such a truly imperial avenue when it was finished. Driving down the middle of it in their shining automobile, they were the centre of attraction. Past parliament, Burgtheater, town hall, university and Börse they motored back to the Franz Josefs Quai and then, at Herr Geipel's request, up the Rotenturm Strasse to the Hotel Meissl & Schadn on the Neue Markt. There he dismissed the dream car. It was not his but belonged to the makers, who had given him a demonstration run, hoping that he would buy it for 17,500 kronen. It was a great deal of money, but Max was so carried away that he could not understand why Herr

Geipel, who was so rich, said he would have to sleep on the proposition.

Over coffee in the hall of the hotel it became clear that Herr Geipel was not really interested in automobiles. He talked about the Ring and how far-sighted Emperor Franz Josef had been to level the city wall and build this magnificent street, flanked by those splendid buildings, in its place. He explained the way the paving stones had been laid and said he was thinking of doing something like it for Asch, his home town, some day.

Vienna always inspired him, he said. It was the greatest city he knew. Its population was approaching two million. And who were the Viennese? Natives from Lower and Upper Austria, the valleys and mountains of the Tyrol, Salzburg and Carinthia, from the Hungarian plains, the industrial towns and farmlands of Bohemia and Moravia. Jews from Galicia, Poles, Slovaks and Ruthenians with a sprinkling of Mohammedans from Bosnia and Serbo-Croats from the sunny shores of Dalmatia came to buy, sell, work, play, study, see relatives, petition or intrigue. They came and went in a continuous stream. Many stayed and merged with the Viennese, all added variety and cosmopolitan flavour to the life of the capital in whose multiracial parliament they were represented.

There were, of course, politicans among them who would like to break up the great Empire into a number of little national States so that, instead of one united government, there would be a dozen little ones who could all have their own presidents, Ministers, trade barriers and even national armies to try to get the better of each other—a fine prospect for the politicians but a poor outlook for the people. But he was sure it would never happen. Nobody took these noisy hot-heads seriously.

For the first time Max felt the thrill of being part of the metropolis. In the past he had thought of himself as a mere visitor everywhere, except in the textile quarter, but now, after his triumphant ride round the Ring and the inspiring talk with Herr Geipel, the whole of Vienna belonged to him.

Henceforth he would change his routine. He would stay in Vienna over Saturday and Sunday. He would visit the museums, promenade with the fashionable people on the Ring, and—well, perhaps just once—venture into the Hotel Sacher for a cup of coffee and a slice of the famous Sachertorte. If he was to double the family business he had to become a man of the world and hold his own not only with the Jewish wholesalers in the textile quarter but with Vienna's business magnates and the country's important industrialists. Father might raise his eyebrows, but he would learn to understand.

Max admired the Habsburgs, who had governed Austria for six centuries. There was no other royal house like them. Austria was the heart of Europe and the most beautiful land. The Germans across the border might think of the Austrians as easy-going and inefficient, but what did they know about keeping a dozen different races happy, each of whom spoke its own language? The citizens of no country were freer and happier than the Austrians. Perhaps the English were equally free, but England was a long way away. Of the Monarchy's neighbours, Germany and Russia were police States, Roumania, Serbia and Italy turbulent troublemakers and Turkey and France traditional enemies.

Max thought himself fortunate to be an Austrian. He had inherited little of his father's ponderous gravity, which invariably sought the difficult and passed the easy by, a Bohemian characteristic. Temperamentally he took after his mother, and a keen sense of humour, coupled with a talent for music, made him popular with everyone. His capacity for hard work was relieved by a lightness of touch which often bordered on genius.

In the autumn of 1905 he married Berta Geipel, a daughter of the oldest and most respected family of Fleissen, who, as he used to claim with a twinkle in his eye, only fell for the way he played the zither. They spent their honeymoon at Stuttgart in southern Germany, and Max combined it with a visit to C. Terrot Söhne, the knitting machine makers. To give his bride a treat he hired a motor carriage for the short trip from Stuttgart to Cannstatt. Berta said she loved the ride, and that settled the matter. He had to have an automobile. For a very long time his father would not hear of it, but eventually he gave in, and in 1908, two years after I was born, came a red four-seater Dixi from Eisenach in Thuringia. It remained the only motor car in Fleissen for many years. Max was my father, and the account of his memorable ride round the Ring with Gustav Geipel was one of his favourite stories.

Perhaps I should explain that the Geipels of Fleissen and the Geipels of Asch were only distant relations, but since each family had a Wilhelm and a Gustav, all rather unusual characters, they were frequently confused with each other. Tempting though it is to relate some of the amusing incidents they were involved in, they do not belong in this book and I shall record only one example of the eccentricity of Wilhelm Geipel of Asch, a cousin of Gustav and also a wealthy bachelor.

The Hotel Meissl & Schadn in Vienna was a popular meeting place for industrialists, especially from Bohemia, and many a deal was concluded there over a cup of coffee. One day Wilhelm Geipel walked into the dining room wearing a crumpled suit and a grubby scarf, and ordered a Salzburger Nockerl. It would take at least half an hour, said the waiter, hoping to get rid of the unwelcome guest. But Wilhelm said he would wait, and lit a cigar. When told that smoking was not allowed he blew a cloud in the head waiter's face. This brought the manager on the scene, who requested him to leave quietly, or he would be thrown out by two strong men. Wilhelm got up. 'I'll go,' he said, 'but it'll be you who'll get thrown out!' Then he bought the hotel and promptly sacked the manager, the head waiter and the waiter who had annoyed him. As far as I know, Meissl & Schadn belonged to the Geipels until the end of the second world war.

To return to the Pasolds. Max was an only child, and at the age of twenty-eight, after ten years in the business, his father took him into partnership. At the same time, in 1910, the name of the firm was changed to Adolf Pasold & Sohn. Meanwhile the factory site, awkwardly shaped and in the middle of the village, had been completely covered with buildings. The next extension, the 'new factory', a modern four-storey block, was therefore built half a mile to the south-east, on the outskirts of Fleissen, where Adolf had over a period of many years bought up a number of fields covering an almost square area of some twenty acres. Buying land was a delicate operation, but he was adept at handling farmers. He also knew how to deal with Polish Jews. Ninety-five per cent of the firm's customers were Jews.

Max concentrated on purchasing yarns and other raw materials, on machinery, and on the introduction of modern business techniques, which often brought him into conflict with his father. Not that Adolf was against progress —far from it. He always readily agreed to spend money on improvements, provided they were suggested diplomatically. He was an autocrat, and did not like the criticism of his well tried practices implied in his son's ideas of doing things differently. The fact that Max had become a partner did not mean that Adolf was no longer boss, and he wanted the world to know it.

In the early spring of 1911 the office of Adolf Pasold & Sohn, manufacturers of knitted underwear, was a spacious room with three windows looking out over Amüller's farm and the factory of Josef Friedl Söhne, the firm's largest competitor. It was furnished with two double-sided pedestal desks with high stools, a work table and chair, a copying press and a tray of water. Against the wall stood a tall cupboard filled with correspondence and stationery, and a safe which held ledgers, documents, postage stamps and ready cash. On the left of the front door hung a frame with the firm's registration certificate, on the right a poem extolling the virtues of honesty, industry and punctuality. It ended with the words:

> Six minutes only late each day
> Throws three whole days a year away!

The back door, through which one heard the hum of revolving circular knitting machines, led into the factory.

The senior partner, Adolf Pasold, a heavily built, balding man in his middle fifties, stood at his desk studying the mail. It consisted of a score of hand-written postcards from wholesalers, shopkeepers and pedlars from the four corners of the Monarchy, a letter from Francesco Parisi, the forwarding agent in Vienna, another from a spinner and a report from Sandor Szente, the firm's commission agent in Budapest. Slowly and deliberately the senior partner tore up several postcards which annoyed him and dropped the pieces in the waste paper basket.

The junior partner, Max Pasold, with a shock of blond hair and artistic hands, sat on the high stool opposite, dipping his pen in the inkwell, writing a letter. A graduate of the commercial college at Pilsen, he endeavoured to improve his father's time-honoured business practices.

The book-keeper and general office manager, Albert Hilf, a stickler for tidiness, was entering black figures in a ledger. Behind his right ear was another penholder with a nib for red ink. Written on the opening page of the book were the words 'Begun in the name of God on 1 January 1911'.

The office boy, fifteen-year-old Georg, pronounced Schorsch, was copying invoices by laying them in a thick book, the pages of which he moistened and then put under the hand press. He had a pimply face, turned-up nose, closely cropped hair and large ears which were pulled by everyone.

Four heads were raised as the rustling of paper was interrupted by a sudden rush of knitting machine noise. The foreman, Johann Feiler, stood in the open back door. He was a handsome man in his mid-thirties, with a waxed moustache; his shirtsleeves were rolled up, and from his trouser pocket protruded a screwdriver and a pair of needle pliers.

'We're having difficulties with that trial case of yarn from Leibitschgrund. Shall we return it?'

The senior partner went to investigate. As soon as he had left the room the office boy retrieved the torn postcards from the waste paper basket, stuck the pieces together and gave them to the junior partner.

'Schorsch,' said the junior partner, 'we can save ourselves this trouble. Give me the mail first in future. I'll deal with the offending correspondence before Father tears it up!'

Three days later the senior partner had found out that young Max saw the mail before it came to him. He took the office boy by the ear, marched him out into the road, pointed at the sign above the door and demanded:

'Can you read? What does it say?'

Shaking in his boots, the office boy stammered, 'Sir, it reads Adolf Pasold & Sohn!'

With a ring of satisfaction his his voice the senior partner pronounced, 'There, you see: Adolf comes first, son comes afterwards! I get the mail first, and don't you forget it!'

A few days later a gentle knock on the door announced Isidor Schönberg

The *Kollektion*

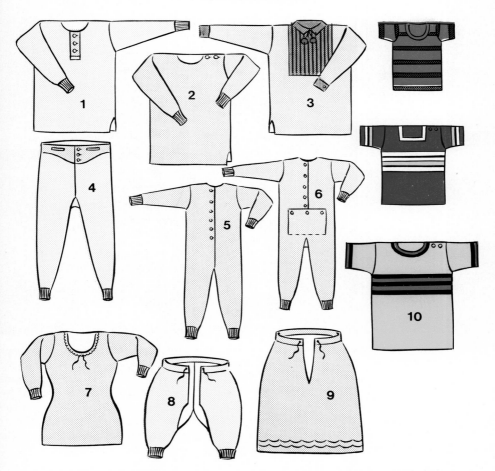

1–2 men's fleecy lined vests, *3* men's fleecy lined vest with woven shirt front inset, collar and cuffs, *4* men's fleecy lined pants, *5–6* women's and children's fleecy lined combinations (back view), *7* women's fleecy lined vest, *8* women's fleecy lined open drawers, *9* women's fleecy lined petticoat, *10* men's and children's summer-weight sweaters in bright colours, called *Ruderleibel*: in modern parlance, T shirts

1 Pilsen market, 1890. Four times a year Bohemia's most important fair was held there. It lasted eig
days and was attended by thousands of traders from all over the kingdom who, so the histori
Johann Gottfried Sommer recorded in 1838, displayed their merchandise in 71 vaults, 469 wood
booths and 210 stalls. They were arranged in alleys and numbered; every alley was guarded by
armed watchman and lit by lanterns at night. Woollen, linen, cotton, silk, leather and metal goo
grain, cattle and produce of many kinds changed hands and it was not only the manufacture
merchants and money-lenders who profited, but also the innkeepers, brewers, bakers and butche
not forgetting the house-owners who let rooms to the visitors

from Krakau, a red-headed Polish Jew wearing a black velvet hat and long black kaftan. He was a faithful customer of the firm and an old friend of the senior partner.

'Come in! I am pleased to see you, Herr Schönberg. You are late this year! How is business?'

'Bad, Herr Pasold, I have had a bad season. Veilchenblum sold at give-away prices and ruined my trade,' complained Schönberg. 'I paid you too much and lost money on your goods. You must quote me a very special price this time to make up for it!'

'We always quote you our lowest price, Isidor,' said Adolf Pasold. 'No one buys cheaper than you. Here, feel the weight of our 400 quality! It's so firmly knitted the pants stand up by themselves. I'll let you have them at 11 kronen and 80 heller a dozen.'

Veilchenblum and Isidor Schönberg

'Ribboinneh shel oilem! Master of the Universe!' exclaimed Isidor. 'I have just been to Friedl, they offer me a better quality for 9 kronen 60 heller!'

Adolf slowly shook his head. 'That is unlikely. If Friedl's pants were cheaper Veilchenblum would not have placed his order with us!'

Isidor was visibly shaken. 'Veilchenblum has been to see you? An order he has given you? May the Lord strike him down! We promised each other that he would not go to you and I would not go to Friedl!'

'Our price is 11.80, Isidor, and I'll book your order as soon as you pay the 90 kronen you deducted from our last invoice,' said Adolf firmly.

'Deducted?' Isidor gasped. 'I have deducted nothing! Herr Book-keeper, you are my witness, I owe you nothing!'

'Herr Schönberg, you owe us 90 kronen plus 3 kronen 20 heller interest,' said the book-keeper. 'I have sent you three reminders already.'

Schönberg became agitated. 'There is some mistake, Herr von Pasold, sir, in your books is a mistake, your book-keeper is trying to rob me!'

Had the senior partner heard aright? He treasured the good name of his old established firm, and this insolent little Jew was besmirching it! His face flushed. With a heavy ledger in his raised hand he took a stride towards Schönberg and shouted, 'Rob, did you say? Out with you, miserable Galician, or I'll throw you out!'

For a moment Schönberg thought of feigning a heart attack, but then decided against it and, protesting loudly, fled into the street. Adolf Pasold wiped the beads of perspiration from his brow and returned to his desk, where he busied himself with the mail.

Two hours later Schönberg's face appeared in the door. 'May I have the honour of speaking to Herr von Pasold, my old friend, Baron Pasold?'

'Schönberg, what do you want?' growled the senior partner.

Schönberg was all smiles. 'Herr Baron, I have come to pay the 60 kronen.'

'Ninety-three kronen 20 heller, Herr Pasold!' said the book-keeper.

'Interest he wants to charge, Sir Adolf! Your book-keeper is a usurer,' pleaded the little Jew.

'Isidor,' asked Adolf, 'are you prepared to pay the 90 kronen?'

'Baron Pasold, sir, may the Lord Almighty forgive me for throwing so recklessly about my hard-earned money! I shall pay.'

Schönberg fumbled under his long black coat, pulled out a small bag from one of his secret pockets and slowly counted nine shiny gold pieces on to the table. He was let off the interest.

Then the two business friends examined the *Kollektion*. It never varied from one year to the next, there were men's underpants and vests, women's combinations, vests and drawers, and children's combinations. And believe it or not, the *Ruderleibchen* with their bright red, yellow and blue stripes looked exactly like the T shirts that became so fashionable half a century later. The price of every garment and of every size was compared with what it had cost the year before, and any variation caused by a rise or fall in the cost of the yarn and by competition was argued about at length.

After prolonged negotiations which were repeatedly broken off by one side or the other, after Schönberg had had a slight heart attack, two glasses of water and many times appealed to the Almighty, and after the senior partner had reached again for the heavy ledger, the contract was at last finalised. Schönberg agreed to pay 11 kronen 50 heller for the middle size of men's pants. The order came to 220 dozen and a value of almost 2,000 kronen. The merchandise was to be at Krakau before the middle of July. Schönberg's customers were by no means all in Galicia. He did profitable business in Russia. The border was only 10 km away, but the goods had to be smuggled across, and that took a little time. They had to be on the market before the cold weather set in.

BORN IN THE FACTORY
1906-12

MY EARLIEST RECOLLECTION is of an enormous *Quarkkuchen*, a cheese flan Grandmother had prepared for some special occasion. It had just come back from the baker and was lying on a large round board to cool. I was about two years old and stood with Grandfather admiring it, when he whispered, 'Jump!' The next moment I jumped with both feet right into the middle of it. He lifted me out, saying, 'Don't let Grandma catch you,' and I hastily scrambled upstairs to safety. We lived in a flat on the first floor of the factory; my grandparents had their rooms below ours. Later the maid brought us a piece of Grandmother's flan, the piece with the imprint of my boots in it.

As I grew older I began to explore. There were a number of buildings, the oldest of which was a two-storey house dating back to about 1800. As the business had grown other buildings were added. They straggled up the side of a hill, all on different levels, and were connected by wooden stairs and gangways. The latest and largest had four storeys and a row of cast iron stanchions down the middle. It was so high that I dared not look out of the windows of the top storey.

The factory seemed vast to me, and the things in it were of absorbing interest. I was not allowed into the machine rooms by myself, but even the cutting, folding and packing departments and the store, where everything was done by hand and I could not come to much harm, were large enough to get lost in. The forbidden sections held the greatest attraction, of course. On the sewing floor, for instance, the line shafts ran under the wooden benches on which the sewing machines were fixed, and it was exciting to see all the wheels whirling, but I did not go too near them in case I got caught by one of the belts. More fun was to be had on the knitting floor. The circular machines hung from girders, and below each machine, revolving on a bearing screwed to the floor, was a large round tray made of tin into which the fabric dropped. When the tray was full the workman stopped his machine, cut off the piece of material, lifted it out of the tray and carried it to the scale to be weighed. Meanwhile I sat in the empty tray and spun round until the rotation made me feel dizzy. And I loved to stand at the boilerhouse door to watch Weller, the boilerman, blow the whistle at lunchtime. Sometimes he would show me the steam engine, with its polished brass knobs and huge flywheel, which he could stop by pressing against it with his stomach after the steam was shut off.

I made spears out of the paper tubes on which the yarn came from the spinners, and Johann Feiler, the foreman mechanic, showed me how our knitting machines worked before I could read and write. He became my confidential friend. I was thrilled to watch the shower of sparks from his grinding wheel, and he always had a welcome supply of broken sinkers, small, pointed blades of steel, with which one could tease the neighbours. On dark winter evenings one pushed them into the putty of their windows and, hiding behind a hedge, made tapping noises by pulling a thread attached to them.

I was fascinated by Grandmother's tales about the days when she was a little girl, and I tried to imagine how Great-grandfather carted his cases of knitted stockings to the market at Pilsen and how he returned with gold ducats well hidden in his belt. The road led through dark forests in which highwaymen were known to roam, and the thought of them sent pleasant shivers up my spine. With my toy bricks I built a trap to catch the robbers. It was a jail with a swivelling roof on which a lump of gold glistened. The gold was yellow plasticine. It drew the highwaymen from the forest. They scaled the wall to steal the gold, the roof gave way and they fell into the dungeon.

In 1912 my parents took me and Silvia, my two-year-old sister, and Marie, our nurse, for the summer holidays to Swinemünde on the Baltic, 500 km away. It was the year of the *Titanic* disaster, and I stood on the beach with my bucket and spade, looked out to sea and felt sorry for the little boys and girls whose parents were on board the liner that never came back. But most of the time I enjoyed myself building castles and canals in the sand. I felt proud for years after to have travelled so far. Few of Fleissen's inhabitants went farther than Eger or Karlsbad in all their lives. No one else in the whole school, not even the teachers, had ever seen the sea, and my schoolmates would not believe that one could look across it and not see land the other side.

Like everyone in Austria I attended State school from the age of six. The school was a large modern building half a kilometre from home on the other side of the valley. We were about thirty children in a class. Boys and girls, bright and dull, Protestant and Catholic, rich and poor, all sat together on the same benches. At the end of the year there were exams, and the vast majority who passed moved up into the next class. I liked being with boys of my own age. Most of them were the sons of factory workers, and I wanted to be as much like them as possible. During the summer months I refused to wear shoes and went barefoot as they did, in the winter I usually 'forgot' my over-coat, however much Mother protested, and I talked only Egerland dialect with my friends, although at school and at home I had to speak High German —or at least our Bohemian version of it.

Two-thirds of Bohemia's population were Slavs who spoke Czech. They lived in the middle of the country and were mainly occupied with agriculture. The German-speaking third, over two million people, lived in the industrial border regions, but also in Prague and the other towns, where they made up a large proportion of the intelligentsia, industrialists and traders. Czech- and German-speaking Bohemians had shared the country, quarrelled with each other and worked peacefully together for close on a thousand years, our tea-cher explained. The people of the Egerland and way beyond it spoke only German, as did the officials at Eger and the businessmen who visited Fleissen. There was a German university at Prague, and technical and scientific books were printed in German. And of course Emperor Franz Josef and his court who governed the Monarchy from Vienna spoke German. Very few people in our part of the country knew Czech. It seemed such an unnecessary lan-guage, used only by the peasants in the interior.

I liked my teachers, was interested in the lessons and, except in singing, found it easy to be top of the class. Natural history was one of my favourite subjects, and after school I explored fields and woods with my friends, caught newts and water beetles in the ponds or fished for minnows in the streams. Mother never knew how often I fell in the water and had to sit in the sun to get dry again. I went home only when I needed my tool box to build some-thing or when I was hungry.

Every form of automation intrigued me. After a demonstration at school of syphoning water from one tank into another I thought I had discovered the secret of perpetual motion. I rushed home and built a small waterwheel which I positioned between two vessels. The water, I thought, could be syphoned from the lower to the upper tank and so, I thought, would keep the wheel turning for ever. The failure taught me a useful if not conclusive lesson. For quite a few years my solution to the problem of perpetual motion was always just round the corner, until I finally conceded that friction made it impossible. But my desire to make things go by themselves remained.

Then Uncle Wilhelm Geipel, my godfather, whom I greatly admired because he held a university diploma in engineering and had done his mili-tary service as ship's engineer in the Austro-Hungarian navy, gave me a Meccano set for my birthday. It proved the best present I ever had, especially with the supplementary sets which came along each year. Whilst I could not construct a knitting machine with them, I built models of winding frames and later a weaving loom on which I wove narrow strips of patterned fabric,

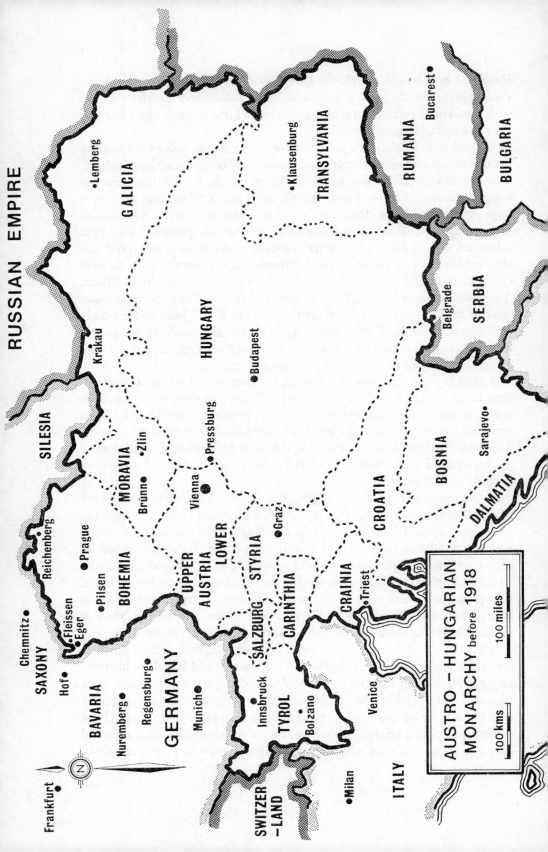

AUSTRO – HUNGARIAN
MONARCHY before 1918

100 kms
100 miles

RUSSIAN EMPIRE

GALICIA

• Lemberg

• Krakau

SILESIA

SAXONY

Chemnitz •

Reichenberg •

Hof •

• Prague
Pilsen •
• Fleissen
Eger •

BOHEMIA

MORAVIA

Brünn •
• Zlin

Vienna •

UPPER
AUSTRIA

LOWER

STYRIA

Graz •

HUNGARY

• Budapest

Pressburg •

KLAUSENBURG

Klausenburg •

TRANSYLVANIA

RUMANIA

Bucarest •

BULGARIA

SERBIA

Belgrade •

BOSNIA

Sarajevo •

CROATIA

DALMATIA

GERMANY

BAVARIA

Nuremberg •
Regensburg •

Munich •

Frankfurt •

N

TYROL

Innsbruck •
Bolzano •

SALZBURG

CARINTHIA

CRAINIA

Triest •

Venice •

ITALY

Milan •

SWITZER
– LAND

hoping to sell them as ties. The machine was a success technically but a failure commercially.

Father's pride and joy was his motor car. The roads were appalling and forced him to drive so slowly that the dogs in every village ran rings round us, barking their heads off. It was most undignified, and I thought up a water spout in place of the radiator filler cap on the bonnet. The idea was to operate it through a wire from the passenger seat. To my great regret Father did not allow me to proceed with the invention, explaining that the water in the radiator was needed to cool the engine and not the dogs.

A passionate motorist, he took Mother and us children to all the beauty spots, interesting towns and old castles within reach. The castles were the most difficult, for they were usually built on hills, and in those days cars did not like going uphill. Often we had to push, and did not always reach our destination. We drove to Karlsbad and tasted the hot springs, to Joachimstal, where the first dollars were coined in the sixteenth century, across the border to Bayreuth and Coburg, and we visited every museum in the area. I did not know whether Father's interest in old swords, guns and suits of armour was feigned or real. Mother claimed he only used it as an excuse for motoring. Be that as it may, these excursions greatly stimulated my taste for history and the pleasure of collecting, which has survived all my life.

Fleissen had originally been a farming community, but the soil was poor, the climate rough and of the seventeen farmers none had more than twenty head of cattle in his byres. During the previous hundred years the village had developed into one of the industrial centres of the Egerland. The leather factory which belonged to my uncles, the Geipels, was famous throughout the Austro-Hungarian Monarchy for the quality of its leather. When I was a boy most of the two thousand inhabitants earned their living there or in one of the many knitting mills. The two largest of them were Lehrmann's and our own, each employing about 250 workpeople. We had both overtaken Friedl. Then followed Braun, Reichel, Stübiger and a number of out-workers who owned two or three machines and knitted on commission for the larger manufacturers. In addition there were some twenty small makers of musical instruments such as violins, cellos and clarinets or parts for them.

They were all family firms and, as was natural in such a small place, most of their owners were related to each other. The knitwear manufacturers especially were in keen competition. All made the same types of garment, bought their yarn from the same spinners, dealt with the same bank managers, sold to the same customers and tried to entice each other's labour away. During the day they did their best to put each other out of business but in the evenings all the deadly rivals sat peacefully together in the 'Goldene Stern',

playing the piano or zither, having a game of cards and drinking a glass of
beer. All except the Lehrmann brothers, whose quarrels with their neighbours were too many and too bitter and who had few friends. They always
had two or three lawsuits going, mainly over rights of way and water, and even
threatened to sue each other. Court cases were to them as games are to other
people: no sooner had they lost one than they started another. The horse
which regularly took old Mr Lehrmann to the district law courts at Wildstein 6 km away was popularly referred to as the 'litigation mare'.

Fleissen lies on the railway connecting Eger with Plauen. This was useful
for long-distance transport and travel. Both towns were important railway
junctions, and the train journey to either took about an hour. For local transport and cross-country journeys in the Egerland, and for moving merchandise
over distances of up to 30 km, however, one used horses, in summer with open
carriages or carts and waggons, in winter with sleighs. Father motored whenever he could, which was rather daring, for there was always the risk of a
puncture or a more serious breakdown, and if it was important that he reached
his destination he fell back on the horses. Nor could the car be used when the
weather was too bad or there was snow on the road. We had one or two pairs
of horses as long as I can remember. Most of the time they collected cases of
yarn from spinners at Asch, Haslau, Liebenstein, Neuenteich, Schloppenhof,
Königsberg and Leibitschgrund and took our merchandise to Fleissen railway station.

Our trade was seasonal, and the spring season was relatively unimportant.
People did not wear knitted underwear during the summer. Almost all the
goods we manufactured during the year were despatched to our customers
between July and September; in the meantime they were packed in wooden
cases and accumulated in our store opposite the railway station. I felt proud
that we had a warehouse in such a strategic position and loved to ride to it,
sitting on top of the cases which our horse-drawn waggons took there. While
they were being unloaded I strutted down the gangway in the middle of the
store and counted the cases already stacked. They were marked in large
black letters with their destinations and the customers' initials. Salzburg, I
read, Vienna, Trieste, Brünn, Muncacs, Debrecin, Laibach, Tarnopol and so
forth, and felt incredibly rich. I knew nothing about overdrafts, of course, and
that our indebtedness to the bank mounted in direct proportion to the growing
stocks.

It was the foresight of past generations, the driver told me, that had created this warehouse, and I was deeply impressed. But when I said so to Grandmother she chuckled. 'Foresight? Sit down and I'll tell you how it happened.

'When the railway was built in 1863 Fleissen refused to have a station
because the farmers were afraid it would lower the price of corn. So the trains

steamed past without stopping, and your great-grandfather Johann Adam Wilhelm Pasold thought that on Sundays and in the evenings after work the people of the village would like to watch them. They would want to sit and drink a glass of beer while they watched. And so, he thought, it would be a very good place for an inn. That was why he bought the site. But there were very few trains, and people soon lost interest in them, and so the inn was not built. It would have been better if Johann Adam Wilhelm Pasold had spent the money on another knitting machine instead of sinking it in that useless piece of land. For forty years the goats grazed on it, but then at last Fleissen got a station, and, as luck would have it, next to our site. Meanwhile we needed a warehouse, and that was the ideal place for it. But it was too small. So we bought part of the adjoining hill and levelled it. The warehouse was built just before you were born.

'But that wasn't all. While digging the foundations they struck water, which was the next best thing to striking gold. Laying a pipe all the way to the factory would be expensive, of course, but it could be done if our factory well should ever dry up. So you see,' she said, with a twinkle in her eye, 'Johann Adam Wilhelm Pasold's far-sightedness paid off in the end.'

Once or twice in years to come when our water supply was threatened we almost had to lay that pipe. In spite of the worries this situation caused I always remembered Great-grandfather's 'foresight', and it never failed to amuse me.

In the autumn of 1912 we moved to the large villa which Father had built opposite the new factory. It stood in the middle of a four-acre site on which trees were being planted, flower beds laid out and grass seed sown to turn the field into a garden. This aroused in me a passing interest in gardening. I brought some small trees home from the forest and planted them, but all died, except one silver birch which over the years grew into a majestic tree, and the thought of it gives me a greater feeling of nostalgia than the memory of almost all our once treasured family possessions that now lie behind the Iron Curtain.

3

THE
GREAT WAR
1914-18

THE VAST MAJORITY of Austrians, irrespective of whether they spoke German, Hungarian, Czech, Slovak, Polish, Yiddish, Croat or any other language, although often at loggerheads with each other, were loyal subjects of the Monarchy, but it was only natural that such a mixture of races should provide fertile soil for political agitators. The Slavs in the south-east, the Balkans, were particularly troublesome. Despite centuries of experience the central government in Vienna found it not easy to keep order in this hotbed of intrigue. Liberal-minded but much misunderstood, Franz Ferdinand favoured giving Austria's subject races a greater degree of political freedom. This might have pacified the malcontents, and Serb politicians would have lost their support for the Greater Serbia they dreamed of. To forestall him they had the archduke murdered at Sarajevo by the Black Hand, a secret political organisation operating in the Balkans. The assassins escaped to Serbia. Vienna demanded their extradition, then issued an ultimatum, and when this too was ignored, declared war. And these, as my professor of history taught me years later, were the events that led the world into catastrophe.

I was only eight at the time, and did not understand the connections, but I waved as enthusiastically as all the people of Fleissen to the young men who, bedecked with flowers and led by the local band, marched to the railway station, where they entrained for Eger to join the 73rd regiment. It consisted almost exclusively of men from the Egerland, and was famous. 'We'll be back in six weeks,' they joked. Most of them never came back. Their bones lie in the Serbian mountains, on the Russian plains and in the valleys of the Italian alps.

Once Armageddon had begun it could not be stopped. Our brave soldiers had hardly crossed the frontier in pursuit of the murderous Serbs when Russia, the protector of all Slavs, declared war. We stood in danger of being crushed by the Muscovite steamroller, but fortunately our wise statesmen had made a pact of mutual assistance with our neighbours, Germany and

Italy. The Germans helped us push the Russians back, but the Italians made excuses. Then war broke out in the west between Germany and France. The French wanted revenge for the defeat of 1870. The Germans tried to by-pass the French fortifications and march on Paris through Belgium, but the Belgians resisted, and this brought Britain into the war against us—much to everyone's regret, for the Austrians and the British liked each other and got on well together. Grandmother had told me that King Edward VII spent many of his summer holidays at Marienbad, not forty kilometres from Fleissen, because he was so fond of Austria.

Our teacher was very disappointed. The British claimed to be gentlemen, yet here they were cutting off our food supplies with their illegal blockade. If their war aim was to sink the German navy, let their sailors go ahead and try, for battleships had guns with which to defend themselves. But why make war on defenceless women and children? British politicians had no right to complain when the Germans retaliated with submarines and Zeppelins. 'May God punish England,' said the people of Germany. In Bohemia there was no hatred, only sorrow. Our teacher was glad that Austrian and British troops would not have to shoot at each other because our soldiers, fortunately, fought in the east and south, whereas the British were in the north-west.

The sentiments of the adults were reflected in the war games of the children. I was given the splendid uniform of a Hungarian Honved officer for Christmas—red trousers, pale blue jacket with rows of gold braid across the chest, and a helmet and sword to match. I wore it to fight the Serbs, and always won. The difficulty was to recruit Serbs, and I usually had to bribe my schoolfriends to play their part.

I much preferred to be Admiral Beatty, who, having penetrated with the British fleet into the Adriatic, was attacking Triest. Wearing my sailor hat, I floated in a wooden tub on the Geipels' shallow millpond, being bombarded by Austrian shore batteries, 35 cm Škoda howitzers to be exact. The water reached precariously near the brim of my tub, and the shells were logs which my friends aimed so that the splashes should sink it. There was nothing objectionable in being a British admiral; on the contrary, he was a sporting fighter, but, being the enemy, he had, of course, to be sunk.

But no soldier or sailor ever quite equalled a Red Indian chief. I had discovered Fennimore Cooper's *Leather Stocking*, a volume of some 500 pages which I read and re-read until I knew it almost by heart, and none of my later heroes matched Chingachgook and Uncas, the last of the Mohicans. Unfortunately Red Indian outfits were not on sale during the war, and I had to make my own, sawing tomahawks out of bits of timber and painting them with silver paint.

Italy sat on the fence, waiting to see who was most likely to win. In 1915 she broke her treaty obligations to Austria and Germany and entered the war on the side of the enemy. A disgraceful breach of faith, said the teacher. Helmut Amarotico, the brainiest boy in the school and my best friend, was Italian, and I felt very upset when his father was interned and he was beaten up by the other boys. My parents helped me to resolve my conflict of loyalties. 'It is his misfortune and not his fault that he is Italian,' they said, to my relief. 'You are his friend and must stand by him in his hour of need; this is not betraying Austria.' Helmut and I have remained firm friends to this day, well over half a century, although in the 1939–45 war we were again in opposite camps. Ironically that time the Italians sided with the Germans, while I had become British.

The shortages grew more serious every week, money bought progressively less, and the population was urged to invest in War Loan. Contrary to the official communiques and the newspapers, Father believed that the war could go on for a long time. To provide food for the family, especially milk for my baby brothers—Rolf, born in August 1914, and Ingo, in January 1916—he bought the Kreul Hof. It was a small farm of about fifteen acres, some of which was meadow and woodland, with four cows, two or three calves and some chickens and ducks. The purchase price was 36,000 kronen, a considerable amount of money at that time. The shrewd old woman who owned the farm drove a hard bargain. She would accept only 16,000 kronen in cash; for the rest she demanded a two-storey house we owned. It stood on a piece of land which, the water diviner claimed, contained a subterranean spring, and, water being the precious life blood of Fleissen's industry, Father did not want to part with it. A compromise was struck; the old woman got the house and we kept the small piece of land between the road and the millstream where the subterranean spring was reputed to be.

As the war progressed and food became desperately scarce we had to give up most of our crops, milk and eggs, but something was always left over. We had no butter, very little meat and the small ration of coarse bread we received was made from Hungarian maize, but we had enough potatoes, beetroots, some corn, occasionally a rabbit, and we never went hungry. Most able-bodied men were called up; the women, the old and the maimed worked in the factories; there were not enough hands to do the farm work, and for two or three weeks in September the schools closed so that the children could help get the harvest in. The Pasolds were no farmers, but Mother was a Geipel, and her family, in addition to manufacturing leather, had farmed for generations. Quite naturally, therefore, she took an active interest in the Kreul Hof. No sooner were my lessons and homework done than she expected me to help on the farm, grazing the cows, picking potatoes, turning hay or bundling sheaves of oats—none of which I liked doing. I much preferred to escape to the woods to catch lizards for my terrarium or to accompany Helmut on his excursions to the remoter villages in the Egerland, foraging for black market eggs, flour, lard or a slice of pork.

The store rooms of our factory were empty. The regular merchandise had long been sold and could not be replaced, the stocks of raw materials were exhausted. All seconds and thirds, the imperfect fabric, the spools of faulty yarn, faded trimmings, bad sewing thread and all the odds and ends which had accumulated over the years were used up. We had never been so bare of any kind of goods, and consequently our bank balance had never been so large. Father and Grandfather were worried. The value of money was declining steadily, and they saw the firm's working capital evaporating. They knew that some day the war would have to end and that money would then be needed to get the factory back to regular production and fill the empty stores with raw material. They bought War Loan, of course, like all loyal citizens, but to put all the firm's liquid funds into government paper, however hard they were pressed to do so, would have been reckless. So they decided to buy some property which they thought would hold its value. Grandfather visited estate agents and found two attractive buildings that were for sale, the Mattoni House at Franzensbad and the Kraus House in the Schanzstrasse at Eger. Both were let at reasonable rents. After much discussion and some sleepless nights they were bought.

Several times Father was called up and said farewell to us in his badly fitting field grey Austrian uniform, but, a true Pasold, he hated being a soldier and never got farther than the barracks at Prague, from where he returned after a few days with his deferment papers and a government contract for army underwear in his pocket. 'I'd be no use at the front,' he said. 'I couldn't shoot at anyone.' He was more useful in other ways. Britain's blockade cut our supply not only of food but of all essential raw materials that came from overseas, such as copper, tin, hides, rubber, cotton, etc. The greatest economy had to be exercised and substitutes looked for. Textiles became so scarce that the bloodstained uniforms of the dead, friend and foe alike, were sent back from the front, washed and disinfected, and then cut up and made into new garments. It was gruesome and dirty work, but clothes were desperately needed, and we were glad to be able to keep the factory going.

Cutting these old uniforms wasted a great deal of cloth, for many of the pieces left over were too small to be of any use. In 1916 Father therefore bought from a dealer in second-hand machinery a plant for breaking fabric clippings into fibres. A cotton spinner who closed down his mill for lack of raw material sold us a condenser carding set and two mules—self-actors, as they were called. Although they had no previous experience of spinning,

Father and Johann Feiler erected the machines, and after a series of failures spun coarse yarn from the reclaimed fibres, which, however uneven and lumpy, they used successfully as backing thread on the knitting machines. The authorities were pleased, and Father had no more trouble with call-up papers.

For Helmut and me the blood-stained uniforms held quite another interest. Before the pieces of cloth could be fed through the breaker all metal had to be removed to avoid damaging the teeth of the machine or striking sparks which might set it on fire. Helping to cut off buttons and hooks, we looked for badges, ribbons and medals for our war museum. Then I discovered that Uncle Wilhelm received truckloads of leather straps, belts, cartridge containers and leather equipment of various kinds for reconditioning. Before passing it to the workpeople in his factory his examiners removed any ammunition that had slipped through. He kept it safely locked up in a chest in his office, and we paid him frequent visits, begging him to show it to us. While one of us diverted his attention the other quickly pocketed some of the cartridges. It was bad enough that we were stealing, and from my favourite uncle at that, but the thought of two small boys having whole magazines of live rifle and revolver ammunition of the Austrian, Russian, Serb and Italian armies, a partly loaded machine gun belt, two hand grenades and several detonators still makes me shudder, especially when I remember the complete lack of respect with which we handled these deadly things.

Helmut was twelve years old, and I was eleven. Sitting with our friends round the fires on which we roasted the small potatoes we found in the fields after the harvest, we threw one or two of the cartridges into the flames and delighted in the bangs with which they exploded and in the whistle of the escaping bullets. Objects which were rare enough to be added to our permanent collection we made 'harmless' by opening them up and removing the charge. We loosened the bullets by knocking them against a stone, poured the gunpowder out of the cartridges into a bottle, then made a fuse by soaking a thread in oil, buried the bottle, lit the fuse and waited at a safe distance until our bomb blew up. On one occasion some of the powder went off in Helmut's face, covering it with small black burn marks and singeing his hair and eyebrows. There was trouble when he got home, but he never confessed how it happened. Perhaps it is best for parents not to know everything and to trust their children's guardian angels.

Uncle Alfred, who had always been so jolly, was killed on the Russian front, and Uncle Gustav was wounded. An increasing number of children at school wore black armbands showing that their fathers or brothers had died in the war. There was much sadness, and tears were shed in many homes. The fallen had given their lives so that we could live. They had died for the Austro-Hungarian Empire, for Bohemia, for the Egerland. Our heroic armies and those of our gallant allies, although outnumbered ten to one, were winning everywhere, for they fought for right and justice and against lies and the dark forces of evil, teacher explained. There were reverses, of course, but reverses happened in every war, and the few we suffered were clearly unimportant, as everyone could see from the small print in which the newspapers reported them. That was how I saw the war at the age of eleven.

We knew nothing about the enemy within, about the Czech Mafia and the underground activities of Kramař and Rašin. We were not told that, while the Monarchy fought for its very existence, the Czech politicians Dr Masaryk and Dr Beneš had fled from Prague with forged passports and, via Italy and Switzerland, gone to France, Britain, Russia and America, canvassing for the destruction and permanent partition of the Austro-Hungarian Empire. It was high treason, of course, for they were Austrian subjects. Masaryk influenced Western opinion, 'using as few lies as possible', as he later wrote in his book. Ignorant of Central European history and problems, Western statesmen aided the Slav nationalist programme, and the two succeeded beyond expectation. They were in regular communication with the malcontents in Bohemia, and their secret propaganda was so effective that tens of thousands of Czechs in the Austrian army deserted to the Russians and formed a legion to fight against the Monarchy. I was too young to know whether the people of Fleissen were aware of any of this; I certainly was not. To our teacher and class the war was a very straightforward issue between right and wrong, and my parents, as far as I remember, never talked about it.

In 1916 our old emperor Franz Josef died and was succeeded by his nephew, Karl. Black flags hung from Fleissen's buildings, and we attended a memorial service. Shortly afterwards Father returned from a visit to Prague in jubilant mood. He had heard confidentially that Karl was offering peace to the allies and the Czechs were with him. We hoped and waited. But peace would not have suited Masaryk and Beneš. They stepped up their anti-Austrian propaganda abroad, and Beneš hurriedly sent secret despatches to Prague, imploring the Czechs to provoke the Austrians into initiating persecutions to provide him with propaganda material. Clemenceau, the French 'tiger', supported him. He wanted to break up the Monarchy and establish Czech and Polish States in Germany's rear. The peace negotiations came to nothing and millions more had to give their lives.

On the home front conditions went from bad to worse. Father's car—it was his third Dixi—had long been commandeered by the government. Johann Feiler had had to take it to Eger and give an army driver fourteen days' instruction how to handle it. The church bells had been taken away to be melted down into guns or ammunition. There was nothing to eat, no coal to keep us warm, no clothes to wear, and people could buy nothing with their money except War Loan certificates. Leather had disappeared; our shoes for the winter were made out of an inch-thick wooden sole and an upper part of coarse plaited straw. The memory of these shoes makes me think of an episode my parents never heard about.

My school friend Georg Hablawetz and I went skating on the Schnecken-teich, a lonely lake in the woods half an hour's walk from Fleissen. I loved the stillness of the forest in the winter, with every snow-covered pine looking like a Christmas tree. There was no one within miles. The ice on the lake was as smooth as a table top, except for some gently rounded mounds here and there which were easily avoided. We enjoyed ourselves, racing up and down the lake, following closely upon each other's heels. I had just overtaken Georg, and thought it would be fun to skate over the mound immediately ahead of me, but for some reason changed course and passed alongside. It was about six inches high and some four feet in diameter. When I glanced over my shoulder my friend had disappeared. Where the mound had been gaped a dark hole. Skating up to it, I saw his boots kicking in the icy water. The thick wooden soles and the straw made his feet come to the surface and kept the rest of him under. Now the ice began to crack all around me. Instinctively I lay flat on it, spreading my legs and arms, caught one of the boots, and, over the breaking edge of the hole, pulled him on to firm ice. The mounds were large bubbles of gas which had risen from the peaty bottom of the lake and formed blisters on the surface which were covered by only a thin layer of ice. Georg had lost one of his skates in the hole. I pushed him to the shore, carefully avoiding the other blisters, and then we ran all the way back to the village. He was shaking with cold, his face was blue, his jacket and trousers turned to solid ice, and I wondered whether he would live. He was too scared to go home, so we went to his uncle, who could be relied upon not to tell. The uncle was a baker, and on his oven Georg was thawed out. He missed two days at school but suffered no ill effects.

About that time Helmut and I tried smoking. Tobacco was rationed and difficult to obtain, but dried rose petals, we were told, tasted almost the same. In fact they tasted awful in our home-made pipes. Then Helmut got hold of some cigarettes made of real Turkish tobacco, or so it said on the packet. But to our disappointment they tasted worse, and made us cough. Hadn't Herr Fischer, our favourite teacher, explained that tobacco was bad for the lungs and that non-smokers could run faster? Neither of us has smoked since.

I had a mould to cast tin soldiers, but I had no tin. There were two rubbish dumps in hollows on the outskirts of the village which Helmut and I frequently visited to look for anything useful. The people of Fleissen had little to throw away, but occasionally we found old iron pots or sheet-metal buckets with holes in them. If enamelled they were useless, but if they were

The old Pasold cottage at Fleissen, built by Valentin or Johann in
the last quarter of the seventeenth
century

2a The chest of the Knitters' Guild
of Fleissen. The guild's documents
and valuables were kept in it. The
ceremonial opening of the chest by
the Master signified the beginning
of the meeting, when members
present were solemnly adjured to
'take off their caps, cease smoking,
and behave in every respect
decently and respectfully'. It was
'before open chest' that all official
business was transacted and new
members were admitted

3b The Knitters' Guild of Fleissen was founded in
1786. Emblem and chest are still in the author's
possession

4 The type of weaving loom used by Johann Peter Pasold and his son Johann Georg in the eighteenth century

5 The stocking frame invented by the Englishman William Lee in 1589 was an incredibly complex machine for the time. Mainly of iron, it consisted of some 2,000 parts

6 A century and a half later it was modified in the small Saxon town of Olbernhau in the Erzgebirge, the slur-cock mechanism being replaced by a wooden drum with cogs. In this form the stocking frame was introduced to Fleissen in the second half of the eighteenth century

7 In 1861 Johann Adam Wilhelm Pasold bought a circular knitting machine with eight feed-wheels

8 Fleissen: the village square in 1891, from a contemporary pen drawing

9 Christoph Adolf and Magdalena Pasold, the author's grandparents

10 Max Walter Pasold as a student at Pilsen and 11 on becoming a partner

2 Fleissen in 1898. The tall chimney belongs to Friedl's factory, the only one in the village that was power-driven. Immediately in front of it is the factory of Christoph Adolf Pasold

3 When Christoph Adolf's son Max Walter joined the firm it was renamed Adolf Pasold & Sohn, a large extension was built and a steam engine installed. It too now had a tall chimney

Vienna, capital of the Austro-Hungarian Monarchy, 1900.
14 (*above*) The Opera. *15* (*inset*) Emperor Franz Josef I. *16* (*below*)
Traffic in the Graben. Small wonder young Max was impressed

7 Vienna, 1904–05. The Hotel Meissl & Schadn in the 'Neue Markt' was a favourite meeting place
f industrialists from Bohemia

18 Max Walter and Berta Pasold, the author's parents

19 The author, aged one year

20 At the wheel of Father's Dixi in 1909

covered with a thin layer of tin or zinc we carried them home, broke them into small pieces and melted the layer off on a shovel in mother's kitchen stove. I usually waited until Cook made baked potato dumplings, which needed a sharp fire. The yield was small, but the soldiers we cast out of the recovered metal we traded in at school for small pieces of lead, tin or zinc, provided the deal showed a profit in weight, and gradually we built up two small armies. A modern rubbish dump with its abandoned motor cars, broken television sets, old bedsteads and plastic bottles would have meant more to us than Harrods' toy department can possibly mean to a little boy nowadays, however heavy he may be with pocket money.

With our armies of toy soldiers we fought wars. We arranged them in battle formation and then shot them down with blowpipes—short lengths of metal tubes which Mother used as curtain rods. For ammunition we used berries from shrubs in the garden. They were just the right size, and the red juice on the fallen soldiers looked most realistic.

I became a very good shot with my blowpipe. Starting with a length of two feet, I gradually shortened it to nine inches so that I could carry it in my trouser pocket. It was a handy weapon at school, for its range comfortably covered the classroom, and it was much more accurate than a catapult. Shooting pellets of chalk when the teacher's back was turned, I could position a full stop or decimal point anywhere I chose on the blackboard. The little pipe remained my companion for years. Sometimes I wish I had it still.

I was an avid reader in those days. Graduating from Grimm's and Andersen's fairy tales to *Robinson Crusoe*, which I read and re-read a dozen times, I continued with Greek and Norse mythology and then began to devour Father's library. It was filled with travel books, biographies and historical novels, and I read them all, even if I did not quite understand them. At school and later at college I was lucky in having two history teachers whom I respected and loved, and I always looked forward to their lessons. But I liked it best when Grandmother Pasold talked to me about the past. She had an incredible memory and kept me spellbound many a winter's evening with tales about the days when she was young.

The war, with its casualties, shabbiness, hunger and cold, dragged on. It was in its fourth year now, and seemed to be lasting for ever. I could hardly imagine what peace would be like. We were lucky, I thought, to be so far from any fighting. The nearest front was more than 400 km away. People had lost interest in the war, in winning it, or in the future. Their minds were on finding enough food, a few potatoes or a beetroot, to keep alive until tomorrow. The farmers had been called up, the work in the fields was done by the children and the old, and at night the farmer's wife protected the crops with a shotgun. Not even the news of the Russian revolution caused much stir. Our teacher explained that this would enable the Central Powers to move their forces from the east to the west and defeat the French and the British, but it did not seem to work out that way. The British had developed a dangerous new weapon, the tank, against which there was little defence, and well equipped, well fed and rested American troops were now appearing in battle-torn and war-weary Europe. There was no hope that the war would ever end.

Then suddenly it was over. Combined Italian, French and British forces won the decisive battle of the Piave. The Austro-Hungarian army ceased to resist, and disintegrated. The soldiers threw away their arms and went home to their hungry families. The Monarchy was defenceless. Prague was garrisoned by Magyar troops, who left to return to Hungary. Their arms were picked up by the Sokols, the politically orientated Czech nationalist organisation of gymnasts, and on 28 October the independent republic of Czechoslovakia was proclaimed. Were we to be part of it? No, said our teacher. President Woodrow Wilson of America promised peace based on self-determination, which could only mean that both the Czech- and the German-speaking Bohemians had the right to independence.

What was going to happen to our Egerland and other large non-Slav territories? I heard much talk of our joining up with the truncated new Austria, and even of becoming a small, self-governing State which, in addition to Eger and Franzensbad, would include Karlsbad and Marienbad. We would have liked this very much, but Prague stopped both schemes by sending troops, and a number of civilians lost their lives. I was twelve when we sang the Austrian anthem for the last time at school. The picture of Emperor Karl was taken down from the classroom wall and that of President Masaryk, who meant nothing to us, was hung in its place. We were no longer Austrians, said our teacher, his voice trembling with emotion. I was bewildered. The wicked Serbs had started the war, and I knew from the illustrated papers that our soldiers had won almost every battle. How could it be that we were now to become Czechoslovaks against our will? No one seemed to know, one rumour was followed by another, and our fate hung in the balance for a very long time.

4

WE ARE
NO LONGER AUSTRIANS
1918-21

THE MONARCHY DID not fall apart because of senile decay but was torn asunder by brute force. Its end was not as inevitable as many writers of history would have us believe. They merely repeated the propaganda put out by the 'victorious' successor States who had good reason to present a distorted picture. Austria's collapse was in fact brought about by the combination of military defeat, cunning Slav politicians, and the support they received from the misguided Western allies.

It is not the purpose of this book to go deeper into the complex racial, social and economic problems of central Europe than is necessary for essential background. Before 1918 people and merchandise passed freely between Prague and Triest, Uzhorod and Innsbruck. Trade flourished, protected by the central government at Vienna, and economic conditions were stable. Except for a handful of fanatics neither Czechs nor Poles, Croats or Slovenes had any intention of breaking up the Monarchy.

Historical comparisons are invidious. Circumstances are never quite the same, but if I may be permitted to draw a remote parallel (without wishing to point a moral) between the present situation in Britain and that of Austria two generations ago it may be helpful to the reader. The various Celts of Scotland, Ireland, the Isle of Man and Wales have grievances, be they real or imaginary. Their politicians clamour for a greater degree of autonomy and a larger share of the kitty, but not one in a thousand of these dissatisfied Celts would want to go so far as to wreck the United Kingdon. This, roughly, was also the mood of the Slavs in Austria.

To rouse them a Serb underground organisation trained teenage assassins and incited them to commit a series of murders. The purpose of these outrages was to provoke Vienna to take retaliatory measures against her Slav subjects and make them angry. The technique proved successful. Propaganda and the Monarchy's loss of prestige due to her military defeat did the rest.

To begin with, Kramař, Dmowskí, Jovanović, Masaryk and other extremists, although supported by Serbia and Tsarist Russia, had not dreamed that their rocking of the boat would capsize it. Preoccupied with fighting Germany, the Western allies took little notice of the few agitating Austrian Slavs and remained relatively friendly towards the Monarchy. But when Russia was eliminated from the war by the Bolshevik revolution the Entente's attitude changed, and it actively encouraged these fanatics to disrupt the Austro-Hungarian Empire. Some of the moderates now joined the radicals, success whetted their appetite, and Austria's defeat enabled them to realise their increasingly ambitious programmes.

By hard work, the manipulation of figures, able persuasion and luck, Masaryk and Beneš won the treble chance in the political football pool. President Wilson was more interested in the large Slav vote in the USA than in doing justice to the people of far away Central Europe. The destruction of the Monarchy came as a shock to its war-weary inhabitants, irrespective of race, and to most of her politicians. Those who could climbed on the band-wagon. Washington and London congratulated themselves on having liberated Austria's enslaved nations, and Paris on having turned them into grateful vassal States. Subsequent events—Munich in 1938 and the Communist take-over of 1948—have since proved how hollow these achievements were. For thirty years now the unfortunate inhabitants of those 'liberated' ex-Austrian provinces, whilst 'enjoying national independence', are paying the terrible price for the follies committed in 1918 and the early '20s.

The Czech leaders claimed the whole of Bohemia, Moravia, Austrian Silesia, large slices of Hungary, and later also Carpatho-Ruthenia for their newly formed Czechoslovak republic. It was to be a model democracy, another Switzerland, they told the world. A well chosen catch-phrase which did not fail to impress. But the Swiss cantons had, over a period of centuries, formed themselves freely and voluntarily into a federation. In Czechoslovakia, by contrast, millions of people were forced at bayonet point to join the State they disapproved of.

It seemed that the right of self-determination of minorities applied only to the Czech, not the German- or Hungarian-speaking parts of the Monarchy which the Czech legionaries held occupied. Contrary to the promises, there were to be two classes of citizens, conquerors and vanquished, and instead of the much condemned multi-racial Austro-Hungarian State there was to be a multi-racial Czechoslovakia with over four million people in it who did not want to be Czechoslovaks.

It appeared that the provisional government in Prague had the support of the Western powers and, in addition, enough troops to impose its will on the defenceless minorities. We now heard that during the war Masaryk and Beneš had organised Czech Legions in France, Italy and especially Russia by

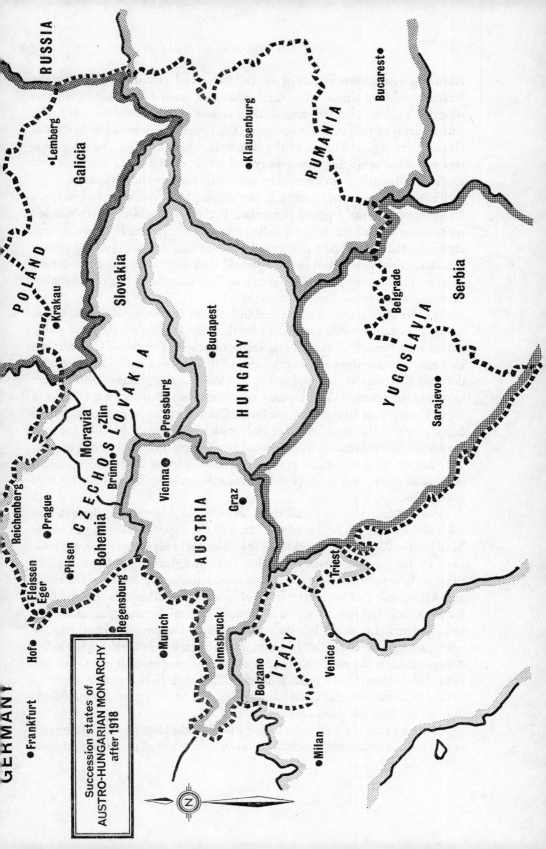

GERMANY

RUSSIA

•Lemberg

Galicia

POLAND

•Krakau

Slovakia

Bucarest•

RUMANIA

Klausenburg•

Budapest•

HUNGARY

Belgrade•

YUGOSLAVIA

Serbia

Sarajevo•

Moravia

Zlin

C Z E C H O S L O V A K I A

Reichenberg

•Prague

•Pilsen

Bohemia

Brünn•

Pressburg•

Vienna•

AUSTRIA

Graz•

Triest•

Fleissen

Eger•

•Regensburg

Hof•

•Munich

•Innsbruck

Frankfurt•

Bolzano•

ITALY

Venice•

Milan•

Succession states of
AUSTRO-HUNGARIAN MONARCHY
after 1918

N

recruiting deserters, prisoners of war and Czechs who lived abroad. When the Austrian soldiers threw away their rifles and went home the legionaries returned to Bohemia fully armed, thus providing the newly born republic with an army of well over 100,000 men. The largest contingent was in Russia. Cut off from central Europe by the Bolshevik revolution, the Czech legionaries seized the trans-Siberian railway and, living off the land, slowly pushed east to Vladivostok, from where they eventually returned home by sea.

Reflecting the general feeling in the village, I did not want to become a Czechoslovak. I was a proud Bohemian. Perhaps I would not have minded quite so much had the new republic been named Greater Bohemia. It was especially the 'slovak' part that vexed me. Not that we had anything against the Slovaks politically, but in the Egerland they were known as *Rastelbinder*, hawkers of pots and pans, mousetraps and brushes made from pig bristles. Were we to be lumped together with them?

At heart Father agreed with me, but he knew there were weightier issues at stake. Czechoslovakia seemed to be the only reasonably sane and stable State in the turmoil of central and eastern Europe. The rise of Communism in Russia, the mutinies and the collapse of the Austrian and German armies defeated all authority, law and order. The disillusioned, hungry masses were easy prey for agitators. There were Communist *coups* and civil war all around us, in Hungary, in Bavaria and not forty kilometres away over the border in Saxony, where the notorious Max Hölz with his motorised band of 800 men plundered and murdered. There would be Communism in Bohemia too if it were not for the government at Prague, a small team of hard-headed Czechs of peasant stock, and their brutally nationalistic, if undisciplined, force of legionaries.

Besides Masaryk and Beneš there were Švelak, the farmer, Šramek, the Catholic, Klofač, the leader of the left, and the Slovak Stefanik, the young Minister for War who was accidentally shot down in his aeroplane over Pressburg by his own trigger-happy legionaries. And, most important of all in those early days, there were the industrialist Kramař, the leader of the right, and Rašin, who had both been in trouble with the authorities all their lives for their anti-Austrian activities. Both were arrested for high treason in 1915 and condemned to death but later amnestied by Emperor Karl and freed— only to continue immediately plotting the destruction of the Monarchy. Austria was not the ruthless police State its enemies made it out to be, but nevertheless these Czech politicians had risked their lives for their dream of national independence and were not prepared to let their young republic fall into the hands of the Communists.

Father was not the only industrialist who thought Communism the greater of two evils. The economic situation and the political and psychological temper of the masses at that time are well described in *The Financial Policy of Czechoslovakia during the First Year of its History*, which was written by Dr Rašin, the Minister of Finance, in 1921:

... Among the working classes the opinion was openly expressed that the moment had come for them to seize the mastery, and that their former masters would now become their servants. Throughout the whole of Europe the working classes were imbued with this false idea, which was fostered by the Communistic experiments of the Bolshevist Republic. This feverish condition of the masses did not break out in Czechoslovakia in direct revolutionary action but found expression in that empty Bolshevism which teaches that high wages, strikes and reduced output must eventually succeed in expropriating capital.

Revolution was in fact simmering below the surface, and before Dr Rašin had finished writing his book there was an attempted Communist *coup* in Czechoslovakia which the government put down with great determination. But apart from maintaining order and protecting public and private property the young republic was faced with the urgent task of getting production going again:

This was certainly a gigantic task in a country that had been robbed owing to the blockade of all means of maintaining the fertility of the soil; there was no artificial manure, the stock of cattle had been reduced to a third of its pre-war proportions, there were no teams for the proper working of the land—industry had been undermined, all copper and brass parts having been removed for the production of munitions, all industrial activity diverted to the output of munitions, lead requisitioned for rifle ammunition, steel for the casting of guns, wood for the trenches, the execution of safety work in the coal mines had been stopped. In every sphere of economic life the war had made itself felt with devastating effect.

Directly connected with the task of restarting industry was the pressing problem of the creation of an independent currency. Like the other successor States, Czechoslovakia continued to use the banknotes and small coins of a Monarchy that no longer existed. To prepare and legislate for a currency of her own, print new notes and exchange them for the ones in circulation was a mammoth task and took time. Meanwhile the printing presses in Vienna, over which Prague had little control, poured forth more and more of the rapidly depreciating communal money. It was Dr Rašin who planned the separation of Czechoslovakia's currency from the Austro-Hungarian krone and carried through the complex operation with great efficiency and at lightning speed.

On 25 February 1919 the National Assembly in secret session empowered the Minister of Finance to call in all banknotes in circulation in Czechoslovakia and confiscate 50 per cent of them, the remaining 50 per cent to be validated by a stamp and returned to their owners. On the night of 25 February the entire frontier was sealed off by the army, all frontier traffic was stopped, and next morning stamping began at the banks, which were designated as temporary government departments. At the same time all securities, bonds, dividend warrants, policies and claims were registered, with those not declared being forfeited to the State. The registration embraced goods, stores, fittings, mortgage claims and real estate and provided the basis for a wealth tax.

These drastic financial measures had immediate and gratifying results. While inflation in Germany and Austria continued apace and the governments of both countries tried to keep up with it by printing ever more banknotes, the international value of the Czech krone began to climb.

The separation from the Austro-Hungarian standard resulted in the Czech krone being quoted independently on the European exchanges, and from this time onward Czechoslovak business life found expression on the international market.

. . . from 29 February to 17 May 1919 the mark fell from 52 Swiss francs for 100 marks to 36 Swiss francs, the Austrian krone from 25½ to 23, while on the other hand the Czech krone rose from 26 to 33½ and remained at about 30 francs (per 100 Kc) up to 23 July in spite of the fact that in June the republic had to deal with the Hungarian–Bolshevist incursion. But from this time onward it fell steadily, in complete dependence of the decline of the mark and the Austrian krone, till, on 2 February 1920, it reached 5·65 francs . . .

What had gone wrong? Financial manipulations alone, however successful, could do no more than provide a temporary breathing space. Only the efficient use of the country's productive resources could bring about a lasting improvement in the economy, and these resources were not being used properly. Czechoslovakia was by far the wealthiest of all the successor States. She had inherited at least 60 per cent of the fallen Monarchy's industries: sugar, malt, beer, spirits, textiles, shoes, glass, timber and wooden goods, machinery, etc. But her factories were geared mainly to supply the territories of the old Austro-Hungarian Empire, a common market of more than 50 million people. Most of these were now lost; the new republic had only 14 million inhabitants. New outlets had to be found, export markets developed, and that required time, the will to work and competitive prices.

But neither the politicians nor the masses were willing to face these facts. The cost of production rose daily. People spent more than they earned, and to close the gap demanded higher wages. The socialist government ranged itself on the side of the workers. Without support from the authorities the employers lacked the strength to refuse labour's demands. They made wholesale concessions and passed the increased cost on to the consumer. Prices and wages began to spiral, and the value of the Czech krone tumbled.

In June 1920 my uncles, the Geipels who owned the leather factory, the largest industrial undertaking in Fleissen, dismissed a workman for bad time-keeping. This started a strike. Workers remaining at their posts were beaten up by the strikers, who had been reinforced by hundreds of unemployed coal miners from Königsberg and Falkenau some 20 km away. Uncle Gustav requested police protection for those willing to work, but the chief of the Okresni Vybor, the government office at Eger, refused with the words 'The people's will is God's will'. Armed with shotguns, my uncles barricaded themselves in their villas, while the factory across the road stayed closed.

A week later Uncle Wilhelm's workers struck in sympathy, incited by a village politician whom I will call Kraut. During the war he had been the leading Austrian nationalist, and smashed the windows of my friend Helmut's home because the Amaroticos were Italians. Now he had become a prominent socialist.

Uncle Wilhelm was not greatly worried. Business was bad, he was short of leather and of orders, and intended to use the enforced stoppage for a business journey to Prague. His office staff was still working, and on his way to the station he called at the factory to dictate a few letters. But no sooner had he passed the picket and entered the building than stones began to fly and every pane of glass was broken. He looked out at the crowd through the broken windows. 'Come out,' they shouted, 'or we'll come in and get you!' He sent the frightened office staff home through the back exit and then fired two revolver shots in the air to alert the gendarmes. While the mob broke down the front door Uncle Wilhelm took the lift to the top of his six-storey building and from the flat roof climbed up the factory chimney. A very athletic thirty-two-year-old, armed with a loaded revolver he felt confident that he could hold the roof until the gendarmes arrived.

Down below the mob smashed the furniture and set about lighting the furnace to smoke Wilhelm out. Then four gendarmes and two civilians, Kraut and Schimmer, who claimed to represent 'the people', climbed on to the roof and called on him to come down. They would guarantee his safety provided he surrendered his revolver. Putting his trust in the heavily armed gendarmes, he handed over the gun and followed them downstairs. The offices were in a shambles. He was surrounded by shouting men and women, the gendarmes disappeared and Kraut demanded that he sign a declaration recognising the Socialist Workers' Council, a body he had not heard of before. When he protested that this was blackmail someone from behind hit him over the head with a chair, and as he lay on the floor among the broken glass others jumped on him. Then he heard someone say, 'He's dead,' and he lay quite still.

No one wanted to be involved in a murder. The crowd cleared the offices;

only Kraut stayed behind and phoned my uncles Friedrich and Otto to
threaten that they would be next. But the mob had cooled its temper and dispersed. Two men carried Wilhelm across the road to Aunt Hulda's house,
where I arrived a few minutes later. We had heard the shots and the rumour
that he had been killed. Knowing that the strikers would not hurt a fourteen-
year-old boy, Father let me go to investigate. I shook in my boots as I made
my way through the crowd, but was overjoyed to find Uncle alive. He even
recognised me with a faint smile.

The authorities did nothing to restore order, and the strike petered out on
its own. Uncle Wilhelm recovered, only to have a nervous breakdown a few
weeks later, and his factory remained closed for months. The cunning Kraut
lay low for some time, while the career of Schimmer, the other ringleader,
ended abruptly when he was killed in a shooting affray between his band of
smugglers and Czechoslovak frontier guards.

Industrial unrest and local eruptions continued in many parts of the country and slowed down its recovery. Dr Rašin, if not all his colleagues in the
government, saw very clearly what was happening.

Neither capital nor the capitalists were destroyed or expropriated by this 'dry
Bolshevism'. The workers did not acquire any capital. They did indeed raise their
standard of living, but they spent every bit of their high wages. The only sufferers
were the people with small independent means, pensioners, owners of rented houses
and all who had fixed incomes, which sufficed to buy only a tenth or a twelfth of
what they had covered in peacetime.

. . . The increase in wages . . . and prices . . . fostered discontent among all classes
and . . . brought such confusion that businessmen found difficulty in making
calculations of any kind . . . The immense jumps in wages caused a sudden rise in
the standard of living of the broad masses, and in the pursuit of pleasure nothing
was too dear . . .

Compared with the standards we are used to nowadays the luxuries and
pleasures indulged in by the masses of Czechoslovakia were extremely
modest: a bottle of beer and a sausage after years of starvation, an overcoat,
an extra piece of furniture and perhaps a violin or a bicycle. Yet in the aggregate the home consumption of these things pulled the country down. They
should have been exported to strengthen the republic's financial position.
The astute Dr Rašin knew that without confidence in the currency it was
impossible to put the economy on a sound basis. Instead of concentrating on
production and the creation of new wealth industrialists were preoccupied
with the preservation of their existing resources; the country drifted and
valuable time was lost:

. . . Czechoslovak currency was in an unhealthy condition, and its improvement
could only be brought about by strict maintenance of internal order, by the exercise

of economy in State expenditure without disproportionate growth in the incomes of the people, by raising the productive capacity of the nation and by placing a restriction on all unnecessary consumption and especially on the importation of superfluous articles of luxury from abroad. It was of the first importance that our production should exceed our consumption in order that we should be in a position to use the surplus for purchasing raw materials and other necessaries abroad . . .

Rašin's pleas for harder work and more stringent economies met with considerable opposition from the left, but the world crisis and growing unemployment gradually brought the politicians and the people of Czechoslovakia to their senses. They learned the hard way that efficient production, exports and a stable currency were essential for the country's survival. At last they began to understand that these conditions could not be brought about by egalitarian doctrines of sharing out and consuming the diminishing wealth, but only by greater personal effort, less State interference in business and the encouragement of private enterprise:

The feverish malady which attacked the Czechoslovak Republic in the second half of 1919 and which led to the depreciation of the krone began to abate in the last six months of 1920, after the defeat of the Bolshevik armies in Warsaw, and influenced by the crisis in production which had affected not only Czechoslovakia but the whole world . . .

. . . it was recognised that to allow State marketing in every class of goods to continue was out of the question, and that freedom of trade and free competition must again come into play. The control of meat and fats was discontinued altogether and that of corn and flour restricted. One government control office after another was liquidated.

. . . unrestricted trade was greatly welcomed by all classes of producers, the working classes not excepted. It was also welcomed by consumers, who realised that free competition improves the quality of goods and gradually reduces prices.

Painful though Dr Rašin's measures were, industry and commerce supported them but remained bitterly opposed to the government's ruthless political dictatorship. For over 500 years trade and industry had been developed and controlled mainly by German-speaking Bohemians. They now accused Prague of violating the terms of the amnesty by refusing to extend the right of self-determination to the country's minorities. Some hoped that the ancient legal status of the Egerland, which was historically not part of Bohemia but had been only pawned to the Bohemian Crown in 1322, would sustain her claim for a degree of independence. For almost three anxious years we did not accept our inclusion in the new State as final. But force prevailed, and we remained Czechoslovaks whether we liked it or not.

It was not the best beginning for that model democracy, that 'other

Switzerland', Masaryk's professed dream republic, in which equal citizens of different tongues would voluntarily and happily live and work together. Such a concept could not be built on force. Did not the Czech nationalists and their foreign supporters realise that the German- and Hungarian-speaking minorities, more than four million unwilling subjects, would only wait for the opportunity of breaking up this artificially created republic to regain their freedom, with outside help if need be, in the same way as the Czechs had broken up the Monarchy with Russian, French, American and British help? The act of folly and injustice committed in the excitement of victory was to bear bitter fruit for all concerned twenty years later.

The press was censored, of course, but the people of Fleissen were no great newspaper readers, and although we had the *Egerer Zeitung* every day I do not think we took it very seriously. Politics were discussed on Sunday mornings after church when we met my uncles and their families at Grandmother Geipel's house.

Uncle Otto was very outspoken in his condemnation of Czech megalomania. Kramař and Beneš took advantage of the simple-minded Slovaks, stole Magyar territory, violated the rights of the German-speaking minorities, quarrelled with the Poles and grossly deceived the French. Out of a pack of lies they constructed a Central Europe that would collapse like a house of cards in the first gust of wind. We'd live to see it fall and bury its architects under the debris. Someone ought to warn the Western powers. As far as the government's monetary reforms were concerned, Uncle Otto fancied himself as Fleissen's financial genius who could have done much better than Dr Rašin. And secretly he could not forgive the Czechs, those uneducated peasants, for abolishing all titles, including his *kaiserlicher Rat* (Imperial Counsellor), an award he had received for services rendered to the Monarchy.

Uncle Gustav took a more conciliatory view. Having lived for several years with a Czech family in Prague and learned to speak Czech, he saw both sides. He was also the expert on international affairs, for he had been three times to India and Africa, where he made expeditions into the interior to buy hides from the natives. His opinion was listened to with great respect. Was it conceivable, he asked, that Germany could afford to lose her colonies, pay the enormous reparations demanded by the victors, recover from her other war wounds and become a military power again? The French and the British seemed to think so; that was why they had created Czechoslovakia and Poland in Germany's rear. Should the Germans ever threaten the West again these two vassal States were expected to attack them from behind, so the theory ran. They had signed a sacred pact to this effect, but just suppose, Uncle Gustav mused, that Germany should one day turn on the Poles and the Czechs instead. Would France and Britain go to war to help them? And because of this phony pact our right to political self-determination, President Wilson's noble notion, was denied.

Politics apart, the Geipel enterprises were burdened with large sterling debts which now had to be repaid. The drop in the value of the krone had increased these liabilities more than fivefold, and since the firm's liquid assets were invested in War Loan, which had become valueless, my uncles were very worried.

Uncle Friedrich was better versed in local topics, and invariably thundered against Burgomaster Kraut and his Reds who were plunging the village into debt with their grandiose road building schemes. Kraut secured the votes of the unemployed loafers by providing easy jobs for them, lined his pockets by placing the orders at inflated prices with contractors who bribed him, and presented the bill to industry in the form of ever higher rates. The other target of Uncle's wrath was Dr Adolf Lehrmann, who, it seemed, had much influence with politicians in Prague and used it to make life difficult for the Geipels.

Father thought all politicians were opportunists who promised one thing and did another, but since he had to concentrate on running his business and was not prepared to get involved in politics he had to make the best of conditions as they came. As it happened, he approved of Dr Rašin's drastic measures. And instead of getting worked up like my uncles he found it more rewarding to watch and to keep a jump ahead of events. He thus paid off the firm's large tax arrears with Austro-Hungarian War Loan certificates the day before the new government declared them invalid, a cruel blow no one else had expected. Father's move was a scoop, and the whole village was jealous, for it saved our firm a great deal of money.

I listened carefully to the conflicting views and in turn agreed with each of them. It was all very confusing and rather above my head, except Uncle Friedrich's outbursts about Burgomaster Kraut. But I kept very quiet and felt guilty. My friend Helmut Amarotico had told me that his father paid Kraut a commission to get profitable contracts. Having been interned for four years, he had to make up for lost time. Everyone knew that Kraut was a rogue. The funds of the local co-operative society had inexplicably disappeared before he became burgomaster. Being a very plausible talker, he had wriggled out of the incriminating situation. It was said that he took bribes from all and sundry, and I could not understand how a man of his reputation could hold an official position. Perhaps the Okresni Vybor at Eger backed him because he had the support of the local socialists and was therefore a convenient counterweight to the troublesome farmers and industrialists who were critical of the government, and especially to the influential Geipels, who were reputed to be reactionary and anti-Czech.

Listening to these discussions, even if I could not always understand them, relieved the dreariness of Sunday morning. I hated having to wear my best clothes, the church was chilly, and the pews were uncomfortable. Fleissen had been a Protestant stronghold for almost four hundred years, and my elders felt passionately about religion, but I would have preferred to play with my pals in the fields. Although I secretly worshipped the silver-haired Reverend Alberti, a most dignified old gentleman, I followed his sermons like a series of not very interesting fairy tales. There was little connection between conditions and people in the Holy Land and those at Fleissen. The chanting of the choirboys before and after the sermon and especially the dragging melodies of the psalms sung by the congregation at snail's pace, accompanied by the unpleasant sounds of the organ, made me unhappy. Did God like this kind of music? I could not believe it. There was, however, no escape. Mother saw to it that I attended the service regularly.

The afternoon was my own. Grandfather had bought three stallions from the disintegrating Austrian army, and our coachman, who had been in a dragoon regiment, gave my sister and me riding lessons. Silvia refused to carry on after a nasty fall, and as exercising three horses was too much for me I invited my school friends to help. Playing cowboys and Indians in the woods and shooting from the saddle with bows and arrows was great fun. In the winter, before the snow lay too deep, we galloped over the frozen fields, imagining we were Cossacks on the plains of Siberia. I also enjoyed riding behind my parents' sleigh through the glittering white forest when the newly fallen snow swallowed the sound of the horses' hoofs and one heard nothing but the tinkling of the bells on the harnesses. But the following spring Father bought me a bicycle, which left me even less time to exercise the stallions, and they were sold.

I had never seen anyone balancing on two wheels at Fleissen: there was no rubber for tyres during the war. Only once, when my grandparents took me to Karlsbad, did I see a man on a bicycle. Perhaps it would be truer to say that I heard him as he clattered over the pavement on his machine. Each wheel consisted of two metal rings with many small steel springs between them instead of the tyre. But my bicycle was better and had rubber tyres. It was more difficult to ride than a horse, and I fell off far more often. Nowadays toddlers are brought up on scooters and fairy-cycles and are used to mechanised transport almost before they can walk, but I had to discover by experiment and learn the hard way.

I loved my bicycle. One could do so much more with it than ride it. There was a tool kit with which to adjust the handlebars or the height and angle of the saddle. One could reposition the bell, take off the chain and soak it in oil, adjust the handbrake, balance the wheels, pump the tyres up harder or let them down and practise mending punctures. The ball bearings in the hubs of the wheels were marvels of precision and the back-pedalling brake a masterpiece of ingenuity. Best of all, one did not have to exercise the machine if one did not feel like it. Shortly after I had my bicycle Uncle Wilhelm bought one for himself, and then Helmut got one, and we went on excursions to Franzensbad and Eger. We rarely crossed the border, because the customs procedure of putting a lead seal on each bicycle and the paperwork were so cumbersome. None of this rigmarole was necessary with a horse.

Franzensbad, the smallest of the three famous spas of western Bohemia, is only 10 km from Fleissen. My grandparents usually went there for the weekend to go to the theatre or to have coffee under the trees in the Kurpark, listen to the band and watch the people promenading up and down in their fashionable clothes. Visitors who took the water, holidaymakers, foreigners and actresses mingled with local dignitaries, industrialists and landowners. They brought their wives and daughters, and most of them knew each other, stopped for a friendly chat or were at least on nodding acquaintance.

One Saturday morning Grandfather sat at his desk in the office signing letters while Rolf and I amused ourselves with old envelopes and a large rubber stamp. Grandfather was bald, and as he bent over, his shiny pink top looked so inviting that I could not resist stamping ADOLF PASOLD & SOHN on it in mauve ink. 'Don't disturb me,' he said, without realising what I had done. 'It was only a fly, Grandpa. We're trying to catch it,' said Rolf, laughing.

Have you any idea how well a large stamp in bright mauve ink shows up on a bald head? Just try it! We left, expecting that Grandmother would see the stamp the moment Grandfather came home and would wash it off. But she had gone out. He ate the lunch she had left for him and then took the train to Franzensbad, where he spent the afternoon in the Kurpark sitting at a small table in the front row enjoying the music. Why was everyone laughing? It was not until he returned home in the evening that Grandmother saw the stamp. So that was the explanation of all the amusement in the park. He had been the cause of it, and not one of his friends who had smiled and chatted had told him. He was furious.

I was sorry when I heard about it on Monday morning, and apologised, though pointing out the publicity value for the firm, but Grandfather was so cross that he would not speak to me for three days. Then he forgave me and laughed.

In spite of the considerable difference in our ages my brothers and I had much fun together. When I was thirteen Rolf was five and Ingo only three, but we made a good team. Silvia, our sister, who was ten, felt less inclined towards pranks, and we left her to play her girlish games with her friends.

Some of the escapades I organised were not without risk, and the implicit confidence my brothers had in my leadership was hardly justified, but with unerring instinct Mother usually arrived on the scene at the critical moment and saved the situation. We had many a scare but never came to any real harm.

There was the time when we tried to make a lift. Our house consisted of a basement, ground and first floor and a very spacious loft. Looking from the loft down into the garden almost made one dizzy, it was so high. To go up and down this height in a basket would be quite an achievement. Ingo weighed least, so he'd try the journey first. We found a length of rope, but it reached only half-way down, and we lengthened it with treble thicknesses of string and a piece of cord from an old curtain. We tied the end to the two handles of a baby basket, sat Ingo in it and lowered it out of the window. He was much heavier than we expected, and both Rolf and I had to hold on to the rope with all our strength as we paid it out in a series of jerks. We thought it was a pretty long rope but came to the end long before the basket touched ground, and we were not strong enough to pull it up again. All we could do was hold on, without being able to relax sufficiently even to look down to see how far short we were.

Mother was in the drawing room playing the piano when something made her look up. There, outside the window, about 8 ft above the rose bushes was a basket swinging to and fro with her youngest in it. Within seconds she was in the garden, waiting with outstretched arms below the swinging basket just beyond her reach. Her shouts brought the gardener running, and with the help of a step ladder Ingo was released. He thoroughly enjoyed the experience.

An adventurous little boy, Ingo was quite fearless and often got himself into positions from which he had to be rescued. Once he climbed over the carved wooden bannisters on the upper landing in the hall, and Mother found him dangling from a narrow ledge, literally hanging by his fingertips, screaming for help. Another time he wriggled his head between some iron railings, and one of the bars had to be cut to get him out. Some years later he cycled along the top of the brick wall of a factory building under construction and fell with his bicycle from the first storey into a ditch, escaping with no more damage than being winded and buckling two wheels.

When December came the snow began to fall, and by Christmas it was a foot deep. Fields, gardens, roads and forest lay under a white blanket. Waggons and carts gave way to sledges, and instead of squeaking axles and the sound of iron-clad wheels bumping over potholes the tinkle of little bells on the horses' harness warned pedestrians, for sleighs slid swiftly and silently through the snow. The mill stream was frozen, from the roofs hung

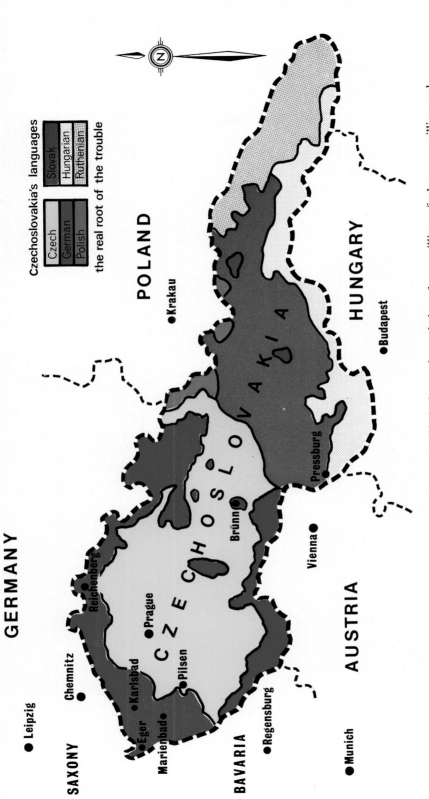

According to the official census taken in 1930, Czechoslovakia had a total population of 14·5 million, of whom 7·4 million spoke Czech, 3·3 million German, 2·3 million Slovak, 700,000 Hungarian, 550,000 Ruthenian, 160,000 Yiddish, 80,000 Polish and 10,000 Rumanian

21 Castle Seeberg, two hours' walk from Fleissen, a favourite spot for schoolboy outings

long icicles, and the children had snowball fights and built snowmen and snow huts. I loved the winter.

Christmas was the most important festive occasion of the year, with a decorated tree and lighted candles in every house. On Christmas Eve, wearing our best clothes, we sang 'Silent night', with Mother accompanying us on the piano, then the sliding doors to the drawing room opened and we collected our presents.

My first pair of skis were a Christmas present. Since no one at Fleissen had the faintest idea how to use them, I tried to learn the Telemark and other now outdated manoeuvres from a book, but the long, unwieldy boards with their Huitfeld bindings and my totally unsuitable boots and clothes defeated all my efforts. The snow was too deep and heavy, the slopes on which I practised were not steep enough. Every time I fell, snow slipped down my neck and trousers; I got soaking wet and thoroughly discouraged. It was not until the following winter at Asch, when I saw others ski, that I began to make some progress.

The snow usually lay until March, then it began to melt, and for two or three weeks the roads were covered ankle-deep in slush and mud until the sun gained enough strength to lick them dry and I could use my bicycle again.

At the beginning of May I found a baby deer in the ditch by the side of the road. The little fawn was only a day old and could hardly stand on its spindly legs. Since I could not see its mother anywhere, and there were dogs not far away, I carried the helpless little thing home in my arms and gave it some warm milk from a bottle. It must have been very thirsty, for it drank and drank. Then I put it in a basket, covered it with a rug and let it sleep. Within a few days it had grown strong enough to stalk about in the garden. I put its basket in a spinney under a pine tree, but it preferred Mother's beds of runner beans and settled there. Twice a day I fed it with the bottle. I needed only call 'Hansi!' and the little fawn came hurtling to the front door. It was so tame that it followed me about, and it loved to play with Rolf and Ingo, who treated it as one of the family, stroked it and raced with it round the house. But alas, babies grow up, and Hansi became a full-sized deer. It no longer drank milk. Instead of eating grass it nibbled the buds of the flowering shrubs and the young shoots of Mother's vegetables, and did so much damage to the fruit trees that the gardener was afraid they would die. Hansi would have to go.

I coaxed it out of the garden, across the fields into the woods where it belonged, but it followed me back to the village. It stood outside our garden gate, pleading with sounds not unlike those of a kitten, and looked at us out of its big, brown eyes. We could not lock it out, it was so tame that it would have fallen victim to a dog or a knife within hours. Nor could we bring ourselves to shut it up in a confined space. The awful decision had to be taken.

Hansi had to die—as painlessly as possible. Never again, I promised myself, would I take an animal out of its natural surroundings. With heavy hearts and tears in our eyes we called butcher Böhm. We gave him the meat, the skin was stuffed. I kept it in my bedroom for many years, and often thought of that happy summer as I stroked Hansi's soft coat.

About that time Helmut and I learned to swim, again with the help of a small instruction book. We must have been incredibly clumsy, for it took us a whole summer to learn the breast stroke and another to swim on our backs. We practised in our lake in the woods, and once at least I would have drowned if my governess had not pulled me out. It was fortunate that she came with us that day. Her job was to teach Silvia and me French and English.

As soon after the war as it became possible to buy a car—an Austrian car, of course, for Father would not consider any other—we made the long train journey to Vienna to select one. I believe it was during the 1920 Easter school holidays. At the border we apologised to the Austrian immigration officer as we showed our provisional Czechoslovak passport. It was sad but not our fault that we were foreigners now. I had never been to Vienna and looked forward to seeing the imperial castle, St Stephen's Cathedral and the Danube, but for Father it was a sentimental visit. The capital of the old Austro–Hungarian Empire was more to him than just a city. He had been at home in it for so long he loved it, and now we no longer belonged. I saw him wipe more than one secret tear from his eye as he showed me the sights, and I shared his sadness.

After various road tests we ordered a six-seater Steyer, a beauty of a car. It was an open tourer with a six-cylinder engine and a pointed radiator designed to cut through the air like a knife. The speedometer dial was calibrated up to 100 km/hr (63 m.p.h.), and although no one would want to drive at such hair-raising speeds the salesman assured us that, given favourable conditions, the car was in fact capable of approaching them. All being well, it would be ready for collection from the works before the summer.

Of course we also visited the showrooms of all the other makers and looked under the bonnets of their cars. I was thrilled to see the Amilcar, a tiny, beautifully streamlined single-seater French racer, but even more beautiful was the agent's receptionist, an angel with big blue eyes and golden hair who had just stepped out of heaven. To a country boy of fourteen this Viennese girl was the personification of everything pure and beautiful, and I could not take my eyes off her.

When Father and Johann Feiler collected the Steyer from Austria I could not go with them because I had to be at school and so missed the excitement of that first drive, but I was allowed to paint the international identification letters next to the number plate of the new car. In the olden days it would have been an 'A' for Austria, but now we heard that we had to show 'CSR' for Czechoslovak Republic. Father was livid, and told me to design a monogram of the three letters which was difficult to decipher. He was not going to advertise our 'Rastelbinder nationality' to all and sundry. But my design was not acceptable to the police, and in the end we had to fix the standard letters 'CS'.

During the summer holidays we made a long trip south. The road was bad and dusty; we met very few other cars, and always waved if we saw one. It was unthinkable that parking even in city centres could ever become a problem. We took spare petrol in cans from the garages in the larger towns, for there were no petrol stations. The speed limit through the villages was 15 km/hr. We were plagued by dogs, held up by chickens and geese, and the farmers would not keep to their side of the road. But these were trifling annoyances compared with the joy of driving in the new car. Father and Feiler took turns at the wheel, while Mother, eleven-year-old Silvia and I sat in the back.

On the first day we drove as far as Nuremberg, where we looked at the old castle, the torture chamber, and had sausages at the Bratwurstglöckl. The following night we spent at Munich and visited the Hofbräuhaus. Then, driving along Lake Starnberg, the Alps came in sight, and towards evening we reached Garmisch, our holiday goal. The snow-covered mountains made an unforgettable impression on me. I could hardly believe they were real. I had, of course, seen pictures of the Alps, but I had also seen pictures of Father Christmas, of St George fighting the dragon and of Zeus on Olympus and had found out years ago that pictures were no proof that these things really existed. Yet here was the Zugspitze towering above me in awe-inspiring, indescribable grandeur, just as I had seen it on picture postcards. I was quite overcome.

Garmisch was then still a village. Most of the farmers wore leather shorts, the women wore dirndls and in the evenings they danced *Schuhplattler*. There were tourists, to be sure, but they were in the minority and our car was one of three parked in the square. We spent two very happy weeks there.

5

AT THE
TEXTILE COLLEGE
1920-24

AT FOURTEEN I TOOK the entrance examination for the textile college at
Asch. It was an excellent school. There were only four others in Europe that
were comparable. They were at Chemnitz and Reutlingen in Germany, at
Troyes in France and at Leicester in England. Asch was a town of 20,000 inhabitants and the centre of the textile industry in western Bohemia. Although
only 15 km from Fleissen it seemed much farther because there was no direct
railway and the road climbed 650 ft over a 2,300 ft-high ridge, twice crossing
the Czechoslovak–German frontier.

I lodged with Frau Ludwig, a widow who took students as boarders. The
pupils were mostly from Czechoslovakia, but some came from Vienna,
Jugoslavia, Hungary, Poland and even Norway. We were nineteen boys in
the class and two girls. I was one of the youngest pupils in the college and
had been only to a village school. Most of the others came from towns and
were so much more experienced than I, it was no wonder I was shy and a little
scared of them.

After a while I became aware of broad but quite distinct groups into which
the students could be divided. The group I had most in common with were
the sons of industrialists. We were no geniuses but, on the whole, I think we
had a more practical turn of mind and worked harder than the somewhat
older sons of doctors, lawyers, schoolmasters and civil servants, some of whom
had changed in mid-stream from a humanistic education to the textile
college and thought themselves intellectually superior. Many were members
of the 'Verbindung', a forbidden, semi-secret students' organisation, modelled
on those at universities. They met at out-of-the-way inns, where they wore
coloured caps, drank beer, made political speeches and fought duels with
rapiers to uphold some strange code of honour. I had no desire, nor did they
ask me, to join them.

We also had five Jews in the class, sons of professional men and merchants.
Four were German-speaking Bohemians, the fifth was Hungarian. For some
reason obscure to me they were a group by themselves. What was it that made

them different? They looked and dressed like Gentiles. The Verbindung was anti-semitic, but I was not too sure what this meant. One morning I heard that there was trouble; the Jews had been disrespectful and were to be punished. Word was passed round that no one was to speak to them. Any Gentile who talked to a Jew would himself be boycotted. I was too young and lacked the moral courage to defy the powerful majority and stand up against this curtailment of my personal freedom, but I felt so outraged that I refused to talk to anyone, Jew or Gentile, as long as the boycott lasted. It fizzled out after two days and was never repeated in all my four years at college.

When I told Father about it at the weekend he shook his head. Most textile manufacturers were Gentiles, while the wholesalers and retailers were Jews. Did these young fools not realise that they needed each other? It had not occurred to me that hardly any of our customers were Gentiles. I had thought that only the Galicians, with their beards and curls, their black velvet hats and their kaftans were Jews.

Of the five in our class, two were rather stupid, two were intelligent but much too worldly for me, which left Ladislaus Turan, or Lazie, as everyone called him. He was the Hungarian, the son of a doctor, a compulsive talker with an inexhaustible vocabulary, an extrovert and so very different from myself. Perhaps that was the reason why we got on well together. He sat next to me and, being much better at French and algebra, helped me with my exercises when the professor was not looking. In return I helped him in physics and engineering.

Tuition was entirely in German. We spent forty hours a week at lectures and in addition were expected to do about six hours of homework. There was no time for sports. The curriculum fell into three parts, firstly subjects of general knowledge such as literature, geography and history, algebra, geometry and physics; secondly commercial subjects such as book-keeping, shorthand, commercial law, English and French; and thirdly technical subjects such as textile technology, colour chemistry and pattern composition. I especially enjoyed drawing engineering designs on my large drawing board, of which I was secretly very proud. To be top of the class was not as easy as it had been at Fleissen, but although weak in mathematics and algebra I was usually among the first three.

The college was divided into a weaving and a knitting section. Weaving was a larger, more highly thought of industry than knitting, and almost all professional men and civil servants who wanted their sons to go into textiles let them study weaving. We had in the knitting section only sons of knitwear manufacturers, although from the speed with which knitting technology and machinery developed it was apparent that the future belonged to us knitters, and we felt a little sorry for our colleagues of weft and warp faith who were so short-sighted.

After eight weeks of lectures we always had two weeks of intermediate examinations. My technique for securing good marks was simple. While some of the other students dreamed or surreptitiously read novels I concentrated on the lessons, even those I did not like, since I had to sit in class anyhow. As soon as the lectures were over I volunteered to be examined, hoping that I would still remember most of what we had been taught. It was also partly bluff, a show of self-confidence which impressed my professors. Once my beastly exams were over I relaxed for two weeks in complete safety while my less crafty friends burnt the midnight oil.

Walking to school one morning, I came upon a small crowd of agitated people—among them one or two of my fellow students—outside the Okresni Uřad, the Czech administrative headquarters. Curious to know what the commotion was about, I joined them, when suddenly shots were fired. Cordoning off the road, a row of legionaries were advancing, shooting at the cobblestone pavement ahead of them so that the bullets ricocheted. Quickly the crowd dispersed, and I ran to the college for shelter as fast as I could. Seconds later our chemistry professor, old Herr Pichler, was pushed through the door with rifle butts. The poor man broke down and cried. His beautiful alsatian, which always accompanied him to the college, had turned to defend its master and the legionaries had shot it.

What was the cause of the excitement? Back in 1779 Joseph II, the son of Empress Maria Theresia, had visited Asch, and to commemorate the occasion the citizens had erected a bronze statue of him. The fact that he was the Monarchy's most liberal and enlightened ruler meant nothing to the Czech legionaries: he was a Habsburg—reason enough to topple him over during the night. Outraged, the people of Asch re-erected the damaged monument and anchored it with heavy chains. The legionaries made another night attack on the statue, and when the wary but unarmed citizens hurriedly rose from their beds, trying to protect it, the hooligans lost their heads and fired at random into the crowd, killing three and wounding about a hundred others. In the morning there were pools of blood in the streets, and I felt sorry that behind my double windows I had slept soundly through all the shooting and only witnessed the breaking up of the protest demonstration afterwards.

We did not do much work that morning. Two legionaries watched opposite the college, and whenever we appeared at the windows, shaking our fists at them in the intervals between the lessons, they raised their rifles and we quickly ducked, but there was no further shooting.

Demolishing Austro-Hungarian monuments was only one of the many petty irritations which incensed the population. Czechoslovakia repeated all the mistakes in dealing with her minorities which the Monarchy had made, but the Czechs were more determined than the easy-going Austrians and made the pendulum of history swing further in the opposite direction. Flushed with their newly won independence, they effectively crushed any goodwill the German-speaking Bohemians bore the young republic. Bohemia was our homeland too. We had lived, worked and built here for twenty generations and helped to make the country what it was. And all these generations had spoken German.

Street names like 'Kaiser Strasse' had to be renamed Hauptstrasse (High Street) and the names of hotels and other buildings which offended Czech ears had to be changed. Three of the inns at Fleissen were in this category: the 'Stadt Wien' became Gasthaus Zrenner, the 'Kaiser von Osterreich' was renamed Zum Schwarzen Ross (Black Horse) and the 'Stadt Berlin' became the Rathaus Restaurant. Long before the war the Austrian authorities had erected in the Egerland a series of heavy cast iron road signs at level crossings which were, for some obscure reason, in German and in Czech. They said 'Achtung auf den Zug' and underneath 'Pozor no Vlak' ('Beware of the trains'). Nobody in the Egerland could read Czech! A team of workmen now had to cut the iron plates in half and remount them so that the Czech lettering was above the German.

The republic's very existence depended on her foreign trade, but no foreigner understood Czech. All export negotiations had to be carried on in an internationally known language. Since Czechoslovakia's intelligentsia and business community and almost half her population spoke or at least understood German, it should have been made the country's alternative 'national' language. But this was quite unacceptable to the Czechs. They preferred French, which hardly any of them understood. If one spoke to a Prague policeman in German he replied, 'Nerozumný německý' ('I do not understand German'). If one spoke to him in French he asked, 'Sprechen Sie deutsch?' The situation was ridiculous.

Of the languages taught at the college, English was compulsory while Czech and French were voluntary subjects. Many of the pupils took lessons in French but few availed themselves of the opportunity of learning Czech, and to my great relief Father said I need not bother with it. 'Look west, my boy, not east,' were his words. It was a matter of priorities. The long hours we worked left little time for subjects that were voluntary, and Czech was considered unimportant by commerce and industry. The textile college was, of course, a State school and our professors were civil servants, but the Ministry of Education could do little to enforce the teaching of Czech. There were not enough teachers in the country who knew the 'national' language. The shortage was especially severe when it came to men with higher degrees or specialised technical knowledge. Of the nine professors at our college only Professor Hauptmann could speak Czech. Similarly, there were no textbooks in Czech. It was therefore largely for practical considerations that most schools, especially those of higher education, carried on teaching in German during the early years of the republic.

On two afternoons each week we worked on the knitting machines with which the college was well equipped. Besides modern Terrots, Stibbes and other circulars, hand and power flats, Jacquards, Raschels and a large Schubert & Salzer fully fashioned machine, we had half a dozen wooden and iron stocking frames which were a hundred years old and the direct descendants of William Lee's original invention. They gave a good deal of trouble. We had to cast the needles into small blocks of lead, I believe four at a time, screw them into the frame and then align them in a horizontal row so that the sinkers would pass nicely between them. Once a frame was set up it was fun knitting shapes and patterns on it to match the designs we had drawn.

Professor Steffe, who taught textile technology, encouraged us to think how machines could be improved, and anyone who had an idea was called to the blackboard and asked to draw it and explain it to the class. I am afraid most of my inventions were more original than practical, and I remember one occasion when, tongue in cheek, I took up half an hour of the class's time drawing a most elaborate piece of equipment intended to ensure the production of perfect fabric. Whenever a stitch dropped, causing a ladder, a spring-loaded lever felt the hole, pulled a wire and released a weight which fell on the careless workman's head to alert him. The idea pleased my classmates but I had to stay behind for a couple of hours and wind twenty bobbins of thread to teach me to take lessons more seriously.

Most of my attempts at inventing, however, were earnest efforts, and it was my ambition to become as famous as James Watt, Marconi or Edison. I wanted to take out a patent for something. Inventors seemed to me the greatest benefactors of mankind. I wished I lived in America, the country of Henry Ford, which I imagined was inhabited by a nation of inventors whose aim was to make everything automatic. It was frustrating that Europeans could not appreciate the brilliance of my revolutionary ideas. They lived in the past and obviously knew no better, but my time would come.

Lessons on Saturday began at eight, as always, but ended at twelve. The afternoon was free. During the first two years at Asch I usually went home for the weekend. After a hurried lunch at Frau Ludwig's I set off on the two-hour walk to Fleissen. The road led down into the valley at Niederreuth and up the long hill to Oberreuth, where it crossed over into Saxony. One showed one's identity card to the Czechoslovak frontier guard and proceeded downhill to Bad Brambach, where one checked in with the German customs and then out again. Shortly before Fleissen the road re-entered Bohemian territory, and there the identity card was inspected once more by a Czechoslovak customs official. On Sunday afternoon I made the journey in reverse. In the summer when the sun shone and the road was dry, albeit dusty, the long walk was quite enjoyable and I often brought a schoolfriend home, but in the winter, with a foot or two of snow on the ground, it could be a very tiring trek. Sometimes Mother insisted that I went by train, a very roundabout journey via Franzensbad, where I had to change. It took at least three hours. At other times Father sent me back to Asch with the horses and sleigh. On one occasion the snowdrifts at Oberreuth were so deep that the horses could not get through, and I sent the sleigh back, battling on in the blizzard on foot. Mother was worried when the driver told her, especially since she could not telephone to find out whether I had arrived safely. There was no telephone service on Sundays.

One day I had a message from Father asking me to meet him at Bad Elster on Saturday afternoon. Bad Elster, a small spa across the border in Saxony, was a little over an hour's walk from Asch. It was summer, and Father sat in the Kurpark; the band played, and he was having coffee with a business friend who wore a smart brown suit and smoked a cigar. Although Father introduced him as Mynheer Schönberg from Amsterdam, I could not quite believe that this short, red-bearded man who had the accent and gestures of a Galician Jew was a Dutchman. As I listened to their conversation the picture unfolded.

It appeared that Schönberg was an old customer of ours whose business had been at Krakau before the war. When the Russian army advanced into Galicia in 1914 he had not waited to be evacuated to one of the refugee camps set up by the Austrian authorities but made his way across Germany and slipped over the border into neutral Holland. There was money to be made in Holland, and Schönberg had wasted no time. He was now better off financially than he had been at Krakau, and this was only the beginning. The Dutch were a wealthy nation, they could afford to buy vast quantities of knitted underwear, and he was going to provide it. He would build up a large, respectable business in Amsterdam. And as he said 'respectable' he tapped the table with his podgy fingers. But he had a problem. He was stateless. To come to Bad Elster he had crossed the Dutch border into Germany without a passport, which was risky enough. He was not prepared to do it too often, still less would he cross another frontier to go to Fleissen, for if he were to be picked up he might be sent back to Galicia, and that was now part of Poland. What he wanted was a dependable supplier whose merchandise would enable him to get established and with whom he could do business by correspondence. That was the reason why he approached his old friends Messrs Adolf

Pasold & Sohn. He was ready to place an order for 5,000 dozen men's and women's underwear then and there.

It was a fantastic quantity, and Father was very interested, but it seemed that he too had a problem. It would take many months to make all this merchandise. Meanwhile it had to be financed. And suppose, just suppose, that Mynheer Schönberg was sent back to Poland or met with some other accident, what then would we do with these garments which were manufactured especially for Dutch requirements? What guarantees, what references could Mynheer Schönberg offer?

'None, except my word,' replied the Galician, 'and 500 guilders on account.' He pulled a wad of grubby notes from his pocket and, before counting them on the table, turned to look at me with his shrewd, watery eyes. 'You must come to Holland, young man. We'll send you to the Dutch East Indies for a while,' and with these words he had me firmly on his side.

The deposit was quite inadequate to cover such a large transaction, but Father accepted it. 'We have known each other for a long time, and I trust you,' he said, and wrote a receipt on the back of the concert programme. He dated and signed it and gave it to Schönberg, who put it in his wallet. Then the details of the order were discussed, but I was too excited to pay much attention. For me the beeches, birches and chestnut trees of the park were turning into palms, Beethoven's seventh symphony into the war cries of dancing natives and the roar of tigers.

Father and I had cold supper on the terrace of the Wettiner Hof and then rode in our open carriage at a slow trot through the gently rising valley of the Rauner Grund towards Fleissen. It was a beautifully mild evening, the full moon lit the winding road and Father softly whistled one of the melodies the band had been playing in the park. I wish I had inherited his ear and hands for music. He needed to hear a tune only once and was able to play it on the piano or zither.

'Do you think Schönberg sells much in the Dutch East Indies?' I probed.

Father laughed. 'Of course not. He doesn't even know where they are. But he may well do big business in Holland, and we shall back him, although Grandfather won't like it much. He once took an export order and was swindled. That was before the war, but he's never forgotten it. Times have changed. We must export if we want to survive,' he said, and went on:

'For the past two years we've been restocking the empty shops of Czechoslovakia, but they will soon be filled. What then? Before the war we supplied the whole Monarchy, but the powers who won the war have in their ignorance broken up this prosperous trading area into six separate States, none of which can economically stand on its own feet. The new little Austria has been left with all the mountains and with Vienna, once the capital of an empire, a city which is much too large for her to feed. Hungary has more maize and pigs than she knows what to do with, and Czechoslovakia has inherited most of the Monarchy's industry, with no market for it. Meanwhile Roumania, Poland and Jugoslavia are building up industries of their own.

'Among them these countries now have five times as many politicians and civil servants as we had before. They produce nothing except more regulations, restrictions and customs barriers, and the petty nationalism and racial hatred are far worse than they ever were under Austrian rule. Still, Czechoslovakia has fared better in the share-out than any of the other successor States, and we must be grateful—but we need outlets for our products. Teplitz, Asch and Fleissen, the knitting centres of the old Monarchy, are all in the new republic. Our home market is much too small. We must forget the south-east and export to the wealthy nations in the west and the north. We must support Schönberg.'

Most of what Father said was familiar to me, but it had never been put so clearly, and I had not realised how much the future of our firm was affected by this state of affairs. Now I understood why he was so anxious to secure Schönberg's business, and I appreciated the significance of the large export order.

And it really was the beginning of our export trade. We made and delivered the 5,000 dozen as promised, the Dutch liked our underwear, and Schönberg paid up on the due date. He must have done well out of the deal, for his next order was for 10,000 dozen. Somehow he managed to solve his passport problem and now became a regular visitor to Fleissen. Of course he did not buy only from us. Lehrmann and Braun offered him lower prices to break into the business, and some of his orders went to them. But he too soon had competitors. It was not long before other Dutch traders became aware of his growing turnover. They found out where the goods came from, visited Fleissen and Asch, and the business became highly competitive at both ends.

Listening to Father talking about business or meeting one of our customers always made me realise that the purpose of going to school was to prepare myself for the work I would have to do when I joined Adolf Pasold & Sohn. For a few days I would bear this in mind when I listened to the lectures, and concentrate on mathematics, book-keeping and colour chemistry, but then the college atmosphere and schoolboy topics won again, and I studied not because I thought what I learned would be useful to me later but in order to pass my exams with a minimum of effort.

Some of my more mature classmates smoked, drank, pawned their watches and went out with girls. I knew that I was too green to compete with them, nor was I attracted by their way of life. I preferred to mix with the less sophisticated boys and chose my friends from among them, but this did not altogether protect me from getting into mischief.

Frau Ludwig's rooms were on the first floor of a two-hundred-year-old house in the centre of Asch. It had a heavy front door made of oak and a huge key that weighed a quarter of a pound. I knew where the spare key was kept, and as my bedroom opened on to the corridor I could provide access for my pals without arousing the good widow's suspicion. I also had a *Kachelofen*, one of those cosy stoves built of glazed tiles which one finds in most old houses in central Europe. Since coal was still scarce, Father supplied me with a special ration. My den was therefore comfortably warm, even on the coldest winter night, and I organised gaming parties. We played cards for increasing stakes until one night I lost 150 Czech kronen, half a year's pocket money. It took almost that long to pay off the debt, and I have never again played for money.

About a year after our meeting with Schönberg two other buyers from Holland appeared, the hostile brothers Jessaia and Emanuel Lissauer. They smoked large cigars and did their best to spoil each other's business. Since both bought substantial quantities, and every manufacturer liked to sit on two stools, we supplied both. Whenever we accepted an order from one, the other threatened to take his custom elsewhere, but as both did business with all the larger manufacturers and tried to intimidate each of them in turn the effect was more comical than serious.

Then came buyers from England. Quite possibly it was Lehrmann who made the first sale to London, and this time Father cut in by quoting keener prices. There were three of them, the dynamic Mr Stern, the bald-headed and excitable Mr Israel, and the impassive Mr Singer, who was so impartial that he refused to accept even a luncheon invitation from a supplier and ate at the inn at a table by himself. Before long most of the knitters of Fleissen and Asch shipped an ever-growing proportion of their output to Britain.

If Fleissen doubled in size during the next decade it was due to the business these three *Engländer* brought to the village. We owed our prosperity largely to them. They were competitors, and avoided meeting on their business journeys, but they never said an unfriendly word about each other, which was in marked contrast to the tirades our other customers indulged in. All three were in their fifties, German by origin, and had as young men emigrated to England, worked hard and established successful importing houses. I did not know their histories at the time, but from what I heard about the size of their transactions, which were many times bigger than Schönberg's, the very correct manner in which they dealt with manufacturers, the promptness with which they settled their accounts and the respect and even awe in which they were held by everyone, I concluded that they were great men indeed and that the major part of Britain's textile trade went through their hands. Fleissen was in a state of excitement whenever one of them arrived.

By far the most impressive and popular of these buyers was Alfred Stern. He wrote out contracts for enormous quantities. 'How large is your production?' used to be his opening question to prospective suppliers, and within the hour he would put down orders which would keep a factory going for six months on double shifts.

'Mr Stern has arrived,' Father would announce. 'I understand he is at present negotiating with Lehrmann,' and his voice would quiver a little.

'He has ordered 30,000 dozen and is now on his way to Friedl,' Grandmother would correct him. She had a rapid news service all of her own and was able to provide a running commentary on the movement of buyers in the village.

'Stern is here,' said the workers in the factories to each other, aware that their jobs depended on his orders. The children on their way to school shouted, 'We've seen Mr Stern,' half expecting to be given the day off to celebrate the important event. 'Stern has come,' chirped the sparrows from the roof-tops. They were the only ones who could afford to whistle.

Among all the other things Mr Stern could do well he excelled at packing parcels, a skill no doubt acquired in his youth. On his factory visits he would challenge the packers to compete with him. He took off his jacket and in a given time packed more and tidier parcels than any of them, much to everyone's amazement and admiration. Everyone doffed his hat to him when he walked through the village, and all the manufacturers felt highly honoured if sometimes he joined them for a meal or a game of cards at the inn.

The envious, old established but less mass production-minded factory owners of Asch, who secured only his smaller orders, jokingly referred to the great man as 'Herrgott von Fleissen'. An exaggeration, but he certainly deserved to be described as the patron saint of Czechoslovakia's knitting industry. In my boyish fancy I thought he must be as well known and respected in London as in Fleissen, and imagined that he was invited to state banquets, lunched with the lord mayor and frequently conferred with the Prime Minister. It may well have been the glamour surrounding this most unusual man that kindled the desire in me to go to England. I concentrated on learning English, and took a special interest in history and geography lectures on Britain and her empire.

Orders for ten, twenty and sometimes thirty thousand dozen of a single, simple type of garment were the dream of any manufacturer. Endeavouring to satisfy the demands of a handful of large export customers, we lost interest in the multifarious requirements of two thousand little drapers and small wholesalers in the home market whose business we once used to covet. There was not the time any more to barter with them over their individually tiny and complicated orders. We cut down on the production of vests, pants, combinations, petticoats, cardigans and the variety of other garments with trimmings, buttons and tapes in order to concentrate on the mass production of elasticated knickers. And most of our competitors did the same. The 1920s were a period of drastic change for Fleissen's knitting industry. The village became one of Czechoslovakia's largest exporters and earners of foreign currency, and even if British Ministers had never heard of Alfred Stern, Dr Eduard Beneš certainly had.

I was, of course, away at the textile college at that time. Having overcome my homesickness and made some friends, I no longer came home every weekend, but when we met, Father usually related what he thought would interest me about the business. Afterwards Grandmother filled in the tit-bits and gave me colourful descriptions of the personalities who were involved. During the summer holidays, which lasted two whole months, I always spent some time in the factory, and so I kept in touch.

We sold over 90 per cent of our output abroad, mostly to England and Holland, but not everyone was happy. Our old customers throughout Bohemia, Moravia, Slovakia and Ruthenia found it increasingly difficult to place their orders and were very cross with us. Grandfather was on their side. Exports were all very well, he said, but some day something would go wrong and we would need the home market again. Meanwhile we would have lost the connections and goodwill which took several generations to build. There was a good deal of disagreement between him and Father over this issue, but Father usually won.

It may seem strange that we apparently made no attempt to sell to France, with whom Czechoslovakia had such close ties of political friendship, or to Germany, which was at our doorstep. Both countries had large enough knitting industries of their own and safeguarded their home markets by high customs barriers. The fact that Czechoslovakia was France's greatest admirer and staunchest ally did not induce Paris to relax her traditionally protectionist policies. And the Germans had not bought our textiles when Bohemia was still part of the Austro–Hungarian Monarchy, so why should they buy them now? They imported large quantities of raw materials from Czechoslovakia— for instance, coal, timber and china clay—but were reluctant to buy industrial products such as knitted goods from us *Böhmaken*, as they called us somewhat unflatteringly. Besides, Germany was on the road to bankruptcy.

The four years I spent at the textile college were happy ones, and I was sorry when the time came for the final examinations in the spring of 1924.

As always, I volunteered to get the series of ordeals over as quickly as possible. We were not told the results for some time, but once the die was cast there was no more I could do, and while my friends continued to worry and study and delay their examinations to the very last day I spent the remaining weeks in a happy state of serenity. Some years earlier I had taken up photography as a hobby, and it now became my ambition to photograph all our professors in their most characteristic attitudes and compile an album of them, to give to the school as a parting present. Without being caught, I 'shot' one after the other at blackboard or desk. Today, with high-speed film and a camera that fits into a pocket, it would be child's play, but with my large 1920 plate camera it was not easy. Only the Head escaped me. In the end I plucked up courage, knocked on his study door, confessed my secret ambition and begged him to pose for me. He was delighted, and I got my picture. The album created much hilarity as it went from hand to hand at the official farewell party.

My closest friends were Ernst Eckert from Marienbad, a good-looking lad with blue eyes and fair hair, Robert Übler, son of a yarn agent at Asch, who had wavy brown hair and was very artistic, Ladislaus Turan, the volatile Hungarian Jew who was brilliant at mathematics and languages but could not get interested in machines, and Kurt Linke, son of a fabric glove manufac-turer, who was very self-conscious because he was the smallest boy in the school. We all passed with flying colours, and, to celebrate, arranged a private party to which we invited our favourite tutor, Professor Hauptmann, who taught languages. Having been well treated by the British as a prioner of war, he was an anglophile. I admired him. The most understanding and kindest of men, a gentleman in the truest meaning of the word, he greatly influenced my outlook, and during four years as his pupil I caught his enthusiasm for every-thing Anglo-Saxon.

He was proud of us, he said, and confident that we would prove a credit to the school, that we would help to make the world a better place, and he wished he could meet us again in twenty years' time when each of us had made his mark in industry. We had tears in our eyes when he shook hands with us and wished us well. But our emotion did not last long; we were young, and the future beckoned.

It is a blessing that people do not know what fate has in store for them. In May 1945, twenty years and eleven months later, I passed through Asch in the uniform of a British lieutenant colonel, surrounded by the misery that was the aftermath of the second world war. Czechoslovakia had only just been 'liberated', and in the prevailing chaos I failed to find out what had happened to my friends. Enquiries a year later revealed that Ernst and Robert had been called up and killed fighting for the Germans, Lazie had disappeared in a German concentration camp and Kurt was still a prisoner of war, while his family was being driven from their home and factory. Professor Hauptmann, I was told, had been beaten to death by the looting, raping and murdering mob that went under the proud description of 'freedom fighters', for some offence he had not committed. One of the many thousands of cases of mistaken identity.

6

THE GREAT INFLATION
ACROSS THE BORDER
1919–24

TO WATCH THE collapse of the German mark in the early 1920s was an experience I have not been able to forget to this day. I have ever since looked warily beyond the coloured slips of paper called banknotes, at the governments who issue them and treated all money with suspicion. Countries are governed by politicians. How many politicians have the economic common sense we expect from a businessman or banker? Governments are so wasteful that they can stay in business only by continually defaulting, by devaluing their currencies and thereby cheating their citizens, not necessarily by decree but by promoting or at least permitting creeping inflation. The fact that long periods of inflation are interrupted by short spells of deflation during which the purchasing power of money sometimes actually rises may temporarily obscure this sad truth but does not alter it. We are not far wrong if we assume that in 'normal' times and in 'respectable' countries money loses on average as much as 5 per cent of its value per annum. In other words, a pound note issued one year is worth only 95*p* the next. Inflation is a form of additional taxation imposed by the government on the people, especially on the savers, but only a few of us recognise it as such. We have learned to live with it, and put up with it as long as the decline is not too steep.

To see how inflation got out of control in Germany was a frightening spectacle. Sitting just across the border, in the front stalls, as it were, we followed the disastrous course of events with fascination and felt sorry for the victims. Having relations there made it seem all the worse. Uncle Richard Stübiger had emigrated from Fleissen to Saxony in the good old days before the war and become a naturalised German subject. His business and home were now in Brambach. Fortunately he was only forty, young and adaptable enough to weather the storm, but it was a hard struggle.

Germany was exhausted and utterly broken by the 1914–18 war and almost five years of blockade. There was no food and no real money, industry had no raw materials, millions of hungry unemployed clamoured for bread and for work. The country was unable to raise the enormous sum of £6,600 millions reparations demanded by the victorious allies. Payment had to be made in gold or foreign currencies, and this inevitably led to the complete collapse of the mark. When the French failed to squeeze blood out of a stone they occupied the Ruhr, Germany's most highly industrialised area, bringing coal production virtually to a standstill and thereby further aggravating the defeated enemy's economic difficulties.

No fewer than thirty paper mills worked day and night for 1,700 printing presses churning out mountains of million- and billion-mark notes the value of which evaporated as soon as they were issued. Salaries and wages doubled and quadrupled every week, prices spiralled and any money not spent today was practically worthless tomorrow. Yet government and law courts insisted that 'mark equalled mark'. It was not only people who had retired on their life's savings, those with fixed incomes and pensioners who lost their all, but also the landlords who could not put up rents, the businessmen who could not replace stocks quickly enough, the farmers who sold their crops for cash; in fact most of the middle class population was in this deplorable state. Savings of 50,000 marks which had represented a considerable fortune before the war and promised their owner and his dependants comfort and security for life now hardly bought a box of matches. Many people, especially the lone and the elderly, starved to death or committed suicide.

From July 1914 to November 1918 the international value of the mark had fallen by 50 per cent, and in January 1919 the American dollar was worth

Value of $1 in marks, 1919–23

1919	January	..	..	..	.. 8
1920	January	..	..	..	.. 50
1921	January	..	..	..	.. 65
1922	January	..	..	..	.. 200
	August	..	..	..	.. 650
1923	January	..	..	..	7,260
	February	..	..	..	41,000
	June	..	..	..	74,750
	July	..	..	..	160,000
	August	..	..	..	1,100,000
	September	..	..	..	9,700,000
	1 October	..	..		242,000,000
	10 October	..	..		2,975,000,000
	19 October	..	..		12,000,000,000
	31 October	..	..		72,500,000,000
	1 November	..	..		130,000,000,000
	10 November	..	..		630,000,000,000
	20 November	..	..		4,200,000,000,000

eight marks. This was, however, only the beginning of the disastrous erosion of the purchasing power of German money. The final collapse started with the military occupation of the Ruhr by the French on 11 January 1923, as the accompanying table shows.

This fantastic situation was exploited by German and foreign currency operators. Dutch, Swiss and Scandinavian businessmen, Czechoslovak industrialists and East European Jews were quick to realise the exceptional opportunities. Speculating young bank clerks became overnight steel barons and owners of large shipping companies, and whole streets of houses changed hands for ridiculously small sums of dollars, guilders, sterling or Czech kronen. Only amateurs actually changed their foreign currency into marks. The more astute operator merely deposited his dollars with a bank as security against which he borrowed marks. Since the value of his deposit in terms of marks doubled almost every few hours, his liability rapidly wiped itself out and he could go on borrowing ever larger amounts *ad infinitum*. He used the same technique in reverse to purchase merchandise, shares, real estate or family heirlooms. An apparently generous offer in marks tempted the starving owner to part with his property, but by the time the purchase price was paid, sometimes weeks later because legal formalities had to be completed, inflation had reduced it to a pittance. And the situation in Austria was not very different from that in Germany.

Foreigners were super-beings from another planet who ate caviar, smoked real cigars, had the prettiest girls, lived in luxury hotels and made profits out of everything they touched. Speculators in foreign currencies raked in fantastic gains. Out of the successful opportunists emerged a class of money-squandering newly-rich who filled the nightclubs, drank champagne and wore fur coats. Their wealth appeared to be inexhaustible, but in fact most of these fortunes were dissipated by their reckless owners as quickly as they had been made.

Living so near the border, my friends and I made excursions into Germany and indulged in modest buying sprees. Having kronen in our pockets made everything on sale there incredibly cheap. For my weekly pocket money of five kronen, the price of a small slab of chocolate at Asch, I bought in Germany a dynamo set, two tyres and a pump for my bicycle. One had to be careful, of course, not be be caught by the Czechoslovak frontier guards on the way home. Most of them were rough legionaries who did not hesitate to use their rifles.

The collapse of Germany's and Austria's currencies was one of the outstanding phenomena of the early 1920s, and one would have thought that Professor Güttler at the textile college, whom we nicknamed Moses because of his beard and biblical appearance and who was our lecturer on financial subjects, would have seized upon it to explain the causes and effects of inflation to us. He could hardly have found a better example or a more interested audience, but he let the opportunity go by unused. Perhaps he would have needed a Mount Sinai from which to contemplate the scene. As happens so often, contemporaries can be too close to historical events to be able to assess them. Our textbooks described monetary systems based on the gold standard, and said nothing about inflation. We had to learn from experience, and several episodes stand out vividly in my memory.

In August 1922 I spent a holiday in the north of Germany with my parents and my sister. Father motored us in the six-cylinder Steyer to Warnemünde, a small port and seaside resort. During the day we were on the beach or looked at the ships in the harbour, in the evening Father and I sat in a local tavern listening and talking to fishermen, sailors and sea captains. It was a strange and fascinating world for us landlubbers. We became friendly with the owner of a small fleet of tramp steamers which plied between Rostock and other Baltic ports. When he discovered that we were foreigners he immediately took us for millionaires and offered us his fleet. The price he asked, converted into Czech kronen, was so modest that Father could have paid the whole sum then and there out of the reserve he had brought with him on the holiday. We looked over one of the boats next morning and were impressed with its size. I was excited. A fleet of cargo ships trading between foreign countries —it sounded most romantic and I was disappointed when Father shook his head. 'Cobbler, stick to your last,' he said.

We were lucky to get out of the next episode with no more than a scare. Invited by an estate agent, Father and I went to Leipzig to view a large corner building, a cafe and office block called Glas Palast. The owners were two Polish Jews who had acquired it not long before and wanted to sell again at a reasonable profit for Czech kronen. We agreed on the price, lawyers and notary public confirmed that everything was in order, Father deposited the money in the joint names of the owners and himself and then waited for completion of the purchase. Leipzig was the centre of Germany's fur trade. I dreamed of an office in the Glass Palace and of travelling to Canada and Alaska to buy pelts. Two months went by, but the vendors never completed the contract. It transpired that they had sold the building to six different buyers, received from each of them the deposit of the purchase price in foreign currency and pledged all these deposits as security for overdrafts with which they financed more profitable speculations. Father had to engage another lawyer to get his money back.

Some people made currency-smuggling their business, which was dangerous; others coined easy money by dealing quite legally in foreign exchange.

I heard a good deal about these financial operations and caught the speculation fever. There were various techniques which all seemed to be based on selling marks forward. This was too involved for me. I was a bull, I wanted to buy something that rose in value, not sell something that fell and which I had not even got. Besides, German marks were boring, there were more romantic currencies about, such as dollars, pounds, francs or guilders, which had the solid ring of wealth about them. If the value of the mark declined because Germany had lost the war, I reasoned in my innocence, then surely the value of England's currency must rise because she had won it. So I scraped together my fortune, bought a pound note for 320 kronen and patiently waited for it to rise in value. But I waited in vain. After holding it for two years I eventually got out at 165 kronen. It was not a very encouraging transaction for a budding financier when mere office boys quadrupled their capital in a matter of weeks.

During the summer holidays in 1923 I spent a month at Schubert & Salzer's, the famous knitting machine engineers at Chemnitz. Somewhat to my surprise, Father put me up at a small commercial hotel, not at all the type of establishment he usually chose. Noticing my disappointment, he said, 'I want you to see how travelling salesmen live. You'll have to deal with them all your life.' That very evening in the dining room a young man from Bolton spoke to me. He was trying to sell fine-count cotton yarn, 120s and finer, to the Saxon fabric glove industry, and I felt immensely gratified that the English I had learned at school enabled me to carry on a halting conversation with him. It was the first time I had talked to a real Englishman, and after this memorable experience nothing would have induced me to change my modest hotel.

Father had arranged with Schubert & Salzer that I would work in the section where the circular machines were assembled and tested before being dispatched to customers. My instructor was a young mechanic who, as far as I could judge, was a good engineer but lacked the time and talent to explain what he did and why. To keep me busy and prevent me from interrupting him with too many questions he let me clean the machines before they were covered in grease to prevent them getting rusty in the heavy wooden cases in which some of them travelled half way round the world. I am afraid I did not learn much about the finer points of adjusting knitting machines, but on Saturdays my instructor remembered that I had come to Chemnitz to learn, and so he took me to the cycle track and took great pains to make me understand the finer points of cycle racing.

I was much more interested in motor-cycles than in pushbikes, and longingly studied a shaft-driven, single-cylinder K-G machine in a shop window I passed every day to and from work. When I first saw this dream machine its price was way above my reach, but although the dealer marked it up every day, trying to keep pace with the rapidly falling value of German money, converted into my Czech kronen it became daily cheaper, and I became more and more excited. But before it dropped to the level of my pocket the motor-bike was sold.

Later Father bought me a motor-cycle, a red Ardie with a two-stroke engine, two gears and a V belt drive. I was very, very proud of it, although it was underpowered and the V belt slipped in wet weather or when I had to change down on a hill. I used it to travel between Asch and Fleissen at weekends, always taking the long road via Franzensbad. The direct route through Germany involved documentation at all those customs posts, which was very tiresome. Besides, my Ardie refused to climb the steep road to Oberreuth and carry me as well. I had to jump off and run by its side most of the time. Had my schoolmates found out, my reputation as 'that daring motor-cyclist on his powerful machine' would have been lost at once.

Our business grew and we had to increase capacity. Since our knitting machines came from Germany, perhaps we could now buy some at bargain prices. Five well known firms made suitable types of spring-needle circulars, Terrot, Haaga, Fouquet & Frauz, Schubert & Salzer and Roscher. All needed work and wanted our orders, but to build a battery of machines took several months, and with the value of money falling every day they were unable to quote firm prices in marks. By demanding payment in dollars or gold they shifted the currency risk to the buyer and took away his chance of profiting through the inflation. We could have afforded to buy two or three machines on such a basis, but we needed twenty. Father therefore tried an advertisement for second-hand machines in a German textile journal. In response to it a man named Bierlich came to visit us. I was home from school for the Whitsun holidays and listened to his discussion with Father.

At first I disliked the bald-headed, talkative little man who spoke with the Saxon accent that sounds so unpleasant to Bohemian and Austrian ears, but as he told his story I began to feel sorry for him, and in the end I quite took to him. He had been foreman in a knitting mill at Chemnitz before the war, earning good money and, wanting to be his own master, had invested his savings in two Terrot circulars on which he knitted fleecy fabric for various manufacturers out of the yarns they supplied to him. But now trade was bad. The firms for whom he had worked were not able to keep their own factories going. He wanted to sell his machines to buy food for his family. The price he asked seemed reasonable. I could see that Father also felt sorry for him. 'We'll come to Apolda to have a look at your Terrots,' he said, 'and if they are as good as you say, we'll buy them.'

A few days later, at five in the morning, Father, Johann Feiler and I, wrapped in our leather coats, sat in the open Steyer at the German frontier waiting for the barrier to be raised, and, after having our passports and the carnet stamped, drove into the rising dawn. It was the first trip of many. Perhaps this is why I remember it so well. There was a nip in the air; our headlights lit up the deserted road as we sped through Brambach towards Adorf and Ölsnitz. Broad daylight now; haze lay over the meadows, dew glistened on the grass and trees, and occasionally we passed a farm cart. By the time the towns came to life we were driving through the woods and over the hills of Thuringia. In Jena we stopped for breakfast, and at 9 a.m. we rang Mr Bierlich's bell.

His machines seemed to be in good condition. Carefully Johann Feiler unscrewed one sinker wheel after another, checked each bearing, looked for damage to the brass rings and for hammer marks on the cover plates. 'All perfect,' he whispered. While Feiler continued with his examination Father and I sat with Bierlich in the living room adjoining the workshop and closed the deal. 'What will you live on?' Father asked, 'when your machines are gone and you have eaten up the proceeds?' The little man shrugged his shoulders. Something would turn up, he hoped; perhaps he could become a salesman. Did he know of any other knitters who wanted to sell their machines? asked Father. Bierlich thought there were quite a number in the villages and small towns of Thuringia and Saxony. They all needed money, and what was the use of hanging on to their machines? There was no work for them. German manufacturers could no longer compete with those of Czechoslovakia in cheap, fleece-lined goods.

'You can become our buying agent,' said Father. 'We want up to twenty machines. Find good ones for us and we'll pay you 10 per cent on every purchase.'

Bierlich grasped his hand. 'I knew it,' he exclaimed. 'A real Saxon always falls on his feet!'

But I felt suddenly unhappy. I had seen Bierlich's wife and children and his old mother. No doubt the other knitters whose machines we were going to buy also had families to feed. In the car on the way home I questioned Father whether he thought we did right to take advantage of their misfortune. 'I am glad you feel like this,' he replied, 'but they cannot eat their machines, and if we don't buy them, Lehrmann or Braun or some manufacturer in Poland will. The German people are paying the penalty for losing the war—and remember, we Austrians lost it too. But for the grace of God and the cunning of the Czech politicians we might share the fate of those poor knitters. Think of it next time you grumble about the Czechoslovak republic.'

It was a sobering thought. While conditions across the frontier went from bad to worse, industry in Czechoslovakia showed signs of prosperity. As a matter of fact there were remarkably few grumblers on our side of the border at that time. Although Czech- and German-speaking Bohemians did not love each other any more than they had done in the past, all were quite happy to share Czechoslovak citizenship and currency.

Father was right. As soon as the news leaked out that we were importing used machines from Germany other manufacturers set forth to do the same. The rapid expansion of Czechoslovakia's knitting industry in the 1920s was carried out with second-hand machinery from neighbouring Saxony and Thuringia. Germany's loss was our gain.

Bierlich proved a jewel. We bought through him not twenty but forty circulars which doubled the capacity of our knitting department. We could not have afforded new machines, and the second-hand ones we bought were better than new. Most of them were built between 1910 and 1914 from good pre-war materials. The post-war machines were made of iron, aluminium and other *ersatz* instead of good brass. Design had not changed; the life of a well maintained spring-needle circular was thirty years and more. We never bought a single machine without thoroughly inspecting it. Having a car made it easy to cover the territory from Sonneberg in the west to Chemnitz in the east. In the summer these trips were enjoyable outings, and the hazards of winter rarely stopped us. With the help of chains and shovels we ploughed our way through the snowdrifts of the Erzgebirge. Our less enterprising competitors went by train and usually took three days for a cross-country journey which we did in one. And, being first, we picked the best machines.

The frightening disintegration of Germany's economy and the threat of Communism at last brought the politicians to their senses. In December 1923 Dr Schacht became president of the Reichsbank. Montagu Norman, the Governor of the Bank of England, had faith in him, and with the aid of British and Dutch credits the mark was stabilised. The miracle was achieved, but Germany had suffered more lasting material and moral damage through the ordeal of inflation than through the war. It helped to prepare the ground for Hitler's later rise to power.

Germany took years to recover from the effects of the inflation, and the small knitters continued to sell machines long after the stabilisation of the currency. A 24 gauge 48 in. diameter circular with eight feedwheels fetched about 2,500 marks. Few of these knitters were as lucky as Bierlich. Most of them became factory workers again, and I hope that in one way or another they all managed to keep their families alive. Father always paid in Czech banknotes, and never failed to advise the recipients to hold on to them as long as possible and not to exchange them for marks. Strange as it may seem to us today, there were apparently no currency restrictions. Even at the height of the inflation one took unlimited amounts of money in notes or cheques in any currency from one country to another.

The acquisition of so much second-hand plant had the result that Bohemian knitwear factories were filled with circulars of every gauge and diameter. Of course we would have preferred to buy ᴀew machines once the German inflation was over and makers could again obtain brass and good steel. We actually bought one every year or two, but for the price of one new circular we could get three second-hand ones which together produced twice as much as the one new machine. They varied in diameter and gauge, make and condition, and were much more troublesome to operate, but who could afford to buy the kind of plant he would have liked?

Today, with the lessening of manual skill, the continual shortening of training periods and the frequency with which employees change their jobs, ease of operation is an important factor when selecting a battery of machines, but in the 1920s it was the capital cost that usually decided the issue. If carefully tended, old machines made just as good fabric as new ones. Man had brains to think, hands to work with, but little money to buy expensive, foolproof, automatic plant. In far-away, wealthy America, perhaps, but not in poor Czechoslovakia.

Fleissen knew that opportunity rarely knocks twice, and when it suddenly came to the village the local manufacturers grasped it with both hands. They were not to be defeated by lack of capital. Production had to be doubled and quadrupled overnight. Since they neither had the money to order rows of new machines nor could wait to have them built, they ventured every available krone on the second-hand knitting plant that Germany's economic collapse threw on the market. Had they not done so, Fleissen could never have become one of the world's largest suppliers of fleecy knickers.

7

A YEAR
IN ENGLAND
1924-25

MANY BOHEMIAN INDUSTRIALISTS sent their sons to England and their
daughters to Switzerland to finish their education, and my parents followed
this pattern. I was eighteen, had passed my final examination at the textile
college and was looking forward to going to London, when I met a girl, a pretty
brunette who was a year younger than I. She was fascinated by my motor-
cycle and then by the adventures she imagined I was likely to meet in London.

My motor-cycle was not powerful enough to carry two, so we went on
bicycle rides together. She was a little dare-devil with laughing brown eyes,
but since I was convinced that all pretty girls were good girls I felt it was my
duty to protect her. Steadfastly I refused to take advantage of a series of
tempting situations. More than once the tyres of her bicycle mysteriously
lost pressure on lonely paths through the woods, and when she missed her last
train I made her cycle to Asch, where I delivered her safely at her front door
shortly after midnight. The border was closed by then and I had to cycle
back to Fleissen the long way, arriving home on Sunday morning at 4 a.m.

It never occurred to me that she contrived these little accidents on purpose.
I thought the nocturnal ride through the forest had strengthened her confidence in me and cemented our friendship, and was surprised and disappointed when she dropped me for a middle-aged man with a more powerful
motor-bike and a moustache. He was at least twenty-four! Girls were quite
unpredictable, it seemed.

For the previous four years I had kept diaries, mainly of the amusing incidents that happened at school and the trips we took during the holidays. I
filled the last few pages, describing my tantalising outings with Else, then
made a parcel of the four books, tied it securely with string and sealed it with
red sealing wax. Aunt Hulda had given me a little seal with the initials EWP
for my birthday. I used it with such determination that it broke. Then I hid
the parcel away, resolving not to open it until I was fifty and then read the
diaries to my grandchildren. The broken seal I decided to throw into the
middle of the English Channel.

Since I was to stay in England for a whole year, I had special clothes made by a tailor at Franzensbad who was an international expert on men's fashions. I remember a 'plus-fours' suit of genuine English material with large grey and black checks, probably designed and woven in Yorkshire specifically for export. The suit was too loud and conspicuous to be worn in Bohemia, the tailor agreed, but it was just the thing for England, as I could see from his journals.

And so the day came when I said farewell to Mother and the family, to our relatives and friends, and set off with Father and Uncle Wilhelm for London. Neither of them had been to England before. It was 1924, the year of the British Empire Exhibition, and we joined a small conducted tour of about a dozen businessmen, starting from Leipzig. The prospectus stated that the tour's three objectives were to show us modern and traditional London, the great exhibition, and the City, which was the world's commercial and financial centre. A Mr Balque who looked like Mr Punch led the party.

The train journey across Germany and Holland in a sleeper and the Channel crossing on a still, sunny day were exciting but much as expected. It was not until we reached Harwich that the surprises began. I had learned at school about England's 'narrow gauge' railways, but had not imagined trains with such miniature coaches. Nor had I ever seen so many knives, forks and spoons as were laid out on the little tables in the brightly lit dining car. They tinkled like bells as we sped towards London through endless green meadows with cows grazing in them. All this grass was a most unfamiliar sight. Back home only the damp land in the valleys, along the banks of streams and rivers, was left as meadow; all dry land between the forests was ploughed and planted with corn, potatoes or beet, and the cattle were mostly in stables.

Liverpool Street station came as a disappointment. It was much smaller than the station at Leipzig, and the taxis which took us to our hotel looked outright ridiculous. They were so old-fashioned that they reminded me of Father's old Dixi. He only laughed, but I felt let down. England was the land of my dreams: I wanted everything here to be the most splendid, efficient and best. The Imperial Hotel at Russell Square, although not as modern as I had expected, appealed to me. Its semi-dark lounge had tall marble pillars and something that gave it a mysterious, almost Eastern atmosphere. The tables in the dining room were again laden with silver cutlery, and breakfast, with grapefruit, porridge, bacon and eggs, marmalade and tea made us realise what a rich country Britain was and how well people lived here. The excellent impression was only spoilt a little by the more than ordinary waiters who had dirty fingernails and, I felt, did not treat us with the reverence due to distinguished visitors from a foreign country. But I would not hear of it when Father remarked that the service in the hotels at Karlsbad and Marienbad was better and the plates were cleaner.

The following days were packed with new impressions. Mr Balque took us down Southampton Row and Kingsway to the Law Courts, Fleet Street, St Paul's, the Strand, Trafalgar Square, Whitehall and the Embankment. Some of the way we walked, stopping here and there and entering buildings of special interest. Now and again we took a bus, and from its open top viewed the swirl of traffic around us, which was quite breathtaking. At street crossings it was directed by policemen. How we admired these imperturbable supermen in their tall helmets and dark blue uniforms who with quiet efficiency controlled the pandemonium of omnibuses, vans, cars and motorcycles, horse-drawn vehicles of all kinds and pedal cycles. And we admired the skill of the drivers, who were continually dicing with death. To experience this fantastic traffic was alone worth a visit to England.

We were impressed by the Houses of Parliament but less by Buckingham Palace, which failed to compare with the royal palace in Vienna or the Schloss at Schönbrunn. We walked in Hyde Park and were amazed to see men riding horses on an ordinary weekday afternoon when surely they should be working at their desks. We listened for a while to the orators at Speakers' Corner without understanding what they said, visited Selfridge's and from there took another bus along Oxford Street. After cocktails at the Cafe Royal we had dinner at the Trocadero and then looked at the lights of Piccadilly Circus and Leicester Square and at the painted ladies. The more enterprising members of our party went to a nightclub, while the rest of us strolled back to Russell Square through the warm summer evening. Uncle Wilhelm used the opportunity to talk to me about the temptations and wickedness of big cities and, as a warning, told me what happened to him when he was a young man and first went to Prague to study at the university. He worried unnecessarily. I was terrified of painted ladies.

The Empire Exhibition was at Wembley, and we went there by Underground train. We had all heard of London's Underground and looked forward to travelling on it, but we had not expected anything so fantastic. To sink down deep into the earth in a huge lift and see the station below, with its curved walls, was an experience in itself. We heard the roar of a distant train grow louder and die away again. And then our own long streamlined train came thundering out of the yawning darkness of the tunnel. It was as round as the tunnel itself. As if by magic a number of doors all opened at once, in a matter of seconds the well lighted coaches swallowed the waiting passengers, the doors shut behind us, the train accelerated and we hurtled through the darkness at a speed that was impossible to guess. The station at Holborn where we had to change almost took our breath away. There were several railway lines crossing each other at different levels, and the many passages, stairs and platforms made our party stick closely together for fear of becoming separated and getting lost in this subterranean world, the wonders of which almost exceeded those on the surface above us—*how* high above us we did not know. We could hardly believe the map that showed the vast extent of this system of underground trains and marvelled at the skill of the engineers who built it and the courage of the men who financed the scheme. 'What people, what a city!' Father said admiringly, and I could have embraced him.

The exhibition overwhelmed me. I remember it vividly, and will try to describe the colourful, bustling spectacle I saw, but the lasting impact it had on me cannot be conveyed in words. The nostalgic picture of this mightiest of all empires as displayed at Wembley is so deeply engraved in my subconscious that its influence still lingers after all the years that have since passed.

The two enormous Palaces of Engineering and Industry dwarfed all the factories of Fleissen put together. It seemed hardly possible that they were built and equipped only for a temporary exhibition. The cost must have been fabulous. There was the biggest sheet of plate glass in the world. It was so flawless that had it not been for its huge ebony frame I would not have known it was there. Engines of every kind, steam and electric, a 16 in. gun weighing more than a hundred tons capable of throwing a giant projectile over twenty miles, and on the other hand heavy armour plate bearing the marks of gunfire, which fascinated the layman. Locomotives of every type could be boarded. I admired the foolproof signalling board of the Metropolitan Railway, and a ball four times the size of a football which floated on the vertical air stream of an electric fan. There were models of ships and of the ports of London, Bristol and Liverpool and of the Manchester Ship Canal. Father marvelled at a fully automatic powerhouse, and Uncle Wilhelm tried to calculate the electricity consumption of a huge electromagnet which picked up two tons of scrap iron at a time. One could see the whole process of biscuit manufacture, from the thick sheet of dough on an endless band at one end of the ovens to the chocolate-covered products at the other. The Queen's table linen was exhibited next to Irish point lace, silks and woollens and Coats' sewing thread. There were innumerable textile machines, and a film showed the whole process of cotton manufacture. We could have spent weeks in those great halls.

But the splendid pavilions of Canada, Australia, India, South Africa and of all the other British overseas possessions interested me even more. The Canadians showed a life-size model of the Prince of Wales, complete with his horse, on his ranch in Alberta, entirely made of butter. The Australians demonstrated wheat harvesting, dairy farming and wine making and sold apples of a size we had never seen before. All the visitors to the Australian pavilion seemed to be munching apples. The South African pavilion was built in Dutch style; part of it was devoted to lifelike models of wild animals in their natural surroundings, and one could have lunch in a real South African dining car. The most exciting exhibits were those of gold washing and sifting in running water and the seeking for diamonds. Thousands of tons of real diamond-bearing blue soil had been shipped from the Cape for this purpose, and one could watch the stones that were found being cut and polished.

The more exotic the pavilions the more they thrilled me. The main entrance to that of Burma was copied from a pagoda at Mandalay, guarded by a monster pair of leogriffs. Within the gates one walked through the street of a typical Burmese village where native women rolled cigars, young men played a ball game called chin-lon, and dancing girls from Rangoon gave song and dance performances. In the walled city of West Africa negroes carved bowls, forged ornamental ironwork, turned potters' wheels, made objects of brass, embroidered and wove on four different types of primitive looms. It was divided into four compounds in which the various races, the Hausa, Yoruba, Fanti and Mendi lived under native conditions, and their houses were built of sun-dried bricks. The colonies of Nigeria, Sierra Leone and the Gold Coast each had a separate pavilion where tribesmen and their wives were at work on their special crafts. The Hong Kong pavilion was designed in the picturesque style of a gateway to a Chinese city, every part of which had been made in the colony; one could watch Chinese girls tend silkworms, unwind cocoons and prepare the fine threads for weaving, and the food in the Chinese restaurant was prepared by a former chef of the imperial palace at Pekin.

Beside the New Zealand pavilion there was a Samoan house built of breadfruit tree and coconut palm wood, bound with fibre. The reconstructed life-size tomb of Tutankhamen revived ancient Egypt. I watched a working model of the pitch lake of Trinidad. In the domed and towered pavilion of Malaya the gardens, trees, grass, flowers and birds were made of rubber. There was a panorama of Singapore, a shop selling straw hats and basketwork made by Malay girls, and three men in native costume worked a tin mine. Ceylon had copied an old Sinhalese temple. But the most beautiful, the most romantic of all was the Taj Mahal at the end of the lake, the entrance to the pavilion of India.

India held an irresistible fascination for me. Again and again I returned to this palace of Eastern mystery, sniffing the incense of the Orient that wafted from ornamental brass burners, to study the beturbanned, brown-skinned craftsmen and traders, their movements, gestures and dress. Were they Hindus, I wondered, or Muslims? Did they chew betel? Could they charm snakes, lie on beds of nails, make ropes stand and climb up them? A bearded merchant, Mr Singh of Amritsar, gave me his card and I treasured it for years.

There was also an amusement park, an enormous one, with roundabouts, water chutes, miniature trains, shooting galleries and a giant switchback.

Schoolboys splashed in cockleshell boats on the artificial lake, crowds of people picnicked on the lawn. It was pandemonium, and with so much else to see we did no more than walk through it. Surprises met us at every turn, and when, in the glare of the evening illuminations, Mr Balque, our guide, pointed at the full moon and said to me, 'It looks almost like real,' I believed for a moment that it wasn't.

More than seventy British dominions, colonies and dependencies were represented at Wembley in an area of 220 acres. Nigerians in their colourful robes, cowboys from Calgary, dusky East African beauties, Indians, Malays, Chinamen, Australians, New Zealanders and Fiji islanders in an endless variety of human types, colour of skin and national costume, and in a profusion of tongues with which the tower of Babel itself could not have competed—yet all were members of one great empire, united under one king and flag, linked by the English language, financed by sterling, ruled by British justice and protected by the Royal Navy. How proud they must all feel, I thought, and how I envied them.

After two days at the Empire Exhibition Mr Balque showed us some more of London. This time we went east. We rode past the Prudential building in Holborn and looked at the statue of the Prince Consort greeting the City, visited Smithfield, saw the Mansion House, the Bank of England, the Royal Exchange, Lloyd's, which had grown out of a coffee house and was now insuring the farthest corners of the earth, the Tower and London Bridge. We took a boat trip through the Pool of London, marvelling at the many ships. I was in my element. There could be no doubt that London was the place for me, the most important, busiest, most exciting place in the world. In the early evening we visited Chinatown, keeping closely together and giving a wide berth to suspicious-looking figures lurking in dark doorways. We drank Jamaica rum in a pub that was frequented, so Mr Balque whispered, by seafaring men, smugglers, dope pedlars, prostitutes and cut-throats. There would be drunkenness and fighting later on, so he said: better not stay too late. I saw two Chinamen disappear up a narrow staircase, and wondered whether there was an opium den on the first floor. Father thought I had read too many adventure books. 'You are not to come here when you are in London on your own,' he insisted, overrating my urge to explore and my courage. I had seen quite enough.

The day Father and I went to the City on our own to call on customers proved an anticlimax. With great expectations we set off from the hotel in a taxi shortly before 8 a.m. for the textile quarter, the area bounded by Cheapside, Aldersgate Street, Barbican, Chiswell Street and Moorgate. Both Father and I had learned at school that Britain's textile industry was the most advanced and the largest in the world. The countless ships we had seen in the

Pool of London carried cotton goods from Manchester and woollens from Leeds and Bradford to South America, India, Australia and Japan. And most of the firms engaged in this enormous international trade, manufacturers as well as merchants and agents, had offices in London. Moreover the textiles that came from overseas, the fleecy knickers made at Fleissen, for instance, were shipped to London, from where they were distributed throughout the British Isles and, no doubt, the empire. We expected the textile quarter to look like the pictures we had seen of Manhattan.

But instead of wide avenues lined with skyscraper office blocks and modern warehouses the taxi took us into a rabbit warren of narrow streets and alleyways filled with primitive carts drawn by horses. Could these dingy four-storey houses and this slow-moving traffic really be the London of such famous firms as Stern's Hosiery Co., Israel & Oppenheimer and A. T. Singer? It was half past eight now, and not a single office we called on was at work yet; not even the bosses had arrived. We did not allow, of course, for the fact that they and most of their staff had to travel an hour to get to work, nor would we have accepted that as an excuse.

We were even more bewildered when, after waiting for half an hour, clerks and businessmen began to arrive, and we saw the inside of some of these buildings, with their narrow staircases, dark offices, open fireplaces and pedestal desks at which men stood writing invoices in longhand. For every calculation in £ s d they referred to little books called ready reckoners and they paid their suppliers by innumerable cheques, each of which cost 2d, and the recipient lost the interest while it was being cleared. By contrast, our office back in Fleissen, that out-of-the-way Bohemian village, was twice as light and we had central heating throughout. We used typewriters for everything except book entries. Calculations under the metric system, especially if weights or measures as well as sums of money were involved, were much faster and more accurate. And we made all our payments simply through postal giro. Could Britain maintain her position as the world's greatest trading nation using such old-fashioned methods?

'We don't find it easy,' admitted Mr Alfred Stern. 'This is a great country for tradition, and change comes slowly. We have a government commission that is studying the metric system. It has studied it for many years, and one of these days, no doubt, we shall take the plunge. I would prefer it to come a little sooner, but fortunately the British Empire is so wealthy that it can afford to take its time. London's great merchant and finance houses, the Bank of England, the Stock Exchange and Lloyd's combine more wealth and influence than all the Continental capitals put together.'

'Wages are too high in Britain, and the people are too conservative,' said Mr Israel. 'Our workmen earn two pounds a week, and your manufacturing methods are ahead of ours. That's why we have to buy cotton underwear in Czechoslovakia, stockings in Germany and gloves in Italy while there are two million unemployed on our doorstep. Still, I must not complain. Imports now provide my livelihood.'

It was the war that robbed British industry of its leading position in the world, claimed Mr Singer. While Britain fought, her overseas customers built factories to make the goods she could not supply. Many of her export markets were lost for ever, in fact trade now flowed in the opposite direction. Britain imported textiles—fleecy knickers, for instance, which Fleissen and Asch manufactured more cheaply than Leicester. 'But make no mistake,' he said. 'This country has vast resources and great powers of revival.'

Father felt he had to put the record straight. 'The war broke up our country and disrupted our industry more than yours,' he protested. 'But who am I to pass judgement? I am glad we can supply you.'

The old-fashioned City had come as a shock to me, I had to admit, but listening to these businessmen I soon regained my enthusiasm for everything British. Tradition was the key word that explained everything. Anyone who doubted Britain's power, ingenuity and enormous resources need only go to Wembley, as we had done, look at an atlas or travel on London's Underground. I could not understand Father's cautious reservations. He had the highest regard for the engineering skill of the British; they built the finest spinning machines in the world; why could they not replace the antiquated hoists in the City warehouses by modern lifts instead of parading in fur hats and red coats? Was it tradition that stopped them? he asked, and thereby showed his regrettable lack of respect for Britain's glorious past.

On Saturday, after lunch, Father and I took a taxi to 28 Frognal, the boarding house at Hampstead which Mr Israel had recommended and where I was to spend the next twelve months. It was run by two middle-aged ladies, Miss La Roche and Miss Ramsay, who showed us the lounge, a pleasant room with a bay window and a large open fireplace enclosed by a semicircle of settees and easy chairs. It had potted plants in it, but in the winter, they explained, there would be a roaring log fire. We saw the dining room with four tables each for four people, and were then taken upstairs to the second floor to my bedroom. It was furnished with a wardrobe, a bed, two chairs and a washstand with a basin and a jug and had a small fireplace with a gas fire. There was no running water, but the window looked out over the little back garden, and I thought I would be quite happy there.

We were introduced to one of the guests, a tall, good-looking young German named Dr Roth, the son of another of Mr Israel's business friends. He was about four years older than I, and jokingly promised to keep an eye on me. Before Father left we went for a last stroll. The parting seemed to come almost harder to him than to me. He wanted to say so many things, give me so much good advice, but the words failed him, and we walked side by side in silence. Then two boys knocked over a corrugated iron dustbin, and among the rubbish tumbling out was half a loaf of white bread. Father stopped.

'I've never seen such waste in any other country,' he said. 'Bread is the Almighty's most sacred gift to man. Are these people not afraid to be punished for the way they treat it?'

Father had never mentioned God to me before. He was self-conscious about the subject, and although he went to church regularly I was not certain what he believed. I had inherited the Central European conviction that bread was something sacred, but I did not know what to reply, and we continued our walk, making light conversation. The things we both wanted to talk about remained unsaid, but in thought I promised Father not to let him down, and hoped he understood. He took a taxi to rejoin his party to catch the night boat for the Hook of Holland, and I returned to my boarding house to unpack and meet the other guests.

Besides Dr Roth, who came from a small town in Württemberg and, like myself, wanted to perfect his English, there was Willy Hess—little Willy, as he was referred to, a young newspaperman from Berlin. He was nineteen, only a year older than I, but to hear him talk one would have thought there was not much London could teach him. Ten Kate, a tall, curly-haired Dutchman, was learning the tea trade in the City and intended to become a planter in the East Indies. Ben Rosenberg from Copenhagen, a commission agent, competed with Willy Hess for the favours of Miss Raphael, who worked as a secretary in a bank, and there was a young couple, Harry and Ella Clayton, from Manchester. Mr Clayton was about twenty-six and a glove buyer at Hitchcock Williams Ltd in St Paul's Churchyard. Being the oldest of us all, married, and the only Englishman, he was condescending in a fatherly kind of way, and I got to like him in spite of his bumptiousness. I also liked Ella, who entertained us by playing the piano and singing popular dance tunes. The names of the other three or four I have forgotten.

After a few days of exploring the neighbourhood and settling in I joined a course of English tuition for foreigners at Pitman's College in Southampton Row. The students in my class came from the four corners of the world, and the mixture of languages in which they conversed made me think of the League of Nations. How I wished that my friends at Fleissen and Asch could hear them. I usually lunched with a young Spaniard, a Swiss and a Persian at a small restaurant round the corner. They intrigued me immensely, but I did not seek their company after lessons, hoping from one day to the next that I would get to know some English boys instead. Pitman's taught many subjects besides languages, and most of the pupils were English, but to my great disappointment they did not seem to be interested in foreigners, and I was too shy to try and make contact in these unexpected circumstances. I felt bewildered. In Czechoslovakia and Germany foreigners were always made such a fuss of, everyone wanted to meet them, they were invited to people's houses and given the best of everything. It did not seem quite fair.

I spent four hours daily at the college, and two evenings a week I took private lessons from Mr Salter, a retired schoolteacher. Besides coaching me in spelling and grammar he talked about the British way of life and how much it differed from that of foreigners. He had once spent a holiday at Ostend and penetrated as far as Bruges, which had confirmed his preconceived ideas of the Continent and its people. No doubt Father would have disagreed with much of what he said, but Mr Salter was such a kindly and wise old man (at least fifty, I thought) and so fair-minded that I could not possibly argue with him. Greeks, Spaniards, Frenchmen, Austrians and Norwegians all seemed very different races to me, with completely different characteristics and customs, but to Mr Salter they were simply Continentals. Only the British were a race apart, and although he was far too well-mannered to say so there could be no doubt that they were altogether superior. There were only two kinds of people in Europe, and God had conveniently separated them from each other by the Channel. As a matter of fact, Britain was hardly part of Europe. I thought it best not to contradict.

But I was here to learn, and Mr Salter's views, unpalatable as they were, could not be dismissed lightly. It did not take me long to sense that they were held by other English people—the kindly Misses Ramsay and La Roche, for instance—and I would have liked to know the secret of British superiority. How was it defined? In terms of intelligence, integrity, morals, courage, sporting achievements or table manners? Assuming Continental equality, which I knew did not exist, a British pastrycook would presumably be thought superior to a Czechoslovak one. The Prime Minister of Great Britain would be thought superior to the head of the government at Prague. But would a British pastrycook be considered superior to a Czechoslovak Prime Minister? And in what way? Where was the line drawn? I was determined to find out.

'British propaganda!' laughed Ten Kate when I raised the subject at Frognal. 'The Channel has effectively prevented progress from reaching England,' said Willy Hess. These two certainly did not believe in Continental equality. Hess called the Dutchman a Kaaskoppe and Ten Kate referred to the German as Moffenbonz.

Having learned English for four years at the textile college, it did not take long before I was able to carry on a fairly fluent conversation. On Sunday morning I usually went for a walk on Hampstead Heath with Mr Clayton, who wore an impressive pair of plus-fours with tassels which made mine look like a schoolboy's knickerbockers, and talked about football. It was the national sport, he said. If I wanted to understand the English I had to know the finer points of the game. Unfortunately I did not even know the difference between soccer and rugby. Kicking a ball had never given me a thrill, let alone sitting on a hard bench watching others; but, not daring to confess, I patiently listened to his lectures. I would have much preferred Mr Clayton to tell me something about Lancashire, his youth, or his work as a glove buyer, but failed to make him change the subject. Nor did he ever ask a single question about my home or country. I gathered he shared Mr Salter's views of the Continent. 'The wogs begin at Calais,' I had heard him say to one of his friends who came to visit him, and whilst I did not know what wogs were it did not sound very complimentary.

Then I met Barbara, Miss Ramsay's seventeen-year-old niece. She was still a schoolgirl, and the first person in England who wanted to know about Czechoslovakia. She had not the faintest idea where it was but liked the romantic sound of the unpronounceable name and expected it to be a wild, mountainous region inhabited by brigands, barons, ogres and—well, were there any fairy princesses? She seemed a little disappointed that I had neither horns nor a beard. I looked so ordinary, only my halting English and strange pronunciation and, of course, those extraordinary knickerbockers gave me away. But she tactfully avoided mentioning them, and said my English was very good. Had people in—what was that funny name again?—ever seen a motor car?

I did not know whether to feel angry or amused. It seemed incredible that she could be so ignorant. Had they no geography lessons at her school? But her curiosity was so obviously genuine that in the end I felt flattered. Here at last was someone who was interested in me and the country I came from—and such a pretty girl at that. I told her all I could and very nearly fell in love with her.

We met almost every weekend. Sometimes she came to stay with Miss Ramsay, and we went for walks on Hampstead Heath, had tea at the Brent Bridge Hotel or saw a film at the cinema at Golders Green. She was the first girl I ever kissed, but when we met next time and I tried to kiss her again she would not let me. She was a Girl Guide and it appeared that the Guides disapproved of kissing: they thought it was sloppy. What a pity! I soon got to know the bus route to her home. She lived at Herne Hill. Her father was the London agent for a Northampton shoe firm. Her mother made me feel so welcome that I soon felt one of the family. Stuart, her sixteen-year-old brother, was a little young but a nice lad and good companion, and the three of us explored the surroundings of London. By bus, train, Underground or steamer we visited the places of interest, from Crystal Palace, Hampton Court and Windsor Castle to Epping Forest, Greenwich and Box Hill. It was a much more pleasant way of learning the language than sitting at Pitman's during the week.

Four hours a day at the college, fortunately, left ample time for other pursuits. I learned to find my way about London, seeing the sights and competing with Dr Roth, who also attended the English class, to discover the fastest route from one place in town to another without using taxis. We might start at Baker Street station or Nelson's column, walk off in opposite directions and then each find our way by bus, on the Underground or on foot to the main entrance of the Law Courts or to Speaker's Corner at Hyde Park, trying to get there first. Back at Frognal, we then wrote essays about our routes and what we had seen on the way. I also played tennis with Willy Hess and took boxing lessons at the Polytechnic, but was not much good at either.

I discovered a small theatre at Hampstead, saw a number of plays there and became a Bernard Shaw fan. After the performance the audience would stand to attention while the national anthem was played, and no one moved until the last note had died down. This was the regular practice in all theatres, and I admired the self-discipline and patience of the British. They never appeared to be in a hurry, always showed consideration for others, and if anyone pushed it was invariably a foreigner. I was equally impressed by their good manners on buses and on the Underground, however tight the squeeze might be.

I made my first radio set. The crystal with whisker and a pair of earphones cost £1 and the wire mattress of my bed provided the aerial. We had learned the principles of wireless telegraphy at college. Professor Pichler had tried to give us a demonstration with a glass tube with metal balls in it but could not get it to work. My crystal—it was called a detector—worked perfectly. I lay in bed with the earphones on and detected not just dots and dashes but real music which mysteriously penetrated walls and closed windows in the form of invisible waves to be caught by my mattress.

Towards the end of November we had two days of fog. It was thick and yellow and brought all road traffic to a standstill. I had been eagerly waiting for it, and was thrilled. No one could claim to know London unless he had experienced fog. It was as essential as Big Ben or bacon and eggs, and I wrote enthusiastic letters home describing the pea souper, as it was called, and the open flames that were burning at road junctions.

Christmas came, and most of the guests at Frognal went home, but Dr Roth and I had a more ambitious programme. We were going north to far-away Scotland. We took the Royal Scot to Glasgow, a grey city of stone buildings and clanking tramcars. Looking at the sights, the headquarters of the famous firm of J. & P. Coats was pointed out to us. We knew them as the world's largest cotton thread makers, but had somehow expected them to be located in Manchester. Who could have foretold then that one day I would become a director and sit in the boardroom in that very building!

From Glasgow we went down the Clyde to the Isle of Bute, to stay at the Hydro Hotel. There was no snow and to our surprise no Christmas tree. And we had language problems. The Scots spoke English, or so we had learnt at school, but their English defeated us. The weather was mild and wet, and we spent the first two days playing table tennis. We could have felt bored, had the thought of being on a Scottish island not filled us with excitement, and we accepted the grey sky and the rain in good part.

On New Year's Eve there was a gala dinner. Some of the men wore kilts as part of their dress suits. We sat at our gaily decorated small table, not sure what to expect. Half-way through the meal which had started so formally the conversation around us livened up, crackers banged, paper hats appeared, streamers flew through the air and balloons burst. Soon we were in the midst of the paper battle. We threw streamers and blew the whistles we found in our crackers. Then the dancing began, one of the ladies at the next table invited us to join their party, champagne began to flow, we tried to do Highland reels and at midnight we sang Auld Lang Syne. The whole large roomful of people became one jolly party, and it was very late before we went to our beds.

Next day everyone talked to us, we were asked to come for walks and were invited to cocktails. How different these Scots were from what we had expected. Living so much farther north we thought they would be even cooler and more reserved than Londoners, yet here they were going out of their way to make us feel at ease. They enquired where we came from, what had brought us to the Isle of Bute, joked with us, gave us their addresses and asked us to visit their homes. How charming they all were! If only we could have understood them a little better. One man in particular—Jimmy Baird was his name —made everyone laugh, but he spoke such broad Scots that we could hardly make him out. He was a draper, we gathered, and came from Wishaw, near Glasgow. He gave me his business card, which I posted to Father, asking him to send samples of our underwear to T. Baird & Sons. And so began not only a valuable business connection but a wonderful friendship which has lasted almost half a century. The Baird brothers came to mean a very great deal in my life.

Before leaving Scotland and its hospitable people we spent a happy evening with the Turnbull family. We had met them on New Year's Eve, played table tennis and danced with the daughters—two lively girls a little younger than we. Mr Turnbull held an important position at the law courts—he was a judge, I believe—and had a large house in Glasgow. It was very kind of them to give us a farewell party.

'There is a large Christmas parcel waiting for you,' Miss La Roche greeted me on our return to 28 Frognal. 'It has been sitting in the hall for a whole week and we are all very curious to see what is in it!'

I took the parcel into the lounge and unpacked it in front of the blazing fire. Out came a selection of fleecy knickers for small, medium, large and extra-large women, all nicely labelled, in various qualities and colours. The unusual spectacle created considerable hilarity among the residents, and I felt embarrassed. It had never occurred to me that there could be anything funny about Directoire knickers. Of course they were women's under-garments, but what was wrong with that? I saw them as merchandise, products of an intricate industrial process. What did laymen know of the manufacturing skill that went into the technical details of these garments? There was the shape, length of leg, position of gusset, weight of fabric, evenness of surface, gauge of stitch, composition of yarns, firmness of fleece, double-needle ruching at the knee, single-needle ruching at the waist, width of overlock seam, strength of elastic and so forth, the outcome of years of patient development work.

Father sent them because he thought I ought to have a comprehensive range of our products by me, just in case I saw some business opening. To make me go to the City now and again and keep in touch with our customers he henceforth sent all correspondence and samples to me and asked me to hand them over personally. I soon overcame my feeling of embarrassment when these parcels arrived, in fact I displayed the knickers in the drawing room, pretending to be a commercial traveller and giving a mock sales talk as my contribution to the evening's entertainment. Next morning I would take them by Underground to Aldersgate Street and deliver them with Father's messages to Mr Stern, Mr Singer and Mr Israel.

These calls also served the useful purpose of reminding those busy men of my continuing presence in London, and they occasionally responded by inviting me to have lunch at their homes on a Sunday. By far the most beauti-ful was Mr Stern's, Templewood House on Hampstead Heath, where he entertained business friends, industrialists, members of Parliament and other important persons. I was too shy to say much more than Yes or No on those occasions, but I took in and remembered long afterwards every word that was said.

Father was concerned lest I might get into trouble in the big metropolis with too much free time on my hands. He wanted me to gain business ex-perience and arranged for me to work at the office of Israel & Oppenheimer's.

So I quit Pitman's and went to the City. Being a student, I had no work permit and could only take unpaid employment. Not that this mattered, but as a consequence nobody at the office took me seriously, and since Mr Israel did not want me, the son of a supplier, to know from whom else he bought, how much he paid for our competitors' goods, what profit he added or to whom he sold, I was not given the chance to learn much. I was put in a corner of the counting house, as the office was called in those days, and given a book from which I had to copy out figures, write statements and address envelopes. I had taught myself to type back at Asch, faster and certainly much more legibly than I could write, but there was no spare typewriter, and I had to do it all in longhand. It was a most boring job, and the only happy hour of the day was the lunch break, which I spent reading Bulldog Drummond in the lounge of the Manchester Hotel, where I had coffee and a sandwich. Father meant well, but the few months I sat scribbling in that office were an utter waste of time. I ought to have spoken up, but, realising that Mr Israel was only doing Father a favour, I did not want to make a nuisance of myself.

At Easter I took Barbara and Stuart for a short holiday to Fleissen. They liked our house, which was much larger than theirs, and were intrigued by its many cellars and the double windows, but thought our garden very badly kept. They missed the lawn. The snow had only just gone, and through the sparse grass the brown earth showed. My lake in the woods looked much like any other pond and was tiny compared with Virginia Water, and the forest itself, well, yes, it was big and dark, but the trees were all very similar—not like those in the parks of London. City dwellers, unaccustomed to natural beauty, I told myself. We looked at things through different eyes. And they were foreigners here who missed much of the atmosphere, not understanding the language. It was amusing how emphatically they denied being foreigners. They were British; it was Czechoslovakia that was full of foreigners who did not understand. We had much fun, and the visit was over far too soon.

The Ramsays returned to England by train and boat, the way we had come, but I had found out that one could fly from Amsterdam to London and decided to try it. I had never flown before and, to put it mildly, felt very apprehensive as I walked to the waiting airliner. It was a Fokker, larger than a motor lorry, and was made of wood and canvas. Painted on its sides and wings were the letters H-NACJ. Behind the engine, which had a four-bladed wooden propeller, was the open cockpit for the pilot and a closed cabin for about eight passengers. Seeing that I was on my own, the pilot offered me the seat next to his, which I accepted with alacrity. A mechanic gave me a leather coat and helmet and a pair of goggles and strapped me into my seat. The engine sprang to life, the aeroplane roared across the grass field, I held on with both hands to my seat and the side of the cockpit, and then the earth dropped away below us.

We climbed to the dizzy height of 3,000 ft into a cloudless sky. It was a beautifully still afternoon. Out of the corner of my eye I watched the pilot. He seemed relaxed, and I had confidence in him. Now and again he looked at his map, then he gave it to me and showed me where we were, following the Dutch and Belgian coastline towards Calais. I wished he would concentrate on his flying instead of bending over me.

After about two hours I saw Cap Gris Nez ahead. The pilot rotated a wheel, paying out the trailing aerial, a long wire with a weight at the end, and tapped out a message in Morse code. I wondered whether he was telling someone that we were about to leave land and cross the Channel. Then suddenly the left wing rose steeply. I held tight, afraid the aeroplane was turning over. But it righted itself again; we had only changed course, and were now heading out to sea. Anxiously I studied the pilot's profile, but he seemed calm, and I felt reassured. For fifteen endless minutes I saw only water, then a thin line became visible on the horizon, the white cliffs of Dover bathed in the late afternoon sun. It was an inspiring sight.

Soon there were green fields below us; we flew over small towns and large country houses set in beautiful grounds. England looked like a huge, well kept park. We appeared to be following a long, straight railway line with now and again a miniature train on it. Again the aerial was lowered and a message tapped out into the ether. I was now completely at ease and thoroughly enjoyed the remainder of the flight. Well before sunset we landed at Croydon, barely four hours after leaving Amsterdam. It seemed incredible, and I felt elated. One of these days, I promised myself, I would fly again.

Little did I realise how lucky I had been with this, my first flight, and how much aviation in the '20s depended on the vagaries of the weather. I was to find out on a business trip nine months later, when flying from London to Amsterdam in January 1926. Rain and high winds delayed our departure, and when at last the pilot decided to brave the elements the journey was so rough that I was terrified until I became sick beyond caring whether the aircraft broke up in mid-air. I stayed in bed for two days afterwards and did not go near an aeroplane again for several years. Flying was more of an adventurous stunt in those days than a serious method of transport, and even courageous men took to the air only in case of extreme urgency. A pilot's job was considered even more hazardous than that of a trapeze artist.

I was now a little more at home in London and made better use of my time, sitting at the Law Courts trying to follow legal arguments, listening to debates in the House of Commons, going to the theatre, visiting museums and exhibitions and watching sporting events. I saw Lacoste take the tennis championship from Borotra at Wimbledon and applauded Mlle Lenglen. They played so incomparably better than Willy Hess and I that we thought it best to pack our rackets away. I watched motor racing at Brooklands, and went with Barbara and Stuart to the Derby.

Backing horses was a fool's game, I lectured, and I did not think much of people who indulged in it. Most of them claimed that they won, but I did not believe them. One could hardly expect to have the entertainment and get paid for it, and to prove it I put 2s on a horse of Barbara's choice. To my consternation and her delight we won £2. I was suspicious. Having been brought up to distrust easy profits, I elbowed my way through the crowd and asked the bookmaker for the money. He was busy; would I call at his office in the morning? So that was the catch! 'Sorry,' I said, 'I want it now!' To my surprise, he paid up without any further ado. It seemed all wrong, almost like cheating, I thought, that we should have made 38s just by sticking a pin in the programme, instead of having to work for it. True, the amount did not represent a fortune, but suppose I had put £5 on that horse? The Ramsays could not understand, and shook their heads. 'We wish you had,' they laughed.

I tried hard to behave and react like the English, but drew the line when it came to sport. The vast majority did not actually play, they watched, and I just could not raise the necessary enthusiasm. Britain, it seemed to me, was a country of three balls: cricket, golf and football. The importance grown men attached to them astounded me. Mr Ramsay, a keen golfer, would have given up ten of his best customers for a 'hole in one'. And who would think that cricket could justify headlines on the front pages of national newspapers like 'Can England survive?' 'England desperate' or 'No hope for England'. Most sporting events, so it seemed, were held on ordinary weekdays, and I was surprised that thousands of spectators found time to flock to them. Had they no work to do? It was quite unthinkable for a football match at Eger or Asch to take place at any other time than the weekend, while in England people sat around on Sunday feeling bored.

For a while I went back to Pitman's and took commercial subjects in the hope of making friends among the English pupils, but once again I failed. I had little in common with them, and they were not interested in me. I now discovered how badly many of them spoke, and for the first time I became aware of a kind of class distinction that did not seem to exist among other nationalities. Back in Bohemia people spoke High German or lapsed into their local dialect at will. The dialect varied according to the part of the country they came from, but had little to do with social status. In Britain, on the other hand, the working class and the middle class seemed to be permanently separated from each other by the different way in which they pronounced their words. They understood but could not speak each other's English, nor did they want to. And to make matters worse there were local dialects in addition, each apparently with a class tag. A Scots pronunciation did not lower a man's status, whereas a Lancashire one did. It was all very complicated.

To be invited by Mr Stern was always a very special treat. I admired him more each time I met him. He excelled in everything he did. I knew no one else with so much knowledge, personality and energy. Other businessmen seemed pygmies by contrast. Not that I had met many, or could judge their business acumen, but it was not difficult to tell that their general level of education left much to be desired, and I felt somewhat disillusioned. Czecho-slovak industrialists were men of calibre, although, admittedly, none of them was of the stature of Mr Stern, but Britain's leading men obviously had more important things to do than occupy themselves with commerce. Having to administer such a vast empire, they were presumably colonial governors, diplomats, Foreign Office officials, international bankers, explorers, admirals or heads of the secret service. Commerce was left to the second- and third-raters, I thought, and that explained why in Britain anyone engaged in manu-facturing was somewhat looked down upon, whereas in Czechoslovakia he was looked up to.

But why was farming thought to be more genteel than manufacturing? I had hardly seen any real farms, mostly meadows with cattle grazing in them summer and winter. Why should wealthy industrialists want to become gentleman farmers, dress up in fancy costume and ride to hounds? Not so long ago the English were the greatest industrial nation in the world: they had invented the steam engine, the locomotive, the spinning jenny, the knitting frame—why did farmers not want to become gentlemen manufac-turers and take a pride in machinery? My friends only laughed when I asked such questions.

The last ten days of my stay in England I spent with the Ramsay family at Herne Bay, where they had taken a house for the summer holidays, and then, in the middle of August 1925, I packed my bags and returned to Fleissen. It was a sad farewell. I would have given almost anything to be able to stay in England. London was the hub of the world. Everything that was worthwhile happened there. Nothing ever happened in the backwoods of Czechoslovakia. Besides, my education was not finished, and there was so much more to learn.

My friends assured me that I spoke English very well, but it was not nearly well enough for me. When I compared my sentences with those of Michael Arlen, my favourite author at the time, I could have despaired. He was an Armenian yet wrote such excellent English. How I would have loved to be able to express myself as well as he did. And I would have liked to acquire at least a working knowledge of French and Spanish, but not just from books. I was thirsting for travel, to see other countries and get to know other peoples. Instead I had to go back to Fleissen, where there were only four slow trains a day and no buses at all, no Underground system, no illuminated signs, no banks or shipping companies with romantic-sounding names, no traffic policemen; there was not even a newspaper boy.

From the deck of the steamer I took a last photograph of the white cliffs of Dover, then I tore myself away and tried to think of what lay ahead.

8

WORKING
WITH FATHER
1925-27

I WAS, OF COURSE, glad to see my family again. For a few days I was made a fuss of, which confused me. I felt self-conscious walking about the village. Everyone knew I had just returned from London and stopped me to ask questions. At first I found it difficult to answer in Egerland dialect without, occasionally, using an English word, and was afraid this would be taken for affectation.

Great changes had taken place. Father took me over the new factory block opposite our garden, which was almost completed. A large boiler, a new 150 h.p. steam engine built by the Brünn Königsfelder engineering works and a 120 kW generator were in the course of erection. Proudly he showed me his full order book and all the knitting machines he had bought during my absence. We went for a run in the new car, a large open Buick which had cost 120,000 Czech kronen, and he let me drive it. He wanted my help in the business and said that, as I was now nineteen, the time had come for me to shoulder some responsibility. If I was to run the factory one day I had to get used to living at Fleissen, which was a much more interesting place than I realised.

Did Father guess what I felt? He seemed to rely on me. To confess that I had no intention of living permanently at Fleissen and that I should therefore never want to take over the firm would be a terrible disappointment to him. How could I even think of letting him down after all he had done for me? Torn and unhappy, I went for long walks in the fields and the woods, hoping in vain to find peace. Some day I'd have to tell him, but not yet. I'd first stay for a few years and work in the business, as Father wanted. He was not going to cut me off from the world. Would he have sent me to London if that had been his intention? He wanted me to keep in touch with other countries. I was to do the firm's export correspondence under Georg Hoyer, one of the head clerks, a slightly balding man in his middle thirties whom I still remember with respect and affection. Hoyer was in charge of costings and sales, and I sat by the side of his roll-top desk and typed letters in

English. At first he dictated them to me in German, later he only discussed the salient points of a transaction with me and trusted me to convey them in suitable phrases to our clients.

Whenever possible, Father and Grandfather made me sit in at business discussions and when they had visitors. In this way I got to know many of our customers and suppliers. Spinners and their representatives came to see us almost weekly; machine makers from Germany, builders, bankers and insurance agents were regular callers. I observed how prices were negotiated, purchases made, complaints dealt with, how overdrafts were arranged, currency risks covered and doubtful propositions stalled. If I did not quite understand the purpose of some transaction I would go to Grandmother and let her explain it to me. I was not at all shy with her, and she had the gift of making everything look so simple.

Several hours a day I spent in the factory, preferably with Johann Feiler, the technical manager. He knew more about the mechanism of knitting, sewing and brushing machines, electric motors, gears, shafts and pulleys, steam engines and pumps than even Father. Together they once invented a cutting machine for which they secured a patent, but, I was told, it caused so much waste that Adolf Pasold & Sohn finished the year with a loss and the machine was scrapped. Feiler always had one machine or another stripped down for repair and improvement. Being with him was fun. He taught me how to use a drill and a blowlamp, how to cut screws and harden steel. Going through the factory with Father was less enjoyable. He invariably found something that was not as it should be and left me to put it right. The yarn cases were not stacked properly, the floor was dusty and soiled the fabric, the cutting patterns were frayed, there was too much thread wasted in the sewing department, a steam trap leaked, the lift was not used efficiently. If there was nothing wrong he would make me check the stock of buttons, needles, elastic or packing paper and work out when fresh supplies were needed. These were jobs I disliked.

One of the first things I had to learn was to distinguish between the different types of fabric and the yarns from which they were knitted. We made only cotton underwear. The principal yarns were 40s, 36s, 20s and 16s carded. There was also 30s marl in pale yellow called macco, and pale grey, blue and pink, then a soft spun 12s which was a mixture of 97 per cent natural and 3 per cent dyed fibres to give a mottled effect, and finally various grades of condenser yarn which were spun in 9s metric, which approximately equalled 6s English count. The latter went into the left side of the winter-weight fabrics and were brushed to provide the fleece. They came in different qualities made from pure Indian cotton, which was the most expensive, to the off-whites, light greys and dark greys spun from cotton waste. We did not use wool and knew little about it. Hardly anyone in Czechoslovakia wore wool underwear, not only because it was too expensive but because it would not wear and wash as well as cotton.

For the home trade we made men's vests with sleeves and long underpants, women's vests and drawers, and combinations that buttoned down the back for women and children. There were two qualities. No. 400 was the heavier, No. 200 the lighter. Both were made of 30s marl yarn in pale shades on the outside, with thick white fleece made from pure Indian cotton inside. It was the thickness of the fleece that determined the quality: the thicker the better. Our winters were long and cold, and for cotton underwear to be warm it had to be thick. Grandfather was so proud of quality No. 400 that he used to claim that the pants made from it stood up by themselves.

Directoire knickers, which were at first made only for export, were by now the largest and most important part of our trade. Our local customers laughed at them, but gradually they began to sell in Prague and in some of the other towns, if only in modest quantities. Almost the whole of our output, at that time well over 100,000 dozens per annum, went abroad. The fabric for the winter knickers was knitted from two threads of 36s and a backing thread of 9s condenser yarn spun from waste. The lightest and cheapest quality was No. 534, a code which meant that it had 34 stitches per 5 cm, and a dozen pairs of women's knickers made from it weighed 5 lb. The next heaviest and more expensive quality was No. 644 with forty-four stitches per 5 cm, and a dozen weighed 6 lb. And finally the heaviest and best of our qualities was No. 752. It had fifty-two tight stitches and weighed 7 lb. The fabric for summer knickers was plain stockinette made from single 16s or 20s without any condenser yarn. We knitted about fifty pieces daily. They were collected by three competing dyers, bleached, and left white or dyed cream, beige, grey or saxe; those knitted with dark grey condenser were dyed navy.

When the pieces came back from the dyers they were checked for shade and weight, and if a colour did not match the pattern or the loss of weight was excessive there was trouble. Trouble never ended. There were faulty dyeings in almost every batch. Being knitted on circular machines, the pieces were in the form of long tubes until cut into garments. Summer-weight fabric was returned by the dyers in neatly calendered rolls, ready for the cutting table. The much bulkier winter-weight material came back in bundles which we straightened out and brushed. Four passes over a Gessner wire card brushing machine gave it a lovely thick fleece. None of this was basically new to me. From the age of six I had been continually in and out of the factory. Father always encouraged me to look at new machines and explained how they worked. I had learned a good deal about knitting and general business practice at the textile college, but there was much I did not know.

Now I learned how price rings are broken by sowing the seed of suspicion among the contracting parties. To avoid competing against each other the three dyers had agreed to charge the same prices. For a while we gave each of them a share of our work. Then, suddenly, we would send the waggon of one of them away empty and give all our pieces to the other two. Within a week the dyer who got no work came to see us. Were we not satisfied with his colours? The colours were all right, we replied. What then was the reason? Could it be that the others charged lower prices? We shrugged our shoulders and smiled. Would a secret discount of 3 per cent, payable in cash, restore the balance? 'Try it,' we suggested, and for a few weeks gave him all our work, sending the waggons of the other two dyers away empty until one of them broke and offered a bonus of 5 per cent.

Using similar tactics, we obtained better rates of interest from the bankers, lower freight rates from the forwarding agents and keener prices from suppliers who feared competition. And, of course, our customers used the same technique with us. We all knew it, yet, like hope, suspicion slumbers for ever in man's breast, waiting to be kindled and exploited.

I learned, but whenever I got a little above myself in youthful over-confidence something happened that cut me down to size. There was, for example, that contract I placed for fuses. Father had gone to Prague for two days to see some Ministry, and at his suggestion I sat meanwhile in his chair, when the slick salesman from an electrical appliance firm called. He had a new kind of fuse, six fuses, in fact, in one unit, which could be turned like the drum of a revolver. Intrigued, I gave him an order for twenty-five units. When Father returned and saw the contract he sent for me and asked if I had read the small print on the form.

'It's some standard clause,' I replied, 'not worth reading. The order comes to only 100 kronen.'

Father looked at me. 'You had better read it,' he said. I had signed a contract for no less than twenty-five gross fuse units of six fuses each, more than we could use in ten years. The total amount came to 14,400 kronen—quite an amount of money in those days, when a skilled sewing machinist earned ninety kronen and a knitting machine operator 150 kronen per week. I have read the small print on contract forms ever since.

Competition was keen, prices were cut and profit margins on large contracts were as low as 5 per cent. Some of the smaller manufacturers even sold at cost, hoping that by the time they had to execute the order yarn prices would fall and the transaction would subsequently show a profit. Turnover was everything. Fleissen's knitting industry worked double and treble shifts,

and at night its lit-up factories were an even more impressive sight than
during the day.

We had to work shifts to make money. Manufacturers ploughed almost all
their profits back into their business. Not a year passed without one of them
enlarging his buildings or plant. The chimney stacks were built higher, horse
carts were replaced by motor lorries, one after another the quaint old houses
were pulled down to make room for multi-storey factory blocks. Not that this
was the general picture of Czechoslovakia's textile industry. Far from it.
Many firms in other parts of the republic were not nearly so prosperous.
Fleissen was an exception, and was looked upon as an economic miracle like
Kunert's stocking empire at Warnsdorf. They were surpassed only by Bata's
world-famous shoe town of Zlin. The success of all three of them was the
result of a high degree of specialisation. Fleissen's knitting industry manufactured little else but Directoire knickers, millions of them, and mass-
produced them with surprising single-mindedness of purpose. The keen,
century-old spirit of competition between the leading families was also
evident among the hard-working population, whose restless diligence was
aptly illustrated by the picture of a bee in the left bottom quarter of the crest
of Fleissen. I could hardly have wished for a better place in which to get my
training.

But in the evenings I felt lonely. There was no one I could talk to about
the world outside without being thought a bore or giving the impression that
I wanted to show off. Not even my favourite Uncle Wilhelm or my old friend
Helmut were really interested in London and after a few sentences would
change the subject to some local topic and talk for hours about the growth
rate of trees in the Bohemian forest, or the delay in the delivery of a letter
because the new postmaster understood insufficient German. We went for
long walks through the woods together, but while they talked I was thinking
about ways and means of escaping from Fleissen and starting a business in
England.

We had about eighty circular knitting machines in 24, 25 and 26 gauge and
a variety of diameters from 36 in. to 64 in. Most of them had eight feedwheels.
The small-diameter machines had only four or six, whereas the large ones
had ten or twelve, and one monster had twenty-four. And each had its
peculiarities. To knit fabric of uniform texture and square yard weight on
this greatly varying plant required considerable skill on the part of managers
and operatives. What they could not achieve, of course, was uniform width
or length of the tubular pieces of fabric. We had not even a calendar, only a
rolling machine without steam on which we did our best to stretch the elastic
fabric back to its natural width after the dyeing, drying and fleecing processes
had pulled it long and narrow. A most unsatisfactory way of doing it.

When the pieces were rolled we stacked them in the fabric store, where they matured sometimes for months before they were needed by the cutting department. To run the factory efficiently it was essential to keep the knitting plant fully employed irrespective of the fluctuating intake of orders, and the store sometimes held a buffer stock of a thousand rolls or more.

Since we made garments of many different sizes and some could be cut with less waste from a given width of fabric than others, it was very important to have some control over the width. If the cutting waste was 8 per cent

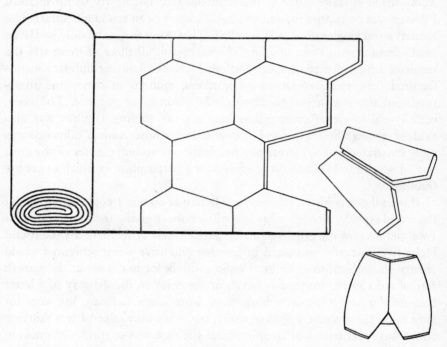

When cutting Directoire knickers waste was avoided by carefully matching the width of the fabric to the size of the pattern

instead of 4 per cent it wiped out a large slice of a manufacturer's profit. We needed a steam calendar, but what type? Calendering was considered part of a dyer's job and was wrapped in the mystique with which the dyeing fraternity surrounded everything it did. After much discussion we decided to buy a calendar with a felt blanket, the wrong machine for our type of work, I am afraid. It was much too cumbersome and slow. A cheaper calendar with steel rollers and a simple steaming device would have been more suitable.

We had some thirty cutters, all women, who worked with hand shears, cutting the individual garments out of a single layer of the tubular fabric.

Each of them had her own table with a wooden top measuring approximately 6 ft by 15 ft. One after another they went to the store to select rolls of the most suitable width and length for the particular size and quantity of garments they had to cut. Two men pulled the pieces out of the stack and carried them to the cutter's table. It was tedious work, and, thinking back, I marvel at the exemplary uniformity of our fleecy knickers.

Calendaring fabric to the required width was all very well, but it did not always stay that width, and some garments lost their shape after they had been washed a few times. The great variety of our knitting plant had come about through purchasing so much of it second-hand. Had we standardised on certain diameters and gauges we would have had to buy new machines, and that we could not afford. Our competitors were, of course, in the same predicament, and the thought occurred to me that by exchanging machines among us, always concentrating those of similar diameter and gauge in one of the competing eight factories, we could achieve a considerable degree of rationalisation. I realised that seasonal changes and fluctuations in orders would sometimes favour one manufacturer, sometimes another, and that, to keep peace among them, profits would have to be pooled. Why, the most sensible solution would not be a cartel but a merger. We could then afford a dyehouse of our own, and a spinning mill. Managerial duties could be shared out, each member of the team could concentrate on fewer functions but on a larger scale, and I would set up an office and warehouse in London and be responsible for selling the output of the whole combine. We'd all make 15 per cent profit instead of 3 or 5 as at present.

Father was amused. 'If you can get the others to agree, I'll play,' he laughed. Mr Ehrlich, the manager of the Anglo-Czechoslovak Bank at Eger, to whom I explained the scheme, hoping he would finance it, became quite excited. His enthusiasm seemed to guarantee success, and in my mind I began already to plan the layout of the London warehouse. But when I presented my ambitious scheme to the three brothers Braun, the friendliest and most co-operative of our competitors, they treated it as a joke. Technical difficulties apart, did I seriously believe that the eight textile manufacturers of Fleissen who had fought each other for a lifetime could be brought under one hat? That they would trust each other? That fox and rabbit would live peacefully together? And when they mentioned 'fox' they glanced in the direction of Lehrmann's factory. Clearly I did not know much about human nature! They so utterly destroyed the project that I did not dare take it to Friedl or Lehrmann. And that was that.

My next disappointment came when I failed to interest anyone in an automatic cutting machine which I had invented. Cutting with hand shears and paper patterns was obviously out of date; Father and Johann Feiler had realised this twenty years ago. The fact that their machine had been a failure proved nothing. My ingenious invention was based on a different principle, a series of small circular knives with keys sliding on a common shaft. Path and angle of each knife was determined by an interchangeable cam. The knitted fabric was to be fed full width at one end and the cut shapes would come out at the other. It was a large, complex machine which could, I calculated, cut more knickers in a day than we made in a week.

Evening after evening I sat over my drawing board, working out the details. Father thought I was wasting my time: the machine was far too big and complicated to function. But I would not listen. I wrote to all the machine builders I could think of, described my invention without disclosing too much of its secret mechanism, and offered to share the profits with them if they would, at their expense, construct a prototype. All my efforts were in vain. The engineering firms lacked enterprise and vision, and I, like all frustrated inventors, felt misunderstood and disillusioned. Today I know that their judgement was right. Even if my machine had worked it would not have been a commercial proposition. Other inventors designed mechanical cutters which were much simpler and better than mine.

By the time I was twenty-one I dealt with all but the largest of our foreign customers entirely on my own, and only issues of principle and price were resolved by Father or Hoyer. The transactions which were my responsibility were by no means small, as my two score of British, Dutch and Scandinavian customers bought some £30,000 worth of goods from us per annum, almost a third of our total turnover.

Father continued to attend personally only to the few most important of our clients who came to the factory. They were Mr Stern, Mr Singer and Mr Israel from London, who all spoke perfect German. Young Harry Millington from Manchester, who could not speak German, always brought Mr Kirsch, his Chemnitz buying agent, with him and so, to my regret, deprived me of the opportunity of translating. Millington was by far the most difficult customer, and we did not care very much for his business. Although he knew less about the merchandise and placed smaller orders than the others, he always tried to buy more cheaply. Then came the brothers Lissauer from Amsterdam, competitors who hated each other. Each told us in turn how the other cheated him and warned us to be careful. Finally there was old Schönberg, with his pointed little beard and red-rimmed eyes. Father never forgot that he was our very first export customer and was always pleased to see him.

Grandfather and Hoyer concentrated on the many hundreds of home-trade buyers who had done business with us for generations. Some were wholesalers from Prague, Reichenberg, Brünn or Pressburg, but most were Galician Jews whose curly locks dangling in front of their ears, black velour hats and long black coats left an indelible picture in my memory. They haggled for hours over price, cash discounts and interest rates, and to trade successfully with them required years of training.

The highlights of those years were my business journeys abroad. The journey from Fleissen to London and back, second class train and sleeper, first class on the boat, cost about 1,500 kronen (£9 5s). I wore a tweed suit and the kind of sports cap which I thought was the outward sign of a world traveller. It was an exhilarating experience to stand at the window of my second class compartment and watch the factory chimneys of Fleissen disappear as the train wound its way uphill through the pine forest towards Brambach. At Leipzig, where I changed, I had dinner. There was usually a wait of a few hours. I admired the station, the size of which never failed to impress me. It was said to be the largest in Europe. The bustle, the lights, the faint smell of steam and soot, the sound of whistles and of the metal wheels of trolleys which echoed in the enormous hall provided the foretaste of adventure ahead. Leipzig station seemed like the threshold of the magic outer world. About 10.30 p.m. the gate to the platform opened, at which the night express for Holland was waiting. I put my bags on the sleeping car for Amsterdam, and always tried to secure an upper berth because I thought it less likely that I would be robbed there while I was asleep, and then came an enjoyable hour or so of strolling up and down the platform, having a good look at my fellow passengers and the coloured hotel labels on their luggage, wondering where they came from, what their business was and whether they were as seasoned travellers as I thought myself to be. I read the names of the towns on the Wagons-Lits coaches and watched the attendants in their smart uniforms getting ready for the departure. At last the great moment came, the mighty express pulled out into the night, the adventure had begun.

At Bentheim, almost too early in the morning, passport and luggage were inspected. It was now broad daylight and far less romantic. I had breakfast in the dining car and then counted the telegraph poles flitting past as the train sped through the flat Dutch countryside, with its canals and occasional windmills. Arriving at Amsterdam, I booked in at the Victoria Hotel across the bridge opposite the Central Station, which was near enough to lug my bags without having to spend money on a taxi. Within half an hour I had unpacked my samples and, with a price list worked out in Dutch guilders in my pocket, was on my way to the offices and warehouse of Jessaia Lissauer & Zonen in the Heerengracht.

Instead of an order I usually found a complaint waiting for me. How was it that Emanuel Lissauer, the wicked brother and deadly competitor of Jessaia, had received his goods first? When I explained that Emanuel had placed his order first, Jessaia blew a cloud of smoke in my face and said it was wrong of us to supply such a charlatan at all. Were Jessaia's orders not worth twice as much? I coughed and replied that both were extremely valuable. Then I was taken to the warehouse and the attack switched to the quality of the goods we had delivered. It was not up to our usual standard. The elastic in the waist of our fleecy knickers had thinner strands of rubber. Yes, I said, but there were more of them and it was in fact an improvement. The fleece was flatter than last year, less woolly, and the navy colour was too pale. Being technically better informed than mere merchants, I was usually able to prove that our goods were up to sample, and only very rarely would I make a concession. After some rapid exchanges in Dutch which I could not follow I was told that there was little prospect of any further business. I was shown samples from Lehrmann and Braun which were better and cheaper than ours. Would I go back and tell my father?

I was on my way to England, I explained, and would probably sell the next four months' production there. Should any be left when I returned to Fleissen, I would certainly talk to Father. Some more rapid Dutch. Would I go back to my hotel to check my prices and come again tomorrow?

Next day the order book would lie on the table, and Jessaia, surrounded by four cigar-smoking assistants, would page through it, reading out the quantities he had already placed in Chemnitz, Stuttgart, Asch and, yes, also in Fleissen. He had bought enough—except that he could perhaps do with another 5,000 dozen fleecy knickers for the autumn, something like our No. 644 if I would reduce the price by 5 per cent.

'Sorry,' I said. 'We are almost sold out of 644, and Stern in London wants to place a repeat contract.' After some hesitation Jessaia wrote out an order for 1,000 dozen 24 in., 1,000 dozen 26 in. and 500 dozen 28 in., to be delivered in navy, saxe and grey, and we agreed on a price concession of $1\frac{1}{2}$ per cent.

My negotiations with Emanuel Lissauer, Fleesman, S. I. de Vries and de Vries van Buuren followed similar lines. For one reason or another our goods were never quite right and our competitors could always do better. Fleesman usually came right to the point, and I knew he meant it if he said he was not going to buy. The de Vrieses, on the other hand, instead of getting down to business bored me with lectures about their integrity and the impeccable standing their firms enjoyed in the trade, which was rather a waste of time, for I kept myself well informed about the commercial and credit rating of all my customers. They wanted to impress on me that they were much higher-class than the Lissauers, and whilst they might not place quite such large orders it was an honour to be on their list of suppliers. I liked Schönberg's approach much better. He peered at me out of his watery eyes across the table in his dingy little office, stroked his goatee beard and said in a mixture of guttural German, Yiddish and Dutch, 'Mynheer Pasold, we are both in business to make money.'

After a few days of coming and going, comparing and arguing, I collected orders for some five to six thousand dozens, my estimated target. Father would be pleased.

We also had an agent in Amsterdam, a very decent, hard-working man named Odewald. He sold our goods to some of the big retail stores who refused to deal through importers and prided themselves on buying direct from the manufacturers. Since the quantities they bought were comparatively small, they had to pay a higher price which also included 5 per cent commission for Odewald. Occasionally there was trouble. The Lissauers or Fleesman would complain that Odewald had sold to one of their customers and I went to his office, usually after business hours, and did my best to straighten matters out. Frequently Odewald's nephew, a gay young man-about-town, would call for me in the evening with his beautiful girlfriend to show me as much of Amsterdam's night life as I could stand without being tired out in the morning. Why could I not stay another night, he urged, there was so much more to see and do. But I was anxious to get to London. My job completed, I packed my bags and took the boat train to the Hook of Holland.

9

BETWEEN MOORGATE
AND ALDERSGATE STREET
1925-27

NOW CAME THE part of the trip I was most looking forward to, a week or ten days in my beloved England. But before I could set foot on the shores of the promised land I had to brave hazards like a prince in a fairy tale. The Channel had to be crossed, and the Pasolds were poor sailors. Was it because we had lived for six hundred years in Bohemia, which is such a long way from the sea? I dreaded the crossing, and if it was at all rough I was sick. Taking vigorous exercise on deck, facing the wind and breathing deeply only made me feel worse. Why wasn't the Channel Tunnel being built which they had been talking about for so long? Later I found that I felt better down below, lying on my back in warmth and darkness.

Having conquered the waves I had to face a team of steely-eyed immigration officers. Silently they examined my Czechoslovak passport. 'What is your business, and how long have you come to stay?' they demanded. 'Can you prove it?' I pulled out my file of business correspondence. 'What is your address in England?' 'I stay with the Ramsay family at 66 Ferndene Road, Herne Hill. They are friends of mine.' The officer stamped my passport. 'Granted leave to stay for two weeks,' he said and waved me on. I do not know why I was always so apprehensive, there never was any trouble.

On the train journey from Harwich to London I relaxed. It felt wonderful to be back in England. The grass was so green, there was cattle in the fields, I read the advertisements on the hoardings, and as we reached the suburbs and dusk fell I could see into some of the brightly lit rooms in the endless rows of houses. They were modest homes, and I wondered if the people in them appreciated how lucky they were to live in Britain and be able to work in London without permits and time limits. I would gladly have exchanged our large house and garden at Fleissen for one of those little flats in Bethnal Green.

The Ramsays could not have been kinder to me, and during the middle of the 1920s their home was mine whenever I came to London. Barbara, Stuart and I were great friends, and I think secretly Mr Ramsay was just a little afraid that I might want to marry his daughter. In his quiet way he was very proud of being British. To have a foreigner as a friend was quite permissible, in fact it intrigued him and impressed the neighbours, but to have one as a son-in-law would be a very different matter. Fortunately he was soon able to relax. Barbara became engaged to a local boy.

I used to share Stuart's bedroom, and in the mornings we went together by Underground from the Elephant and Castle to the City, where he had secured a job as junior clerk at Erlanger's bank, and I spent all day and every day seeing customers. I never went farther west than St Paul's. One did not go to the West End to earn money, only to spend it, and that did not tempt me. I loved the City. It had smells, noises and a traffic pattern all its own. Taxis and vans crawled through the narrow alleyways, backed into cul-de-sacs and mingled with push barrows and horse carts carrying cases bearing markings from all corners of the world. The people in the City were real, from the newspaper boy outside Aldersgate Street tube station, the commercial travellers with their sample cases, the buyers who always popped across the road for a coffee, to the gentlemen in striped trousers and bowler hats who strode along Moorgate and who, I imagined, thought only in millions.

My first call was usually at Nicholl Square, the headquarters of Stern (Hosiery Manufacturers) Ltd. They were by far the largest importers of hosiery and underwear in the British Isles. The modest entrance to their premises gave little indication of the tremendous volume of business done there. Two flights of narrow stairs led from a small courtyard to Mr Stern's private office, part of which was taken up by an impressive, richly carved desk laden with papers. On a side table were bronze statues and other *objets d'art*, and on the wall hung a coloured photograph of the great man in a white suit and topee riding in a rickshaw in China. Right now he sat in his throne-like chair signing cheques, as almost always when I called. He looked up, smiled, pointed at one of the three normal-sized chairs facing his own and carried on with his signing. When he had finished he got up, shook my hand, asked how Father was and then said, 'I have a bone to pick with you.' He rang the bell. 'Charles, show Mr Pasold the consignment of 534 his people have sent and explain why the matter is serious!'

I followed the young man upstairs.

'My name is Davis,' he said. 'I'm one of the salesmen. You've invoiced three cases of saxe blue knickers as navy. Fortunately we discovered the mistake before the goods went out to our customers.'

I apologised, made a note and promised it would not happen again. To make me appreciate the trouble we had caused by the wrong description of the merchandise he took me over the five-storey building to show me how the organisation worked. It had the goods lift in the middle, which was unusual. On the top floor was the general office with the book-keeping department, called the counting house, where a number of clerks stood behind pedestal desks entering figures into ledgers and girls typed invoices and letters. The next two floors served as warehouse for socks and stockings and as sorting and assembly areas for orders. It was here that our error had been discovered. On the second floor was Mr Stern's private office and an impressive show-room with long tables on which hundreds of samples were neatly laid out in rows, among them our qualities 534 and 644. Considering that Stern's business with us added up to £40,000 and more in a single year our samples occupied remarkably little space on his counters. If this was the average ratio, then, I quickly calculated, his total turnover must run into several million pounds.

My estimate was not far off the mark, as I discovered years later. Stern's annual sales amounted to close on £3 million. Approximately one third of this merchandise, especially women's and girl's underwear, was imported from Czechoslovakia. Another third, mostly men's vests and pants, came from Japan. The remainder—stockings, half-hose and a variety of other knitted garments—were made in Germany, Italy, Poland, Belgium and in Stern's English factories.

First floor, ground floor and basement were used for storing bulky goods, such as fleecy lined underwear, and as packing rooms. From here about ten trolley boys supplied the London wholesale houses. The parcels were loaded into wicker baskets mounted on swivelling wheels and pushed through the labyrinth of narrow streets and passages to Cook & Son at St Paul's Church-yard, Pawson & Leaf's, Foster Porter's, the Fore Street Warehouse Co. and half a dozen other famous firms in the City. Stern also supplied, of course, the wholesalers in the large provincial centres, such as Wilkinson & Riddell in Birmingham, Watts's in Manchester, Arthur's in Glasgow, etc. The wholesalers then sold in turn to the thousands of independent retail shops up and down the country.

These wholesale houses had enormous purchasing power, and their lead-ing buyers were the gods of the drapery trade. Mr Stern wined and dined them in London and took some of them on trips to the Continent, after which he invited them to come to his showroom and place their orders. Meanwhile Mr Ratcliff, his second-in-command, descended with a vast range of samples upon those in the provinces who would not come to town. Fleecy knickers were bulky, and the duplicate sets of the many different qualities, sizes and colours from the various manufacturers took up a great deal of room. The range filled a dozen or more large hampers which were collected from Nicholl Square by one of the four railway companies, the LMS (London

Midland & Scottish), the GWR (Great Western), and so forth, depending on the destination. They were collected with carts drawn by horses. These hampers travelled in a goods van on the same train as Mr Ratcliff. At the other end they were conveyed, again by cart and horse, to the wholesaler's warehouse, sent by chute down to the basement and from there taken by lift to the underwear department. They were then opened in Mr Ratcliff's presence, and the buyers made their selection and put down contracts for the quantities they wanted.

Stern's employed altogether about eighty people, including travellers. The head packer, who was in charge of the department, earned 27s 6d a week. The salary of a competent clerk was 20s. The weekly income of the head porter was 15s and of the porters and trolley boys 12s 6d. Excellent wages, Mr Davis assured me. He himself earned 25s plus another 5s commission. For 30s one could buy a man's suit!

Obviously he did not think he was giving away any secrets, but I felt guilty. From my spell in Israel & Oppenheimer's office I knew that manufacturers were not meant to pry into the importer's business. Mr Stern had always played fair with us, so I felt in honour bound to do nothing he might disapprove of. I worshipped him. Quite probably Father and especially Grandmother would be interested to know about Stern's trading methods and how he sold such fantastic quantities of merchandise, but I resolved to keep to myself what I had just heard and seen.

'The matter is serious,' repeated Mr Stern when I returned to his office, 'very serious. We cannot check every consignment and have to rely on your invoices. Make sure you describe your merchandise correctly in future.' Then he smiled, and I felt a little easier. 'I know you won't let it happen again. And now enough of business. I'll take you home to dinner!'

We sped in his little open car towards Hampstead Heath. He was a very fast and skilful driver, and I wished Father could share the thrill of zigzagging through the traffic with him. Rounding a corner, he snatched the *Evening Standard* from a paper boy, read the headlines and at the same time told me, in response to my questions, how his trade with Japan had begun.

'We used to buy our underwear from Germany,' he explained, 'but the business ceased when war broke out in 1914, and I sent Ratcliff to Japan to have the merchandise copied. It took him some time to find manufacturers who could make what we wanted, and even longer before he could obtain satisfactory counter samples. The Japs failed to understand the hurry. Had he not taken six long weeks to get to Osaka? Why was he so impatient to complete his negotiations when time passed so pleasantly in the company of Geisha girls? At last the samples were ready. He placed contracts for several hundred thousand pounds and departed for England via America. On 7 May

1915 his ship, the *Lusitania*, was torpedoed by a German submarine off the Irish coast and over a thousand people died. Ratcliff clung to a raft for twelve hours and was picked up, but his precious samples were lost. Without samples it was impossible to take orders. However, this turned out to be a blessing in disguise, for when the goods arrived from Japan eighteen months later prices had trebled and our profits were fantastic.'

Mr Stern was so carried away that he failed to notice the signal of a policeman. The officer caught up with us in the crawling traffic and pulled out his notebook. But Mr Stern spoke first.

'Young man,' he said in an authoritative voice tempered by a fatherly smile, 'I can see that you do not know who I am. You are new to the force?'

'Sorry, sir,' replied the policeman, unable to resist the dominating personality of this extraordinary man. I was not in the least surprised to see him put away his book and wave us on. Had I been in his place I would have done the same.

'Good fellow,' said Mr Stern approvingly as we drove away. 'We have the best police force in the world, the most helpful members of Parliament, an intelligent civil service and by far the shrewdest customs men. They open everyone's bags except mine—but then, I never have anything dutiable.' I agreed with him, although, on reflection, as a non-smoker and non-drinker I never carried anything dutiable either, but the customs always opened my bags.

'You will be here for ten more days?' he enquired when I took leave of my host and hostess after dinner. 'Come and see me again at the office when you have made all your other calls. I want to show you something before you go home.'

The following morning I called on A. T. Singer. He owned 1 and 2 Addle Street, a forbidding-looking building which I never entered without some trepidation. Mr Singer was our second largest customer. In addition to qualities 644 and 752 Directoire knickers in navy, saxe and white, we made for him fawn-coloured vests and pants for men and two ridiculous-looking types of undergarments for women which were called divided skirts and open drawers. Both were made from tightly knitted silver-grey fabric with white fleece inside; the former had a buttoned flap and buttoned knee bands, the latter had ribbed cuffs below the knees and a draw tape in the waist. I carried samples of all these garments nicely ticketed and folded in my bag in case I should be asked for them.

Mr Singer enjoyed the highest reputation, and being financially very strong usually paid his suppliers in advance if they needed money. It was said that the interest he collected came to more than the profit he made on his trading. A tall, heavily built man with a large red face and a moustache, his grey hair cropped like Field Marshal Hindenburg's, he wore a high, stiff collar and an immaculate, somewhat old-fashioned black jacket and striped trousers, and looked as forbidding as his four-storey building. Although he seemed to like me I was afraid of him.

In his austerely furnished office he told me the story of his life. He had been in love with a girl back in Germany, but she would not marry him because he had no money, and so he came to London to forget her. He warned me against the wickedness of the metropolis. It had not improved since he was a young man, many years ago. His opportunity to make a fortune had come at the end of the war, when he had bought large stocks of army underwear from the American government. It found a ready sale in threadbare Britain, whose clothes cupboards were empty. With a gleam in his eye he related how he had made the fantastic profit of £80,000 on one large shipment. He worked hard, gave good service to his customers, and by the time the market collapsed his reputation was established. He then switched his purchases to the continent of Europe. Directoire knickers suddenly became the great fashion. He bought them mainly from Czechoslovakia.

I wanted to know why fleecy knickers were not made in England. I had learned at the textile college that Leicester's knitting industry was famous. Mr Singer explained that there seemed to be very few of the Terrot-type knitting machines in Britain on which fleecy fabric could be made, apart from Pownall's plant in Manchester. Besides, the huge fleecy knicker trade had developed only since the war, and British manufacturers did not move so fast. They were still rubbing their eyes while Asch and Fleissen got on with the job. How was I getting on myself? Did I like working in the factory? Was Father pleased with me?

Working in the factory was all right, I said, but Fleissen was unbearably small and remote, and some day I hoped to start my own business in London, where there were so many more interesting opportunities. He thoroughly disapproved. Surely I would not abandon our old established family firm and start from scratch in this noisy, overcrowded city! How could I think of exchanging the hills and woods of Fleissen for the dirty streets and the fog of London? 'I want to do what you have done,' I replied. 'The fog doesn't put me off. It's exciting.' He shrugged his shoulders. 'Times have changed,' he said. I had obviously displeased him, and regretted having revealed my secret ambition.

He did not want to see my samples. He would shortly be at Fleissen and would discuss the autumn business with Father. My face fell, and he must have noticed it, for he asked Mr Burgess to come in. 'Mr Eric would like to take an order back with him,' he said. 'Write out a contract for 100 dozen divided skirts—no, make it 200.' I was used to very much larger quantities, but hid my disappointment and said politely, 'Thank you, Mr Singer. Father will be pleased.' When I asked him what kind of people wore these funny garments, he smiled. 'Fisherwomen at Grimsby,' he replied as he walked to the door with me.

I felt sorry for Mr Singer. Poverty had been the curse of his youth, and he had worked day and night to make money. Now he was rich, but his wealth had not brought him happiness, and he felt cheated and lonely. He did not even use his money except to make still more. He lived in a small semi-detached house at Palmers Green, from where he commuted to the City by bus. He owned no car, could not drive, and never took a holiday. I could not understand him.

Saturday was half-day in the City. The faces in the Underground became alive, people read the sports pages and joked with each other, and the atmosphere in the offices was noticeably relaxed. The clerks wore black or navy, to be sure, but of the departmental managers, directors and partners many appeared in grey or brown lounge suits, or even in sports jackets and flannel trousers. Mr Ramsay daringly wore plus-fours, but his was only a small office and it was in Oxford Circus, not the City.

In the afternoon I went shopping with Barbara to Brixton. We enjoyed the ride on the open top of the bus, and she pointed out landmarks to me. 'There's the house of Bessemer, the steel millionaire.' I showed off by explaining the Bessemer process of making steel, about which I had learned at the textile college. It did not impress her. In the evening I went with her and Stuart and their friends to Wimbledon Palais de Danse. Mr Ramsay very kindly let us take the car, and Barbara drove it, which gave her considerable status. I was used to the small dance floors of the hotels at Franzensbad, Karlsbad and Bad Elster, where at tea time ten couples or so would shimmy or foxtrot to the strains of 'Valencia' or 'Ramona', but Wimbledon was enormous, it was larger than the largest factory floor I had ever seen. To dance on this floor felt like taking a girl for a walk on Clapham Common. One had to be careful not to lose the way back to one's table. While the girls had ice cream the young men talked about motor-cycles and the TT races. Stuart said little; his was only a 250 c.c. side-valve BSA, which, however, he loved dearly. As the owner of a 680 c.c. Zenith, which I shall describe in a later chapter, I commanded some attention. It was a heavy machine, but of course had only a side-valve engine. 'Because of the easier maintenance,' I explained. 'Czechoslovakia has bad roads and few service stations.' No one knew or cared where Czechoslovakia was. One of the lads, the son of a garage proprietor, had a 500 c.c. overhead-valve Norton, in fact he and his girl had come to the dance on it. Everyone kept respectfully silent when he spoke.

One Sunday afternoon I took Eileen Joyce to tea, a charming girl with beautiful hands, rather shy at first but full of fun when one got to know her better. She was younger than I, but quite a little lady, so very different from Barbara, the tomboy. An Australian, she had studied music at Leipzig and was now continuing her studies in London. Unfortunately I have inherited none of the Bohemian's natural talent for music, and refused to go to concerts with her. Beethoven and Bach could not make me forget the discomfort of the hard wooden chairs which seem to be a speciality of concert halls. She in turn failed to appreciate the music of motor-cycle engines, or the thrill of booking an order for fleecy knickers. We lost touch. Time went by, Eileen became famous, her pretty face smiled down at me from countless hoardings, but I never heard her play. Many years later she gave a concert at Slough, and I went. The applause seemed never-ending. She was surprised and pleased to see me backstage. When I told her how little she had changed in all the years since we last met, and how I admired her for holding the audience in raptures 'even though she played the same exercise four times', she laughed and said I had not changed either.

But I must come back to my story. With renewed hope of clinching some orders I set off for the City on Monday morning. Failing to see two of my customers with whom I had appointments—the one had forgotten and gone out, the other was too busy and asked to be excused—I called on Israel & Oppenheimer's. The atmosphere was explosive. Mr Israel was in a temper. Something had gone wrong in the glove department. Waving pieces of paper, the excitable little man rushed from one glass-partitioned office to another. He was the managing director and very much a dictator. The cause of the commotion seemed to be Mr Oppenheimer, the director in charge of gloves, who had been too lenient with a wayward supplier. He sat at his desk with a very flushed face, paging through files of correspondence. 'Hello, Eric,' called Mr Israel as he dashed past me in the corridor. 'No time to see you, I'm afraid. Ask Leslie to take you to lunch.'

Leslie, his son, a good-looking lad of my own age, was more interested in girls than in business. Glad to get away from the office, he took me and young Elliot, the assistant underwear buyer, to a little restaurant and related his adventures in Paris, where he had just been to learn French. A wasted morning as far as I was concerned—worse, in fact, for I got into trouble with Elliot. Anticipating that some of Mr Israel's wrath might fall on him, he thought it advisable to prepare for this eventuality by taking a tough line with me. He picked on the two-needle finish at the waist and legs of our knickers. His customers complained that the elastic jumped out and was more difficult to rethread than when inserted by the old single-needle machines. When I asked whether he would accept a little wider overlock seam that would grip the ends of the elastic more firmly, he blew up. He was not there to solve the manufacturer's problems. He would just send us debit notes. The week was not starting very well!

One of my most troublesome customers was the London Knitwear Co., of Clerkenwell. The premises from which they operated were a semi-derelict ground floor and basement, and I was glad that Father never saw them. He might well have closed the account. The whole firm consisted of three people: a retired accountant who put up the money, whom I met only once, when he suggested that I might take over half the shares to provide more capital for the company and whose name I have forgotten; Captain Da Costa, the managing director, a character who looked and talked like a barrow boy; and a young man in brown overalls who did everything from typing letters and invoices to packing parcels and shifting cases. They knew nothing whatever about knitted goods, relied entirely on my guidance and never questioned quality. That part of the business went very smoothly, but Da Costa had continuous feuds with our forwarding agents. They delivered late, broke the wooden cases, damaged the goods or had them stolen. In the end I got tired of the acrimonious correspondence and insurance claims and told him to make his own arrangements to get the merchandise transported from the railway station at Fleissen to his basement in Clerkenwell. He did, but the claims continued.

As I sat in Da Costa's office listening to yet another tirade against the carriers who handled our consignments, and against shipping and forwarding agents in general, the young man in overalls announced a Miss Swift. Da Costa called him an idiot, apologised to me, visibly embarrassed by the interruption, led the lady between the wooden cases to the far corner of the room and talked to her in a low voice so that I could not follow the conversation. She was obviously a customer, and he did not want me to discover her identity. I turned away and looked out of the window into the dirty yard where three urchins played football. When she had gone Da Costa got out his order pad and wrote a contract for 5,000 dozen fleecy knickers, 534 quality, payment to be by a three-months bill of exchange. I refused to take it. 'Don't buy more than you can pay for,' I said. 'Talk to your bank manager, and I'll come back the day after tomorrow.'

We found a compromise. Da Costa promised a 20 per cent cash deposit and we were to deliver the goods to the London shipping agents, who would release them as and when payment was forthcoming. And to eliminate any possible misunderstanding I took Da Costa by bus to King William Street and we saw the shipping agents together.

A year or two later I learned accidentally that Miss Swift was the buyer for Marks & Spencer, a small but rapidly growing chain of shops selling cheap underwear. Manufacturers did not like to supply them direct, and the trade was done by middlemen like Da Costa. I believe Marks & Spencer's were his only connection and that the thousands of dozens of fleecy knickers we sold to the London Knitwear Co. during the 1920s all went to them.

Another of my customers who had money problems was Langleben & Davidson Ltd of Jewin Street. Since I would not give them extended credit, they placed orders only for small quantities with me, a thousand dozen of Directoire knickers at a time. They bought substantial quantities of our merchandise from Stern at slightly higher prices. He accepted three-monthly bills from them which he prolonged in case of need. It would have been best for us not to trade with them at all, but since the large customers rarely gave me an order and preferred to deal with Father at Fleissen I had to do business with some of the smaller firms, however difficult it might be, otherwise there would have been no justification for my journeys to England. I sometimes called on them daily until a small contract was finalised.

The last day of my visit came, and I had to see Mr Stern again. When I sat opposite him, with the grand desk between us, he said, 'Eric, you are a lucky boy. I am going to show you something no other manufacturer at Fleissen has yet seen. It's going to be the biggest thing since Directoire knickers were invented, but you must give me your word to tell no one except your father.' He paused and studied me for a few seconds. The silence seemed eternal. Then he nodded: 'Yes, I can trust you,' and continued almost prophetically, 'We are heading for a revolution. Short skirts and Directoire knickers are only the beginning of women's emancipation. Have a look at this!' He unlocked a drawer. Slowly, almost reverently, he unwrapped a pair of pale peach-coloured fleecy knickers and held them up to me with both hands. 'Flesh, the new colour,' he said. 'And with artificial silk stripes!'

It was a gaudy-looking pair of bloomers. Most of the dye had been absorbed by the cotton, leaving the artificial silk thread with which every fourth row of the fabric was plated a shiny, silvery line. 'I like the effect,' I said. 'We can knit this kind of material, we have used artificial silk before, but it will cost more than cotton.' Mr Stern was not listening. 'They are beautiful,' he said. 'We developed them together with Marschall, Frank, Sachs in Chemnitz. I will give orders to only three manufacturers in Fleissen, and you can be one of them if your price is right and you do the right shade of flesh. But of course I shall also order navy, saxe and cream. I make, however, one condition. You must not supply knickers with artificial silk stripes to anyone else this coming autumn. Stern's Hosiery must have the market to themselves. Next season you can sell them to the others, even to Langleben & Davidson, if you like.'

I blushed and wanted to explain, but he would not let me and said with a smile, 'You may think London is a very big place, but as you see I know what

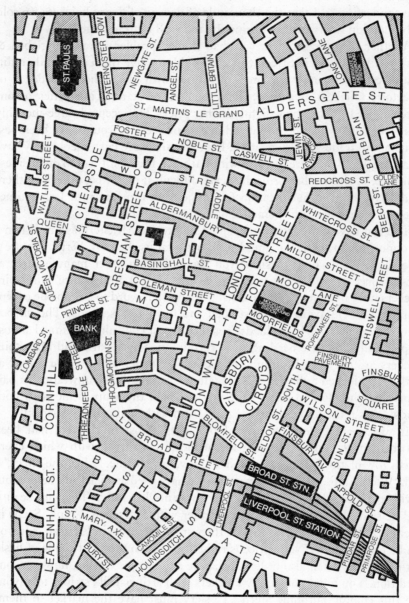

The textile district of the City of London in 1926

goes on in the trade. Please remember it.' Then he wished me a good journey and said that he would himself be in Czechoslovakia before the end of the month. Would I ask Father to prepare samples and prices of flesh-coloured knickers with artificial silk stripes?

My time was up. I had to go back to Fleissen. It felt like going into exile, and only my duty to Father and the knowledge that in a few months I could come again kept me from deserting. For the return journey I chose the short sea crossing from Dover to Calais. It took only two hours, but even they could be agony if the sea was rough. My face glued to the window of the boat train, I watched the trees, the smoke from the chimneys and the washing on the clothes lines waving me goodbye. From their movement I anxiously tried to assess the strength of the wind and anticipate the size of the waves. Only when the ordeal was over, the Channel lay behind me and I sat in the Orient Express on firm French soil was I able to think again about other things. I summarised the results of my visit to London. Did they justify the cost of the trip? Would Father approve of the orders in my briefcase? What mistakes had I made and what had I learned?

None of the large importers, the ones whose business kept us going, ever gave me a worthwhile order, I reflected. They all travelled regularly to Asch and Fleissen to place their contracts. The fact that I spoke English and called on them in London did not seem to give us the slightest advantage over Lehrmann, Braun, Friedl or Korn, who spoke only German and stayed at home. Worse, our customers did not seem to welcome my visits. They probably felt that eventually I would go with my samples to the wholesalers. The only orders I picked up were from smaller, financially weaker, less desirable firms, and, I disliked admitting it, we could well have done without their troublesome business.

Looking back today, I am surprised that it never occurred to me to study the windows of the expensive shops in London's West End, where fashion trends usually showed first. I too could have predicted that flesh would become our most popular shade for the coming season. But I did not take shops seriously. Those at Fleissen, grocers', butchers' and bakers', were of no help. The shops at Eger where the country people went to make their purchases on Saturday afternoon gave no lead either: they catered for the peasant population. The well-to-do had their clothes, frequently even their underwear, made by tailors. True, some of the fashionable shops at Karlsbad and Marienbad, which were open only during the season, compared with those of Bond Street, but the merchandise they showed was only for the extravagant international clientele. I saw no connection between it and the goods we manufactured.

In fairness to myself I must say that all Fleissen shared these views. Any suggestion that we might learn something from shopkeepers would have seemed ridiculous, especially since we all worked mainly for export markets. The manufacturers of Fleissen did not bother their heads about styles or consumer reaction. We never thought of designing or developing a garment. That was the British importers' concern. We were not in the least interested to know why England suddenly wanted flesh-coloured knickers. Without batting an eyelid we would have made a million pairs of bloomers with only one leg, and made them well, had Mr Stern asked us to do so.

It was a very different matter when it came to machinery layouts, better manufacturing methods, ideas of increasing productivity or ways of saving waste. These were terms Fleissen understood. German and American techniques were copied or adapted. We were industrialists, we built factories, operated boiler plants and steam engines, laid out production lines with conveyor belts and power-driven machinery, followed the cotton market, bought raw material and turned it into finished merchandise, and we did it on a very large scale. What were shops in comparison with industry? Almost frivolous places where people were induced to spend their hard-earned money. We thought the retailer did little more than sell inefficiently in singles the knickers, vests and pants which we manufactured efficiently in their hundreds of thousands. Our mass-production methods were far in advance of those used in British factories, our hard-working labour force was very co-operative and took great pride in their jobs, the garments we made were of remarkably consistent good quality and we beat the whole world on price.

But what we gained through able factory management, hard work and long hours we partly lost again through our failure to appreciate the importance of fashion, styling and merchandising. My year in London had taught me nothing in this respect. I would have needed a guiding hand to point out what Fleissen lacked. One well spent afternoon in the West End of London would have been of more benefit to me and to our business than the three months I had sat in Israel & Oppenheimer's office. Incredible as it may seem, another twenty years had to pass before I fully appreciated how important it was for a manufacturer to establish close contact with the shopkeeper and through him with the consuming public, instead of relying on middlemen for information.

Father was pleased with the orders I had taken and the information I brought home. Not that he said so; it was not in his nature to praise, least of all his own children, and I did not expect it. The Pasolds are not very demonstrative. Besides, I had only done my job, and not exceptionally well at that, as I was fully aware, but Mother told me that Father was secretly proud of me. And he spoke well of me to my uncles and to friends and acquaintances whom he met in the evening. That made it all the harder to think of leaving him and starting up in England.

FLEISSEN'S BUSINESS COMMUNITY
1925-30

ALTHOUGH LITTLE MORE than a village, Fleissen had become one of Czechoslovakia's outstanding earners of foreign currency and, after the city of Eger, the largest payer of taxes in the Egerland. The most level-headed, hard-working and technically progressive community in the whole of western Bohemia, it vibrated with business activity. Of the four largest enterprises, three were owned and directed by teams of brothers. As chance would have it, almost all of them were at that time in their forties, which, no doubt, contributed to the virility of the village. Each manufacturer's every move was followed by the population with keen interest. The merits of every extension project, new machine or change of production technique was widely discussed and the likely effect on the firm's progress weighed. And fortunes fluctuated as the years went by, providing a never-ending topic of conversation.

The factories were all multi-storey buildings. Fleissen was all hills and slopes, with few level pieces of land large enough for even a medium-sized production unit all on one floor. Very little land came on the market, and the price was so high that one simply had to make the best use of it by building upwards. To own a single-storey north-light factory in which one could spread and lay out machinery in the most efficient sequence was the unfulfillable dream of every manufacturer.

The largest concern was still that of the Geipels, whose leather factory exported mainly to the USA. In addition they owned close on two thousand acres of agricultural and forest land and had embarked on a scheme of intensive cultivation and soil improvement, using waste products from the tannery as fertiliser. The partners of the firm were the brothers Friedrich, Otto and Gustav, while Wilhelm, the youngest, my godfather and favourite uncle, controlled the leather stamping plant. Between them the Geipel enterprises employed some 800 people, most of them men, but since their business was so different from the manufacture of textiles its growth could not readily be compared with that of the other firms. There was the impression that the knitters were expanding faster and that the gap was narrowing, but

Fleissen had no means of guessing the size of the Geipels' turnover, which in the best year exceeded the fantastic figure of 50 million kronen and showed them a profit of 5 million. This was more than the profit of all the knitters added together. No wonder they could carry out these extensive agricultural developments, drainage and road building schemes. My uncles gave, however, not the slightest indication of such earnings. Admittedly they lived well, and Uncle Gustav collected works of art. He had done that as long as I could remember. And they had a car, a Minerva, but three large families shared it. Friedrich, Otto and Gustav each had the use of it two days a week and alternately every third Sunday, an irksome timetable which nevertheless was strictly adhered to.

Next in size to the Geipels came the Lehrmanns, who were slightly ahead of us although we would not admit it. Of the four brothers, Bernhard, Fritz and Hans were working in the concern, while Dr Adolf Lehrmann was a sleeping partner who kept in very close touch. His official position was that of '*Oberrat* and *Bezirkshauptmann*', administrative head of the district of Marienbad, an important government post of authority. In his student days at Prague University he had met Eduard Beneš. He spoke Czech reasonably fluently and entertained the men from the Ministries lavishly whenever they spent a weekend or longer holiday at Marienbad, one of Czechoslovakia's loveliest spas, in a beautiful setting of mountains, large forests and trout streams. He laid on shooting and fishing parties for them, and was the perfect host. Through Beneš's personal intervention he secured a large long-term loan from the Živnostenská Banka which enabled his brothers to expand the business rapidly. Their labour force now approached 600. Moreover for a senior civil servant the doors of most government departments were open, and Dr Lehrmann used the influence he had with the officials of the Inland Revenue, Ministry of Trade and Industry, water authorities and even with the courts to foster his business interests. No other firm at Fleissen enjoyed such exceptional advantages.

Although civil servants had considerable discretionary powers, it would not be true to say that corruption was worse in Czechoslovakia than in most other eastern Central European States. Everyone knew that they were underpaid and that many of them supplemented their meagre income by showing favours to open-handed 'clients'. The lower ranks, especially in the provinces, were satisfied with very small bribes, twenty kronen, perhaps, or a goose. Only if a transaction had to be referred to a higher official at Prague did it tend to become expensive.

Bribing a government official was a punishable offence, but not one case in a thousand came to light. The powers that were did not want cases of bribery reported in the press, and all newspapers, even the Communist *Rude Pravo*, toed the line. It was too risky to upset the authorities, who could retaliate by exercising such strict censorship over a paper that it suffered severe financial losses or might have to cease publication. Gifts to obliging government officials had not been unusual under the Monarchy either, and one understood that the war had lowered moral standards. Many of Czechoslovakia's officials had been civil servants under Austrian rule. Additional ones were selected not on merit but for political reasons, because they spoke Czech, and some were ex-legionaries who had to be found jobs when their units were disbanded and replaced by the regular army. Anyone who knew his way about government departments and had 'connections', especially if he could speak some Czech, was able to achieve a good deal with comparatively little money—and Oberrat Dr Lehrmann had all the necessary attributes.

A more sinister civil service practice was the preferential treatment given to Czech-owned enterprises. In the eyes of the nationalists far too great a proportion of the country's industry was owned by German-speaking Bohemians. The politicians tried to redress the balance by helping to make Czech firms grow faster. They gave them government contracts and discriminated in various other ways in their favour. This was, of course, not an openly declared policy; on the contrary, the government denied that any such policy existed, but the facts spoke for themselves. There was no need for Ministers to issue specific instructions: the officials knew their masters' wishes and used their own initiative to implement them, frequently with an eye to personal gain. Some firms fought back with lawyers and appeals, others were more adaptable and played the game. A few crisp banknotes at the right moment or some favour shown to a government official resolved many a conflict between nationalist ambition and business interest.

The four Lehrmann brothers were pastmasters at adaptability, from Ministerial and church level down to village politics. Adolf, a high-ranking civil servant, masqueraded as an avowed Czech nationalist. At his suggestion the firm made a brave attempt to qualify as a Czech enterprise by 'importing' one Czech-speaking boilerman—the only Czech workman in the village—and showed thereby considerably more political realism than its competitors. Adolf was a Protestant. Brother Hans was a devout Catholic, a close personal friend and political supporter of the priest, Bernhard a freethinking conservative and Fritz an agnostic who supported the socialist party. They were thus well equipped to deal with all contingencies arising from changes in governmental or local politics. All four represented the firm in turn, according to circumstances and the face it wanted to show. But at times they also fought each other, and the whole village chuckled when a peasant once found a notebook headed 'Die Schandtaten meiner Brüder' ('Disgraceful deeds committed by my brothers') which belonged to Dr Lehrmann and which he hurriedly retrieved by paying the lucky finder a handsome reward.

By 1926 Fleissen was tired of the socialists who had burdened the village with debts and of Burgomaster Kraut's irregularities. He had committed perjury so often that the court would no longer accept his sworn affidavits and published an announcement to this effect. I never heard of such a case before or since. A conservative mayor was elected, and it was thought that Kraut would now be without a job, for nobody would want to employ him. To everyone's amazement Lehrmann's appointed him within the week as their personnel director and used him to represent them in dubious transactions, honouring his signature or repudiating it as it suited them. If the complaints became too loud he was demonstratively dismissed by one of the brothers, took an enforced holiday and was then re-engaged by another. They paid him well; his experience and utter lack of scruples made him ideally suited to the job, and he seemed to enjoy it. This illustrates the kind of competition we were up against. Kraut caused Father and me many a headache in years to come.

We followed in size closely behind Lehrmann's, with more than 500 employees. The growth of Adolf Pasold & Sohn since the war was wholly due to Father's efforts. He had no brothers with whom to share the burden of management or even discuss some of his problems, far less to open the back doors of government departments. To the best of my belief he never bribed anyone, I do not know whether for moral reasons, out of pride, or because he did not want to expose himself to blackmail. The responsibility of making decisions and carrying them out was his alone. Professional advice, for what it might be worth, was easier to obtain in a city than in a place like Fleissen where one had to rely on one's own ability and judgement. Father had to be a textile man, engineer, accountant, financier, lawyer, organiser, buyer, salesman and negotiator. He had to know what went on in the world, keep in contact with other businessmen, government officials, village politicians and be the friend and leader of his workpeople, a formidable task for any one man. True, Grandfather at sixty-nine and Grandmother at sixty-seven still worked full-time in the firm and were remarkably enterprising, but they were used to the conditions of the Austro-Hungarian Monarchy and found it hard to adjust themselves to post-war Czechoslovakia. The world had changed for the worse. Grandfather was disappointed over the carelessness of the young. 'Waste not, want not' was his motto, and he walked through the factory picking up ends of string a foot long which he knotted together and gave to the packers for tying parcels. He shook his head about the government introducing the forty-eight-hour week and doing away with Saturday afternoon work when so much remained undone. We had no clocking system, but Grandfather was usually at the factory himself just before 6 a.m., and anyone late—not that it happened often—was severely rebuked. Some of the new ideas were too socialistic for his liking, but not all of them were bad. He approved whole-heartedly of the newly introduced national health insurance scheme, which, incidentally, operated successfully and at a profit. The authorities understood that income had to exceed expenditure and over the years built up large reserves which they invested in profitable public works, increasing the funds still further. And there were other innovations. Grandfather continued to express his opinion, but felt uncertain and no longer wanted to lead. The reins now lay solely and firmly in Father's sensitive hands. Although out-numbered by the many partners of his rivals, he more than held his own. But he needed help, and relied on me. I was now twenty and ready to do a man's job!

Our annual sales had climbed to over 15 million kronen, and in a good year our profits approached a million, sometimes even more. Profits were important to plough back into the business in order to maintain our trade against the growing competition not only from Czechoslovakia but from Poland and especially Japan. Every manufacturer tried to produce better garments at cheaper prices, and this he could do only by continually increasing the efficiency of his factory. Whoever made most money was in the best position to modernise his buildings and buy better plant earlier than his competitor, thereby stealing a march on him.

Everyone watched the race between Lehrmann's and ourselves. The odds seemed to be slightly in favour of Lehrmann's. We had, unfortunately, no means of finding out what figures they returned to the Inland Revenue, far less what their real profits were. Grandmother's information service failed when it came to financial matters. Nobody knew but the Lehrmann brothers themselves, and the figures they leaked were always false. It would have been interesting to compare our results with theirs, but even had we been on friendly terms we would not have told each other the truth. Nobody ever did where profits were concerned.

Both Lehrmann and ourselves—in fact all the knitters at Fleissen, and most of those at Asch and Teplitz—produced their fabric on circular spring-needle machines which were built by Terrot, Fouquet & Frauz, Haaga and Roscher. The basic design used by all four was identical. Only the finish varied. This Terrot-type circular, as it was called, was made in a wide selection of diameters, from the smallest two-loopwheel machine to monsters of over ninety inches, accommodating up to two dozen loopwheels. They came in a variety of gauges from 16 coarse to 28 fine. Machines of 48 in. diameter with eight loopwheels and a gauge of 24 fine were the most popular. Most of them were equipped to knit only plain summer-weight and fleecy winter-weight fabric; only a few had stripers, press-patterns and other attachments. Since we had all acquired our machinery over a period of twenty or thirty years, mostly as second-hand bargains, the profitability of each firm's operation depended to some extent on the skill with which it used its oddly assorted plant, for we all made the same type of product, Directoire knickers, and we all sold in the same market.

A good way behind us came the Braun brothers. They had about 300 workers. Rudolf was in charge of finance, Hans of production and Adolf of sales. Apart from their own business and an insatiable curiosity about the activities of their competitors they had few interests. No manufacturing secret was safe from them. They planted spies in their rivals' factories and made good use of the bits of information that came back. There was no one more adept at stealing the ideas of others than the Brauns. Having smaller resources than Lehrmann's and Pasold's, they were intelligent enough not to compete with them for Stern's large contracts, but cut and finished their garments a little differently and catered for other buyers. They were the only firm who installed warp looms in addition to their Terrot-type circulars. Adolf travelled extensively in Holland and Scandinavia, selling to wholesalers and large retail stores rather than to importers, and in this way secured higher prices. We were on friendly terms with them and rarely had any arguments.

Friedl's was a sad story. At the beginning of the century Fleissen's largest textile concern, famous throughout the Monarchy, a firm which even in those early days exported some of its knitted garments to Britain, it had steadily declined since Gustav Friedl's death. Of the four brothers who should now have worked together, two were not interested and took their money out. Ewald, the third, spent more time shooting and fishing than at the factory. This left the burden on Adolf's shoulders, who, hard-working though he was, lacked the ability and the capital to keep the business on an even keel, far less to participate in the race with his thrusting competitors. The still impressive building in the centre of the village was filled with out-of-date machinery, the wheels turned slowly, one after another the faithful old customers died off, and the new, progressive buyers transferred their custom elsewhere. The firm was a blot on the map of the village.

Carl Korn was a newcomer from Germany and therefore thought to be slick and slightly suspect. He had married one of the Friedl daughters but after some disagreement with the firm was paid out and started on his own. He built an attractive small factory, employed about fifty people and made fleecy knickers, like most of Fleissen's knitters. His largest customer was Stern. Korn was an enigma. He sold at lower prices than the large manufacturers, who predicted that he would go bankrupt. In response he only smiled and said his overheads were low and his trading results very satisfactory. But his business experience was limited, he knew only how to operate in a falling market, usually sold the year's output in advance and postponed covering his raw material requirements to the very last moment. By the time he bought his yarns the price had fallen, and on balance the transaction showed him a profit. All went well for a number of years. He built up a reputation as a very astute businessman and particularly impressed my uncle Otto. Then came an unexpected rise in cotton prices. Carl Korn went bankrupt and disappeared as mysteriously as he had come, abandoning his wife and leaving hardly any assets for his creditors. It was then that Otto's secret participation became known. My financially so clever uncle, who was envious of the apparently large profits made by the knitters, had been completely hoodwinked. Without telling anyone he had put a million kronen in Korn's enterprise and become a sleeping partner. Now he had lost the lot, and the people of Fleissen laughed. A leather manufacturer had no business meddling in textiles!

Korn's factory was bought by Adolf Geipel. He was no relation; Geipel was a common name in the village. Adolf was ambitious and able, but his health was not very robust and he was short of capital. Within a few years he killed himself with overwork and worry. As for Reichel, Stübiger and Fischer, each employed about twenty workers in addition to the members of the family, who all slaved long hours in their businesses. Too small to export their merchandise, they supplied mainly the home market, but they all had expansion plans.

It would not be true to say that the people of Fleissen had an inferiority complex. Perhaps they could not compete with townspeople in education and refinement, but they were tougher and did not mind working harder. Like most country folk they distrusted easy profits, convinced that success had to be earned. They believed in giving value for money, in large turnover and small returns.

Maximum effort and stringent economy were taken for granted; it was only the result that counted. If there was an oil stain on a piece of fabric the knitter got into trouble not only for soiling the cloth but also for wasting oil. No bobbin was taken off a machine until the last yard of thread had been used. No letter was sent if a postcard would do. Envelopes were made not of white but of cheap coloured paper, and when they had served their purpose were used to scribble or make calculations on before they were sold to a waste-paper merchant. No telegram contained an unnecessary word. Every scrap of material, empty box, piece of cardboard, string, wire or timber was utilised. Manufacturers pondered from morning to night how to produce more cheaply and where to save—but never at the expense of quality. If buyers were to lose confidence in the value and consistent standard of Fleissen's merchandise its flourishing knitting industry would sink back into the obscurity from which it had so very recently emerged. Grandfather, who was fond of quoting proverbs, impressed upon me a hundred times: 'Money gone, much lost—name gone, everything lost!'

As far as I could judge, competition among the musical instrument makers was just as keen. Most of them were skilled craftsmen, all specialists working in their homes. Some made the gracefully shaped bellies, backs and ribs of violins and cellos, others carved nothing but finger-boards, necks and scrolls, some only bridges or bows, and some spun the strings. The parts were then assembled into complete instruments, varnished and tuned. I knew little more about this trade than that each instrument was a work of art and that most of them were bought by middlemen and exported.

Then there were the farmers, who could no longer compete with the wages paid by industry. The more progressive of them introduced machines and released labour. The others found the going very difficult, and although they and their children worked hard most of them had to sell off one field after another to make ends meet or, with heavy hearts, mortgage the farms which had been in the possession of their families for generations. The buyers were local manufacturers who had long-term expansion plans and snapped up every square metre that came on the market. Negotiations were carried on in strict secrecy, and no property deal was disclosed until the vendor and purchaser had been to the land registry at Wildstein and recorded the change of ownership. Since my grandparents were on even more intimate terms with the people of the village than Father, they usually found out first if a farmer wanted to sell a piece of land, and Grandfather conducted the negotiations.

People in Bohemia considered land as their most treasured possession, and any change of ownership was an almost sacred transaction. A square metre of poor agricultural land, covered by snow three months of the year, located on the outskirts of Fleissen, fetched about 2.50 kronen. This was the equivalent of 10,000 kronen or £60 an acre, five or ten times as much as the price of a similar field in the United Kingdom. This staggering difference between Continental and British land values has often puzzled me in later years, and I have many times been surprised and quietly amused when people in England, let alone Scotland or Wales, have argued that land in the island had become too expensive. It all depends on what one is used to.

Every working man in Bohemia had the ambition to own a house with a small vegetable garden, a chicken run and a shed in which to keep a pig, a couple of goats and some rabbits. Since there were no speculative builders, he had to find a piece of land and build himself. Finding the land was the most difficult part. To build a small detached house with a kitchen and a living room downstairs, two bedrooms and a loft upstairs, and a cellar to keep coal and potatoes in for the winter cost about 25,000 kronen. A family, if they were all working, could live quite respectably on their income and save 100 kronen or more in a week.

Living respectably meant having bread, sausage and coffee or a bottle of beer for lunch, which was the main meal of the day. This did not take long to prepare and, bearing in mind that there were no fewer than thirty different kinds of sausages, was not nearly as monotonous as might appear. The evening meal consisted of boiled potatoes or potato dumplings with cream cheese and a salt herring or buckling. Wives and daughters were skilled at sewing, knitting and mending, and made clothes last a very long time, and, while fashion was of secondary importance, everyone's suit or dress was clean, tidy and had no buttons missing.

After school the children went in the forest to look for mushrooms and the various delicious kinds of edible toadstools, picked blackberries and cranberries for bottling and collected firewood, and at weekends they were joined by adults. Men who worked night shifts in a factory spent part of the day digging up the stumps and roots of trees which were left in the ground when sections of the pine forest had been felled, and cut them up into logs. It was heavy work, for there were no tractors in those days. When an area was cleared of roots the owner had to level the soil and replant before he could obtain permission from the Forestry Department to start felling another section. Although most forests were private property, the State looked upon them as a valuable national asset and made sure that they were maintained in good order. More than half of Czechoslovakia was covered by forest, and large quantities of timber were exported.

During the previous fifteen years Fleissen had grown to 3,000 inhabitants, and in addition more than a thousand men and women came from neighbouring villages to work there. They came on foot, in summer and in winter, for the day shift or the night shift, walking on the paths that led through the forest and between the fields. Some of them walked several miles each way, leaving home at four in the morning to arrive in time for the early shift at six, and in winter time, when the snow lay a foot deep, they had to start even earlier. But they never complained and were happy to have regular jobs. Canteens were unknown, so they brought their food with them, or another member of the family would bring it at mealtimes in a small bag or tin can; in the summer they would eat it sitting on the narrow grass verge along the factory fence, and in winter inside, on the stairs, in the boilerhouse or wherever it was dry and warm. As the factories expanded most of them provided dining rooms furnished with rough wooden tables and benches, and a stove on which workers who lived too far away to go home for their meals could heat up the food they brought. And as the workpeople became a little more affluent an increasing number bought sausages from local butchers.

Apart from the farmers the village was booming, and innkeepers, shop-keepers, bakers and butchers did well. Take the butchers. There were five of them in Fleissen, and Josef Böhm was the most prosperous. He slaughtered twenty oxen, fifty cows, a hundred calves and two hundred pigs a year, and made over half of all this meat into sausages. His annual turnover reached the astonishing figure of 200,000 kronen and showed him a profit of 50,000. To the tax authorities he declared a turnover of 100,000 and a profit of 25,000 kronen. He had such an honest face and such simplicity of manner that they invariably believed him. At the rate of 20 per cent his tax assessment came to 5,000 kronen, which, tongue in cheek, he pleaded he could not afford to pay. After being granted time to find the money and eventually threatened with legal seizure of his goods and chattels, he would do a deal with the officials and settle for around 2,500 kronen. We shall hear more of Herr Böhm later.

Readers who are not familiar with the philosophy and tactics of Central European tax authorities between the two world wars may welcome a few words of explanation. The tax men knew that some liabilities would inevitably slip untaxed through their fingers and did not attempt to devise a watertight system. To operate it would have required an enormous civil service. Half the population would have had to work in the tax departments while the other half would be busy hiding its wealth instead of getting on with production. On balance everyone would lose. 'Live and let live' was the accepted motto, but it would be equally true, if less kind, to call it 'catch as catch can', for the tax men could be very tough if they felt like it. One of their favourite methods was to keep a suspected tax defrauder 'incommunicado' for a week or two at an hotel while the officials ransacked his home and office. Tormented by fear of what might be found, the victim usually broke down after a few days and confessed or offered some acceptable compromise.

Bank deposit books offered welcome if not complete protection against the prying eye of the tax inspector. It corresponded in effect to the present notion of the 'numbered account' so many Englishmen dream of these days but are not allowed to have. Czechoslovak banks accepted cash from any stranger and opened interest-bearing savings accounts without checking the identity of the depositor. As a receipt they issued bank deposit books with any desired name or number on it. The bearer of the book could claim the money without having to prove that he was in fact the legal owner. As a protection the de-positor could only make withdrawls against a code word which was not shown in the book and which the drawer had to quote before the money was handed over. Bank deposit books were as negotiable and as anonymous as bank-notes, with the added advantage of earning interest while in the owner's pocket and of not being cashable in case of loss unless the finder or thief knew the code word. The peasants in particular trusted their savings to bank deposit books, happy in the knowledge that not even the bank manager could add up how much money they had in his bank. There was no limit to the amount that could be deposited in any one book or the number of books held by one and the same person. They were issued for the convenience of the public and had the government's blessing. Without them most small savers would have hidden their money under the floorboards and the larger ones used other devices to protect themselves against the inquisitiveness and greed of the tax men.

Interest was added and the credit balance brought up to date whenever the book was presented to the bank. Interest was income and had to be declared to the Inland Revenue, but in practice many owners forgot, secure in the knowledge that they could not be traced. Anonymous bank deposit books were part of Czechoslovakia's way of life. Wives hid the savings from their household money in them, farmers their takings from cattle auctions, civil servants their bribes, politicians their party funds and businessmen their undisclosed profits.

It was the established, if illegal, practice of the clothing trade to sell seconds without invoicing them. The prices were cut to the bone but the buyers paid cash for which they wanted no receipt, neither party paid tax, and that made the transaction worthwhile. Grandfather sold whole truckloads full of imperfects as job lots to his friends, the Polish Jews from Slovakia and Ruthenia, stuffed the money in his pockets and later paid it into one of the bank savings books.

Old habits die hard. The reader will be intrigued to know that anonymous bank deposit books as I describe them are still in regular use in Austria today and—even more surprising—have recently been reintroduced in Communist Hungary.

Nothing showed more characteristically the different mentality of the Reichs-Germans across the border and the German-speaking Bohemians in Czechoslovakia than their attitude to taxation. Whilst the Reichs-Germans had clear-cut regulations for everything and were sticklers for observing them, the Bohemians, Czech and German-speaking alike, had inherited the Austro-Hungarian talent for bartering and compromise. Having lived together, sometimes in harmony, sometimes fighting each other, for 800 years, sharing the same administration and the same history, they had grown very similar in habit and outlook. In Germany anyone caught evading tax was treated as a criminal and shunned. In Czechoslovakia he was thought unlucky. He did a deal with the authorities, paid the penalty, and everyone laughed. There was little stigma attached to being fined: nobody could win all the time!

Officials in Germany were soulless beaurocrats who only knew their printed instructions and, in blind obedience, carried them out to the letter. Our civil servants, by comparison, used a wide measure of discretion, and one could reason with them, but somehow or other they extracted the revenue the government needed. In spite of Czechoslovakia's heavy defence expenditure, which, as later events proved, was a complete waste of money, the country's finances were sound and regularly showed a healthy surplus.

Direct taxation, which was not very steeply graded, took about 20 per cent of declared, or 10 per cent of actual, incomes. This is, of course, an over-simplification. The system was as complex as it is in most civilised countries, and a man's tax liability depended on his trade, type of income and other circumstances. I neither knew nor would I remember all the provisions. It took a good tax lawyer to work his way through the complicated legislation.

As a matter of principle one never accepted a tax demand without querying it and making an appeal The authorities were used to this and compromised. The Exchequer relied mainly on indirect taxation, especially on the 2 per cent turnover tax collected every time goods, even semi-finished products, changed hands. This encouraged vertical integration in trade and industry, and cut out unnecessary middlemen. A knitted-goods manufacturer, for instance, who spun his own yarn, knitted his fabric, dyed and finished it himself, made his own accessories such as elastic bands, assembled the garments and supplied the retail shops direct without going through a wholesaler saved 2 per cent of the value of each of these operations. And if he sold his goods overseas he saved even the last 2 per cent, for there was no turnover tax on exports.

Whatever one might have held against our predominantly social democrat politicians, they knew that the profit motive and free competition were the best incentives to keep industry virile and efficient. As long as manufacturers had confidence in the good housekeeping and integrity of the government they automatically ploughed their profits back into the business in the form of better plant and machinery and new buildings. Those who did not soon fell back in the race and went bankrupt. By looking after the interests of their firms industrialists enriched the country as a whole and raised everyone's living standards. Czechoslovakia's economy was sound, and not even her most critical German- or Hungarian-speaking subjects could fault it.

At times it was very interesting to live in Fleissen. There were weeks when I was excited and happy to be at the hub of all this stimulating competition, bustle, planning and creation, but on my lonely evening walks I suddenly felt again that I was wasting my time. Life was passing me by, Fleissen's petty activities were but tiny vibrations set off by the big things that happened in the world outside, the real world. I felt like a bird in a cage. If only I could make out a good case for opening an office in London.

It seemed incomprehensible to me that Father, the Geipels and the other leading men of Fleissen who had travelled and seen a good deal of the world appeared quite content to live and die in the village. During business hours they were industrialists of stature whose interests and influence extended to distant London, Amsterdam and Stockholm, who studied cotton reports from Bremen, Alexandria and New Orleans, who were informed about developments at Snia Viscosa of Turin and on whose desks lay the *Prager Börsen Courier*, the Czechoslovak equivalent of the *Financial Times*. But in the evening these important men of international affairs shrank to the size of pygmies. They merged with the tradespeople and the workers, spoke their language, shared their jokes and occupied themselves with purely local matters which hardly made a ripple beyond the borders of the Egerland. It was frightening to think I would become like them if I stayed at Fleissen too long. My feet would sink ever deeper into the tough local clay and be held by it. The horizon my eyes scanned so longingly would recede into the distance and my ambitions remain unfulfilled dreams.

My parents, confident that I would outgrow my youthful restlessness, pretended not to notice so as to give me time to settle down. I was too self-conscious to talk to them about my uncertain plans, but unburdened myself to Grandmother. She disagreed with me. What was wrong with Fleissen? Why did I want to live in England? She knew it only from hearsay, but what was so wonderful about that windswept, rain-sodden island on which millions of open fires belched black smoke into the atmosphere, wrapping everything in thick fog?

'Britain is a green and sunny island,' I corrected her, 'the country of freedom, fair play and the highest moral standards. Its people are not forced to serve in the army as they are in Czechoslovakia, they have to pay no import duty on things they buy abroad, they do not need to fiddle when paying taxes, they can travel through half the world without a passport, sterling is everywhere as good as gold and an Englishman's home is his castle—not even a policeman is allowed to enter it!'

Some of this I knew from my own experience and judged with the maturity of my twenty years. As for the rest, I merely repeated what I had heard from English friends or read in Rudyard Kipling's books, but I said it all with great conviction.

Grandmother smiled. 'A stint of army discipline hurts no young man. Our import duties are not high and serve a useful purpose. It is easy to get a passport, we can take our capital abroad freely and change it into any currency we like. And have you ever seen a policeman in our house? We work during the week and spend our Sundays as we want, at church, football, the theatre, on the dance floor, in the cafe, the beer garden or the forest. And we can eat and drink when and what we like. That's what I call freedom and fair play. But not so the English. They are regimented. They are not allowed to drink when they are thirsty, not even the adults. The government tells them the hour they can quench their thirst. And then, like naughty children, they drink more than is good for them. Football is the national sport, I am told, yet they are not allowed to enjoy it on Sunday when there is time, so tens of thousands watch it during the week when they ought to be at work, which disrupts industry. Is this freedom, liberty or licence? I am not surprised that we can manufacture Directoire knickers cheaper than they can!'

I was very fond of Grandmother, but I simply could not make her see. It was futile to argue with her about things she did not understand. Like so many Continentals, she did not even appreciate that England was not synonymous with Britain.

11

THE
LAUGHING VILLAGE
1925-30

I WOULD NOT like the reader to gain the impression that the inhabitants of Fleissen were interested only in money. They worked hard, and financial success meant a great deal to them. They were careful, they saved as large a part of their earnings as possible or ploughed it back into their businesses. But they also relaxed and enjoyed themselves.

There was no organised entertainment apart from the dance on Saturday night, no racing or bingo, not even a regular cinema, let alone football pools. Television had not yet been invented, but a few families had large, clumsy radio sets which screeched. Most people arranged their own inexpensive amusement, and make no mistake, they had plenty of fun. In the evening they met at the various inns, drank a glass of beer, ate a portion of goulash and played cards for minute stakes. Many of them were talented, if home-taught, musicians who played the violin, zither, clarinet or piano. And a well developed sense of humour found expression in never-ending practical jokes from which no one was safe and which kept the village laughing.

While the Goldene Stern was the most popular inn with the manufacturers and the tradespeople, it was by no means a preserve of the well-to-do. Anybody could spend an evening there, and a number of working men, peasants, knitters and tanners usually did. They were respectful towards those who had more money and a wider horizon, but that did not inhibit them or make them feel in the least inferior. Given time, they meant to be manufacturers themselves—albeit small ones—or their children would be. Meanwhile they earned and saved.

Father and Grandfather spent almost daily an hour or two at the Goldene Stern in animated conversation with fellow manufacturers: with Rudi Friedl, the yarn agent, Dr Löw, the village doctor, Schmidt the chemist, Roderich Geipel, a dealer in musical instruments, and many others. At the next table Uncle Otto and his pals played skat, a popular card game. One evening he pulled his gold watch from his waistcoat pocket, laid it on the table and said, 'At ten we'll break up!' He drank another glass of beer, left the room for a few moments to answer a call of nature, and when he came back his valuable watch had gone.

'Meine Herren,' he announced in a stentorian voice which brought the lively talk in the room to a sudden halt. 'My watch has disappeared. It is an heirloom. Whoever has taken it, please hand it back. I'll treat the matter as a hoax—provided the culprit pays for a barrel of beer!'

He looked from table to table. The smoke from a number of cigarettes curled towards the ceiling. Nobody moved.

'This is a shattering experience,' he said. 'Frau Müller [the innkeeper's wife], please have the doors locked. I demand a search!'

The village policeman, who was enjoying a glass of beer on his evening off, and the excise inspector, Wallenta, from Wildstein, a frequent and popular visitor, were chosen as searchers. One by one they went through the pockets of the guests; the tension mounted, until, to everyone's consternation, they found the watch on Father Vogel, the parish priest. The good man was dumbfounded. He turned first pale and then purple as he met the stares of thirty pairs of eyes, not knowing how to protest his innocence.

Uncle Otto's booming voice broke the silence. 'I am scandalised!' he thundered. 'I would not have thought such a deplorable lapse could happen among friends!' He fumbled with his watch, attached it to the chain, slowly put it away and then continued: 'How dare you, all of you, suspect the good Father Vogel of such a misdemeanour! I myself slipped the watch into his pocket to see what you would do. Shame on you, on all of you! My apologies, Herr Vogel. Will you permit me to suggest a punishment that fits the crime? Frau Müller, please roll out that barrel of beer. It's on me, and don't unlock the doors until these heathens have emptied it!'

Then he turned to my father. 'Max, let's have some music!'

Father sat down at the piano, Uncle Otto conducted, and thirty voices sang 'Trink, Brüderlein, trink', finishing with 'Hoch soll er leben', the equivalent of 'For he's a jolly good fellow', raising their glasses to the man of the Church.

A regrettable indiscretion with a young woman at Eger had caused Vogel's transfer to Fleissen, by way of punishment. The lusty son of an Egerland farmer, priesthood was not of his choosing—he had succumbed to the stronger will of an ambitious mother. He could drink with anyone, and after the shock to which he had just been subjected a little relaxation was called for. So he gave himself special dispensation to consume eight glasses of beer instead of the customary four. Occasions like this were all too rare; one had to make the best of them. And a good time was had by all.

Uncle Otto was very fond of playing skat and became impatient if one of his cronies kept him waiting. 'Why can't you be on time?' he demanded when butcher Böhm arrived thirty minutes late on Saturday night. 'You know it takes four to play!'

'Beg your pardon, Herr Geipel,' replied Böhm respectfully. 'There has been an accident. Lame tailor Zölch has slipped and fallen in the pond at Schnecken [the adjoining village]. I helped fish for the body until after sunset, but we could not find it. Only his wooden crutch was floating on the surface. The pond is being drained overnight, it'll be half empty by morning.'

The trio were shocked by this tragic news. 'Poor old Zölch,' said Uncle Otto, and then he banged the table: 'I've always said there'd be an accident! For two years I've pleaded with the council to protect the footpath with railings, but these stubborn clodhoppers wouldn't listen! Now it's happened, just as I said it would. Poor Frau Zölch, such a hard-working woman.'

'God rest his soul,' said butcher Böhm. 'One must take these things philosophically,' and he did his best to cheer the others up, but the thought of the drowned man out there in the pond cast a shadow over the game.

Early on Sunday morning Uncle Otto was on his way to Schnecken. He wanted to be there when the body was found, and he had two 50 kronen notes in his pocket to give the widow before he proceeded to church. The sun shone and the birds sang as he strode between the fields of ripe corn. The harvest promised to be good. It was difficult to think of death on such a morning. He had just turned the corner at the first farmhouse in Schnecken when he heard a tap and shuffle behind him, and a friendly voice called out, 'Good morning, Herr Geipel! Nice morning for a walk!'

Uncle Otto swung round. It was none other than the lame tailor who doffed his hat to him. Uncle realised that he had been taken in, but the relief of seeing the old man alive and well was greater than his anger. He chatted with him for a while without disclosing what had brought him there, pressed one of the 50 kronen notes in the surprised tailor's hands, and turned back towards Fleissen, speculating how to get even with Böhm. He felt exceptionally righteous as he listened to the sermon that morning.

The pond was drained shortly afterwards, but for another purpose. Böhm, Amarotico and several others had rented it for raising carp, a delicacy which ranked next to roast goose. The little fishes they set out in the spring of the previous year had grown large and fat and were now ready for the table, so the pond was emptied and the carp were shared out. Of the four large fish which were Amarotico's share, one made a delicious meal for his wedding anniversary; the others he hid in a large rainwater tank in his garden to await future festive occasions.

By chance Böhm heard about this. During the night he brought a net, lifted the three large carp out of the tank and replaced them with smaller ones. Next day, when Amarotico fed his fish, he was surprised how insignificant they looked all of a sudden. Could it be that they had shrunk? Or was it the angle of the light in the water? He felt a little uneasy, and decided to ask his friend Böhm, who, after all, was a butcher and knew something about fish.

'Josef, have you ever heard of carp shrinking?' he asked, not confessing what was bothering him for fear of looking foolish.

'Of course not,' laughed Böhm. 'Fish grow, they don't shrink. I've only once heard of fish contracting—in rainwater, someone said, but I've not seen it myself. Must have been some old wives' tale.'

Amarotico went home to have another look at his carp. There was no doubt they had shrunk. Why take chances? He called his children. 'Elfriede, Lucie, Roland! Give me a hand with these buckets!'

They baled out the tank until there was only a foot of water left, then they filled it up again from the pump across the road. It took best part of the afternoon.

That night Böhm returned with his net, lifted the small fish out and put the large ones back. Next morning Amarotico inspected his carp. Incredible as it might seem, they had grown to their original size again! So it had been the rainwater, after all. He shook his head in wonderment. 'We live and learn.'

At the Goldene Stern that night Amarotico told his remarkable experience to an intensely interested round of amateur fishermen, who had been tipped off by Böhm beforehand. Theories of the strange phenomena caused by rainwater were exchanged, and Amarotico spent a most gratifying evening. But the following day, when the story leaked out, his leg was pulled without mercy and he swore to take revenge on Böhm.

Butcher Böhm had to travel all over the Egerland to buy cattle. He therefore acquired a small car, a Škoda, and learned to drive. When the time came to take his test he loaded a leg of pork for the examiner and, accompanied by the friend who taught him, drove to Eger. Ing. Štribrny, the examiner, usually combined a driving test with inspecting a boiler at some remote village, for this was also one of his duties. Since he had no motor vehicle of his own, driving tests were the only means of conveyance to cover his territory. With much crashing of gears, scattering flocks of chickens and twice having to call on Ing. Štribrny for assistance to push the car out of swampy patches in the road, the task was satisfactorily accomplished and Böhm passed his test. It was too late for the licence to be issued that day, but he could collect it the following afternoon.

Böhm was a very contented man. His heart overflowed. He went to the

Goldene Stern to celebrate and to boast a little. Amarotico was not at the party, but the others, without Böhm's knowledge, called on him on their way home and told him.

Still smarting from the leg-pull over the shrinking carp, Amarotico was brooding on how to get even with Böhm, and now saw his chance. He took the morning train to Eger, where he had to do some business, and while he was there saw a policeman he knew.

'Will you be on duty this afternoon?' he enquired.

'Could be. What's on your mind?'

'I want you to arrest butcher Böhm of Fleissen. He's coming to Eger this afternoon, driving his Škoda without a licence. Hold him for an hour to frighten him.'

The policeman did not like the suggestion, suspecting it might get him into trouble, but Amarotico was persuasive.

'There'll be no trouble,' he assured him. 'Böhm is an old friend of mine, a good sport who enjoys a joke. And I'll buy you ten glasses of beer!'

Meanwhile, back at Fleissen, Frau Böhm was helping her husband into his new leather coat. He donned his sports cap and, to make his triumph complete, schoolmaster Pfeifer and the organist, Krämling, came for the ride. The journey took about an hour. All went well, and Böhm's skill was greatly admired by his companions, neither of whom could drive. By the time Eger came in sight he was bubbling over with self-assurance. There was now only the bridge to cross. But on it stood a large policeman holding up his hand.

'May I see your driving licence?' he asked politely.

'I'm just on my way to the Okresni Uřad to collect it,' replied Böhm confidently.

The policeman raised his eyebrows. 'So you have no licence?'

'I passed my test yesterday but it takes a little time to issue a licence, and I was told to come back today.'

'You may or may not have passed your test, I have no means of knowing. It is beside the point. The law requires you to carry your licence when in charge of a motor vehicle!' Out came the notebook. 'Your name and address, please.'

Böhm became agitated. 'It's not my fault that government officials don't work faster. Those clock-watchers should have given me my licence yester-day!'

'So now you see fit to insult the civil service of the republic. And before witnesses! Kindly repeat what you said,' and the notebook was at the ready.

Böhm remonstrated, and when Pfeifer and Krämling supported him the policeman took their names and addresses too.

'I arrest you for obstructing an officer of the law,' he said. 'Leave the car and come with me to the police station.'

The matter was getting out of hand. Changing his tactics, Böhm slipped a 20 kronen note in the policeman's pocket. The effect was totally unexpected.

'Attempting to bribe an officer! You'll probably get eight days for that.'

It certainly was Böhm's unlucky day. He usually got on so well with people, and with the law in particular. How could he have landed himself in such a situation? There was nothing the three men could do but go with the constable to the station. They had hardly walked a hundred paces, when they were suddenly hailed by Amarotico from the other side of the street: 'Hullo there, where are you three off to?'

They tried to explain, but the policeman would not let them. 'No loitering. Move on!' he commanded.

Amarotico stopped him. 'Hold it, constable, these gentlemen are friends of mine!'

'And who are you?' demanded the policeman.

'I am Amarotico, the builder. Surely you have heard of me, a personal friend of the chief of police! What are these gentlemen accused of?'

'Beg pardon, sir.' The constable saluted. 'I had to arrest him' (pointing at Böhm) 'for being in charge of a motor vehicle without a driving licence, for insulting the republic, for obstructing the law and for attempting to bribe a police officer. The other two for aiding and abetting!'

'Serious charges,' admitted Amarotico. 'I'll talk to the chief of police and recommend you for promotion. Meanwhile you had better release my friends. I'll vouch for them!'

'As you wish, sir,' replied the policeman, and saluted again. Turning to the law-breakers, he said, 'You may go,' and walked away.

Schoolmaster Pfeifer was the first to regain his speech. 'Herr Amarotico,' he said, shaking him by the hand, 'I shall never forget what you have done for me. To be involved in such a scandal! I would have lost my job!' And the organist forgot his grammar and stammered, 'Me too!'

Böhm had a lump in his throat. 'Vinzenzo,'—he swallowed once or twice—'you are a friend indeed! And after that silly joke with the fish! I had no idea you knew the chief of police!'

'One does not boast about one's high connections,' Amarotico replied modestly. 'It was lucky I came along just at the critical moment!'

The three motorists took their saviour to Brandner's Delikatessen Bar, where they treated him to crayfish mayonnaise, artichokes and a bottle of Italian wine. Böhm collected his licence from the Okresni Úřad, then the four of them squeezed into the small Škoda and drove home.

It did not take long for the truth to leak out, and the people of Fleissen laughed for days. Böhm laughed with them. Amarotico and he were now quits again, but the schoolmaster and the organist, who took themselves rather seriously, felt their dignity had suffered and were not amused.

Not long afterwards Amarotico received a letter from the provost of Maria Kulm, a holy shrine and pilgrim centre famous for its miracle cures, inviting him to quote for laying 200 square metres of terrazzo flooring, 'quality, design and colour scheme to be in keeping with the great church'. Terrazzo floors were Amarotico's speciality. Given time, he hoped to make them as popular in Bohemia as they were in his native Italy. He was not the only one in the field. Wunderlich of Eger, whom he hated from the bottom of his heart, competed with him, but this contract would put him way ahead of his rival. Proudly he showed the provost's letter to his friend Böhm.

'Josef, this is a great honour. Are you by any chance going to visit Maria Kulm in the near future?'

As it happened, a farmer not far from Maria Kulm had offered Böhm a pair of oxen, and he was going to look at them later that week. He would be glad to give Vinzenzo a lift.

The next few days Amarotico spent in a state of animated anticipation, preparing for his interview with the provost. He filled two sacks with carefully selected stones to serve as samples, arranged colour combinations and sat over his drawing board sketching patterns. Thousands of pilgrims would see this floor, and he wondered whether he could incorporate his name, albeit unobtrusively, into the design. It would be a wonderful advertisement for him, and he drew various alternatives.

Böhm frowned a little when he saw the sacks, but Vinzenzo said it was essential to take them, so he agreed. As they drove along the winding country road towards Maria Kulm Amarotico confessed to a considerable degree of nervousness. He had never met a high dignitary of the Church and had no idea how to address him. He was also a little afraid. More years had passed than he cared to remember since he had last attended Holy Mass or been to confession. In fact he had in recent years come to think of himself more as a Protestant, and his conscience troubled him. But Böhm reassured him.

'Bow, make the sign of the cross and say, "Praised be Jesus Christ our Lord",' he advised. 'That's sure to please the provost!'

They arrived at the Church of the Holy Shrine and pulled the bell rope. A monk-like figure opened. To be on the safe side Amarotico bowed, crossed himself and praised the Lord before he asked to be taken to the provost, at whose request he had come. At first the figure in black took him for a pilgrim, but when he saw the two sacks he demanded to see the invitation. Just then the provost himself came along. Amarotico bowed, praised the Lord once more and handed over the impressive-looking envelope.

'It's about the 200 square metres of terrazzo,' he explained.

The provost glanced at the letter, then the blow fell. 'My good man,' he said, 'this was not written by us. It is not our paper!'

'But your Holiness,' stammered Amarotico, 'the envelope bears the postmark of Maria Kulm!'

The provost smiled. 'Could someone have played a joke on you?' And the monk-like figure shut the gate.

Amarotico was crestfallen. 'Josef, who could have done this to me?' and after a moment's reflection: 'Nobody else but that scoundrel Wunderlich! But he won't get away with it! I'll ask Dr Zentner, my solicitor, to write him a letter. Let's go to Eger at once.'

Böhm found it hard to keep a straight face. He did not know who had sent the spurious letter—more likely the schoolmaster, the organist or even Otto Geipel, he thought, than builder Wunderlich. However, he kept these doubts to himself. Amarotico was too angry to listen to reason. The oxen had to be looked at, and Böhm inspected them so thoroughly that when the job was done it was too late to go to Eger and see the solicotor. By the morning Vinzenzo would think the better of it.

And Vinzenzo did. It was never established who wrote that letter.

Salt was a State monopoly in Czechoslovakia. It was dirty and expensive. In Germany it was sold as ordinary commercial produce, clean and cheap. No wonder smugglers brought it across the border by the sackful. Butchers used a great deal of salt. Böhm bought a little in Czechoslovakia as a cover, but most of his supplies were of the pure kind and arrived during the night. The authorities knew it, of course, and when they caught him he was fined. The fines were quite heavy and hurt, but on balance it still paid to use smuggled salt.

The tax on meat became due with the killing of the animal. Once cut up and partly made into sausages it would have been too difficult for an inspector to prove its origin. Böhm and his apprentices were therefore on the job as early as 4 a.m. One morning the bell rang at 6 a.m. and when Böhm opened the door he saw, to his surprise, District Inspector Wallenta in his horn-buttoned jacket and green hunting hat, with rifle slung over his shoulder, and carrying a heath-cock he had shot.

'Good morning, Josef. I heard noises and thought you might give me a cup of coffee.'

While Böhm talked to Wallenta in the front room the little apprentice scrambled upstairs in the backroom with a newly slaughtered calf which he was trying to hide. But it was too heavy for him. He slipped, boy and calf rolled against the door, it sprang open, and Wallenta saw what was happening.

'Josef,' he said, 'let me see the book, and if this calf is not entered I must fine you!'

It was not entered. While the two men had coffee together they bargained over the amount of the fine. The tax on a calf was 36 kronen and the penalty could be ten times that much, but Wallenta thought 100 kronen would be appropriate. Böhm wriggled and in the end got away with a 'disciplinary fine' of 20 kronen.

'Josef,' said Wallenta, 'the cup of coffee was an excuse. I am here to warn you. An excise commission is on the way from Prague. It'll be at Fleissen tomorrow. Are your books in order?'

'To the best of my knowledge and belief they are,' replied Böhm, and added, 'Had you come two hours later that calf would have been entered too!'

'I know,' said Wallenta, with the slightest twinkle in his eye. They shook hands and parted.

An excise commission from Prague! Tomorrow! The information was worth far more than the bagatelle of 20 kronen. Böhm sent one of the boys post-haste to his salt supplier, telling him to hold back delivery of the ten sacks of contraband salt on order. He carefully scrutinized his books, in the evening had a drink with Father Vogel, moved two untaxed carcasses into Amarotico's cellar, went to bed, said his prayers and slept the sleep of the just.

Next day the commission arrived, three officials from headquarters accompanied by Inspector Wallenta, all in uniform, complete with peaked caps and silver braid. They found the books in good order and then, prior to searching the premises as was their custom, Inspector Wallenta asked formally, 'Herr Böhm, before commencing our routine inspection, have you hidden anything dutiable you wish to declare?'

'I have hidden nothing, Inspector, you are welcome to see for yourself!'

The officials searched the building from loft to cellar, opened all the cupboards, looked under the beds, found nothing, expressed their satisfaction and departed. Then they moved on to inspect the books and stocks of the other butchers, bakers, millers, innkeepers, tobacconists and tradespeople who dealt in or used dutiable commodities. When they had gone Böhm sent for the ten sacks of smuggled salt. They were delivered on Friday night, and he fondly patted the bulging canvas bags as he stacked them in the room behind the shop.

On Saturday morning, just before lunchtime and out of the blue, the government sleuths returned and found the salt. Böhm was caught. He tried in vain to find a plausible explanation. The sacks were counted, then the commission withdrew to have lunch at the inn over the road. Completing the act of official administration could wait until the afternoon.

Meanwhile Böhm and his apprentices shovelled twenty kilos of salt out of each bag and, not knowing where to hide it, dumped it into a large wooden barrel in which they sometimes kept fish and which happened to be empty. Then they topped it up with water. When the officials came back they weighed the sacks.

'Herr Böhm, these sacks weigh only eighty kilos! Either you are trying to swindle us or your German suppliers have given you short measure.'

'Neither, sir! If I may explain, with respect, our stretch of the frontier is so rough and hilly, no smuggler could carry more than eighty kilos!'

For a split second Böhm's and Wallenta's eyes met. He knows, Böhm realised; but Wallenta said nothing. The commission sat down to calculate the fine.

'The maximum,' Wallenta requested, to Böhm's horror. It came to 5,000 kronen, the price of a whole railway truck full of salt! In spite of his pleadings the commission remained adamant, and what was worse, they demanded immediate payment. If only he had time to think.

'But it is Saturday afternoon,' he argued. 'The bank is closed!'

'Take the money from your bottom drawer, borrow the cash from your neighbours, but pay—or we are back on Monday morning. One of us will sit in your shop and watch you all week if need be!'

This was a prospect Böhm could not countenance. He fell back on the bottom drawer and counted the notes on the table.

Excise Inspector Wallenta was a very exceptional civil servant. He could not be bribed, as was generally known. It was his pride to live on his salary—entirely adequately, as he thought. His wife, who was liked by everyone, was an excellent housewife who managed surprisingly well on a modest budget. What her husband did not suspect was how little she had to pay for the best joints, the freshest bread, eggs and butter, the whitest flour and the juiciest fruit. Knowing his old-fashioned principles, she thought it best not to tell him.

His passions were shooting and fishing. Not that he could have afforded the luxury of a shoot or a trout stream of his own. Being a good shot and generally popular, he was often invited by his many friends, which he greatly appreciated but for which he granted no favours when it came to official duties, nor did his hosts expect any. He disliked fining people and frequently looked the other way if he thought there were extenuating circumstances, but few succeeded in pulling the wool over his eyes. The State paid his salary, and in return he saw to it that the interests of the State were protected—within reason, of course.

Wallenta was not only gifted with a sixth sense that enabled him to scent out the most skilfully disguised duty evasions, it was also said that he had supernatural powers where animals were concerned. He understood and could communicate with them in their language, and I was told by experienced and thoroughly reliable hunters that at least twice he willed stags to follow him from the forest right to the edge of the village, and only when he lifted the spell did they turn and, terrified, race back to the shelter of the woods.

A few weeks after the unfortunate salt episode Böhm and Wallenta sat together on the bank of Böhm's trout water, which gurgled through meadows and forest, casting their flies.

'Was it really necessary to fine me the maximum?' asked Böhm. 'The heaviest fine I've paid in all my life. Three years' salt savings gone down the drain!'

Just then Wallenta hooked a large trout which had outwitted him for the past hour, taking three flies off his line without getting caught.

'There,' he said, as he lifted the struggling fish out of the water. 'You've asked for it; you've got away with far too much!'

'Josef, I'm worried about you,' said Wallenta one day when he called on Böhm. 'What's going on? We've not caught you once these past two months. You're up to something!'

'I've reformed—gone straight, as you might say, since paying those 5,000 kronen!'

Wallenta looked at him sideways. 'I believe you, of course,' he said, 'but my colleagues don't know you so well, and the Excise Department at Eger is becoming suspicious. I'll have to fine you for something. Can't you think of some evasion, some misdemeanour you have committed?'

Böhm shook his head. 'Not a thing!'

'Josef, think harder,' pleaded Wallenta. 'It looks too suspicious if your name is missing from the penalty list two months running. I'll have to impose some fine on you, for your own good—or would you prefer Prague to send another commission?'

'Not a commission! I haven't recovered from the last one!' said Böhm with feeling, and then he remembered a few transgressions which satisfied his friend and put his name back on the list.

I could go on recounting similar episodes. The other inhabitants of Fleissen played much the same practical jokes on each other and were equally involved with various officials. If I have written in such detail of just these few characters, it is for the very good reason that Vinzenzo Amarotico was our immediate neighbour. His eldest son Helmut, my best friend, married Inspector Wallenta's daughter. And Josef Böhm was our butcher and also a close neighbour. His daughter Marianne is now the wife of my cousin, Udo Geipel—so I knew of all these incidents at first hand and laughed about them when they happened.

12

FIVE
SCOTSMEN
1925-28

THE SAMPLES I had asked Father to send to T. Baird & Sons and my correspondence with Jimmy Baird, whom I had met on that Christmas holiday on the Kyles of Bute, led to regular business. The Bairds were drapers, with only five shops, and could not buy the larger quantities we were used to, but they were the first account I had opened, and to encourage me Father allowed me to quote prices which were only 5 per cent higher than those paid by Stern. Had they bought through the normal channels, from a wholesaler who was supplied by an importer, they would have had to pay at least 30 per cent more. No wonder they preferred buying from us direct. And it tickled Father's vanity to have a customer in far-away Scotland, where noble lords still lived in castles and where the natives played bagpipes and wore kilts. None of our competitors shipped goods to such an exclusive and outlandish destination.

'Why don't you go to see your Caledonian friends on your next visit to Britain?' he suggested.

I needed no urging. The farther I could travel the better, and before long I stood in front of Baird's sizeable shop in Kirk Road, Wishaw, which was their headquarters. There were no fewer than five Baird brothers, although only Tom, Jimmy and Colin, handsome men in their thirties, worked in the business. John, the eldest, lived in semi-retirement in a cottage in the country, and Willie, with the blessing of his brothers, had emigrated to America during the slump, convinced that there was no future in Britain. The Bairds were tall and lanky, wore tweed suits with large checks, and seemed genuinely pleased to see me. I had to have tea and biscuits in the small, wood-panelled private office, and was then introduced to Miss Smith, the cashier, the sales staff, some of the customers who were in the shop, and to Andrew, the warehouseman, whose job it was to unpack the cases from 'Sheskoslovakee', as he called it. In London I might be ignored as just another alien, but to these Scots I was an object of interest and curiosity. If only I understood them better, so that I could follow the humour of their conversa-

Music festival at Fleissen in 1924. Procession of visiting bands through the village, headed by the reception committee, *22a*, and visiting clubs, *22b*. Music was taken seriously in the Egerland, and the manufacture of musical instruments an important export industry

23 The Mattel Mill, near Wildstein, in the Egerland

24 Oberndorf, near Franzensbad

Harvesting in the Egerland

Typical Egerland farm

27 The old mining town of Schlaggenwald, the home of Balthasar Pasold

28 Altenteich, on the road from Fleissen to Franzensbad

Asch: the main street

Asch: the textile college

31 Karlsbad: Theatre Square. The Hotel Imperial in the background

Marienbad : Goethe Square

Franzensbad : the main street, flanked by cafés and restaurants

34 The family in 1923: our parents, Silvia, Rolf, Ingo and the author

35 The family home at Fleissen

36 The 'new' factory of Adolf Pasold & Sohn was completed in 1925. It was built on the outskirts of Fleissen, where there was plenty of room for expansion

tion. Strangely enough, they did not seem to have the slightest difficulty in understanding me. They wanted to know about our factory and about Fleissen, and when the time came for me to return to Glasgow they would not hear of it. I had to meet Mr Colin's charming wife, Min, and stay the night in their house.

Next morning at the store, observing the Bairds at their respective jobs, I thought how very different their temperaments were in spite of their great family likeness, and how harmoniously they worked together. This was how I wanted to work together with my brothers when they grew up. Tremendous strength lay in operating as a team.

Most in evidence was Mr Jimmy, an enthusiast and an extrovert. He was responsible for the fashion department, a comparatively recent and highly successful venture. If he had his way he would convert the whole store into a fashion house. He bustled about, directing and advising the staff, who clearly thought the world of him, greeted customers by name and chatted with them, gave encouragement here and cracked a joke there. It amused me to hear him say to one of the shop girls:

'Lassie, see yon wee wifey? Hurry to serve her, she's our breakfast, dinner and tea!'

Not only yours, I thought; Father's and mine as well. Seeing our knickers being sold in singles was a new experience. I was fascinated to watch the expressions of the women who bought them, and to think that some of the money they took out of their purses found its way over a thousand miles into the hands of our knitters and sewing machinists, who used it to buy bread for their families and kept butcher Böhm in business.

Meanwhile Mr Jimmy had turned to a lady who was fingering a coat. 'Mrs Mackintosh,' he said, 'this is not for you. I wouldn't let you buy this coat even if you wanted to!' His humorously reassuring presence permeated the store.

Mr Tom, a powerfully built man of few words, scared me a little, although he was kindness itself. The main burden of the business seemed to rest on his broad shoulders. He was the rock, the central pillar round which all else revolved. Fashions were all right, and he gave brother Jimmy full credit, but T. Baird & Sons' trade was founded on the solid base of staple products which were not subject to the whims of fashion, such as piece goods, household linen and underwear. The fashion business was a risky one. If one was unlucky and bought the wrong style or colour from those crafty manufacturers in the south the merchandise had to be cleared at half price. It did not always follow that Wishaw would buy tomorrow what London bought yesterday. There was no accounting for taste. But Tom accounted accurately for the firm's cash. He was the treasurer and had the key to the safe.

With visible pleasure he fingered a crisp, white Bank of England fiver. I showed him a green Czechoslovak 100 kronen note, with the pictures of President Masaryk and Prague with Castle Hradčin. 'Pretty, but is it actually worth 12s 3d in "real money"?' he teased. He always treated these outlandish fancy bits of coloured paper with suspicion. Kronen, roubles, drachmas were all devised by foreigners to confound each other with their decimals and confuse the British traveller. And the honest Scots were exploited even by the English. A good Scottish pound note was worth only 19s 6d south of the border! The trouble with the Bairds was that I never knew when to take them seriously, and their accent only made matters worse.

Mr John, the senior partner, took little interest in the daily conduct of the business. His sole purpose in coming to the office that morning was to talk to me about Europe, especially the emergence of the new Central Europe, a subject that intrigued him. He seemed remarkably well informed about Czechoslovakia, and even knew about 'good soldier Schwejk', which surprised me, for most people in Britain had difficulty in locating our country on the map 'somewhere between Germany and the Black Sea'. Were we happy now that we had independence, he asked?

'Independence? We?' I had not expected the question put in this form. 'I am Austrian by birth, not Czech,' I protested. 'We lost our independence!'

'Surely all Bohemians were Austrian by birth?' replied John. 'Why did they break away from the Austro-Hungarian Monarchy and proclaim the Czechoslovak republic?'

'Only the Czech-speaking Bohemians did. The German-speaking minority, more than three million of us, wanted to remain Austrians. We were forced with bayonets to become Czechoslovak citizens, and the Allies let it happen because it suited their book. You can hardly call that independence!'

Mr John was well read and a penetrating thinker. 'Is language the main difference between you?'

I had to think for a moment or two. 'Having lived together for so many centuries, Czech- and German-speaking Bohemians have become very much alike. They acquired each other's habits, intermarried, many of their names got mixed up; if it were not for the language you could hardly tell them apart. But would *you* waste your time learning Czech, a difficult language understood by no one outside the republic and by only two thirds of the people in it?'

Mr John sighed. 'Half the trouble in this world is caused by people not understanding each other. We always resolve one injustice by creating another. No settlement arrived at with bayonets can last.'

'Father thinks it will last as long as Czechoslovakia is more prosperous than Germany and Austria. Should that ever change who knows what might happen, but I see no reason why it should.'

Mr Colin showed me the stock rooms, the shelves of which were stacked with a great variety of knitted and woven merchandise. He took down a box here and opened a paper parcel there to let me see the contents: men's and women's underwear, pullovers, jerseys, pyjamas, shirts and socks. They were made of wool and cotton, and there were women's knickers, slips and stockings of artificial silk. Most of these goods came from manufacturers in Leicester and Nottingham, such as Morley's, whose trade mark was a flying wheel, Wolsey's, Brettle's and other famous firms.

I felt the garments, spread them out on the table to study how they were cut and sewn, and looked at the prices at which they were bought and sold. They were marked in code. One had to remember the words 'Speak Truly', the letters of which the Bairds used in place of the figures 1 to 10. Anyone not familiar with the code words could not read the prices. It was a new and interesting experience for me to see what other manufacturers produced and how their value compared with ours.

Some of the goods, especially the more expensive ones, bore trade marks; others, such as our fleecy knickers and the cheaper general run of underwear, both British and foreign, came without any mark of identification. The trade marks intrigued me. Many of them—Wolsey's cardinal, for instance— looked most decorative. But those nicely woven labels cost money without actually improving the quality of the garments. Why was the public willing to pay for them? I assumed it was the public who paid, for however wealthy these great concerns might be, ordinary commercial practice would surely still apply? We had learned the principles and laws governing trade marks at the textile college, superficially at least, but I had forgotten, and felt ignorant. No one at Fleissen knew much about the subject or was interested in it. Back home, prices were so keen and all-important that the cost of any such embellishment would make the goods unsaleable. Customers would have the labels removed and demand the money instead. Did British retailers prefer to deal in branded goods? What difference did an attractive label make to sales? Should we have one designed for our fleecy knickers?

Mr Colin did his best to enlighten me. He preferred to think in terms of value and satisfaction rather than just price. Value not merely in a narrow, material sense. A well chosen and advertised brand name made good merchandise even more desirable and therefore more valuable. It was not so much a matter of a pretty label as of the image it created in the consumer's mind. 'Take Chilprufe,' he said, 'the best trade mark I know. It stands not only for consistently superb quality, but many people believe the garments to be actually proof against chills. A Chilprufe vest gives the wearer a feeling of well-being and protection no unbranded garment can provide.'

'Beautiful,' I agreed, fingering the fine wool. The brand name promised

more than it could fulfil, and I strongly disapproved of corrupted words—
English spelling was confusing enough already—but I did not want to
interrupt Mr Colin's lecture.

Whether branded merchandise need necessarily be dearer than unbranded
was debatable, he continued. Manufacturers usually claimed that the extra
sales they achieved by advertising their brands more than covered the
expense. The cost of the labels was negligible in this context. Vastly greater
sums were swallowed up by the nation-wide publicity campaigns, press
advertisements, posters, showcards and other means of creating a favourable
image for the trade mark. It was right that manufacturers should thus stimulate demand for their branded products, and for retailers to stock them and
display them in their shop windows. But a number of makers had the nerve
to fix the prices at which their products were to be sold over the counter, and
Mr Colin thoroughly objected to this interference in a retailer's business. The
firm of T. Baird & Sons had become the leading drapers in Lanarkshire by
giving better value than its competitors, notably the Co-operative store, and
Baird's would continue to sell branded merchandise below the prescribed
prices. They would not let any supplier dictate to them. This was the reason
why they refused to handle some nationally advertised brands and promoted
unbranded merchandise instead.

I could not follow his argument completely—the subject of retail price
maintenance was too unfamiliar to me—but I realised how strongly Mr Colin
felt about it. He wanted to sell his goods at the lowest possible price to the
public. 'Large turnover, small profit—just like my Father,' I thought.

'Now, to come to your fleecy knickers,' he said. 'Merely to attach a pretty
label would achieve nothing. Traders in Scotland and England would react
in the same way as those in Czechoslovakia. They wouldn't stock any branded
goods unless the manufacturers supported them with advertising.' And Mr
Colin thought it unlikely that my Father would let me embark on such an
expensive campaign.

'Cheer up,' he laughed when he saw my disappointment. 'You ought to
feel pleased that you can sell your vast production without advertising.' No
doubt he was right, but the thought of a trade mark appealed to me very
much, and I would have liked to have some valid excuse for registering one.

Mr Colin clearly thought me more knowledgeable than I was. His references to the intricacies of distribution surprised and confused me. I had
imagined shopkeeping to be so much simpler. Taking merchandise from a
shelf and handing it over the counter to the consumer had seemed such a dull
occupation in comparison with manufacturing that I had never given it any
thought. I wondered whether Father, Grandfather and the other manu-

facturers at Fleissen were as ignorant about retailing as I was. We produced our goods to specifications laid down by London importers. The fleecy knickers we made all looked alike—so much so that it was difficult to tell whether they had come out of Lehrmann's, Braun's, Friedl's or our own factory. The importers wanted it that way. Wrapped in half-dozens in neutral paper, they were packed into standard wooden cases and shipped through a forwarding agent to England. That, as far as we were concerned, was where the excitement ended. The goods then became the responsibility of the importers who sold them to wholesale houses, where they were broken down into small consignments and distributed to the shops. I never realised the complexity and romance of this seemingly simple sequence of events in which the trader who took short cuts could so easily come to grief. The operation of T. Baird & Sons became all of a sudden an intriguing mystery.

Mr John noticed my bewilderment. 'Let's start at the beginning,' he said. 'I'll tell you how the drapers did their trade before the war, when the Old Man was alive, and how it has developed since. You'll then understand the present business much better.' He made me sit in an armchair by the fireplace, asked one of the shop girls to bring tea and biscuits, and lit his pipe.

'Twenty years ago you saw far less ready-made underwear in the shops than today. Most women made their own and their families' or had it made by their tailors and dressmakers along with the rest of their clothes. The material they bought by the yard from the draper. He sold suitings and dress fabrics, shirtings, wool flannels and satins, knitting wool, thread, buttons, hooks, press studs, stays, braid, ribbons, ties, stockings, shawls, plaids and similar wares. Flannel came in three colours. Red was used for ladies' petticoats, drawers and nightdresses. Navy was made into vests, shirts and drawers for coal miners, while farmers and steelworkers preferred general-purpose grey. Cotton shirts, called Oxfords, were off-white with coloured designs, those made of wool had stripes of various widths and were used for making Lama shirts. Glazed cotton satins in self-colours or printed with Paisley designs were used for quilts and household goods. All came in single widths of 39 in. Fashion garments, blouses, jackets, coats and dresses appeared in drapers' windows about 1910, but the trade didn't amount to very much, and only developed after the war.'

Mr John then described how after their parents' death, shortly before the end of the war, the five Baird brothers decided to disregard their father's will and pool their inheritance. The total fortune, consisting of the shop at Wishaw, young Tom's shop at Motherwell, stock in trade and cash came to £2,000. Instead of sharing it out according to their ages in the proportions their father had intended, they decided to create a chain of five shops—a far-sighted concept for those days—which they would own in equal parts and manage jointly, each concentrating on one particular aspect of the business. This gave them considerable purchasing power. Like their father before them, they always paid cash for everything they bought, thus securing the lowest prices and keeping their financial independence. Drawing little money for themselves, and satisfied with unusually small profit margins, they were able to offer the public better value than the other drapers, and as a result put many of their competitors, one after another, out of business.

After the war came the swing to factory-made garments. Brother Jimmy began to travel less frequently to Manchester to spend the firm's funds on piece goods, and more often to London, where a fashion industry was springing up, to buy ever larger quantities of ready-made apparel. In addition to its reputation for value T. Baird & Sons acquired a fashion image that attracted buyers even from fifteen-miles-distant Glasgow.

Then, in 1926, came the slump and the miners' strike. The break began at the top, at the manufacturing and wholesaling end of the trade, where, within a matter of weeks, prices tumbled by 50 per cent and more. But the tens of thousands of small retailers up and down the country, unwilling to face up to the inevitable losses, refused to sell the goods they had on their shelves below cost, until their businesses ground to a standstill. The Bairds' shops were all located in the heart of the Lanarkshire mining area, and felt the brunt of the strike more immediately than shops in other parts of Britain. Moreover Jimmy's close contact with the mainly Jewish makers of fashion goods in London made him realise at an early stage what was happening. Looking beyond the losses, he saw the enormous trade to be done if one had the capital to buy this cheap merchandise and pass it on to the public.

So the Bairds slashed prices to clear their stocks and obtain cash. The first loss was the best! The reductions were so drastic that they caused a stampede on their five shops, and the police had to keep the crowds in order. In one week they sold out all their merchandise for the sum of £20,000, and their rivals, especially the manager of the local Co-operative Society, thought they had gone off their heads.

The money safely in the bank, they could now go about re-stocking their empty shelves. Tom, Jimmy and Colin set off on their greatest-ever buying spree. First they proceeded to Manchester, where panicking wholesalers were desperately trying to reduce their commitments and clear their bulging warehouses by accepting almost any offer a purchaser cared to make. Goods costing a thousand pounds coming in from the factories in the morning were sold in the afternoon for three hundred. It was rumoured that the piece-goods buyer of S. & J. Watts had so much merchandise on order that his firm lost £250,000 in the process. The Baird brothers emptied his department at give-away prices. Then they continued to Bradford, Leeds, Leicester and

London, placing orders and paying cash wherever they went. Their shops
were not large enough to accommodate all the merchandise purchased with
the £20,000, and deliveries had to be spread over several months.

While other drapers hesitatingly and slowly reduced their prices, losing
almost a year's trade, the Bairds' shops were crowded and did record business. This exceedingly successful operation doubled their capital and their
self-confidence. Always independent, they now became a law unto themselves.
Gone were the days when they would buy all their supplies through regular
wholesale channels or sell branded goods at the makers' recommended prices,
and a growing number of manufacturers who had contracted with the powerful Wholesale Textile Association to supply only wholesalers found ways and
means of doing business with T. Baird & Sons direct. It was a fascinating
story. Not only the Bairds' business but shopkeeping in general took on a new
aspect. I was amazed that there could be so much excitement in the life of a
retailer.

Just then Jimmy came in with half a dozen back numbers of the *Draper's
Record*, the trade's weekly magazine.

'Here,' he said, 'take them with you. Read them on the train going home;
you'll find them informative. Meanwhile don't believe everything brother
John tells you. We retailers are very small fry in comparison with the wholesalers. They are the wealthiest and most powerful traders in the land, placing
large contracts with the manufacturers, to whom they pay cash, while tying
thousands of retailers to themselves by giving them extended credit, thus
competing with the banks. But T. Baird & Sons take good care not to be tied
to anyone. The combined buying power of our five shops is substantial. We
pay cash and won't be dictated to by anyone.'

'It's been tried often enough,' laughed Tom. 'I remember when I was
about fifteen Father used to sell Paton's knitting wool below the prescribed
price. One day their salesman came and said he would no longer stand for it,
but Father told him to think again. Having paid for the wool, it was his to do
with as he liked. And to prove it he presented two skeins to a surprised old
lady who had just come into the shop. We haven't touched Paton's wool
since.'

We also visited the branches. At each of them I shook hands with the
manager, was introduced to the sales staff and to some of the customers. We
looked at the stocks, and to see our familiar parcels of fleecy knickers on the
shelves filled me with pride. There were no complaints, the Bairds were very
satisfied with our merchandise, and Mr Tom wrote out an order for 150
dozen spread over our most expensive qualities, 644 and 752. I was surprised
that one could sell so much in five shops. If only I had a hundred customers

like the Bairds I could establish an office and a small warehouse in London. But how was I to find a hundred such customers?

I had to stay for the weekend. My hosts had a special treat in store for me. On Saturday afternoon they took me to see the football match between Rangers and Celtic, or was it Motherwell United against the All Blacks? I had not the least idea what went on, but pretended to be interested, and cheered whenever they cheered. After the match we returned to the Wishaw store, for Saturday was the most important day in the retail business, and in the evening the week's takings were totalled up. The branch managers telephoned their figures. Each had tried to beat the previous week, the corresponding week of the previous year, and the sales of the other branches. The Baird brothers were almost as excited as they had been at the football match.

On Sunday Colin and Min took me to lunch with brother John. The sun shone and Scotland looked beautiful, much wilder than England, yet the colouring was softer, and the heather laid a faint purple overtone upon the distant hills. We motored to the upper reaches of the Clyde, where John Baird's house stood on the bank of the shallow, fast-running water which was at least fifty feet wide and, Colin explained, provided excellent brown trout fishing. Were the light not so bright, we should find brother John in his oil-skin waders standing in the river with his rod.

I looked forward to meeting this unusual man again. He was playing the piano when we arrived. We stood and listened for a few minutes until he noticed us, jumped up to welcome us, and introduced me to his wife, Betty. They were the gentlest and most relaxed of couples, lovers of books and paintings, and I felt thoroughly at ease with them in their comfortable, tastefully furnished home. John was so much easier to understand than his brothers. His soft, quiet voice, his well chosen words and the ideas they expressed made me hang on his lips. We talked about farming, religion and politics, about the General Strike of the year before, how much it had cost the country and how little it had achieved. The hours flew.

John was the philosopher of the family. Four years in the trenches in the midst of mud, death and futility had done something to him. He no longer wanted a part in the bustle of business and of making money and preferred to live peacefully by the side of the river. It seemed a strangely detached, negative existence which, especially at my age, I found difficult to reconcile with his exceptional gifts. Such a life, I thought, would be hardly imaginable in Czechoslovakia, but then this was a different world. Scotland, with its eerie lochs and misty hills, its glens and clans, its bagpipes, sporrans and dirks, its shortbread and haggis was not like other countries. If I lived here perhaps it would cast its spell over me.

In the morning, after an early breakfast, Colin drove me to Glasgow to catch the train for London. I did not know how to thank him and Min for the happy time they had given me. What wonderful people they were! And when we said farewell at St Enoch Station I knew that we would remain friends for life.

The train for London was almost empty. The only other passenger in my compartment was a distinguished-looking man of about fifty who was sitting in the window seat opposite mine reading *The Times*. After watching the Scottish scenery for a while, I took out the back numbers of the *Draper's Record* which Jimmy had given me, and marked what I thought would interest Father. There were, first of all, the wholesalers who advertised woven underwear and who might some day become my customers. I knew it was incorrect to describe this merchandise as 'woven', for all of it was made from knitted rib, plain stockinette or fleecy knitted fabric, but for some strange reason the trade always referred to underwear made from knitted material as woven. British terminology could frequently be confusing, I had discovered.

I then studied and marked the announcements of the manufacturers, our potential competitors. The largest advertisers seemed to be Wolsey. I saw their trade mark, the cardinal's head, in every issue. Their merchandise was presumably so well known that they did not have to list it in detail. They merely repeated each week that they had a comprehensive selection of wool and artificial silk underwear. Their factory and head office were at King Street, Leicester, and they had a warehouse in London, at 129 London Wall. They also maintained branches at Birmingham, Belfast, Cardiff, Dublin, Edinburgh, Glasgow, Leeds, Liverpool, Manchester and Newcastle. What an organisation! I tried to imagine their factory, a huge modern building, no doubt, rows and rows of the latest knitting machines, and of course a dye-house and a spinning plant, all driven by a high-efficiency steam turbine. But Wolsey's were not the only giants in the industry, as was obvious from the many other advertisements.

Suddenly I became aware of the old gentleman opposite. He had put down his paper and was watching me. When I declined a cigarette, he pointed to my journals and said:

'Everyone seems to go for artificial silk nowadays. There's bound to be a reaction.'

Was he in the trade? A salesman, I wondered, an agent, a merchant or perhaps a manufacturer?

He seemed to read my thoughts. 'Let's say I'm an engineer. My firm develops textile machinery,' he volunteered. This information immediately established a bond between us as far as I was concerned. He spoke the clear English of the south which sounded like music in my ears. The next few hours passed very quickly. We talked about warp looms, Milanese machines and Raschels, about Jacquards, flats and circulars, and whether Terrot- and Tompkins-type loopwheel machines would be superseded by the Deutsche Rundstuhl made by Schubert & Salzer of Chemnitz, which was especially well suited to knit artificial silk. Would cotton ultimately be replaced by artificial silk?

'Never,' he smiled. 'Just look at this, it's so much better than artificial silk!'

He took a lady's vest from his briefcase. It was unusually soft, yet substantial, and felt very pleasant. I had never seen such finely knitted wool material before.

'Not wool,' he laughed. 'It's interlock! One hundred per cent cotton!'

Cotton? I could hardly believe it. Professor Steffe, back at the textile college, had explained the Scott Williams interlock machine to us but had not made it appear very important. I never knew that it produced such beautiful fabric, and now had a close look at this miraculous vest. It was made of the most perfectly spun yarn I had ever seen and must be very expensive. Was this the reason why neither the Bairds nor Mr Stern or any of our other customers had mentioned interlock to me? Or were the garments too strictly price-controlled to be of interest to them? I looked for the label. It said 'Vedonis'.

'Please tell me more,' I asked the old gentleman, who watched my reactions with amusement. And he obliged.

'It is a long story,' he began. 'A patent for interlock fabric was first granted in America in September 1908 to Robert Walter Scott, the inventor, and his partner, Louis Napoleon Devon Williams. A further patent for the machine which became known as the Scott Williams was granted in 1909. A number of American firms secured manufacturing rights. But the price-cutters got hold of the merchandise, and before the fabric got going in the States it was killed by competition. No one could make enough profit to develop an interlock industry. Then George Spencer, an English hosiery manufacturer, realised the potential of the invention, but failed to come to terms with the British agents for Scott Williams. Having met Robert Scott, he decided to make the journey to America and apply personally for a licence. It was granted in 1910, and by a strange coincidence Spencer's old friend, Herbert Lancashire, of J. B. Lewis & Sons, the makers of 'Meridian', turned up in Robert Scott's office on the same day and also obtained a licence to manufacture interlock in Britain. The two men agreed then and there that the field was large enough for both their firms to prosper, provided they each specialised in their own type of production. J. B. Lewis & Sons were to concentrate on the men's trade and George Spencer & Co. on the women's and children's.

If either party were to manufacture the other's products it would sell them at higher prices. This agreement, I may say, is still scrupulously observed.

'On their return to England a new company was formed jointly by Lewis's and Spencer's known as the Scott Knit Fabric Co. Ltd, whose sole object it was to collect and pay royalties to the patentees and discuss with the principals all matters relevant to the patent. It was not until 1925 that Simpkin Son & Emery of Hinckley and R. Walker & Son of Leicester joined the Scott Knit Fabric Co. Both Wolsey's and Morley's, by the way, had been offered the right to manufacture interlock in 1911 and had turned it down, believing the fabric to be "impracticable".

'In the early days of manufacture a 10 in. interlock machine cost $580 and a 20 in. machine $705. The technical difficulties were enormous. Production was slow and troublesome, the machine needed to be improved and partially redesigned, suitable needles had to be developed, and the greatest problem of all was to obtain the right kind of cotton yarn. Eventually, through close liaison with Dee Mill, the perfect hosiery twist was achieved.

'The war caused a serious setback, and afterwards it took time to get supplies of the correct materials, and particularly needles for the machines. The heavy development expenses had hardly been recovered by 1925 when the patents were about to expire. Application was therefore made for a five-year extension, the case was heard by Mr Justice Tomlin, and the application was finally granted. The cost of a 10 in. machine had in the meantime risen to $901 and a 20 in. machine to $1,224.

My acquaintance paused, and as he settled back in his seat his eye caught a full-page advertisement in my *Draper's Record* which read: 'Next to myself I like VEDONIS'.

'George Spencer's,' he explained. 'An effective slogan.'

'So Meridian and Vedonis are the two interlock brands?' I enquired. 'Are both sold in the shops at fixed prices?'

'You bet! Interlock could never have been developed in this country had the price structure not been firmly maintained.'

Very much influenced by the Bairds' opposition to manufacturers who imposed retail price maintenance, I ventured to disagree. If a trader chose to cut his profit and reduce the price of his goods it was no one's concern but his own, a public-spirited act in fact, which was bound to increase demand and so benefit the manufacturer.

'Steady! Traders' motives are not always so pure when it comes to cutting the prices of branded merchandise. Suppose there are two drapers in the High Street, Brown and Smith, who are rivals, of course. Brown does a large trade in Vedonis underwear, stocks the complete range, spends money on advertising and displaying it and depends on it for his livelihood. Smith, on the other hand, sells mainly unbranded goods. To create the impression that he offers better value, and to entice Brown's customers to come to him, he occasionally buys small quantities of Vedonis which he sells at cost or even below. This gets him publicity, and when people are in his shop he tries to sell them unbranded garments on which he makes his normal profit.

'Brown is not able to retaliate by reducing his prices because Vedonis accounts for too large a slice of his trade. He therefore goes to the manufacturer and asks for a price concession—a quantity discount, most likely. So we have now reached the stage when the manufacturer has to protect Brown by refusing to supply Smith, or when he begins to finance a price war between his clients In the end neither he nor they have any profit left. Vedonis is discredited and dropped by the trade. Many a good product has been ruined in this way.'

The sequence of events could not have been explained more logically, and I became uncertain. I was just about to relate the tale of Thomas Baird senior making a present of Paton's wool to the old lady when the train slowed down and stopped. We had reached Nottingham. Without telling me who he was— and I had not the courage to ask him—the old gentleman wished me a good journey and alighted, leaving me wondering. Which side was right? The manufacturer who, having invested his ingenuity and capital in creating a good name for his product, refused to let it be debased and the trade of his customers ruined by a price-cutting minority, or the shopkeeper who, having paid for the goods, claimed they were his to do with as he pleased? It was an interesting but purely theoretical problem for me then. Little did I realise how many real headaches it was to cause me in years to come.

The shops were closed when I arrived in London, but the first thing I did next morning was to take a bus to the West End and buy an interlock vest to take back to Father. Doubts returned about it being really all cotton, but I had not the heart to cut this beautiful garment to make a flame test. Again I wondered who the knowledgeable stranger in the train could have been who so modestly described himself as an engineer. Mr Spencer himself, perhaps? Had I missed the opportunity of securing a licence to manufacture interlock in Czechoslovakia? How I wished I had asked him.

Father was as impressed with the vest as I had expected. We cut a sleeve off and, with difficulty, unravelled some of the yarn. It was 100 per cent cotton and of superb quality. Nothing like it could be produced in our country; only Lancashire was capable of spinning such yarn It would have to be imported, like the yarn for the Czechoslovak fabric glove industry, and that was much too dear for our type of trade. We pursued the matter no further.

13

CAREFREE
DAYS
1925-29

I TALKED FATHER into letting me buy an English motor-cycle for seventy guineas. When word came that it had been cleared through customs I could hardly sleep with excitement, and was off on the early train to Prague to collect it. What a machine! It had a 680 c.c. side-valve JAP engine, a three-speed Sturmey Archer gearbox, semi-racing handlebars and a beautiful maroon-and-silver saddle tank. The engine had to be run in, so I curbed my desire to open the throttle, and rode no faster than the prescribed 45 km per hour, which brought me to Karlsbad by evening. Bursting with pride, I arrived at Fleissen next morning, and Father admitted that he had never seen a motor-cycle like it. He rode it two or three times down the road and back again while I watched apprehensively lest he should make a wrong move and damage my precious possession. I have always been an anxious owner.

My Zenith was not an inanimate machine. Gripped firmly between my knees it became part of me. The throbbing of the engine was music in my ears, and the Castrol oil in the faint blue haze from the chromium-plated exhaust pipe the sweetest smell I knew. The response of the tremendous force of twenty-five horses to the slightest movement of the throttle was immediate and gave me a sense of control and power I had never experienced before. The acceleration was terrific. I had to hold tight to avoid sliding off the saddle and being left behind as my mount leapt forward, yet a slight turn of the twist grip and it became as gentle as a lamb. Going into a bend at speed, changing down, leaning over until the foot rest almost scraped the surface of the road and roaring away at full throttle gave me a thrill greater than I could describe.

Father, a keen motorist himself, loved to watch competitions but thought it was too dangerous for me to take part in them. I found the temptation irresistible, and, in order not to upset him, entered for hill climbs and less advertised road races farther away from home, hoping he wouldn't get to hear about them. I was too cautious, and my side-valve Zenith in spite of its impressive speed, not fast enough to win any races but occasionally my picture appeared in motoring journals, and then there was an inquest.

One day Grandmother had a talk with me. She told me how worried Father was about my motor-cycling escapades. He knew that he could not stop me, because he had been just as daring when he was a young man, but his horse and bicycle were not as dangerous as my motorbike. She opened her hand and showed me a ladybird. At first I thought it was alive, it looked so real, but it was made of glass and enamel. 'Let me sew it on your jacket,' she said, 'so that you will come to no harm. It will protect you.'

'Don't be so superstitious, Grandmother,' I laughed.

'Superstitious or not,' she said, 'I believe it, and so does your father, although he may not admit it. You wouldn't be sitting here and there would probably be no Adolf Pasold & Sohn if it were not for the little beetles. Your grandfather's grandfather, so the story goes, left his weaving loom to take up knitting because of a ladybird. They've brought the Pasold family luck for more than a hundred years.'

'This is the twentieth century,' I replied. 'How can you believe such nonsense?' But I liked the little ladybird and let Grandmother sew it on to my breeches above the left knee where it showed when I sat on my bike. Everyone who saw it tried to pick it up and I had much fun with it.

Unfortunately I was alone with my motor-cycle in our part of the world. It had cost over 20,000 Czech kronen including import duty—as much as a cottage—and few young men could raise so much money. I knew of only three other motor-cycles within a radius of twenty miles, all belt-driven German Wanderers, and all belonged to sober family men twice my age who used them for business journeys. I had nothing in common with them. One was Herr Müller senior, an elderly yarn agent from Asch with a drooping moustache, who called on us regularly. Sometimes when it rained he sent his son Robert, a young man with an impudent face and aggressive manners which put me off. When I got to know him better and discovered what a nice chap he was we became friends and rode out together at weekends. This was much more fun, although I was rather self-conscious because of the disparity in the performance of our machines. He saved and borrowed, and two years later when he had scraped enough money together he too bought an English motor-cycle, a McEvoy. I sold the Zenith and bought a Brough Superior with a chromium-plated tank and twin exhaust pipes. Both machines were thoroughbreds, with 680 c.c. overhead-valve engines. We removed the insides of the silencers and thundered up the winding roads in the hills, through woods, valleys and villages, making windows rattle and leaving clouds of dust behind. We had leather waistcoats and leather breeches made to measure, and felt like modern versions of medieval knights on their chargers.

Some of my happiest recollections are of weekend runs through Franconia and Thuringia when the autumn sun played on the yellow, red and brown foliage of the trees, when dew lay on the meadows and the deserted roads through the woods were covered with dead leaves which swirled in the slip-stream behind us. The crisp October air filled our lungs and we sang with sheer exhilaration as we drank in all this beauty and clocked up the miles. We visited a castle, an interesting bridge, some lake or looked at a new power station. We ate hearty meals at village inns while a crowd of admiring youngsters surrounded our powerful, outlandish bikes. Seeing the letters CS below our numberplates and guessing that they stood for Czechoslovakia, most people in Germany expected us to have horns and wear fur coats, and we were amused to see their surprise when they discovered that we looked quite ordinary and spoke German as well as they did. How could they be so ignorant about conditions on the other side of the border, which was, after all, barely fifty miles away? Saturday night we spent, maybe, at some old mill, with the sound of the rushing water of the mill stream lulling us to sleep. At the crack of dawn we were on the road again, and by sunset on Sunday we were home, tired and dusty, but happy with what we had seen, the mileage we had covered and the dangers we had braved. What joy it was to be young!

One of my favourite weekend targets was the castle of Schwarzburg, beyond Saalfeld. Picturesquely situated on a peak in vast pine forests, a corner of it had been converted into a hotel and restaurant which served delicious blue trout, venison or wild boar with Thuringian dumplings and cranberry sauce. The bedrooms were wood-panelled and smelled of pine, and from the cosy dining room with its heavy wooden beams and the tiled stove in the corner one looked into a large, light-green meadow down below, sur-rounded by thick dark-green forest as far as the eye could reach. We sat there and enjoyed the stillness after the speed of the ride, the roar of the engines and the rush of air. If we were lucky we saw a stag with its family of does come out of the darkness of the woods and graze in the moonlight. I wished I were a poet so that I could put the peace of those hours into words and preserve it for ever.

In May 1928 Robert and I went on a grand tour. We took our bikes through southern Germany, the Tyrol, Switzerland and northern Italy. It rained when we left, and by the time we had our carnets stamped by the Czech and the German customs officials at the border between Eger and Waldsassen we were dripping wet. A motor-cycle is not the ideal means of transport in pouring rain and on muddy roads. It rained all day and the following day, the Alps were hidden in cloud and the valleys filled with drizzle. The water ran down our necks and up our sleeves, it obscured our goggles and hurt our eyes. It rained all week, and Garmisch, Landeck, Martinsbruck, Pontresina, and Maloja pass, Bellagio and Como all looked the same. The mud on the road was several inches deep and treacherous, the potholes were full of water, and

PLAUEN

ÖLSNITZ

SAXONY

Graslitz

Adorf

Rossbach

Bad Elster

BOHEMIA

HOF

Shönbach

Leibitschgrund

Rehau

ASCH

Brambach

Fleissen

Steingrub

Hörsin

Schwarzenbach

Schnecken

Schönberg

Klinghart

Liebenstein

Voitersreuth

Wildstein

Maria Kulm

Haslau

Altenteich

egerland

Seeberg

to Karlsbad
–Prag

Franzensbad

BAVARIA

EGER

Stabnitz

Losau

to Marienbad
–Pilsen
–Prague

0 2 4 6 8 10   20 kms

0   5   10 miles

the rain poured incessantly from the clouds, the sides of the mountains, the trees and the roofs of the houses. Each night we hoped that our clothes would be dry by the morning, and each morning we set forth again in the rain.

Riding too fast along the slippery road by the side of Lake Como, I skidded with my heavy machine and fell in the mud twice in one afternoon. In Como I was following close behind a tram when suddenly the earth opened in front of me and I almost crashed down a ten-foot-deep hole that gaped between the tramlines. Men were laying a sewer. Perhaps it was the ladybird on my breeches that protected me. Then water got into the petrol, causing engine trouble, and finally I had to mend a puncture in the pouring rain. We stayed two days at the luxurious Park Hotel at Locarno to recover.

The return journey over the Gotthard Pass, along Lake Lucerne and through the Black Forest was not much better. We never saw the sun, yet we enjoyed every minute of our two weeks' holiday. We did not even catch a cold. Father hoped in vain that I would now give up my motor-cycle in favour of a car. Several other young men had acquired motorbikes, my cousins Egon and Heinz Geipel a Rudge and a BMW, my friends Kurt Linke a Matchless and Hermann Hübner an OEC, and there were now Nortons, Douglases, FNs, Indians and Harley Davidsons in the neighbourhood. Robert and I had become well-known figures in the local motor-cycling community, and the competition from these newcomers made me all the keener. I gladly borrowed Father's car in the winter and in bad weather, but in the summer and autumn when the roads were dry I liked my Brough Superior much better, and refused to part with it.

My brother Rolf thought it a privilege to be entrusted with cleaning and greasing the Brough, and did it most conscientiously. Father was so impressed with his diligence that, much to my surprise, he bought him a small motor-cycle, a 175 c.c. McEvoy, when he was fourteen and had passed the entrance examination for the textile college at Asch. As far as I remember one did not need a driving licence for motor-cycles, and Father believed a bike with such a tiny engine would be a mere toy. Little did he realise how much power British engineers had succeeded in packing into those small two-stroke engines. He treated Rolf's entry for the Niederreuth–Asch hill-climb as a harmless joke, and had the surprise of his life to see him ride such a superb race that he won first prize in the junior category. Rolf's win caused a minor sensation in motoring circles, and he felt as proud as a peacock when he was photographed on his machine wearing a huge crash helmet and the victor's wreath of oak leaves round his neck. It was well deserved. I never came first in any race.

Occasionally, but not very often, we took girlfriends on the pillion. On balance, their presence and the picnics they laid on were poor compensation for slowing us down and making our mounts less controllable. Not many girls knew how to sit tight and lean over with the machine going through bends. Once, with Lotti, a friend of my sister's, on the pillion, my Brough caught fire on the long, straight road behind Eger. We were going flat out, and I did not know that anything was wrong until Lotti's stockings scorched and she began fidgeting. As I slowed down the flames shot upwards, enveloping us both. Slamming on the brakes, I turned into the ditch by the side of the road, the blazing bike fell over, and we were thrown clear. There was nothing I could do but watch helplessly as the petrol tank burst and the fire gradually burned itself out. Apart from some burns and scratches and our ruined clothes we were all right, but the motor-cycle was a sorry sight. Fortunately my fear that it would be a total write-off was unfounded. A large consignment of spares from Brough's at Nottingham and several weeks' work by two devoted mechanics made it thoroughly roadworthy again, but some of the scars remained, and it looked less beautiful. Moreover Rolf was now so busy cleaning his own bike that he had little time for mine, and I could not arouse any enthusiasm in Ingo to take over. He was more inclined as he got older to borrow my machine and ride it when I was not about than to clean it.

It is natural to love the country where one was born and has spent one's youth, and I hope to be forgiven if I think of the rolling countryside of western Bohemia, with its lofty hills and dark pine forests, its quiet valleys and gurgling trout streams, its yellow cornfields and picturesque farmhouses and its forbidding old castles as one of the most beautiful parts of the world. The visitors who came each year to Karlsbad, Marienbad or Franzensbad, to the pearls in this exquisite setting, will surely bear me out. They had been coming for the past two hundred years, not only to sip the health-giving waters that gush in hot or cold springs from the ground but to rest and enjoy the scenery, the food, the concerts, the elegant shops, the promenades, to see and be seen.

Before the first world war these famous spas and their surroundings were the playground of the international upper crust, the illustrious, the fashionable and the rich. At Karlsbad the crowned heads of Europe and their hangers-on, Russian aristocrats, Hungarian landowners, American millionaires, celebrated actresses, poets and composers strolled up and down the Alte Wiese, as the narrow shopping street was named that leads along the river Tepl to the Hotel Pupp, in those days one of the largest and most luxurious hotels anywhere. The steaming Sprudel, that mysterious geyser throwing its healing waters in irregular jerks some fifty feet high into the air, the Hirschensprung commemorating the discovery of the hot spring by Charles IV when stag hunting in 1349, and the Hotel Pupp with its thick carpets and silently perfect service were the embodiment of Karlsbad.

The springs of Marienbad contain salts with different healing properties, but the town, with its parks, hotels and shops was equally beautiful. One took coffee with whipped cream on the terrace of the Belvedere in the morning, ate delicious Bohemian specialities for lunch in the ornate dining room of the Weimar Hotel—provided the doctor permitted such indulgence—and danced waltzes, polkas and polonaises to champagne and gipsy music at the Bristol at night. It was Edward VII, the King of England, who had made Marienbad famous. He regularly met the rulers of Europe there to negotiate international agreements, besides taking the waters and shooting with the local landowners.

Visitors to Franzensbad, the smallest and least fashionable of the three resorts, usually lived somewhat more modestly. They took mud baths and drank Glauber Quelle, promenaded with their glasses in the Kurpark listening to the band, made excursions to near-by Castle Seeberg, sat at little tables in the Kaiserstrasse to watch the passers-by and spent the evening at the theatre.

After the war, in the 1920s, things were no longer what they used to be. Measured by the Almanach de Gotha and *Burke's Peerage* the visitors were of a lower class, the scene had become more democratic, but it stayed dignified, and outward appearances changed little. These select resorts were not for the masses. Everything remained spotless, buildings and lamp posts were always freshly painted, all glass and brass was polished, the pavements, the parks and even the woods looked spring-cleaned. Every dying tree was removed, every dead flower replaced without delay. People were tidy, but if anyone did drop a cigarette-end or a piece of paper it was immediately picked up by a park keeper. And one never saw a broken bottle, tin or box in the countryside.

The clientele was much the same as one met at St Moritz, Deauville and Baden-Baden. Diamonds, mink coats and chauffeur-driven Rolls-Royces, Cadillacs and Minervas were still much in evidence. The rubber-tyred wheels of handsome carriages still rolled noiselessly over the smooth asphalt and the gentle clatter of horses' hoofs lent an atmosphere of unhurried, old-fashioned respectability, but royalty and aristocracy were largely replaced by politicians, industrialists and members of the *corps diplomatique*. It was surprising how many motor cars one saw with CD plates. To be vice-consul of some remote Central or South American republic was a status symbol which could be bought if one knew the right people and had enough money. A sprinkling of curly, bearded Orthodox Jews in their black robes and occasionally a maharaja or some wealthy Egyptian added an Eastern touch to the picture. To complete it perhaps I ought to describe the sick who came in their thousands and found cure or relief, but I was young and healthy myself, and hardly aware that the people who promenaded, sipping from their glasses, to the strains of an orchestra had faulty digestions, gall bladders, kidneys or livers.

I had no means of comparing post-war conditions with those before 1914, and was not particularly interested in the nostalgic memories of my elders. When I 'discovered' the three spas the scenery was as beautiful, the hotels were as comfortable and the menus as delectable as ever they could have been. Perhaps champagne flowed a little less freely now, but five o'clock tea dances had been introduced instead, which suited me much better. Every hotel in the town or on the wooded slopes that commanded such an attractive panorama had open-air dance floors and bands that played the latest two-steps, foxtrots and tangos. And for the price of a cup of coffee and a slice of Pischinger Torte mit Schlag one could dance for two hours.

Needless to say, I could not come on my motorbike, even though it was a Brough Superior. Motor-cycles clashed with the sophisticated elegance of these health resorts, and the police confined them to certain streets. No hotel commissionaire would have let me pass in boots and leather breeches. One was expected to wear a well-cut, neatly pressed suit, pointed shoes, brightly coloured socks and tie to match. Besides, the girls who sat well on the pillion, Paula and Mia, did not look their best on a dance floor. I needed a more decorative girlfriend, and that was how Sonja came into my life.

Father was happy to let me borrow his second car. He saw in this transformation not only a sign that I was growing up but a welcome opportunity, as he thought, of getting rid of that dangerous motorbike. He offered to put his hand deep into his pocket, if I gave it up, to buy me a sports car, a two-seater Buick cabriolet with two dickey seats. When I rejected his generous offer he bought me the car all the same, hoping for the best. It gave me great joy and no trouble for five years, but for acceleration and speed it could not touch my Brough.

Sonja had black hair, flashing blue eyes, a shapely little figure and danced the tango like a dream. She also played the piano and had a beautiful voice which could fill a whole church, as it did when she sang solo at my sister's wedding. Sonja lived at Schwarzenbach, a small town across the border in Bavaria, where her father owned a brewery. To visit her I had to cross the border from Bohemia into Saxony, from Saxony into Bohemia and from Bohemia into Bavaria, clearing customs six times, and the same again in reverse on the homeward journey. Taking her to Karlsbad and back involved two more frontier crossings, four more customs clearances. It was hardly possible to accomplish all that in a day and still have time for a hurried meal and a dance however early I set off on Sunday morning. We needed a whole weekend for these excursions, a day and a half, but that required a chaperone.

I talked to Grandmother, who was very understanding. She liked Sonja, and came with us for the first weekend. The next few times she just pretended. Making sure everyone saw us leave together, she drove with us as far as Franzensbad, where she spent the afternoon at the concert in the park, to return quietly home by train in the evening, while Sonja and I explored Karlsbad or Marienbad. 'Behave yourselves,' she smiled, 'and people will soon get used to seeing you two together. You're young only once: make the best of it.' And she was quite right. No one ever raised an eyebrow, only Mother told me off if I came home too late on Sunday night.

The memory of those carefree weekends is among the happiest of my youth. We danced on the open-air terraces of all the exclusive hotels, ate cake and ice cream in every little *Konditorei*, again and again feasted upon roast venison, pork, goose or duck at the romantic shooting lodge on the Glatzen and afterwards sat in the sun, listening to the birds and the gentle breeze in the branches of the majestic pine trees which surrounded the opening in the forest. We visited Metternich's Castle Königswart, swam at Tippelgrün, admired the flower arrangements in the parks, watched the races and went to the theatre.

Sonja, a German citizen, could hardly believe that she was abroad. Only the stamp on her passport and the fact that we drove on the left-hand side of the road reminded her of it. Czechoslovakia was supposed to be a foreign country, yet everyone everywhere spoke German. Why did one hardly ever hear a word of Czech? I had to explain that western and northern Bohemia were not and never had been Czech in all the eight hundred years of their history. Not 2 per cent of the population were Czech. We were Bohemians, of course, and proud of it, but Austro-Bohemians. We had become Czechoslovak subjects through the peace treaty, against our will, without a plebiscite, at the point of bayonet and gun. I knew how effectively this act of violence had been played down by Czech propaganda in England, but was surprised that Masaryk and Beneš had succeeded in misleading even the people of neighbouring Bavaria.

'So this ought to be part of Germany?' Sonja enquired innocently.

'Heaven forbid!' I retorted.

She seemed perplexed. 'If you want to be neither Czech nor German, what on earth do you want?'

I laughed. 'Emigrate to England and become British, to get away from this petty nationalism. The British treat their subject races more intelligently.'

'And leave all this behind?'

'Not altogether. I'd spend my holidays at Karlsbad and Marienbad. I'd have a British car with a GB plate on it and be a distinguished foreign visitor instead of a second-rate Czechoslovak citizen.'

She did not know whether to take me seriously. 'And the people who live here—who have built the towns and villages, own the hotels and farms, plough the fields and plant the forest? Tell me what they would like to be,' she demanded.

'Independent,' I replied. 'Austrian, or at least remain German-speaking Bohemians and continue to quarrel with the Czechs, as they have done for centuries. But they want to quarrel on equal terms. The country belongs to both, and they need each other.'

This was too involved for Sonja.

'Few foreigners understand,' I agreed. It was the very complexity of the situation that had enabled Masaryk and Beneš to get their way with the Western powers. The Austro-Hungarian Monarchy should never have been destroyed, Czechoslovakia never created, at least not in its present form. But why cry over spilt milk? Things had to be accepted as they were.

There was little to complain about. With so many foreign visitors present, the Czech officials were on their best behaviour. Karlsbad, Marienbad and Franzensbad were windows through which the world viewed Czechoslovakia, and the government saw to it that no shadow fell on the skilfully presented picture of a model democracy. In other parts of the republic less exposed to foreign eyes the atmosphere was not quite so congenial.

Summer passed, the leaves began to fall, the dance bands returned to their night clubs in the cities, one after another the hotels in the resorts closed their doors for the winter. Now my Brough Superior came into its own again. I put on my leather breeches with the little ladybird, Robert arrived on his McEvoy, Paula and Mia reappeared, there were six weeks of glorious motor-cycling weather until the rain came, then snow, and another year was gone.

We always had a hilarious New Year's Eve party, and in February came Carnival, with its tomfoolery. We danced in fancy costumes, wearing masks and false beards, pretending to be someone else. The snow lay for almost three months, and most of my weekends were spent on skis. Nothing could compare with the run home at night through the lonely forest of ten thousand snow-covered Christmas trees steeped in the silvery light of the moon, with not a sound to be heard except the swish of my slender boards sliding through the powdery snow. Then, towards the end of April, I felt once again the powerful acceleration of my faithful Brough, and in May Sonja and I were once again on our way to Karlsbad in the car, to see how the season had opened. They were carefree—well, almost carefree—days.

That summer, or maybe it was the summer after, my friends Colin and Min Baird came from Scotland for a visit, and we took them in the Buick for a happy fortnight's motoring through Bavaria, Austria and Switzerland. They had not been to that part of the world before, the weather was glorious, and we had such a happy time that one evening, sitting by the fountain in the square at Garmisch, Sonja and I almost became engaged. But fate, in the shape of a knobbly-kneed old peasant in leather shorts and green braces, intervened. He had come to fill his bucket. This interruption brought us back to earth. The spell was broken and never quite returned.

14

LESS CAREFREE
DAYS
1925-29

ONE OF THE greatest worries of my youth was the army. Czechoslovakia had compulsory military service: every young man who was medically fit had to serve for eighteen months. I hated the very thought of it. The Pasolds are no soldiers, and I was no exception. Besides, I could not afford to waste the precious time, I had work to do. What point was there in serving in an army that could never fight a real war, except perhaps against Poland? In a war against Germany, Austria or Hungary one soldier in every three would be a potential deserter, if not worse. Was it reasonable to expect that the millions of German- or Hungarian-speaking inhabitants would fight to defend the Czechoslovak Republic, a State into which they had been forced against their will, any more than Dr Beneš had fought for the Austro-Hungarian Monarchy? I simply could not take the Czechoslovak army seriously. However well equipped, it was a farce.

Dr Beneš had evaded military service by leaving the country to study in Paris and Dijon, but the conscription laws were stricter now than they had been under Austrian rule. I would have to leave the country for good, to emigrate, and even this was made very difficult. The validity of passports issued to men of military age was strictly limited. In any case, I could not run away because of Father and the family business. The only possible escape for me was to be medically unfit.

Grandfather had been lucky; he was 'bought off', a regular practice at that time in Austria. The Monarchy needed money as well as soldiers. Uncle Otto cut the sinews of his trigger finger, and Father was rejected because of an enlarged thyroid gland. But there was nothing wrong with me, I was perfectly healthy and not prepared to mutilate myself. The medical examiners would need to be persuaded to classify me as unfit and I could think of only one way of doing that. To my dismay Father shook his head and flatly refused to bribe anyone, even if it meant losing me for eighteen months. I had to look elsewhere.

Some of the boys with whom I had been to school relied on an overdose of strong black coffee to give them the symptoms of a weak heart, others looked forward to playing at soldiers. It seemed their only hope of ever seeing another part of the world, if only the Slovak mountains. I found out that the prospective recruits were examined by two army doctors—different ones each time to make bribery more difficult—assisted by Dr Stein, the chief medical officer for the Egerland. My best chance, it would seem, was to make a cautious approach to Dr Stein through my uncle Friedrich, who knew him.

'I'll have a chat with him,' Uncle promised, 'but Stein won't take money. Find some attractive present whilst you're in England. He's a chain-smoker.'

Arriving in London on a Saturday evening after an exceptionally rough sea crossing, I booked in at the Imperial Hotel in Russell Square and, feeling ill, went straight to bed. On Sunday morning I phoned for a doctor. He arrived in plus-fours. He had a golf appointment and was in a hurry. 'Appendix,' he diagnosed. 'We'll have it out in the morning.' I protested and asked to see an x-ray. It showed among all my intestines a completely normal appendix. I had only been very seasick. The bill came to seven guineas and gave me quite a shock, but also an idea.

'Doctor,' I said, 'converted into the currency of my own country this is an awful lot of money, and having incurred the expense unnecessarily I am afraid to face Father. Please write on a sheet of your notepaper an explanation of this photograph and say that my inside was very upset by the movement of the boat. Please make it look important by using long words and complicated sentences so that Father will forgive me. And please write the receipt at the bottom and sign over the twopenny stamp.'

Dr MacPhearson thought it a little unusual, but, with an understanding smile and a hand that was difficult to read, he obliged. I left contentedly with the large x-ray picture and the impressive-looking medical opinion under my arm, and went to a jeweller's shop, where I bought a gold cigarette lighter. Only then did I take my bag of samples to the City to call on our various customers.

Uncle Friedrich approved of the handsome lighter and roared with laughter when he saw the medical evidence of my delicate inside and heard how I had obtained it. 'Capital, capital!' he exclaimed, slapping his thighs. He wished he could see the examiners' faces when they studied the report. They could not possibly ignore the considered opinion of an eminent London doctor without the risk of looking foolish or displeasing their superiors. Of course, a certificate from Paris would have been even better, but London was quite good enough. I felt relieved, and only hoped Uncle was not treating the matter too lightly: for me it was deadly serious.

The examination took place two months later at Wildstein. Young men from several villages, some boisterously noisy, others with tense, worried

faces, assembled at various inns awaiting their turn. I joined the party from
Fleissen: sons of farmers, clerks and factory workers, about twenty in all. We
had to undress in an ante-room and were called in alphabetical order to appear
before the military commission. It was headed by a fierce-looking major who,
after listening to the medical evidence, decided whether a man was fit to
become a soldier. First the mayor of Fleissen inspected our birth certificates
and other identification papers and confirmed that each of us was in fact the
person whose name was on the register. Then we were examined by the two
army doctors, and if they could not agree Dr Stein acted as arbitrator. Two
orderlies kept the records.

My name was called, I stepped forward and my height was measured.
Without a word of explanation I handed my x-ray to one of the army doctors
as if expecting that it would speak for itself. Holding it up to the window, he
scrutinised it for a considerable time while I stood, stark naked, to attention.
No doubt he knew all about the trick with the black coffee but was clearly not
used to x-ray photographs. 'Very interesting,' he remarked at last, and without admitting his failure to discover the abnormality (there surely must be
one, otherwise there would not be this x-ray picture!) passed the photograph
of my inside to his colleague, who seemed equally perplexed. 'Very interesting, pane kolega,' he agreed, scratching his head. Then Stein had a look at it.
'Excellent definition,' he said. 'Now let's see the report.' I produced Dr
MacPhearson's letter, with the Harley Street address embossed at the top,
which made the desired impression. It appeared that all three men knew a
little English, and I followed with baited breath their efforts to read the unfamiliar foreign handwriting, afraid that at any moment they might ask *me*
the nature of my complaint. Seasickness would hardly be a valid reason for
declaring me unfit for service in the Czechoslovak army. But I need not have
worried, they were busy showing off trying to see who could decipher and
translate most words—'disturbed equilibrium . . . oesophagus . . . diaphragm
. . . violent movement . . . inflammatory condition of the stomach . . . enlarged . . . intestinal tract . . . severe . . . liable to recur' they read out, until Dr
Stein ended the guessing competition. 'Certainly not fit,' he muttered, as if
to himself, and the two medicos in uniform readily agreed.

'Neschopen—untauglich,' pronounced the major. There were another
thirty men to be examined, and he wanted to be through by lunch time.

I did not know or care what they entered in the register besides 'neschopen'. The sun shone twice as brightly as I drove home to bring my parents the
glad tidings and phone Uncle Friedrich. When I met him alone a fortnight
later he grinned. 'Dr Stein likes the lighter and wants you to bring the x-ray
photograph and the report again next year.' So the seven guineas proved a
good investment after all. I was free, for a while at least, and I could make

plans again. The valuable year I had gained must be used to the best advantage. There was scope to do more business in Scandinavia, I felt sure. I had engaged agents in Denmark, Sweden and Norway; now I would go and visit them on their home ground, see customers with them, observe their sales techniques and assess for myself the potential of the three markets. Without delay I went to Eger to have my passport renewed and applied for the necessary visas.

Having been rejected by the army once unfortunately gave only temporary respite. One had to go through this ordeal three years in succession, and only when certified as unfit for the third time was one finally in the clear. However, my luck held. Aided by my x-ray photograph and Dr Stein's diplomatic influence I got safely through the remaining two medical examinations.

Few of the friends with whom I compared notes and who had all tried to keep out of the army succeeded so completely. Hermann Hübner, for instance, the son of a knitwear manufacturer at Asch, a highly intelligent young man whose father was dead and whose mother struggled hard to keep the business going, had to waste his precious time in the uniform of a private doing office work which a girl of fourteen could have done. Among other things it was his job to keep the 'Kmenovy list', recording the personal data of every soldier born in 1906. Whenever one of them died he had to stamp the word 'Zemřel' across the entry. It was such a simple procedure that Hermann decided to 'die' himself as far as the military were concerned. He put the magic stamp across his own name, and while this did not get him out of uniform immediately it at least made sure that he was not called up again in subsequent years for manoeuvres, refresher courses and periods of further training but was henceforth left in peace.

How well I remember my first business calls in Copenhagen, Stockholm and Oslo. It was a new experience for me to meet 'buyers', as they were called. Back in Czechoslovakia the proprietor himself or one of his partners placed the orders. In England and Holland too I negotiated only with the owners of the importing firms who were our customers. Every one of them was an 'entrepreneur', a character and a sturdy individualist who thoroughly understood the merchandise he handled, knew what he wanted and got on with the deal. With the exception of Alfred Stern, these importers sat at worn old desks in workshop-like offices, unaware of personal status or the impression their premises made on visitors, but intensely jealous of the good name and reputation of their firm.

Our trade in Scandinavia was different. We sold to wholesale houses and large retail concerns, such as Illum, Kooperativa Foerbundet, Boehlke, etc, and the buyers I met were not the proprietors but employees who were less concerned with the firm they worked for than with their particular department and, as each of our agents warned me in turn, with their own importance. They sat in smart offices behind polished desks with glass tops, had to be treated with deference, and at Christmas expected a box of cigars. Most of them kept us waiting to show how busy they were. They liked to impress and be flattered, a technique quite foreign to me. I found it most difficult, and preferred to talk about the features of our goods, quality and value. And I very much doubted Father's willingness to give away cigars. It was well that our agents went round with me, otherwise I would have sold very little.

In Copenhagen I contracted my first bad debt, a very substantial one. The report we had at Fleissen about the financial standing of the firm in question was not confidence-inspiring, but in my eagerness to build up our Danish business I ignored it and accepted a large order. The customer subsequently got into difficulties and we lost half our money.

Our agent, Fritz Larsen, a tall, handsome Dane with a pleasant personality, was popular with the buyers. He seemed to live well, and in the evenings took me to all the best restaurants and showed me the Tivoli and the other sights of Copenhagen, a gay and very attractive city. Through him I met another Else, but she was quite a different girl from the one back at Asch who had tried to lead me astray. She had just lost her mother and was now an orphan. I felt terribly sorry for her, she looked so beautiful in her black dress, and when she smiled a dimple appeared in one of her cheeks. I went to the cemetery with her to lay some flowers on her mother's grave, and on Sunday she took me by train to the small town of Helsingör, made famous by Shakespeare's *Hamlet*, and showed me the old castle of Kronborg. I liked her very much, and we wrote letters to each other for a year or two before we lost touch.

There was nothing Nordic about our Swedish agent, Jacob Müller. He had black hair, bulging eyes and talked with his hands, joked with the buyers and pulled their leg, but always let them have the last laugh. They obviously enjoyed the visits of the volatile little man, and he extracted surprisingly large orders from them. The trouble with both the Danes and the Swedes was that they were showmen who, to impress manufacturers with their purchasing power, always bought more than they needed and then, half-way through the season, tried to wriggle out of part of their contracts. But Müller usually found other buyers for the unwanted merchandise, and we were never seriously embarrassed.

He made good use of my presence. This was my first visit to Sweden, he explained. I had come all the way from Czechoslovakia to make the personal acquaintance of our most valued customers, to hear their wishes and consult them about next season's trade. It all went down very well, and most buyers reached for their order books and wrote out an order to prove that they were gentlemen. Müller called only on firms in Stockholm, Göteborg, Norrköping,

Bôras, Malmö and other fair-sized towns, sold to them at our lowest prices, which included 3 per cent commission for him, and ignored the small stores in the country. He was by far the most successful of all our agents.

Stockholm was a beautiful city. The sun shone, small boats rode on the water, the people were well dressed and looked happy. On Sunday I explored the outskirts and came to the zoo. After a while I became aware of a girl, a striking blonde, who seemed to be following me about. She asked the time, we looked at the camels and tigers together, and then went to have dinner. At the next table sat two Latins who made eyes at her, and she started to flirt with them. 'Italians,' I thought, getting a little annoyed. Would I mind if she made a date with them for the following evening? she asked. I did not mind.

'You can have spaghetti with them right now,' I said, walked back to the Grand Hotel and went to bed.

Jacob Müller was intrigued when I related the episode to him next morning. He reckoned he knew every girl in town but could not place my blonde from the description I gave him. How was it that he had missed her?

'Her name is Quinia,' I said. 'She claims to be a Finn.'

Müller was satisfied. 'That explains it,' he said. 'She can't have been in Stockholm for very long!' And we picked up our range of samples to start the day's work.

Olaf Engelhardtsen, our Norwegian agent, had a sales approach all his own. He was so dignified that he would not carry the bag with samples himself but sent a boy with it ahead of his visit. He strutted about the customer's premises as if he owned them, and in his expansive way treated the buyers as his equals. He was obviously a man of standing and substance who commanded considerable respect. The fact that I had come to Oslo was of no consequence. He had things well under control and needed no assistance. And he too was a very good agent.

Perhaps it was Norway's geography that determined Engelhardtsen's sales technique. His salesmen called on all the little shops in the fishing villages, the hamlets in the fjords and the valleys up to the Arctic Circle. Their travelling expenses were high, and they carried only the price lists that included commission of 5 per cent and 10 per cent respectively. These prices also showed us 5 per cent and 10 per cent more profit, which was justified because the orders were small and there was a good deal of extra work involved.

I returned to Fleissen with vivid impressions of northern Europe, its people and its trade. Many Swedes and Danes spoke German; the Norwegians were better at English. To time a business journey to Scandinavia correctly was practically impossible. The Swedes bought very early, almost before our samples were ready; the Danes placed their contracts a month later, and it took another two months before the Norwegians decided to write out their orders. They came when there was hardly enough time left to manufacture the goods and the Swedes were already beginning to agitate for next season's samples. But it was all very interesting, and I thoroughly enjoyed my trip.

As I had expected, Father flatly refused to let any presents be sent to buyers. When Grandfather noticed my disappointment he beckoned me into his office.

'These buyers hold positions of trust and must be adequately remunerated by their employers,' he said. 'If they are honest men they will be loyal to their firms and not be influenced by presents, so you'd be wasting your money. And if they are dishonest we do not want their business.'

'But Grandfather,' I remonstrated, 'I gave a cigarette lighter to Dr Stein, and everyone gives presents to government officials. It's the same thing, surely!'

'Not everyone, not your father, for instance. Besides, it's a very different matter with civil servants. The government deliberately underpays them, expecting those members of the public who seek their services to make up the difference. There is some justice in that, for most taxpayers never trouble government officials and are only too glad to keep away from them: why should they pay their salaries?'

And there the matter rested. I am glad to say that our business with Scandinavia flourished without cigars.

Meanwhile Father had made me his deputy. Aware of my youth and in-experience, I realised that I did not deserve this exalted position and felt so self-conscious that I kept it a secret from my friends, even from Helmut and Robert. I wanted to work my way up and not be promoted because I was the boss's son. Nor did I call an office, a telephone or desk my own, and sat wherever there was a vacant chair. I had, however, two drawers in Grand-father's desk where I could lock up my papers.

The season's sales and purchases completed, Father took time off for a long-overdue thyroid operation and then went with Mother to the south of France to recuperate. The factory was running well. The weather was beautiful, and notwithstanding Father's absence I urged my grandparents to take their usual holiday at Karlsbad. Surely I was old enough to be trusted to look after the business on my own for a while! So now I was in charge.

Having worked late one evening, I was just locking the office when a stranger came to the door. He had bushy brows and wore a cap and an old raincoat with the collar turned up. Could he have a word with me in private? He spoke with a north Bohemian accent. There was something compelling in his voice, and after a moment's hesitation I let him in and offered him a

chair. Was I certain that we could not be overheard? Quite certain, I reassured him, wondering what he might have to say. He pulled out a crumpled
certificate from which it appeared that he was the secretary of the miners'
union at Falkenau, some ten miles away.

We looked upon trade unionists as revolutionaries, Communists plotting
to abolish the capitalist system. There were none at Fleissen, at least we knew
of none, but there were Socialists, and that was bad enough, for Socialists
were Communists in embryo. The coal miners at Falkenau had the reputation of being Communists. My visitor claimed that they were planning to
create labour unrest in the factories at Fleissen as a prelude to the setting up
of a trade union branch. The campaign would begin with a strike; the decision whether it would be at Lehrmann's or at Pasold's had not yet been taken.
Both firms had one or two secret supporters of the Communist Party among
their employees. He said he had access to the confidential membership lists
of the party and knew who the potential troublemakers were. Provided I got
rid of them immediately, the strike would not take place at our factory.

Nonsense, I thought, our workpeople were pleased to have safe jobs and
earn good money. They would not listen to agitators. There were no Communists among them, and they wanted no trade union. The man was obviously an impostor. The typed scrap of paper he had shown me did not even
state his name. He must have found out that Father and Grandfather were
away and thought he could intimidate me.

I laughed. What did he want from me? 'Money,' he replied. 'If you pay
me 100 kronen I'll tell you who the Communists are, so that you can get rid
of them, and for one krone per person per year I'll keep an eye on your employees in the future.' I opened the door. 'Get out!' He looked me in the face
for the first time. 'You'll be sorry,' he hissed, and went.

A week later, when I had almost forgotten the incident, two of our knitters,
lads of about twenty, came to see me and asked for higher piecework rates.
The yarn was inferior and caused machine stoppages, they claimed. I looked
at the yarn and found nothing wrong with it, but after the lunch break they
were back. From the way they behaved I concluded that they had been
drinking. The whole knitting department supported them, they said. I explained that Father was away recuperating from his operation and that he
would look into the matter when he returned at the end of the month. This
did not satisfy them; they demanded an immediate increase. 'Go back to your
machines,' I replied firmly. 'I cannot change wage rates in Father's absence!'

Shortly after they had gone Johann Feiler appeared in the office. 'All
knitting machines are stopped,' he said. 'There's trouble brewing, but I can't
get to the bottom of it.' Before he could say any more the factory ceased to
hum. The motors had been switched off; it was suddenly as silent as on

Sunday. Then came the sound of many feet walking downstairs. From the office window we watched our workers pouring out through the gates, not only the knitters but the winders, the sewing machinists, the cutters and the packers as well.

Schreiner and Hoyer came to the private office, followed by the departmental foremen. Why had everyone walked out? Was it a strike? Who was behind it? I very much wanted to know. It was hard to believe that it could be those two immature knitters who were causing the trouble. The news spread through the village like wildfire. Strike was an ugly word. Everyone remembered the strike at the leather factory during those tumultuous days after the war, when shots were fired, the office furniture was smashed and Uncle Wilhelm was almost killed. It was the only strike Fleissen had ever experienced, and nobody wanted another one. Whilst we discussed what to do two gendarmes with rifles and bayonets fixed arrived and patrolled in front of the factory. They were there to maintain law and order. But there was no trouble: we could see no pickets, our people had gone straight home. They were too ashamed to be seen in the street, it transpired later. But I did not know that at the time. The sight of the two warlike gendarmes made me very tense, and I was prepared for the worst.

Apart from the half-dozen clerks in the office and the departmental foremen no one turned up for work the next morning, and I sent Father a telegram to the south of France. Two days later he arrived. When I told him about the mysterious stranger who claimed to be secretary of the mineworkers' union he said he was glad I had shown him the door, but he did not want to know anything about the strike itself. He felt upset and humiliated that it should have happened at our factory. As soon as our workpeople heard he was back they returned. The stoppage was over. 'Now let's forget all about it and make up for lost time,' he said, and that suited everyone. No questions were asked, nobody was dismissed, the piecework rates were not changed, and the whole village was relieved not to have come under the domination of outside troublemakers. I felt guilty for a long time for having brought Father home. He was still very weak. Somehow, I thought, I had mishandled the situation, although I never quite understood what I had done wrong.

Some months later I met Hans Braun, part-owner of Fleissen's third largest knitting mill, who was always well informed about local affairs. He insisted on buying me a glass of beer, and then began to talk about the strike. 'You saved my firm money by throwing that union official out,' he said. 'Lehrmann's were first on his list, but they paid up. Had you done the same we would have had to pay too or the strike would have been engineered in our factory. Thanks to you we neither paid nor had the strike.'

I felt foolish, but swallowed my pride and asked him to tell me more.

'Unions need income,' Hans Braun explained. 'The more members they can recruit the more subscriptions they collect. Union bosses are politicians. They want power, and the larger the membership they control the greater the power they wield. Fleissen is a thorn in their side. It is the most prosperous industrial community of western Bohemia, expands faster, pays higher wages, has more contented workers than any other within a radius of 150 kilometres, and it has no unemployed. Wherever the unions canvass for members, Fleissen is held up to them as an example of success due to the absence of union interference. Small wonder they try to disrupt our tranquillity.'

As the people of Fleissen saw it, the purpose of socialism, communism, trade unions and collective bargaining was to drive a wedge between the work-people and their employers to prevent them from talking to each other and settling occasional differences except through a middleman, a shop steward, in whose interest it was to keep them apart. The factory owner and his employees had been boys and girls together, sat on the same benches at school, and called each other by their Christian names. Why should they let someone come between them? Besides, the shop steward would be a Red, and the people were disillusioned with socialism. The corrupt Red council that held sway under Burgomaster Kraut in the years immediately after the war and plunged the village into debt had left a bad odour behind. In a modest way the people of Fleissen were capitalists who worked and saved towards a house and a small garden of their own. An ambition which might take a lifetime to realise, but they considered it a life well spent. Trade unions had nothing to offer and gained no foothold, nor was there ever another strike.

15

TWO SPINNING MILLS
AT ONCE
1926-29

THE COST OF a knitted garment could be broken down into three approximately equal parts. One third was the cost of yarn, one third wages and salaries, one third everything else, such as dyeing, accessories, packing materials, heat, light, power, maintenance and replacement of buildings and machinery, insurance, transport, bank interest, selling expenses, commission, profits and taxes. Competition saw to it that each item of expenditure was continuously scrutinised to discover whether it could be reduced. Yarn being the largest single item, manufacturers spent much time comparing the samples of various spinners, looking for the cheapest quality they could economically use on their knitting machines, studying crop reports and buying when they thought cotton prices, which fluctuated daily, were at their lowest. Half the success of a manufacturer's operation depended on how lucky he was in buying the right yarn at the right time. Father usually covered his requirements for six, twelve or even eighteen months ahead. They were weighty and at times very worrying commitments.

We used two types of yarn, which were supplied by separate spinners. One type was spun from American cotton and, although only 16s and 40s count, was generally referred to as fine yarn. It was used for knitting the basic fabric. The other was much coarser, 6s count, spun by the condenser method from Indian cotton or various kinds of waste. It served as backing yarn and, when brushed, gave the fabric a thick fleece and made it feel soft and warm.

Generally speaking, the fine spinners were larger, wealthier concerns than the condenser spinners, and both ranked very much higher than the knitters. We looked up to them with respect and envy. Anybody who was able to raise 60,000 kronen could buy a few old circular machines and start a small knitting plant, but spinning on such a small scale would have been quite uneconomic. To build and equip a spinning mill, especially for fine yarns, cost millions. Every enterprising knitter dreamed of the day when his or his children's business would be big enough to produce its own yarn and be independent of those powerful and seemingly dictatorial spinners.

I must now return to October 1926. Cotton prices had been falling steadily, with a depressing effect on business. We were still working two shifts completing old contracts, but no new orders were coming in. It was so quiet—had all our customers suddenly died? Or were they placing all their orders with Lehrmann's? Were Lehrmann's able to sell at lower prices because they spun their own condenser yarns?

We had scrapped our waste spinning machinery after the war when cotton became available again, reasoning that our plant was too small to be efficient and that it was more economical to buy our condenser yarn from a number of spinners who were competing fiercely against each other. Lehrmann's, who had copied us and also installed a waste spinning plant, took the opposite view. Instead of scrapping theirs they enlarged it to make it competitive. They continued to break up and re-spin their waste clippings, while we sold ours to waste merchants. In addition to waste they had recently started to spin condenser yarns from Indian cotton. It seemed to pay them, for we heard that they were negotiating with Schwalbe, the spinning plant makers, for still more machines. These rumours worried us. Lehrmann's could not be allowed to forge ahead unchallenged. We had to take a closer look at condenser spinning. Once again Father and I were at the border before the crack of dawn waiting for the barrier to be raised, and after a brisk run and a short stop for breakfast were at Schwalbe's factory at Werdau in Saxony by 8.30 a.m. The sales director refused to disclose whether he had booked any orders from Czechoslovakia but did his best to sell us a spinning plant. An ideal little unit consisting of four three-card sets with eight mules—self-actors, as they were called—together with the necessary openers and preparatory machinery would cost 200,000 marks, he said. The cost of transport and erection, the land, the building and the power plant had to be added, of course.

We shook our heads. With business as slow as it was we had not the courage to spend that kind of money, nor did we believe that such expensive plant could pay us even if operated in three shifts.

The sales director tried to be helpful. If new machines were too dear we might like to look at a condenser spinning mill in the town which was for sale, part of the Wilhelm Kauffmann enterprise that had gone bankrupt. It was equipped with Schwalbe machines throughout. The largest creditors were the Deutsche Bank at Chemnitz, who had tried to sell the mill as a going concern but had found no bidder. The obliging salesman phoned Chemnitz and obtained permission for us to visit the plant.

Every machine was working. There were bale breakers, openers and blowers, twelve beautiful three-card sets, twenty-nine self-actors, a dye-house for loose cotton and a large modern dryer, all in excellent condition. It was a joy to see, and we were glad we had come. After this visit the second-hand machinery we saw at dealers and in other mills looked old and uninteresting.

On the way home we talked of nothing else but the Kauffmann plant, and with every mile farther away it became more desirable. What a pity they would not sell the machines piecemeal. There was to be another auction in January; the bank was prepared to lower the price to about 220,000 marks. A spinning mill in Germany was of no use to us, and we had no intention of making a bid, but decided to attend the sale. Who could say, perhaps there might again be no buyer for the going concern and the machines would be sold off singly after all.

We had pictured a condenser plant of very modest size, two three-card sets and four self-actors to begin with, but no doubt Schwalbe's sales director was right when he said that such a unit was too small to operate efficiently and we would need to double it. Again and again we discussed the project, made calculations of what it might cost, pegged out the site at Fleissen where we thought of erecting the building so that it could easily be extended and wondered where we could find the right man to run the plant. We had some experience of spinning rough yarn from wartime waste, but knew nothing about the intricacies of selecting and buying raw Indian cotton and converting it into lofty condenser yarn. We needed expert advice.

Father telephoned Direktor Walsch, the manager of Krumbholz, the fine cotton spinners at Leibitschgrund. He had been to see us a year earlier in response to a complaint about the excessive moisture content of a consignment of yarn Krumbholz had delivered. How well I remembered his visit. The dispute was settled amicably and he gave us a credit note, but he took me down a peg by proving that my method of determining surplus moisture was not strictly correct. I did not like him very much.

It seemed that Walsch was even more anxious to talk to us than we were to him. Before Father had explained what we wanted to consult him about he said, 'I'll have the horses out right away—be with you in a couple of hours,' and put the receiver down. Half an hour later Herr Krumbholz phoned, and I took the call. 'My mill is not for sale,' he said in an agitated voice. 'Don't waste your time.' I was taken aback. 'We aren't in the least interested in your mill,' I replied. Father laughed when I told him.

In due course a coach drawn by two steaming horses arrived, and Direktor Walsch, a heavily built man, burst into our office. Without waiting to hear what Father wanted, the floodgates opened and out poured a long tale in rapid Silesian accent. For years, it appeared, Leibitschgrund had been running at a loss. Krumbholz had cooked the books and persuaded Baron Zdekauer, the merchant banker, to advance ever larger loans. He now owed him between 7 and 8 million kronen. Zdekauer intended to foreclose on his mortgage and sell the mill. He would ask 5 million but come down to 2 or $1\frac{1}{2}$, in fact it could be bought for a song.

'I fear you are under a misapprehension,' Father interrupted. 'We do not want to buy Leibitschgrund: we seek your advice on a condenser plant.'

At last Walsch understood, but he did not give up. 'I know nothing about condenser spinning,' he said, 'but surely a fine cotton spinning mill would suit you much better. Ours is just the right size for you. Come over tomorrow and have a look at it, a visit commits you to nothing,' he persisted.

Next day we were on our way to Leibitschgrund. Half an hour's drive in the Buick brought us to the picturesque valley, with its gurgling trout stream and the dark, eighty-year-old pine forest stretching from the banks of the crystal-clear waters of the brook up to the ridge of the hills and many miles beyond. A little farther down where the valley opened into a long, narrow meadow the mill, with its tall chimney stack, nestled on the right bank, surrounded by the tiny village that belonged to it. And as we drove over the wooden bridge into the factory yard we met the gamekeeper in his green hat and horn-buttoned jacket, gun over his shoulder, followed by a red setter.

Direktor Walsch took us first through the spinning shed half-way up the hill, an old-fashioned single-storey north-light building with a wooden roof and narrow spans. It was closely packed with flat carding engines, all made by Platt Bros. of Oldham, which seemed in fair condition, and antiquated self-actors, altogether some 12,000 spindles spinning an average count of 30s. They clearly needed to be replaced by ring frames. All this machinery was driven from an overhead line shaft. The cotton dust in the air made us sneeze, and the din was such that we could not hear ourselves speak.

Then we visited the weaving mill, a large, comparatively modern building with light, spacious workrooms. It consisted of ground floor and three upper storeys, and housed 360 weaving looms, yarn preparation equipment, yarn store and packing department. If anything the noise here was even worse than in the spinning shed. We wondered how the workpeople could stand it, and imagined the relief they felt when after the day's toil they escaped into the stillness of the woods. Krumbholz sold only about half his yarn production. The remainder was woven here and the grey cloth disposed of to merchant converters, a money-losing business.

The powerhouse made us gasp. A huge upright steam engine of 1,000 horse-power built by Ringhofer in Prague in 1896 drove the line shafts of both factories through a complex system of ropes and pulleys. We could hardly believe this kind of transmission still existed at a time when industry had long changed over to motor-driven line shafts and progressive manu-facturers were already talking about individual motor drives. Yet here towered this sparkling engine with its majestic height of some 25 ft, slowly turning at 350 revolutions a minute, dignified as a Roman emperor. There was, in fact, not a single electric motor in the whole of Leibitschgrund. Walsch noticed our surprise.

'You may think we are old-fashioned,' he smiled, 'but this is a most efficient power plant.' We thought it imprudent to argue with him. In fairness I must say that I saw similar engines and rope drives in Lancashire thirty years later and was assured that they still worked economically.

The whole valley with its 500 acres of beautiful pine forest belonged to the factory. So did the workmen's houses, the school, the inn and the tiny chapel. So too did the large house in which Herr Krumbholz lived, with its flower beds, fountain and vegetable garden, its outbuildings and stables. And the brook with the trout in it, the pond, the mill stream and the 15 h.p. turbine which drove the dynamo providing the electric light. We were bewildered by the mixture of loyal diligence, old-fashioned feudalism and industrial hopelessness.

Herr Krumbholz avoided us, but we had the eerie feeling that he was anxiously watching from some hiding place wherever we went, and felt deeply sorry for him. His son had preferred the short-lived glamour of an Austrian officer's uniform to the management of the business, came to the remote valley only to organise shooting parties, and disappeared again in the social whirl of Prague or Vienna. Overtaken by an age he did not understand and events he could no longer master, the old man was still envied by every unsuspecting traveller who passed through Leibitschgrund admiring the idyllic setting of the seemingly prosperous concern, but he knew that his days of ownership were numbered.

Baron Zdekauer, whom we met after our tour of inspection, was a tall, distinguished-looking man of middle age. Wearing a deerstalker, a jacket with green lapels and cuffs, and leather knickerbockers, he gave the impression of being a local squire rather than a banker from the capital. He came straight to the point: the property was for sale at a price of 5 million kronen. Father replied that this was totally unrealistic as far as we were concerned. The baron smiled, took note that we were not interested in his proposition, said goodbye, and left us to drive back to Fleissen, which we did, lost in thoughtful silence.

Another visit to Werdau brought an unexpected change in the situation there. We heard that Herr Schärf, a local manufacturer, had suddenly shown interest in the Kauffmann property. On the spur of the moment we called on him, and met with an icy reception. He had been wrongly informed that we were potential bidders against him. But he thawed when Father explained that all we wanted were some of the machines. Did Herr Schärf need them all, or would he consider selling us some if he should buy the property?

'You can have all the machines,' answered Schärf. 'I only want the land and buildings.' He hesitated for a moment as if a thought had struck him. 'The bank are aware of the development scheme I have in mind and think they can hold me to ransom over this mill. If I withdraw suddenly they'll panic and sell it to you for a much lower figure. You can then take the machines and I'll give you 100,000 marks for the empty shell,' he suggested.

The plant was much too large for us. We could, at best, use only half of it, but perhaps the remainder could be sold. We consulted a dealer in second-hand spinning equipment, a man named Franz Müller, with whom we had established contact. He offered to dispose of any machines left over after we had had our pick. Being able to sell them singly, he thought he could get a good price for them. We would retain the best machines, and, provided all went well, they would cost us very little by the time the transaction was completed. The proposition was worth considering, and we decided to sleep on it.

Trade continued to stagnate without any improvement in sight, yet here we were negotiating for two spinning mills at once. Was it not reckless to think of risking our capital on even a single venture at such a time? But the smoke from Lehrmann's chimney reminded us that we could not afford the comfort of caution. The pace of competition was getting hotter every year. We could not afford to slide back and lose the race. Were we to bid for the condenser mill at Werdau, with all its uncertainties, or try to do a deal with the baron?

The machinery at Werdau had the advantage that it was almost new, and we could build a modern factory for it right next door to our knitting mill. But that would take time, and then we'd have to find and train labour, which would not be easy. This plant would, of course, only produce condenser yarn; we'd still have to buy our fine yarns. Leibitschgrund, on the other hand, was a fine cotton spinning mill in full production, and could begin to supply us immediately. True, the yarn it spun was of poor quality, but we were satisfied that it could be much improved by installing a new cotton cleaning plant. Leibitschgrund was much the larger project. For a while we vacillated between the two, then Father produced a brilliant scheme.

'Let's buy both,' he said. 'Let's sell off the 360 weaving looms at Leibitsch-grund, put new floors in the building, and install the condenser plant in it.' He knew it would fit, because he never walked through any factory without unobtrusively stepping out its length and width. 'The power plant is there; we teach the weavers to spin condenser yarn, and we use the waste from the fine cotton mill as raw material for it.' It all added up perfectly, and in this way Leibitschgrund could become economically viable.

'Have we enough money to buy both concerns?' I asked.

'It'll depend on the purchase price,' replied Father. 'There's also the cost of the new cotton cleaning equipment, the removal of the weaving looms and erection of the condenser plant, and other conversion expenses. Leibitschgrund runs at a loss at present and will continue to do so for at least another year. We shall have to find that money too. I've talked to the Bohemian Union Bank at Asch, and they'll tide us over the difficult period.'

'How much do you think we can get for the 360 looms?' Grandfather wanted to know.

'Just enough to pay for the new floors,' Father guessed. 'They're narrow, outdated machines and can only be sold to some backward country like Roumania.'

Our next move was to resume negotiations with Baron Zdekauer. We went to see him at his bank in Prague, and after a day's hard bargaining he dropped his price to $4\frac{1}{4}$ million. Since Father would not go above $1\frac{3}{4}$ million the meeting ended in deadlock. Direktor Walsch's efforts brought us round the conference table again a week later, this time at the Hotel Post at Karlsbad. The baron came down to $3\frac{1}{2}$ million; Father slowly climbed to $2\frac{1}{2}$ but would not go one krone higher. Again deadlock. Then, as we parted at the door, Zdekauer weakened and said, 'I'll accept $2\frac{3}{4}$ million if you decide now.' Father asked for a week to consider, and, visibly tired, the baron agreed.

We were quietly congratulating ourselves that Lehrmann's, our traditional enemies, had kept out of the combat, when two other contestants appeared unexpectedly. One was Schütz, a textile concern in northern Bohemia, the other Fischer, the largest knitters and spinners in Asch. Before the week was out they had both visited Leibitschgrund and conferred with Krumbholz, who was still the legal owner. The news was very perturbing, and I suddenly realised how disappointed I should be if we lost the mill and estate in that beautiful valley to a competitor. I was aware of the conflict within me. My urge to emigrate and settle in England was as strong as ever, and I was afraid that Leibitschgrund would make this more difficult, for the reorganisation would mean a great deal of extra work for us all and tie me even more firmly to Czechoslovakia. But I also knew that it was vitally important to make Adolf Pasold & Sohn as competitive and self-sufficient as possible, and my personal interests had to take second place.

Outwardly Father remained completely calm, but I sensed that under the surface he was as anxious as I not to be beaten at the last moment. Without delaying further he closed the deal at $2\frac{3}{4}$ million, subject to Herr Krumbholz signing the contract. In addition Zdekauer extracted 125,000 kronen from us for stocks of coal, oil, packing cases, paper, the five-ton lorry that plied between the mill and the coal mine at Falkenau, two pairs of horses, and other items. The date of the take-over was to be 1 February 1927.

With Leibitschgrund virtually in the bag, we attended the auction at Werdau on 27 January and, since we were the only bidders, the Kauffmann property was knocked down to us for 200,000 marks. At the rate of eight kronen to the mark this represented 1·6 million kronen, but fortunately we had to find only half this amount, for Schärf kept his promise and immediately deposited his 100,000 marks for the land and buildings. Franz Müller helped us to select the seven best three-card sets, sixteen self-actors, a bale breaker, a Crighton opener and a willow, and we told him to sell the remainder of the plant. It realised some 70,000 marks, much more than we had dared to hope, but of course we did not know this at the time.

After a slight delay which gave us some anxious days Krumbholz signed, and we took over on 5 February. The news that we had bought Leibitschgrund caused a sensation in the textile industry of western Bohemia, and for weeks was the main topic of conversation among manufacturers and agents. Take-overs were rare, and the wildest guesses circulated as to how many millions we had paid, but the actual purchase price remained a closely guarded secret. Our confidential clerks gave away no information, nor did those of the other parties concerned in the deal. Employees were, on the whole, very loyal and seldom broke a confidence. They usually stayed with the same firm for life. They were glad to have permanent jobs, and did not move around as people do these days.

While Father and Grandfather were chuckling over the curiosity and ill concealed envy of our competitors the amazing history of Leibitschgrund made the round of the inns. I wanted to hear it in detail, to write it down, and Grandmother, who was usually well informed, promised to tell it to me. 'See me this evening,' she said. 'It's a long story. I won't play cards for once, and will talk to you instead.' And after supper she waited for me in her armchair.

'In the old days, when a weaving loom stood in every cottage,' she began, 'people spun flax on their hand wheels and wove it into linen. Then cotton came from the East, mainly from Turkey, and many of the weavers changed over to the new raw material, for there was great demand for the cloth made from it. Cotton yarn could not be spun on their wooden hand wheels, it had to be bought from a spinning factory across the border at Adorf, in Saxony, which had large English spinning machines made of iron. The import duty on cotton yarn was high, and much was therefore smuggled. The smugglers carried it in bundles on their backs through the forest. But the customs officials came to the cottages of the weavers, and any weaver who could not prove he had paid duty on the yarn or bought it from a Bohemian mill was fined heavily.

'In 1826 a man named Wenzl Sandner who was a merchant in Prague bought an acre of land in the valley of Leibitschgrund for 224 gulden and built a cotton spinning mill on it. The machines were imported from England, and a waterwheel provided the power. During the day the spindles turned and the inquisitive customs officials could watch how the yarn was spun, but when they had gone the smugglers came out of the forest with their loads and the mill was busier in the dark of the night than in daytime. Then something must have gone wrong, I don't know what,' said Grandmother, 'for in 1835 Sandner disappeared and Franz Richter became the owner.

'He seemed to do well, for he enlarged the mill, bought more spinning machines from England, and installed weaving looms, but he was always in trouble with the neighbouring farmers. There was no road through the valley then, and the only access to the mill was the cart track along the ridge of the hill. Sometimes in the winter it was blocked by snowdrifts, or in the spring too soggy with the melting snow, and Richter's waggons passed over the adjoining fields. This led to endless quarrels, and he was beaten up more than once. When the farmers refused to let him repair the track at his own expense the cunning mill owner resorted to a trick. He invited the bishop, who was planning to visit Graslitz, to travel through Leibitschgrund and bless the enterprise, its workpeople and their neighbours. The unsuspecting prelate consented to make the detour, and when the farmers heard of the great honour to be bestowed upon them they hurriedly repaired the road for the bishop free of charge.' Grandmother winked—she was Roman Catholic herself, the only one who had married into the staunch Protestant Pasold family in more than three hundred years, and she was as amused as I. 'But now comes the most fantastic part of the story,' she continued.

'Richter became too greedy. When Austria fought against Bismarck in 1866 he had government contracts, and it was said that the cotton cloth he supplied to the State found its way back to the mill to be delivered and invoiced again. Before he could be apprehended he died and was buried, leaving the business to his widow and his trusted book-keeper, Krumbholz, who, incidentally, came from Fleissen. But some of the people who had been to the funeral whispered that the coffin had been empty and that Richter had left the country in one of those large, round returnable packing cases in which spinning machines came from England. The mystery was never solved. The widow made over her share of the mill to Krumbholz, who became the new owner, and she retired to Prague. There, three years later, she met a bearded gentleman from America and married him. His name, by some strange coincidence, was also Richter.

'Johann Krumbholz worked hard, and under his management the firm continued to grow, but his son was educated in Prague and became more of a gentleman than a manufacturer. He began to neglect the mill. When the

Monarchy provided an easy market not enough of the profits were ploughed back into new buildings and machinery. Then came the 1914–18 war, followed by the tough trading conditions in Czechoslovakia, and the rest you know yourself. I'm sorry for the poor old man,' she sighed, 'although he had brought about the downfall himself. And now once again Leibitschgrund has a new master. I wish I could look into the future to see how it will all work out.'

I enjoyed my talks with Grandmother Pasold: she knew so much and explained things in such a simple way. How strange it must feel, I thought, to look back over such a long span of time and so many changes. She was born in 1859, Grandfather in 1857, the middle of the previous century, which seemed a long, long time ago and made one think of Napoleon, if not quite of Julius Caesar. How well my grandparents had adapted to our modern, mechanical age, and I admired them for it, even if the finer points were lost on them. One could hardly expect them to know, for instance, the effects of pre-ignition in an internal combustion engine or how the valves in a radio receiver worked. They could not ski, drive a car or dance the two-step, but I thought none the less of them for that. Not that Grandmother was always right, of course. She genuinely believed that some day—and it would not be very long—I myself would be as old as she was now, and that I might be as bald as Grandfather and prefer to sit in the park at Franzensbad listening to the band instead of careering about the countryside on my noisy motorcycle. That, surely, could never come true. It was admittedly logical that everyone should grow old in due course, but deep down I felt that it could not apply to me. I ran my fingers through my thick shock of hair, flexed my muscles and thought, 'Never.'

We had all been toiling quite hard in the past, but now those of us in responsible positions at the Fleissen factory had to shoulder additional duties to help Leibitschgrund, and to free Father so that he could devote most of his energy to the task of reorganisation, which he tackled in a well thought out order of priorities. Not everything that needed doing could be done at once. The number of technicians, engineers, carpenters and bricklayers available was limited, delivery dates for new machinery varied and had to be spaced so that the buildings were ready when it was due to arrive, and arrangements had to be made for the necessary funds to be there at the right time. It was essential that sales and production at Fleissen meanwhile continued to run smoothly and that the growing yarn supplies from our own mill balanced the tapering-off supplies from outside spinners.

The first step was to get to know the people who lived and worked at Leibitschgrund, to identify and get rid of the shirkers, the dishonest and the disruptive elements who had contributed to the run-down of the enterprise, and to give the others fresh faith in the future. It was not easy to do this, for the entire population of the village was related and intermarried, and we had to proceed with caution. After some initial misunderstandings and trouble, however, the great majority were impressed by Father's impartiality and firmness, which was in striking contrast to the vacillating favouritism practised by Krumbholz. He soon gained the workers' confidence, and in due course we could not have wished for a more co-operative labour force.

The leaking roofs were mended, buildings repaired, a new bridge was built, the mill stream cleaned out, and the ash which was piled up in a huge heap just outside the boilerhouse was cleared away and used to prepare the base for a large new single-storey warehouse. Since Leibitschgrund was surrounded by forest, it was to be built as an attractive timber structure to tone in with the valley. All this was not only in the interests of operating efficiency, it also proved to the workers that we meant business and that we intended to improve the amenities.

There had to be much coming and going between Fleissen and Leibitschgrund. Our three-ton lorry and the horse carts were continually on the road, and Father made the journey daily by car. It was a rough and tedious trip. The track along the ridge of the hill had fallen into disuse, and the 'new' public road through the valley was in very poor condition. It consisted of a chain of potholes, and broken springs were the order of the day. We complained to the local council, saw the Okresni Uřad at Eger and sent petitions to Prague pointing out that in the interests of employment and of keeping industry going, export industry at that, the road should be mended. Like Richter eighty years before us, we offered to pay for the repairs ourselves, but all to no avail; officialdom did not respond. Maybe someone was waiting to be bribed. In the end Father bought stones and gravel, recruited a gang of workmen and put the repairs in hand himself. This swiftly brought the law down on him. Our gang had used some of the overgrown heaps of gravel which had been lying by the roadside for years. Believe it or not, he was accused of stealing government property, a serious criminal offence, was committed for trial, and lost his case in court. Fortunately his appeal succeeded, and the prison sentence was commuted to a fine.

Direktor Walsch succeeded in disposing of the 360 weaving looms to the Balkans, as Father had expected, and as soon as they were dismantled the badly worn floors of the multi-storey building were renewed. Franz Müller supervised the dismantling, packing and loading of the condenser plant at Werdau and its erection at Leibitschgrund. He also found a foreman, who began with the training of some of the now unemployed weavers as soon as the first three-card set and the first self-actors were in working order. Father employed the others in a vast tidying-up operation throughout the mill buildings and the village.

With these initial measures under way, he concentrated on the difficult task of improving the operating efficiency of the enterprise. Money was draining away at a frightening rate every week, every hour, and to reduce the losses, let alone turn them into profits, required tireless exertion. Many of the changes that had to be made to do away with time-honoured malpractices and wastefulness were unpopular with the workpeople, but slowly, very slowly, they began to understand that their own prosperity depended on that of the mill, discipline improved, and output began to climb.

The next stage was to improve the yarn we produced. The quality of the 16s to 40s cotton counts was atrocious. The twist was much too hard, and the remnants of cottonseed in the yarn caused so many knitting machine stoppages and needle breakages at Fleissen that we had to pay our knitters higher wages. It was not the fault of the spinners but of the antiquated cleaning equipment we had taken over from Krumbholz. A cable trolley took one cotton bale at a time from the store in the valley to the opening room at the spinning shed half-way up the hill. There were no adequate facilities for mixing, and the blowing room was a dark hole. The whole department had to be redesigned and equipped with modern machines. Father built a large new opening and blowing room in the valley, scrapped the cable trolley and instead blew the loose cotton through a long sheet-metal pipe up the hill into four new mixing chambers. The old self-actors with close spindle spacing which had produced pin cops for the weaving mill were replaced by ring frames, although Direktor Walsch held the traditional view that hosiery yarn had to be spun on mules. Experiments were made with other types of cotton, especially Peruvian, which proved very suitable. The twist was made softer and other changes were introduced which, in the aggregate, improved the quality of the yarn considerably, but in spite of all efforts it was never quite as good as the yarn we could have bought at only slightly higher prices from our old suppliers. Fischer's of Asch, for instance, whose spinning capacity far exceeded the demand of their own knitting mill and from whom we had bought regularly in the past, produced cleaner, softer and more even yarn than Leibitschgrund.

But if our fine cotton mill with its high proportion of old machinery did not measure up to the standard of the modern mills in the neighbourhood, our condenser plant presented a very different picture. It was as good as new and a pleasure to see. The seven three-card sets from Werdau had been erected on the ground floor of the multi-storey building, from where bobbin-hoists took the sliver bobbins to the self-actors on the first and second floors. On the top floor the cops of yarn were packed into large wooden cases in which they were then transported to the winding department at Fleissen. Right from the start, when all the operatives were still learners, the condenser yarn we produced gave our knitters no trouble.

We began by breaking up and re-spinning the small pieces of waste that fell under the tables in our cutting department at Fleissen. In the past we had sold them to waste merchants, large international organisations such as Bunzl & Biach of Vienna or Sapt of Stuttgart. Waste was big business; it provided the textile, paper, furniture and other industries with valuable raw material. We sorted our waste clippings into white, light, mixed and dark shades and re-spun them separately. The white were the most valuable, the dark the cheapest. Only about 5 per cent of the fabric we cut became waste, and we therefore bought in the waste clippings of our competitors. But they refused to sell them to us direct for fear of giving away the composition of their fabrics, and we had to buy them through the same waste merchants we had sold to in the past. We also bought willow and comber waste, which came from spinning mills. In addition we used substantial quantities of raw Indian cotton, which produced the best and most expensive condenser yarn. Buying all these various types of raw material was a complex business, and needed skill and experience. A wrong purchase would start a chain reaction throughout our vertically integrated organisation and prove very expensive.

Father did all the buying himself. American and Peruvian cotton for the fine spinning mill came from merchants in Bremen and sometimes from Liverpool. He made the selection in consultation with Direktor Walsch, who was, of course, a lifelong expert in this field. But Walsch knew nothing about condenser spinning, and there Father had to rely largely on his own judgement and advice from dealers. He liked me to be present when the salesmen came and untied their hundreds of samples, each consisting of two handfuls of the various grades of cotton or waste neatly packed in small rolls of blue paper. They were spread out on desks, tables and chairs, and the selection was made by a process of elimination. The chosen samples were divided in half, packed in separate parcels and sealed by both parties. One half was kept by the buyer, the other by the seller, to serve as evidence for arbitration if the bulk shipment should not come up to sample.

All these transactions took place in Father's private office. He got so absorbed in them that time and again he was an hour late for lunch or forgot about it altogether, much to Mother's dismay, for she worried about his health. At last she threatened to hold me responsible for making him keep regular hours. But this was easier said than done: I could not possibly interrupt the negotiations and tell the salesmen to go away when it was lunchtime. Some other method had to be adopted, and I remembered one of my schoolboy devices. Father sat with his back to the wood-panelled wall, facing visitors across his large desk. Immediately behind him stood a bookcase, and above it hung a picture. I tied a length of thin string to a cardboard disc, lowered the disc behind the bookcase, led the string in the groove between two wood panels up over the nail that held the picture and down again, and from there through a series of hidden wire hooks to my corner of the office. Then I stencilled on the disc:

When I unobtrusively pulled the string the disc rose from behind the bookcase; when I let go it disappeared again. The effect on the salesmen was electrifying. When the message mysteriously appeared they hurriedly concluded the deal and took their leave, with Father suspecting nothing out of the ordinary. He frowned when he discovered the gadget, after I had operated it successfully for several weeks, but then laughed and let me continue to use it.

Being present at selection, price and delivery negotiations gave me valuable experience, especially since I also saw how the selected grades of raw material behaved later in the spinning process, how the resulting yarns ran on the knitting machines, and how the finished garments looked and handled. Few textile men were so intimately connected with the whole production cycle. Father was fully occupied with Leibitschgrund, and I was now responsible for most of the sales. To be well informed about technical details was most useful in my dealings with customers.

Spinning our own condenser yarns undoubtedly made us more competitive, but in retrospect I am not sure that the acquisition of Leibitschgrund was an equally sound move. Many years passed before the fine cotton spinning plant made any real contribution to the progress of our business. Father did not live to see it. Constantly overworking to modernise the old-fashioned enterprise undermined his health. His premature death was largely caused by strain and worry. The ultimate financial success of the operation was the result of later technical developments for which the credit must go to my brother Rolf and my brother-in-law, Willie Nebel. Their courage and tenacity achieved what to Father and me had seemed impossible. But I must not run ahead of the proper sequence of events.

16

WHITE BEAR
SWEATERS
1927-29

THE LEHRMANNS WERE not to be beaten. No sooner had we bought Leibitschgrund than they decided to build a fine cotton spinning mill at Fleissen.
It was a little smaller than ours, but they equipped it with brand-new high draft
machines—a costly undertaking—trained local labour and ran the plant in
treble shifts. There could be no doubt that it was a very efficient operation,
more efficient than ours, and to have it adjoining their knitwear factory gave
them an added advantage. They were very dangerous competitors.

In contrast to Adolf Pasold & Sohn, who had abandoned their original
factory long ago and moved to a level ten-acre site on the periphery, the
Lehrmanns stayed with their enterprise in the middle of the village. By
negotiation, patience, intimidation and cunning they acquired all the surrounding cottages, one after another, and gradually extended their site to
about four acres. Its odd shape and slope made a clean factory layout impossible. The buildings were too close together, not at right angles, and their
floors were not on the same level, but the property had the great advantage
of being on the stream.

Lehrmann's next move was to build a dyehouse. They were fortunate
enough to have a spring in their factory yard which provided a steady flow of
precious clean water, but if this proved at times insufficient they supplemented it during the night from the stream. They had trouble with the
disposal of the effluents, though, because they had not enough room for an
adequate filter plant and emptied most of their dirty water into the stream,
again during the night. The farmers below the village objected, but their
court actions had little effect. The fines were small, because frequent even
more obnoxious discharges from Geipel's leather factory had killed all the
trout long ago. However, we liked to believe Lehrmann's difficulties to be
greater than they really were.

We knew little about dyeing. It was more of a craft than an industry.
Dyers liked to shroud their activities in mystery. They passed their secret
recipes on from father to son, and rarely allowed anyone to look inside their

works. Dyehouses were primitive. There was nothing in them to delight the engineer, no precision machinery, no polished metal, gears or dials. Rows of clumsy open wooden vats with wooden winches driven by flat leather belts from a rusty line shaft, one or two belt-driven centrifuges, an untidy array of iron pipes and valves were hidden in the fog caused by clouds of steam belching from the vats and reducing visibility to a yard or two. Condensation dripped from the ceiling and the rusty ironwork, deep puddles covered the floor, and the atmosphere was oppressive. The heart of every dye plant was a large, Lancashire-type boiler which consumed vast quantities of coal and water and supplied the heat that brought the dye baths to the boil.

Rough, half-naked men with brawny arms stained by yellow, red and blue dye manhandled the heavy pieces of wet fabric, rinsed and centrifuged them and hung them over wooden poles in large drying chambers, where they were left for two or three days. Summer-weight fabric was then calendered, winter-weight merely bundled, because it had to be fleeced before it was rolled, and most knitters preferred to do the fleecing themselves. The cost of transporting the bulky loads of fabric from the knitting mills to the dyehouses and back again—distances of ten kilometres or more over bad roads—was included in the dyers' charges.

By doing their own dyeing the Lehrmanns saved the cost of transport, but was that enough to justify the troublesome operation? We heard much about their water and effluent difficulties. The whole village talked about faulty dyeing, lack of expertise and breakdowns in plant, and we consoled ourselves with the thought that their venture could hardly be profitable. We did not suspect that these woeful stories were put in circulation by the wily Lehrmann brothers themselves to discourage us from thinking about dyeing.

One morning Grandmother brought the news that Lehrmann's were negotiating for the Lower Mill, and a few days later the purchase was confirmed. This gave them the mill stream and a claim to water which could not be challenged even by the Geipels, who owned the Upper Mill. The two firms now had a stranglehold on Fleissen's water, and the war between them intensified. Each accused the other of extracting more than its fair share. We were glad not to be involved in their litigation and laughed whenever we saw a *Kommission* of gesticulating lawyers, court officials, witnesses and representatives of the contending parties on the bank of the stream looking for hidden pipes or checking the degree of pollution.

But our laughter had a hollow ring. We did not want a dyehouse, we said— a case of sour grapes if ever there was one. How could we think of dyeing when we hardly had enough water to keep our boiler plant and steam engine going! Both wells on our factory site were drying up: the situation was getting desperate. Something had to be done, and soon.

We had two water-bearing plots of land in reserve for just such an emergency, both about half a kilometre from the factory. One was by the warehouse at the railway station, but a survey revealed technical difficulties which made the laying of a pipeline impracticable. The other adjoined the mill stream. We dug a test hole where the water diviner indicated, and struck a rich vein. Water was pouring into the hole, coming not from the direction of the mill stream but from the hill. The council gave us permission to lay our pipeline in the public road leading to the factory, we built a pump house, fitted a motor-driven pump and remote control gear, and within a few weeks the installation was complete. At long last our water supply was secure, so we believed.

Lehrmann's ignored our construction work. They let us finish the expensive job without opposition, but on the day we started pumping they obtained a court injunction against us, claiming that the water we were extracting was theirs. It was seeping from their mill stream into our well. Father offered to have the bed and banks of the stream concreted at our expense, but the Lehrmann's asked for nothing less than to have the well filled in.

The lawsuit lasted several weeks. A *Kommission* came, and experts were called. A number of holes were dug in a circle round the well to determine which side the water came from. Chemicals were put in the mill stream and the water from our well was tested to see whether traces of them had seeped through. Both tests disproved Lehrmann's claim. The court decided in our favour, but such was the influence Dr Adolf Lehrmann wielded behind the scenes that we had to concrete the mill stream and, in addition, were refused costs in the lawsuit. Father paid gladly. The water supply was vital to us. Our opponents had not succeeded in closing it down, but the court investigation had revealed the yield of our well and reassured Lehrmann that it was insufficient for a dyehouse.

Much time had elapsed since we became the owners of Leibitschgrund, and we wondered why the authorities were not demanding the usual stamp duty of 8 per cent of the purchase price. We hoped they had mislaid the file. The later we needed to pay the better, for we were short of money.

Then one day Father had a note summoning him to Eger for an interview with Ober-Finanzrat Dr Brückner, of the stamp duty office. He came back snorting with indignation. Brückner was not satisfied that the $2\frac{3}{4}$ million kronen we had declared represented the true purchase price. It seemed much too low. Investigations had shown that before we took over the enterprise it was insured for more than four times that value. Was Father prepared to pay stamp duty on, say, 10 million?

We knew the reason for the discrepancy. In order to mislead Baron Zdekauer and secure ever larger loans from the bank Krumbholz had made fictitious entries in the books, overvalued stocks, plant and buildings, and increased the insurance to the quite fabulous amount of 12 million. Unaware of these facts, Dr Brückner wrongly concluded it was the real value of Leibitschgrund. He thought the figure we had declared was only a fraction of the sum that had actually changed hands. The 10 million was a try-on in the hope that it would make us disclose the real purchase price or lead to a compromise.

Father's sense of justice was outraged, and he flatly refused to pay one krone more than was due. He was not to be intimidated by government officials who acted purely on unfounded suspicions. If Dr Brückner did not believe us let him prove otherwise!

'Do you think Brückner wants to do a deal?' I asked. 'What I mean is, does he want to be bribed?'

Father threw up his arms. 'Bribe him for the privilege of paying the correct stamp duty? Are you out of your mind? I shall appeal and appeal, I'll go to court, and if need be to the President of the Republic!'

But Dr Brückner was equally adamant. He would not budge from his figure of 10 million. The case was referred to Prague, and back again to Eger for further investigation. We had two *Kommissionen* at Fleissen going through our books with a fine-tooth comb. Their presence in our office was most disconcerting. Father had to open the safe, which they searched in the hope of finding incriminating documents or evidence of some hidden transaction. They went through our cupboards and the drawers of our desks, read our correspondence, studied our bank accounts and made copious extracts. They interrogated Father, Grandfather and myself, Albert Schreiner, the head book-keeper, and a number of clerks, prepared statements of what we said and made us sign them. Direktor Walsch at Leibitschgrund and his staff received similar treatment. Sometimes the examiners disappeared without comment, but after a few days they were back to continue with their searches. We were not worried about the outcome of the stamp duty investigation, but Dr Brückner was conducting a war of nerves. There was no knowing what his sleuths might unearth. We must surely have violated this or that regulation some time or other, and any irregularity he discovered would be welcome. As it happened, nothing was found, but Father had many a sleepless night while the search continued.

The worrying stamp duty affair dragged on and kept us in suspense for two years, then something extraordinary happened which brought it to a most unexpected end, as we shall see.

With Father occupied at Leibitschgrund, the whole of the export business, with all its problems, was left to me. Trade had improved. The temporary setback of the previous autumn had been overcome, but competition had increased and selling become much harder. Knitted underwear made in Poland and in Japan appeared on the British and Dutch markets at very cheap prices. The spectacular growth of Fleissen's knitting industry, which was based entirely on the production of Directoire knickers, made other Czechoslovak manufacturers envious. They changed over to the production of knickers, and in addition a number of new makers sprang up. With the growing popularity of knickers, distribution did not remain in the hands of the old established importers in England, Holland and Scandinavia. More merchants entered the field, some of whom traded at cost or even below in order to break into the market. Bankruptcies followed which had an un-settling effect on the trade. Since 90 per cent of our total output was exported, the responsibility of finding enough orders to keep the factories going without selling to financially weak buyers kept me on my toes. I had to travel abroad more often, which I welcomed, although many of the journeys were any-thing but pleasant. Invariably I had to straighten out troubles and try to collect money from slow payers.

One day a letter arrived from Mr Stern in London. It was marked 'strictly confidential' and asked Father and me to attend a meeting at the Hotel de Saxe in Prague. We went, not knowing what to expect, and found some thirty knitwear manufacturers assembled. All our competitors from Fleissen and Asch were there, as well as the knitters from Teplitz, Schönlinde, Warns-dorf and Deutschbrod. Mr Stern sat at the top table, and after the doors had been locked to keep out intruders he impressed upon us that not a word of what he was going to say must be passed on to anyone.

'Gentlemen,' he began, 'I have taken this unusual step of asking you to come here because I have to talk to you about a very serious matter. The livelihood of every one of us is at stake.'

Uttered in his most sombre voice, these words chilled the audience into breathless silence. Mr Stern was generally admired, highly respected and probably the largest customer of every manufacturer in the room. The matter must indeed be serious.

'Britain has a growing unemployment problem,' he continued. 'There are moves afoot to restrict imports of knitted garments. British wages are much higher than those on the Continent: manufacturers in Leicester and Notting-ham cannot compete, and their factories are standing idle. They are clamour-ing for anti-dumping legislation and protection in the form of import duties. Their demands are being discussed in Parliament, and they stand a good chance of succeeding unless we counter with well reasoned arguments. Import duties will raise the cost of living! We must canvass members of Parliament and the press to win public opinion to our side, and we must prove that you are not dumping. Dumping means selling below cost. You must prepare a breakdown of your wages and prove that you make a profit on your exports to Britain. We must engage high-powered lawyers. This will cost a great deal of money. We British importers are putting up a large sum, but we cannot finance such a costly operation alone. Your future is as much at stake as ours, and I appeal to you for generous contributions to our fighting fund. I will give you no receipts for your money, nor will you be told how it is being spent. You will have to trust me, and I have to rely on your secrecy. If it leaked out that foreign manufacturers are financing the fight to maintain Britain's free trade there would be headlines in the newspapers and we would lose our case.'

The vision of import duties and the loss of our British trade made us all reel. Mr Stern could not have presented his case better or more dramatically. There was not a person in the room who did not spontaneously offer generous support.

He explained that before coming to Prague he had already held a similar meeting with the Saxon manufacturers in Chemnitz, and that he would now do the same at Stuttgart and repeat it in Poland and Italy.

Father sent a credit note for £100. There were no currency restrictions in those days, and we did not have to ask the National Bank for a permit. And that was the end of it. For the time being the free-traders won their battle, and exports to England continued. We never knew whether Mr Stern's activities influenced the victory.

Mother was worried about Father's health. He was a passionate motorist, but now he took Wollner, the chauffeur, for his daily visits to Leibitschgrund instead of driving himself.

'I need to think about the business,' he said, 'and I can't do that properly while driving the car. Half an hour each way adds up to five or six hours a week, and I can't afford to lose them. The Lehrmanns, Brauns and Geipels all live within a few minutes' walk of their factories. How could we hold our own against them if I wasted 10 per cent of my time steering round potholes and avoiding children and dogs?'

'Must we keep up with them?' I blurted out, and immediately regretted the question.

'You know the answer yourself,' said Father. 'There is no place for slackness in industry. Ease off and you go to the wall, like the Friedls or Krumbholz.'

I knew he was right, of course, but I continued: 'You are all crazy, you remind me of the sorcerer's apprentice. The factories you build to make money so that you can afford a better life become treadmills in which you labour like slaves. Why don't all the manufacturers of Fleissen agree to ease off a bit and make a little less profit or charge slightly higher prices?'

'How would you word such an agreement?' laughed Father. 'It could never be implemented—firstly because those who mean to expand would not accept it, secondly because Fleissen would lose out to Asch. And if the manufacturers of Asch also agreed to work less, Bohemia would lose out to Saxony and Württemberg, and so forth. Czechoslovakia competes with Germany, Europe with America. The war for economic supremacy, or at least survival, goes on relentlessly, continuously, throughout the world. Industrialists are immensely important people and just as dedicated as surgeons or research scientists. The country's living standards depend on our effort and ingenuity, the stability of the Czech krone on our exports. It is a privilege to be an industrialist, and tremendously satisfying to organise the work of a thousand people so that the combined effort provides a livelihood for them and their families, and a surplus to develop the business. How can you talk of slowing down in the face of such a challenge?'

'Do you believe,' I countered, 'that the Lehrmanns work the way they do because it is good for the country?'

Father shook his head. 'Of course not,' he replied. 'A businessman's motive is to make money, but that doesn't reduce the value of his work for the country. By catering for the needs of the consumer, employing labour and paying taxes he benefits the community, whether he intends to or not. To remain competitive he can only use a small part of the profit for himself; most of it must be ploughed back into the business in the form of new equipment and working capital. This applies to the Lehrmanns just as much as to us. They also have to invest and risk their capital, use their intelligence and work in the treadmill. The amount of money they can draw for their personal use is insignificant in comparison with the sums drawn and spent by employees in wages and by the nation in the form of taxes.'

What Father said was true, but it was not what the people believed. Having grown up with working class children, I knew how the masses felt. They may have looked upon large employers of labour as benefactors when Father was my age, but now, confused by socialist slogans, they thought of employers as capitalist exploiters. Moreover educated people—doctors, lawyers, civil servants and politicians—were jealous of businessmen's profits, forgetting the risk element, and that most of the money had to be ploughed back into the enterprise to keep it healthy, while professional men could spend their income on themselves and their families. Did I really want to be an industrialist in these circumstances?

True, I was happy among boilers, engines, pipes, shafts and wheels, making things. I loved to sit over my drawing board designing production layouts. Competition was exciting. To follow Father and double the size of the concern was a challenge, but it would mean that I would have to become a slave like him. If only I could design a push-button factory which needed no more than a handful of workers: the thought of employing another thousand people with whom I could not possibly maintain personal contact did not appeal to me. I would lie awake at night, worrying about finding work for them, while they thought me a grasping profiteer. Surely there were more congenial ways of earning one's livelihood!

'No one will thank you, Father, for killing yourself with too much work, and since we can't slow down you'll have to delegate more,' I suggested. 'Let's try to find a factory manager for Fleissen, someone to work like Direktor Walsch does at Leibitschgrund. That would relieve you a little.'

'Engage a stranger as second-in-command? Are you implying that you intend to persist with your plan of emigrating to England?'

'It won't be as bad as it sounds,' I replied. 'I shall remain responsible for disposing of the output of Adolf Pasold & Sohn. I can do that better from an office in London than from Fleissen. Selling to wholesalers direct instead of through importers will give us better prices.'

Father remained silent for a while. 'Fortunately I have two more sons,' he said at last. 'I'll have to wait for them to help me run the factories. When are you thinking of leaving?'

'Not for a year or two. Not until Leibitschgrund is on its feet,' I reassured him, deeply sorry that our conversation had taken this turn. To upset Father was the last thing I wanted to do, but I had to tell him that my mind was made up. As a merchant I could do a large trade with a small number of employees. I could hand-pick my team, be in close daily touch with them, and pay them good salaries. I dreamed of an office in the heart of the City, a dozen smiling clerks, a warehouse and a few travellers selling on commission. I would work harder than any of them so that our factories would never be short of orders and our labour force would always be busy on double shifts.

A fortnight later Father returned to the subject, and I could see that he was at last taking my plans seriously. 'Do you think you can forsake Fleissen and live happily in a foreign city?' he asked.

'The world is so large and exciting, and London is the centre of it,' I replied. 'How can one compare it with this remote village? The people here are decent, hard-working folk. I have great respect for them, but their interests are too narrow and I feel lonely. Then there are the continual language squabbles. Do I have to learn Czech—a pretty useless tongue, as you say yourself—only to remain a second-class citizen in spite of it? Why should I? My Czechoslovak passport means nothing to me. England will be my real home.'

Father's eye wandered over the cornfields to the wooded hills on the horizon. 'Politicians and governments come and go. They do not last as long as a family firm. You cannot throw up the sponge every time someone happens to come to power with whom you disagree. It has taken generations to build this business. The fathers and grandfathers of the people who work for us now have worked for your grandfather and great-grandfather, and their children will come to us for jobs when they are grown up. You have a responsibility to them.'

'Of course I feel responsible, but when you were a boy your father employed barely a hundred people. You knew them all by their Christian names, and their brothers and sisters and parents as well. The firm was one large family. Now we employ eight hundred you still know most of them, but I don't and never shall. The bigger we grow the less of a family we shall be. Besides, the world is changing, paternalism is on the way out. Workpeople no longer look on the boss as a father figure. The socialists see to that!'

'I do not want to leave the family firm,' I continued. 'I hope you will let me be a partner, but I want to live and work in London, the capital of the British Empire—of Canada, India, Australia and most of Africa. Just think of the enormous population and the wealth of those countries. I can do business with all of them from London, but never from Fleissen. The idea of setting up an office there for Adolf Pasold & Sohn is not very original: most of the large Bohemian manufacturers had sales offices in Vienna before the Austro-Hungarian Empire broke up. To have our own sales organisation will give us an advantage over Lehrmann! Think of the Rothschilds,' I added. 'They were five brothers, and it was only because each of them went to another country and they continued to work together that they became rich and powerful. We ought to do the same. In six or seven years Rolf and Ingo will be old enough to join the firm, and you will still be a young man. Then there will be four of us, not counting Grandfather and Grandmother. Let me go to London and one of your other sons to some other international centre, and between us we shall keep the whole of Fleissen busy. Some day we'll buy out Lehrmann and Braun.'

Father smiled. 'That sounds much better, but now let's not talk about it any more. If you still feel this way in two years' time I'll help you to get started in London.'

We banked with the Asch branch of the Böhmische Union Bank, as did most of our competitors. Father went to see Direktor Huder, the manager, on average once a fortnight and took me with him at increasingly frequent intervals. They discussed money matters, the rate of interest on our credit or debit balances, depending on the time of the year and the state of trade. We were usually overdrawn in July and August, when the warehouse was full of merchandise, and liquid in early spring, when customers had paid us, before we had paid our taxes. Father sold sterling, Dutch guilders and Scandinavian kroner which we received for our exports and bought dollars to pay for the raw cotton we imported from America. Sometimes he handed over a brief-case full of banknotes, the spoils of some cash transaction with a customer who had bought a parcel of seconds and wanted no invoice. This money was entered in a bank savings book.

One talked freely to one's banker. He never divulged one client's secrets to another. The discussions ranged over a much wider field than finance. Czechoslovak businessmen expected and got advice on nearly every subject under the sun from their banker. And every discussion gave the banker extra insight, some new angle, a better understanding of industrialists and their problems. He learnt when spinners held off buying cotton because they expected a break in the market, for how far ahead the weavers had orders on their books, which type of knitting machine proved the most profitable and what building schemes were coming to fruition. He was well informed about trends in trade, the labour situation, cotton and wool prices, foreign exchange movements, tax dodges and contemplated government counter-action.

The banks' head offices in Prague were in touch with the Ministries of Finance and Trade, with employers' associations and trade unions, and often had prior warning of changes in legislation and other measures. They com-municated their confidential knowledge to the branch managers, who passed it on to those of their clients to whom it was likely to prove useful. Con-versely they reported the mood of industry back to Prague. By virtue of their unique position of respect and trust the banks were used as clearing houses and means of anonymous contact between business community and authori-ties. Through them both sides leaked and filtered off-the-record messages, requests and warnings to each other.

The padded double door of Direktor Huder's private office created a re-assuring atmosphere of discretion and security, which was just as well, for one looked from the visitor's side of his desk out through the window and across the street right into the Departments of Excise and of Inland Revenue. A chilling sight! Fortunately they were far enough away to ensure that one could not be recognised, and there was no danger of lip reading. Mr Huder seemed an exceptionally able man, and I was fascinated listening to him. He appeared to have a dual personality, father confessor and devil's advocate rolled into one, and he could change from one role to the other according to the need of his client. Businessmen with a heavy conscience, knowing their secrets would be safe with him, came to confide in him, to be first admonished and then helped to extricate themselves. The timid, on the other hand, he encouraged even if it meant being somewhat elastic in the interpretation of the rules. He helped his clients, with the full knowledge of head office, to circumvent official restrictions. If he carried out chancy transactions for them he charged a risk premium. And through his mediation many a breach of financial regulations was settled out of court with a warning or a fine.

Not that we had this kind of trouble. The late '20s were a period of economic freedom. One could move one's capital about without let or hindrance, and taxes were ridiculously low compared with present British rates. Czechoslovakia was prosperous. The advice we sought was in connection with our deal with Schärf and the machinery at Werdau, the purchase and development of Leibitschgrund, and lesser commercial transactions. Later, in the '30s, when industry and trade were hampered by currency restrictions, it was different. Direktor Huder acquired an additional dimension. His opportunities of rendering valuable service to his frustrated clients multiplied. I do not know whether his superiors in Prague would have approved of some of his daring operations had they known about them, but I had too many other problems to cope with by then to ask such questions.

Four large banks with branches throughout the republic and a number of small ones competed with each other. The borrowing and deposit rates were agreed between their head offices and were, at least in theory, all the same, but the additional services they provided depended largely on the individual branch manager. His personal resourcefulness and initiative often weighed as much with the client as the name and reputation of the bank.

The chamber of commerce to which we were affiliated was at Eger. I do not know why we hardly ever used it, but have an idea that we regarded it, quite wrongly, as a semi-government institution and therefore never quite trusted it.

Of course, we were also members of the local manufacturers' association, a voluntary advisory organisation without executive powers, whose offices were at Asch. No one took it very seriously. The members were independent individualists who rebelled against authority on principle. Having to obey government departments was bad enough. They did not want yet another body to tell them what to do. The chairman was usually one of the smaller industrialists, some enthusiast who put his heart and soul into his term of office and retired after two or three years a disillusioned man. The more important manufacturers refused to let themselves be nominated and hardly ever attended the meetings. They were too busy with their own affairs to bother about those of others. Notoriously uninterested members were the Fleissen industrialists. They came only if trouble was brewing that affected them, and only to listen to what the others had to say, hoping to pick up some useful piece of information. When they spoke it was mainly to interrupt or contradict, and if they put their names to some laboriously hammered out agreement they did not adhere to it.

The people of Asch and the Egerland, including the educated ones, were singularly tongue-tied. They had no time for elegant phrases, nor did they know how to shape them. 'Deeds, not words' was their admirable motto, but it put them at a great disadvantage when it came to political or legal debates. They lacked the salesman's easy flow of persuasive language. This made association meetings a bore. I never heard anyone make a good speech. On reflection, even at college all the boys who talked well came from other parts of the country or from abroad, while the locals, and I was one of them, expressed themselves in clipped sentences and monosyllables. Although an avid reader and able to write imaginative compositions, words failed me when I spoke. I would have been scared to death to speak in public.

The interests of the whole of Czechoslovakia's German-speaking textile industry, by far the largest sector, were represented by the Textile Federation, whose headquarters were at Reichenberg. We paid our membership fees, of course, and in turn received the federation's bulletins, but otherwise had little contact with it.

The most spectacular rise of any enterprise in the republic was that of Bata. Within less than the span of a lifetime the Czech shoe manufacturer Thomas Bata, the cobbler, as he liked to be called, had made a bustling ultra-modern industrial town out of the village of Zlin. Rows of huge standardised multi-storey factories sprang up almost overnight, accompanied by streets and squares of workmen's houses, blocks of flats, schools, a hospital, a cinema and a hotel, set among trees and flower beds, all designed, built and administered by Bata's own organisation. His shoe production was highly mechanised, nothing was done manually that could be done equally well by a machine or conveyor belt. Each manufacturing department ran as a semi-independent unit, making its own profit or loss, in which the employees participated. The people worked like ants irrespective of hours and earned very good wages. Labour relations appeared to be excellent, and one never heard of any trouble. Managers and foremen, imbued with the same enthusiasm as their boss, thought of nothing but shoes. How could they make better and cheaper shoes and more of them? One of the features that impressed me most, although I never saw it myself, was Mr Thomas Bata's private office, which was built into a large lift. At the touch of a button, it was said, he ascended or descended, together with his personal assistants and secretaries, complete with desks, filing cabinets, telephones and typewriters, to any of the ten production floors in the main factory building.

Bata exported millions of pairs of shoes all over the world. They were so cheap that even the natives of India and Africa could afford to buy them. And he owned a chain of about a thousand shoe shops throughout Czechoslovakia. Every large village seemed to have one. Admittedly his shoes were not of high quality, but they were quite serviceable and cost less than half most other makes. His method of pricing was unusual for those days. A pair of sandals, shoes or boots might be 29, 39 or 59 kronen, always just short of the round figure, which made them appear even cheaper than they were. A mild form of deception, we felt at the time, and did not quite approve of it. The quantity and assortment each shop had to sell was calculated by head office on the basis of the population and living standard of the area. If it could not sell all, the factory took the balance back and debited the shop manager with a per-centage. If it sold more, the manager earned a handsome bonus. To be manager of a Bata shop was a risky but coveted position. These men worked all day and half the night, and it was the accepted view that they either be-came rich or had to shoot themselves. It was the consumer who benefited most, and after him the government, for whom Bata's exports earned much foreign currency. But the local cobbler, the old man who had made my shoes when I was a boy—and there were thousands like him—went out of business.

We supplied the factories at Zlin with fleecy fabric for shoe linings. One day, while Father was away, Mr Bata himself came to Fleissen. He wanted to see how we did the brushing. I took him to the finishing department, and to my surprise he crawled right under the machine and lay on his back on the dirty floor, not minding in the least that his suit got covered with cotton fluff and his face and hands with black grease. He had hard hands and a firm grip and was very down-to-earth, not at all as I had imagined the country's greatest industrialist to be. My chest swelled with pride when he said he thought highly of Adolf Pasold & Sohn, for I knew he was not given to flattery. After this meeting I ranked him with my other heroes, with Alfred Stern, Henry Ford and the mysterious Swedish match king Ivar Kreuger.

Shortly afterwards I paid my first visit to Zlin. On my return I was so full of the great Bata manufacturing organisation, bubbling over with what I had seen and thought we ought to copy, that Father could hardly conceal his pleasure at my enthusiasm. Only a few weeks earlier I had declared that I wanted to be a merchant with just a handful of employees! But he was too diplomatic to remind me of my inconsistency. How could we best emulate Bata? he asked.

My imagination had been fired by books about Henry Ford's conveyor belt systems and flow production methods, and now I had seen the same principles employed at Zlin. If motor cars and shoes could be made in this way, why not knitted underwear? It seemed to me that the layout of our factory was out of date. Our manufacturing departments did not follow each other in logical sequence. Too much energy was wasted on moving material about unnecessarily. We kept our yarns in the basement, took them by lift to the third floor to be wound and knitted, then took the fabric back to the basement for fleecing, and up again to the second floor for cutting and sewing. Gravity chutes delivered the bundles of sewn garments to the floor below, where they were folded and packed. The latter arrangement was sensible, but it seemed stupid to carry the fabric to the basement and up again. I wanted the fleecing machines to be moved to the second floor.

Father disagreed. Since most of our fabric was sent to the dyers, it had to make the journey down and up in any case. The basement was the best place for the heavy, dust-making fleecing machines.

But I would not listen. Some of the fabric was fleeced without being dyed, and fleecing machines should be installed in the cutting department, where a powerful extractor fan would take away the dust. 'Think of the winter!' Father reasoned. 'Your fan would suck the warmth out of the building. Heating is expensive. And there's the fire risk!' Sometimes the broken hook of a needle from a knitting machine became embedded in the fabric. When the fast-rotating wire cards of the fleecer struck it there were sparks and the cotton dust caught fire.

However, I was adamant. 'Why did you send me to the textile college? Why do I study modern techniques? What use is it for me to come with new ideas if you won't let me apply them?'

So Father gave way. Moving the machines proved costly. The fan sucked out the warm air but not the dust, which settled in a thin layer on all the cut garments, and the cutters complained about noise. We had to build a wall round the offending machines. This obstructed the view and the flow of the fabric. In the end Father had the fleecing and finishing departments transferred to a separate building, 'to secure a reduction in the fire insurance premium' as he put it, and to everybody's relief, including my own, the fleecing machines returned to the ground floor.

The next piece of 'modernisation' I introduced against Father's advice was a large sheet-metal tube which connected the knitting department on the third floor of the main factory with the first floor of the finishing building. The 4 ft diameter pipe crossing the yard looked impressive. I intended it to serve as a gravity chute for the 50 lb lumps of fabric, but whenever the outside temperature dropped condensation formed in the tube and the fabric refused to slide. So I had the tube lagged and the lagging protected against the weather. This was an improvement, but there were always complaints about the draught. Father never once said 'I told you so', but I felt unhappy every time I saw the contraption.

The greatest potential for saving labour lay, of course, in the cutting and sewing departments, for they employed the largest number of workers. Once again I took out my drawing board and attempted to simplify the complex automatic cutting machine I had designed a year or two earlier, but was defeated by the inconsistent widths of our fabrics, caused by the great variety of diameters and gauges of our knitting machines.

I had a little more success in the sewing department. Mounting two sewing machines in tandem on the same bench and connecting them with a foot-operated clutch, I made it possible for one girl to operate both together, attaching strips of woven fabric to the front of men's undervests and adding a decorative fancy seam at the same time. The arrangement worked well, and Father liked it, which restored my self assurance. But technical improvements alone had not put Bata where he was. The vast publicity campaign he ran continuously in the press and on hoardings played an important part. We ought to advertise, I advised, and laid on the table some of the familiar full-page Bata advertisements showing illustrations of shoes, the incredibly low prices at which they sold and the addresses of the Bata shops.

Father and Grandfather shook their heads. They did not realise how out of touch they were, I thought. They could not assess the irresistible power of publicity in our modern world. I knew better. I had read books on the subject and seen how much money British businessmen spent on advertising, not only in newspapers but on posters, buses and illuminated signs. We ought to have an illuminated sign on top of our factory!

'Advertise what and to whom?' Father asked. Our products are not branded and our customers are merchants who would object if we were to put our name on the garments they buy from us. We have no control over the price they sell them at and cannot tell the consumer where our goods are to be found. And remember, we export almost 90 per cent of our output. How can we possibly advertise?'

'It seems we shall have to open a chain of Pasold shops,' I replied.

'If we did that we would compete with our customers, and they would stop giving us orders. Moreover we know nothing about retailing. And do you think we could keep shops going just by selling the limited range of underwear we make? The fact that we manufacture so few types of garments and mass-produce them in such vast quantities is our strength.'

I thought this very unsatisfactory.

'On the contrary,' Father protested. 'We don't need to waste money on advertising and distribution. Let's spend it on improving our manufacturing techniques.'

There was no point in prolonging an argument I could not win. Father held all the aces, but I was far from convinced that he was right. In fact I was sure that advertising paid and that some day I would find the approach that suited our business. And I would have that illuminated sign on the factory roof yet!

The opportunity of trying my hand at a publicity campaign came sooner than I expected, as a sequel to somewhat frustrating events. We believed in specialisation. Our factory was laid out to make only our standard type of merchandise. The style of men's underwear never changed, and when it came to Directoire knickers the only changes in the past three or four years had been the introduction of rayon stripes, a pocket, the addition of helio and pale green to the range of colours and the gradual shortening of the legs. And we disliked even these minor changes, because they interfered with the smooth flow of our mass production, the secret of our success.

Only Jacob Müller, our lively Swedish agent, demanded 'something new' now and again. In the spring of 1928 he had asked for samples of Directoire knickers knitted from marl yarn. It seemed a good idea. Marl yarn consists of a mixture of white and dyed cotton fibres which give the resulting fabric a mottled effect, so there is no need to dye it in the piece. Leibitschgrund was not equipped to spin marl, and we bought some to experiment. For the fleecy inside of the knickers we used condenser yarn spun from our reclaimed waste fabric clippings, which were sorted in colours to blend with the marl. To prevent excessive fly we added a little oil when we spun condenser yarn. This gave the fabric a distinct odour which disappeared with dyeing. Marl fabric was not dyed, but we thought the faint smell would evaporate and hoped for the best.

Unfortunately Jacob Müller misjudged his market. The Swedes did not want marl underwear—perhaps they did not like the smell—and we were left with the trial quantity of knickers we had made and a few hundred kilos of marl yarn. It was not a tragedy. This sort of thing happened in every business. I was sure that I could find some other outlet for the merchandise. Our Dutch and British customers to whom I showed the knickers would not buy them at any price. Only Captain Da Costa, the managing director of the London Knitwear Co., who knew least about the trade, was interested. He had a client, he said, who was always looking for something different. Would I leave the samples with him: he hoped to place a large order within a few days. It transpired later that his client was Miss Swift, the chief buyer for Marks and Spencer's. Perhaps she had had a cold and did not smell the oil in the yarn, for she gave him a trial order for twenty-five dozen. Da Costa feared that I might not accept such a trifling order and optimistically wrote out a contract for 2,500 dozen, 'to begin with', as he said.

I patted myself on the back. Perseverance had paid, I thought as I caught the boat train from Liverpool Street station. The small stock of marl yarn we had was quite insufficient for such a quantity of knickers. Not suspecting that Da Costa was gambling, I ordered enough yarn to make 5,000 dozen. Our supplier had to spin it specially, and I did not want to be caught short when the repeat orders came from London.

But I had not reckoned with the nose of Mr Simon (later Lord) Marks. In fact I did not even know of his existence. He was not suffering from a cold. He smelled the oil before the twenty-five dozen were unpacked. The resulting chain reaction reached me in the form of a laconic telegram from Da Costa cancelling his order. I threatened to sue him for damages, for our goods were exactly as sampled, but the London Knitwear Co. had only a very small capital and no money in the bank. If I pressed our claim the company would simply go into liquidation. To settle the dispute Da Costa offered me a seat on the board and, for £200, the majority shareholding. Needless to say, I declined and let the matter drop. Instead of a few hundred kilos of marl yarn I now had a few thousand to find a use for, and that was no longer a laughing matter.

Experiments made by Andreas Pleyer, who had graduated from the textile college at Asch three years before me and was now in charge of our knitting department, produced a new kind of fleecy 'double chaineuse' marl fabric in two shades, one silver grey, the other light brown. Both had vertical stripes created by alternating loops of helio and dark grey condenser yarn, of which Leibitschgrund usually spun a surplus. To find an additional use for it would be welcome. As the material was not dyed, it had, of course, the characteristic oily odour, but it looked and handled well, was easy to knit, and the high proportion of condenser yarn made it remarkably inexpensive.

We cut samples of men's cardigans and sweaters from it and trimmed them with bias binding, which we decorated with a zigzag seam—a technique I learned at Uncle Richard Stübiger's apron factory at Bad Brambach. He also loaned me suitable folders to attach to our sewing machines. Horn buttons gave the cardigans an attractive, somewhat Tyrolean appearance. The sweaters we fitted with zip fasteners, which were then still an intriguing novelty and an important sales point. Made of brass, they were coarse and heavy compared with those we use today, but no man could resist playing with them as with a fascinating piece of precision engineering.

Both garments represented a radical departure from our customary type of product but fitted well into our manufacturing set-up. Father, Grandfather and Grandmother liked the look of them and thought they would sell in Czechoslovakia. Perhaps a little rashly, I was promised a free hand in pricing and marketing the new lines. To Father's consternation I added a profit of fifteen per cent to the cost price, three times as much as his usual rate, and pleaded for his consent to the registration of a trade mark and its promotion through an advertising campaign. He thought these 'American ideas' were not applicable to our industry and I would be wasting hard-earned money, but, not wanting to go back on his word, he allowed me to spend an amount of 10,000 kronen on the operation.

But how could I prevent Lehrmann's from copying our new garments, cashing in on the demand created by our publicity campaign, cutting prices and ruining our trade? I tried to remember what I had learned at the textile college about the protection of fashion designs. If one could protect printing patterns by registering them with the chamber of commerce, why not knitted fabrics or whole garments? On investigation I found to my disappointment that the subject was so involved and the law so complex that I was about to give up in despair, when an idea struck me. If I could not understand the regulations, and the chamber was not sure about them, then our competitors would not understand them either. Perhaps Lehrmann's could be hood-winked into believing that the merchandise was protected.

I deposited with the chamber of commerce at Eger two sealed packages containing samples of our goods, together with cuttings of all the fabrics we had knitted during the experimental stages. This procedure was supposed to give a degree of legal protection for the limited period of one year, after which the packages were opened and the contents made available for public inspection. I saw no reason why one should then not deposit a fresh, slightly different lot of samples, and so forth, and meanwhile put on the garment labels the words 'Protected by law'. Bluff seemed my only means of defence. A determined imitator prepared to take specialised legal advice would not be fooled for long, but it was worth trying, and, as we shall see, it worked.

The choice of a suitable brand name is always difficult. All the good ones that come to mind are already registered by someone else. A trade mark should be distinctive, have pleasant associations, suit the product and be easily remembered. People do not all react the same: some remember pictures better than words, and vice versa. I therefore searched for a combination of the two, preferably the picture of a popular animal with thick fur to suggest warmth and an easily pronounceable name. I paged through the six volumes of Brehm's *Tierleben*, the well known illustrated zoological bible, and sketched from it the picture of a polar bear. But if I gave it the German name the Czechs would not like it, and if I used the Czech word it would be unpopular with the German- and Hungarian-speaking population. So I solved the dilemma by registering the words 'White Bear', which were easily understood by everyone and, being English, offended nobody. On the contrary, they lent our goods distinction. The blue label I designed proved very effective. Besides the trade mark it bore the small inscription 'Made in Czechoslovakia' and in addition 'Protected by law', to warn off Lehrmann, leaving it ambiguous whether the name, the design of the garment, the construction of the fabric or all three were protected.

We appointed Mosse in Prague our advertising agents. Preparing a publicity scheme with them was a new and exciting experience. In view of the small sum of money available the campaign could be only a modest one, but, even so, our advertisements would appear in all the important newspapers, and I was tingling with excitement. The fact that Czechoslovakia had Czech, German, Slovak and Hungarian papers presented no difficulty. The illustrations of our cardigans and sweaters and the trade mark in English remained the same throughout, only the text was drafted in the language of the publication in which it was printed. A problem did arise, however. How were we to indicate the surprisingly low price of approximately ten kronen at which our White Bear garments could be bought in the shops? To quote figures would lead to trouble with the shopkeepers, for we had no influence over the varying profit margins they added.

In the middle of the night came a brainwave which I sketched on my bedside pad. It showed a sweater, the trade mark and the slogan 'Costs no more than a simple meal'. In the corner was a small picture of two sausages and a portion of sauerkraut on a plate, with a knife and fork, a slice of bread and a glass of beer. Somewhat to my surprise the idea still made sense in the morning, Mosse liked it, and it became the main theme for this and our future advertising campaigns. If only we had shops of our own, like Bata, I thought. Then we could advertise prices the public could rely upon. But Father would not even discuss the subject and asked me never to mention it again, in case it came to the ears of some buyer.

Cardboard showcards to be displayed in shop windows and on counters were prepared for distribution to our customers, and as a constant reminder of the campaign, we made up doggerel like

> Don't just send a Christmas letter,
> Give instead a White Bear sweater!

which we printed on our stationery, envelopes and wrapping paper. My friend Lazy Turan, who had been to the textile college with me and now had a job in our office, was particularly good at thinking up amusing rhymes, and produced them with equal facility in German, Czech and Hungarian.

Although only a modest campaign, it struck the right note and made a remarkable impact. Czechoslovak newspapers carried few advertisements, and any new name among the regular ones immediately caught the reader's eye. The attractive illustrations and the striking trade mark aroused considerable interest, and, while the starting orders were small, I was delighted that we received so many. Father, however, remained sceptical; Grandfather thought the operation wasteful and rather undignified; the knitting industry regarded our advertisements with mild amusement, and Lehrmann openly ridiculed them.

While the sale of fleecy knickers became more difficult as the years went on, the demand for White Bear cardigans and sweaters gathered momentum. Our competitors became envious, and would have copied our merchandise had it not been for the sealed samples at the chamber of commerce which, tongue in cheek, I renewed every year. Only Lehrmann's tried a cheap imitation, but the quality and finish of their sweaters were poor and they made a psychological mistake in choosing 'Esquimau' for their trade mark. Who could pronounce it or knew what it meant? The French word may have sounded good in the ears of a small group of chauvinist francophil Czech politicians, but the consuming masses preferred the solid ring of Anglo–Saxon reliability, especially in connection with a men's garment. The reader may think I make too much of this, but in a country as sensitive over languages as Czechoslovakia it was very important to get the trade name right.

Looking back to that first publicity campaign, I recognise it as a milestone in the history of our firm. It came, quite accidentally, at the right time and helped us to survive the crucial years that lay ahead.

17

TRANSATLANTIC
ADVENTURE
1929

AMERICA WAS SETTING the pattern for mass production, and its conveyor belts had become the symbol of the new industrial efficiency. I read all I could about them, wondering how they could be applied to the production of knitted garments, and when, in spring 1929, the Czechoslovak Textile Federation planned a tour to the USA to visit weaving and knitting mills, Father allowed me to put my name down. About the same time my friend Willy Hess, with whom I used to play tennis in London, wrote that he was going to India for his newspaper to write a series of articles on cotton. Jokingly I suggested he should come to America instead, they grew cotton there too, and to my pleasant surprise Willy changed his programme and joined our group.

We sailed from Bremen in a 20,000 ton liner—the first time either of us had been on a big boat. The crossing took about ten days. Through Willy I met another newspaperman, Arthur Rundt, a freelance journalist who was on the way to Alaska, where he hoped to dig up remnants of the gold rush of 1898 and find some of the pioneers who might be left behind. Also there were villages of Red Indians down the Yukon river, genuine ones, which he intended to visit and write about. He was a friendly man of about fifty who had seen the world. Whenever I had the chance I sat in the deckchair next to his and made him talk about his adventures. One day he asked me what I intended to do after my factory visits. Was I staying on in America for a while? Could I drive a car, ride a horse, swim and type? How good was my shorthand? Could I handle a gun in case of need?

'Tolerably well,' I replied, wondering what he was getting at.

'Would you like to come to Alaska as my secretary? You'd get no pay, but my journey is sponsored by the Canadian Pacific Railway Company. I have free transport on all their trains and ships, and free accommodation in their hotels for myself and a secretary—all first class, of course. The job's yours for the asking. I think we'd get on all right together.'

Did I want the job! I could hardly speak for excitement. This was too good to be true, but my inborn caution rang its little warning bell. I thought there must be a catch somewhere, and asked for a day or two to think about it. Who was this man Arthur Rundt? What proof had I that he was a respectable newspaperman and not some dangerous impostor? Perhaps the purser could tell me. I would go and ask him and put my cards on the table.

'You're a lucky young man,' said the purser. 'Mr Rundt is a well known writer.'

Willy Hess sent a radiogram to his paper to double-check on the mysterious journalist and received an equally reassuring reply. I wondered what Father would say. I had his permission to stay in America for a month or two after the official visit if I could build up business connections there, but searching Alaska for Red Indians was a very different proposition. In the end I decided not to tell him until it was too late for him to stop me. After a sleepless night I accepted Mr Rundt's offer.

'Splendid,' he said. 'I have some film work to do in New York while you visit factories. Let's meet in four weeks in Chicago.' And we shook hands on it.

America was in the grip of Prohibition and I knew that Chicago was the city of bootleggers and gangsters, the headquarters of Al Capone. No doubt Mr Rundt had chosen it for a purpose—a promising start to our adventurous journey.

The skyline of Manhattan impressed me tremendously. Skyscrapers were ugly towers of reinforced concrete, I had been told, but nothing was further from the truth. They were the most exciting, the most graceful buildings I had ever seen, and the mere thought of the calculations and the engineering skill required to construct them made my head spin. I shall not weary the reader with a description of the geometrical arrangement of the streets and the sensible numbering of the houses, the shops on Fifth Avenue, the lights of Broadway, the drugstores, the rush of the traffic and the Negro bootblacks. There was much that surprised me. Since it was so much farther away from Europe, I had expected New York to be more Anglo–Saxon than London, instead of which I found it less so. It felt more like a vastly expanded Leipzig or Hamburg built vertically, and while the inhabitants spoke English, they behaved and reacted like anglicised Dutchmen.

We saw the stock exchange and the cotton exchange in operation, visited the head offices of various textile concerns and were given a luncheon by the chamber of commerce. Then we went by night boat to Fall River, where the worthies of the town and representatives of the local manufacturers' association met us at the pier with heart-warming speeches of welcome. Someone had to reply—and suddenly everyone looked at me. As the only member of the delegation who spoke English well enough, I was asked to propose a vote of thanks.

I had never made a speech in my life and wished myself a thousand miles away, but before I could look for somewhere to hide I was levered to the front, facing the mayor and the reporters with their pencils and cameras at the ready. Inspiration, I had always thought, came spontaneously to orators when they faced an audience. It never occurred to me that they prepared their speeches beforehand. Bathed in perspiration, I stood and waited, a frightened dwarf trapped between these captains of industry from both sides of the Atlantic. But no inspiration, no elegant phrases came, least of all in English. I was desperate. Attack seemed the best form of defence. Trying to be witty, I raised my voice and blurted out a challenge.

'Gentlemen,' I heard myself say, 'back in Europe people believe that everything is bigger and better in America and that all your work is done for you by conveyor belts. You are reputed to have the longest and fastest conveyor belts in the world. We are told that the raw material goes in at one end and the dollars come out at the other. This, we are told, is the source of your wealth. We want you to prove it!' And, forgetting to express the delegation's gratitude to our hosts, I returned to the back row while my listeners stood in bewildered silence. Then I realised my omission, stepped forward again and said:

'We are surprised that you have left your beds so early this morning to meet us. It was not necessary. What we have come to see are your conveyor belts, and we thank you most sincerely for letting us look at them!'

On reflection I wonder why the good citizens of Fall River had anything further to do with us. Perhaps they felt that I meant well, but my appallingly tactless little speech must have embarrassed them. They had no conveyor belts, as we soon discovered. Their factories were very well equipped and they were justly proud of them, but after the breathtaking skyscrapers of New York they came as an anticlimax. I was a little disappointed to find that their spinning and weaving sheds were as noisy, their dyehouses and finishing plants as foggy and wet, as those in Czechoslovakia.

I was far more impressed with the method a building contractor used to remove a four-storey house. It stood in the square, opposite the club where our hosts took us for a sandwich lunch. The contractor threaded a steel cable through a window on one side of the ground floor and out the other, attached the ends to a heavy lorry and simply pulled the building down. It was gone when we came out of the club forty minutes later, and we marvelled at American speed and simplicity. This could not happen in Czechoslovakia. The regulations would not allow it. Besides, the job had to be done by hand so that the contractor could save every brick, beam and window frame. Bulldozers and similar machinery, of course, did not exist in those days, and we Europeans still treated bricks and mortar with respect—until the second world war taught us otherwise.

We visited textile mills and machine factories at Providence, Boston, Utica, Philadelphia and Reading, where we saw a number of interesting knitting plants. None of the latter approached my picture of a modern, near-automatic mass-production unit. All made a large range of goods; none had taken product specialisation as far as we had done at Fleissen. Some of the methods they used were ingenious, and I filled my notebook with sketches, but I realised that few of them could be applied in Czechoslovakia, where wages were so much lower than in the USA. How we had misjudged these ruthless American businessmen! They were kindness itself and showed us everything we wanted to see, but there was no real application for conveyor belts in the production of textiles. The motor car industry told a different story. An assembly plant of General Motors at Detroit had a complicated system of conveyors half a mile long. It was a pity we hadn't the time to study it in detail.

Meanwhile Willy Hess talked to spinners, yarn agents and cotton brokers, and in the evenings showed me the articles he wrote for his newspaper. He could not tell a cotton thread from a wool one, but that did not matter, he assured me. A good journalist was able to write well about everything, from microbes to meteors, from high finance to low comedy, without having to know anything about them. It was his skill in making contacts and asking the right questions that mattered.

'Do you understand all you write?' I asked, laughing.

'Not everything,' he confessed, 'but the textile men I write for are experts —they'll understand it.'

Perhaps he was right, but the thought of 'little Willy', who was only a year older than myself, reporting on the state of the American textile industry and the prospect of the cotton crop amused me. Unsuspecting businessmen like Father carefully weighed every word they saw in print. Would they still take these articles seriously if they knew the author?

We spent one weekend at Niagara Falls at a hotel filled with honeymoon couples, another on the sands of Atlantic City, and one in Washington, where the Czechoslovak embassy laid on an official reception for us. Then the delegation went home and I proceeded to Chicago, the city of the bootleggers. I read in the papers that a man was shot the morning I arrived, but to my disappointment I never actually saw a gangster the whole week I was there. I now started trying in earnest to sell underwear for Fleissen. My attempts in New York had failed, our Directoire knickers (they called them bloomers) did not suit American taste, and unfortunately I met with no more success in the Middle West. Even if we changed the quality and style to meet local requirements the import duty on cotton goods was so high, and the customs regulations so weighted against the foreign supplier, that it was best to forget the USA as a potential market. Perhaps I would have more luck in Canada. I packed my samples and hopefully sent them to Vancouver before going to meet Mr Rundt at his hotel.

'I have news for you,' he greeted me when I met him. 'We're going to Hollywood.'

'But you've engaged me to stalk Indians in Alaska!' I replied, unable to conceal my disappointment.

He seemed surprised. 'Don't you want to see California and live for a few weeks with film stars in the world of make-believe? We'll go to Alaska afterwards.'

'Why do we have to go to Hollywood?'

'Because of the revolution there. We want to find out whether Hollywood believes the silent film is finished and the future belongs to the talkies. I have undertaken to write a series of articles on the subject,' he explained. 'We'll interview producers, stars and technicians.'

I was not interested in film stars, but had little choice, and to pacify me Mr Rundt promised to break the long train journey in Arizona, where we could look for Red Indians in the Grand Canyon. The railway cars of the Santa Fe line were laid out on the open plan. There were only a few separate compartments, and my boss had booked one of them so that we could work undisturbed. He dictated short stories which dealt with life in New York and were intended for European readers. I took them down in shorthand, read them back to him and then typed them. When he asked how I liked them, and I replied truthfully that I did not, he laughed.

'Wait until you see them in print on good paper in a glossy magazine,' he said. 'That'll make all the difference. They'll read well.' The better I got to know him the more he impressed me, and I felt flattered when he invited me to call him Arthur.

After crossing from New Mexico into Arizona we left the train and took an automobile to a small hotel which was built like a ranch. The next few days we spent in the saddle exploring the Grand Canyon, the vast, unlikely hole in the ground which I can best describe as a magnificent mountain range in reverse. But the Red Indians were a disappointment. Our guides were two tame 'chiefs' of the Hopi tribe, misshapen little men who were decked out from head to waist in feathers to impress the tourists and bore the romantic but inappropriate names of Black Eagle and Roaring Bull. If Fennimore Cooper, the author of *Leather Stocking*, my favourite boyhood book, could have seen them he would have turned in his grave.

Our train took a whole day to cross the Mojave desert. The air was hot and laden with fine sand which settled in a thin layer on my papers and type-writer, on tables and cushions, and we bit on it in our food. I was glad when we arrived at Hollywood. We checked into the comfortable Beverly Hills Hotel and then contacted Joe Schildpatt, an old friend of Arthur's. Joe, a good-looking young actor who hailed from Vienna, was then at the zenith of his short-lived fame. He was rolling in money and knew everyone. Would he advise us how best to approach the giants of the film world, the leading pro-ducers, directors and stars to secure interviews?

'You don't ask them for interviews,' advised Joe. 'They have to come to you. We'll "leak" to the press that Europe's most famous newspaperman is passing through Hollywood—incognito, of course—and when his identity is discovered it's none other than the celebrated Dr Rundt.'

'Steady, Joe,' protested my boss. 'You know I hold no degree.'

But Joe was adamant: the degree was essential. This was Hollywood, and every self-respecting European was a doctor. There was no need to worry, no one would check, and he, Joe, would get suitable visiting cards printed. His enthusiasm was catching. Film people craved publicity; they would queue to see the influential Dr Rundt if they thought he would write about them. The lesser lights would come to the hotel, then the giants would get to hear of us and send their chauffeur-driven Cadillacs. And he rehearsed us on how to receive and deal with the visitors.

Dr Rundt was not to take any telephone calls. They were to be transferred to me, and I was to refuse all appointments. This would make the news and publicity seekers all the more eager, and they would try to gatecrash. Dr Rundt's door would be locked, mine would be open. Joe showed me how to indicate that my boss was in, by taking a protective stance in front of the communicating door, and how to hold visitors at bay. I was to keep them waiting for at least fifteen minutes before I ushered them into the presence of the great man, who would receive them in his pyjamas to prove that he did not care and was not expecting anyone. His untidy room would be littered with papers, books and journals, all displaying articles by Arthur Rundt. And I was to treat my boss with immense deference. Never, never was I to intro-duce myself as 'Dr Rundt's secretary', but always as 'secretary to Dr Rundt'.

No royal command performance could have been rehearsed more tho-roughly. Joe acted for us in turn the parts of the impetuous gatecrasher, the obstructing secretary and the famous doctor from Vienna, and made us repeat them until he was satisfied. Our first visitor phoned, was refused, and stormed into my room within hours of the press notice. Had he been sent by Joe to give us confidence? I have forgotten the names of our many callers and do not know whether any of them eventually became box office draws, but our act worked like a charm, and soon the Cadillacs whisked us through the well guarded gates of the famous studios and fabulous hillside residences.

Our visit could not have been timed better. An atmosphere of apprehension, almost of crisis, hung over the movie capital. What would sound do to the industry? Producers were worried, technicians revised their techniques, actors took elocution lessons. Would Britain accept films with American sound tracks? Would foreign actors lose their jobs because of their accents? Would Europe accept talkies in English, with French, German or Italian captions? Who would pay for the conversion of all the cinemas to sound? Had sound come to stay, or was it only a passing craze? The importance of overseas markets was suddenly fully realised. This played into our hands. The film industry was worried about the risk of losing exports and sought the support of the European press. Hollywood's giants were as anxious to talk to us as we were to interview them. They wanted publicity.

Douglas Fairbanks gave us lunch. He was all in favour of sound: it would conquer the world. We spent a relaxed afternoon in his magnificent swimming pool. Charlie Chaplin was less confident. How was he, the clown who relied on the effect of the baggy trousers, bowler hat, stick and jerky movements, to introduce sound into his films? He invited us to dinner and let us watch the shooting of an evening scene in *City Lights*. Maurice Chevalier was not sure whether his French accent would be a handicap or an advantage. Warner Brothers, the pioneers of the talkies, were bubbling over with excitement, while Cecil B. de Mille talked about the need for soundproof stages and muffled cameras. I do not remember the name of the sound engineer, or should I call him sound magician, who was upset because the gentle tapping of an actor's cigarette on a gold cigarette case caused explosion-like bangs on the sound track. Sound was full of surprises. We readily saw the many problems and were glad they were not ours.

It was impossible to take this crazy city, with its celluloid heroes, seriously, and I felt no qualms about joining the general game of bluff as I rushed from one studio to another arranging interviews and blowing my boss's trumpet in my capacity as his devoted secretary. Invitation followed invitation, we went from party to party and hardly found enough time to write our stories. Joe was cock-a-hoop. Having graduated from the stage, his voice and diction were perfect, and he thought talkies were created specially for him. He was more than generous. He loaned us one of his Cadillacs to go down the coast road to Mexico, an unforgettable drive, but I did not think much of Tiajuana and its gambling machines. He seemed surprised when we returned the car in one piece, unscratched in fact. His trouble was that he had too much money and did not know how to spend it. He bought half a dozen pedigree mastiffs but after a couple of days decided he did not like dogs and let them go, just by opening the kennel door. His marriage was breaking up. I sympathised with his pretty wife, the daughter of a steel magnate. Joe showed us a priceless pearl necklace. If he wanted a woman and she was reluctant he gave her the necklace as a present.

'I'm surprised you still have it,' I said innocently.

Joe laughed. 'Oh, I take it away from them afterwards.'

The continual parties got me down, and when my boss triumphantly waved two tickets for a premier at the cinema that looked like a Chinese pagoda, the world's most famous, where the stars immortalised themselves by embedding their footprints in the pavement, I declined to go. 'But this is one of Hollywood's great occasions. You'll not get a second chance in your lifetime to see so many beautiful women, diamonds, expensive furs and naked shoulders,' he pleaded. 'Every star will be there. Some people would give their left hand for a ticket.'

'No, thank you,' I replied stubbornly. 'I'm sick of film stars and I won't sacrifice two hours' sleep for such a spectacle.' So I went to bed and missed this unique experience.

The story got around and earned me the doubtful reputation of 'the man who had never seen a film'. I was fast asleep, dreaming of dancing with Sonja on the terrace of the Hotel Bellevue at Marienbad, when Arthur shook me.

'Wake up, I say. Wake up!'

'What time is it?' I asked sleepily.

'Three o'clock in the morning. Get up. We've got work to do. There are twenty thousand dollars to be made, but speed is of the essence!'

Sitting on the edge of my bed, he outlined the situation, which seemed so fantastic it could have arisen only in Hollywood. Stupendous Spectaculars, one of the leading film companies, were in a jam, and Mr Spiegel, the producer, was offering this sum to get them out of it. (Lest the reader jump to conclusions, let me add that these two names bear no resemblance to the real ones.) When sound pictures began, everybody thought in terms of musicals, and Mr Spiegel decided to steal a march on his competitors by engaging Paul Whiteman and his orchestra. That was months ago. The contract did not start until 1 June, which gave the company plenty of time to think up a suitable plot and get the script prepared. But in the rush of things Paul Whiteman had been forgotten. Now that he had arrived there was neither plot nor script. He sat waiting on the beach, with his famous band of eighty men, while Stupendous Spectaculars had to pay him a fortune. No wonder Spiegel was anxious to buy himself out of this costly predicament. Ideas men, authors and script writers were working overtime.

'I've thought of a plot,' my boss explained eagerly. 'The band plays on a luxury liner which collides with an iceberg and sinks. Whiteman and his musicians are swallowed by a whale. They set up their orchestra inside it. The syncopated whale dances through the waves of the ocean and has a Lorelei effect on all shipping . . . but you'll see how the story develops as I dictate to you.'

I took down, tore up and retyped for a day and a half. We hardly had time to eat, until eventually the script was completed. Joe thought it was terrific and that we could start spending our prize money already, but he was in too much of a hurry. The three of us rushed to the studios of Stupendous Spectaculars. By now, Dr Rundt's reputation was such that Mr Spiegel received us personally.

'This film will make Stupendous Spectaculars the greatest movie company on earth,' Joe blurted out. It was the wrong thing to say. The little man behind the huge desk eyed him coldly.

'Stupendous Spectaculars *is* the greatest movie company on earth.' He flicked through the typescript, reading a paragraph here and there.

'I don't like it,' he said at last.

'You'll make a big mistake if you turn it down,' Joe almost shouted. 'I'll guarantee it'll be a success!'

'And how do you propose to implement your guarantee, young man?' asked Mr Spiegel, deflating the cheeky actor.

We were unlucky. Since our job was finished, we packed our bags and departed on the night train for San Francisco, leaving Hollywood's madhouse atmosphere, Paul Whiteman, Mr Spiegel, Joe, Charlie Chaplin and their problems behind us. It was high time. Even Arthur, the most rational of men, was showing symptoms of hallucinations.

When I woke, the train was nearing the city of the Golden Gate. I threw the window open to let in the sunny morning, and the sea breeze and sang with happiness. We had an introduction to a businessman in San Francisco, a fruit exporter,whom we interviewed to write an article about peaches, oranges and pineapples. What a relief it was to listen to someone who knew that two and two made four. He restored my faith in the sanity of the human race.

Our next stop was Vancouver, where my first call was on the general manager of Canadian Pacific. The training I had received in Hollywood made me by-pass all underlings and go straight to the top. I finalised the details of our trip to Alaska with him, secured the two best state rooms on the boat and earned a pat on the back from Arthur. The CPR practically owned Canada, there was nothing they could not do, and it was therefore important to get on the right footing with them from the start.

For the next few days I reverted to my job as commercial traveller. My consignment of samples had arrived safely from Chicago, I cleared it through the customs, and then called on potential buyers. What an anticlimax it was to sit patiently in their waiting rooms, answering their questions with a deferential 'Yes, sir, certainly, sir' or 'No, sir' and say 'Thank you very much' when they gave me some trifling order. But I did not mind, as I was anxious to establish a business connection with Canada, which would please Father. He was sure to have received my letter meanwhile in which I told him about my expedition to Alaska but not where he could contact me, and I had a bad conscience whenever I thought of him.

When I had shown my collection of knickers to the leading wholesale houses and satisfied myself that business could be done I engaged an agent, left my samples with him, and became once again the influential secretary of Arthur Rundt, the great, elusive newspaperman. A small delegation of CPR representatives saw us off as we boarded the SS *Alice*, the steamer that was to take us north, and of course we sat at the captain's table.

Between countless islands covered with pine trees many of which were four or five feet thick we sailed for 500 miles along British Columbia's wooded coast to Ketchikan, our first port of call in Alaska, and, with some 6,000 inhabitants, the country's largest town. Alaska covers an area six times that of Great Britain but had then only 60,000 people, half of them whites who lived in the towns, the other half Eskimos and Red Indians in tiny settlements spread all over the vast territory. We visited one or two Indian hamlets and were amused to see their grotesque totem poles, but the inhabitants were disappointing. Could one take redskins seriously who wore knitted jerseys and cloth caps? They wouldn't know a tomahawk if they saw one.

Sailing northward, the channels opened into great lakes, then closed to narrow gorges between the islands. The water was so transparent that one could see the bottom of the sea. In places it was a thousand feet below us, in others there were great sharp rocks which reached almost to the glassy surface and threatened to rip open the hull of our steamer should it stray from its course.

We passed a number of glaciers on our way north. Most of them lie motionless on the shore; only the Taku Glacier, which closes the end of the picturesque, twenty-mile-long Taku Fjord, is alive. Its millions of tons of ice, a sheer wall over 200 ft high and a mile wide, are under enormous pressure and push into the crystal water at the rate of ten feet a day. Between floating icebergs turned into huge sapphires by the morning sun we cautiously steamed within half a mile of it, and then challenged the giant with a short, shrill blast from the ship's siren. When the sound waves hit the glacier it angrily responded with a thunderlike explosion, hurtling blocks of ice as large as skyscrapers into the sea.

Four days after leaving Vancouver we arrived at Skagway, at the head of the Lynn Canal. In the late 1890s adventurers came to Skagway in their thousands, trekked over the mountains to the headwaters of the Yukon and floated on rafts down to the newly discovered goldfields of the Klondike. Skagway became a large transit camp, a bustling shanty town, with its two main streets named Broadway and Fifth Avenue. But when the gold became scarce and the miners stayed away the deserted saloons and dance halls and many of the wooden shacks collapsed. Now there were only a few hundred people left, and 'Goldie', whom we met at the coffee bar, was one of them. He had given up mining long ago and now earned his livelihood hunting bears. Whilst waiting for the train that would take us over the mountains was there anywhere we could walk to get a view of the town and the fjord? Goldie shook his head. Apart from the road up to the White Pass there was not a track, not even a footpath, out of Skagway. Where could it have led to?

Turning and twisting, our wood-fired train crawled up the side of the mountains towards the pass, stopping now and again to catch its breath, and after a picturesque journey of seven hours delivered us safely at White Horse, the northern terminus.

The flat-bottomed boat named *Casca* which was to take us some 400 miles downstream looked just like Noah's Ark, except that it had an engine and a paddlewheel, and the only animal aboard was a young grizzly bear. Sammy was the crew's pet and had the run of the ship. The playful little ball of wool seemed to take a special liking to Charles Lewis, a rather nervous, middle-aged American who did not care for animals and feared for his trousers. His wife had left him. To forget her he had sold his business, invested his capital in stocks and shares and gone travelling. Listening to his story helped to while the time away. There was nothing to do and little to see but hills, woods and scrubland, and every eight or ten hours a few log cabins which were marked on the map as towns. The largest of them was Fort Selkirk, with a population of perhaps fifty. While the *Casca* delivered provisions and mail, and loaded logs—the fuel for her boiler—Sammy was locked up, and we stretched our legs ashore.

It was a long, slow journey, and the passage through the Five Finger Rapids, although a little frightening, came as a welcome relief. Once or twice moose crossed the river in front of us, and we were fascinated to watch a large bear on the bank fishing for salmon. We passed within a stone's throw, but it took not the slightest notice of us, splashing in the water with its front paw. The master, a dour Scots Canadian, told us that the Athapasca Indians set fishing wheels in the river which were turned by the current, scooping up pink salmon and throwing them into a wooden box, thus laying in food for the winter for themselves and their dogs. In parts the Yukon, the 'father of rivers', was now a mile wide. It had many sandbanks, and between them channels of fast- or slow-running water which made navigation hazardous. In 1929, long before the highway was built, the river provided the country's only means of communication: in summer by boat, in the long winter months when it was frozen, by sledge and dog team. Floating downstream, we lost all sense of time. So near the arctic circle the sun hardly set before it rose again, and even at midnight we could read without a light.

Dawson City, our destination, had the atmosphere of a ghost town. At the beginning of the century more than 30,000 inhabitants thronged its busy streets, millionaires drank and gambled in its noisy saloon bars and amusement halls, and trade flourished. But when most of the gold was gone the population shrank to 800. They were mainly people who lacked the energy to return to civilisation, elderly men who eked out a modest existence. Weeds grew in the thoroughfares, most of the houses had stood empty for years, the windows were broken, the roofs were collapsing and no one cleared away the debris. We were relieved to find that the hotel was comfortable and the food good. There were eggs, flour, potatoes, butter, fish, a variety of things in tins, smoked bear and always fresh moose steak.

Gold mining had become an industrial operation. The manager of the Canadian Klondike Mining Co., to whom we had an introduction, was away at White Horse, so we made friends with Jackson, one of the foremen. He showed us the old-fashioned method of washing gold dust out of sand in a hand basin, which no longer paid, because the rich deposits had all been exhausted. We then saw the huge power-driven dredgers, cranes and bucket conveyors used by the company to dig the gold-bearing sand out of the river in bulk, the high-pressure water jets which loosened the hillsides of earth containing the yellow metal, and the large mechanical sluice boxes in which it was isolated. The nuggets and gold dust were then stored in padlocked metal boxes in the company's depot, an ordinary blockhouse.

Arthur's newspapers were more interested in human stories than in modern mining methods, and a few evenings at the Arcade Cafe provided enough material to keep my typewriter clicking for many hours. The old gold diggers were only too willing to talk about themselves and the good old days, for nothing worth talking about had happened since. They would have us believe they had all been millionaires who lost their gold gambling, or filling girls' shoes and stockings with nuggets, throwing gold dust in women's hair or being robbed of their fortunes at the point of a gun. Their stories were thirty years out of date, but in between their romancing Arthur extracted the information he was seeking about their present dreary lives which were so completely devoid of both gold and women.

And where were the redskins? It was primarily because of them that we— or at least I—had come to the Yukon Territory. We had not met any so far.

Jackson seemed a little surprised. Did we really want to meet them? They had nothing in common with the white man. The tribes lived by hunting, trapping and fishing as their forefathers had done. This was music to my ears. At last we were on the trail of the braves who had so heroically defended their heritage against the greedy whites and, rather than bend to so-called civilisation, withdrawn to the wilderness of north-western Canada and Alaska.

Could Jackson take us to an Indian village? He could, but he was not going to. Why not? He just did not want to. The redskins were perfectly peaceful, he assured us. There was no risk of being scalped, and it was quite safe for us to visit them, but he was not coming. Could he find us horses and a guide? It was better to take a boat, he explained. Moose Hide, the nearest village, was only a few miles downstream.

'Secretary, go and find a boat,' said my boss, 'a motor boat!'

Easier said than done. The one and only motor boat belonged to Williams, the undertaker, who was busy digging a couple of graves. For five dollars we could hire it, but we would have to go on our own. Moose Hide was on the right bank of the Yukon and not difficult to find. I examined the craft. It was old and one pulled a rope to start the engine, but it looked sound, and I took it.

Williams scratched his head. He would have to ask for a deposit of fifty dollars, the value of the boat, just in case we should miss the village, for there were whirlpools beyond. He hoped I understood. I did, and thought it best not to mention the whirlpools to Arthur. I loaded an extra tin of petrol and reported that everything was ready.

Would the boat hold one more? 'Sure,' I replied, glad that Jackson was coming after all. But it was Lewis who wanted to come, and before I could express my misgivings he arrived. I wondered whether he could swim. If he couldn't he was sure to back out of the expedition when he saw the boat. But I had misjudged him, and he laughed as the gravedigger threw him an old lifebelt 'without promising that it would float'. A sharp tug on the rope, the engine started, and we were off. This, I felt, tingling with anticipation, would be the crowning adventure, the climax of my journey through America. Little did I suspect the fiasco we were headed for.

I kept in the slow-running water close to the shore, looking out for rocks, sandbanks and driftwood. The craft handled well, and we had an enjoyable ride. Charles Lewis opened a bottle of firewater. He had brought two, one for the chief. It was beyond my understanding how anyone could drink the stuff. Sooner than expected, the Indian hamlet came in sight, an untidy cluster of log cabins. We pulled our boat on to the shore next to the canoes that were lying there and climbed the bank to the village. At first it seemed deserted, but there was smoke, and then we saw eyes peering at us out of the dark window and door openings.

'Hello, there,' called Arthur. 'Come out and let us look at you. We're friends!'

A solitary figure appeared, an elderly, bareheaded man in fancy dress who announced in halting English that he was Chief Isaak. It was hard to imagine anyone looking more peaceful. I felt terribly disappointed. Accepting one of Arthur's cigars and the bottle from Lewis, a broad grin came over his wooden face and he allowed us to take his photograph while his warriors and their squaws hid from the evil eye of the camera. They refused to be photographed. I bartered with the chief over a pair of moccasins, letting him get the better of me, which pleased him immensely, and after taking a few pictures of the petrified village we made a show of returning to our boat.

'Start the engine and get ready to push off!' I shouted to my companions, then ran up the bank and photographed the curious crowd who had come out to watch our departure. There were angry howls as most of them turned and fled, but I was so disillusioned by these chickenhearted Redskins that I no longer cared if I upset them. I ran back to the boat, pushed it away from the bank and jumped in. Then I noticed that the engine was not running. Again and again I pulled the rope, but it would not start. Helplessly we drifted downstream. There was petrol in the float chamber. I blew through the jet and cleaned the collector brushes—then suddenly I remembered the whirlpools, and my heart missed a beat.

Arthur added to my apprehension by informing me that the Indians were taking to their boats and coming after us. Raising my head as I gave the rope another jerk, I saw that Lewis had drawn a revolver, but fortunately just then the engine fired. I headed out into the middle of the river and turned upstream. Being chased by redskins in the wildernes of north-west Canada might sound romantic, but it was in fact most undignified. They resembled gypsies rather than warriors, and it was all my fault that we found ourselves in this humiliating situation. But worse was to come.

Watching the Indians, who were now left a good distance behind, I was not looking where we were going. Suddenly we struck a sandbank, and the engine began to race. I jumped out to refloat the craft, but found to my dismay that the pin which held the propeller on the shaft had sheered and fallen out. We were stuck in the middle of the Yukon, miles from anywhere, with three canoes of redskins in pursuit. They were paddling hard against the current and made only slow progress, but they were drawing nearer. Lewis panicked and wet his pants. Arthur took the revolver from him and left him to his bottle. Frantically I searched the sand for the missing pin, then pulled a nail out of the boat instead and it fitted. With the help of a stone I bent the protruding end to prevent it from falling out and, almost under the noses of the gesticulating Indians, we refloated the boat. The engine started at the first pull of the rope and we were away, completing the homeward journey without any further excitement, and felt relieved when Dawson City came in sight.

Lewis was convinced the redskins would have scalped us had they caught us. I suspected they were after my camera, while Arthur thought they meant no harm but were only trying to help us. We shall never know. All three of us felt rather sheepish about the escapade and kept it to ourselves, but my boyhood illusions of Red Indian romance and Wild West heroism which had been created by my old friend Fennimore Cooper and other fiction writers was gone for good.

Before airlines shrank the world to its present size Dawson City was a very long way from Europe, fully four weeks of continuous travelling by day and night—if one was lucky enough to make all connections without waiting. Fortunately we were in no hurry, but the journey up the Yukon seemed endless, and through the Five Finger Rapids the Ark had to pull itself by winding in a steel cable which was fixed to the rocks above.

Charles Lewis was returning to civilisation with us. Anxious to know what had happened during his absence, he bought an American newspaper as soon as we reached White Horse. When he saw the stock market quotations he became very agitated and cabled his broker, switching all his investments. Later, on the train to Skagway, we discovered that the paper was three weeks old. Lewis almost jumped out of the window, but even if he stopped the train there was nothing he could do in those lonely mountains. My acquaintance with stocks and shares was purely theoretical. Father needed all his money in the business and never touched the stock market, but there is something inherently funny about a speculator caught on the hop, and I fear the poor man got little sympathy from us. On the contrary, Arthur used the incident for an amusing article. One man's meat is another's poison. Lewis left us at Skagway, and we never heard how his speculation turned out.

On our way south we stopped for a day at Juneau, the capital of Alaska, with a population of 5,000 and an old taxi displaying a placard: 'The president of the USA rode in this car: why not you?' After looking at another glacier and some more totem poles we returned to Vancouver, wondering whether either of us would ever come back to this beautiful part of the world.

Canada is a vast country. We looked at it from the luxurious observation car of the CPR as we steamed east, first winding our way through the valleys of the Rocky Mountains to Calgary, then crossing the seemingly endless wheat, cattle and cowboy region via Medicine Hat, Moose Jaw and Regina to Winnipeg and the lakeland of Ontario to Toronto, the industrial centre. The railway personnel had received instructions to look after our comfort, and we had a compartment like a state room in which we could work and have our meals served in private. As so often, I marvelled at the influence Arthur wielded with the CPR.

'How did you acquire it?' I asked. 'Your articles make interesting reading, but they're by no means sensational. They deal with such ordinary things.'

'My stories are read by tens of thousands of Europeans, most of whom are hardly aware of Canada. I arouse their interest by making the country and people come alive. Canada is growing up, and anxious to assert herself in the community of nations. Her statesmen want to act on the international stage. They can do it much better against a background of fireside homeliness than by boasting. I help to provide that background.'

'That may be good for Canada,' I conceded, 'but why should the CPR be so eager to pay the bill?'

'Because they are much more than a railroad and shipping company—they're the country's backbone, its largest landowner. Whatever is good for Canada is good for the CPR. The expense is trifling compared with the good-will my articles create.'

'You're not very generous. You've mentioned the CPR only twice, and very casually, in the five stories I've typed!'

Arthur smiled. 'Ours is a gentle craft and finely balanced. If I overdid it my newspapers would object, and don't forget they pay me for these articles. I mustn't bore my readers.'

He was certainly an exceptional man. How could I ever thank him for all I had seen and learned as his secretary? And I praised my good fortune that he had befriended me. I wished I knew more about him. He had a wife back in Vienna and a son somewhere in America, but he never talked about them or about himself and remained a mystery to the end.

I believe the Royal York Hotel at Toronto, where we stayed, was at that time the largest hotel in the British Empire. We sat in the hall, the most spacious I had ever seen, over a last cup of coffee before Arthur caught his train for New York, and then I was alone. He had been more like an uncle to me than a boss, and I felt lost without him. Once again I made the round with samples, trying for orders. There were several wholesalers in the town, but by far the largest firms were Eaton's and Simpson's, two mail order houses and store groups, who fought each other. One could supply only one or the other. I called on both a number of times, and in the end secured a small order from Simpson's. It was the beginning of a lasting business connection.

In Montreal I succeeded in booking several trial orders. This encouraged me to engage an agent, a military-looking gentleman with a moustache who called himself Colonel Drew and who was recommended to me by the chamber of commerce. He represented a Yorkshire worsted mill and a Swiss silk manufacturer, and laughed heartily when he saw my samples of ladies' bloomers, but after I had explained some of the technical points and we had called on a few wholesalers together he agreed to take the agency on my terms and a rate of 5 per cent commission.

I liked Canada, its vastness and the drive and enterprise of its people. Everyone talked about the future. The very air was stimulating. And Canada was British. In spite of the large French population I felt so much more at home here than in the USA. Being able to do business and thus take part in the economic life of the country instead of looking at it merely as a visiting sightseer also affected my attitude. Had my mind not been so firmly made up about settling in England I would have liked to become a Canadian.

The head office of the CPR was in Montreal, and I called there to convey Arthur's thanks to the director of the press department for all the support he and his public relations people had given us. To my delight he continued to treat me as a colleague. He secured one of the best cabins on the SS *Montcalm* for my return journey to Europe and told the captain and the purser to look after me, for I was an important journalist. He said it so convincingly that I almost believed it myself.

The first officer was waiting to welcome me as I boarded the ship, visibly surprised to see someone so young. I felt a bit of a fraud, but pulled myself together, determined to act the part. Then Colonel Drew came to see me off. Walking round the deck, we unexpectedly met an old friend of his, Sir Herbert Ames. They had served together in France during the war. 'From Czechoslovakia? How interesting! I hope to see something of you on the journey, young man,' said Sir Herbert as I was introduced. 'Knock on my cabin door any time.'

We were well down the St Lawrence river when the *Montcalm* slowed down to take four men aboard who had come alongside in a speedboat. I watched from the upper deck, wondering who they could be, when the purser sent me an invitation to join a small private party in his cabin. Full of my own importance, I swaggered downstairs.

'Meet some of your colleagues from the press,' he said as he presented the four men for whom we had just slowed down. They were reporters from leading Canadian newspapers. I could have sunk into the ground. The game was up. They would discover in two minutes that I was not a real journalist. Meanwhile they did the talking. A very important person was on board, it was whispered: he was on his way to Geneva to represent the Canadian government at a crucial conference. But Sir Herbert eluded the press: he did not like being interviewed.

'Sir Herbert Ames?' In a flash my courage returned. 'Let me introduce you to him,' I said modestly.

The reporters got their interview and disembarked, satisfied, at Quebec City. The ship's officers were suitably impressed, and my stock stood high with everyone for the rest of the journey, except with Sir Herbert. I carefully kept away from him.

The Atlantic was smooth as a millpond. Sir Herbert departed at Cherbourg, and about ten days after leaving Montreal we docked at Hamburg early on Saturday morning. Provided I caught the 8 a.m. express I could be at Fleissen that night. But passengers were not allowed to disembark until the ship was cleared by the medical authorities. Waiting for them meant missing my train. This would not happen if Arthur were here; he would make me do something about it! The thought stirred me into action.

'Captain, these dispatches are for the Sunday papers!' I pretended, waving my briefcase. 'What can you do to help me?'

It was not true. Arthur had posted all his articles in New York weeks ago, but to my surprise the trick worked. The captain had me put ashore in a rowing boat while the other passengers watched enviously as they waited for the doctor.

I caught the express, and Father met me with the car at Plauen in the evening. He never said a cross word about my expedition to Alaska. Now that I had returned safely I think he was quietly pleased about my initiative and that I had seen so much of the North American continent. Our business with Canada never grew very large, and I had an unpleasant difference with Colonel Drew, who claimed commission on the orders I took before he became our agent. I forget how it was settled, but we continued to ship our knickers, if in modest quantities, to Montreal, Toronto and Vancouver for many years to come.

18

END OF
AN EPOCH
1929-30

IT TOOK, ON average, a year and sometimes longer before a bale of raw cotton entering our Leibitschgrund raw material store left the Fleissen factory in the form of a consignment of knitted garments. We normally carried a stock of some four hundred bales of American 'middling'—sufficient to keep the fine spinning mill going for three months—and had a further three hundred bales or so on order for forward delivery. Fluctuations in cotton prices had an important bearing on the financial results of our business. In theory they should not have had, for we normally balanced the orders we received for finished goods with corresponding purchases of raw material, but in practice things did not quite work out that way. If cotton prices fell there were always customers who tried to get out of their contracts under some pretext or other in order to buy cheaper elsewhere, and we were left with the expensive cotton. To counteract this risk one could 'go short', but if the market then rose un-expectedly customers insisted on getting every dozen they had contracted for. One had to cover cotton at the higher price and got caught that way.

Buying cotton for Leibitschgrund could be a worrying job. The fine yarn mill used up to 1,600 bales of American 'middling' per annum. A large amount of money was involved. One had to watch the market. Prices fluctu-ated daily, and choosing the right moment when to buy needed skill and luck—mostly luck! Sometimes I wondered whether studying crop reports, world consumption figures and statistics was worth the effort. All too often one drew the wrong conclusions from them. Why not ignore forecasts? It might be safer to average prices by buying a hundred bales every few weeks irrespective of market trends. But Father disagreed. A businessman had to use his head, he said, and made me plot the daily New York quotations on graph paper, from where I then transferred the monthly highs and lows to a summary chart which also showed our purchases.

Twice during the past two years the price of 'middling' had fallen to 18 cents per lb. Each time Father had made a profitable purchase and regretted afterwards that he had lacked the courage to buy a larger quantity. So when in August 1929 the price fell once again to 18 cents he placed a forward order for 500 bales, which, together with the somewhat larger than usual stocks in the warehouse, covered our needs for a year.

In September it looked as if prices were hardening. The old pattern seemed to repeat itself, and Father rubbed his hands. If cotton merchants and grapevine informed us correctly Lehrmann had missed the crucial moment to buy and, we hoped, would have to pay more later. But in October the market weakened, and in November the price of 'middling' fell to $17\frac{1}{4}$ cents. Surely it could not go any lower? The bottom must now have been reached and prices would begin to climb again. This was a time when courage would pay, we thought, and bought a further 150 bales. In December it dropped to $16\frac{3}{4}$ and in February to $15\frac{1}{2}$ cents, and each time Father bought another 150 bales to average the previous purchases, until we had forward commitments for more than twelve months, in addition to the stocks in our warehouse—an all-time record. Lehrmann's were now also buying, we heard, but were fixing prices for only part of their purchases. We could not understand what they were waiting for.

Father was usually a cautious buyer and made remarkably few mistakes, but he certainly made one on this occasion. And it was not only American 'middling' he bought too dear. In addition he made a forward purchase of 200 bales of Indian cotton for the condenser mill. I am, however, running ahead of the story, so let us return to the autumn of 1929.

Towards the end of September Arthur Rundt telephoned. Could I meet him at Karlsbad? Father came with me to make his acquaintance. We had lunch and coffee at the Hotel Imperial and looked down upon the multicoloured autumn foliage of the beautiful resort and its steaming Sprudel below us. Arthur had a proposition. He planned to zigzag through Russia and Siberia next spring and summer, cross into Manchuria and China, and come back by way of Vladivostok. The Communists and Peking had promised every assistance. Would I be his secretary on the same terms as last time?

It was a most tempting offer. In my mind I saw the Kremlin, the Trans-Siberian railway, Cossacks cantering across the Steppes, block houses, the Chinese wall, mandarins and pagodas. Father, too, seemed quite carried away but did not try to influence me one way or the other. The decision was mine, and I found it very difficult to decline. But, to my lifelong regret, I did. I'd had enough holidays, now I wanted to work. And I was impatient to start my venture in England.

My plans for opening an office in London were well under way, and we agreed that from January 1930 onwards I could divide my time between it and the factories in Czechoslovakia. But someone would have to do my work at Fleissen during my absence. Once again I urged Father to engage a factory manager, a *Direktor*, and this time he gave way, although reluctantly.

The legal status and the functions of a *Direktor* in most Continental countries must not be confused with those of a company director in Britain. In Czechoslovakia the title implied merely that the bearer managed an enterprise, or a substantial part of it, on behalf of, or together with, the owners. Direktor Walsch, whom we had taken over from Krumbholz, was an experienced cotton spinner, a good technician and administrator, a wily negotiator and of considerable help to Father at Leibitschgrund. Unfortunately he had the reputation of beating his wife, which set a bad example to the workpeople; but nobody is perfect.

Were could we find a *Direktor* for the knitwear factory? Professional managers were quite usual in spinning mills but rare in the knitting industry. Most knitters managed their factories themselves. The choice was extremely limited.

If one had an unusual problem one consulted one's bank manager, who acted as general adviser to all his clients. Ours told us of a knitting mill about to go into liquidation. Direktor Engelhard might become available. We interviewed the short, somewhat pompous man with the pointed beard. He was fifty, held good references, had been in the knitting trade all his life and gave the right answers to our questions. Although Father hesitated, I had my way and we engaged him. His duties were to commence with the new year.

Herr Direktor Engelhard, used to a much smaller factory than ours, felt he had never had the chance to prove what was in him. He would show that he was cut out for big business. It came more natural to him to talk and think in millions than in ten thousands. To his disappointment Father was cautious and did not promise to hand over the management of the whole plant to him right away. He would entrust him only with transport, the yarn store and the winding department and in addition make him responsible for negotiations with the dyers, which did not involve too great risks. I thought he underestimated the man's ability, but being less than half Engelhard's age I found it difficult to weigh him up. He was obviously a glutton for work, had a firm hand and commanding voice, and, given time, would, I hoped, be able to take over most of the daily business routine. True, there were moments when I had doubts, but I conveniently overlooked them. The wish was father to the thought; hope swayed my judgement.

Our financial year ended on 31 December, and before I could leave for England I had to help with stocktaking and then compile the results. It was always a period of hectic activity, and we used to get part of the work done during the preceding weekend. Mid-day Saturday, when the factory stopped, Grandfather, Father, myself and the heads of the various departments began counting and weighing, and by Sunday night the static stocks of raw material, accessories and finished garments were recorded. Goods in the process of manufacture were counted on the last day of the year. Each man wrote out sheet after sheet of paper and Father made the round every few hours collecting them. By New Year's Eve he had a drawer full of white, blue or yellow slips covered with figures and descriptions.

I spent a week analysing the figures and preparing a summary. Father gave me a price for each item. It was a matter of judgement. If trade was promising, or cotton looked like rising, the goods were worth more than if a depression was approaching. It took me another two tedious weeks, multiplying, checking and adding, before I was able to hand him a list of the detailed and total value of the stock. Father usually had a shrewd idea what it would be and guessed the year's results with remarkable accuracy, long before Schreiner, our chief book-keeper, had drawn up his accounts.

The value of the stock, which amounted to several million kronen, was a closely guarded secret, for it provided the key to the firm's true profits, and not even Schreiner was allowed to know those. Father carefully locked the list in his private safe and waited until the books were balanced and the accounts prepared 'on the assumption that the stocks were the same as the year before'. He then decided what profit to declare to the Inland Revenue, and I had to adjust the stock records accordingly.

It was important to keep the tax people happy. They liked to see steady profit figures. Violent fluctuations aroused their curiosity and made them start unpleasant investigations. Every prudent trader therefore created a secret reserve, a cushion, in his stock records. He could then level out the uneven performance of his business by reducing or increasing the reserve. Balance sheets were prepared primarily for the benefit of the tax authorities and did not mean much to us. Nor did they to Direktor Huder, our bank manager. He preferred to rely on Father's verbal report.

During the second half of the 1920s the output of our factory steadily increased and our annual sales climbed to a peak of just under 20 million kronen, with a record profit of $1\frac{1}{2}$ million. I had not been in business long enough to realise fully what good years they were and took the rising curve for granted. But 1929 turned out to be the last of the series of 'normal' years as I knew them. The world market prices of cotton and other raw materials declined, the purchasing power of the krone increased, and our merchandise became steadily cheaper. Wages remained practically the same but bought more. While the volume and sales of our production grew, our turnover figures began to fall.

As always when prices fall, buyers refused to make forward commitments but operated from hand to mouth. Not enough orders were placed to keep the industry fully employed. Manufacturers cut their profit margins, competition got tougher and the quality of the merchandise suffered. The picture in Britain was much the same. As the price of fleecy knickers fell there was a gradual lowering of quality for which the consumer was at least partially to blame. A few years earlier women had paid 1s 11¾d for a pair of knickers, but when one shopkeeper cut the price to 1s 9d to get a larger share of the market the others had to follow suit. A year later the price was down to 1s 6d. Job lots and bankrupt stock came on the market at even less. Women, naturally anxious to obtain the best value for their money, shopped around, and the price of a pair of fleecy knickers fell to a shilling. In the slump of the early '30s one could buy them from bazaars and stalls at 9d and even 6d.

The importer added 7½ per cent to the manufacturer's price, the wholesaler added 15 per cent to the price he paid, and the retailer's margin was 30 per cent. In order to make a profit the shopkeeper put pressure on the wholesaler, who in turn demanded price concessions from the importer. So he had to buy more cheaply from the manufacturer, even if this meant a slight reduction in quality. The fabric was knitted a stitch looser, a slightly cheaper condenser yarn was used and the garment was cut a little smaller. The average weight of a pair of women's fleecy knickers in 1925 was eight ounces, but by 1930 it was to drop to five ounces. Fashion also played a part, for women preferred ever lighter, shorter and closer-fitting underwear.

No. 752 quality knickers continued to hold pride of place in our range, but we got few orders for them. We had to charge 84 kronen (10s 3d) per dozen, which meant that the shopkeeper in Britain asked about 1s 6d for a pair, and not many women were prepared to pay that sort of price any more. The demand was now for much lower qualities. Our production capacity was equivalent to 6,000 dozen 534 quality women's knickers a week, which, at an average price of 60 kronen (or 7s 3d), added up to an annual turnover of 18 million kronen. They sold in the shops for 1s a pair. We actually made on average only 4,500 dozen knickers, and used the remaining capacity for the manufacture of vests, pants, singlets, drawers, divided skirts, bathing suits, sweaters, cardigans and other garments. They were traditional lines for our home market, but many of them also sold abroad.

Here is an attempt to reconstruct the overall situation in the late 1920s. It can be only a much simplified approximation, for most of the records of that period have been lost and I have to rely on my memory, and on rough entries in old notebooks, for many of the figures. The picture varied substantially from one year to the next, especially from 1930 onwards, when falling cotton prices and dwindling sales had a disastrous effect.

Turnover of Adolf Pasold & Sohn (kronen)

1927	18,800,000
1928	18,200,000
1929	19,950,000
1930	16,700,000

| | Markets (%) | | |
	Summer garments	Winter garments	Total
Britain	20	50	70
Holland	2	8	10
Scandinavia	3	2	5
Others	2	1	3
Home	3	9	12
Total	30	70	100

The value of the monthly production varied only slightly between 1,400,000 and 1,600,000 kronen, but since the garment trade is seasonal our dispatches fluctuated considerably from one month to the next, and the pattern was approximately as follows (in kronen):

Summer garments		Winter garments	
January	750,000	June	1,400,000
February	1,500,000	July	2,000,000
March	1,750,000	August	2,400,000
April	1,100,000	September	2,200,000
May	900,000	October	1,600,000
		November	1,400,000
		December	1,000,000
	6,000,000		12,000,000

No. of employees (m male, f female)	Weekly earnings (kronen)	Total (kronen)
235 spinning (m/f)	100–120	1,300,000
35 winding (f)	100–120	200,000
35 knitting (m)	200	350,000
20 mending (f)	100	100,000
5 fleecing/calendering (m)	120–140	30,000
50 cutting (f)	120	300,000
180 sewing (f)	100–120	1,000,000
100 folding (f)	100	500,000
10 packing (m)	140–150	70,000
10 foremen/women	250–350	150,000
10 office staff (m)	150–250	100,000
10 others (m)	150–250	100,000
700 employees	Average 120 weekly	

Total 4,200,000

Health insurance, etc 300,000

Annual total 4,500,000

Of the 700 employees, two thirds were at Fleissen, the others at Leibitsch-grund. The knitters were all men who worked in double and, when needed, treble shifts. The sewing machinists normally worked in two shifts from 5 or 6 a.m. to 2 p.m., and from 2 p.m. to 10 or 11 p.m. according to requirements, and on Saturday morning. Most of the spinners also worked in two shifts. Almost everyone was on piecework, and earnings varied according to individual performance. I can only quote averages.

Taking the average weekly earnings as 120 kronen, and converting it into sterling at the then current rate of 164 to the £, we arrive at approximately 14s 7½d a week or £36 11s 3d a year. The turnover of 18 million kronen represented £109,750: approximately £156 per employee.

	lb	Kronen
Annual sales value equivalent to 300,000 dozen of 534 quality fleecy knickers at 60 kronen per dozen, weighing 5 lb	1,500,000	18,000,000
Annual consumption of American cotton, about 1,500 bales costing approximately 18 cents per lb	750,000	4,500,000
Waste clippings and spinning waste (own and bought) and Indian cotton for condenser yarn	1,200,000	2,000,000
Coloured yarn, beige, clerical grey and marl which Leibitschgrund could not spin and had to be bought in	150,000	1,000,000
Less manufacturing waste, 50 per cent of which was reclaimed and re-spun at Leibitschgrund	600,000	
Total	1,500,000	7,500,000

	Kronen
Approximately 75 per cent of our fabric was piece-dyed. Cost of dyeing	1,400,000
Sewing thread, elastic, trimmings, buttons, woven fabric and other accessories	1,500,000
Wages of 700 employees (Fleissen and Leibitschgrund), average 120 kronen a week	4,200,000
Health insurance, etc.	300,000
Salaries, insurance, interest, coal, oil, depreciation, repairs, maintenance, packing material, postage, selling and travelling expenses and all other overheads	1,800,000
Turnover tax (comparatively low because none payable on imports, exports and internal transactions between Fleissen and Leibitschgrund)	100,000
Profit	1,200,000
Total	18,000,000

A profit of 1,200,000 kronen represented £7,300, and was a substantial sum in those days. The owners of the firm (Father and Grandfather) paid themselves no salary but took what money they needed out of the profit and put the remaining 80 to 90 per cent back into the business.

We felt uneasy about the degree to which we depended on exports. Our business had become too vulnerable to changes in the pattern of international trade, due to the rapidly growing competition from Japan, for instance, and our efforts these past few years had not been directed at expanding our sales, which would have made us even more vulnerable, but at becoming more self-sufficient. We wanted to build a strong, vertically integrated manufacturing organisation that could meet any competition. And this objective we were achieving step by step. Spinning our own yarn added nothing to our turnover but, once the programme of modernising Leibitschgrund was completed, would make us more competitive and increase our profits.

Profits were important. It was a matter of comparing our results not so much with those of the previous years as with the figure we estimated Lehrmann's had earned. If our profits should fall short of theirs, then they would have more money than we to spend on improving their plant, and that would be fatal for us. It would then be only a matter of time before they put us out of business. We simply could not afford to fall back in the race.

Owing to circumstances beyond our control, turnover and profit fell drastically after the peak of 1929, but it would be wrong to conclude that Adolf Pasold & Sohn were stagnating. Far from it, as will be seen, but the world depression could hardly have come at a more unfortunate stage in our development.

Towards the end of January 1930 I left for London, where I had rented 600 square feet on the first floor of 41 Jewin Crescent, in the middle of the textile area of the City, and to impress Father reported that it was only five minutes' walk from the Bank of England. I subdivided the premises into a showroom, two tiny offices and a small store, bought some second-hand furniture, a typewriter, installed a telephone and screwed a brass plate with the name E. W. PASOLD on the entrance. Then I appointed a firm of auditors who had been recommended by a friend and went to open a bank account. But I had left it a little late: it was past five o'clock, and the Midland Bank, which I thought was the best for some reason I have long forgotten, was closed. So were Barclay's and the Westminster, only the Fore Street branch of the National Provincial was still open, and Mr Powell, the manager, seemed in no hurry to go home. 'It may be late and a small account,' he smiled, 'but we are always happy to do business.' A man after my own heart. The National Provincial have remained our bankers ever since.

The customers of Adolf Pasold & Sohn were importers who bought from us ex Fleissen. They estimated their requirements for the season and placed their orders nine months in advance to give us time to manufacture the merchandise. But my London office would be selling to wholesalers who were not planning so far ahead and who expected to have repeat orders delivered almost by return. To be able to give this service I had to carry stocks in London. My premises in Jewin Crescent were far too small. I could not afford a warehouse of my own, but negotiations with various forwarding agents led to a satisfactory if somewhat costly arrangement. My goods would be stored at the docks until I called them off.

I needed a trustworthy deputy to look after the business in my absence and to act as salesman, clerk and warehouseman. Although my friend Stuart Ramsay was only nineteen, I offered him the position, but his father thought it offered insufficient prospects and advised him to stay with Erlanger's, the bankers, where he was a junior clerk. I felt disappointed, for Stuart was an honest, hard-working lad whom I trusted implicitly. We would have got on well together. An employment agency gave me a list of applicants. The selection was small, and my choice fell on a young man of twenty-two—let us call him Mr Finch—who had been employed in the Chemnitz office of a Lancashire cotton spinner and spoke fluent German. I didn't like his man-of-the-world attitude, but he seemed competent, and I thought we would get used to each other. Since he was to be in charge of the office, I left it to him to engage the staff, a solitary typist.

One hurdle remained. I had to tell the importers that I was starting a business in London before they found it out for themselves. Would they object to my selling to their customers? Lying awake at night, I dreaded to think what would happen if they should divert their trade from Adolf Pasold & Sohn to Lehrmann's. Father needed their orders. It would take years before my organisation could secure enough business from the wholesalers to keep our factory going. If it came to the worst, if I lost the goodwill and support of the importers, I would have no choice but to abandon my venture.

Filled with apprehension, I climbed the stairs to Mr Stern's private office. He seemed tense. The usual smile was missing from his face. No doubt he had already heard of my establishing an office in London and thoroughly disapproved. Before I could open my mouth he waved me into the chair opposite his own and began to talk. Instead of coming straight to the point, as I expected, he talked about the crash on Wall Street and the repercussions it was having on business in Britain. But I was too preoccupied with my own problems to appreciate the complicated interplay of world trade. What was he leading up to? Was he trying to discourage me from going on with my project?

'This may not be the best time to start a business,' I said when he paused, 'but I could not do it sooner. You have always been very kind to me, and if you guide me a little our interests need not clash.'

'Clash?' It took him a moment to connect. 'Oh, you're referring to the little office my boys tell me you are opening round the corner!' He seemed amused. 'I dare say there's room for both of us. Let me wish you luck. You'll need it, with those thunder clouds on the horizon! Quote wholesalers high enough prices—they'll buy much smaller quantities and place their orders much later than I do. You'll have the risk and expense of carrying stock for them in London. You must pay your salesmen commission and allow discounts. You'll have handling, packing and freight charges to get the goods from London to the provinces. All that will add up, and presumably you'll want a profit as well. My big organisation can operate more cheaply than you can, and you may find it hard to compete, but I'm sure you'll pick up a little business.'

Mr Stern was a sport. His words lifted a great weight from my shoulders. Thankfully I pressed his hand and promised to keep him informed of my progress. The Wall Street panic and its effect on Britain's trade seemed remote to me. I would not let them interfere with my programme. Customers were usually gloomy about the future, it was part of their technique.

Greatly encouraged, I called on Mr Singer. Telling him would not be easy. He knew about my ambition to set up in London. I had confided in him years ago, and he had advised me against it. But to my surprise he had forgotten. He could not have taken me seriously, and I almost felt a little hurt. If only he had known sooner, he said. He was about to retire and was giving his business to three of his employees. It would henceforth be called Matheson Burgess & Co. The Co. was Mr Colmer, a young man not much older than myself. Had he known about my plans maybe I could have taken over the firm of A. T. Singer instead of building up a business of my own, which would take me twenty years. But it was too late now!

I was shocked. Mr Singer was one of our best customers. I could hardly believe that he intended to retire and that I had missed, by such a narrow margin, the opportunity of acquiring his old established firm. The house of A. T. Singer would have been big enough to handle the whole output of Adolf Pasold & Sohn. The thought seemed altogether too staggering to contemplate, and I could only stammer how sorry I was and that I wished the new firm every success.

Mr Heldmaier, a comparatively new customer, said he did not mind in the least where I sold my goods. If my activities proved damaging to his business, then of course he would cease buying from Adolf Pasold & Sohn, but he did not anticipate that would happen. I was such a tiny fish in a very large pond. The danger came from elsewhere, from Japan. It was rumoured that Stern's imports of cheap Japanese knickers exceeded those from Czechoslovakia.

The reception I had from Mr Israel was less comforting. 'You can't sell the same merchandise to us and to our customers too,' he barked. 'Either you deal with the importers or you go direct to the wholesalers!'

My assurance that I would charge higher prices to wholesalers did not satisfy him. 'You must not offer them the same lines you sell to us! I don't mind if you supply them with something different. Knit knickers for them in another kind of stitch! Offer them petticoats, gaiters or something else your machines will make—anything, provided it's different from the merchandise Israel & Oppenheimer buy from you!'

No doubt Mr Israel was right. Supplying importers and wholesalers with identical merchandise was bound to lead me into trouble sooner or later. Perhaps I could interest the wholesalers in our marl men's wear, which was finding such a ready sale in Czechoslovakia. The slightly oily odour of the fleece would matter less in outer garments than in underwear.

While Mr Finch called on wholesalers in the City and Jewish traders in the East End with one range of samples, I toured the provinces with the other. Baker Baker of Bristol gave me a trial order for summer-weight Directoire knickers for quick delivery but would not look at the marl garments. I had better luck in Birmingham, where Larkin's placed an initial contract for 200 dozen men's marl slipovers. It made my day. The buyer thought they would sell well—wrongly, as it turned out—and he would soon send repeat orders. None of the other wholesalers in Birmingham were prepared to see me, but my old friend George Peacock, who directed his growing chain-store empire from West Bromwich, made me welcome as always. His shops sold a wide variety of merchandise, and he seemed to select and buy it all himself without assistance from a buyer. He made decisions easily, almost casually I thought, and without reference to any records. How could he carry the many prices and continually changing stock figures in his head? Pushing the marl slipovers and jumpers aside, he flicked through my samples of fleecy knickers and offered me a contract for 8,000 dozen at a slightly lower price than I was asking. Tempted though I felt, I refused it. The upkeep of the office at Jewin Crescent had to be earned, and that could not be done by cutting prices. He shook me warmly by the hand as I departed. Perhaps we'd do a deal next time.

Ryland's of Manchester gave me an order for 250 dozen fleecy knickers, but I was far more pleased with one from S. & J. Watts for fifty dozen marl slipovers. Admittedly the amount came to less than £20, for the price of a dozen slipovers was only 14s, but I felt encouraged and hoped that repeat orders would follow. None did. From Manchester I went north to Newcastle and on to Glasgow. Like all commercial travellers I wasted many hours anxiously watching the clock in customers'—or more often only potential customers'—waiting rooms while buyers, that fortunate species of *homo sapiens*, oblivious of the value of my time, gossiped or went out for a cup of coffee. And when they noticed me at last most of them said they were too busy to look at samples and sent me away. Only one in four allowed me to open my bag. Yet I felt confident and happy. This was how Mr Stern and Mr Singer had started, I told myself. I knew it would take patience to break into the wholesale trade, and every account I opened was a victory. I travelled by train from one city to another, always after business hours, and sat every evening in a different hotel bedroom writing order copies and business reports, which I posted off to Jewin Crescent.

At Arthur's in Glasgow I had a somewhat unnerving experience. The buyer picked a pair of 534 quality o/s knickers out of my range, fingered them, took them to the window and told his assistant to bring one of the I. & O. samples. I could see at a glance that it was one of ours. He compared them and then turned to me.

'Are all the knickers you sell made in your own factory?'

'They are, sir,' I replied. 'We make hardly anything else but Directoire knickers.'

'How is it that I can buy them from a London importer a penny cheaper than from you direct? Importers don't give money away!'

'They buy a little cheaper because of the huge contracts they place,' I replied apprehensively lest I got myself into deep waters. I. & O., I suspected, was short for Israel & Oppenheimer, and I was on a collision course.

'Right,' said the buyer. 'If I gave you a large contract, say for 500 dozen, would you reduce your price by threepence?'

'Unfortunately I couldn't, sir. Five hundred dozen is not a large quantity for us.'

'Not a large enough contract?' There was a note of incredulity in his voice. 'Cut your price by twopence, then, or at least by a penny-halfpenny. I can't drop my regular supplier and buy from you unless you offer me an advantage!'

He was, of course, quite right. Perhaps I could reduce my price by a penny-halfpenny for such an order. It was a substantial one for a wholesaler, and I badly wanted to open the account, but if Mr Israel were to find out that his firm had lost a sale because I cut the price he would send for me. Better not ask for trouble, I thought regretfully, shook my head and carried my bag of samples downstairs.

Having called on all the wholesale houses whose names I could find in the telephone directory, shown my samples to the few buyers who were willing to look at them, taken two small orders and reluctantly concluded that there was no ready market in Glasgow for my marl merchandise, I went to Wishaw on Saturday morning, 1 March, to spend the weekend with my good friends the Bairds, who were anxious to hear how I got on. When I told them I had opened eleven accounts and sold altogether fifteen hundred dozen on my journey—a disappointingly small quantity, to my way of thinking—they congratulated me on what they described as an excellent effort. Some day, they predicted, I would need to employ a hundred clerks, warehousemen and travellers. I would not be content with the small, efficient team of ten I talked about. Pasold would become as well known a name as Stern. What a cheerful bunch of optimists they were!

To relax with the Baird brothers after the lonely fortnight among un-interested strangers was a wonderful tonic. Jimmy pulled my leg, John thought I took business much too seriously, and Tom gave me good advice and an order for 200 dozen pairs of knickers. I was glad to have it, although I realised that if I continued to supply T. Baird & Sons, who were, of course, retailers, I was risking my connection with the wholesale trade which I was so laboriously building up. Just as Mr Israel the importer objected to my selling to wholesalers, so the wholesalers would claim that I was taking away their legitimate trade by supplying the retailers direct. I could only hope they would not find out. Had I not supplied Peacock's chain-store organisation for two years now without hearing a word from anyone about it? True, I had nightmares sometimes, but all business was fraught with danger, and one might as well give up if one was not prepared to accept risks.

I stayed at Colin's house. He and his wife Min treated me as one of the family, and Colin delighted me with his inexhaustible store of quotations from Burns, Proust, Butler and a whole series of authors I had hardly even heard of. All were somehow relevant to my circumstances, and although quoted in jest made me see myself in better perspective. Colin read a great deal, but how could he retain all these morsels of wisdom in his head and reproduce them at the appropriate moment? It was a rare gift, but then, he was a most unusual man. Back at the store a canny Scots draper who judged the value of a pair of underpants to a penny and had a quick eye for a bargain, in the tranquil atmosphere of his beautiful home, which Min kept in a permanent state of spotless comfort, he was a man of letters, an intellectual who talked about a wide range of subjects with absorbing interest. I admired him greatly and considered myself fortunate to have such a friend.

In the evening I received a letter from my sister Silvia, which had followed me from hotel to hotel, with the disturbing news that Father was ill and had to have an operation. I retired with a heavy heart and had a restless night. Early on Sunday morning fell the blow which brought all my dreams to a sudden end. I was still half asleep when Colin came to my room, sat on the side of the bed and read me a telegram: 'Come home. Father died'.

The shock almost stunned me. What could have happened? Father had seemed well when I bade him goodbye in January. Had he driven himself too hard? He had not wanted me to leave him, but I had been selfish and persisted. Remorse overcame me. The train was well on the way to London before I mastered my grief sufficiently to take a rational view of the situation. I would now be responsible for looking after Mother and the family. Silvia was twenty-one, and a very sensible girl, but Rolf was only fifteen and a half. Ingo, the youngest, had just had his thirteenth birthday. And how would Grandfather and Grandmother bear the loss? There could be no doubt that I would have to take over the management of the family firm and abandon all hope of ever living in England. Would I be capable of keeping the concern going? Was I man enough to follow in Father's footsteps? The thought was too presumptuous to contemplate. I could but try and do my best not to let him down.

On the train I wrote two letters, one to George Peacock, in which I told him what had happened and that I would accept the order for 8,000 dozen knickers at his price if the offer was still open—for it was vital to have work for the factory—the other to Mr Finch, appointing him general manager of the young enterprise at Jewin Crescent and entrusting him with the safe-guarding of my interests.

The journey from Wishaw to Fleissen took a day and a half and seemed endless. A hush lay over the village when at last I arrived, for Father had been very popular and greatly respected by everyone. Mother looked older, but she never lost her self-control, and set us a wonderful example. 'He need not have died,' she told me. 'He was run down. A sore throat developed into tonsillitis, Dr Löw took out the septic tonsils, and then pleurisy set in which was diagnosed too late. He was so weak he had no will left to live. I won't let you see him. Remember him as he used to be when he was happy and well!'

The funeral procession was an ordeal we would have preferred to avoid, but Father had also belonged to our workers and to all the people of the village, and they wanted to walk behind the hearse to the cemetery with us, through the slush of early March, or silently line both sides of the road. After the funeral Grandfather told me solemnly that I was now the head of the family and of the firm, and the fate of both lay in my hands.

It was the custom to wear black for a month, and I remember wearing a black tie and armband for a whole year.

19

BATTLING
FOR SURVIVAL
1930

MANY OF THE villagers had disapproved of my decision to abandon Fleissen and make my home in England, but now I had returned, and that was enough to make them forgive and forget. Father had been idolised by our employees, and the affection they bore him was transferred to me. They did everything they could to help me take control of the business. Direktor Walsch and Direktor Engelhard assured me of their loyal support, and even our competitors seemed sympathetic and left us in peace for a while.

My brother Rolf, who was in his second year at the textile college, insisted that his place was at my side in the firm and refused to continue with his studies. Immediately after the funeral he started work as my personal assistant, taking dictation in shorthand, which he had learned at private lessons the year before, typing letters and keeping confidential records. He worked in the sample room preparing ranges, took charge of the stock of manufacturing sundries and made himself useful in the factory, learning as much in a month about yarns and fabrics, about knitting, fleecing, cutting and sewing as I had learned in years. Fortunately he had been interested in the factory ever since he was a small boy, and his numerous questions about business had often made Father laugh. I was impressed with the grasp he had of technical and commercial matters but felt it was deplorable that his studies should have ended so prematurely. He did not seem to think so himself. He had never liked school, and much preferred to work in the firm.

There had been significant changes in the curriculum since I had left the college. School hours had become even longer and stretched from eight to twelve and from two to six, with no time for sports or games, and there was homework to be done. Czech, unfortunately, had taken the place of English as a compulsory language. With so much else to study, Rolf could take evening classes in English only twice weekly. Anxious not to waste Father's money, and being lucky in having a good teacher, he had learned enough to write simple business letters by the time he joined me. In the summer I sent him to London for two months, where he stayed with our friends the

Ramsays at Herne Hill. During the week he worked with Mr Finch at the office in Jewin Crescent, learning as much of the language and the City as he could. However, I am running ahead of events, so let me return to the early spring of 1930.

The respite our competitors granted us did not last long. Business at Fleissen was a continuous battle for survival. No quarter was given or expected, and now that Father was dead the Lehrmanns made another attempt to bring our factory to a standstill by cutting off its water supply. Their cunning *Direktor*, Kraut, claimed that over the centuries the mill stream had gradually shifted its course and that its original bed lay 6 ft to the south, right over our well. As owners of the Lower Mill they demanded that it be moved back to its original position. If they could prove their contention our well would have to be filled in. And so, within weeks of Father's death, I had a lawsuit on my hands.

Things looked grim, and I was very worried. So, incidentally, were the authorities. It was no secret that Dr Lehrmann took a personal interest in this case, and one had best not displease him, since a word from him in high places could, and frequently did, speed or stop the promotion of a civil servant. But it was also appreciated that our factory could not carry on without water and that the employment of 700 people was at stake. Lehrmann's tried to overcome official hesitation by giving assurances that they would, within a reasonable period, find work in their expanding enterprise for any of Pasold's employees who might lose their jobs. There was a labour shortage at Fleissen, and it would have suited them very well to take our skilled winders, knitters, cutters and sewing machinists.

A government *Kommission* arrived, officials from the water board, the land registry at Wildstein and the Okresni Vybor at Eger, to study the situation. In my anxiety I took the stern expressions on the faces of all these civil servants as a bad sign, whereas in retrospect I believe they hoped for some compromise solution that would get them out of a real difficulty.

'Dobré jitro, Ing. Kubischta. Má úcta pane dottore. Jak se maté, Dr Slaviček? Dobré, pane kolego Novotny. Timto zahajuji jednání ve veči Lehrmann contra Pasold . . .,' after which introduction in Czech the investigation was conducted in German. This was the usual procedure so that the contending parties could follow and take part in the arguments. Some of the older civil servants also found German easier, for, in spite of their Czech names, they had only a limited command of the Czech language.

The two Jewish lawyers, Dr Hahn for Lehrmann's and Dr Freundlich for Pasold's, having shared a taxi from Eger and discreetly left it well out of sight, were now visibly straining to get at each other's throats. At that time all the important lawyers in the Egerland were Jews: only bagatelles were entrusted to Christian solicitors. Watched by a crowd of onlookers, the *Kommission*, accompanied by the mayor of Fleissen, three Lehrmann brothers and myself, tramped up and down the muddy bank of the mill stream, arguing and gesticulating for several hours. How could a mill stream change its course? Through floods and droughts and the action of the icefloes in the spring, said the one; through deliberate interference by the miller or the owners of the adjoining land, said the other; through widening of the footpath, said the third. Not one of them cast more than a cursory glance at the plan.

The two lawyers dominated the scene by hurling invective at each other and at the opposing firms. This was quite customary, and done to impress the clients. Open-air performances of this kind drew a considerable audience and gave the legal profession a welcome opportunity to advertise itself. Unfortunately Dr Hahn had much the louder voice and larger vocabulary, and my fear that we were losing ground seemed to be confirmed by the ill disguised smirk on the Lehrmanns' faces. Then a heavy shower drove us to take shelter in the Rathaus restaurant in the market square. Although it was mid-afternoon the members of the delegation ordered goulash, the standard fare of Czech civil servants on such occasions, as I had ample opportunity of observing during the years to come. The Lehrmanns drank small beer and the mayor and myself had coffee. Parties of officials frequently came to Fleissen to investigate land, water, tax, duty or other problems and were a welcome source of income to the local innkeepers. While everyone ate and drank the debate continued with undiminished vigour. His mouth full of goulash, Dr Hahn proved a more effective debater than the abstemious Dr Freundlich, who scowled behind a large glass of mineral water and to my dismay hardly spoke. Was he already exhausted? Was there no hope left that we might win?

As soon as the rain stopped we returned to the mill stream. Would none of the civil servants examine the evidence? Were they intimidated by that screaming opposition lawyer? Overcoming my shyness, I raised my voice to make myself heard above the din and demanded to see the map. Triumphantly Dr Hahn produced the vital document for me to inspect. The crumpled plan, a certified copy of the entry in the *Grundbuch*, the large book kept at the land registry in which all property and its owners were recorded, looked genuine enough. There was no doubt about it, the old mill stream had a bend whereas now it was straight. The position of our well had been pencilled in recently and seemed correct. My heart sank. Yet something seemed odd— and suddenly I realised that the drawing was upside down: north and south were reversed. The old bed really lay on the opposite side, some twelve feet to the north of the well. Only Kraut could have thought up such a cunningly simple piece of deception. And who could say that it was not a genuine mistake? Now I knew why he was not present.

At first there was laughter when I pointed out the mistake, which meant that the mill stream was in fact running over our land and we could demand that Lehrmanns should remove it. Then the members of the *Kommission* silently studied the plan. They were visibly uncomfortable. Ing. Kubischta, the representative of the water board, dictated a short protocol. I looked for the Lehrmann brothers to see their faces, but they had quietly disappeared. The lawyers stood together whispering, Dr Freundlich muttered something to me about a public scandal and a report he was going to send to Prague, then he left almost arm-in-arm with Dr Hahn in the direction of the waiting taxi. The civil servants pulled out their watches and found they had to catch their train. The onlookers dispersed; the comic opera was over. Within minutes I stood alone by the well, feeling much as David must have felt after slaying Goliath, and wondered what would happen next.

But nothing did. Dr Freundlich sent his bill, a modest one, and said the case was closed. It was in nobody's interest to embarrass the civil servants, and I, of course, was too harassed all round to turn the tables on Lehrmann, tempting as it was to do so. Relieved and content to know that our water supply was safe, I hid my pride at having emerged victorious, but felt a little surprised and even hurt that my uncles, the Geipels, who had such vast experience in water matters, had been so reticent and let me fight this battle alone. Had they not promised at Father's funeral that they would always come to my assistance? What I did not know until much later was that they, as well as the Lehrmanns and Marr the dyer, had, unknown to anyone, laid pipes connecting their works to the stream and were secretly drawing ever larger quantities of public water for their tannery and their dyehouses. They were convinced that somehow we were doing the same. The last thing the Geipels wanted was to be involved in a dispute about water which might have led to a general exposure. I had much to learn.

The Wall Street crash, the repercussions of which I had underestimated in my youthful inexperience, and the growing world crisis were affecting business. Our British customers in particular were reluctant to commit themselves forward, and the contracts they placed were small. Sales in Holland, Scandinavia and overseas also dropped, and it looked as if worse was to come. Stern, the largest buyer of all, gave most of his business to Lehrmann's, who seemed to accept any order they could get, irrespective of price. They introduced a ruthless economy drive, cut the salaries of their clerks and the wages of their workpeople and sold their goods for less than it cost to manufacture them. In this way they kept their factory on three shifts while we and the other firms, who adopted less drastic measures, were cutting back production and working shorter hours.

Czechoslovakia tightened her belt, and although her industry relied heavily on exports her internal economy remained relatively sound. I remembered Grandfather's words of warning that it was the home market we would have to turn to in our hour of need. We decided to compensate for our falling foreign trade by recapturing as much as possible of the local business we had neglected and left to others during the past six years of export boom. But our old customers in Bohemia, Moravia and Slovakia could not forget their bitter resentment over the preference we had for so long given to sales abroad. They wanted me to repent. Cap in hand I had to beg them for the favour of supplying part of their requirements. It was I, Mr Pasold personally, they wanted to upbraid and fulminate against before placing their trivial contracts. How grateful I was for every small order that helped to provide work for our employees, and how anxiously they enquired after the results of every one of my business journeys. I had only one trump card in my hand, our White Bear merchandise, which was becoming increasingly popular with the Czechoslovak public and which no one else could supply. It was the one section of our business that continued to yield a good return.

Grandfather still came to the factory every day but no longer took part in its management, and gave advice only when I asked for it. He was seventy-three, and never recovered from the shock of Father's death. He lived in the past. The petrol engine which was replacing the horse, the miracle of radio waves carrying music and the human voice over a thousand miles, the glamour of artificial silk, and all the other achievements of the new age of which I felt so proud and which seemed to give me the right to feel a little sorry for the generation before me as out of touch and old-fashioned, meant nothing to him any more. Without Father to enthuse about it, progress had lost its purpose.

In June he died, and before he closed his eyes for ever asked with a fading voice if the firm was all right and how large its reserves were. I often wish I had told him 'Ten million' or any other large sum to reassure him, but I felt one had to be truthful to a dying man and refrained from mentioning a figure, replying that the value of our reserves depended on trading conditions.

Father's and Grandfather's probates were surprisingly simple. Their wills had been drafted by Dr Zuckermann, the ablest lawyer in Eger. They mentioned no figures and were such short and seemingly vague documents that I was afraid the authorities would not accept them without a detailed examination of the estates. But I was wrong. Dr Zuckermann, who seemed pleased to see the large notebook I brought to our meetings in which I recorded in shorthand every word he said, asked me to have complete confidence in him and do exactly as he directed. I never experienced a smoother, more efficiently conducted procedure. Mother inherited the villa we lived in, Rolf, Ingo, Silvia and I a quarter each of the business assets with the obligation to keep Mother and Grandmother. The three brothers were to become equal partners in the firm, and while Rolf and Ingo were minors I was to manage the enterprise. Silvia's share was to be paid out in cash over a number of years. For some special legal reason I never fully comprehended the death duty on both estates, if I remember correctly, came to less than 100,000 kronen, and I gladly paid Dr Zuckermann's substantial fee.

My taking over the firm's management stirred the stamp duty office into renewed action. Ober-Finanzrat Dr Brückner was not prepared to wait any longer for payment of the duty we owed in respect of the purchase of Leibitschgrund. Determined to follow Father's line, I ignored the demand and consulted Uncle Gustav. He introduced me to Dr Scholle, an eminent tax lawyer at Prague who, so he assured me, had excellent connections in the highest places. Had Father come to him at the start, said the lawyer, he could have brought influence to bear, but now the matter could no longer be settled by private arrangement. Too many officials knew about it. All he could do was to persuade Dr Brückner to refer the case to the district court and put me in the witness box to save his face, but he warned me not to be too optimistic. The court was not likely to reduce Dr Brückner's demand very much: it might even increase it.

The case was heard in the ancient court room of the old castle at Wildstein. The thick walls, tiny windows and vaulted ceiling conveyed the atmosphere of a dungeon rather than a court of justice. I stated under oath that we had paid not more than $2\frac{3}{4}$ million kronen for Leibitschgrund, while the tax officials claimed that their evidence, though not conclusive, indicated a purchase price of more than 10 million. Wagging his finger at me, the judge threatened to have me locked up if I was not telling the truth. I retorted that he had not the power to send an innocent man to prison, whereupon the old man peered at me through his brass-rimmed spectacles and snapped, 'Don't be so cheeky, young man. Plenty of innocent men have sat in jail down the ages! Will you compromise at 7 million kronen?'

I looked at the iron bars in front of the little windows. 'In view of what you have just said,' I replied, 'it would appear that I have no choice.' To my surprise he shook my hand as I left, and with the faintest trace of a smile wished me well.

The stamp duty amounted to 8 per cent of the purchase price. I had committed Adolf Pasold & Sohn to the payment of 560,000 kronen, whereas the correct figure should have been 220,000 kronen. Could I have done better by serving a term in jail? Not that I fancied the idea, but I could not afford the time. Too many other urgent problems needed my attention, and I hoped that Father would have understood and approved of my compromise.

And now comes the best part of the story. Three weeks after the court session a young official brought the demand note. Since it was for such a large amount, he insisted on handing it to me personally and made me sign for it. I glanced at the paper. It requested payment of 56,000 kronen, certainly a very large sum in the eyes of the young official, but not what I had expected. Could it be that somebody somewhere along the line had forgotten a nought? It seemed too good to be true. Hiding my surprise, I promised remittance without delay. The man left satisfied, and I took the note to Albert Schreiner, our chief book-keeper.

'Let's not get too excited just yet,' I laughed. 'They're sure to discover their mistake before long.'

'I am afraid they will,' replied Schreiner, scratching his head. Expecting that we should have to pay duty on 10 million, we had created a reserve of 800,000 kronen in the books and in the balance sheet we gave the tax authorities. If we now cancelled the reserve, questions were bound to be asked.

'Don't cancel the reserve,' I suggested. 'Let's pretend to be stupid. As good citizens we believe in the infallibility of the Czechoslovak civil service. It's not our job to check the accuracy of its calculations. Treat the 56,000 as part payment.'

'And carry the balance of 744,000 forward in the books for ever?'

'Not for ever,' I replied. 'Only for five years—unless, of course, the authorities demand further instalments before their claim expires.'

For the next few years we lived in constant fear lest some inspector should find the missing nought, and my heart beat faster whenever I saw an excise man in our waiting room, but incredible as it may seem the stamp duty office never discovered its mistake, and the Inland Revenue never queried the reserve we showed in our annual balance sheets. After five years we wrote it off, kept our fingers crossed and heard no more. How I wished that Father could have shared the happy ending of this wretched affair.

Father used to devote more than half his time to the management and modernisation of Leibitschgrund, but business had now become so difficult that my presence was required at Fleissen. I could hardly devote two afternoons a week to the spinning mills, and left their day-to-day administration in the hands of Direktor Walsch. He knew his job and was not afraid of hard work, but his handling of labour left much to be desired. Had it not been for the general recession in trade and the fear of unemployment we might have had trouble with the unions several times. And I had to intervene not only in labour disputes. A side of human relations that was quite new to me demanded my attention. Most of the workpeople at Leibitschgrund lived in the firm's houses, and I had not been aware of the many family and matrimonial problems that arose in such a closely knit and comparatively isolated community. The inhabitants had been accustomed to take their grievances to Father, but they were not prepared to discuss the intimate details of their private lives with Direktor Walsch. I was their ultimate employer and landlord, and now they brought their troubles to me. They would wait for me in the evening when I was getting ready to return to Fleissen. I did my best, but felt acutely conscious of my incompetence. To mediate between men and women twice my age was at times very embarrassing. How grateful I was to be spared responsibility for the home life and connubial bliss of our employees at Fleissen!

During the first half of the year it looked as if the price of American middling cotton would settle down at around fifteen cents a pound, but in June it began to slide again and continued to fall until in September it touched ten cents, the lowest in twenty years. Not since before the war had cotton been so cheap, yet we had to take in and spin consignment after consignment at an average price of seventeen cents.

And as cotton prices fell the recession worsened. Traders everywhere hesitated to place orders and delayed paying for the merchandise they had received. Banks refused to give overdrafts and called in the loans they had made. Financially weak manufacturers sold off their stocks below cost in order to get money with which to pay their weekly wages. This unsettled the market still further. The public demanded cheaper goods. Merchants tried to get out of their high-priced commitments. Every dozen that was not delivered on time was cancelled. Every delivery a customer could fault was returned. The greatest problem was now to secure enough business to keep our machines turning, which involved me in much hurried travelling.

While I tried to be everywhere at once, Rolf concentrated on economy measures in the factories. Thrift came naturally to the people of Bohemia. They rarely wasted anything in prosperous times, but now they were doubly careful. They knew that their jobs, the employment of the whole enterprise depended on good housekeeping and conscientious hard work. Not a needle, not a yard of thread, not a sheet of wrapping paper was wasted; no letter was sent if a postcard would do, not an electric light was kept burning unnecessarily. Small in themselves, these savings added up. Similarly, in the aggregate, the hundreds of major and minor decisions taken on all levels every day made the difference between smooth or inefficient operation.

If ever we needed the help of an able administrator it was now, but I had

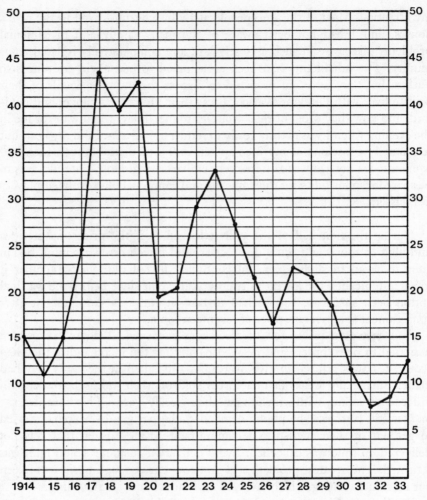

Average price of American cotton 'middling' in US cents per lb from 1914 to 1933. Continually falling raw material prices made business hazardous for the textile trade, and especially for spinners

to admit to myself that Direktor Engelhard was not the man. The job he had taken on was beyond him. He realised it himself and attempted to cover up his deficiences. Twice daily he stormed through every department of the factory, shouting at foremen and workpeople. For the rest of the time he buried himself in papers, pretended to study production figures which he carefully initialled, or signed letters. He had a mania for signing his name. It was dangerous to leave any unsigned mail on the desk, for if Engelhard saw it he would sign it whether he knew anything about the subject or not. This applied also to letters typed in English, although he could not read them.

Rolf considered Engelhard's monthly salary of 3,000 kronen a totally un-justifiable expense and wanted me to dismiss him, but this was easier said than done, for he had a contract. Unless Engelhard proved dishonest or grossly negligent there was nothing I could do. Then Engelhard blundered in a way that made me doubt his sanity. He placed an order for two million labels, I forget for what purpose, and reported proudly how clever he had been to get them at a specially favourable price, owing to the large quantity.

'But that's ten times more than we need!' I remonstrated.

'Exactly,' replied Engelhard triumphantly. 'But I didn't tell the printer that. Two million are cheaper than two hundred thousand—it's the mass production that does it. We simply throw the remaining one million eight hundred thousand away!'

I was speechless. Clearly he would have to go. How could we get rid of him? Was extreme stupidity a valid reason for dismissal? I would have to consult our lawyer, but first I had to undertake an urgent business journey. When I returned, Engelhard had gone. Without saying a word Rolf had made him hand in his notice simply by following him round the factory like a shadow, silently standing behind him when he sat at his desk browsing through his papers, looking over his shoulder while he signed letters, even waiting outside the toilet door while he retired for a few minutes, keeping an accurate log of the Direktor's activities. After a week of this treatment Engelhard's nerve broke and he asked to be released from his contract. We paid him a year's salary as compensation and parted friends.

By the end of the summer we had hardly any orders left and began to work short time at both Fleissen and Leibitschgrund. I walked through the village at night, counting the lighted windows of our competitors' factories. They also became fewer. We were now manufacturing mainly for stock. Anxiously our employees watched the warehouses filling up. They would not have worried so much had Father and Grandfather been alive: they had been through difficult times with them before, but how safe were their jobs with me, a twenty-four-year old, at the helm? The responsibility weighed heavily upon me, for I knew that there was now no alternative work for them any-where. Their and their families' livelihood depended on my ability to keep the factory going. I tempted the importers in Britain with special offers at reduced prices, sent telegrams to Jewin Crescent urging Finch to try harder, bombarded our agents abroad and at home with letters requesting extra efforts, and personally visited as many customers as time would permit, begging for orders and promising delivery by return. But the results were meagre, as our clients found it hard to reduce their own stock and were not in a mood to buy.

Only sweaters and cardigans continued to sell, and the demand for them almost exceeded our capacity. It was astonishing how popular the White Bear label had become in the short span of twelve months. Had the advertising campaign been so effective, or was it the style, quality and value of the merchandise that made the public buy? Certainly there was nothing on the home market to compare with it. Unfortunately only about a quarter of our knitting machines were capable of producing White Bear fleece fabric. They worked flat out in shifts, of course, together with the button sewers, buttonhole and binding machines in the sewing department, while most of our plant merely ticked over.

Like all the other knitting mills in the village, we were laid out to manufacture mainly Directoire knickers, and only large export orders could keep us adequately employed. We waited eagerly for the buyers from England, who came later than usual this year. The first was Mr Israel, who disappointed us by buying only half as much as we had expected, and I wondered whether my opening the office at Jewin Crescent was making him give his business to other suppliers. Fortunately an order from Peacock, which came by mail in response to one of my letters, made good the shortfall. We missed Singer's business. He had concentrated on somewhat higher-priced merchandise and been our largest customer for 644 quality. Matheson Burgess & Co., his successors, lacked drive and funds and lost most of the trade to the newcomer Louis Heldmaier. He was a cautious operator. Instead of placing large forward contracts he bought consignments of samples, and as he booked orders from his customers he passed them on to the manufacturers. We received a continuous stream of small orders from him, and although over the season they added up to a substantial quantity we were never sure what to expect, which made production planning difficult. We were not used to doing export business in this way.

But where was Mr Stern, the largest buyer of them all, the man whose order book and fountain pen controlled Fleissen's prosperity? Repeated rumours that he had been seen in the village proved false. The suspense mounted. When he arrived at last we were in for a shock. Instead of visiting us, he spent the whole day at Lehrmann's, from where he telephoned me to say he was too busy to see us on this occasion. He would be back in a fortnight and would call on us then. Meanwhile would I entrust our samples and prices to young Ratcliff, his twenty-two-year-old assistant. I was thunderstruck. What could have gone wrong? Again I thought of Jewin Crescent. Had Finch done something to upset our relationship with Stern? The thought raced through my brain. If Mr Stern was too busy during the day, could I possibly see him for a few minutes in the evening, I asked? Could I drive him to his hotel at Franzensbad, Eger or Asch? He thanked me but declined.

The Lehrmanns increased their production capacity by building yet another factory

Lehrmann's car was taking him to Marienbad and on to Prague, he explained. His voice sounded natural and friendly.

Perhaps there was a simple explanation. I could think of no valid reason why Mr Stern should not go to Prague in Lehrmann's car. And Marienbad lay on the direct route! Yet an inner voice told me that something out of the ordinary was going on, something that was not in our interest. To add to my fears, Grandmother's private information service brought the startling news that Stern was negotiating a deal with Lerhmann's for more than 150,000 dozen knickers. If this should prove true and the contract be signed it would be the largest ever placed with the Bohemian garment industry. Why should Stern contemplate such a huge commitment? Did he think the market had reached bottom and cotton prices were going to rise? How much more could he buy? Would there be any orders left for us, or would our employees have to find work at Lehrmann's?

I knew that Lehrmann's had also covered cotton for a year ahead, but they had been luckier than we. They had made their purchases later than Father, and instead of buying at firm prices had gambled on a falling market. This had saved them hundreds of thousands of kronen. They could therefore still make a profit if they sold their goods for less than it cost us to manufacture ours. It was hard to compete against them. If only I could have discussed the situation with someone, but Rolf was too young and Mother was mainly concerned that he and I should not kill ourselves with work and worry as Father had done. My uncles, the Geipels, were interested in nothing but hides and leather. Only my talks with Director Huder of the Böhmische Union Bank helped a little. He listened patiently and said:

'You both work hard, but like all young men you have to gain experience. The four Lehrmann brothers, on the other hand, are all in their forties and fifties. Accept that you have to consolidate and fall back in the race. For some years the gap must widen, but don't lose faith. Your time will come!'

A few days after Mr Stern had telephoned, Harry Millington called and wrote out a sizeable contract, but the price he beat me down to was so low that it hardly covered our overheads. I would not have accepted it had we not been desperately short of work and had I not been afraid of losing Stern's business. Again and again I checked our costings, the weight of our garments and the percentages of waste, implored our employees to be still more careful and pressed the dyers to reduce their charges. When Mr Stern came to see us two weeks later as he had promised I quoted prices which were far below our production costs, but the order he gave me came to a mere 10,000 dozen.

And now I shall digress a little to let two of Stern's ex-employees fill in some of the gaps. The first is Charles Davis, an old friend of mine, whom I met when he was a young salesman and who now lives in retirement. He has this to say:

'The Sterns came to England at the beginning of this century, I believe from Westphalia. At first they were commission agents, selling underwear for German manufacturers. During the 1914–18 war they made large profits importing similar goods on their own account from Japan, but Alfred Stern's great chance came after the war, when the British government sold off its surplus stores of American- and Canadian-made army underwear to the highest bidder. Alfred contracted for huge quantities, acquiring pure wool vests that had never been unpacked for as little as 5s a dozen. He resold them to wholesalers throughout the country. The market had been starved of such merchandise, and firms like S. & J. Watts of Manchester, Bell & Nicholson of Birmingham and Arthur's of Glasgow were eager to have them. Probably some of the best customers, offering to pay over the odds to secure extra supplies, were the Jewish traders in the East End of London. They paid 26s to 30s a dozen, 'a cut price, specially for my friends', according to Alfred, the

37 I declined Father's offer of a car in exchange for my Brough Superior

38 Rolf at the age of fourteen, having just won a hill climb on his 175 cc McEvoy

39 Left to right: Cousin Günther Geipel, Rolf and the author at Pörtschach, on the Wörthersee in southern Austria, where we spent some of our happiest holidays in the mid-'30s

40 The leather factory of our uncles, the Geipels, at Fleissen, and, *inset*, their house in Vienna. From the firm's letter head

42 Friedl's knitwear factory

43 The school at Fleissen, built 1910

41 Our cousins Udo and Heinz Geipel as lieutenants in the Czechoslovak army. Military service was compulsory, and they spent two years in the crack 28th regiment at Prague

44 The Goldene Stern, whe Fleissen's manufacturers met in t evening for a chat and a glass of be

The spinning machinery at Werdau was dismantled and dispatched to Leibitschgrund

ADOLF PÄSOLD & SOHN
WIRKWARENFABRIKEN
FLEISSEN
Telephon Nr. 4

White Bear
TRADE MARK

46 The famous sweater, made from yarn spun at Leibitschgrund

47 Leibitschgrund had been sadly neglected by the previous owners. We modernised the spinning mill and improved the employees' houses

48 Prague, the capital of Czechoslovakia, seat of the government and Ministries

49 Unfortunately it was mostly unpleasant business that took us to Prague, and we were seldom in mood to admire the beauty of the city

Eger, railway and shopping centre,
as the seat of the district departments
the government administration for
western part of the Egerland

The court of justice and the jail were
the old castle at Wildstein. The ap-
oach to it was sometimes referred to
the 'bridge of sighs'

Rundwirkmaschinen-Fabrik

Gebrüder Haaga

Gesellschaft mit beschränkter Haftung

GRÜNDUNG 1884

Stuttgart

BÖHEIM-STRASSE 42-44

Telegr.-Adr.: Fouquet Rottenburgneckar • • Fernspr.: S A. 30
Girokonto: Deutsche Bank u. Disconto-Ges. Zweigst Cannstatt
Postscheck-Konto: Stuttgart Nr. 426.

Fouquet & Frauz A.G.

FABRIK FuF ZEICHEN

*Älteste
Rundwirkmaschinen-Fabrik
Deutschlands*

Rottenburg
am Neckar.

GEGRÜNDET 1874.
FERNSPRECHER: REUTLINGEN S. A. 3157.
DRAHTANSCHRIFT: **ARBACH REUTLINGEN.**
POSTSCHECK-KONTO: STUTTGART NR.2987.

BANK-VERBINDUNGEN:
\\ REICHSBANK - GIRO - KO
DEUTSCHE BANK u. DISCONTO-GESEL
FILIALE REUTLINGEN

Maschinenfabrik Arbach G.m.b.H. G. Grözinge

REUTLINGEN,
WÜRTTEMBERG

TELEGRAMMADRESSE:
GESSNERWERK AUESACHSEN
FERNSPRECHER:
Nr. 3245, 3246, 3247.
CODES: PRIVAT, ABC 5th EDITION
MOSSE + MARCONI

ERNST GESSNER, AKTIENGESELLSCHAF
TEXTILMASCHINENFABRIK

Aue i.Sa.,

52 Letter heads illustrated with pictures of factories reflect the stability of bygone days. Adolf Pasold
Sohn as well as Pasolds Ltd regularly purchased machinery from these engineering firms in German

The town hall at Reichenberg, in the north of Bohemia. Our application for a licence to export machinery to England was supported by the Textile Manufacturers' Federation, whose headquarters re at Reichenberg

54 Our factory building at Langley nearing completion

55 On 12 June 1932 our team of young 'experts' from Fleissen crossed the Channel to erect the machinery at Langley and begin training local labour. Left to right, top row: Gustav Passler, Ernst Schreiner, Franz Bergmann, Alfred Passler; in the middle, Franz Pöllmann; bottom row: Rolf Pasold, the author, Georg Wollner

56 Alfred C. Hurst, MBE, London agent

57 G. L. Watkinson, of the Bo later Sir Laurence Watkinson

salesman. His prosperity grew, his reputation was never tainted, and when I joined Nichol Square in 1923 he had over half a million pounds in the bank.

'To my mind he was an adventurer at heart who played for very high stakes, a showman abounding with an energy and enthusiasm that was catching, a generous and outstandingly able man, but not always a good judge of character. He was often taken advantage of by unscrupulous people with schemes that failed.'

My second informant is 'young' Ratcliff, whom I was fortunate to meet again after an interval of almost forty years. We spent a pleasant evening reminiscing.

Ratcliff recalled that Stern's business ran into difficulties in 1930. Expenses were high and competition was keen. Prices had been steadily declining over the past year or two while Alfred Stern, the optimist, entered into vast forward commitments, and his warehouses were bulging with merchandise in anticipation of the dreaded import duties the protectionists were clamouring for and the free-traders were fighting against. His investment in Klinger's of Edmonton, probably Britain's largest rayon hose manufacturers, was frozen. The knitting mill at Huntingdon, which he owned, operated at a loss. Misguidedly he had taken a financial stake in the development of the Maratti circular warp loom, an intriguing but unsuccessful invention, and he had been talked into buying a cotton plantation in Abyssinia. His resources were overstretched, and his indebtedness to the bank was substantial. He now favoured suppliers who gave credit.

Lehrmann's very ably took advantage of this situation. Using his official position as District Governor of Marienbad, Dr Adolf Lehrmann took Alfred Stern to Prague and introduced him to his old friend Dr Beneš, the leading statesman of Czechoslovakia. It was a clever move that ingratiated him with both men and greatly benefited his firm. The business tycoon from London and the Minister were favourably impressed with each other, and once again Beneš used his influence with the Živnostenská Banka to secure quite exceptional overdraft facilities for the purpose of financing Lehrmann's exports to Britain. It was arranged that Stern, who had always paid by cheque, would henceforth settle his liabilities with three- or even six-month bills. Stern undertook to buy the whole of Lehrmann's available output, and Lehrmann undertook to supply no one in Britain besides Stern.

This caused Millington's, who were Stern's most serious rivals, to increase their purchases from us. I would have much preferred to deal with Mr Stern, but, knowing nothing of his special arrangement with Lehrmann, I declined to grant extended credit. However badly we needed orders I insisted on prompt payment by cheque, a principle inherited from Grandfather which proved its worth, as we shall see. Lehrmann's prices were lower than ours but our merchandise was superior. Some of Stern's clients demanded it, threatening to take their custom to Millington's if need be. This was the reason why Stern gave us the order for those 10,000 dozen and why he continued to give us business, albeit on a much reduced scale. He was now fully committed to Lehrmann's. I had, of course, no notion of all this at the time.

Our order book was far from healthy, but we now had enough work to keep all our people fully employed for at least six weeks, which enabled me to make a long-overdue business journey to Scandinavia and England. My first port of call was Copenhagen, where, accompanied by Fritz Larsen, our Danish agent, I made the round of the wholesalers and stores, selling lightweight knickers and cotton stockinette bathing suits with and without skirts, for spring delivery. The quantities were not large but I was grateful for even the smallest order. Every dozen helped to keep the factory going.

The ferry took me to Malmö, where I met Jacob Müller. After making a few calls locally we proceeded to Göteborg and then to Boras, the centre of the Swedish knitting industry. To judge by the size of the factories I saw there, Fleissen had little to worry about. Continuing our journey we visited Jonköping, Linköping and Norrköping, by train, of course, for commercial travellers had not yet discovered or could not afford motor cars. Taxis were not always available, and lugging my heavy case of samples gave me a healthy appetite which made the famous Swedish *smörgasbord* taste truly delicious.

We booked an order from nearly every firm we visited, and my spirits rose. Müller was a superb salesman who knew his customers. Treating one with deference, joking with another, driving a hard bargain here, apologising, explaining and persuading there, he invariably won not only a contract but also the buyers' thanks and future goodwill. It was sheer joy to watch this virtuoso. How I wished I had his ease of manner, quick retort and thick skin. Having done a good deal of selling these past years, I fancied myself as a salesman, but now I realised that selling was a vocation and I would always remain an amateur.

Six months ahead of the Danes, the Swedes were already placing orders for next autumn. I could see that 'fleecies' had lost much of their popularity. There was now a growing demand for knickers made from two layers of summer-weight fabric in contrasting colours, a type of garment no other country was wealthy enough to buy. Müller exploited my presence to the full. It was not often that a manufacturer from such an outlandish place as Czechoslovakia came to call on his customers personally. I had to clarify technical points that mystified him and some of the buyers, listen to complaints and suggestions and, most important, make price concessions which he on his own had no power to grant. The world depression was casting its shadow over Scandinavia too. Generally speaking, the Swedes did not seem to worry too much, and still bought freely, but they used the financial crisis as a means of forcing my prices down, and I was in no position to refuse business. Our workpeople expected me to bring back a bag full of orders. Employment was more important than profits just now. I spent the last three days of my visit in Stockholm, where I landed two substantial contracts, one with Ahlen & Holm, the other with Kooperativa Förbundet. Then I made the long and tedious journey to England.

The sun shone and there was a nip in the autumn air as I surfaced from Moorgate tube station at 8 a.m. It was good to be back among the bustle and the familiar smells of the City. Doors were being unlocked and nameplates polished. I felt in unison with the army of determined-looking men with rolled umbrellas and the neatly dressed but mostly plain girls hurrying towards their desks, ledgers, telephones and typewriters. Turning into Jewin Crescent, the little brass plate with my own name on it greeted me. 'Welcome home,' it seemed to say. With my handkerchief I wiped a smudge off its shiny surface, collected the small bundle of mail from the shelf inside the entrance, ran up the narrow stairs to the first floor, two steps at a time, and let myself in.

The small office was tidy and clean. On the counter in the showroom lay our ticketed samples in a neat row. To my surprise the stock room was almost empty. Finch must have made substantial sales during the past ten days, for the list I compiled just before my departure from Fleissen indicated a stock of over 500 dozen. Contentedly I settled down to read the mail. There were two small cheques, an advice note from the forwarding agents, an invoice from Fleissen, a telephone account and a letter from the Houndsditch Warehouse Co. asking me to call on Mr Rose, the underwear buyer, to discuss a 200 dozen order. My visit had started well! To bring myself up to date I studied the correspondence files. Here and there a letter seemed to be missing, but business appeared to be running smoothly and there was no sign of trouble anywhere.

At a quarter past nine the typist arrived—rather late, I thought, and made a note to speak to Finch about it. She was new, she explained; Mr Finch had engaged her only two weeks ago.

Where was Finch? I had written to let him know I was coming and expected to find him at the office. The girl confirmed that he had received my letter, but she had not seen him since, and if she might just mention it, her wages for the week had not been paid.

'Perhaps he's ill, ' I said. 'Find his address, and if he doesn't arrive within half an hour, phone his landlady. Meanwhile I'll go and see the Hounds-ditch Warehouse Company. I can only stay in London for a few days, and time is valuable.'

'You're not the Mr Pasold I know,' said Mr Rose, the buyer, when I told him I had come in response to his letter. 'Are you his brother?'

'The gentleman who normally calls on you is Mr Finch. I apologise if there is some mistake,' I said. It was always wise to put a buyer in a friendly mood by apologising to him for something or other.

'He comes here frequently,' said Mr Rose. 'A balding young man in his early twenties. Always took him to be Mr Pasold! He never told me his name was Finch.'

Mr Rose wanted 6d per dozen off the price, which I refused to concede. After some bargaining we agreed on 4d, and he wrote out the order. On my way back to Jewin Crescent I thought about Finch and his pretending to be Pasold. I would have to tell him very firmly not to mislead customers. The deception, however harmless it might appear to him, must cease forthwith.

A more unpleasant surprise awaited me at the office. The girl had tele-phoned Finch's landlady and been told that he had packed his things and dis-appeared. She did not know where he had gone. Would we pay the rent he owed her?

It seemed unlikely that Finch intended to come to work. The petty cash box was empty. I scanned the books. They looked tidy and, apart from the missing entries for the past ten days, were up to date. But I wondered about the large amount that was outstanding. Our customers did not usually keep us waiting for payment. I phoned Clarkson & Hyde, the auditors, and asked them to help me assess the situation. For the next few days one of their accountants carefully checked all the entries, compared them with the in-voices and payments we had received, obtained a statement from the bank and ascertained from our customers what amounts they still owed us. Whilst he was thus engaged I continued with my business calls. Worried as I was, I had to go on selling because the factory needed orders.

Before the investigation was completed one of the partners of Clarkson & Hyde came to see me. It appeared that over £600 was missing, and he feared that Finch had misappropriated the money. More time was needed, however, to determine the exact amount that was involved.

So Finch was a thief! I was shocked that he should have taken advantage of my involuntary absence due to Father's death to rob me. The scoundrel must not be allowed to make good his get-away while the accountants deter-mined the exact amount of the deficiency. The police had to be put on to him at once. Within half an hour I was sitting opposite an officer at Moor Lane police station and telling my distressing story. The man in blue took it down and then, to my surprise and disappointment, suggested that I should find Finch, engage a lawyer and let him prosecute.

Engage a lawyer? But this was a criminal case, not a civil one! There was little hope of recovering anything from Finch even if I found him. Much as I wanted him to go to jail, I was determined not to throw good money after bad. Surely it was for the police to catch criminals and bring them to justice! In any case I had no time to play Sherlock Holmes. I was expected in Czechoslovakia, where urgent work waited for me.

The officer sympathised. Things were not as simple as I seemed to think. Being a foreigner, I clearly did not understand that the police had to abide by certain regulations. However, they would keep a look out for this man Finch.

Disillusioned, I returned to Jewin Crescent to make up my mind. I wanted to stay and fight, but the factories at Fleissen and Leibitschgrund had priority. All my time and strength were required to keep them going. Direktor Huder's advice to consolidate was right, I thought. I had no choice but to let Finch go, and write off my losses. To find a new manager in his place and start all over again would demand more of me than I could give. The young enterprise that meant so much to me had to be liquidated. It seemed that I was not meant ever to live in England. Sad and lonely, I drafted a letter to our customers, telling them that the London office was being closed and that all business would in future be conducted from Fleissen.

After disposing of the remaining stocks and samples, making arrangements for the sale of the furniture and putting the premises in the hands of the estate agents, I completed my business calls and took every order I could get, almost irrespective of price. Then I did two days' hard selling with Odewald in Amsterdam and returned home.

In due course Clarkson & Hyde made a full report. Finch had embezzled altogether some £900. It transpired that he had been backing horses and using the petty cash to pay for his losses. When this no longer sufficed he embarked on a more ambitious scheme to defraud me. Pretending to be Mr Pasold, he opened an account with the Yorkshire Penny Bank in Cheapside, signed my name and gave business houses who knew me as references. Having thus deceived the manager, he proceeded to pay customers' cheques into this account and then drew the money out for his own purposes. As expected, we heard no more of the young man and never recovered a penny, but five years later, in March 1935, the police phoned to enquire whether we knew his whereabouts. He had since stolen from another firm, and they were issuing a warrant for his arrest. Unfortunately we could not help them, but I hope he was caught and got the punishment he deserved.

I did not feel proud of my first year at the helm of the firm. Whilst it was not my fault that we were over-bought in cotton and that the price had fallen, I reproached myself for losing the bulk of Stern's business to Lehrmann's. And had I kept an eye on Finch this latest calamity would not have happened. Could Adolf Pasold & Sohn sustain such losses for long? The responsibility for the survival and success of the family firm was mine, and it lay heavily on my young shoulders. Was I man enough to steer the battered ship safely through the tempest? How I missed Father's and Grandfather's guiding hand.

When Schreiner and I prepared the balance sheet for this disastrous year I fully expected it to show a substantial loss, but to my great surprise and relief we broke even, probably owing to the profits we had made on the rapidly growing sales of our White Bear sweaters and waistcoats.

20

STERLING
DEVALUED
1931

CZECHOSLOVAKIA WAS HIT hard by the world depression. The exports on which her industries largely depended fell dramatically. By the end of 1930 more than 10 per cent of the country's organised labour force was out of work, and during the following two years the officially recorded unemployment figure rose to a frightening 30 per cent. But this was by no means the true total, since it omitted the vast number of workers who did not belong to a trade union. Only union members were recorded: the rest were not entitled to unemployment benefit, although 80 per cent of the money was provided by the taxpayer and a mere 20 per cent came from union subscriptions. The government subsidised the unions so heavily for political reasons.

Unemployment figures, counting trade union members only

		Approx %
December 1930	239,000	10
January 1931	310,000	12½
February 1931	344,000	13½
December 1931	486,000	20
March 1932	634,000	25
December 1932	750,000	30

Total exports (kronen)

1928	21,185,000,000
1929	20,485,000,000
1930	17,460,000,000
1931	13,118,000,000
1932	7,399,000,000

Adolf Pasold & Sohn's exports (kronen)

1928	15,071,367·67
1929	15,488,295·48
1930	16,190,674·36
1931	10,974,649·83
1932	3,605,812·00

Bankruptcies

1928	1929	1930	1931	1932
518	645	886	1,052	1,416

We were now only in the early months of 1931. The worst was still to come. As trade slowed down, goods in shops and warehouses remained on the shelves unsold and tills stayed empty. Banks reduced overdraft facilities, retailers and wholesalers cut down their orders or refused to accept delivery. Prices fell and the number of bankruptcies rose. Shift working came to an end almost everywhere. Fleissen, whose blazing lights had for so long been beacons of prosperity, now lay in darkness. Only the lonely private offices remained lit into the small hours of the morning, for, as always, the slower the wheels turned the harder the owner worked and the greater were his worries.

Hardly any of Fleissen's workpeople were union members. They had nothing but their modest savings and their cabbage patches to fall back on if they lost their jobs. Yet even now they had more faith in their employers than in shop stewards. The strong family spirit prevailed. Freedom from union interference, the failure of a few agitators to drive a wedge between employers and employed, enabled each firm to use its own initiative and find its individual means of salvation. Our industry kept going. Mass unemployment as experienced in many parts of the country never came to our corner of western Bohemia.

I cannot say whether that winter was really as cold and long as I remember, or whether it only seemed so to me, and to the workpeople who, on short time and concerned about their jobs, came daily from the surrounding hamlets and villages, laboriously wading through the snow on foot. It lay two feet deep in the woods, on the fields and in our garden. Exposed stretches of the road between Fleissen and Leibitschgrund were closed by snowdrifts higher than a horse, and the few men wrapped in old coats and scarves, whose job it was to dig a passage through them with hand shovels, had a well nigh impossible task. So had Wolf, the driver of our five-ton diesel lorry, who daily brought a load of cases of yarn and took bales of raw cotton and waste clippings back to the spinning mill. He was a giant of a man, an old hand at ploughing through snow with heavy lorries. Accompanied by Klier, another heavyweight, and equipped with chains, spades and a sackful of sand, he sometimes took all day to battle seven miles each way through the blizzard.

Leibitschgrund was all but cut off from the outside world. Nestling in the frozen valley, surrounded by pine forest, the mills and houses lay under a mantle of glistening white powder snow, and icicles several feet long hung in irregular rows from their roofs. Coming upon it out of the wintry woods the place looked like a picture on a Christmas card, and its beauty never failed to make me forget, for a few happy moments, the worrying business that brought me there. I chose days for my visits when it was not snowing or blowing. Even so, I repeatedly stuck in snowdrifts and my car had to be dug out. Sometimes I went with the lorry and stayed the night with Direktor Walsch. We spent the evening poring over graphs and figures which told of the rapidly filling yarn store. It seemed uncanny how every department achieved production records just when demand was lowest. Leibitschgrund was now spinning more than our factory at Fleissen consumed, and we had to curtail output. Could we keep the spindles turning by selling yarn to our competitors? Never an easy task, it was doubly difficult now when they too were on short time and spinners all round were fighting for diminishing orders. By perseverance and by cutting prices we secured some small business from underwear manufacturers at Fleissen and Asch. A cold winter had one compensation, especially if it came early. It was good for the underwear trade. Frost in November and snow three weeks before Christmas brought a welcome spate of repeat business for fleecy knickers, vests, pants, combinations, sweaters and cardigans. These rush orders kept some of our machines going until the end of January.

Time and again we tendered for government work. Czechoslovakia's large army, gendarmerie, State police and the uniformed customs officials guarding her 4,000-kilometre frontier had to be clothed, but in spite of all our efforts we failed to secure a single contract. It was not that Hlawatsh and Horowitz, our hardworking agents at Prague and Brünn, lacked the necessary 'contacts' in the Ministries, but it seemed our factories were in the wrong part of the country. The Czech purchasing departments preferred to obtain their supplies from firms located in predominantly Czech-speaking districts.

To supplement the reduced earnings of our people we let the men shovel snow, paint ceilings and walls, mend floors and clean idle machinery. The girls were put on sorting waste, re-winding yarn, mending and other useful jobs, sharing them out as fairly as we could. Time and again I was afraid we might have to shut down altogether, but thanks to the steady demand for White Bear sweaters and cardigans the worst never happened, and we scraped through this dreadful period without dismissing any of our employees.

Most firms were on short time; only Lehrmann's still worked to capacity. Stern's huge, long-term contracts took up two thirds of their total output. They were thus in a strong position, and by virtue of their favourable cotton purchases and own dyehouse were able to undercut us in every market, ruining the price of fleecy knickers both in Holland and at home.

Unfortunately, like the whole of Fleissen's knitting industry, we depended on the knicker trade for full employment. Our factory was not laid out to mass-produce much else. The increasing orders for our White Bear merchandise, delighted as we were with them, caused major complications. They consumed marl yarns, which we had to buy from other spinners, while our own spinning machines were underemployed. Nor could we rectify the imbalance in our knitting plant. With great trouble we converted a number of single-chaineuse circulars to produce the double-chaineuse fabric from which the sweaters and cardigans were made, and kept them running day and night. Meanwhile the remainder of our knitting department had not enough work to operate even a single shift fully.

Had I been able to overcome the technical difficulties I would have converted a larger part of our plant to the production of White Bear garments. It was profitable business. Our customers were pleased with the goods and did not haggle over price—a welcome change. Stimulated by a few thousand showcards and an occasional advertisement, demand ran ahead of our limited supply. If only we could think up some equally popular product made of other than double-chaineuse fabric to employ the many circulars that stood idle. Something with long or complicated seams to provide work for the largest possible number of sewing machinists. Something that could be exported, preferably to England, the only country whose businessmen placed really large orders.

We tried fancy bathing suits cut from two or three different pieces of cotton stockinette in contrasting colours, with appliqué work and embroidery. Perhaps sports shirts in 'Köper', a light piqué fabric, might sell. They were cheaper than woven ones. The cutting and sewing of collars presented difficulties. Our girls were not used to such accurate work, but in the end they mastered it, and the shirts looked attractive. We made samples in bright yellow, red and blue. We also tried men's and boy's track suits, or training suits, as they were called in Bohemia, of navy blue fleecy fabric in 644 quality. The suit consisted of a sweater with zip front and slip-on trousers with elastic waist and ankles. We even experimented with a ladies' lightweight jumper made of marl stockinette. Not that we thought it would sell, but it added a little variety to the range. I packed this collection of novelties in my sample bag and set forth on yet another journey to Amsterdam and London, where I met with indifferent success. Knickers still sold best, but at prices which hardly covered our costs. Sports shirts and bathing suits aroused moderate interest, and I succeeded in booking several trial orders, which pleased me. But I had no luck with any of the other lines. Nobody wanted track suits, and few buyers gave the marl jumper a second look.

Before my return to Fleissen I saw Salo Rand, a friend who hailed from Gablonz in Czechoslovakia, an importer of imitation jewellery. His office was in Fore Street, in the heart of London's textile area. I asked if I might leave my samples with him until my next visit to London. Salo was happy to oblige. If I was thinking of appointing an agent now that Finch had flown he would recommend Mr Hurst on the floor above. It could be worth my while meeting him.

I declined, but Salo insisted. Mr Hurst was a friend of his. I ought to meet him, if only to look at his daughter, the prettiest girl in the City of London. And he dragged me upstairs. Peggy Hurst opened the door. She really was a strikingly attractive young woman. I liked her laughing blue eyes and her slim, graceful figure, and felt sorry when she immediately withdrew to a small inner office, leaving us alone with her father, a nervy little man of about fifty with a nose that seemed too large for his face. He represented two German manufacturers, one of whom made gloves, the other stockings. They took up only part of his time, he explained. An agency like ours was just what he wanted. He knew every buyer in the trade. Would I give him a chance to prove how well he could sell?

I told him that I visited England three or four times a year and saw customers myself. We needed no agent. Our prices were too keen to allow for a commission. But A. C. Hurst was not to be put off. He could sell more than I, he argued, and at higher prices, so that his 5 per cent commission would in fact be paid by the customer. Why would I not let him try? What could I lose by it? At that crucial moment Peggy brought us each a cup of tea.

'All right,' I said. 'I'll give you the agency for marl jumpers, but I handle all the other merchandise myself.'

Rewarded by a smile from Peggy and a slap on the back from Salo, I retreated with a somewhat guilty conscience, for I knew that marl jumpers were unsaleable. I would not need the sample any more, and gave it to Hurst only to shake him off. In the evening I departed for home and thought no more about the incident.

Then something unexpected happened. Mr Hurst sent an order for marl jumpers from Foster Porter, followed at short intervals by others from Bradbury Greatorex, Sharp Perrin, Pawson & Leaf's, the Fore Street Warehouse Co., Cook Son and a number of other well known firms. Their orders varied between twenty-five and 100 dozen. Within the span of about four weeks he booked just over a thousand dozen, all for speedy delivery. I was dumbfounded. How could he sell our jumpers to every leading wholesaler in London, and at 15s 6d a dozen, when I had failed to secure a single order at 14s 6d?

I found out on my next visit. It was Peggy who got the orders. The sample I had left with Mr Hurst just fitted her, and she wore it when calling on outerwear and fashion buyers, carrying the shade card in her handbag. She had grown up with her three sisters in a large house at Stanmore, in an atmosphere of tennis parties, golf, dogs and art. When her father lost all his money on the stock exchange and could no longer afford to pay a clerk and a traveller she

joined him, albeit reluctantly, in the City. A pretty girl, she hated the mono-
tony of the office until our jumper provided a challenge for her. With her
elegant figure, persuasive voice and impeccable manners, she knew how to
model and to sell. The cheap jersey looked like *haute-couture* on her, and the
strange, soft marl handled like wool. It created a stir on the golf course, she
told the wholesale buyers, who in those days were all men. When they heard
that the garment could be retailed for as little as 1s 11d they reached for their
order books. Success bred success. Peggy bubbled over with enthusiasm; her
large blue eyes became quite irresistible. Small wonder I could not compete
with her technique.

I remember walking along Cheapside with her, when she suddenly caught
my arm. 'Look,' she exclaimed. 'One of our jumpers. How nice it looks!'
And we had to follow the unsuspecting girl who wore it, until she was
swallowed up by Post Office Underground station. It may seem strange that
we should have felt so elated. The thousands of jumpers we delivered were
obviously being bought by the public, yet actually to see one in the street was
a fascinating experience. But neither Peggy nor her customers were satisfied
for very long with just one style, and demanded 'something new', which did
not please me at all. We had hardly got into our stride manufacturing this
type of jumper and looked forward to making it for years ahead, as we did
with our fleecy knickers.

'You may be able to mass-produce underwear,' Peggy protested, 'but not
fashion goods. People don't want to see the same old thing all the time!'

Were we expected to make a different style of jumper every season? I
could hardly believe she really meant it.

'Not one,' Peggy corrected me. 'Several. We need to vary the colours, have
three-tone marl, try fancy neckbands, wider welts, a tie in front or a bow at
the back, short sleeves and perhaps batwing shoulders.'

If this was fashion business we were crazy to undertake it. We neither had
the flair, nor could we continually adapt our machinery and production. Had
we not been so desperately short of work I would not have given the proposition another thought. Alas, we needed orders.

'In that case,' I suggested, 'you had better come to Fleissen yourself, show
us what you want and try to understand the limitations of our plant.'

Peggy's visit to Fleissen coincided with my sister's wedding. The sun shone
out of a blue sky when Silvia married Willie Nebel on 23 May 1931. My friend
Sonja sang solo in church. There was no microphone, but her beautiful alto
voice filled every part of the large building and brought tears to my eyes. I
felt very proud of her. She stayed with us for the weekend, and in order to give
her and Peggy a treat I decided to take the two girls to Karlsbad on Sunday.

We made an early start. It was a beautiful spring morning, the birds were singing and the three of us set forth in my open Buick, which Wollner, our chauffeur, had polished specially for the occasion. I chose the long route via Graslitz, through the dark pine forest and enchanting valleys of the Ore mountains, to show Peggy some of the beauties of western Bohemia. We had coffee at the village inn of Hirschenstand and lunch at historic St Joachimstal, whose silver mines had produced so much wealth in the sixteenth century. We promenaded along the Alte Wiese at Karlsbad, tasted the health-giving water of the Sprudel and danced from four to six on the splendid open-air floor of the Hotel Imperial. A short stop to admire the picturesque castle and the old town of Elbogen, perched high above the Eger river, and late dinner at Franzensbad concluded the programme. I enjoyed myself tremendously. The car ran well and everything went according to plan, only the girls seemed on edge. I did all I could to entertain them and went out of my way to show them the sights, but the harder I tried the more strained the atmosphere became, until they hardly spoke and only eyed each other coldly. Such a waste of a beautiful day, I thought. Women were strange creatures.

Peggy did her best to think up new jumper styles, but to my dismay I had to reject all her suggestions because they were too costly, and she became disheartened. It was out of the question to raise the price above 15s 6d a dozen. Cotton jumpers had to retail at no more than 1s 11d to sell in worthwhile quantities. There were wool ones on the market at the next popular price, which was 2s 6d. Then a traveller from an embroidery firm called, and among his large range of appliqué motifs we found an inexpensive swallow with outstretched wings. Sewn on the front of our jumper it looked very pretty. A thin line in the neckband, knitted in a colour to match, and—hey presto!— we had created the 'new look' which, we hoped, would help fill our order book for the coming season. Combined with a separate skirt cut and sewn from matching marl fabric, with elasticated waist, it made a set that could be sold at 31s a dozen wholesale, a smart jumper suit to retail at 3s 11d.

Thrilled to have shared in the development of the new line, Peggy hurried back to London, where her zeal was rewarded. Few buyers could resist giving her a contract. The bird suit, as it came to be called, proved one of our great successes for the autumn season.

Willie Nebel, my new brother-in-law, was thirty. His father had been an import–export merchant at Leipzig, his mother a Fischer from Asch. Orphaned at an early age, he was studying at the University of Graz in Austria when his uncle, Gustav Fischer, the well known textile industrialist, urged him to become his confidential secretary. Willie abandoned an academic career and went into business. I liked him, and we got on well together. Would he take the job of assistant manager at Leibitschgrund and live there with Silvia, I asked him? If Fleissen was a God-forsaken little place, Leibitschgrund had still less to commend it, apart from scenic beauty. In the winter it made one think of Siberia. To an educated, widely travelled young woman with interests as varied as Silvia's it must have appeared like exile. However, after consulting his young wife Willie accepted the challenge, and his presence at the mill soon took a heavy load off my shoulders.

I had now headed the firm for a year and a half, customers and suppliers we were getting used to the young man behind the large desk in the private office, and I was beginning to find my feet. It was, however, the memory of Father that influenced most of my actions. Before every important decision I consulted him in imaginary discussion. Daily I would ask myself how he would have dealt with this or that situation, and tried to do what he would have done. But when it came to buying or selling foreign currencies, an important feature of our business, I thought I knew better. We had to pay dollars for the raw cotton we imported. Our customers paid sterling, Dutch guilders and Scandinavian kronor for the goods we sent them, while the running expenses of our factories, our wages and our taxes had to be paid in Czech kronen. Exchange rates had kept pretty steady during the past few years, but since there were time lags of nine months or more between entering commitments and receiving or making payment Father always sold or bought currencies forward. We were manufacturers, not speculators, he used to say.

Selling sterling forward seemed to me to imply lack of confidence in London's financial integrity. This was preposterous. Surely Britain was incomparably sounder and more trustworthy than Czechoslovakia. I knew both countries and their people, I thought, and had not the slightest doubt that it was safer to hold pounds than Czech kronen. Let Lehrmann sell sterling forward, Pasold's would put their trust in the Bank of England. The fact that other businessmen did not seem to share my confidence made me all the more defiant.

Early in September I took a holiday, the first in two years. I motored with Helmut Amarotico and Heini Hofmann to Salzburg and Reichenhall, where we stayed at the Hotel Luisenbad, a favourite retreat of my parents. While we were there the papers printed headlines 'Mutiny in the British navy'. The front pages were filled with reports of naval ratings preventing the Atlantic Fleet from raising anchor at Invergordon, forcing the commander-in-chief to cancel the exercises and stay in port. With serious faces people discussed the dramatic news at street corners. The fleet! The most powerful weapon of the British Empire! Could it be true? My friend Heini was nine years older than I, and fancied himself as an expert on international affairs.

'England is in a bad way,' he said. 'She has 2,700,000 people out of work, and now the Navy revolts. How long can the Empire last?'

I felt like hitting him. Refusing to believe this ballyhoo, I dismissed the startling information as cheap sensationalism on the part of newspapers. Stunts like this increased circulation figures and enabled them to charge more for advertisements. The Navy was as sound as a bell, and so was the Empire, I declared. On Sunday 20 September we returned home.

On Monday morning the news broke that Britain had gone off the gold standard. As the telephone lines were jammed, I jumped into the car and drove to the Böhmische Union Bank at Asch to find out what it all meant. Direktor Huder confirmed my worst fears. I had never seen him so agitated.

'The Bank of England has suspended exchanging gold for pound notes. Sterling is no longer worth what it was,' he explained at intervals between hectic telephone conversations. 'Britain has mismanaged her affairs. You might compare her with a commercial enterprise that is unable to meet its obligations. The creditors will lose money.'

I was shattered. Britain not able to honour her commitments? We had some £10,000 owing to us by British firms, and I had not sold a single pound forward!

'How much do you think we shall lose?' I asked.

Huder shrugged his shoulders. 'Impossible to say. At the moment we have a buyer for £3,000 at a discount of 12 per cent. Would you like to sell? You may find the rate will deteriorate further if you wait, but if you do the deal and it recovers, don't blame me!'

After a moment's reflection I decided to sell and incur the loss of £360. Who could say what might happen during the next few days?

Nature seemed strangely out of tune with these momentous events as I drove back to Fleissen. The warm September sun lay over the countryside, the birds sang, and the farmers worked in the fields oblivious of the catastrophe that had fallen upon the world. Britain not able to maintain the value of her currency, I kept repeating to myself. Britain, in whose integrity I had implicit faith, the country I felt so proud of, that meant more to me than the rest of the universe put together! And not a single pound sold forward! What was going on in London? Would customers still take the goods they had ordered? There was no market for such quantities of knickers anywhere else. Would they pay higher prices? Did they expect us to bear part or all of the loss? In the evening came a cryptic telegram from Stern, reading 'Continue production'. This reassured us somewhat, but there was, of course, little else we could do. We could not send our workpeople home and close the factory. Next day, when I managed to contact Mr Hurst on the 'phone, he dissuaded me from paying a hurried visit to England. It would be premature and achieve nothing. 'Stay where you are,' he advised. 'We're as much in the dark as you are.'

On 2 October came the first ray of hope in the form of a letter from George Peacock, offering to share the fall in the value of the pound with us. He would pay 10 per cent more for all goods invoiced after 28 August. A generous offer, which I gladly accepted and which encouraged me to go to London to negotiate similar arrangements with other customers. But apart from Alfred Stern, my friends the Bairds at Wishaw and one or two more who were ready to compromise, I met with little success, especially from the smaller importers and the wholesalers. 'We placed our contracts in sterling,' they said, 'and a pound is a pound.' From their point of view they were, of course, right. The pledge of the Governor of the Bank of England printed on every note, 'I promise to pay the bearer on demand the sum of one pound', was meaningless.

It astounded me to see how little impact the devaluation made on the British scene. If something unpleasant had happened, the man in the street did not want to know. It could hardly be of such consequence as to affect him. There were still twenty shillings in the pound, and that was all he cared about. Let the foreigner panic. The football results seemed far more important. Nor were my better educated English friends greatly perturbed. Most of the world's trade was carried on in sterling, they claimed; why bother about Czech kronen? And I sensed that they felt just a little sorry for me. Was it supreme imperturbability or sheer ignorance, I wondered?

By contrast the *Pfundsturz*—the crash of the pound, as the devaluation was called—and its likely consequences remained for months the principal topic of conversation in Fleissen's factories and offices, in the inns, the villas of the rich and the cottages of the poor. My uncles, the Geipels, kept very quiet. Their hides came from India, and were paid for in sterling, while they exported their leather to America and received dollars. It was said that they made a fortune, although they would not admit it. Our competitors, especially the Lehrmanns, had prudently sold most of their sterling forward. Their combined losses were probably less than those sustained by Adolf Pasold & Sohn alone, which made our relative position all the worse. While I was licking my wounds they were mainly concerned with the future of exports to England, on which the livelihood of the village depended to such a large degree. Would the trade continue? In addition to the severe financial setback this worried me too, of course.

All told, the devaluation cost Adolf Pasold & Sohn well over £2,800, or almost half a million kronen. This may not seem much today, but in 1931, when our skilled workmen earned the equivalent of £1 in a fifty-hour week, it was a very substantial sum, a large part of a year's profits.

The deep impression made on me by these events never quite wore off. Not that I admired and loved Britain any the less, but I remained wary of her financial stability. For all her greatness, tradition and wealth, she was as subject to economic laws as other countries, even if the English did not understand or want to admit it. Her celebrated bankers, politicians and statesmen, notwithstanding their striped trousers and top hats, were as fallible and suspect as those of humbler lands. Of course, I kept these thoughts to myself and, especially at Fleissen, staunchly defended Britain and everything she did.

The sterling devaluation had repercussions on other currencies. Czechoslovakia, hurriedly and perhaps needlessly, reintroduced the defensive foreign exchange control measures which had been lifted in 1928. We were in the tow of France politically and the soundest country in Central Europe economically. Our krone was strong. The gold cover had risen to 48·8 per cent, which was greatly in excess of the statutory 30 per cent. Apart from complicating travel and the business of exporters and importers, these controls achieved little, I thought, unless one accepted form-filling by a multitude of clerks in industry, banks and government departments as a welcome alternative to unemployment. Restrictions were a challenge to every Czechoslovak, whether he spoke Czech, German, Slovak or Hungarian, to circumvent them. The tens of thousands of ordinary people crossing the long, wooded border every day took money backwards and forwards. Hotel porters and bartenders dealt in foreign exchange. The regular flow of dollars sent home by emigrants was diverted to the highest bidders in the black market. Businessmen established currency reserves abroad, the small army of consular and embassy officials made lucrative use of diplomatic bags, and there was not a bank manager worthy of the name who could not procure guilders, francs, marks, zloty or gold coins for good clients without permit. Although most transactions were small, in the aggregate they must have added up to a large turnover. But it was a two-way traffic, done for easy profits, and there was no flight from the krone.

Englishmen, on the other hand, could move their capital freely from one country to another without asking or telling anyone. The very idea of restrictions seemed preposterous to them, and few of my British friends believed me when I told them that I had to apply to the Czechoslovak National Bank for an allocation of foreign currency before I could travel abroad.

'Not allowed to take your money where you like?' they asked incredulously. 'How typically Central European!' Their comments did not please me. Surely they had little cause to be so smug. It was Britain who had got herself into financial difficulties and upset the equilibrium, not Czechoslovakia.

Britain's greatest problem was her growing army of unemployed. Her industries were clamouring for protection, and well before the end of 1931 it was a foregone conclusion among my business acquaintances that free trade was a thing of the past and that import duties would be imposed in the near future. On what kinds of goods, and at what rate, nobody could tell me.

Devaluation had made our exports to England difficult enough. If, in addition, an import duty of 5 per cent should be imposed we might still be able to trade, but some buyers expected 10 per cent and even 20 per cent. Should their predictions prove correct our business would come to an end. The consequences for Fleissen would be disastrous, but where would the British get those millions of dozens of fleecy knickers from? I gathered there were very few Terrot-type knitting machines in the country. Even on treble shifts they could supply only a fraction of the demand. British manufacturers did not have a reputation for being very efficient. How could they be, working with their archaic yards and inches, hundredweights and ounces, pounds, shillings and pence! I knew how cumbersome the system was in commerce, and it must be a much greater handicap in industry. Surely—the thought flashed through my mind—this would be the right time to establish a factory, an ultra-modern knitting mill, in England! But of course, any such scheme was out of the question. We could barely cope with Fleissen and Leibitschgrund. Still, the idea was exciting, and I discussed it with Willie and Rolf.

Then we heard that Fischer's of Asch had decided to manufacture in Britain. They were negotiating for the lease of an old factory at Edmonton, in the north of London. Direktor Wunderlich was to be in charge, and sales were to be handled by Heldmaier, the well known importer. That clinched the matter. If Fischer's could establish a plant in England so could we. They might get off to a flying start, but we would overtake them. It was clearly a mistake to rent an old building in a country that had so many old factories already. And Wunderlich was over forty. To hope that such an old man, however able, could manage the factory successfully when he could scarcely speak English was surely wishful thinking. Heldmaier would have the whip hand, and he was a merchant, not a manufacturer! We would build a factory, a modern, single-storey, north-light building, the type Father had always dreamed of. And we would manage it personally, Rolf and I between us. We would commute between Fleissen and England while Willie took complete charge of Leibitschgrund.

Mother was horrified when we told her of our plan. She pleaded with me that we already had far too much to do. Rolf was only seventeen, and other boys of his age were still at school. We ought to wait and see how Fischer's got on, and if they did well, in two years' time, we could look for a factory to rent. England would not disappear in the meantime.

But I was adamant. 'Trade doesn't stand still. Speed is essential. It's now or never,' I declared. 'And I don't want to rent a factory. I shall build one to suit our special requirements.'

Rolf was completely on my side, and so, to my delight, was Grandmother.

The old lady had tremendous spirit. In spite of her seventy-two years she was in the business all day and every day, and knew what went on not only in ours but in all the other knitwear factories at Fleissen.

'Go ahead,' she said. 'I have faith in you and Rolf. This is a venture the Lehrmanns won't have the courage to imitate. Not one of them can speak English!' And her eyes flashed. She must have been very beautiful when she was young.

'Your Father might still be with us if he had not worked himself to death,' Mother sighed. 'I could not restrain him from sacrificing his health for the business, and now I have failed to prevent his sons from doing the same. I can only pray for you. But if you have made up your minds to manufacture in England, then do it on a worthwhile scale. Don't waste your time starting with the ten knitting machines you talk about. Make it twenty. Double the size of the factory!' Mother was wonderful.

Two days later I left for London to discuss the project with Mr Hurst. I found him a very worried man. Afraid that tariffs would terminate his sales of foreign goods and ruin his livelihood, he was all in favour of manufacturing in England. His services were at my disposal. He would do anything to be of assistance, anything short of providing capital—for he was rather hard up, he confided. Should he begin by seeing estate agents about renting a factory at Leicester or Nottingham?

I had no intention of manufacturing in the Midlands, the traditional home of Britain's knitting industry, where the natives would, no doubt, want us to adopt their old-fashioned ways. 'Let's look for a twenty-acre site within an hour's journey of the City, build a modern factory and train our own workers,' I said.

The little man cleared his throat. He did not want to offend me. 'I don't pretend to know much about factories, but isn't this going to cost a lot of money? Surely you can't mean twenty acres? It's a huge area.'

'Exactly 80,937 square metres,' I replied. 'We shall need space for expansion. In years to come we may employ a thousand people, as we do in Czechoslovakia.'

Mr Hurst looked at me sideways. 'Well, you must know best, but it seems to me you're tackling things the hard way. I'd start small and buy more land when the business warrants it.'

'It'll be too late then,' I countered. 'We'd be held to ransom by the neighbours.'

He changed the subject. 'What range of goods will we make? How many different styles of jumpers?'

'None,' I said. 'We shall make only fleecy knickers to begin with. Complicated garments like jumpers must wait until our labour is trained.'

'But we can't keep a whole factory going by selling only knickers!'

'Of course we can,' I replied confidently. 'The demand is enormous, and if imports are stopped we shan't be able to churn out enough.'

I am afraid this was only one occasion of many when Mr Hurst must have thought me stubborn and overbearing. He was a salesman, anxious to secure an early supply of attractive British-made merchandise. A factory meant little more to him than a necessary encumbrance on which as little money should be spent as possible. I, by contrast, was a technocrat. This super-plant was to be the embodiment of all my dreams, the ultimate in technologi-cal achievement. It was to have everything Fleissen lacked. Creating and running it would be the main purpose of my life, the resulting merchandise and its disposal no more than a side issue. Although not in agreement with me, Mr Hurst had little choice but to fall in line, for he could not afford to risk losing the agency of the new factory. He would search for sites, he assured me, that met the conditions I had outlined and show them to me on my next visit, immediately after Christmas.

Fully aware that Mr Hurst was right when he had said I was choosing the hard way, I did not underestimate the difficulty of starting a new enterprise with completely 'green' labour, and intended to make all operations as simple as possible. We would manufacture only one product, fleecy knickers, in just one quality and one size and, if possible, in only three colours. The machinery, most of which would have to come from the Fleissen factory, because we could not afford to buy new plant, had to be selected with this purpose in mind and the whole production layout planned for it. No easy short cut, such as renting an old factory, could lead to success, I told myself.

There was the problem of financing the venture. The new factory would have to be paid for, and it was not just a matter of finding the money but of converting it into sterling now that exchange controls had come into force. The complication worried me, but I did not let it deter me. We would over-come it—all in good time! The ninety circulars we had at Fleissen were made up of a multitude of diameters and gauges, each producing fabric of a dif-ferent width and size of stitch. To make standard merchandise on such a varied plant took a thoroughly competent team of departmental managers and foremen and an experienced labour force, none of which we would have in England for years to come. I therefore earmarked all the 44 in. diameter 24-gauge machines for the new factory, much to the dismay of Johann Feiler, our works manager. They formed the only large battery of reasonably uniform circulars we had, and Feiler naturally did not want to lose them. He agreed with the logic of my reasoning, but this did not lessen his sadness. His machines were like children to him. He had accompanied Father on all his buying trips, and remembered the circumstances when each of them was purchased. He had nursed them, was proud of them, and now the best of them were to go.

Planning the sewing department came next. The changes in the technique of making up that had taken place since Father's death seemed revolutionary. The German firm of Dürkopp had introduced a conveyor belt flanked on both sides by sewing machines on individual stands, each with its own motor. Hippmann, a small engineering firm in Czechoslovakia had copied the idea and supplied three such conveyors to Lehrmann's, where the tough Direktor Kraut had the unpleasant task of making two hundred unwilling sewing machinists work on them. Had it not been for the continuing reports of Lehrmann's labour troubles I would have introduced moving belts into our sewing department long ago. The mere thought of any kind of conveyor belt excited me. Now, with the new factory project ahead, I delayed no longer and also placed a contract for three conveyors with Hippmann, without disclosing that one of them was intended for England. Its capacity matched that of the twenty knitting machines.

The cutting department presented a special problem. It was unthinkable that we should cut fabric in single layers on individual tables with hand shears as we did at Fleissen. I wanted to cut a dozen layers at a time with a motor-driven knife. The fact that no one, as far as I was aware, cut fleecy knickers or other bulky knitted goods in this way proved nothing. But a dozen thicknesses of wide, tubular fabric could not be laid accurately on top of each other by hand. A machine and a very long table were needed. Reckless as most young men of twenty-five, I hid a small bundle of 1,000 kronen notes in the upholstery of my car and drove across the border. The hills and woods of Bavaria, Franconia and Württemberg were steeped in the glorious tints of autumn, faint mist lay in the valleys, and I sang happily as I sped towards Reutlingen. Almost fifty years have passed since then, yet I remember that drive as if I had done it yesterday. Strange that some quite unimportant incidents should remains so vivid in one's memory. At Reutlingen I outlined my plan to my old friends the textile machine engineers of Arbach. They undertook to build a special laying machine for me, and I paid cash in advance.

Then I talked to Mr Hippmann. Could he build me a twenty-metre-long cutting table, the top of which would not warp and have no joins in which scissors, knives or fabric would catch? He assured me that he could, and I gave him the order.

We needed a fleecing machine. A day spent with Gessner at Aue in Saxony, the leading makers of this type of plant, revealed that their latest model was no better than the three machines we had at Fleissen except for individual motor drive and roller bearings. So I decided to take the newest of our three fleecers to England and ordered only conversion parts for the individual drive. I also placed a contract for a small calendar with heated rollers.

Our bottle bobbin winders had run on double shifts for many years and were too worn to be used in the new factory. I therefore went to the makers, Grosser, at Markersdorf, near Chemnitz, and ordered two new ones for which, once again, I paid in Czechoslovak notes. This completed the production plant.

Rolf meanwhile prepared a list of the hundred-odd pieces of ancillary equipment such as a card grinding frame for the fleecing machine, a lathe, tools, spares, bobbins for the winders, needles and initial supplies of yarn, elastic, sewing thread and so forth. It was his responsibility to ensure that all would be ready when needed. For the time being, however, our plans were to remain secret. There would inevitably be protests from various quarters as soon as the news leaked out that we were setting up a factory in England. The less prior warning our rivals and other potential opponents had the better.

Came the first snow, and then Christmas. Mother made a brave effort to re-create the festive atmosphere of bygone years when Father was alive, the music box played 'Silent night, holy night', and the candles flickered on the slowly revolving Christmas tree while Rolf and I lay on the floor trying to design the perfect factory layout on our drawing board. Ingo, home on vacation from the textile college, was rather young to take much interest in our planning and, before we could find him a job, disappeared to go skiing with his pals. On the afternoon of Christmas Day my old friend Helmut Amarotico, now a successful young architect, left with me for London. 1931 had been a busy year for him, and he was now taking a few days off to look at the factory sites which Mr Hurst had located. He had never been to England and was looking forward to the journey.

21

WE DISCOVER
LANGLEY
1931-32

ON BOXING DAY morning our express train steamed across Holland. After eating a hearty Dutch breakfast with cheese and sausage in the dining car we discussed once again the topography of London and its surroundings. I had drawn on my map a circle of twenty-five miles radius from Trafalgar Square. The site we were looking for had to be within this circle and fulfil the following requirements:

1 It had to measure at the very least 32,000 square metres, about eight acres. To begin with, the English factory would be merely a branch of Fleissen, but it was my secret ambition to make it, in time, the centre of the Pasold enterprise. That would need space.

2 It should be so located that I could divide my day between working in the factory and calling on customers in the City without losing too much valuable time travelling.

3 An ample supply of soft water was essential, in case we should want to build a dyehouse of our own at some future time. Water was the lifeblood of industry.

4 Equally important were facilities for the disposal of effluents, large quantities of discoloured water containing waste chemicals and some cotton fibres, preferably without having to build a costly purification plant.

5 Good road and rail connections, and the possibility of laying in a railway siding should the need arise. Since most of our merchandise went north, we had to look for a location north of the Thames.

6 Finally, a supply of labour in the neighbourhood, not skilled textile workers but young people we could train.

In the evening we arrived in London, took rooms at the Strand Palace Hotel and treated ourselves to a Christmas dinner consisting of turtle soup, roast turkey and plum pudding. The bill came to 6s for the two of us. I had chosen the Strand Palace not only for the good value it offered but also because it was London's newest hotel, and I wanted Helmut to see its advanced architecture, chromium plating and lighting effects. Too costly, of course, and altogether too showy even for an ultra-modern industrial building, but we sketched some of the features, hoping to capture just a little of the glamour for the entrance hall of the new factory.

When we called on Mr Hurst next morning he showed me a number of advertisements for clothing and knitwear factories which were for sale, some within walking distance of his office. Why go to the trouble and expense of building if we could buy a ready-made manufacturing unit at a bargain price?

I was not interested in old factories. Our profit margins were extremely tight. To survive against Japanese competition we had to have the most up-to-date plant. It had to be designed specially, I explained. Could we now go and inspect sites?

So Mr Hurst took us to see Leopold Farmer & Sons, the estate agents and factory specialists, at Gresham Street, and introduced us to one of the partners. The grey-haired gentleman waved me into an armchair. 'I am intrigued,' he smiled, 'to meet two such enterprising young men. At Mr Hurst's request we have prepared particulars of industrial sites within twenty-five miles of London, but do you want to spend your capital building a new textile mill when old established ones are going bankrupt every week? You can acquire their buildings, plant and trained labour for a song. We have many garment factories, among them several knitting plants, on our books. Most are in the Midlands and the north, but there are two or three in London which might suit you.'

'You pay me a compliment, Mr Farmer,' I replied, 'by suggesting I would succeed where others fail. It is not economical to run these old factories. Britain has far too many of them, which is why she is losing her trade to foreigners. I believe I can build a much better plant than those you have on your books.'

'So you want a modern factory!' Mr Farmer rang a bell. It was answered by a pleasant young man, a Mr Wood, one of the firm's salesmen. 'Take my friends to Slough and show them the new factories on the estate!'

As we headed west Mr Wood described the trading estate we were about to see. It had started as a dumping ground for old army lorries. After the war the land, well over a hundred acres, was acquired by an enterprising commercial company which converted the derelict storage sheds and workshops into factories and let them to industrialists. It now also constructed factories to clients' special requirements and supplied heat and electricity from a central boiler and powerhouse. There were railway sidings, a restaurant, sports and social clubs, several banks, even a branch of the Inland Revenue, and—yes, of course—an ample supply of water. In short, Slough's trading estate had everything a budding manufacturer with limited capital resources could wish for. A novel and inspired concept, I had to admit, but I had other ideas and was prejudiced against this conglomeration of industrial activities.

Motoring along the Great West Road, my attention was caught by the striking factories on both sides. Neither Helmut nor I had ever seen such impressive elevations, and I made Mr Wood stop the car to give us time to admire them. The name of the suburb was Brentford. Land with road frontage —a small piece was still available—fetched the prohibitive figure of £2,000 per acre. It was not for us, but I decided then and there to engage the architects, Wallis Gilbert & Partners, who had designed these magnificent buildings, to give us a hand with ours.

By comparison the tightly packed factories at Slough looked like barracks, and they disappointed me. 'If you are willing to pay, we can build to your own specifications,' the estate manager suggested, 'and we will reserve an acre of adjoining land for extensions, provided you undertake to utilise it within two years.'

'One acre? Two years? I have to look twenty years ahead.'

'If you outgrow one factory we'll provide you with a larger one somewhere else on the estate.'

I declined the offer. 'Moving would be too costly. Much as I admire your ingenious scheme, I am afraid it does not suit me.'

The factories on the estate could only be rented, which did not seriously interest me, but not far away from it, on the southern side of the railway bridge, there was a triangular site for sale which merited inspection. I turned it down because it measured only about three acres (if I remember correctly it was later bought by the Rheostatic Company), but I was tingling with excitement. The search was now on in earnest. The following day we explored building sites in the Watford and St Albans area, but saw none we liked. They were all too small, of an odd shape, on awkward slopes or inaccessible, and nowhere could we be sure of a reliable supply of soft water. After an equally fruitless day spent at Enfield and Potters Bar I asked to be taken to Cheshunt, where Mr Heldmaier had recommended a supposedly ideal plot with abundant water. It turned out to be a waterlogged meadow by the river Lea. Welwyn Garden City, which we visited next, made a very different impression. I liked the orderliness, the well planned roads, tidy lawns, sports field, neat rows of houses and wooded lanes. A number of small, modern factories, dominated by the imposing Shredded Wheat plant, gave the place an atmosphere of harmonious vitality. All this had clearly not just grown but was the creation of some master mind.

We saw a vacant ten-acre site and consulted the manager of the estate office about it. He could not sell the land, but to my surprise offered to lease it to us for 999 years. What tomfoolery was this? Did he expect us to build our factory on a site we could not own? Patiently he explained the difference between leasehold and freehold. Welwyn Garden City would not be such a well laid out town had its development not been controlled. And this was possible only if all the land was owned by a central authority. Surely a lease of 999 years was long enough for anyone?

Leasehold was new to me, and I did not like it. As far as I knew, all land in Czechoslovakia was freehold, and I was not willing to make the future development of our enterprise dependent on the co-operation and goodwill of a central authority, however well intentioned and enlightened it might be at present. Supposing, by some ill chance, someone like Dr Adolf Lehrmann gained control. What might happen then? There was no more to be said. Regretfully we returned to London, hoping we should have more luck at Edgware, Elstree or Barnet.

Some of the sites we saw during the following days were attractive, but none fulfilled all my requirements, and although Mr Hurst called me a perfectionist who would never be satisfied I refused to compromise in a matter of such far-reaching and lasting importance and stuck firmly to my six basic conditions.

The least problem seemed to be the supply of labour. There were plenty of people unemployed, and school leavers went straight on the dole. The availability of soft water, on the other hand, presented the greatest headache. True, there were now effective methods of softening water, but they were expensive and would unnecessarily raise the cost of producing our merchandise. Less cost-oriented industries seemed content to take their water from the mains, and I spent a good deal of time studying the chemical analyses which local councils kept on their files, or taking samples of their water with me in bottles and having them analysed, but in every case the degree of hardness was too high for my liking.

Discussing with Helmut in the evening the haphazard manner in which we went about our quest, I hit on an idea. The degree of hardness depended on the composition and structure of the subsoil. Before inspecting any more sites we ought to consult the Geological Museum. I had been there several times, looking at specimens, during the year I spent at Hampstead, for collecting stones used to be one of my boyhood hobbies, and I vaguely remembered seeing a section of the strata below London. Perhaps this might tell us where we were most likely to find the water we were looking for.

The geologists at South Kensington were very helpful. They showed us the sectional model of what they called the London basin and explained the fascinating phenomena caused by its peculiar shape. The basin consisted of gault, impervious rock with the Chiltern Hills and the North Downs forming the raised rim. It was filled with chalk, partially covered by clay. Rain falling into it penetrated the chalk and the water became hard. Rain falling on to the hills outside the basin seeped under the impervious rock into a thin, irregular deposit of the so-called Lower Greensand, where it formed a reservoir of soft water, which could be tapped by drilling through the gault. It was necessary to drill to a depth of about a thousand feet, but if one was lucky and struck the Lower Greensand the soft water gushed out under its own pressure at the rate of thousands of gallons an hour, depending on the diameter of the bore-hole. There were several artesian wells of this description in the Hanwell and Hayes area, and Horlick's had one at Slough. It was therefore reasonably safe to assume that we would find the Lower Greensand, and in it an almost un-limited supply of soft water, between Hayes and Slough.

This was exciting information, which narrowed our search considerably. We unfolded the map on which I had drawn the circle of twenty-five miles' radius round London and coloured in the likely Greensand sector. Guided by it, Mr Wood took us to Hayes to show us the Aeoleon factory which used to manufacture pianos in the days when every self-respecting working class family had to have one as a status symbol. It now stood empty, a huge red-brick building complete with boiler plant, and was for sale at £80,000, a fantastic sum of money, although it had perhaps cost more to build. One of its many floors would have provided more space than we could use. The thing was a white elephant as far as we were concerned, and I declined the proposi-tion that we should acquire it and let off the floors we did not want. (Years later the building was acquired by Kraft Cheese.) From there we drove to Park Royal, another industrial estate, and then followed the Western Avenue to its very end at Perivale, where we paced out a large site next to the Aladdin lamp factory. The ground belonged to a jovial gentleman named Sweeny, who invited us to lunch and told us, with a twinkle in his eye, that he was popularly known as the Duke of Greenford because of all the land he owned. Some day the Western Avenue would be extended and the site would gain an important road frontage, he said. The price he asked, if I remember correctly, was in the neighbourhood of £500 an acre, and I said I would sleep on it. Greenford, I thought, had distinct possibilities.

We then intended to inspect a site at Uxbridge, but the driver lost his way in the winding, narrow lanes lined by hedges and trees whose branches some-times met overhead and formed tunnels. The sun shone and it was hard to believe that Fleissen lay under a mantle of snow while here cattle grazed in green fields. Helmut was very taken with the English countryside. And where was the famous fog he had heard so much about? We came through the picturesque little village of Fulmer, with its old church and cottages. At the bottom of a hill the gravel road crossed a stream, not over a bridge but through a ford, as it must have done for hundreds of years. This was enchanted fairytale land, and I simply could not imagine a modern factory in such an old-world setting. Driving over a narrow hump bridge across a sleepy canal and then under a viaduct, we came out of the woods and orchards of Iver Heath into open country, with some old farm buildings on the right and a railway station on the left. The wide expanse of grassland adjoining the railway looked invitingly flat, and I told the driver to stop.

Mr Wood drew my attention to a builder's hoarding advertising several hundred houses to be erected. The land, he said, was not for sale. It was his job to sell me one of the sites on Leopold Farmer's list. Mr Hurst also became a little restless. We had so many sites to see which were for sale: why waste time over one that was not?

'But it's the best we've seen,' I insisted, 'and if we make the owners an attractive offer it will be for sale. They can build their houses somewhere else.'

'You can't put a factory on land that is scheduled for residential development,' Mr Wood explained. 'Look at those houses under construction!'

I hardly listened. Here lay the site I had dreamed about, an almost square meadow of some twenty acres, I guessed, stretching from the hard road on which we stood, alongside the busy main line of the Great Western Railway, to that second row of poplars to the east. And it was, of course, where the geologists had said we were most likely to find the soft-water-bearing Lower Greensand. The fact that the site adjoined Langley station, and that there was a ship canal only two hundred yards away, made it even more attractive. Provided there was a way of disposing of dyehouse effluents, I had found the perfect location—and within twenty miles of London!

'Not allowed to build a factory merely because the land happens to be scheduled for housing? Come, come, gentlemen, industry must have priority. How else can people earn their living? You saw the queues outside those labour exchanges! We bring employment. Our factory would be welcome even on the village green.'

Mr Hurst fidgeted with the keys in his pocket, a sure sign of disagreement. 'I very much doubt it,' he said. 'Things don't work that way, not in England. Country folk dislike factories.'

But Mr Chesterman, the dapper little stationmaster whom we questioned about the village and its inhabitants, became quite agitated when I mentioned the factory. He would inform head office at once. The GWR wanted to transport our goods and raw materials, and we could rely on its powerful support. Meanwhile it might be prudent not to talk to the local people about our project. He could think of a scheming small clique who were sure to cause difficulties.

A confidential interview with Mr Boxall, the manager of Slough labour exchange, confirmed what I expected. The area had a serious unemployment problem which was aggravated by the many Welshmen who came in search of work. Apart from the brickfields and a small bacon factory Langley was a purely agricultural village. There were hundreds out of work, and if we needed more they would come from Slough on bicycles or by train. Mr Boxall very much hoped we would build our factory at Langley.

This encouraged us to call at the offices of Slough Urban District Council and consult Mr Duxbury, the town clerk. Forbidding and cool at first, he thawed visibly and became co-operative as I outlined our plan. Had we seen the industrial buildings to be let on the trading estate? I said we had and did not like them. We wanted to construct our own factory, an attractive building to be designed by Wallis Gilbert & Partners or architects of similar standing. Was the land at Langley definitely scheduled for housing? And if permission to build a factory could be granted, how were we to dispose of industrial effluents—dyehouse effluents in particular?

No, the land in question was not zoned for any specific purpose. Mr Duxbury thought a factory such as I described would particularly please the people who lived on the eastern side of Slough, since the town's major industrial development was over to the west. As for effluents, he saw no reason why they should not be discharged into the public sewer, provided they did not interfere with the proper functioning of the treatment plant.

Use the public sewer? As simple as that? I could hardly believe my ears. This would indeed be the ideal solution. I had to strike while the iron was hot and extract a firm promise from the town clerk before he changed his mind! 'We shall need a binding undertaking in writing from the council, confirming what you have just said about the public sewer, before we decide to build a factory. The dyestuffs we use are inorganic and quite harmless: we do not dye wool, only cotton,' I hastened to assure him, 'and while we might discharge a substantial volume, thousands of gallons a day, it is nothing worse than discoloured water.'

Mr Hurst need not have kicked me under the table. I knew quite well that I was behaving in a horribly un-English manner, but fortunately the town clerk did not seem to mind. He could not commit himself, he said, and would refer my request to the appropriate quarters.

As we drove towards London Mr Hurst admonished me. I had been unnecessarily awkward. Why not cross our bridges as we come to them? He had made enquiries and found that it was not customary for garment manufacturers to do their own dyeing. There were plenty of commission dyers, and we would probably never want to have our own dyehouse.

'Perhaps not,' I replied. 'But what if we do? Water supply and effluent disposal are essentials for a textile plant, and this is the time to make as sure of them as we can.'

I felt elated. At last we were making progress. We had found our site, and with railway company, labour exchange and town clerk on our side I did not take the possibility of local opposition very seriously. One by one we would surmount the other hurdles, of which, I realised, there were still many. To begin with, we had to get that building firm to sell us the land at a price we could afford. It had to be paid for in sterling, which would not be easy in the face of Czechoslovak currency restrictions. But I did not worry—one thing at a time. We sped along the Great West Road, past those breathtaking modern factories with their brilliant neon signs. Coty, Pyrene, Firestone, Maclean's and Jantzen, I read. Set well back from the road, each stood in its own beautifully kept grounds, planted with ornamental shrubs which hid electric lights floodlighting the impressive elevations. This was the industry of the future. Not that I dreamed of building such a palace—I knew my limitations and those of the underwear industry—but it was exhilarating to look at the achievements of others.

Poor Mr Hurst. In retrospect I think he must have been a very worried man. I knew his business and income had virtually ceased, but I did not realise how hard up he was. He pinned his hopes on the factory I was going to establish, a workshop of manageable size, he imagined, employing twenty girls in some existing building which could be rented cheaply and where production could begin without much delay. Yet here was I, a self-opinionated young foreigner, wasting everyone's time looking at vast sites in the country, talking about a dyehouse that would use a huge volume of water and discussing fancy elevations of factories owned by industrial giants. Mr Hurst thought I had no sense of proportion, and he wondered where I was going to get the capital for my grandiose ventures. Indeed, if I had so much money why did I bother to spend it on a factory? I certainly puzzled him.

Two days later we heard from Mr Wood that the builders who owned the land at Langley were willing to sell. They asked £4,500 for the seventeen-acre site, which Mr Hurst thought outrageous. He was quite taken aback when I said I was happy to close the deal provided the council scheduled the land for industrial purposes and gave us a document confirming that we could discharge dyehouse effluents into the public sewer.

'You don't know enough about land values in this country,' he protested. 'A field of that size should cost much less.'

'I am an industrialist, not a land speculator, and price is not my first consideration, but compared with the cost of land in Czechoslovakia £265 per acre seems ridiculously cheap. It works out at only eight kronen a square metre, less than the price of linoleum. I would have to pay more than twice that much at Fleissen.'

'If you found such a site at Fleissen, Asch or Eger you could not buy it for five times that money,' Helmut, for whose benefit we were speaking in German, supported me. 'Why is it, Mr Hurst, that building land in the neighbourhood of London is so cheap?'

The ensuing argument produced neither an explanation nor agreement. Values were relative, and it seemed the price of land, as of everything else, was determined by supply and demand. If I thought an out-of-the-way field in the village of Langley was worth so much Mr Hurst could only shrug his shoulders. I would never see my money back. He was sure that J. D. Arthur, his solicitor, would be of the same opinion.

I was puzzled about the need for a solicitor. In Czechoslovakia a purchase was concluded by vendor and buyer shaking hands and signing the land register. But in England, it appeared, the vendor's ownership, recorded on ancient parchments known as title deeds and going back over generations, had first to be investigated by a lawyer. The quaint procedure tickled Helmut's sense of humour, but I was far from pleased with this unexpected delay and expense.

J. D. Arthur was a wizened little man who looked like an owl. He sat in the midst of dusty bundles of paper in a small, dingy office at Blackfriars. While he immersed himself in the history of the Langley site to establish beyond any possible doubt the vendor's good title, Helmut and I were finalising the details of the factory with Wallis Gilbert & Partners. It was to be a single-storey building consisting of three north-light bays, each thirty metres long with a span of nine metres, giving a total working floor area of 810 square metres. At right angles with the bays was to be a two-storey office block of twenty-seven by six metres, with an impressive reception hall and staircase in the centre. Helmut sketched an elevation which was modern without being extreme and which, built in red-brown facing bricks, would tone in well with the trees and cottages of Langley village. The architects converted our metric measurements into feet and inches and prepared specifications and detailed drawings to invite tenders. Studying the office layout, I noticed two toilets, and on enquiring was told by Mr Wallis that they were for men and girls respectively.

'Girls? We'll have no girls in the office!'

'Not even a typist?'

'No,' I replied firmly. 'There will only be a clerk. He will type all the letters, and the office boy will type the invoices. A girl in an office is only a distraction. We tried it in Czechoslovakia, and it did not work out.' Fortunately I did not get my way. The council insisted on two toilets.

Ingenieur Koch, a very able young German engineer in the architects' employ, discussed the electrical wiring, heating plant and pipes with me, and how to raise the steam we needed for our calendar. Fascinated by a revolutionary new heating system known as Caliqua which was proving highly successful on the Continent, I took my courage in both hands and decided to have the first Caliqua installation in Britain. The idea was to heat water to well above boiling point—in our case, to 160°C or 320°F at a pressure of 8 a.t.ü. or 120 lb per square inch. A rotary pump forced it through an arrangement of pipes and radiators which extracted the desired amount of heat, and returned the now slightly cooler water to the boiler. Because of the pressure all pipes were made of drawn steel and were not flanged and screwed but welded together, forming, with boiler and pump, a permanently sealed circuit. This did away with wasteful exhaust steam, troublesome steam traps and leaking joints. Best of all, there could be little corrosion of the boiler tubes, for it was the same water that kept circulating. Hot water could be controlled more accurately than steam, the pipe diameter could be smaller, and there were other advantages. Wherever steam was needed—at the calendar, for instance —a small calorifier could raise it on the spot. And since only the best was good enough for the new factory, the oil-fired boiler had to be fully automatic. In 1931 this was something to get excited about. The fact that water could be made to stay liquid at temperatures high above boiling point continued to intrigue visiting American industrialists until the late 1950s.

The Caliqua system was to play an important part in the development of our manufacturing processes both in Britain and in Czechoslovakia.

Following the report made by the Langley stationmaster to his head office, we received a telephone call from Paddington. Would Mr Pasold and Mr Hurst please go to see Mr Lampitt, the general manager of the goods section of the Great Western Railway Company? Remembering what I had learned as Dr Rundt's secretary on our visit to Hollywood, my reaction was to let Mr Lampitt come to see us, but Mr Hurst was shocked by my suggestion.

'You do not realise that Mr Lampitt is a very important person. We mustn't offend him, he can be extremely useful to us.'

'Mr Lampitt hopes we shall be useful to him,' I retorted. 'He wants us to locate our factory alongside his railway line so that the GWR get our business, and not the LMS or the LNER. It's the wrong tactics for us to go to his office, but since you feel so strongly about it let us proceed to Paddington.'

Mr Lampitt did not beat about the bush. Competition among the railway companies was keen. He wanted us on his line and queried whether there was anything he could do for us. I was ready for this question. 'Five things,' I said. Could he prevail upon Slough council to speed up the issue of our effluent permit? The GWR owned two small triangular pieces of ground, about two acres, protruding into the site we were negotiating for. Could he sell them to us? When our machinery arrived from Czechoslovakia could he store it for us until the factory was ready? And finally, could he stop one of his fast trains at Langley for us in the morning and one in the evening whenever we asked for it? Mr Hurst looked aghast, but Mr Lampitt, with an amused smile, promised to do all he could to meet my wishes. I felt sure he meant it. London was, after all, not Hollywood, I reflected.

Of all my problems the only one that seriously worried me was the time limit imposed on my stay in England. The stamp on my passport said 'Granted leave to land on condition that the bearer does not remain in the United Kingdom longer than three months', and that was a concession I had secured only after considerable trouble. As a rule the immigration officers at the port of entry granted visitors only two or three weeks. How could I build a factory in these circumstances? Something had to be done to get the restriction removed, to relieve me of the continuous anxiety. I had to talk to the Home Office. After waiting with Mr Hurst for an hour in the queue outside the Aliens Department we saw a tired civil servant who impassively listened to my story about building a factory, said he had no jurisdiction to vary the condition on my passport and suggested we enlist the backing of the Board of Trade.

In those days the BoT was not the vast, powerful organisation it was to become. Occupied mainly with shipping, it had only recently begun to take some limited interest in trade and industry generally. The great departments in Whitehall looked down on it as an inferior commercial appendix of the government machine. I seem to remember that it was housed somewhere in the City. To my great surprise and disappointment the official who received us appeared to be no more interested in our factory project than his colleague at the Home Office.

'Britain has millions of unemployed,' I argued. 'I shall bring know-how, provide work, pay wages, replace imported merchandise—but only if I am allowed to stay. How else can I build a factory here?'

I met with little encouragement. 'We have plenty of knitting mills and talent in Leicester and Nottingham.' The official yawned, jotted down a few details of my project, in which he clearly had no faith, and said he would pass them on to his superior.

Walking back from this disheartening interview to Mr Hurst's office, I felt very unwanted, and a wave of pessimism came over me. Perhaps one could forgive the civil servants in Whitehall for keeping aloof—they carried the problems of the whole Empire on their shoulders—but if even the commercial authorities, whose job it presumably was to foster industry, took no interest in me and my project was it worth while going on with it? Could a young enterprise take root and flourish in an atmosphere of ignorance, indifference and even hostility? Mr Hurst tried to dispel my gloom, and told me not to worry too much. He suggested we should phone Mr Lampitt and ask him to get us an interview with someone higher up. So far we had only met clerks. A week later we received a telephone call asking us to see a Mr Watkinson at the Treasury. Mr Hurst was much impressed, repeating the word 'Treasury' with a mixture of deference, incredulity and triumph in his voice. He hoped there had not been a misunderstanding. Of all the government departments in Whitehall the Treasury was the most awe-inspiring and for ordinary mortals the least approachable.

Mr Watkinson stood with his back to a large white marble mantlepiece in one of those spacious rooms with stucco ceiling in which high government officials transact, behind carefully guarded doors, the business of state. A man of about thirty-five with an alert face, friendly, searching eyes and quick movements, he was the very opposite of the two lethargic fish we had met before.

'You are very young. Tell me something about yourself and about the factory you want to build.' He came straight to the point. I liked him. He was sympathetic, and the questions he fired at me in rapid succession were very relevant. What made me think I could compete successfully against British manufacturers when I had to pay the same wages as they? Why did I want to build a factory instead of renting one, and why near London and not in the Midlands? How did our machines compare with those made at Leicester? What raw materials did I intend to use and where would they come from? And could I tell him something about our customers? The engaging manner in which he cross-examined me put me at my ease, and I was completely frank with him.

'Forgive me if I say something disagreeable. I do not mean to offend you,' I began, to the horror of Mr Hurst, who kept making warning noises, clearing his throat. 'The United Kingdom is a very rich country, and with the wealth of its overseas possessions pouring into these islands the British do not need to be very economical. The waste that goes on in their homes would shock the people of Czechoslovakia. Good food is thrown away, stale bread goes in the dustbin, clothes that could be mended or altered are scrapped, expensive logs and the best coal are burnt in open fires and the heat goes out through the chimney. I have worked in a City office and seen how money is frittered away writing invoices in longhand that could be typed, not using decimals, making tea, keeping visitors waiting and scribbling on clean sheets of notepaper when old envelopes would do. Yet the firm makes profits. The great wholesale houses seem to prosper, in spite of their appalling inefficiency. I think it cannot be so very difficult to succeed in this country.'

'Go on,' encouraged Mr Watkinson.

'The buildings and streets in the City are so old and badly laid out that most of them should be rebuilt, yet London maintains its position as the world's business and financial centre. Admittedly, I have never been in a British factory, but I have studied some quite famous ones from outside and am sure they cannot operate economically. If, therefore, I build a super-modern plant, equip it with the best available machinery and specialise in making one good product for which there is mass demand, namely our Directoire knickers, surely I must succeed. I may not be more intelligent than my competitors, but I shall have better tools and I shall be working while they are playing golf.'

Mr Watkinson listened attentively, the slightest trace of amusement in his smiling eyes. When I had finished he chuckled.

'You ought to be in Parliament. It would do some of our politicians good to hear you. But it's a mystery to me why you want to come to this country, where you find so much to criticise.'

'No country is perfect. I love and admire Britain and the British people. They may be extravagant by my standards, but they excel in many other respects—industrially, too. They produce the best motor-cycles, spinning machines, fine count cotton yarns, men's suitings and roast beef. I would not dare to compete with them on quality, but cheap consumer goods are also needed, especially when so many people are out of work and money is scarce. I am glad to think I have something to offer which Britain is short of— experience of efficient mass production.'

When Mr Hurst told me later that I had sounded rather pompous I felt foolish, but if Mr Watkinson thought so he certainly gave no indication of it. He enquired what exactly I wanted from the Home Office. What was the trouble about my permit?

'I would like a visa that enables me to come and go as often as I like, with leave to stay in the country for unlimited periods. How else can I build and operate a factory here?'

The smile disappeared. 'I fear that is out of the question. But I am willing to recommend the issue of a permit for twelve months. After that we shall see what can be done. Does that satisfy you?'

I hesitated. 'If this is the best you can do I shall have to be satisfied. But the year will be gone by the time the factory is fully in production, and it won't run on its own. I shall have to travel continually between England and Czechoslovakia.'

'You'll have a busy time, young man,' Mr Watkinson joked. 'Go ahead, build your modern factory, and don't worry too much about getting that permit renewed when it expires. Let's see how you get on. I'll keep an eye on you. And if you encounter any difficulties get in touch with Mr Matthews at the Board of Trade.' With a firm handshake and an encouraging 'We shall meet again' he dismissed us. We had won a friend. Years passed before I saw Mr Watkinson again, but to know that he was watching from somewhere in the background and that I could go to him if ever the need arose was comforting. Without being sure quite where he fitted into the Whitehall scene, I had no doubt that he was one of the men who carried the burden of government on their shoulders, and I resolved not to bother him unless, perhaps, some day there came a real emergency.

Three weeks had passed since we first set eyes on the Langley site. It seemed like three months, and I was eager to complete the purchase—one is not very patient at the age of twenty-five—yet the searches to prove the title and the negotiations with Slough council dragged on. Helmut had departed some time ago, and the requests for my return to Fleissen to attend to urgent business became so insistent that I too had to go, leaving J. D. Arthur and Mr Hurst to tie up the few remaining loose ends, as I thought.

The first news they sent me was of a protest meeting held by the Langley Ratepayers' Association, who had got wind of our project and were trying to stop it. The *Slough, Eton and Windsor Observer* of 29 January 1932 carried the headlines

BOMBSHELL FOR LANGLEY RESIDENTS

FACTORY AT FRONT DOOR OF VILLAGE

FOREIGN MANUFACTURERS OF WOMEN'S GARMENTS?

APPEAL TO COUNCIL MAY BE TOO LATE

PART OF LANGLEY ZONED FOR FACTORIES

To my surprise Mr Hurst seemed seriously perturbed by the situation, whilst I read the newspaper reports he sent with some amusement, refusing to believe that the attempt of a few crackpots to halt the march of progress could possibly succeed. I did not know my England! But as it happened, with the support of the local tradespeople, the unemployed and the railway company, we won the day, and the *Observer*'s headlines on 5 February read:

FACTORIES WELCOMED TO LANGLEY

CROWDED MEETING AT THE VILLAGE HALL

PROTEST AGAINST THE RESOLUTION OF THE RATEPAYERS' ASSOCIATION
FOREIGN FACTORY FOR BUCKINGHAMSHIRE

Then the London *Evening News* took up the story. In a ten-inch column headed 'Factory war—lost and won' it described how valiantly the Langley

Ratepayers' Association had fought against the proposal of Adolf Pasold & Sohn, a large Czechoslovak firm, to build a clothing factory in their pretty village. Unable to prevent the intrusion of commerce into their quiet corner of Buckinghamshire, they had compromised, and the factory was to be set back 100 ft from the road. I chuckled. It was I who had told the town clerk at the outset that we intended to build well back from the road and have a lawn in front of the factory. So Mr Hillier, the association's chairman, was now saving his face by taking credit for our lawn. Well, let him!

Unfortunately the consequences of all this publicity proved costly. A building site that excited so much public interest was obviously no ordinary piece of land. The vendors suddenly remembered that they had promised five acres of it, a front corner in fact, to someone else who was prepared to relinquish his prior rights for £500. Both Mr Hurst and J. D. Arthur, who had at long last concluded his searches, spoke of blackmail and implored me not to pay a penny more than originally agreed. They wanted to call the vendors' bluff and let them keep those five acres. Surely the remaining twelve acres were large enough for our purpose? Perhaps they were, but by now I was so in love with the large square site that I would not countenance having it mutilated. Not that I had the slightest doubt about the blackmail, but English law permitted both buyer and seller to change their minds until the contract was signed. Against the wishes of my advisors, I decided it was better to swallow my pride and pay away another five hundred of my precious pounds than be sorry for the rest of my life. So the conveyance transferring ownership of the seventeen acres from Messrs Perry and Another to Messrs Adolf Pasold & Sohn at £5,000 was sent to Fleissen. Then I had another scare over a clause I did not quite understand. It reserved the mineral rights to the lord of the manor. Who was he? And had he the right to dig up our land looking for minerals? I hesitated, until a letter from J. D. Arthur relieved my anxiety, and I completed the purchase on 17 March 1932. Meanwhile the Urban District Council of Slough and the Eton Rural District Council had finalised the wording of the effluent document, an impressive piece of parchment with a large red seal. Unfortunately invalidated by a later Act of Parliament, it is still preserved in the company's archives.

On 15 April I signed the contract purchasing the one triangular site from the Great Western Railway Company and on 31 December the other, which increased the area of our site to nineteen acres.

To explain where the money came from to pay for site and factory I have to return to the autumn of 1931. Following Britain's departure from the gold standard and the drastic fall in the value of sterling, Czechoslovakia reintroduced defensive currency restrictions, prohibiting the transfer of funds abroad. This left two ways open to finance our enterprise, neither of them very much to my taste.

We could submit our scheme to the Czechoslovak Ministry of Trade and Industry and, if it was approved, apply to the National Bank for permission to remit an agreed sum to England. Direktor Huder of the Bohemian Union Bank, whom I asked for advice, thought this way too time-consuming and risky. The Ministry had to consult the trade. That meant our competitors, who were sure to raise objections. Dr Lehrmann would be their champion and bring his great influence to bear. Huder was doubtful whether a permit would be granted, but if it were, the safeguards demanded by the National Bank to retain control over our activities in Britain would be such as to make efficient commercial operation of the enterprise difficult. Balance sheets would have to be submitted regularly, profits returned to Czechoslovakia instead of ploughed back into the business, the Bank's approval sought before additional machines could be bought or buildings altered, and there might be other irksome stipulations. If I was serious about the project Direktor Huder could not recommend an official application.

'Serious? I'll do anything to build that factory in England, anything short of committing murder. And time is of the essence.'

In that case, replied the banker, it would seem best to choose the other way and finance the enterprise with sterling acquired unofficially. Perhaps he could help. Banks were there to help their clients.

'But I shall need £20,000! Isn't that too large an amount to be found on the black market and smuggled out of the country?'

Direktor Huder winced. 'Nothing as crude as that. I think I can make half that sum available in London in the near future. You can give me numbered Czechoslovak bank deposit books in settlement, so nobody will know about the transaction and there won't be any record of it.'

I stared at him in amazement. He laughed. 'Strictly illegal, of course, and not to be repeated. I'll let you into the secret.'

He checked whether the padded doub'e doors of his private office were firmly shut, and then explained. Some depositors—industrialists, professional men, politicians—liked to keep part of their money abroad, preferably in Switzerland. In order not to lose this business the Bohemian Union Bank had set up a holding company in Zürich (under the name of Libella, if I remember correctly). Recent Czechoslovak government decrees had made this illegal; the company had had to be wound up and the funds repatriated. But Prague had no detailed record of the deposits, and some clients, while agreeable to changing their francs back into kronen, preferred to receive them 'un-officially'. The deal he proposed might help two of his clients while earning the bank double commission. The transfer to London would be made via

New York. There was to be nothing in writing. I would have to trust him.

Needless to say, I jumped at this heaven-sent opportunity. Ten thousand pounds would take care of my financial commitments for the first six months at least, and I felt confident that during that period I would somehow find a way of providing the rest. I was, however, left with a further problem. Sooner or later the officials of the Czechoslovak National Bank were bound to hear of our factory in England and might want to know how it was financed. Would they believe me if I said I had borrowed the money in Britain? I lay awake at night wondering how I could convince them. Was it plausible that anyone would lend me such a sum? The best way of finding out was to try. So on my next visit to England I saw Mr Powell, the manager of the Fore Street branch of the National Provincial Bank, where I had my account, and without telling him about the money which was coming from New York asked him for a loan of £10,000 to build a factory. He was startled. How could I be so naive? Patiently he explained that it was against the rules of the bank to finance such schemes. To cross-check I tried the Westminster Bank, where the manager thought I was joking and politely showed me the door. A similar reception at Barclay's made it abundantly clear that no bank was prepared to lend money to an unknown young foreigner, and that I had to think of some better explanation.

In due course the transfer from New York arrived in London, and I took the night train for Scotland to see my old friend Colin Baird, in whose integrity I had complete confidence. Would he take my £10,000 and open an account in his name with the National Provincial Bank in London, giving me the right to draw? I could then prove, in case of need, that it was a private individual, a friend and not a bank, who was advancing me the capital to establish a factory in Britain. Colin failed to comprehend. The Bairds had never heard of currency restrictions and could hardly credit that such an iniquity existed. Was I really proposing to borrow my own money? And why did I have to pretend that it was Colin's? Of Course he wanted to help me, but ten thousand pounds was a very large sum. How could he explain its sudden appearance to his income tax inspector? We would have to talk to his accountant.

The accountant, a canny Scot, was not worried about the tax angle. That could easily be explained. But what were currency restrictions? He gave me a very old-fashioned look. If the money were really mine why the subterfuge? Surely I could do what I liked with my own money, and the authorities had no right to interfere? I almost despaired. 'They may have no right, as you call it, to tell me what to do with my money, but they have the power to send me to jail for contravening their regulations.'

'Jail? Mr Baird, this is a case for a lawyer, not an accountant.'

It was careless of me to have used that word. Colin, too, looked thoroughly alarmed, but he was not going to let me down, and we went to Glasgow to see his lawyer. For the third time I told my story, explained Czechoslovakia's exchange control regulations and answered questions. The inquisition over, the lawyer delivered his verdict.

'Mr Baird, if you wish to assist your young friend in the way he suggests I have no objection. The transaction may seem unorthodox, but you run no financial risk, you tie up none of your funds and you do nothing illegal or dishonourable. On the contrary, if you save him from going to prison for disobeying such an iniquitous law you are to be congratulated.'

Then he turned to me in the friendly, condescending manner used by the British middle classes of the time when talking to foreigners.

'It seems preposterous that there should be governments which restrict the liberty of their subjects by denying them the free use of their capital—money they have worked for and earned. We in Britain would not stand for this sort of thing, and we cannot condone it in others. Our sense of justice revolts against it. The sooner you shake the dust of the Balkans off your feet and, with the help of such good friends as Mr Baird, build your factory in these islands the better. Good luck to you.'

Although relieved, I disliked being spoken to in this patronising fashion, but the self-righteous lawyer gave me such a warm smile as he showed us to the door that I forgave him for thinking Czechoslovakia was a barbarous region somewhere in the Balkans. I wish the good man were alive today and could see how obediently Britons now submit to equally iniquitous currency restrictions.

Colin was delighted to be able to do what I had asked of him. We opened an account at the National Provincial Bank in his name, and I felt secure in the knowledge of having an alibi in case of need.

It would, of course, be still better if the Czechoslovak National Bank never enquired. Perhaps its curiosity could be forestalled, its questions answered before they were asked. Once again I remembered Dr Rundt and the press. Yes, that was it. People believed anything provided they saw it in print. So I drafted a paragraph describing the factory we were about to build and said it was financed by British capital, without, however, stating details. Mr Hurst gave the write-up to a press agency, and it appeared in a number of British newspapers. To my delight *The Times* printed the following piece:

A large site at Langley, Bucks, has been bought on behalf of a Czechoslovak firm, Messrs Adolf Pasold & Son, on which the firm propose to build a factory for the production of women's garments (knitwear). On account of the currency restrictions in Czechoslovakia the factory will be financed with British capital. The architects are Messrs Wallis, Gilbert & Partners. Building will be begun this month, and it is hoped that the first goods will be turned out in July. Messrs Adolf Pasold & Sohn were established in 1870, and up to the time of the imposing of the tariff they sent between 75 and 80 per cent of their total production to Great Britain and the Empire. Their agents in this country are A. C. Hurst, Fore Street, E.C.2, who will also represent the new factory.

No paper was more reliable and respected than *The Times*. As I had hoped, Czechoslovak newspapers, as well as *Strickerei & Wirkerei,* the widely read journal of the knitwear industry, reprinted the information, and I was never asked to substantiate it.

22

HELD UP
BY RED TAPE
1932

EVER SINCE MY first visit to Zlin I had been an admirer of the great Bata shoe firm, a world-wide enterprise that manufactured footwear on the same principles as Ford made automobiles. Its outstanding success was, in my opinion, mainly due to its flow production technique, made possible by the use of conveyor belts, and to the large chain of Bata shops which cut out the middlemen. There were about a thousand such shops in Czechoslovakia; every small town and even the large villages had one, and they did more trade than all the other shoe shops put together.

If shoes could be sold directly to the consumer, why not underwear? Father would not let me try for fear of upsetting our customers, but after his death I opened shops at Chodau, Graslitz, Falkenau, Eger and Fischern, towns near enough to be serviced by our lorry. I had them all painted in a distinctive blue colour, put the name Pasold in large yellow letters above the door and displayed a sign saying 'Direct from manufacturer to wearer' in the windows. As soon as the combined turnover of these first five shops reached 150,000 kronen, I promised myself, we would open more. Shopkeeping proved, however, more difficult than I expected. The variety of goods we made was too small to offer the public a wide enough choice. To supplement it, we bought merchandise from other manufacturers, but the limited purchasing power of only five shops did not enable us to buy at the lowest prices. Much of the advantage we had hoped to pass on to the consumer was thus lost, and turnover rose only slowly. It would have taken fifty shops for the venture to become a viable proposition. I realised that we did not know enough about retailing to risk an experiment on such a scale and secretly wished I had listened to Father, but, refusing to admit defeat, I plodded on, harvesting the worst of both worlds.

I could not have chosen a more inopportune time to sell to the public direct. Retailers were up in arms against us, and not only in those five places. Lehrmann's spread the rumour that we intended opening shops throughout the republic to take the business away from established traders. Two years earlier, when we could export everything we made, I would have laughed, but now we needed the home market again. This propaganda damaged our prospects of recapturing it. Fortunately our White Bear sweaters had meanwhile become so popular with the public that the trade could not afford to boycott us, otherwise the situation would have become precarious.

In Father's day the bustle of business was spread equally throughout the many departments of our factories at Fleissen and Leibitschgrund. No hand was idle, no one had more to do than his fair share. Yarn deliveries arrived when they were needed; we rarely had too little fabric or too much machine capacity. Father foresaw discrepancies and smoothly balanced them long before they could develop into shortages or surpluses and affect production. His mere presence seemed to make the gears mesh and let the plant run at top speed without apparent effort. Customers got their goods on time.

I lacked his magic touch, but it was not inexperience alone that made the passage so rough. The world depression played havoc with trade, and on top of the devaluation of sterling came the uncertainty caused by Britain moving towards protectionism. During 1932 Czechoslovakia's exports to the United Kingdom fell by 70 per cent. Not since the break-up of the Austro-Hungarian Monarchy had Adolf Pasold & Sohn experienced such catastrophic conditions, and I was ill equipped to meet them, having received my business training during the boom years of the 1920s.

How right Grandfather had been when he predicted that exports would not go on for ever and that our home customers would not forgive us for neglecting their orders! The wholesalers of Reichenberg, Pilsen and Pardubice, the owners of the large stores in Prague, Brünn and Pressburg, the little shopkeepers of Klattau and Pisek and the Polish Jews of Kosice and Uzhorod made me eat very humble pie now that we needed them. Ruthlessly they cut our prices to the bone and forced me to agree to conditions I would have rejected out of hand a year ago. Yet in the face of all these adversities, just when the Czechoslovak enterprise needed my full attention, I was preoccupied with my English factory project. When I looked at Father's and Grandfather's photographs on the wall my conscience was troubled.

I worked hard to serve two masters—on the one hand the old established inherited family concern of which I was the custodian, and on the other my life's ambition, the venture in England. Trying to do justice to both, I gave up everything else. There was no time for reading, my skis collected cobwebs, Carnival came and went unnoticed, and when the spring sun dried the puddles on the roads my beloved motor-cycle remained in the garage. My pals ceased to invite me to their parties, and I neglected and lost my girlfriends.

In 1932 the crisis reached its climax, with a total of 30 million unemployed in the industrial countries of the West.

	No. of unemployed	Percentage of labour force
United States	12,000,000	24
Germany	5,575,000	30
Great Britain	2,829,000	22
Italy	1,000,000	
Czechoslovakia	700,000	28
Austria	378,000	
Holland	271,000	
France	261,000	
Switzerland	54,000	21
Sweden	–	22
Denmark	–	32

Who can trace and weigh the complex causes of that catastrophic slump? It would seem that at the beginning of the century the economy of the civilised world was reasonably, if delicately, in balance. But the nations did not appreciate their good fortune. Commercial, colonial and naval rivalry between Germany and Britain, racial hatred and aspirations in Central and Eastern Europe, fanned by ambitious politicians, led to the 1914–18 war. It changed not only the map but also the structure of world markets and the direction of the flow of industrial and agricultural products. It turned traditional creditor countries into debtors and vice versa. War improved manufacturing techniques, notably in North America, and, when the fighting was over, reckless credit policies financed an artificial post-war boom. Rationalised mass production needed fewer hands and churned out more goods than the growing army of unemployed could afford to buy. Prices of raw materials and agricultural produce collapsed. In Argentina railway engines burned wheat, Brazil dumped her coffee beans into the sea. While storehouses were full to bursting point the people starved. What had happened to the time-honoured law of supply and demand?

It was not allowed to function. Guided by their economic advisers, politicians intervened with import barriers, quotas, preferential tariffs, bilateral and multilateral trade agreements, devaluations, exchange controls and similar measures designed to export their own countries' financial troubles and unemployment to others, thus preventing the ailing world economy from curing itself. This game of musical chairs, in which each nation blames the others for its economic failures and tries to pass on the consequences, is as popular today as it was half a century ago, but it is now played with more skill and a greater sense of international responsibility, or so my economist friends assure me. In the interest of all of us I hope they are right.

The devaluation of Britain's currency in the autumn of 1931 caused a chain reaction. It was quickly followed by Ireland, India, Malaya, Canada, Egypt, Palestine, Denmark, Sweden, Norway, Finland, Austria, Portugal and Japan, making it very difficult to export our goods to any of those countries. Our sales to Scandinavia fell by 80 per cent. To make matters worse, Japan now made an all-out effort to conquer the markets of the world by flooding them with cheap merchandise, and took a growing slice of our trade. South Africa, Costa Rica, Colombia, Chile, Peru, Greece and Siam devalued in 1932, Estonia, the Philippines and the United States in 1933; Czechoslovakia reluctantly fell in line in 1934, Belgium in 1935, and France, followed by Holland and Switzerland, in 1936.

This, broadly, was the economic scene in the first half of the 1930s to which we had to adapt our business. I would have hardly credited at the beginning of the decade, when we still sold 90 per cent of our output abroad, that we could lose most of our export trade and survive. Yet, with hard work and luck, we enlarged the small foothold we had retained in the domestic market. Instead of having to retract we expanded, and became one of the leading suppliers in Czechoslovakia. While we were thus immersed in our problems there climbed out of the chaos of those years Adolf Hitler and his jackbooted storm troopers. But we were now still in the spring of 1932, and I was not particularly interested in politics. I took no notice of Hitler.

Rolf had seen to the dismantling and crating of the machinery we intended to take from Fleissen to England. Well greased and wrapped in waterproof paper to protect it from rusting on the journey, and packed in heavy wooden cases, it filled two large train ferry trucks. They stood on a siding at Fleissen station waiting for the issue of an export licence.

The chamber of commerce at Eger had supported my application to the Ministry of Trade and Industry at Prague. This machinery, I explained, was now surplus because of the recession. It was better to send it abroad in a bid to retain the British market than to let it stand idle. At the Ministry's request I had been to Prague and personally satisfied the officials who had dealt with the case. Why then the delay? Someone in Prague had had second thoughts and had referred the matter to the Textile Manufacturers' Federation at Reichenberg for an opinion. Since I had meanwhile left for London to inspect factory sites, Willie, my brother-in-law, paid two visits to Reichenberg and answered questions, whereupon the Federation recommended to the Ministry that our application be granted.

But wait! Having asked the employers' association it was only right and proper to obtain the opinion of the workpeople as well, said the Ministry, intending to refer the case to the appropriate trade union. Easier said than done. The workers of Fleissen were not members, and wanted no truck with the unions. To extricate itself from a somewhat awkward situation the Ministry agreed to accept the majority vote of the interested textile operatives. I forget who arranged the meeting. It was held at the Egerländer, one of the inns at Fleissen, where about a hundred men—knitters, mechanics, packers and labourers from our and other factories—foregathered at eight o'clock in the evening to decide the fate of our application.

I had not been invited. My presence, it was thought, would inhibit our workers and prevent them speaking freely. But I could not stay far away from such a fateful meeting. Not wanting to be seen hanging about outside the inn, I hid with Rolf in some bushes, anxiously waiting for the result. It was not long before Pöllman, the foreman of our winding department, came running out to tell us that all was lost; the vote had gone heavily against us. Immediate action was needed if anything was to be saved. Ignoring the wishes of the organisers, I elbowed myself into the crowded building, climbed on a table and, pretending not to know that the vote had already been taken, called for silence.

A hundred more or less familiar faces looked expectantly up at me through the wafts of tobacco smoke. 'Men,' I addressed them, outwardly calm but inwardly trembling lest my attempt to sway them should fail, 'you are about to take an important decision. But I see that your glasses are empty. You cannot take wise counsel when you are thirsty. Roll out a barrel of beer. I'll talk to you while you quench your thirst.'

Encouraged by a murmur of approval, I continued, explaining in simple words that Fleissen was about to lose the British market unless something were done to counter the effect of the sterling devaluation and the import duties which were sure to come. Could anyone suggest a better move than to establish a factory in England? Its capacity would be tiny compared with that of Czechoslovakia's knitting industry, but it would show the flag, be an embassy as it were, and ensure that contact with British customers was maintained. It would secure business for the old firm. What made more sense than to equip it with machinery for which there was no longer any use at Fleissen? Rumours that the twenty circulars we wanted to export would soon be followed by others and that the Fleissen factory was to be closed altogether were pure nonsense, I declared. Adolf Pasold & Sohn had not the slightest intention of withdrawing from the battle for survival—quite the contrary—and the two train ferry wagons at the station were part of the campaign. The sooner they could be dispatched the better for all concerned.

Then I called for a vote. All arms were raised. Everyone cheered. I wiped the sweat from my forehead, jumped off the table and shook hands with those around me. No one referred to the previous decision, which was dead now and best forgotten. I ordered another round of beer for everyone, and then, together with the members of the committee and the secretary of the village council, who was there to keep a record, drafted a telegram to the Ministry. It seemed prudent to take no chances. The evening ended in an atmosphere of good fellowship and celebration. Even Kraut congratulated me on my victory, 'won in such a truly democratic manner'.

'Democracy' was the catchword Czechoslovakia's statesmen had used, persistently and with great success, for internal and external propaganda ever since the republic was first thought of. It had become the favourite slogan of every village politician: a convenient word that meant all things to all men, a promise of some indefinable millenium brought about by majority decision and without personal responsibility.

Prague now reacted with exemplary promptness. The export licence was granted forthwith, and two days later, on 15 March, the two trucks were rolling towards the English Channel. Glad to have cleared yet another hurdle, I nevertheless felt uneasy. Kraut had been at that meeting: why had he not spoken out against me? Why had the Lehrmann brothers let me get away with that second vote? They could have lodged a complaint and without much difficulty prevented our machinery from leaving the country. So it was not their intention to discourage me from going ahead with my British adventure. Did they expect it to end in disaster? Most people thought it was bound to fail, including my uncles, the Geipels, who were such experienced businessmen. They warned me that I was taking on too much and tying myself up in knots. But my determination never faltered. I had more urgent things to do than worry about advice. Every week brought more disconcerting news from Britain. It now seemed inevitable that free trade would come to an end, but the question was, how soon? Would our machines reach England in time?

The 20 per cent *ad valorem* import duties came into force at midnight on 25/26 April 1932. With half a day to spare our two train ferry trucks reached Harwich on Monday 25 April, but the congestion caused by all the merchandise which had arrived from the Continent in a last-minute attempt to beat the tariff prevented our machines from being entered for customs clearance. They were not dealt with until the next morning, and so became one of the first consignments subject to duty. Hard luck—and such an unnecessary waste of money. It could have been saved but for the procrastination of the officials at Prague. We could ill afford to pay out £300 in British currency in addition to all the other mounting expenses.

So now we knew the worst. There could be little doubt that Czechoslovakia's exports of underwear to Britain were at an end. To bridge a tariff of 20 per cent in addition to the sterling devaluation seemed impossible, and the reaction was immediate. For months British buyers had placed their contracts on condition that they were free to terminate them if or when import duties came into force. Cancellations came pouring in now from all sides. Fleisen was to learn the real meaning of the crisis.

The bitter price wars of the past seemed like child's play in comparison with what was happening now. Of all our export markets, only Holland had neither devalued her currency nor introduced duties or other import restrictions. Almost the whole of Czechoslovakia's knitting industry therefore now tried to unload its vast surplus production there. Holland and the home market were the only outlets left, and manufacturers, faced with the alternative of dismissing their workpeople, most of whom were already on short time, or of selling their goods below cost, chose the latter course. They outdid each other in slashing prices and granted ever longer credit, getting deeper and deeper in debt themselves. Each tried to be the first to offer customers still more tempting terms in the hope of securing any business that was about before it could be taken by a rival. But the wily Dutch merchants, the bargain-hunting Bohemian wholesalers and Slovak stall-keepers were in no hurry to buy. With Britain out of the market and Czechoslovakia's vast production capacity bursting the floodgates, it paid to wait.

The man in the street, worried about the future, saved every krone he earned. The merchandise in the shops, supplied by manufacturers on credit, stayed on the shelves. People ate less. The baker sold less bread, the butcher fewer sausages, the farmer found no buyer for his corn. Industry deferred building projects, no manufacturer had the courage to buy machines. The crisis fed upon itself. The fewer jobs there were the harder everyone worked. Productivity rose, while consumption fell and trade slowed down. Industrial and trading concerns, finance houses, banks and even insurance companies ran out of money and became insolvent. Bankruptcy followed bankruptcy, and each day brought news of some fresh disaster.

On 12 March the Swedish match king, Ivar Kreuger, one of the financial giants of the post-war period, shot himself. He had played a prominent role in the financial reconstruction of Europe by making loans to half a dozen impoverished governments in return for manufacturing monopolies. Even France and Germany had borrowed money from him, the latter no less than $125 million. The crash of his empire, the International Match Trust, with 250 factories in more than forty countries, reverberated round the world.

This sensational event was soon overshadowed by another and, as far as Fleissen was concerned, much more real catastrophe. In the middle of May the first rumours flew through the village that Stern's of London were in financial difficulties, and a few days later it was confirmed that they sought a composition with their creditors. I was away on a business trip at the time and, when I returned, heard that Dr Lehrmann had chartered an aeroplane from the stunt flyer Arigi to make a dash to London and save what could be saved before the other creditors got there, but that brother Hans had refused to board the tiny aircraft made of fabric, timber and glue, and there had been a scene on Marienbad airfield. I do not know whether they actually got to London or not, but quite believe that they were frantic. Stern's, it was said, owed them more than £50,000.

Almost every underwear manufacturer in Fleissen was owed money by Stern's, including, of course, Adolf Pasold & Sohn, but what were our thousand pounds compared with the colossal sum the arch-enemy stood to lose! Frankly, I did not feel sorry for the Lehrmanns, but I grieved for Mr Stern. Even if he had rather deserted us of late—a blessing, as it now turned out— he remained one of my much admired heroes. How could this brilliant man have got into such trouble? In retrospect I wonder whether his Continental background contributed to his downfall. He made the mistake of drawing a parallel between the collapse of the German mark in 1923 and the fall in the international value of sterling caused by the departure from the gold standard. Lacking the true Englishman's blind conviction that the British are God's own people and that ultimately everything they do always turns out for the best, he foresaw a steady decline of the economy accompanied by a rapid erosion of sterling's purchasing power. To have goods, he thought, would be better than to have money, and so he borrowed and bought, and, being a reasonable if misguided man, shared the cost of devaluation and import duty with the manufacturers who supplied him.

To Millington's, by contrast, a pound remained a pound, and if the foreign manufacturer would not continue to supply at the old price he went without Millington's business. Traders generally—importers, wholesalers and re-tailers throughout Britain—took very much the same line. They would agree to some reduction in the quality of the merchandise but not to higher prices, and if Directoire knickers could not be supplied on this basis they simply refused to buy them. Mr Stern tried to swim against the stream and failed. The bank foreclosed, and his company was insolvent. On 26 May the liqui-dation of Stern Hosiery Ltd was gazetted, but in the event it did not take place. A composition was reached with the creditors. Over a period of some five years they were repaid in instalments, approximately 7s in the £. And truth being often stranger than fiction, Stern Hosiery Ltd eventually became a subsidiary of Pasolds Ltd—but that was very much later.

On 12 June another of my heroes came to grief. Thomas Bata's private aeroplane crashed on take-off at Zlin in bad weather, killing the world's greatest shoemaker and his pilot.

But now back to April, and the introduction of the tariff. According to information I pieced together later, the Lehrmanns, persuaded by Stern, had every intention of continuing to export the major part of their output to England irrespective of sterling devaluation and import duties. British women, so they reasoned, would not suddenly go without the 25 million pairs of Directoire knickers Czechoslovakia had been supplying annually and British industry was unable to produce. All goods were bound to get dearer as old stocks became exhausted. There might be a temporary slowing down of sales, but gradually the public would get used to paying more for underwear as for everything else. Provided, therefore, Stern and Lehrmann meanwhile bridged the gap they could confidently expect to retain the market on which they both depended.

The Lehrmanns were prepared to reduce their already very low prices by 20 per cent, the amount of the duty. They would knit the fabric a little looser, cut the garments a little smaller; their spinning mill, their dyehouse and their knitting factory would all work without profit for a whole year if need be. They would forego half their overheads, and in addition their workers were willing to accept a cut in wages. Similarly Stern's undertook to operate on a basis of only half overhead recovery and no profit, while Mr Alfred Stern would use his charisma and great persuasive powers to make buyers realise the need for higher prices.

Now that Stern's were insolvent, this scheme was no longer feasible, so Lehrmann's chose the only way open to them and threw their production on to the domestic market. Prepared for a price reduction of 20 per cent, they panicked and made it 25 per cent, which brought them orders and enabled them to keep their factory going, while putting a dozen other manufacturers out of business.

I had no intention of entering this price-cutting competition, which could only lead to the ruin of one, or probably both, of us. Since the underwear trade had virtually collapsed, I decided to concentrate all our resources on expanding our business in sweaters and waistcoats. Our White Bear brand had made an excellent name for itself. We never tampered with the quality but improved it every season, and the public had confidence in it. Nor had we ever altered—in those days this meant reduced—the price, and consequently shopkeepers never had to mark old stock down. Our advertisements, modest though they were, helped them to sell the brand, and their only grievance was that we could not supply enough. Now that money was so scarce the demand for hard-wearing, inexpensive garments became greater than ever. Many men went to work in a White Bear sweater, for which they paid ten kronen, to save their jacket of woven cloth, costing three or four times as much, for Sunday.

I felt convinced that the White Bear range of garments could keep our business going, provided we had the courage to do three things. We had to increase the number of circulars capable of knitting double-chaineuse fabric, equip Leibitschgrund to spin marl yarns, and mount a full-scale advertising campaign. These projects seemed almost recklessly adventurous at the depth of the slump, but we decided to go ahead with them.

The news that we were buying machines was at first received with incredulity, and then brought a spate of offers. There were more double-chaineuse circulars on the market than I expected. Most of them hung in the homes of commission knitters, out-workers who, in good times, made fabric for manufacturers with insufficient capacity of their own. When trade slackened the commission knitters were the first to suffer. Few had had any work since sterling was devalued, and now that Britain had imposed import duties and Stern had become insolvent what hope was there for them? They were only too willing to sell their machines, and we soon filled most of the gaps left by the twenty single-chaineuse circulars we had shipped to England. Not that we indulged in a spending spree. Like everyone else we looked at every krone twice before we parted with it. The thought of purchasing new circulars, for instance, never entered our minds. They were much too expensive. But we did buy conversion parts from the makers and turned all idle single-chaineuse machines which were suitable into double-chaineuse ones.

While Rolf and I were thus transforming the knitting plant, Willie tried to spin marl yarns at Leibitschgrund. He sent sample lots of cleaned, loose cotton in canvas bags to Krey & Co., the commission dyers at Schönbach, who dyed them in a wooden vat and dried them in an improvised oven. Willie then carded this cotton, made it into sliver, drafted one coloured sliver together with several white ones and then spun the yarn in the normal way on the mule. Simple though it may sound, there were snags at every stage, with sticking fibres, static electricity, coloured fly and other difficulties, as every cotton spinner who has read this far will have guessed, but I do not wish to burden the layman with too many technicalities. Let it suffice that we solved the problems one by one, and before very long whole lorryloads of brown and grey marl yarns produced in this primitive manner arrived from Leibitschgrund. The yarn was a little uneven, but our knitting machines consumed it without any serious hitch. To our delight the production of sweater fabric rose by leaps and bounds. Nearly a third of our circulars operated in shifts, knitting nothing else.

Now to the advertising campaign. It will be remembered that we registered as a trade mark the picture of a polar bear, together with the English words 'White Bear' instead of the Czech, German, Slovak or Hungarian equivalent. The choice had proved a wise one: the brand name was popular with Czechoslovaks of all tongues. We had steered clear of the dangerous rock of nationalism. The bear on its iceflow continued to convey the strength and warmth of our sweaters and waistcoats; their price was still no higher than that of a simple meal, although sausages, bread and beer had all become cheaper. There was no need to give the campaign a new slant. What was new was its scale. While other advertisers economised and cut or stopped their allocations we trebled ours. It amounted even now to only 30,000 kronen, but at no time would anyone else in our industry have dreamed of spending so much good money on a series of ephemeral illustrations in the press. Czecho-slovak newspapers never carried much advertising, with the notable excep-tion of Bata's, and in the depression year of 1932 less than usual. Our campaign therefore made a quite exceptional impact.

Its success was such that despite our increased production we had to ration the supply of White Bear merchandise, giving priority to those customers who also bought underwear. This helped to keep the other two-thirds of our circulars going, if only on single-shift working. All our double-chaineuse knitting machines worked round the clock, of course, and kept the sewing department busy until nine o'clock in the evening. The complicated seams of sweaters with collars, zips, welts and pockets, waistcoats with bound fronts and sleeves and long rows of buttons and buttonholes took very much longer than the simple seams of Directoire knickers. It was a wonderful sight to see the lights of our factory ablaze while the rest of Fleissen—including, for a change, Lehrmann's too—lay in darkness.

I enjoyed being in the factory at night, among the humming machinery and the workpeople who operated it. Schreiner and Hoyer, our chief clerks, had long gone home, and I could no longer be called to the office to sort out difficulties, answer the telephone, wrangle with suppliers or make excuses to irate customers. There was tranquillity at night, time to watch the circu-lars revolve and gradually fill their trays with fabric, time to chat to the knitters about the marl yarns from Leibitschgrund, time to amuse myself drawing electric sparks with my knuckles from the cotton being brushed on the rotating rollers of the fleecing machine. I enjoyed a peace and content-ment at night which I never experienced in the daytime.

We had reason to feel pleased. Our policy was paying off. The year that had started so badly promised to end well. While our competitors operated below cost, our White Bear business showed a clear profit of 18 per cent, in addition to which Leibitschgrund made 10 per cent on the marl yarns it supplied to Fleissen. Father and Grandfather had never, to my knowledge, operated with such fat profit margins. True, this profit had to make up for the depressed prices at which we sold our underwear, but an overall return of some 6 per cent remained, and I see from a diary entry of 19 October 1932 that in spite of substantial stocks and over 2 million kronen owed to us by customers we had no bank overdraft and paid all our suppliers before their invoices fell due.

The credit for this satisfactory state of affairs was not all due to our own efforts. We were helped by developments over which we had little control. Czechoslovakia's cotton spinners were in trouble. Their order books were empty, their mills on short time. Competition had slashed prices to suicidal levels, while overheads remained. Some of the smaller firms were on the verge of bankruptcy, and it was only a question of time when the larger ones would follow. For two years the Cotton Spinners' Federation had endeavoured to negotiate price agreements among its members, but had failed. Bohemian industrialists were an independent breed. Now, in desperation, they signed at last the document that created a cotton spinners' cartel, fixing minimum selling prices and a quota for each mill. It ended the cut-throat competition and put the industry on a healthier basis.

Leibitschgrund fell on its feet. Its annual quota was fixed at only 350,000 lb, a ridiculously small quantity, but fortunately the restriction applied only to ordinary cotton yarn. The production of specialities, such as mixture, marl and condenser yarns, remained unrestricted, while their prices adjusted themselves upwards to the general level. Since we had recently changed a substantial section of the mill from spinning plain cotton to marl yarns, the cartel could not have come at a better time for us or the rules been drawn more in our favour. Leibitschgrund became profitable almost overnight. How I wished Father were alive to see his dream come true.

The White Bear business continued to grow. And in spite of British import duties Mr Hurst was still sending orders for marl jumpers. We needed larger supplies of marl yarns. The time had come to give up our Heath Robinson method of producing them. Should we not install a modern plant and dye the cotton ourselves? Willie thought we should. There was plenty of soft water at Leibitschgrund, but how could we dispose of the effluents? It was out of the question to discharge them into the trout stream.

I made a quick calculation. 'Supposing we aim at an annual production of 30,000 dozen White Bear sweaters and waistcoats, we shall have to knit 300,000 lb of double-chaineuse fabric. This takes 200,000 lb of condenser yarn and 100,000 lb of marl. The condenser needs no dyeing. The marl, on the other hand, we draft from only one coloured sliver and seven white ones, so there are a mere 12,500 lb of cotton to be dyed. Let's add some for Mr Hurst's jumpers and for other things and make it 20,000 lb—still a trifling weight spread over a whole year. I'm not a dyer, but I think a liquor ratio of ten to one is a realistic estimate, in which case the total weight of coloured water to be disposed of would be 300,000 lb, a volume of 30,000 gallons in a whole year, a mere 100 gallons per working day! We own most of the valley, 500 acres of it. Surely with a little ingenuity we can get rid of this tiny quantity of coloured water without polluting the stream,' I said.

'The north slope of the valley consists of vertical layers of soft slate,'
Willie reflected. 'If we dig a large hole and fill it with pine branches to filter
the cotton fibres out of the water I daresay 100 gallons a day would soak away
—simply disappear into the ground.' This made sense. We dug a few test
holes and then asked Ingenieur Gradl of Eger, a civil engineer and expert on
river pollution, whom the authorities were in the habit of consulting in
difficult cases, to vet our scheme and draw it up in presentable form. A pretty
picture always helped, and a fee paid well in advance of trouble might provide
a friend at court. Farmers and fishermen all along the Leibitsch were very
touchy about their trout water: they would raise a hue and cry, I felt sure, the
moment they heard of the first bucket of dye effluent being emptied into our
trench even if, as I hoped, no particle of colour ever reached the stream.

Ingenieur Gradl positioned his red and white poles, surveyed the site we
had chosen for the effluent pit and drew cross-sections of the valley. They
showed the bed of the brook, the sand, the soil and the sloping laminations of
the slate—convincing evidence of the soundness of our scheme. We felt
reassured.

Notwithstanding all those lessons in colour chemistry at the textile college
my practical knowledge of dyeing was limited, and Willie knew only what he
had read up in books, but we were determined to do better than dye our
cotton in an old-fashioned wooden vat. The engineering firm of Carl Fleissner & Sohn of Asch had perfected a new method of dyeing and drying fibres
in the form of sliver. It had proved so successful that their equipment, made
of stainless steel, was being installed by the leading wool spinners of France
and Germany. Although designed for wool, why should it not dye cotton
equally well? We discussed the proposition with Ingenieur Hans Fleissner.
Trade was bad: he too needed orders, and he offered to design and build
machinery for our specific purpose. On 13 December 1932, as the first snow-
flakes, heralds of the approaching winter, came whirling out of a grey sky, we
signed the contract for the plant. The purchase price came to 110,000 kronen,
and delivery was promised for March 1933.

We have now heard a good deal about developments at Fleissen and Leibitschgrund, but what, the reader will ask, was happening meanwhile at Langley in Buckinghamshire? Had the new factory been completed? Far from
letting matters slide, I travelled at least half a dozen times to England in 1932
and stayed, all told, several months, but it will be less confusing if I deal with
the events there separately.

23

'MADE
IN ENGLAND'
1932

EXCEPT FOR THE finishing touches, the factory building at Langley had been completed in eleven weeks and was ready before the end of May, as promised. I shall never forget the thrill I experienced on seeing it for the first time. The red-brown facing bricks I had selected looked splendid, and the clean horizontal lines gave the building an even more modern appearance than it had on Helmut's drawings. The three bays, although only 9,000 square feet in all—a very modest area by any standard—seemed to provide more space than we would require. I was delighted with the lofty entrance hall, the large north-light windows, the glass-hard granolithic floor and the compact little oil-fired boiler unit with its automatic control. The rubber-floored upstairs offices, with their observation windows into the factory, held out the promise of quiet efficiency. The modern toilets equalled those of any good hotel. Everything was just as planned and of excellent quality. I was overjoyed. This was the happiest day of my life.

The ceiling was white throughout, the upper half of the walls eggshell, the lower battleship blue, as were the steel stanchions, the rest of the steelwork and the doors. I had gone to some trouble over this colour scheme and, back at Fleissen, had spent several evenings mixing grey, blue and white paint until the resulting shade satisfied me. I then painted a few square yards of cardboard and sent cuttings to the engineering firms with whom we did business, requesting them to supply all our machines in exactly that colour so that the whole plant would match. And to all the stanchions I intended to fit brackets to hold pots with bright flowers. We would show the good people of Langley how beautiful a factory could be.

I had not, of course, come to Langley merely to see the new building, but to give final instructions about such details as the exact position and height of the steel girders which were to support the knitting machines, the location of the driving shafts, the electric motors, switches and fuse boxes, the fleecing machine, the steam pipe to the calendar and a hundred and one other things. There was, for instance, a platform weighing machine I had to buy. The pit for it was already prepared. Avery's salesman came to see me, and I told him to supply a scale with the dial calibrated in kilograms and grams.

'You mean pounds and ounces, of course,' he corrected me.

'No, I mean kilograms and grams.'

The surprised look on his face amused me. 'Britain has taken the historic decision to leave the gold standard and abandon her policy of free trade to get her ailing industries going again. The next logical step to make them competitive must be the adoption of the metric system. It cannot be far off.'

Now it was his turn to be amused. 'They've been talking about it ever since I was a boy,' he replied, smiling. 'I fear it may take longer than you expect. Let's put both the metric and the English scales on the dial.'

'Very well,' I said, more to please him than because I thought he was right. The writing was surely on the wall. In the nineteenth century, when everybody had plenty of time, English weights, measures and money may not have been too serious a handicap, but in this modern age, speed and accuracy were important. A Continental schoolboy could equate distance, weight, volume, horsepower, temperature and atmospheric pressure easily in his head, while the incredibly cumbersome English system relied on mathematical tricks, conversion tables and approximations. It was not a day too soon to discard it, I felt, having spent hours during these past few months over such time-consuming calculations. No doubt Mr Watkinson and his colleagues, those able men of Whitehall, were already preparing the change-over.

How wrong I was! Had I known that almost forty years would elapse before Britain began to think metric—and then only within the narrow limits of the temperature scale and of money—I would have lost faith in her future. The British are originators who have immeasurably enriched mankind with their discoveries and inventions, but they are singularly unwilling to learn from those of others. As yet the conversion table manufacturers had little to fear, but in due course the change to the decimal system over the whole range of weights and measures would have to be faced. The mounting cost of the delay must run into untold millions.

At Paddington I inspected the cases containing our machinery which the Great Western Railway Company was storing for us in one of their warehouses. To satisfy myself that it had suffered no damage during the journey or the handling by the customs I opened one of the heavy crates, and found the contents dry and free from rust. The delicate machines had been in their boxes for five long months, and I looked forward impatiently to having them moved to their new home at Langley and to see them running again. Soon we would be offering our customers goods with 'Made in England' labels. The thought of it would have made me sing with joy had the dark shadow of unemployment that lay over the enterprise in Czechoslovakia not been ever present in my mind.

To erect the machinery, get production going and then train local labour we had recruited eight young men and eight girls, volunteers from among our employees at Fleissen. I had brought a list of their names, ages, and qualifications with me, and now asked Mr Matthews of the Board of Trade to help me to obtain labour permits for them. Mr Matthews was a wiry little man, friendly, patient and pedantic. He knew about our factory from Mr Watkinson, who had told him to be of assistance to us, and being a conscientious civil servant he meant to carry out his chief's instructions to the letter. But oh dear, oh dear! Sixteen foreign experts were more than he could recommend.

I explained that it would be difficult enough to operate the factory with a team of only sixteen skilled people and train green labour at the same time. We could not do it with fewer. Expense had prevented us from planning to bring to England a single person more than was absolutely necessary. Mr Matthews listened sympathetically, but refused to give way, and since I knew that without his recommendation the Home Office would issue no permits I reluctantly offered to cross two names off my list. With a sigh he agreed to put the remaining fourteen names forward.

A few days later an official from the Home Office telephoned. Would Mr Hurst and I please go and see him? On his table lay the list with the fourteen names. He frowned. In view of the high level of unemployment he could not let all these aliens come into the country to take jobs which could be done by British workers. If I agreed to reduce the number to eight he would give serious consideration to my application. There was a large knitting industry in the Midlands, and I would have to find the remaining key personnel at Leicester and Nottingham.

'Our machines and methods differ from those used by British manufacturers,' I protested. 'If Leicester and Nottingham could do what we are doing there would be no point in our coming to this country.'

The official glanced up from the list. 'The average age of your experts is barely twenty. I find it hard to believe that some of them could not equally well be replaced by older, more experienced British workers.'

'They may be young, but most of them have been with us for six years or longer. Their parents and grandparents worked for us all their lives. They are a hand-picked team, thoroughly familiar with our way of working, and I can rely on them.'

'Ten permits are the most I can promise you, valid for periods from one to six months. Thereafter your experts will have to return to their own country.'

My heart sank. We had reached another crisis. 'In that case I shall make no attempt to start the factory,' I said firmly. 'It would be doomed to failure. There will be no jobs for the fifty British people we were going to train.'

Without comment the official disappeared into an adjoining room, presumably to consult his superior. Mr Hurst nudged me. 'We can't afford to fall out with the Home Office,' he whispered, afraid I was about to be needlessly obstinate again. 'Take the permits he's offering. A bird in the hand is worth two in the bush.' I knew he failed to appreciate the implications. Watching the clock on the wall, we sat and waited. The minutes seemed endless.

At last the man returned. 'We can do somewhat better,' he said. 'We are prepared to give you twelve permits, of which three will be valid for twelve months, three for six months, three for three months and three for one month, on condition that the activities of these foreign experts are confined to the teaching of British operatives. They must not be employed on production work.'

Could I refuse? I deleted two more names from the list, divided the remaining ones into four categories, and hoped for the best. Out in the street I gave vent to my feelings. 'What do these pen-pushers know about operating a factory! It doesn't occur to them that the foreign workers have to unpack, clean and erect our machinery first, and start it up, then get production going —that is to say, manufacture goods which can be sold. Not till we get orders for our products and the factory is running smoothly can we begin training labour. But it's no use trying to explain things to the Home Office, with its take-it-or-leave-it attitude. Back in Czechoslovakia the whole nation knows that a country's welfare depends on the efficiency of its industry, and that industry must always have priority, but here it's hardly taken seriously. If these officials were Czechs I'd know how to talk to them. They'd use their imagination and interpret the regulations to suit the case, I'd show the customary appreciation, they would share the proceeds with their colleagues at the Ministry of Labour, and, much as I disapprove of these methods, the factory would be running in no time at all.'

'Your Czech officials didn't use much imagination when they held up the machinery at Fleissen station,' Mr Hurst chuckled. 'But don't worry too much. If things don't work out we shall have to ask for more help from the Board of Trade. This isn't necessarily the end of the matter.'

He never spoke a truer word. In due course the Home Office sent the twelve labour permits to Mr Hurst, who posted them on to me at Fleissen, and the British consulate at Prague provided our people's passports with the necessary visas. So far so good; but this was only the beginning of a long-drawn-out and for me very worrying struggle in which I fought for the retention of our essential key workers while the authorities pressed us to send them back to Czechoslovakia long before we had been able to train replacements. To see the whole team being taken away in a police van was one of my recurring nightmares.

I had to smile when I thought of our village lads and girls as 'foreign experts'. Ten out of the team of twelve had never been farther from home than fifty miles or seen a ship larger than a rowing boat. Now, all of a sudden, they were to see the world. With a mixture of eager anticipation and apprehension they looked forward to the journey that was to take them across half the Continent and over the sea to far-away England.

The men were needed first. Wearing their Sunday best, and carrying identical fibre suitcases the firm had bought for them wholesale, they set off with Rolf and me on 11 June. We had much fun on the journey. I remember it as if it was yesterday. Rolf had brought his accordion, and so had Georg Wollner, our chauffeur mechanic, whom we took as a fitter because of his all-round engineering skill. Before very long the strains of 'Egerländer halts enk zam' attracted a fellow traveller to our party, a knitting foreman from Asch who was on his way to Fischer's branch factory in London. We questioned him about it, but although he was glad of our company and stayed with us for the rest of the voyage he refused to be drawn.

Bohemian tunes shortened the long sea crossing from Flushing to Harwich. The dreaded cross-examination on landing passed without hitch. I had some anxious moments when I temporarily lost two members of the party in the labyrinth of London's Underground, but otherwise all went well, and we arrived at Langley tired but in excellent spirits on Sunday night. For a few minutes we stood and admired the outline of the new factory silhouetted against the night sky, but because the hour was late I refused to open up and show it to my eager companions. Then we carried our suitcases along the dark footpath that led from the station across the brickfield to Langley church and the Red Lion. Our lads bedded down in the loft of the four-hundred-year-old inn, while Rolf and I shared a small room at Mrs Molland's, a widow in Meadfield Road who took the occasional lodger. Langley was not laid out to accommodate travellers.

Monday 13 June was the great day on which we took possession of our new factory. Our lads were already waiting as I unlocked the front door at 7 a.m., and after an hour's tour of inspection we got down to work, opening the heavy machinery cases which the GWR had delivered.

The knitters, little Ernst Schreiner and the two Passler brothers, began with the circulars. These large 44 in. diameter machines with their thousands of exposed needles were awkward things to manhandle, but with the help of Georg Wollner, who had the muscles of Goliath, they were lifted safely from their boxes and placed in rows below the steel girders on which they were to be hung later. Pöllmann started to assemble the winding frames in the positions I had chalked on the floor. Bergmann meanwhile unpacked the drum and the rollers of the Gessner fleecer from their crates and laid them out ready for erection. It was a busy scene, and before long the factory floor was covered with machine parts of every description.

The Red Lion provided plain but adequate meals. We walked there every mid-day across the sun-baked brickfield—it was a hot and glorious summer— and in the evenings we bathed in the canal. The water was stagnant and not very clean, but it felt wonderfully refreshing after a day's hard manual work erecting machinery.

The news spread that we had started work. On Thursday came the first applicants for jobs. Some were sent by Slough labour exchange, others, like Jock Watson and Bernard Walker, came on their own initiative. I engaged both, Watson because he was a Scot and his hands told that they were used to hard work, Walker because he tinkered with motor-bikes and was obviously mechanically-minded. I had no idea what wages we could pay them. Mr Colmer, the clerk I had engaged, was not due for another ten days. Wages would be one of his responsibilities; meanwhile, if the two young men wanted to start work, they could. There were machines to be unpacked, lifted and cleaned. Both reported for work the following day and stayed with the firm for almost half a century.

We engaged altogether six young men without being able to tell them how much they would earn. This vexed them, but it was better than having no job at all. Rolf kept a record of the hours they worked, and when Mr Colmer arrived two weeks later he ascertained the general wage level in the area from the manager of Slough labour exchange. We then paid all the learners a rate of 9d an hour; only the gardener, who was a skilled man, got 1s. He had to make a lawn and lay out some flower beds in front of the factory. I was anxious to show the people of Langley how groundless were their fears of industry spoiling their pretty village.

Mr Colmer had first come to my notice several years earlier as a junior clerk at the importing house of A. T. Singer in the City. Wondering where to find a reliable man for the office at Langley, I remembered a chance remark of Mr Singer's, praising the diligence of his young clerk. Since Mr Singer was now dead, and his business had closed down, I offered Mr Colmer the position at a weekly wage of £6, and he took it. He was then thirty and by far the oldest and highest-paid member of the Pasold manufacturing organisation in Britain. His career with us began in the small room with bare brick walls to the left of the present main entrance, which we furnished with three wooden packing cases. The largest served as a desk and had books and type-writer on it, Mr Colmer sat on a smaller one, and the smallest was used as wastepaper basket.

It was a blessing when he came. I had not thought we would need a clerk while we were erecting our machinery, but the many unexpected callers, finding the front door locked, came round to the goods entrance and wasted my time. Representatives of insurance companies, house agents, salesmen, a continuous stream of middle-aged labourers looking for jobs, Mr Chesterman the stationmaster enquiring how soon the first merchandise would be ready to be transported by his railway, a local politician named Trevener endeavouring to get on a confidential footing with me for reasons of his own, and all kinds of strange people whom I felt I had to listen to politely yet be on my guard against.

Mr Trevener seemed disappointed when he found that I had already seen the newspaper articles about the objections to our factory raised by the ratepayers' association, and that I did not think our being at Langley was entirely due to the valiant stand he personally had taken on our behalf. I did not quite trust this mild-mannered little man at first—without cause, as it turned out—and it took a year or two before we became friends. He was later appointed a Justice of the Peace.

A few days after Mr Trevener's visit I received an invitation to cocktails with Mr Austin, the head of the actors' orphanage, who represented the defeated opposition. He tried to impress me with his tolerance. He and his friends were not prejudiced against tradespeople—manufacturers of women's underclothing, for instance—even if they were foreigners from Central Europe, and should I need any advice I was free to call on him. Annoyed by his conceit and condescension, I swallowed my pride and his sherry, said 'Thank you', and never saw him again. Having steadfastly refused to be drawn into politics, local or national, in Czechoslovakia, I was determined to keep out of them in Britain. I had other things to do.

At the same time as Mr Colmer came Adolf Köhler, the works manager. He was a lad of twenty, a graduate of the textile college at Reutlingen in Württemberg, who had been recommended to us by Haaga, the German knitting machine manufacturers at whose plant he had been working to gain practical experience. We had taken him for two months to our factory at Fleissen to show him our way of manufacturing Directoire knickers. He was to take charge of the winding and knitting departments at Langley and help with the erection of the laying-up and cutting table and the sewing conveyor belt. A likable, hard-working young man with a ready smile on his face, he was never afraid of getting his hands dirty. We paid him a weekly wage of £3 6s 8d, the equivalent of 50 Reichsmarks.

Everyone worked long hours with enthusiasm, including Saturday mornings of course. Within fourteen days the two winding frames were in running order, the twenty knitting machines hung on the girders, the electric motors and the two line shafts were mounted, the pulleys were fitted with belts and the first circular began to rotate, no longer freewheeling but actually knitting fabric. Soon a second and a third came to life, filling the little factory with the familiar hum that was music in our ears. Before the end of the week Schreiner and the Passler brothers between them had over a dozen machines running, while the local lads watched, took turns on the winding frames, carried bobbins and, like all learners, generally got in the way. We were patient. At Fleissen we reckoned it took two years to become a proficient Terrot operator.

We had sent some cases of yarn from Leibitschgrund with the machinery so that we could start regular production without being held up while experimenting with British-spun yarns. Someone recommended Nahum's of Manchester as suppliers. They were yarn merchants, and we were a little hesitant, for we thought we should buy from the spinners direct, but when we received Nahum's samples and quotations we could hardly believe our eyes. The cotton yarns they offered us, 24s, 36s and 40s, were much better than our own and at least 25 per cent cheaper. How could this be, when the whole world insisted that Lancashire's cotton mills were too antiquated to compete? Wages in Bolton, Wigan and Burnley were bound to be higher than in Czechoslovakia. On the other hand, why could not British manufacturers, who were able to buy their yarns so cheaply, compete with us when it came to Directoire knickers? I was puzzled. Was it only because we had the edge on them with our condenser yarns? Those spun in Lancashire felt flat and lifeless, whereas ours, though spun from reclaimed waste clippings, were soft and lofty and gave a much woollier fleece. Even if I could not unravel the mystery, it was a most encouraging beginning. We placed a trial contract with Nahum's for several thousand pounds' weight of cotton yarn spread over the three counts, and I wrote a report to Willie, my brother-in-law, telling him that in future we would want only condenser yarns from Leibitschgrund.

Nahum's supplied from stock, and the bulk delivery proved every bit as good as the samples. This first transaction led to regular and very pleasant business. We received excellent service and never had the least cause for complaint. Cotton yarn was our most basic raw material, and to find the supply position so surprisingly simple was a relief.

The reader may ask why I had not informed myself about such important things as yarn prices and wage rates before deciding to build a factory in England. To know them would have been interesting, of course, but not conclusive and perhaps even misleading. Yarn prices fluctuated. It was largely a matter of finding the right spinner at the right time. And wage rates without corresponding output figures were meaningless. To worry about them prematurely served little purpose. Whatever the difficulties, I was determined to establish a factory. It was a long-term venture, not to be influenced by purely temporary considerations.

Of all our problems the most frustrating was getting our fabric dyed. We had found a firm of dyers at Acton, only a few miles away, named Sergeant's, who claimed they were laid out for processing knitted material such as ours. Despite their refusal to let me see more than a small corner of their plant, this sufficed to tell me how pitifully out-of-date it was. However, the old wooden winch dyeing machines were large enough to take four of our pieces at a time; they had plenty of water and apparently no effluent troubles, and so I saw no reason why they should not do our work satisfactorily and at an acceptable price. Little did I anticipate at this early stage the difficulties and the never-ending arguments with Sergeant's that lay ahead in the months and years to come.

Teething troubles, we thought when the shades of the first twenty pieces they dyed for us did not match our patterns. Mr Twinam, the sales director, protested that we were too particular but promised the next batch would be perfect. Reassured, and happy that everything was going according to plan, I left for Fleissen to clear up the work which had accumulated there while I was away. In two weeks I was to return with our five instructresses, who were to teach the Langley girls how to cut and sew Directoires. Meanwhile our lads would have to vacate the Red Lion to make room for the girls.

Rolf turned the large, empty room at the top of the factory entrance hall into a dormitory. We had sent half a dozen iron bedsteads for this purpose in the trucks containing the machinery. The first few lengths of fabric knitted on each circular were invariably faulty and provided material for mattresses, for which farmer Brown, our neighbour, supplied the straw. Empty machine crates were made into primitive wardrobes, and the purchase of an electric kettle completed the equipment of the new sleeping quarters. Henceforth the team lived on the job, taking only their meals at the Red Lion. This reduced the cost from £4 10s to £2 10s a week.

Our factory at Fleissen closed for the annual holidays during the last week in July. This was therefore the best time for me to take our girls to England. Mother came also, to supervise the start of their work at Langley. She had not been to England before, and was eagerly looking forward to seeing the new plant and the country with which I was so intoxicated. Ingo, on the other hand, would have preferred to spend his vacation at home, bathing with his pals from the village or riding my motor-cycle. Not as mature as Rolf had been at his age, nor burdened with Rolf's strong sense of duty, he argued that the new factory would get along well enough without him. But I insisted that he come. He was now sixteen and quite old enough to take an interest in the business. There were many ways in which he could make himself useful at

Langley, especially as he was handy with tools and had already developed a remarkable flair for solving minor engineering problems.

Rolf and his team had made good progress during my absence. Some fifty pieces of fabric, all dyed, fleeced and rolled, awaited us when we got back. Using the cast iron carriage which Arbach had supplied, Köhler and Watson neatly positioned half a dozen layers of material on the twenty-metre-long cutting table. Mother and Miss Feiler, one of the Bohemian instructresses, marked the top layer with the help of paper patterns and then we stood in suspense, watching the motor-driven knife following the chalk marks. The circular blade cut through the thickness of three inches of fabric as if it were butter. A thousand pairs of women's knickers cut by one girl in less than an hour—and just as accurately as with hand shears! I wished Grandmother and our workpeople back at Fleissen could see it. If all the innovations we had planned were going to work so well there would be no other factory to compete with ours.

We were also anxious to try out the sewing conveyor belt. It stood erected, the sewing machines were mounted on their individual stands, but with only four sewing machinists, Cislaghi, Stingl, Deinl and Schnabel, it would have been useless to run the belt. We had to curb our impatience and operate without it until some of the local girls had learned to use power sewing machines, which would take a few weeks. Many came to apply for work. The first to be engaged were seven school leavers, bright-eyed youngsters whom we paid 6d an hour, and three young married women, who got 7d. We did our best to make winders, cutters, machinists, menders, folders and packers of them. For the present they watched while our Fleissen girls worked.

The first consignment of merchandise to leave the factory, fifty dozen women's Directoire knickers, went to West Bromwich. My old friend George Peacock, thoughtful as always, had given us an open order for 500 dozen for delivery at a date and price suitable to ourselves. This made it possible for me to concentrate on getting production going before having to worry about sales. The thought that there could be the slightest need to feel concerned about any possible lack of orders never entered my mind. The quality of the knickers we manufactured at Langley was as good—well, almost as good— as that of Fleissen-made merchandise. Naturally the standard would drop a little as the learners gradually went on production, but I was sure our customers would understand. At long last they were able to buy our Directoires with a 'Made in England' label in them, and they would be delighted.

How well I remember putting the first samples of our Langley products in my bag and, with a song in my heart, catching the early train for London. I was a manufacturer of British goods now, and I felt proud. All doors would be open wide. If Mr Hurst and Peggy did not share my exuberance it was merely, I told myself, because they neither understood what we had achieved technically nor appreciated the potential of the underwear trade. Peggy was positively hostile towards fleecy knickers, and refused to call on customers to try and take orders for 'those awful bloomers'. She would be surprised when she saw the large contracts buyers were going to place!

I had asked Mr Hurst to make an appointment for me to see Mr Draper, the head buyer of the underwear department of Cook & Son. They were the largest wholesalers in town and I was thinking of allocating a part of our output to them. But instead of the cordial reception I expected, and a buyer eager to see the Langley samples, we were kept waiting for an hour without even a chair to sit on while Mr Draper went out to coffee with another caller. Was he not afraid that I might walk out and sell all we could make to other wholesale houses?

'What have you brought to show me?' he grunted when he returned. 'Make it snappy, I'm busy.'

It was hardly the reception I had hoped for, but Mr Draper had probably not got the message correctly and did not realise we had come to show him our first Langley-made garments. Taking a pair of navy blue knickers from my case and holding them up for his inspection, I said triumphantly, 'All British!' although, strictly speaking, they had been made by our Czechoslovak workers at Langley. But he merely shook his head. 'Sorry, gentlemen,' he said. 'I have enough fleecy knickers to see me through the winter,' turned his back and walked away.

To my amazement the reactions from the Fore Street Warehouse Co., Stapley & Smith, and Copestake Crampton & Co. were all very much the same as Mr Draper's. The wholesalers were clearly overstocked with Directoires which Stern and other importers had brought into the country in anticipation of the import duties. And they had all over-bought when Stern got into financial difficulties and threw his huge stocks on the market at reduced prices. Wholesale buyers were gods to Mr Hurst. He had no other clients. His livelihood as manufacturers' agent depended on them. He was permanently at their beck and call, and their word was gospel to him. They confirmed his worst fears. There was no longer a market for fleecy knickers. The sooner we forgot about them and began to manufacture something else, preferably ladies' jumpers, the better.

'A range of jumpers. At least six different styles,' said Peggy when we told her of the disappointing day we had had. Neither she nor Mr Hurst seemed to understand that we were quite incapable of manufacturing anything more complicated than knickers at Langley for a year or two at least.

More perplexed than seriously perturbed by this unforeseen state of affairs, I decided to call on my old friends Roberts & Hohly in Jewin Crescent.

They were pleased to see me and interested to hear that the new factory was now in production. They inspected my samples, said they were not impressed with the dull shades but complimented me on the heavy fleece and enquired after the price. But when I quoted 7s a dozen Mr Roberts laughed. 'Our customers can buy the genuine article for 5s,' he said, dropping the samples back into my open case.

'Genuine?' I did not understand what he meant.

'Knickers made by your own firm at Fleissen, or by Lehrmann's. From stocks in this country—as many as they like.'

'Old stock of Stern's, perhaps,' I admitted, 'but that won't last for ever. Besides, these are made in England.' And I proudly pointed at the label. 'Surely a valuable selling point!'

'You can forget that,' replied Mr Roberts. 'It cuts no ice with our customers. Price is the only thing that matters. The women who wear these things wouldn't pay a halfpenny a pair more because they're made in Britain.'

I did not sleep quite as well as usual that night, and next morning had another look at our figures to see how far we could reduce the price. To calculate production costs anywhere near accurately was impossible at this early stage. Could we base them on the output of our Bohemian workers? How would the performance of the Langley labour compare when it was fully trained? How economical would it be in the handling of raw material? A little extra waste in winding, fleecing and cutting could substantially affect the cost of the finished garment. What percentage of seconds would we get? What would our overheads be? We could do little more than make guesses—intelligent ones, I hoped. But however inaccurate our costings were, it would be quite unrealistic to hope that we could produce our knickers for 6s a dozen, let alone 5s.

A few days later we made the round of the East End, calling on Goldenfeld, Deyong, the Houndsditch Warehouse Co., Skolnick, Noah Cohen and other Jewish firms with whom I had done business in the past. They were smaller and less pretentious than the great, conservative wholesale houses Mr Hurst liked to deal with. The owners were mostly of East European origin, second-generation immigrants from the ghettos of Poland and Russia whose natural talent for bargaining and capacity for hard work had acquired an overlay of Cockney wit and accent, and who occasionally dropped into Yiddish when talking to each other. A fascinating combination. Importers, exporters, traders in bulk and retailers all at the same time and from the same premises, their businesses demanded a dexterity of mind and adaptability of attitude which only the Jewish merchants possessed. They handled a large volume of our type of cheap underwear, and if there was anything they did not know about the 'rag trade' it was not worth knowing. Frequently it was the boss himself who came to talk to us, gesticulating freely with wide-open hands, but if he was out or too busy the buyers and departmental heads, usually his cousins, second cousins, brothers-in-law or other relatives, faithfully echoed his views.

'Fleecy knickers? Wouldn't touch them, not ladies' size. Trade's been killed stone dead by all the inferior stuff rushed into the country before the tariff was put on. Children's fleecies and school knickers still sell, but women want lightweight underwear now, either cotton interlock or artificial silk. Only the very big ones, those who need o/s or ex. o/s, still buy fleecy Directoires, because they can't get anything else. Manufacturers of up-to-date garments don't cater for them. We might give you an order for those if you can beat the price we're buying them at elsewhere, but the quantities we need these days are small. The large trade in fleecies is finished.' And this was pretty well the consensus of opinion in Shoreditch, Houndsditch and Whitechapel High Street.

So much for the 'Made in England' label which I expected would have such magic powers. To my surprise and disappointment it impressed no one. Not a single buyer gave us even a trial order, and we returned to the office at Fore Street empty-handed. But I was still not convinced. Buyers rarely told a potential supplier the unadultered truth, I thought. They usually talked to a purpose. It was hard to believe that fifteen million British women had suddenly given up wearing fleecy knickers.

Peggy protested: 'It didn't happen all of a sudden. The writing was on the wall for years, but you didn't want to see it!'

There was consternation when I reported to Mother and Rolf. If women's fleecy knickers were no longer in demand, the very foundation of our British venture would be swept away. We held a council of war. It seemed that my idea of manufacturing only one size would have to be abandoned, at least for the time being. Our production had to be made more flexible. To do this with untrained labour and only a handful of skilled operatives who would soon have to return to Fleissen was difficult. The factory could not be made to run economically in these circumstances, but in due course, when we were firmly established, I was sure we could revert to my original mass-production plan. Then the operation would become profitable. Meanwhile we had to try and satisfy the whims of our customers, and forget about profits. Mother and Miss Feiler made paper patterns, Rolf had the fabric calendered to the most suitable widths for o/s and ex. o/s sizes, and within a few days I set off for another visit to the East End with a new set of samples, priced as keenly as I dared. We could ill afford to lose money, but I was willing to sell at cost. As I put my samples on Noah Cohen's counter I said confidently, 'Eight shillings a dozen for outsize, nine for ex. outsize.' The young man who had received me disappeared with them and came back a few minutes later. 'We like to buy British and will help to keep your new factory busy. I'll give you an opening order for thirty dozen of each size,' he said grandly, raising my hopes only to dash them again immediately. 'I'll offer you a round price of seven shillings for both sizes. That's what we pay elsewhere.'

'But that's 20 per cent below the cost of production,' I pleaded. 'I couldn't possibly consider such an order.'

'Seven and six, then, to get you started, and if you take my advice you had better accept. We can buy a lot of your goods once you build up a regular connection with us!'

Sixty dozen at a shilling below cost represented a loss of £3. After a moment's hesitation I decided that it was, perhaps, not too great a concession to make to open the account with such an important firm as Noah Cohen, and I accepted. I booked two more orders that day, both small and at prices well below cost, but at least it was a beginning. Although there was no cause for celebration, I took Peggy to dinner at the Waldorf Hotel. It was not often that I went to such an expensive restaurant. Usually we talked business together, but not on this occasion. I was in no mood for arguments. Afterwards we strolled along the Strand to Leicester Square, mingled with the crowd in Piccadilly Circus and looked at the windows in Regent Street. I came to town twice a week, but always went from Paddington Station by Underground direct to the City, and rarely saw the West End. Subconsciously I still thought of it as forbidden territory, to be entered and enjoyed only by the successful. On this warm evening it appeared particularly exciting. A country boy at heart, I was fascinated by the dazzling lights and the traffic congestion, the display of fine merchandise, the cries of the newspaper boys and the revolving hotel doors outside which commissionaires in glamorous uniforms helped bejewelled ladies and men in dinner jackets to alight from old-fashioned taxi cabs.

The experience of the past few weeks had been discouraging, but I was determined to work hard, and some day I too would be successful. Peggy was right, of course. As far as London was concerned the decade of austerity that followed the war had passed. The mere thought of selling fleecy knickers to the women of the metropolis seemed ridiculous. And even the women who lived in the suburbs wanted to dress like their more fortunate sisters in Mayfair. But away from this apparent affluence and sophistication there was another Britain. The industrial Midlands and the north, the agricultural areas of Suffolk and Norfolk, the fishing ports around the coast, the mining districts of South Wales and Northumberland; and there was Scotland. These were our markets. The families of the three million workless could not afford the fineries worn in the more prosperous south. Any day now, I thought, the replies from the provincial houses to whom we had sent samples and quotations would arrive, and they would bring better news. I saw no reason why people in the rest of the country should not buy our knickers as freely as they had done in the past.

Once again I was sadly mistaken. Most of the provincial firms we had written to did not even reply. Some sent a curt note saying they were not in the market, while others returned our samples without comment. A few wrote polite letters explaining that fleecy knickers were no longer popular. Women now favoured lightweight underwear. If we could offer artificial silk locknit, or cotton interlock, they might be interested. Only Ryland's of Manchester sent an order for 200 dozen children's knickers.

And so it went on. We sold a few dozen o/s size here, got a small order for school knickers there, but rarely had enough work to keep the factory going. When there were no orders we made goods for stock, and once in a while some East End jobber, for instance Skolnick, would come to Langley and, after hours of bargaining, buy the contents of our shelves for a lump sum.

At the end of his vacation Ingo went back to the textile college and Mother returned to Fleissen to look after the family home. I divided my time between grappling with manufacturing problems at Langley and acting as commercial traveller, calling with my case full of samples on customers in London and the provinces. And whenever the factory at Langley had sufficient work to keep going for a while I spent some weeks at Fleissen and Leibitschgrund, invariably getting seasick on the Channel crossing. The frequent change of scenery, the mixture of failure and occasional success provided me with much variety. Poor Rolf, on the other hand, tied to the Langley factory, had to fight a slow and tedious uphill battle that would have taxed a man of twice his age and experience to the limit. Virtually in charge without interruption from July to December, he was responsible for production as well as for the training of labour.

It took patience to teach the local youngsters to knit. They were intelligent, quicker on the uptake than seventeen-year-olds at Fleissen, but they treated yarn and fabric as if they had no value, did not worry about waste, and would not keep their machines clean. They knitted much faulty material.

Once a week Sergeant's, the dyers, collected the knitted fabric to dye it navy, saxe or pink. They were slow, expensive, and in spite of repeated promises their shades rarely matched. They too spoiled much material, but they had no competition and we were in their hands.

In Czechoslovakia fleecing, or raising, was still a craft the secrets of which were passed from father to son and jealously guarded. Bergmann, who came from an old family of fleecers, was the only one of us who mastered the tricks of this trade. Loyally he endeavoured to teach them to Jock Watson before his

Home Office permit expired and he had to return to Fleissen. But there was not the time to teach Watson much about grinding card clothing, without which the performance of the fleecing machine could not be maintained. The fabric dyed by Sergeant's felt harsh because of the hard water at Acton. It blunted the cards and was difficult to fleece. Jock's willing but inexperienced hands played havoc with the stretchy material, and many a piece got torn. Too much tension on the calender pulled the fabric long and narrow. Laying it on the cutting table was so tricky and, if not done well, could cause so much waste in the subsequent cutting operation that for quite a while Rolf and Köhler laid it themselves.

In the sewing department the girls were divided into teams. Each girl did only one job, for instance insert elastic in the legs of knickers. The partly sewn garment was then carried by the conveyor to the following girl for the next operation, and so on until it was finished. The teams were paid for the total number of garments produced and the money shared out. The slow girls held up the quick ones, and there were frequently arguments on Friday afternoon when Mr Colmer paid the wages.

Sewing knickers should have been a very simple operation, but with so much unskilled labour we had a high percentage of seconds. Almost every garment that came off the conveyor was a little different from the one before, and some had one short and one long leg. But worse: since we could not get sufficient orders for knickers, not even for o/s, ex. o/s and children's sizes, we had, in desperation, taken to making 'princess petticoats' as well. Anything less fit for princesses was hard to imagine. Awkward, bulky garments made of thick, fleecy fabric dyed peach, they had to be sewn accurately and so caused a still higher percentage of seconds. If only the Home Office had understood that it takes time to turn people with a purely rural background into a skilled and disciplined labour force, how much easier our task would have been. But the civil servants were adamant, and the police came to the factory regularly to check on our foreign instructors. Most of them had to be sent home long before their work was finished. This led to much faulty merchandise and slowed our progress.

It was my job to convince Mr Matthews of the Board of Trade, and Mr Keith and Mr Coleman of the Ministry of Labour, that the success of the enterprise depended on some of our key personnel remaining at Langley a little longer, and to get them to support my applications to the Home Office. In one or two cases I succeeded, but I was told that with the exception of Köhler, Passler and Schreiner all our skilled people would have to return to Fleissen before Christmas.

24

COUNTING
OUR LOSSES
1932-33

NOW LET US take a look at the financial side of the picture. Mr Hurst was in favour of forming a company, and took me to his auditors, Messrs Westcott Maskall & Co., for advice. We saw Mr Baird, one of the partners, a man who inspired me with immediate confidence. He asked many questions about the nature of our business, its history and who owned it. I told him the salient facts and that it belonged to Rolf, Ingo and myself. He agreed with Mr Hurst. The registration of a private limited company was a simple matter, and he would be pleased to attend to it if I wished.

'What exactly are the advantages offered by such a company?' I enquired.

'Primarily the limitation of your financial liability,' explained Mr Baird. 'I don't expect for a moment that it will happen, but should the enterprise fail the company's liability towards its creditors would be limited to the extent of the share capital, and your personal fortunes, be they small or large, would be protected.'

'This protection is of little interest,' I replied. 'We shall pay twenty shillings in the pound whatever happens!'

Mr Baird smiled. 'Well, there are other advantages. Strange as it may seem, a company usually finds it easier to raise capital than a partnership.'

'We have no intention of working with borrowed money.'

'You are three brothers,' Mr Baird continued. 'In view of the difference in your ages I assume you own the enterprise in different proportions. A company would enable you to subdivide or change the ownership from time to time simply by the allocation or transfer of shares.'

'We own the business jointly,' I declared, 'not in three parts. Whatever belongs to one of us belongs to the others too, and we want to keep it like that.'

'I can see difficulties there,' replied Mr Baird, 'but we can deal with them when they arise. To return to our subject, a company might offer tax advantages.'

'Tax advantages? How much tax does one have to pay in Britain?' I asked.

Mr Baird frowned. 'Far too much,' he said. 'The standard rate of income tax is 5s in the £, minus some relief for the first few hundred pounds. Incomes exceeding £2,000 bear surtax, starting with 1s in the £ plus 10 per cent, the scale rising to 7s 6d plus 10 per cent on incomes over £50,000. Company profits, on the other hand, do not attract surtax provided they are ploughed back into the business.'

'If I understand you correctly,' I replied, 'being three partners we could earn as much as £6,000 without becoming liable to surtax. It will take us years to make such profits. We shall therefore need to pay only income tax. Deducting the relief you mentioned, our liability will amount to no more than 20 per cent of our profits. That seems reasonable, but how are the rules applied in practice? Let us say a business earns £5,000. Do the Inland Revenue authorities make a tax assessment on the basis of £10,000 in the hope the firm may settle for £7,500?' I asked.

'Heavens no!' Mr Baird seemed horrified. 'Neither the public nor the accountancy profession, not even the income tax inspectors themselves, would tolerate such methods.' He hesitated for a moment, and then added, '—although I believe they are practised in some parts of eastern and southern Europe. You may rest assured that the British tax authorities will not claim a penny more than they are entitled to.'

'In that case we do not want any tax advantages, as you call them,' I said. 'When we begin to make profits we shall be only too happy to pay the tax that is fair and proper.'

'Well spoken,' replied Mr Baird with a smile. 'I wish more of our clients thought like you. It would make our job much easier.'

The discussion cleared my mind. I saw no good reason for registering a company and said so. 'As you like,' replied Mr Baird. 'It can always be done later if you should change your mind.' And so, for the next six years, almost to the outbreak of the war, our business remained a partnership.

As will be remembered, Christ. Fischers Söhne had also opened a branch factory in England and begun production fully six months before us. They were the largest hosiery and knitwear manufacturers in Asch and one of the leading textile firms in Czechoslovakia. Mr Wunderlich, the general manager of Fischer's, who had been transferred to England, was in charge of the enterprise. They were so far ahead of us because they had rented an existing building, an old textile mill with a dilapidated dyehouse which Mr Held-maier had found for them at Edmonton, in the northern part of London. As one of the best known importers and distributors of knitted underwear in Britain, Fischer's had secured his co-operation by appointing him their sole selling agent. The assistance of such an experienced and resourceful businessman had helped them to get into their stride—or so we thought.

Gustl Fischer, who owned and directed the old established family concern at Asch, was an exceptionally able, hard-working man in his early thirties and a good friend of mine. We had been to America together and found that we had much in common. It seemed natural, therefore, to compare notes about our British ventures. To begin with Gustl was enthusiastic. The thirty-five circulars he had sent to Edmonton could hardly knit enough fabric for all the orders Heldmaier booked. He praised the dexterity of the English trainees, who learned twice as fast as Czechoslovak workers and who, after only three months, had acquired sufficient skill to go on piecework. Wunderlich, whose many years of experience included the management of Fischer's dye plant at Asch, resurrected the old dyehouse, equipped it with vats from the parent firm (wooden ones, of course) and successfully dyed the whole of the plant's output. Production rose to 1,500 dozen pairs of knickers a week, which was a gratifying performance. The only cause for disappointment was that the operation still showed a loss, largely due to the heavy cost of training—a non-recurring expense, Gustl expected.

During one of my visits to England Heldmaier and Wunderlich asked me to have tea with them in town on a Sunday afternoon to talk about their problems and to find out with what success we were tackling ours. London was dead on Sundays. We met at the Strand Palace Hotel, one of the few establishments serving afternoon tea, relaxed in the comfortable chairs and tried to find out about each other's business without giving away too much about our own. Exchanging experiences with Gustl Fischer at Asch, 500 miles away, was one thing, but here a careless word might lose a coveted order. After all, we were competitors. I did not learn much except that the relationship between Wunderlich and Heldmaier seemed a little strained.

Gustl Fischer's expectations did not materialise, and as the months went by his early optimism waned. Workers in Czechoslovakia learned a trade and then stayed in it all their lives, usually with the firm that taught them. There was no such loyalty at Edmonton. The factory lost its operatives as quickly as it trained them, and, surprisingly, not to industries that could use their skills. They left for quite unrelated occupations. Newly trained sewing machinists would suddenly take it into their heads to become shop assistants or waitresses, knitters took jobs as garage hands or simply went on the dole. Of the total labour force of eighty, there was a wastage of no fewer than eight or ten every week. Then there was a strike over a knitter whom Wunderlich had dismissed because of bad timekeeping. Industrial anarchy, Gustl felt, and became dismayed. How could the factory settle down to efficient production in such conditions?

To make matters worse, demand for knitted underwear, which had been so brisk during the first half of the year, was rapidly and unaccountably falling off Wunderlich had to manufacture for stock. Heldmaier was not bringing back enough orders to keep the plant employed, and the prices of those he booked were much lower than the cost of production. That he himself insisted on being paid for every bus fare, telephone call and postage stamp, leaving it to Fischer's to shoulder all the weekly losses, upset Gustl particularly. Were they not in this venture together? The partnership was not working out as my friend had anticipated. Wunderlich and the thirty-five circular knitting machines could be earning money at Asch instead of losing it at Edmonton. He decided to give the British enterprise a few more months and, if there was no improvement, to close the factory and send the machines back to Czechoslovakia.

I was surprised to see the mass of figures Gustl received from Wunderlich. The thought of weekly summaries appealed to me, but his almost amounted to balance sheets, and I questioned whether they were worth so much effort. We had nothing of the kind. Being so closely in touch with the daily work on the factory floor, we needed no statistics to tell us how the business was faring, I claimed. But Gustl argued that our rule-of-thumb methods were not good enough, and we arranged that Wunderlich and Rolf should meet. Here is an extract from the letter Rolf sent me afterwards:

Wunderlich came to Langley yesterday to show me his records and weekly reconciliations. They are too complicated. The simplified form you suggest would suit us better. . . . Fischer's mainly make children's knickers. We compared figures, and it will interest you to know that their fabric production last week was 2,750 lb with twelve knitters, while ours was 2,852 lb with nine knitters. But of course one cannot go by one week. Fischer's have two experienced knitters from Leicester, women, who earn 40s a week. The others are men from Edmonton, trainees, earning between 20s and 35s. The winders get only 12s to 14s, yet Wunderlich talks of reducing wages to meet Heldmaier's prices, which are 2s a dozen below Fischer's cost of production. Am not surprised they have strikes at Edmonton. They had one in the sewing department last week, and in the winding department the week before. . . . Fischer's pay £750 rent per annum. Their turnover in the nine and a half months since they started was £7,640—that is, a mere £200 per week—with eighty employees. They must be losing a lot more money than we are. Wunderlich told me confidentially that, in desperation, and without Heldmaier knowing, he called personally on a number of large retail stores in London trying to book orders, but without success. The man is at his wits' end.

Shortly afterwards Fischer's threw in the sponge and offered us their plant. Unfortunately we could find hardly enough work to keep our own machines going, and declined, but we took over their yarn stocks and contracts at favourable prices. The Edmonton machinery was sent back to Asch. This event, although not entirely unexpected, came as a shock to us, and it caused much comment throughout the Czechoslovak knitting industry. If the proud firm of Christ. Fischers Söhne had failed to make a success of their British venture, how much longer could the Pasold boys hold out? This was the question the people of Asch and Fleissen asked. It worried Mother, but I assured her that we would win through, and she believed me. Then Heldmaier unexpectedly paid a visit to Fleissen and came to see us. Afterwards I reported to Rolf:

Heldmaier was here yesterday. He blames Fischer's for the fiasco, just as Fischer's blame him. Says Wunderlich and his staff were incompetent, afraid of taking decisions without referring everything to Asch. Workers were treated badly, as was proved by the strikes. Wunderlich was too mean to provide sufficient samples and expected him to sell above market prices. I daresay they were both at fault. . . . He claims that business in Britain has temporarily ground to a complete standstill. It is not only fleecy underwear that does not sell, but also interlock, locknit, stockings, knitted outerwear and woven garments. Hall & Earl and the other British manufacturers have no work either. But he doesn't believe this stagnation can last much longer. Who knows, there may be a boom just round the corner. Fischer's should not have taken their machines back in such a hurry. Thus spoke Heldmaier! . . . The purpose of his visit? Having lost Fischer's, he would like to sell for us, but I told him that we have Hurst and are not interested.

Another winter was approaching. The east wind blew the last of the brown and yellow leaves over the barren fields and the people of Fleissen wore their fleecy vests and underpants. Five years before, in the good old days, all the factories would have been working round the clock a month before Christmas, but now only Lehrmann's and we showed a brave front. Our windows were lit up to ten o'clock every night, although very often only a quarter of the machines were actually running.

I well remember a conversation with my friend Helmut on one of our evening walks through the woods. As so often in those years we talked about world mass unemployment. We knew as well as everyone else that it would be with us for ever. How could it be otherwise? The shortages caused by the war had been made good. Modern production methods and increasing mechanisation saved manpower for which no jobs could be found and flooded world markets with more merchandise than people could buy. The hands that were busy had to provide for those that were idle. It seemed all wrong, but this was the pattern, and everyone accepted it. Trade cycles, a succession of booms and slumps, of good times and bad such as our fathers had experienced seemed a thing of the past.

But supposing some day the impossible were to happen and a miracle were to reverse this pattern so that there was more work than people to do it. A ridiculous but intriguing thought—and we amused ourselves trying to imagine what the effects of this unimaginable state of affairs would be. Wages would rise, of course, and, to hold prices down, industry would have to introduce more and more mechanisation. Would the workpeople like that? Would mechanisation become a race in which speed would be limited only by the inventive genius of the engineers? Idle thoughts. We knew that such a situation could never arise, but they provided us with an interesting mental exercise.

About that time Lehrmann's and Friedl's went to war against each other once again, providing Fleissen with a good deal of amusement—a welcome diversion from the ever-present shadow of unemployment. It started with Friedl's digging a trench to which Lehrmann's objected. Friedl's continued digging. So fifteen of Lehrmann's workmen appeared, armed with iron plates and buckets of cement, forced Friedl's men to retreat, and filled the trench in. Before the concrete had set, a strong contingent from Friedl's made a counter-attack, beat off the enemy, cleared the trench and used Lehrmann's material as reinforcement. The mayor and the two village policemen stood by at the scene of battle, but thought it prudent not to get involved in the action.

The legal position was uncertain. The gendarmerie received a telegram from the district governor at Eger instructing them to intervene and stop the fighting, but failed to act on it, for—who could tell?—it might have been a hoax. And in the evening at the Goldene Stern the Lehrmanns and the Friedls sat at different tables, pretending not to see each other, while Carl Marr, the dyer, loudly commended the spirit of co-operation prevailing between Fleissen's manufacturers. 'No sooner does the one begin to dig a trench than the other rushes to his aid with ready-mixed concrete,' he said, and once again the village laughed.

Some light relief now and again was most welcome, for the weekly profit and loss figures we drew up after Rolf's meeting with Wunderlich told a sorry tale.

Every Saturday morning Mr Colmer prepared a financial statement showing how much money the factory had lost or made during the week. As the following example illustrates, we compared the value of the production programmed with that actually achieved, the wages forecast with those actually paid, and the overheads allowed for in our costings with those actually incurred, thus showing in a simple form the week's financial results. But no matter how hard we all worked, there was almost always a loss, sometimes as little as £5, at others £40 and more.

Week		Paid			Costed	
Dec 16th - 22nd 1932	lb/dz	total	d lb/dz	d lb/dz	total	
Winding	1,200	8. 12. 6	1.72	0.70	3. 10. 0.	
Knitting						
Summer	616			2.00	5. 2. 8	
Winter	931	18. 4.11	2.83	1.50	5. 16. 5	
Fleecing						
Calendering	1,857	4. 3. 9	0.54	0.50	3. 17. 4	
Cutting						
Petticoats	20			3.00	5. 0	
Knickers	401	4. 2.10	2.36	1.50	2. 10. 1	
Sewing						
Petticoats	20			11.00	18. 4	
Knickers	433	19. 3. 9	10.16	5.00	9. 0. 5	
Folding						
Petticoats	20			1.75	2.11	
Knickers	433	3. 19. 6	1.11	0.75	1. 7. 1	
Assorting	410			0.25	8. 7	
Packing	475	1. 8.11	0.73	0.50	19.10	
Wages		59. 16. 2			33. 18. 8	
Overheads		40. 0. 0			9. 17. 1	
Total		99. 16. 2			43. 15. 9	

Wages as above £	59. 16. 2	
Office salaries	6. 14. 0	Loss £ 56. 0. 5
All other wages	4. 0. 0	
Insurance stamps	2. 3. 9	
Wages total	72. 13. 11	
Petty Cash Payments	6. 12. 4	Invoices out 483. 1. 6
All other payments	31. 4. 11	Invoices in 333. 9. 3
Total payments	110. 11. 2	
Total receipts	178. 1. 9	

The exceptionally high loss of £56 was due to the nearness of Christmas and the festive spirit which made it difficult for our people to concentrate on their work. And once upset, production took weeks to get on an even keel again. These figures are depressing enough, but they tell only part of the sad story, for they were based on the assumption that all the merchandise we produced was perfect and would be sold at the full price. We made many seconds, however, and often had to reduce our prices, even for firsts, to secure business. The actual weekly loss was therefore always greater than shown. To be faced with these deplorable results at the end of six days' hard work ruined many of my and all Rolf's weekends.

1932		£	s	d	1933		£	s	d
20 October	loss	7	11	1	5 January	loss	45	12	3
27 October	loss	10	5	5	12 January	loss	42	7	11
3 November	loss	7	12	3	19 January	loss	29	8	1
10 November	loss	1	19	9	26 January	loss	24	4	10
17 November	loss	4	19	7	2 February	loss	23	1	5
24 November	loss	10	6	1	9 February	loss	14	19	5
1 December	profit	10	19	5	16 February	loss	13	7	11
8 December	loss	9	1	4	23 February	loss	4	0	10
15 December	loss	44	4	5	2 March	loss	17	5	2
22 December	loss	56	0	5	9 March	loss	22	0	2
29 December	loss	48	1	9	16 March	loss	16	11	10

Never extravagant when it came to personal comfort, we cut our expenses wherever we could. Returning to Langley from a visit to Fleissen, I found that Rolf had given up his board and lodgings with Mrs Molland and moved his belongings to the factory, where he put a camp bed in the spare room next to the office. Left without paint on the walls, curtains, carpet or furniture until such time as we could afford to make it into a private office, the bare room did not look very inviting, but the saving was a welcome 12s a week.

Our money would have run out long ago had I not, by a stroke of luck, been able to arrange for another of those risky 'unofficial' transfers of capital from Czechoslovakia. It was again the resourceful Direktor Huder of the Bohemian Union Bank who came to my rescue, and after a few sleepless nights the transaction was safely concluded. It felt terrible to pour these precious sterling funds into Langley's seemingly bottomless pit, but what else were we to do? We had to grit our teeth, work and save until we turned the corner.

Just about that time Farmer Brown came to see me. 'Let me compliment you on your beautiful factory. I expect it's making lots of money for you.'

'A matter of opinion, Mr Brown,' I smiled wryly. 'What can I do for you?'

'Slough council have made an offer for my land to the east of your factory site, sixty acres along the railway line, to build a housing estate. Might you be interested in acquiring it? At a somewhat better price, say £320 an acre, the land is yours. You ought not to let it go, adjoining your site as it does!' He said it as casually as if he were offering me a sack of potatoes. For a wild moment I felt tempted to make him a counter-offer. Father and Grandfather never missed an opportunity of acquiring adjoining land. But where was the money to come from? Besides, we already owned eighteen acres, an enormous area, and business prospects seemed so utterly hopeless that it would have been madness even to consider buying still more. I tried to console myself with the thought that, perhaps, it would be useful for our workpeople to have an estate of cheap houses near by. Sadly but firmly I shook my head.

'It's very good of you to make me the offer, Mr Brown, but we're not in the market. You'll have to sell to the council.'

I wondered while I said it whether the time might come when I would feel sorry to have missed such a unique opportunity. Today the land is worth over £50,000 an acre, but would we have been able to hold on to it all those years? More likely than not the authorities would have requisitioned it for some purpose or other, or designated it Green Belt.

'You'll get nowhere if you insist on manufacturing merchandise nobody wants,' Peggy commented as Mr Hurst and I returned to the office without a single order after spending yet another depressing day showing our fleecy knickers and petticoats to wholesale buyers. 'Can't you make something on your machines that *is* saleable?'

'Such as?' I asked, tired and irritable.

'Ripple dressing gowns are having a good season. They're made of fleecy stockinette fabric, aren't they?'

'Much too complicated! Our sewing machinists are hardly skilled enough to make the legs of a simple pair of knickers the same length. Just imagine what their dressing gowns would look like!'

'It was only a thought,' said Peggy. 'In any case, I'm told that all ripple stockinette fabric has to be imported from Germany because it can't be made in England.'

I pricked up my ears. 'Can't be made in England? Why not? Who told you?'

'Copestake Crampton's buyer,' Peggy replied. 'Something to do with the water. It's been tried time and again, but fabric dyed in English water won't ripple.'

'What nonsense!' I laughed.

On the train from Paddington to Langley I remembered this conversation. I didn't believe there was a large demand for dressing gowns. The grass in the next field always looked greener. If we'd happened to be dressing gown manufacturers buyers would have asked for fleecy knickers! Besides, one needed special finishing machines to ripple the fabric, I remembered from the textile college. The ripples were formed by passing the fleecy fabric under a vibrating table-top covered with sandpaper. Not a job for us, I reflected, but for a firm of finishers, and dismissed the matter.

A few weeks later we had trouble with grinding the card clothing of our fleecy machine, and I paid a visit to Gessner's of Aue, near Chemnitz, to see whether they could help us. As always, I was taken through their exhibition room, and there I saw a ripple machine. It aroused my curiosity, and when I told them we had been toying with the idea of making ripple cloth they gave me a demonstration. Like all engineering firms at that time Gessner's needed orders and were willing to sell the machine for 2,000 Reichsmarks (less than £200) for immediate delivery—but I felt in no mood for buying machinery.

At the beginning of December 1932 the Langley factory had forty-two employees. Of the five instructors among them who were on loan from Fleissen, the Home Office insisted that three (marked *) had to leave the United Kingdom before the end of the year, although training was far from completed. This would reduce our labour force to thirty-nine and the wage bill to below £65. It would also, as we knew only too well, badly affect output and the quality of our goods, a setback we could ill afford. If only those civil servants would stop harassing us. Why could they not understand that it took time to train labour?

Chief clerk, W. G. Colmer	1
Factory manager, A. Köhler	1
Winding department, seven girl winders	7
Knitting department, G. Passler and E. Schreiner, instructors	2
Six knitters, learners	6
Fleecing and calendering department, two semi-skilled young men	2
Cutting department, Miss Feiler, instructress	1*
One semi-skilled cutter, one assistant	2
Sewing department, Miss Cislaghi and Miss Deinl, instructresses	2*
Fourteen semi-skilled sewing machinists	14
Folding department, three girls	3
Packing department, one packer (male)	1
Total	42

25

BUSINESS
CORRESPONDENCE
1932

WAS IT THAT shiny Maria Theresia taler Grandmother gave me on my sixth birthday that made me a hoarder? Her cousin Thomas had risked his life recovering it from the well shaft into which it had fallen. I used to sit at her feet for hours listening to her tales. There were Great-uncle Christoph's wild escapades. He emigrated to America when the Egerland became too small for him. And I loved to hear about the adventures that befell Johann Adam Pasold at the Castle of Prag, whither he journeyed in 1770 to plead on behalf of the inhabitants of Fleissen, who were in dire trouble for refusing to pay taxes.

That silver taler, a crumpled letter from Great-uncle Christoph with a Chicago postmark, a pink seashell which Uncle Wilhelm, who had served in the Austro–Hungarian navy, brought back from the Dalmatian coast, and two old photographs that fell into my hands, started a collection of much rubbish but also of many interesting relics. Over the years an accumulation of old maps, newspaper cuttings, certificates, inventories, diaries and a hundred other things filled a growing number of cupboards and chests. Some of this material was destroyed during and after the second world war, but most I was able to save, and it now provides a valuable reminder of those days.

For the seven years from the middle of 1932 onwards my records are unique. Rolf and I alternated between Fleissen and Langley, and wrote to each other almost every day, discussing the business of both firms in minute detail. This correspondence, more than fifteen hundred letters all told, is still in my possession and vividly portrays our daily worries, failures and successes. Perhaps I should explain why we changed places so often. Being eight years older than Rolf, I was the head of both firms. Although exceptionally mature for his age, Rolf was still very much the younger brother. He lacked experience, and at eighteen did not have the authority necessary to handle all the situations that arose. He was, however, quite competent to hold the fort at one factory whilst I pushed ahead at the other.

Langley was an outpost, and to develop the business there was a tough and lonely pioneering job. Battling uphill as a stranger in a foreign land, facing nothing but adversities during the day, sleeping on the settee in the room next to the office at night, recording a financial loss as reward for each week's hard work and having no recreation at the weekend was demoralising. It would have been very hard for either of us to endure such conditions for too long at a stretch. At Fleissen, on the other hand, there was the family home with all its comforts, and with Mother to look after us. We had our friends, our motor cars and our motorbikes, could go skiing in the winter and had a number of beautiful resorts near by in the summer. Our business was firmly established, our merchandise well known and stocked by hundreds of customers, we had competent and loyal employees, and if trade was poor and we were worried the situation never became as desperate as at Langley. Even in bad times a spell at Fleissen felt like a holiday.

After a seemingly endless stint at Langley Rolf returned to Czechoslovakia on 24 December 1932 very much the family hero. The Nebels came from Leibitschgrund, and Ingo was home on vacation. It had been snowing for several days, and a white mantle covered the countryside. The house smelt of Mother's and Grandmother's freshly baked *Stollen*, of pine needles and of burning candles. Silvia played 'Stille Nacht, heilige Nacht' and 'Oh Tannenbaum' on the piano, we put all business worries out of our minds and had a happy Christmas.

But the harsh reality could not be banned for long. Boxing Day was spent in the cold, deserted factory, where I brought Rolf up to date about the state of our Czechoslovak business prior to handing it over to him. The picture I could sketch was encouraging. The wheels at Adolf Pasold & Sohn were turning at a reasonable pace, while our competitors were short of work. I felt proud of the large turnover we had achieved in our now almost legendary White Bear sweaters and waistcoats. True, with the end of the winter season in sight demand was declining, but it would revive, without a doubt, and grow still bigger next autumn. There could be little risk, therefore, in letting part of our plant manufacture for stock. There were problems too. We had no equally successful spring and summer merchandise. Our order book for spring 1933 was thin. To keep the remainder of the factory going for the next few months would be difficult. And the warehouse was full to overflowing. We had 800 cases of yarn, in some counts more than a year's supply. Unless a miracle happened I was afraid Leibitschgrund would have to be put on half time or closed altogether for a while. A grim prospect. For the sake of the workpeople this drastic step had to be postponed until the worst of the winter was over, whatever the cost.

Then Rolf prepared me for what I would find at Langley. I knew most of it already from his letters, and few words sufficed. The factory operated from hand to mouth and at a loss. It rarely had work for more than a week. Everything would depend on whether I could secure enough orders to keep going.

As soon as the annual stocktaking at Fleissen was completed I set off for Langley, where I found that the departure of our three Czechoslovak instructresses had left a gaping void. The English girls who took over, teenagers most of them, did not take their jobs seriously enough, and sometimes played truant—Violet Odell, for instance, but in the course of time she became one of our very reliable employees. Here are some extracts from my letters to Rolf.

. . . unforgivable that Ministry of Labour insisted on sending the three girls back to Fleissen before had time to train Langley workers sufficiently. Have checked cutting today. Miss Odell wasted no less than 16% of the material, although cut only one size of knickers out of a whole roll of fabric. This sort of thing is enough to make us bankrupt. My first task must be to reduce cutting waste . . .

. . . was in London yesterday but failed to get any orders. Same story everywhere. Fleecy knickers are no longer wanted, buyers will look only at locknit and interlock. We are flogging a dead horse. Must find something else to manufacture, but what?

. . . Ripple dressing gowns really seem to be big business. Having no central heating, English homes are cold in the morning. Women slip on a dressing gown to make breakfast and do their housework before they dress to go out. Hurst tells me that in Golden Lane, not far from his office, a number of makers-up are kept busy producing nothing else. They import their ripple cloth from Apolda. Say it cannot be made in England for some obscure reason. Seems incredible, but could be that English condenser yarn is not suitable. Had a good look at the German fabric and am sure it is knitted on 24 fine Terrots, same as ours. Enclose a cutting. We ought to be able to make it at Langley. . . . I don't think we can make the gowns. They are too difficult for our girls to cut and sew, but we could make and sell the fabric. This would at least keep some of our knitting machines going. The makers-up buy it in 56in. width. A yard weighs $7\frac{1}{2}$ oz and costs $1s$ $3d$ delivered London. Have made a rough calculation and arrive at a cost price of $1s$ a yard, so there would be $3d$ profit. On the strength of this I phoned Hurst, told him to buy a few yards of German ripple cloth to use as samples, and try to secure business. If we get a large order, am willing to accept $1s$ $2d$ or even $1s$ $1\frac{1}{2}d$. Suggest we then immediately buy the ripple machine Gessner offered. . . . Since the fabric is not made in Britain, we ought to have the market to ourselves, and once we master the technique of manufacturing the cloth we might try to make the garments. Please let me have your views.

. . . Am getting cutting waste under control. Have done the cutting myself for a whole day and my worst effort was 10 per cent, my best 6 per cent. Now Miss Odell is away with a cold, so Köhler or I are having to do the cutting to keep the sewing department going. . . .

. . . Was again in London yesterday. Order position is deplorable. Called on Marks & Spencer's, who say our women's knickers are too dear at $12s$ $6d$ a dozen. Want to see a lower quality for about 9s. Shall try. Have quoted Millington's 5s 9d for children's knickers 12 in. to 20 in. with pocket. They reply will buy 10,000 dozen if at 3s 10d. Quite hopeless. Shall write Peacock again. We have work for another seven days in the knitting and for fourteen days in the sewing department.

. . . Heldmaier is going on a round-the-world cruise, since there is absolutely no business he can do. Says both Swans of Leicester and Hall & Earl are on short time. This shows you the state of the trade. . . .

Heldmaier was fortunate in being a merchant and not a manufacturer. His payroll was small. Operating as he did without a large warehouse, he employed only a handful of people, and they could carry on the business on a reduced scale until conditions improved. But we had to keep the factory going to pay our workers' wages, and in desperation were clutching at any straw.

. . . I think ripple cloth could be our salvation. Whereas the underwear trade is stagnating and fleecy knickers are finished, everyone tells me that the demand for dressing gowns is growing from year to year. Called on ten firms yesterday. Every one of them claimed to use between 1,000 and 4,000 pieces of fifty yards per annum. Assure me they will give us their business at 1s 3d to 1s 4½d a yard provided we can make the right cloth, which they doubt. Say many British manufacturers have tried but failed and therefore the fabric continues to come from Germany. . . . Am confident we shall be able to make it, but how can I convince them? Hurst secured a few yards of Apolda-made fabric which we are showing buyers as sample, but I dare not claim we made it at Langley. Say it comes from Fleissen and we can produce the same quality in England. Am keeping my fingers crossed. . . . Why shouldn't we be able to make ripple fabric if the Germans can? Perhaps English manufacturers haven't the right knitting or fleecing machines. Admittedly our fabric is much wider than 56 in., but if we stretch it lengthwise it will become narrower. The Apolda fabric has also been stretched, so much so that there is no give left in it . . . If you agree, let's order the ripple machine from Gessner at once. There is every prospect of enormous business. We can get a monopoly!

Having posted this letter, I wondered how Rolf would react. He usually turned a deaf ear to any proposition that involved spending money. Would my letter sound too optimistic? He became suspicious whenever I appeared enthusiastic about something. In his opinion I was too gullible and entered into financial commitments far too readily. He would probably stall, expecting that my enthusiasm for ripple fabric would wane. Meanwhile we would lose a season's trade.

Being the boss and so much older than he, I could, of course, have bought that ripple machine without asking. But I treated Rolf as an equal partner from the moment he joined me in the firm. There was a tacit understanding between us that we would do nothing except by mutual agreement. If he was against one of my projects and I failed to win him over to my point of view the project was dropped. And it was often not easy to persuade Rolf. He could obstinately refuse to go along with a scheme or, having come half way, suddenly go back to the start. But in spite of his occasional stubbornness I could not have wished for a more loyal, more dependable partner, and while we may have missed some opportunities because of his caution I daresay it saved us from making many a mistake. Entering the ripple cloth business, a trade about which we knew nothing, would be a gamble, but it had to be taken. We could not afford to lost time, and so I followed my letter up with a telegram: PLEASE ORDER RIPPLE MACHINE URGENTLY.

I hoped that the Germans would accept payment in Czech kronen and not demand precious sterling. This was the reason for ordering the machine from Fleissen, although it was to be sent to Langley. Rolf replied:

... Thanks for your letter and the trial costings of ripple fabric. Sounds interesting. Have checked it and, as far as I can judge, your figures are realistic, except that a small amount should be added for the cost of cutting the pieces.

Received your telegram and am asking Gessner to quote for 1,800 mm and 2,000 mm wide ripple machines. Think the narrow one should do ...

Had I written out the order I think I would have taken the wide machine, to be on the safe side and not to waste time. But Rolf was not to be rushed. And, true to form, he would choose the cheaper narrow machine if reasonably satisfied that it could do our job. Besides, asking for another quotation gave him a little extra time to think, and so I agreed.

... Thanks for letting me know that you are ordering the ripple machine. Hope it comes quickly. Am circularising the dressing gown trade, suggesting that makers-up place no more contracts for ripple cloth abroad, since we shall soon be able to supply from Langley ... Hurst has received a trial order for three pieces from Manchester. The firm claim they use 4,000 pieces a year and say we can have part of their business provided we get the quality right. . . . Pay 1s 3d a yard, no need to quote less. . . . Marks & Spencer's claim they sold 900 dozen ripple dressing gowns last autumn. Sales are heaviest before Christmas but go on throughout the year. Say business is growing, and they offer us their trade at 39s a dozen. Have told them we cannot make the gowns but are prepared to supply their manufacturers with the cloth ... Let's capture the fabric market as a first step. When we have that, we'll engage an experienced designer-cutter and try manufacturing the dressing gowns. Then we'll have work for the sewing department too. Keep your fingers crossed.

Rolf sometimes changed his mind at the very last moment. I was therefore glad to learn from his next letter that he had actually signed the contract. As it turned out later, he had been right to buy the 1,800 mm wide machine. It was the ideal width for our purpose.

. . . I made experiments with fabric knitted on our 44 in. diameter circulars and found that when stretched lengthwise it comes down to your desired width of 56 in. Have therefore ordered the narrow ripple machine from Gessner's, which seems amply wide enough and is 100 marks cheaper. . . . Am enclosing copy of the contract. Got packing case and freight included in the price of RM 1·900. I hope you receive the machine safely and quickly, and even more that you will get the large orders you have been writing about, so that it will be kept busy. . . .

. . . Order position at Fleissen continues satisfactory. We have had a lot of snow and it is very cold, ten or fifteen degrees below zero. This helps to clear winter underwear and ski pants from the shelves of the retailers. . . . Went skiing at Schönberg on Saturday, but pulled my ligament again and had to go home by train.

While we exchanged correspondence Langley once again ran out of work, and the situation became desperate, as is apparent from my next letter.

. . . spent all day yesterday in London calling on customers without securing a single order. Buyers are in a strong position and can afford to wait. As the knitting department had work for only three more days, I slept badly, and this morning telegraphed Peacock: 'Need work, can you help us?' And now some tremendous news: two hours later he phoned and ordered 1,500 dozen fleecy knickers! You can imagine the weight this lifted from my shoulders. Have arranged to work double shifts from tomorrow. This contract will keep us going for two whole weeks, and meanwhile I am sure some more business will come along. Let us hope the ripple machine arrives soon. Saw Customs personally but am not very hopeful about getting it into the country free of duty. . . .

. . . Had a little trouble with Miss Odell, the cutter, recently. She stayed away for two half-days and I had to do the cutting myself to keep the sewing machinists going. So told her she could stay at home for a few weeks if she didn't feel well. She need only tell me and I'd get Feiler to come over from Fleissen again. That seems to have cured her headaches. . . .

Shortly afterwards I was able to send Rolf another report full of good cheer.

. . . more good news: Underhill gave me a starting order for 200 pieces of ripple cloth today, to be dyed in six shades, each piece to be sixty yards. It amounts to about £700. Cabled you '12,000 yards of ripple cloth sold' to reassure you that there will be work for the Gessner machine. I only wish it were here . . .

. . . Roberts & Hohly took seven cases of knickers, old Fleissen stock, and one case of Langley seconds. Prices are poor, as you would expect. . . . Peacock bought the remainder of our seconds. He pays 5s a dozen for all children's sizes and 10s a dozen for the women's knickers and the petticoats. Not a bad price. Thank heaven we now have room to breathe again. . . . Marks & Spencer's are very slow making up their mind and have postponed decision to next week. Maybe we'll still get their order. . . .

We have enough work now to keep us busy for a while, and I can relax. From today we shall be knitting to 10 p.m. I am happy. Just off to the North Star to have a well earned bath. . . .

Rolf and Mother were worried about Langley's lack of orders, and their relief equalled mine. Rolf replied:

. . . have just had your letter of 18 January and your telegram, and am overjoyed. Now there is work for Langley, and if we can make the ripple cloth at the price you have calculated we shall even make a profit. It sounds wonderful. Only a few days ago I said to Mother that I still believed in Langley's eventual success . . . Delighted to hear about Peacock's order. He is indeed a friend in need. But how can he pay such high prices for stock lots and survive in this competitive world? . . . We're in the depths of winter here. It has been snowing again all day, and ski pants are still selling well, as are White Bear sweaters. You will be pleased to hear that Mother has succeeded, by repeatedly rearranging the sewing machines, in raising the production per conveyor belt to seventy-five dozens a day. The growing yarn stocks are the real worry. . . . Let me repeat, your news about Langley comes as a wonderful tonic.
PS.
Dear Eric,
    Since you left for England I no longer worry. I know you will succeed. The letter we had from you today brought us joy. It was good that I knew nothing of your fears. . . . You will be pleased when you see our sewing department. I am sure it is the most beautiful in Fleissen. We are busy from 7 a.m. to 8 p.m., while all the other firms are working short time. . . . Rolf is having trouble with his foot, which keeps him from skiing, and Ingo has had flu. I hope you are looking after yourself and keeping well.
        Mother

When Father and Grandfather were alive Mother used to keep out of the business, but after their deaths she was there almost daily to help Grandmother supervise the cutting and sewing departments, and to make up samples. She took an interest in the incoming orders and shared our many worries, rejoicing with us on the all too rare occasions when things went well. The weeks she spent at Langley showing the local girls how to cut and sew had given her an insight into the difficulties the young enterprise was up against, and secretly she reproached herself for having allowed us to start it. As if she could have stopped us! So we usually kept our worst anxieties from her. I wrote, '. . . You must not worry, even if we do have our troubles now and then. Langley is now sold out until the middle of February, four whole weeks—a very nice feeling!'

From Rolf's next letter I was happy to see that, notwithstanding the heavy responsibility that lay on his young shoulders, he could revert to his eighteen and a half years when the pressure was off and he went skiing with his friends:

. . . Fleissen has booked orders for 750 dozen White Bear merchandise and knickers since Tuesday. Had to reduce our prices for knickers by 5 per cent to be more in line with our competitors—except Lehrmann, of course, who is still cheaper. . . . Temperature fifteen degrees below zero. Snow very deep. Willie got stuck with the car on the way from Leibitschgrund today and had to continue by sleigh. . . . I went to Schönberg on Sunday with the gang, and we had a grand time. Very crowded, a skier on every square metre, knocking each other down. There were so many people, hundreds of them, that the inn could not cope, and we had to find our own food in the kitchen. Ingo knows the old building inside out, even the cellar, from which he fetched bottles of mineral water for everybody. He seemed to be the only one to get all the food he wanted. . . . Ingo has become a champion skier, a real Louis Trenker. We others are mere beginners by comparison, even cousin Egon, with his Alpine technique, not to mention Helmut, who, white as a snowman, was still practising stem turns at 4 p.m. because he couldn't get any lunch until Ingo came to his rescue. . . . Ingo broke a ski jumping, so in the evening he borrowed mine for the run back to Asch. In future he can take yours. The winter looks like going on to April. . . .

It was cold in England too, but that did not worry me unduly. The thought that we would soon be manufacturing ripple fabric, a product the trade actually wanted, and the impatience with which I waited for that first ripple machine made me forget all personal discomfort.

. . . I enjoy living in the factory, but the room is cold and still damp. Shave in the evening in the boilerhouse, it is warm there. Once we have enough orders and the little factory is humming it will be a real pleasure to stay here . . .

. . . Bought an electric fire in London, a large decorative one that flickers, for £2 5s. —wholesale, of course, at $33\frac{1}{3}$ per cent off. Also bought another blanket. It gets very cold now at night, and my teeth are chattering when I wake up in the morning. But it's all very healthy, I am sure . . .

. . . Think I may get an order for 100, perhaps even 200 pieces of ripple cloth from Ackermann's, the South African shippers. Am waiting impatiently for Gessner's machine. Believe one will not be enough, we shall soon need two. . . . We have lost the Marks & Spencer's order for spring knickers to some other maker. Don't mind very much. At 9s a dozen it would only have cost us money . . . . . . Went with Köhler to see a performance at the actors' orphanage last night. Croucher, our young knitter, the one with glasses, has a leading part and plays it extremely well. A superb show, better than the theatres at Franzensbad or Eger. Quite incredible what wonderful actors these youngsters are. It's hilarious to hear a team of chubby-faced six- and eight-year-olds singing the latest dance tunes. I wish you could have been with us. It is now very cold in England. Have burned 100 gallons of fuel oil in two days. Contracted with Shell today for twenty tons to be delivered over twelve months. Price $3\frac{1}{4}d$ per gallon. High-pressure hot-water factory heating works beautifully. Am I glad it's fully automatic! Have frostbite in tip of my right ear. Must have stuck out from under the bedclothes during the night. Am now keeping the electric fire on while I'm in bed. . . .

I could, of course, have kept the office heating going during the night, but that would have consumed fuel oil at the cost of shillings. With me the only person sleeping on the premises such extravagance would have been in-excusable.

In spite of all the troubles and hardship I loved the little factory, the most up-to-date knitting mill in the country, I told myself. During the week I was too harassed to enjoy it, but on Sundays, when there were no workpeople about, when the machines were at rest, when nobody had to be watched and nothing could go wrong, a deep silence lay over the building. It was like being in a cathedral. I walked from machine to machine, patting one, wiping an oilstain from another, and imagined how the place would hum in years to come when the crisis had passed, as pass it must.

I loved sleepy Langley village, with its quiet lanes, old houses and big trees. It had hardly been touched by the hustle and bustle of the twentieth century. The express trains that raced through the little station in endless succession, hurtling towards London or away from it, belonged to another world. I marvelled at the contrast between Langley's tranquillity and the restless atmosphere at Fleissen, filled with fierce competition, fights for water, and frequently noisy lawsuits over a few square metres of land or a right of way. Again and again I walked round the boundary of our large Langley site. There was not a factory site in Fleissen to compare with it, and I wished Father and Grandfather could have seen it. Those peaceful Sundays made up for the worries of the week.

Langley was always foremost in my mind. It was the Langley factory I wanted to develop, but we could not afford to neglect Fleissen and Leibitsch-grund. They were the ones that made the money. I was pleased, therefore, to hear from Rolf that:

. . . Willie bought a brand new 120 kW Škoda generator for 25,000 kronen—a bar-gain. It was made for some firm that went bankrupt. For the dye plant we shall need no more than 50 kW, but it is good to have the reserve. Willie thinks he may be able to drive the whole of the fine spinning room with this generator, but I can hardly believe that. He also bought a Siemens generator for 14,000 kronen and a transformer for 3,200 kronen. Must say the spinning mill operates much more efficiently under his management than it did under Direktor Walsch. Only wish we had enough work for it. . . .

With so few skilled people at Langley I always felt a little uneasy having to leave the factory alone, but it was necessary to go to London at least once a week to see customers. I then reported to Rolf in the evening:

. . . spent all day in the City, and am writing this from Mr Hurst's office. Booked an order from Noah Cohen for 422 dozen spring knickers for delivery March, April,

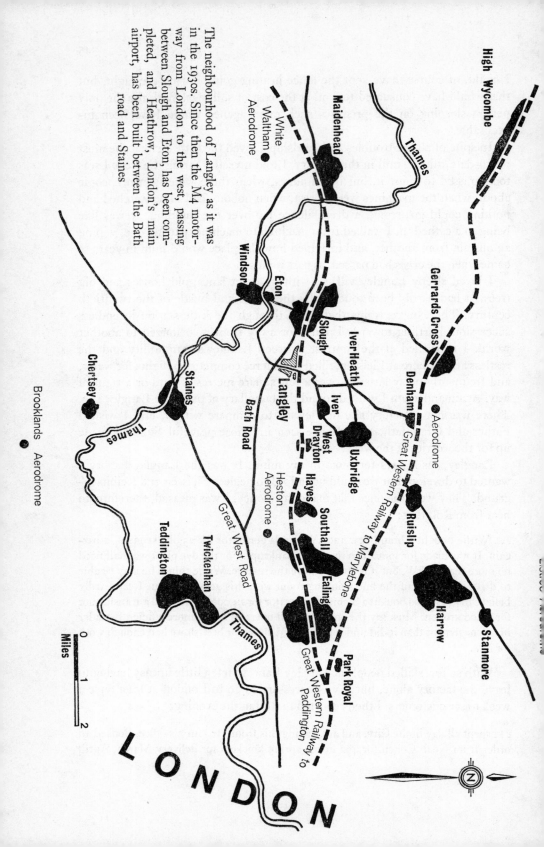

The neighbourhood of Langley as it was in the 1930s. Since then the M4 motorway from London to the west, passing between Slough and Eton, has been completed, and Heathrow, London's main airport, has been built between the Bath road and Staines

High Wycombe

Thames

Maidenhead

White Waltham Aerodrome

Gerrards Cross

Windsor

Eton

Slough

Iver Heath

Denham Aerodrome

Great Western Railway to Marylebone

Ruislip

Stanmore

Harrow

Chertsey

Staines

Bath Road

Langley

Iver

West Drayton

Uxbridge

Thames

Heston Aerodrome

Hayes

Southall

Ealing

Park Royal

Great Western Railway to Paddington

Great West Road

Twickenham

Teddington

Thames

Brooklands Aerodrome

Miles
0
1
2

LONDON

N

May. Bell Top Hosiery Co. order fifty dozen at our price and would place 500 dozen at 7*s* 6*d*, but this is below cost, and I refused. Could book a trial order for ripple cloth from Bloch, South Africa, but dare not make too many commitments until we have the machine from Gessner and prove that we can really make the stuff. . . .

Although getting an order at Fleissen was not nearly such an exciting event as securing one for Langley, I wanted to be kept informed, and Rolf's letters usually gave me a summary of the business taken:

. . . had a good day. This morning's mail brought the following orders:

239	dozen	White Bear cardigans
200	„	White Bear sweaters
370	„	bathing suits (for Sweden)
60	„	ski pants
630	„	knickers
95	„	men's underwear
1,594	dozen	

It is bitterly cold, 18° below freezing. Our chaps are busy with blowlamps, thawing out frozen pipes. Friedl's factory had to close altogether because their well froze, and Lehrmann's refused to let them take a single bucket of water from the mill stream. . . . Ingo and I went skiing on Saturday. Started at 7.30 a.m. and carried on till 6.30 p.m. It was great. Took part in a 4 km race, through the woods up the Kápellenberg, then down and uphill again to Schönberg. Ingo, as usual, was first in his category, with 8 minutes 11 seconds. My time was 8 minutes 12 seconds, Udo's 8 minutes 18 seconds. . . . Mother suggests you make yourself a fleecy night-cap to keep your ears warm. . . .

Langley was as much Rolf's baby as it was mine, and I wrote to him daily, giving an account of everything that went on in the factory:

. . . have introduced piece rates in the winding department. Provisional rates: 0·8*d* per lb for 40s, 0·7*d* for 30s, 0·65*d* for 20s, 0·55*d* for 16s, 0·4*d* for 9s metric. To begin with there was a great clamour and all the winders came running to the office, but now they have agreed to try it for a week. In the knitting department we work from 8 a.m. to 10 p.m. and Saturdays eight to one. Make no exceptions, not even for Kirkby. If he doesn't like it he can quit. The sewing department won't be running efficiently until we have an experienced forewoman to supervise cutting, sewing and folding. I can't do it personally all the time, besides do not know every detail and am too much otherwise engaged. And what happens if Miss Odell really gets ill some day, or gives notice? Her latest new assistant is no use and isn't going to make the grade. Shall try advertising in the *Slough Observer*. A series of three advertisements costs 2*s*.

Am glad to hear that you have such good skiing weather. Make the best of it . . .

And if Rolf did not agree with me he never hesitated to let me know:

. . . I shall be surprised if you can run the winding department on this basis. Admittedly the girls can earn more money on piecework, but will they work hard enough? A forewoman for the cutting, folding and sewing department is all very well, provided she is actually producing, but not if she just wants to supervise. I've had enough of such people and don't want to hear any more about the subject. You can do what you like.

Staying on good terms with Rolf was more important than having a forewoman, so I thought it best to wait, hoping that in time he would change his view. We had no one supervising the sewing and cutting departments, making and grading patterns, instructing girls in the use of the electric cutters and the various types of sewing machines, and grouping them into production teams. Rolf and I had to do it all. We had no one with even the slightest flair for fashion, capable of designing, cutting and sewing a few attractive garments from the limited range of fabrics our machines would knit, garments simple enough to be mass-produced by our semi-skilled labour. Had we found a suitable forewoman the enterprise would have progressed faster, but at the salary Rolf would have approved for such a 'non-productive' person it was impossible to find one.

We usually agreed on most things, but the subject of forewomen and designers was not one of them.

26

OUR FIRST
RIPPLE MACHINE
1933

AT LONG LAST, on 2 February 1933, the ripple machine arrived from Germany. It had really come in record time, within three weeks of placing the order, but I was so impatient to get started on the ripple business that it had seemed an eternity.

. . . the ripple machine arrived at 6.30 p.m. last night. Came by lorry in six large boxes. As feared, no description or drawing included. The only illustration I had, the one out of Gessner's catalogue, the customs kept when I saw them a couple of weeks ago. So when we had unpacked all the parts and laid them out on the floor we didn't know what was what. However, after supper we set to work, Köhler, Passler, Schreiner and I, and tried to put the machine together as best we could. Six times we erected and dismantled the strange mechanism, and at 4 a.m. gave up and went to bed. This morning at eight Köhler ,Watson and I returned to the job, and now it is completed. The last screw is in the correct position. Unfortunately we can't start the machine up until the concrete for the foundation of the motor has set, but on Sunday morning we shall make the first trial run. . . .

Of all the intricate textile equipment devised by man a ripple machine is among the simplest. A heavy cast iron frame rigidly supporting an iron table, the top of which is covered with tough industrial plush; immediately above it, sliding on four adjustable steel pins, a second table the underside of which is covered with sandpaper; a pair of revolving eccentrics to make the upper table vibrate with small reciprocal or rotating movements; a wire card roller in front to pull the fabric slowly between the two tables, another at the back to act as brake and keep fabric taut, and there you have the basic machine. So simple, I thought, that it would not take us long to try the various adjustments and determine which produced the best ripple effect.

We greased the gears, turned the machine by hand to make sure that everything moved freely and then switched on the motor. The top table began to vibrate just as we imagined it should. The bearings stayed cool, we tightened a few bolts, and all was ready to begin our experiments.

The first length of fleecy fabric we put through the machine came out looking exactly the same as before we fed it in, without the slightest trace of a ripple on it. Perhaps the gap between the tables was too wide, so we lowered the top one—without result. We dropped it still further, then raised it. We reduced the speed of the pulling roller, then speeded it up, tightened the brake, increased the throw of the eccentrics until the whole machine shook, then made it progressively smaller so that the movement became hardly perceptible. Try as we might, we could not get the machine to ripple.

On Monday morning Mr Hurst telephoned. 'Underhill's urgently need five pieces of ripple cloth from their order to make samples for their travellers. When can they have them?'

'Soon, very soon!' I replied, and went back to wrestle with the confounded machine, even before dealing with the morning's mail.

By late afternoon I was becoming optimistic. I had succeeded in producing the merest suggestion of a ripple effect when Mr Colmer came rushing downstairs to tell me that Ackermans, the South African shippers, were on the telephone, ready to give us a contract for 100 pieces if we could deliver two sample pieces before the end of the week.

'Say you can't find me and promise to ring back tomorrow,' I said, shaking the strands of hair out of my eyes and wiping my dirty face with greasy hands. 'I think I'm on the right track. Hope to have good news for you by morning.'

After supper Köhler, Passler and Schreiner, the old faithfuls who were tied to their own jobs during the day, once again lent a hand, but we failed to coax the obstinate machine into producing a satisfactory ripple. Overcome with fatigue, we gave up at midnight. Did the fault lie elsewhere? In the way we fleeced our fabric? The loop construction? The twist of our condenser yarns or the cotton from which Leibitschgrund spun them? The dyes used by Sergeant's? But surely not the English water! Whatever the secret might be, until we had discovered it and mastered the problem we could not accept any more business. Having to refuse Ackermans' order, worth £350, made me feel wretched enough, but what was I to say to Underhill's? I did not dare to confess the full extent of our failure even to Mr Hurst and Peggy, and merely said we needed a few more days to overcome mechanical difficulties.

I shall not weary the reader with the voluminous technical correspondence between Rolf and myself that ensued. It did not solve the mystery, but it improved the ripple a little. Two heads are better than one, and putting our thoughts on paper led me to discover and eliminate several mistakes I had made. Gessner's also helped. Their written instructions for operating the machine were too elementary to be of any use, but as luck would have it one of their engineers happened to be in Scotland at the time, and they telegraphed him to call at Langley on his return journey. Not that he knew much about the finer points of manufacturing ripple cloth—machine builders frequently know less about their own machines than the firms who use them—but he gave me a useful hint or two, and little by little the ripple became better. It was nowhere near as good as the German, but Underhill's accepted the sample pieces we supplied and even complimented us on the result of our efforts. Mrs Underhill, the proprietress, was a very understanding lady.

But I could not spend all my time experimenting. We needed orders for knickers and petticoats to keep our people employed. If Mr Hurst could not sell enough I dashed to London, usually to the East End, with my samples and did a deal with some Jewish merchant at cost prices or below. And plenty of other matters also cried out for my attention, keeping me busy. At the beginning of March 1933 I wrote to Rolf:

. . . this morning's mail brought a few orders for summer knickers. Cook's want thirty, Copestake's 180, and Deyong fifty dozen. Just enough to keep us going for a day. . . . Since we introduced piecework in the winding department we need only six girls, and they frequently wind more yarn than the knitters can use. This will rectify itself when the knitting department goes on piecework, but the knitters need a great deal more practice before they can do that . . . As an interim stage to piece rates I have introduced a production bonus in the sewing department. You should see how fast our girls can work all of a sudden. They will soon be as good as the sewing machinists at Fleissen—only we have to watch the quality of their work. . . . Do you remember Miss Jackson, our best sewing machinist, who left two months ago to take a job at the perfume factory across the road ? She has just asked to come back to us. We paid her $6\frac{1}{2}d$ an hour when she left and have now re-engaged her at $6d$. The perfume factory, by the way, has a total labour force of four. . . . Dyeing is still one of our worst problems. Sergeant's have the monopoly and do what they like with us. . . .

Willie at Leibitschgrund also had problems. The combined yarn consumption of Fleissen and Langley was less than his production, and every week the surplus thirty-five cases were added to stock. His warehouse was full, and there were a thousand cases in the basement of the factory at Fleissen—a whole year's supply. The overdraft at the bank was growing. Shutting the mills for a month or two was out of the question because there was no alternative employment for the workpeople. Had it been summer they could at least have gathered blackberries and mushrooms in the woods, but now, in March, the snow was only just melting. Langley got its condenser yarn from Leibitschgrund but bought all its ordinary cotton yarn from Lancashire, where it was better and cheaper, and I wrote to Willie:

. . . you wish to know at what prices we buy cotton yarns in England. Have recently placed a contract for 20,000 lb at:

16s	20s	30s	36s	40s	
$7\frac{3}{4}d$	$8d$	$9d$	$9\frac{1}{2}d$	$10d$	per lb

free delivered Langley. Cases are returnable and not charged. Paper tubes are returnable and the weight is credited in full. Payment within seven days, $3\frac{3}{4}$ per cent discount, thirty days $2\frac{1}{2}$ per cent, sixty days net. You can judge from this that cotton spinning is in a far worse state in England than even in Czechoslovakia. As far as I can make out, most spinners are practically insolvent. They sell below cost to fill their order books, then a number of them get together and ask the banks to finance a merger which is supposed to eliminate the cut-throat competition and make the operation profitable. The banks put up a few million pounds, but the losses continue because of the over-production and the terrific international competition. The former owners are reduced to directors and managers, and no longer worry, for they receive salaries which are assured and the banks have not the heart or the courage to close one mill in every two and put the workers on the street. But, not wanting to throw good money after bad, they provide no capital for modernisation. So there is stalemate. . . . I do not know of a single modern cotton mill in the whole of England. Most yarn is still spun on mules. When it is foggy in Lancashire, which happens quite often, the mills have to stop or the yarn gets black and becomes virtually useless. Only about three plants are air-conditioned. So you see how fortunate Leibitschgrund is to be situated in the midst of its beautiful forest . . . To come to your point, it would be suicidal for you to compete in this market with cotton yarn. Condensers are a different matter, English spinners don't seem to go in for them, but that is because they are not being used . . .

There was little I could do except tell Leibitschgrund to dispose of its surplus yarn in Czechoslovakia. This meant selling it to our competitors, which was always difficult, especially at a time when the whole of the country's spinning industry was short of work. Willie called on the various knitters personally, ate humble pie, and reduced his prices below the cost of production. Our stocks reached the frightening peak of 1,700 cases before there was a change for the better. But we scraped through without having to close the mills.

I could not understand the dearth of restaurants or inns in England. There seemed to be plenty of public houses selling beer at the prescribed hours, but the only food one could get there was stale bread and cheese. In Czechoslovakia even the remotest village had at least one inn serving hot meals, beef, pork, dumplings and frequently fish at any reasonable time of the day or night, and at very moderate prices. Did all English people eat at home? It was therefore welcome news when an attractive hotel opened not far away, and I reported to Rolf:

. . . had dinner last night at the Old Crown at Slough, the new hotel which has been built on the corner of the High Street and Windsor Road, where the old pub used to be. Has a large modern dining room, a cafe, comfortable lounge and the usual bar where you drink your beer standing up. Tip top. Was impressed. Thank goodness we know where to get a meal now . . . I asked to see the bedrooms. Well furnished, running hot and cold water, including breakfast 8*s* 6*d* a day. Mother will be happy to stay here on her next visit. . . .

What I told Rolf in my next letter was premature, to say the least, as we shall see later.

. . . I am sure you will have been pleased to get my telegram 'Ripple now correct'. At last we need no longer be ashamed of our ripple fabric. Saw Underhill and Andrews yesterday. Both are pleased with our sample pieces and ask for speedy bulk deliveries. We know now how to handle the fabric so that it comes out in the correct width, and achieve the specified weight of $7\frac{1}{2}$ oz per square yard—only you have to stand by the machine and watch out that nothing goes wrong. Have various ideas how to mechanise some of the operations, but had to wait until Gessner's engineer had left. Don't want him to see them. . . . As far as I can tell, our production cost does not exceed the estimated figures, and so we ought to be making a profit. Unfortunately the output of one ripple machine is quite inadequate—no more than eight inches a minute. We need more machines. Buyers admit that cotton ripple cloth is very difficult to find. English manufacturers cannot make it, and the Germans sell only in Reichsmarks, involving the reluctant British buyer in the exchange risk . . . The paper boys in London are crying 'War! War!' and the headlines read 'Remember 1914!' According to the British press, Japan and China are as good as at war with each other. The Japanese have bought seven old British passenger liners to use as troop ships, or to cut up and make into shells. It is thought here that the USA and Russia may become involved, and that would lead to another world war. But Britain wants to stay neutral. . . .

Rolf was pleased but cautious. He had, however, given the project some thought, and made a very useful suggestion:

. . . We are delighted to hear that Langley's ripple fabric is now right. Let's see whether we can make it pay before talking about buying more machines. . . . Thinking about ripple cloth, I hit on an idea how you might cut the tubular fabric mechanically into two single layers of equal width. Pass the fleeced tube through the calender, keeping the rollers apart to avoid pressure. Use a 56 in. wide stretcher and fit a knife to each end. I don't know whether straight knives, perhaps with counter blades, or revolving circular ones would be better. You need to experiment. . . . Our newspapers say nothing about war. . . .

Descriptions of machinery and production processes can be tedious. I am therefore endeavouring to keep them as short as possible, but levers, gears, wires and dials, and the degrees of skill with which human beings use them to manufacture things in competition with each other, are the very essence of industry. Success or failure depends very much on a firm's plant and the efficiency of its operation. Less technically inclined readers may not follow the details but will, I trust, get at least the broad picture.

Rolf's idea seemed worth trying. Cutting our bulky tubular fabric by hand in two fifty-yard lengths of equal width was difficult. And the cut material, which was about seventy inches wide, then had to be neatly folded in piles so that it would pass through the ripple machine without creasing. Anything that did away with this cumbersome procedure would be a godsend. A pair of old razor blades screwed to our adjustable metal stretcher served for the first, promising experiments. But now and again the fabric caught and tore. I phoned Gillette's: could they help? Our problem intrigued them, and they invited me to their factory on the Great West Road, only ten miles away. The outcome of this visit was a regular supply of sharp, nine-inch-long steel strips, the intermediate product to ordinary safety razor blades. They cut our fabric perfectly, and I could report complete success to Rolf.

Rolf's inspiration sparked off other improvements—for instance, a simple winding mechanism on top of our calender, which enabled a comparatively unskilled man to cut and roll both layers of material in a single, almost automatic operation. Handling fabric in rolls was much easier than handling it in piles, but, being exceptionally wide, our rolls needed a firm support to give them rigidity and prevent distortion. We solved the problem by importing from Czechoslovakia 200 light steel tubes as used by the aircraft industry. They served the purpose admirably.

Unwinding the neatly rolled fabric again in order to form piles in front of the ripple machine did not seem to make much sense. I took out my drawing board and designed first a simple attachment to feed the fabric from the roll directly under the vibrating table, and then another, much more complicated, to wind it up again on the exit side. Designing the mechanism was one thing, making it quite another.

Bursting with enthusiasm but short of tools, we found an amateur engineer in the village who had a well equipped workshop. With his help we developed and built the various gadgets one by one. Gessner's would have been surprised had they seen the improvement we made to their machine, but unfortunately this had little effect on the quality of our ripple, which still left much to be desired. I had been premature when I claimed that it was now all right. A few pieces would be almost perfect and then, for no clear reason, the waves would get wider and wider or brush off altogether. Sometimes the ripple on one half of the piece would be firmer than on the other, and then again, little balls would form under the vibrating table, marking the fabric with ugly vertical lines. At times I nearly despaired, and even Mr Hurst became impatient.

'If you can get one piece right,' he said, 'surely you only have to repeat what you did exactly and they'll all come out right!'

But it was not as simple as that. 'You're a golfer,' I retorted irritably: 'If you make one perfect shot why don't you hit the ball exactly the same every time? Then all your shots would be perfect!'

I do not, however, wish to create the impression that we had nothing else to worry about than ripple cloth, or Langley's other teething troubles. The factories at Fleissen and Leibitschgrund also had their problems, as Rolf's next letter shows.

... two of our customers are in financial difficulties. Grünspan owes us 7,000 kronen and Goldreich 10,000. I was able to stop the last consignment to Goldreich, 4,000 kronen-worth of summer goods, in the nick of time. Trade is bad, and these twisters exploit the situation at the expense of their suppliers. I wonder how many more will become insolvent. . . . The sliver dyeing plant at Leibitschgrund progresses very slowly. Fleissner is late delivering the machinery and Willie has still not finished adapting the building. He puts me off from one Saturday to the next; meanwhile we shall have to buy another 800 kilos of coloured yarns outside. . . . We still have enough snow left for skiing, but it is getting thin, and the brown earth is beginning to show through. . . .

By now Langley was running short of work again. Our daily production of fabric and garments was larger than the intake of orders. If *only* I could get the ripple cloth business going more rapidly.

... we are knitting only from 7 a.m. to 7 p.m. this week because we have insufficient orders for knickers. To change more circulars over to ripple fabric, and perhaps back again a week later, would be too wasteful. It is now 8 p.m., and the ripple machine down in the dark factory is working away on its own. Needs very little attention. I look at it once an hour and feed it with a new piece of fabric every four hours. Shall now work it flat out for fourteen days, by which time we should get the first reactions from the customers. Can then discuss a second machine. . . . The sewing department works so well now that it's a pleasure to see it. Have formed two teams on the conveyor belt, and a young girl supplies them with sewing cotton, elastic, etc, so that they needn't interrupt production. The machinists are earning up to 32s 6d a week. . . . If only we could get enough orders to keep the factory steadily employed I am sure it would make money. Our Langley workpeople are made of the right stuff, and when they have gained the necessary experience will be a match for Fleissen. . . . Bought a good supply of food in London on Saturday: brown bread, butter, ham, salami, a buckling, oranges and bananas, and gorged myself on Sunday. Just ate and slept and fed the ripple machine and ate and slept. . . . We have had a lot of snow, for England, the past few days. Three inches on Friday! Some trains from the West Country got stuck, others arrived at Paddington fourteen hours late. Miss Crowdy, our packer, went to Yorkshire for the weekend and is marooned there. It is difficult to understand why a few inches of snow should disorganise the British railway system if Continental trains run without trouble through as many feet of snow. . . .

In the long run our only hope of securing more orders was to manufacture more cheaply, and this seemed impossible as long as we depended on Sergeant's for our dyeing. Langley had neither the money to build a modern dye house nor a large enough output to keep it employed. But some day it had to come, and I thought much about it.

. . . Sergeant's will bankrupt us if we go on letting them do all our dyeing. They're expensive, their colours don't match our shade cards, the pieces have stains on them, Mr Twinam is always thinking up fresh excuses, and we frequently have to wait six weeks for delivery. How can we possibly run the factory efficiently in this situation? I know this is not the time, but sooner or later we shall have to do our own dyeing. . . . Had Isler, the borehole specialist, here yesterday. He practically assured me that there is a vast reservoir of soft water—only about two degrees of hardness—at a depth of about 1,000 ft below our land. Drilling a hole, inserting a steel pipe, supplying and fitting valves, etc, would cost £1,200. The water, 50,000 litres a day, would gush under its own pressure to a height of twenty metres above ground level. Isler believes we could dispose of the used water through soakaways on our site, but in any case we have the document from the council allowing us to discharge the effluents into the sewers. Can you imagine more favourable conditions for a dyehouse?

. . . The final figures of the cost of building the factory have now been prepared by Wallis Gilbert & Partners. The balance remaining to be paid is £507, just £250 less than estimated, although the following extras are already allowed for: £50 bonus paid to Chessum's for good workmanship, £85 for the lettering on the roof, the chimney stack and oil tank, alterations to the heating and electrical installation, etc, resulting in a total saving of approximately £600. This is very satisfactory considering that the final bill usually comes to more than the original estimate. . . .

In the spring of 1933 bright yellow and blue knitted cotton sports shirts became so fashionable on the Continent that Fleissen could not produce enough, and Rolf wrote:

. . . sports shirts made from knitted Köper fabric are becoming a big line here. Please return all Köper presswheels which we sent to Langley with the circulars. You have no use for them, but here they are worth their weight in gold. . . . The permits of your three stalwarts will expire this summer. Are the Langley knitters far enough advanced for Passler and Schreiner to return to Fleissen in June? And Köhler? Would he perhaps prefer to return to the land of that clown Adolf Hitler?

The craze for knitted sports shirts had not reached Britain yet. We had other things to worry about at Langley, and I sent all our presswheels to Fleissen.

. . . we are still having setbacks with our ripple cloth, which is why production is only half what it should be, but when all is going well, as it did yesterday—Sunday—

then it's a real pleasure. The machine made perfect fabric all day. The sun was shining and I sat behind the factory in a deckchair with a book and bar of chocolate, left the sliding door wide open just to hear the rumbling and had a quick look every half-hour. Never needed to touch a thing. . . . I'm afraid we can't let Passler and Schreiner go in June. The English knitters are far from ready to run the plant by themselves. They'd smash it up in no time. I hope I can persuade the Ministry of Labour and the Home Office to extend their permits. We need Köhler too, and he likes it here and very much wants to stay in England. . . . Please have a word with Willie about buying more American cotton. With the dollar so shaky I think prices will rise. . . .

Adolf Köhler's was a special case. At the beginning of the century his father had come from Württemberg to London, where he established himself as a 'German baker'. When war broke out in 1914 he was interned, like all Germans, Austrians and Hungarians, and lost his business. After the war he returned to Württemberg a disillusioned man, to start a new life, but soon died. His son Adolf was born in London and was therefore a British subject, but although he liked England and the English, out of a feeling of loyalty to his dead father he wanted to be German and insisted on being given a German passport.

When I asked the British authorities for a labour permit for him they said he didn't need one. As far as they were concerned he was a British subject. But young Adolf, having only recently secured his German passport, protested that he was German. So the officials shrugged their shoulders and gave him an alien's registration book. At first I was dumbfounded by his stupidity, and so were Passler and Schreiner. We would have given almost anything for a British passport—the best passport in the world—while this young idiot refused one! But on reflection I sympathised, even if I could not agree with him. Had Masaryk and Beneš, those Czech intriguers, not taken our Austrian passports away by force and given us Czechoslovak ones in exchange perhaps we too would have felt differently.

There was another, somewhat humorous matter, or so we thought at the time, on which we could not agree with Köhler. He actually believed that that noisy jackbooted Hitler, about whom one read such hair-raising tales in the papers, would put Germany back on her feet. We only laughed and pulled his leg about his rowdy namesake. Good-humouredly he laughed too, but we could not shake his faith in the man. 'Somebody has to bang the table, or the Germans will be treated as second-rate human beings for ever. Mark my word, Adolf Hitler is the first German politician the French and the British will listen to!' he predicted.

But neither I, who knew little and cared less about German politics, nor even Köhler wasted time thinking about Hitler or bothering about his speeches. We had so many more interesting and important things to do, as can be seen from the following letter I wrote to Rolf.

... have engaged a forewoman, a girl of twenty-one from Leicester. She seems reasonably efficient. I gave her a length of ripple fabric and watched her cut and sew a ladies' dressing gown, which she did quite well. Says she has six cutters and twenty sewing machinists under her, manufacturing blouses, jackets, jumpers, etc, all from knitted fabric. Agreed to pay her 45s a week and she is going to start on Monday 27 March. We can always give her a week's notice if she is not satisfactory, but believe me, we need a forewoman. ... You will be glad to know that Peacock has ordered another 2,000 dozen knickers in addition to the 600 last week. Also had an order from Rose for 180 dozen. This will keep us going until the middle of next month. ... Yes, it would certainly be nice if we had a little car, and quite useful for the business to rush sample pieces to the dyers, take a repair job to Slough trading estate, etc, but I am of the opinion that until we are showing a profit we ought to go by public transport. Meanwhile there is no harm in dreaming about a car, but why think of buying one second-hand if the prices of new ones are so reasonable? The small Ford costs £120, the MG sports model £190. They cost almost twice that in Czechoslovakia. I like the Swallow SS best, a six-cylinder, two-litre car that will do 75 m.p.h. and costs £325. Let's wait until we can afford to buy a car like that. ... Things are reasonably under control. Would you like to change places with me about the end of March? I am quite happy to stay on, but I think you will like to see the progress that has been made, and you will find the ripple business, especially, much to your taste. ...

Rolf replied that he was ready for another stint at Langley, and so I returned to Fleissen.

27

A TASTE
OF SUCCESS
1933

SINCE HISTORY BEGAN man has observed and imitated to his advantage the techniques used by his fellow creatures. Craftsmen and artists have copied and improved upon each other's skills and inspirations. Traders have employed fair means and foul to discover their rivals' sources of supply and capture their markets. Methods may have changed through the ages, but the purpose has remained the same. Modern industrialists may no longer steal inventions by breaking into their competitors' factories but circumvent and profit from one another's patents. Nations still go to war over trade. Governments no less than private enterprise engage in industrial espionage. A wicked world? The consumer knows little and cares less about it but is content to reap the benefit.

Immediately upon returning to Fleissen I carried out my intention of going to Apolda, the home of the German ripple cloth industry, to ferret out as many of the manufacturing secrets as possible. I had prepared the ground by writing to a second-hand machinery dealer at Apolda, telling him that we thought there might be a market for ripple fabric in Czechoslovakia and that we were looking for second-hand ripple machines and ancillary equipment. What had he to offer, and could he show it to me?

In fact Czechoslovakia was never a market for German ripple cloth. Traditionally Apolda's exports went to Britain, Scandinavia and overseas, but currency devaluations and import duties had brought this trade virtually to a standstill. The German factories were on short time, some had shut down altogether, almost all were in need of money. The thought of turning out-of-date plant into cash by selling it to ignorant foreigners was an inviting prospect. Selling it to me without giving away know-how! A dozen firms opened their doors, the dust-sheets were pulled off rows of idle brushing, rolling, ripple and folding machines, and I was invited to inspect collections of old iron that looked like medieval instruments of torture.

Without betraying the least disappointment at being confronted with all this junk, I took off my jacket, rolled up my shirtsleeves and made a show of getting down to a thorough examination, checking the wear and tear of bearings, gears and eccentrics. So painstaking was my inspection, and so patent my ignorance of what to look for, that the factory owners usually got tired of watching and decided they could safely leave me in the care of some foreman. This was just what I wanted. I plied my guard with questions, and if he seemed communicative ended by inviting him to my quiet *Gasthaus* for a glass of beer. It would have been imprudent to go to one of the larger hotels and risk being seen.

Before long I had accumulated a wealth of confidential information, manufacturing instructions, production figures and even costings. My briefcase was bulging with an assortment of fabric cuttings. I had specimens of the yarn, small pieces of the emery paper used on the tables, and a short strip of card-clothing which was specially ground for the job. All this would prove invaluable at Langley.

My mission so satisfactorily concluded, I drove back along the winding roads of Thuringia towards the Bohemian frontier. Snow lay on the hills and in the pine woods, but there was a spring song in my heart. I felt pleased with what I had learned. Some of the tricks of the trade might seem obvious once one knew them, as for instance that the fabric had to pass through the ripple machine 'against the loop', in the same direction as it passed over the fleecer. But others were not so obvious and we might never have discovered them on our own. I had little doubt that the information I had acquired would enable us to manufacture ripple coth of a quality equal to that produced in Germany.

Apolda had well over a hundred ripple machines, I reckoned, and Mühlhausen, Weimar, Limbach, the Erzgebirge and Liegnitz probably another hundred. The business was larger even than I expected, and the Germans clearly meant to recapture their export trade, for they would sell only old crocks and retain their more modern machines. But even the plant they considered modern was at least twenty years old. They had not hit on the idea of cutting the fabric mechanically, and of rolling it instead of laying it in piles. My hopes rose. The improvements we were making to our machine would give us an advantage in the cost of production. A modest halfpenny per yard, perhaps, but it was the steady daily saving and not the occasional jackpot that brought success to a business like ours. I felt confident that we had the British ripple trade practically in our pockets.

But to think that we could satisfy the large demand with only one machine seemed ridiculous. I ought to have the courage to order ten new ones from Gessner's right away, I thought. Yet if I did Rolf would think I had gone off my head. He was determined that we should make a success of the one machine before we bought any more, and perhaps he was right. It just meant curbing my impatience a little longer until he too was convinced. That same evening I typed a six-page report for Langley, and next morning went with the samples of yarn I had brought back from Apolda to see Willie at Leibitsch-grund. Could we spin something similar? The yarn was softly twisted 10s to 12s count condenser. We checked the number of turns and studied the fibres under the magnifying glass. They were shortish and rough. East Indian cotton, we decided, but unusually curly, almost like wool in comparison with our Sind.

Cotton is grown in the southern states of the USA, in Peru, Brazil, Egypt, the Levant, Pakistan, Burma, China, Russia and many other parts of the world. As with wine, the characteristics, quality and price vary from district to district, from crop to crop. Cleanliness, colour, length of staple and other features are classified according to agreed standards; there are literally thousands of varieties, and to judge and grade them requires a lifetime of experience. Spinners as a rule 'understood' only the types they used in their own mills, treading warily when experimenting with unfamiliar growths, and we were no exception. We consulted the raw cotton merchants, selected trial lots of several types of rough Indian cotton, among them some bales of 'Comilla' which happened to be in stock at Bremen, and Willie promised to spin them into 11s count condenser yarn the moment they arrived.

From the beginning of April Rolf had taken charge of the Langley factory once again. With enough contracts for knickers and petticoats to ensure full employment for more than two weeks, and Mr Hurst confident that negotiations he was conducting would result in several large orders immediately after Easter, it was Rolf's first experience of working in England without being weighed down by worries. The ripple machine—touch wood—was working well. He made what use he could of the information I had brought back from Apolda, and was pleased with the steadily improving quality of the cloth. Each length seemed to look better and feel a little crisper than the one before. Things were looking up. And when the day's work was done he took to playing the almost forgotten accordion again. The Easter holidays were sunny and warm, and he spent two glorious days exploring the Thames between Hurley and Maidenhead with Köhler, alternately paddling and patching the leaking rubber boat he had brought with him from Fleissen. Life felt good, but alas, not for long.

The business Mr Hurst had been relying on did not materialise. Instead there were cancellations, and I received several most depressing letters from Rolf. He had no more work for the factory and was losing the labour it had cost so much to train. Two sewing machinists had left, more would leave if they could find other jobs, and so would the knitters. It was heartbreaking.

He had again been out with Hurst, calling on the wholesale buyers in the City and the merchants in the East End, but had not sold a single dozen. Nor were the agents we had appointed in the provinces sending any orders. Even the interest in ripple fabric had died down. The last few pieces were about to be delivered, but none of the dressing gown makers was ready to place a repeat order. Was this trade also coming to an end?

I thought of Fischer's. Perhaps they had been right to cut their losses and wind up their British enterprise. But I refused to admit defeat: we would battle on. With Mother and Grandmother I held a council of war. Something drastic had to be done, and we decided that Rolf was to reduce the price of knickers and petticoats by another 20 per cent to secure orders. We would keep the factory going for three more months and use up the yarn stocks. If the situation did not improve before the end of July we would cover the machines with grease to prevent them getting rusty and wait until trade revived, as surely it must. I was, however, still confident that before the worst happened the ripple cloth business would become our salvation. We might have to close the garment section, but not the fabric making. On the contrary, reckless though it might appear, I was in favour of buying additional ripple machines without any further loss of time. There was a second-hand one for sale at Cranzahl, not far from Chemnitz, said to be in excellent condition, the same model as ours at half the price. Then, just as I was writing to Rolf laying down an emergency production programme to keep the factory going for the next few weeks and reiterating my faith in the future of the ripple business, a welcome letter arrived:

Hurrah, hurrah! Underhill's have ordered 100 pieces, Andrews 200 pieces, and Hurst says further orders are on the way. We are sold out for three months! From tonight the ripple machine runs in three shifts. Köhler, Schreiner, Passler and I are going to do night shifts in turn. Each night one of us will sleep on a mattress next to the ripple machine and will be woken hourly by an alarm clock to make sure that all is well. If this arrangement works—and I can't see why it shouldn't—we shall set the alarm to ring every two hours, and later perhaps every three. Whoever does shift work gets two shillings extra for the night. The boys are quite excited. This does not give us work for the sewing department, of course, but I am full of hope again and shall not slaughter knicker prices yet.

What marvellous news! And as the quality of our ripple improved so the repeat business was bound to grow. I could see Langley being snowed under with orders it had no hope of filling. Sleeping on the factory floor next to the noisy machine, working it round the clock, was a brave effort, but would not produce the yardage we should need. I decided then and there to go to Cranzahl and buy that second-hand machine which was for sale. I spent the

GERMANY

- Apolda
- Jena
- Gera
- Burgstädt
- Crimmitschau
- Limbach
- Chemnitz
- Hohenstein-Ernstthal
- Werdau
- Zwickau
- Oberlungwitz

THURINGIA

SAXONY

- Aue
- Plauen
- Oelsnitz

(ORE MOUNTAINS)
ERZGEBIRGE

- Komotau

- Hof
- Adorf
- St.Joachimstal
- Bad Elster
- Graslitz
- Rossbach
- Schönbach
- Brambach
- Leibitschgrund
- Karlsbad
- Asch
- Fleissen
- Hörsin
- Haslau
- Wildstein
- Altenteich
- Schlaggenwald
- Liebenstein
- Franzensbad
- Eger

Egerland

BAVARIA

BOHEMIA

- Bayreuth
- Marienbad

CZECHOSLOVAKIA

| 0 | 10 | 20 | 30 | 40 | 50kms |

| 0 | 10 | 20 | 30miles |

- Pilsen

weekend with friends at Karlsbad, meaning to use Monday, 1 May, for a leisurely drive over the Erzgebirge to Chemnitz, where I had arranged to meet a South African buyer in the evening. On Tuesday morning I would inspect the machine at Cranzahl.

The first of May was a public holiday, but I had not reckoned with the usual political rallies and demonstrations. In Czechoslovakia the socialists were out in force, waving their red flags, shaking their fists at my capitalist motor car, while on the German side of the border I was held up by seemingly endless columns of Nazis with swastikas, glowering at my Czechoslovak number plates. Years of trade depression, unemployment and national humiliation— the fault of spineless German governments and of greedy Jews and foreigners, as Adolf Hitler told them—made gullible millions march to the agitators' tune. It was an uncomfortable journey among all those sweating people tramping the dusty roads. I hate multitudes—except as consumers, of course —and, watching the formations marching past, I wondered who had secured the contracts for supplying their brown shirts. Tired, famished and ill at ease, I reached Chemnitz and then took another hour to get through the crowd to my hotel, where I found the South African, a Jew, white as a sheet. What would they do to him? Would he get out of Chemnitz alive? he wanted to know.

'Take no notice of this nonsense,' I reassured him. 'It will all be over by tomorrow, and you can make your business calls as usual. They want your orders: no one will molest you.'

All was back to normal the following morning, and I felt glad there would be no more marches for another year. The Erzgebirgische Textilwerke at Cranzahl surprised me. I had not expected such a modern, well equipped factory in this remote mountain village. The ripple machine was as good as new, but trade was bad, the works manager explained, and it stood idle. Could one blame the workpeople if they followed Hitler, who promised them work and bread and the return of their self-respect? Germany had six million unemployed before he became Chancellor! But I had no desire to get involved in political discussions. I did the job I had come to do, and in the evening wrote to Rolf:

Have just returned from Cranzahl, where I bought that second-hand ripple machine. It is in tip-top condition, hardly used, and you will be pleased to know that I got it for 1,000 marks.

As soon as the trial bales of rough Indian cotton arrived at Leibitschgrund Willie had them spun. The yarn was not as even as it should have been, for our condenser plant was designed to spin 9s count, and not 11s. Willie had to improvise, but speed was of the essence, and so we rushed two cases of this rather lumpy yarn to Langley with the promise that the next delivery would be better. The following extracts from Rolf's letters which came in quick succession illustrate what happened.

. . . The 11s condenser yarn you sent us runs very badly. The winders complain that it keeps breaking, and ask for higher rates of pay. The knitters are disgruntled over the numerous breakages. You should hear Köhler's language. . . .

. . . After adjusting the thread guides the 11s condenser yarn now runs a little better. I sincerely hope the next delivery is more even. . . .

. . . The first pieces knitted with the 11s condenser yarn have gone to the dyers and are promised back on Monday. . . .

. . . The dyers returned three of the experimental pieces this morning. They look all right. I will report to you later in the day how they behave on the fleecing machine. . . .

. . . We brushed the fabric against the loop, as you say they do in Apolda, and the fleece has come up beautifully. Shall try rippling this evening. . . .

. . . The ripple is outstanding, far superior to any other I have seen. For fabric like this we can get as many orders as we like. You have certainly now found the right grade of cotton, but please see to it that the yarn is spun more evenly. . . .

Yes, we had found the right grade of cotton. The Comilla especially gave beautiful results. Willie overcame his initial difficulties and learned to spin 11s as evenly as 9s. The ripples came out of the machine so crisp and regular that it was a pleasure to run one's hand over the fabric to feel them. If anything our cloth was better than that from Apolda. We now heard nothing but praise from our customers, praise to which we were so unaccustomed that it made us feel almost uncomfortable, praise coupled with the request for larger supplies. What I had predicted was happening. Our capacity was totally inadequate, and although over the next two years we bought eight ripple machines and worked them in three shifts we never caught up on demand.

Had we been able to manufacture nothing but ripple cloth the Langley operation would soon have become profitable. But the factory was laid out to make garments, and on the production of those we lost money, more money than we earned on the sale of cloth. And so the deficit continued, but on a diminishing scale, which was encouraging. We were confident that the time would come when the enterprise could support itself financially.

The knowledge of having introduced a new manufacturing technique to Britain, of making something in the country which, before we came, had to be imported, secretly gave me tremendous satisfaction. It would prove to Mr

Watkinson and his colleagues at Whitehall—if they should ever get to hear about it—that their trust in us had not been misplaced.

For some strange reason our financial year ended on 31 March in England, and not on 31 December, as in Czechoslovakia. The auditors were busy preparing the accounts. The Langley factory had now been operating for nine months and, we estimated, had lost well over £1,000. We were therefore pleasantly surprised when the balance sheet showed a loss of only £700, especially since this included depreciation and bank interest. True, we had not told the auditors that Langley was being subsidised by the parent firm. Fleissen invoiced condenser yarns and other supplies at exceptionally low prices, made no charge for freight, insurance and packing cases, and intentionally forgot to debit the English enterprise for spare parts, needles and bobbins. But even if all this was taken into account Langley had not done as badly as we had feared. Another year or two and, all being well, we would turn the loss into a profit.

Hints about a small car reappeared in Rolf's letters. Not that he suggested buying one now, but even window shopping and the hope that perhaps by the autumn we might be able to afford one were exciting.

'Don't wait for the autumn. Buy it now,' I wrote. 'Mother wants you to have it, too, provided you promise to drive carefully.'

Rolf could not resist this temptation. With his Czechoslovak passport and £250 in his pocket, he went to Coventry. It was out of the question, he told Mr Lyon, the managing director of the Swallow Coachbuilding Co., for him to pay £325, the regular home market price. Since the money was provided by Adolf Pasold & Sohn of Fleissen, a foreign firm, he wanted export terms. A long shot, but to his surprise Mr Lyon offered him 25 per cent discount. So Rolf counted £244 on the table, £6 less than he had been prepared to pay, and became the owner of a shiny red-and-black sports saloon.

The car was a beauty, lower than anything else on the road, a small four-seater with a long, elegant bonnet and a hard top. Sometimes rudely referred to as the 'pregnant banana', the Swallow was the forerunner of the long line of Jaguars that were to become so famous. Decidedly a young man's car, it gave us much pleasure and excellent service for a number of years. When the people of Langley saw it they concluded somewhat prematurely that the worst must now be over at Pasolds, and that the future of the factory was secure. I wonder whether they realised how tightly Rolf controlled the running expenses. He built a garage out of old packing cases and restricted motoring for pleasure to a minimum. I still remember how he and I returned from a business trip to Leicester one evening: pulling up by a garage at Uxbridge, I told the attendant to 'fill her up'.

Rolf was staggered. 'We have only three miles to go and you say fill her up. Who do you think we are? The Rockefellers? Surely a gallon is enough!'

Machinery has always fascinated me, especially if it functions automatically. Most of our attempts at replacing human hands by mechanisation failed, but if occasionally one of our ideas led to success it amply repaid us for all the efforts spent on the many others that did not. It was quite unimportant who had thought of it first. We usually discussed, changed and improved the original concept so often that it would have been difficult to say whether Willie, Rolf, I or some employee had contributed most. It was invariably teamwork, and we shared the thrill. Willie was bubbling over with excitement as he demonstrated the new sliver dyeing plant which had been completed at Leibitschgrund during my absence at Langley. It was not our invention. We had ordered standard wool processing machinery from Carl Fleissner & Sohn of Asch and adapted it for cotton. Sliver is an intermediate product between raw cotton and the finished thread. To the layman it looks like soft white rope about the thickness of one's thumb. Consisting of fibres which are only loosely compacted without being twisted together, it has no tensile strength whatever. At the slightest pull the 'rope' comes apart. Dyeing this flimsy sliver without breaking it in the process seemed impossible, but we accomplished it perfectly in the following ingenious manner.

The neatly coiled 'rope' was compacted by hydraulic pressure on to perforated stainless steel tubes until the soft cotton felt as hard as brick. The tubes were then closed at one end and hot dye was pumped in at the other, forcing the colour through the perforations and into the compressed cotton. After half an hour's pumping while the hot liquid circulated, reversing direction every few minutes, the dyeing was complete and the sliver was rinsed with clean water by the same method. The bundles of wet sliver then slid easily off the steel tubes and were centrifuged. This left them looking distorted beyond repair, yet to our surprise they uncoiled freely. Passing over a pair of warm drums to which the sliver was held by suction, it was dried and wound into tidy rolls without a hand touching it. None the worse for the seemingly rough treatment, it became once again the soft 'rope' that had no tensile strength—but now, of course, it was coloured.

From here the normal spinning process took over again. One could draft and spin coloured sliver, or combine white and coloured in various proportions according to the shade and the degree of mottling one wanted in the finished yarn.

It is not often that a newly developed process works without teething troubles, but this one did. From the very first day it functioned so well that Willie and I were in raptures. Apart from the joy we derived from the sheer

elegance and smooth efficiency of the operation, we knew that we had removed the last obstacle limiting the growth of our White Bear business.
Fleissen would never again be short of marl yarns. But if there were no
technical hitches we had some unpleasantness with farmers and fishermen
lower down the valley who did not believe that the soil absorbed the effluent
from the sliver dyeing plant and suspected that there was a secret connection
between the large soakaway pit we had constructed and the trout stream. They
complained to the authorities, and a *Kommission* of government officials,
lawyers and the mayors of a dozen villages, supported by forty irate farmers,
appeared at Leibitschgrund. The echo of their angry voices resounded from
the hills. Came the lunch interval, during which we all sat peaceably together
in the local inn or on the benches outside, having goulash or sausages and
beer; then the shouting resumed. It can be an unnerving experience to argue
with a crowd of irate peasants. However, the experts were on our side. They
licensed our settling trench and soakaway provisionally for a period of two
years.

A month later someone found a dead trout. Although Willie discovered
that it had been killed by the cooling water from the steam engine, and had
the small danger area screened off to prevent fish getting into it, a second
Kommission descended. After another day's shouting judgement was again
given in our favour. Not that this was the end of the matter. Another dead
trout was found, this time ten kilometres downstream, and, believe it or not,
a third *Kommission* turned up. It had to walk for an hour to reach the dead
fish, only to establish that it had been hooked. By now the officials had had
enough, and when, shortly afterwards, effluent from our soakaway really
seeped through the slate below the soil into the stream they took little notice
of the farmers' complaints. A court case against us dragged on for a while,
and I remember one amusing incident when Dörfler, our loyal gamekeeper,
was called as a witness.

'Your honour,' he said to the judge, 'as you well know, people from all
over the world come to Franzensbad, our famous spa, to take the waters,
especially at a spring called the Glauber Quelle. Its health-giving water
contains Glauber's salt. This is exactly the kind of salt used in our dyehouse.
Far from harming the fish, it will make them grow healthier and fatter than
ever.' No more dead trout were found, and the case petered out.

The sliver dyeing plant proved an unqualified success. Not only could we
now produce all the marl yarns we wanted but they were softer than those
supplied by other spinners, and we could produce them at much lower cost.
This success encouraged me to concentrate once again on improving the
manufacturing technique of our White Bear sweaters and waistcoats at
Fleissen. We reduced prices, sales reached new records, and we earned higher

profits than before, thus providing the money for more ambitious advertising campaigns which in turn increased demand, and we had to install an additional sewing conveyor. The romance of our sweater business was a textbook example of how to create, launch and develop a new product. We did in Czechoslovakia what Meridian, Vedonis, Chilprufe, Wolsey and the other famous English knitters I so much admired had achieved in Great Britain, and I felt tremendous satisfaction.

The White Bear business became a sensation, the envy of the Czechoslovak knitting industry, which, fortunately, did not realise on what thin ice we were skating with our monopoly. It was almost unheard of for a knitted fabric or garment to be registered. I did not believe for one moment that our designs were novel enough to sustain a court action should we ever be faced with one, but the regulations governing design protection were so woolly that not even the chamber of commerce quite understood them. To my relief and never-ending amazement the words 'Gesetzlich geschützt' on the labels and in our advertisements, backed up by the simple device of depositing 'sealed samples' every year, continued to baffle would-be imitators. Tongue in cheek, I repeated the registrations annually, and my bluff was never called. I often wondered what ruses some of our rivals might be using to fool us!

After falling steadily for a number of years, dragging countless growers, merchants and spinners into bankruptcy, the price of raw cotton reached bottom in 1932. But how was anyone to know at the time that it would fall no further? We had been wrong before when we thought the lowest point had been reached at eight and then at seven cents per pound. Throughout 1932 quotations on the New York cotton exchange fluctuated between five and a half and six and a half cents. They could hardly go lower, I reasoned, and a reaction was bound to come, but when? Although stocks in warehouses and mills had shrunk to a minimum, the shelves in the shops were bare of cotton goods, and presumably people's clothes cupboards were by now empty. The trade seemed to have lost confidence in a recovery and only bought from hand to mouth, thus prolonging the stagnation.

Then, from the beginning of April 1933 onwards, cotton prices suddenly began to move upwards, hesitatingly at first, but gathering momentum, and by the end of May they had climbed to above nine cents per pound. I placed substantial contracts at seven and a half cents, replenishing the depleted stocks at Leibitschgrund and Fleissen, and cabled Rolf, urging him to cover Langley's requirements of yarns, sewing thread and even elastic for the whole year. But if I was a bull all my life, invariably expecting prices to rise, Rolf was most definitely born a bear. It was difficult to make him put down a contract for anything. He believed that, given patience, everything could be bought cheaper. I am amused to think that in the forty years that have since passed neither of us has changed very much. I am still liable to commit myself prematurely, while Rolf often ponders too long and sometimes misses the boat.

He did on that occasion. Calling me an alarmist, he gave Nahum's of Manchester an order for 5,000 lb of cotton yarn instead of 30,000 lb as I had urged him to do, and had to pay a higher price for each successive contract while our customers would not pay a penny more for the repeat business they gave us. It was impossible, they claimed, to raise their prices in the middle of the season. However, the cloud had a silver lining. As always when prices harden, people began to buy, and although there was little hope of the Langley factory making a profit in the foreseeable future there were now good prospects of keeping it fully employed. Rolf had been right in refusing to 'slaughter' the prices of our merchandise. Langley would now surely get enough orders without price reductions.

Trade reaction to the climbing cotton prices was much stronger in Czechoslovakia than in Britain. The wholesalers from Prag and Brünn, the retailers from the provincial towns of Bohemia and Moravia, and the Polish Jews from Slovakia who all came hurrying to Fleissen haggled less and bought more than they had done for years. We could not meet all the orders for White Bear sweaters in spite of our expanding output, but other garments had begun to catch the public's fancy too, sports shirts made of knitted Köper, for instance. They had short sleeves, a collar and a patch pocket, and were more comfortable to wear than shirts of woven material. Moreover they were cheaper. Dyed bright yellow, pale blue or bleached white, these new shirts became best-sellers overnight. As the originator had not bothered to protect his idea, or found the procedure too difficult, every manufacturer who had Terrot-type circulars with presswheels and a suitable battery of sewing machines was making them within a few months. Before long, buyers in Holland, Scandinavia and Britain became interested, and soon the factories at Fleissen and Asch began to work shifts again.

Another new garment, a training suit, as it was called, made its appearance. It consisted of a sweater with a zip front, long sleeves and a pocket, and a pair of long trousers elasticated at waist and ankle. Made of fleecy stockinette fabric, mainly in navy blue, it cost very much less than a suit made of woven cloth, could be quickly slipped on or off and was eminently suitable for wear about the house, the tool shed or the garden. In Czechoslovakia these suits rapidly became an essential part of the wardrobe of every man, woman and child. Fleissen's factories were ideally equipped to manufacture them in large quantities, and since it took quite a large piece of fabric to make a training suit, and the seams were long, they provided plenty of employment. The knitting industry of western Bohemia worked its way out of crisis and depression largely at the expense of the weavers.

In Britain too the knitters were taking trade away from the weavers, if perhaps at a slower rate. In addition to sports shirts, which our Langley machinists found difficult because of the intricacies of sewing the collar, we made samples of the training suits which had become so much the vogue in Czechoslovakia and showed them to every wholesale buyer in London who would condescend to look at them, but failed to secure a single order for this 'ugly outlandish fancy dress'.

'I'm looking for a cheap artificial silk blouse: can't you knit one?' asked Mr Newbold of Bradbury Greatorex, whom we supplied with cotton marl jumpers made by our Fleissen factory. The high import duty on artificial silk made foreign merchandise very expensive. As it happened, we had established friendly relations with British Bemberg's, an offshoot of the famous German makers of artificial silk. From time to time their plant at Doncaster produced batches of yarn which did not conform to their normal standards but were completely satisfactory for the artificial silk stripes in Directoire knickers. We thus provided a convenient outlet for Bemberg's, and they supplied us at very favourable prices. This advantage inspired us to experiment, and with the help of our old friend the presswheel we knitted a lightweight fabric entirely of artificial silk. It looked good dyed in pastel shades, and we made ladies' blouses from it which we sold to Bradbury Greatorex and other wholesalers at the ridiculously low price of 15s 6d a dozen. If all went well, which was not very often, we made a profit of 5 per cent on them.

As with the marl jumpers, Peggy did the modelling. For a year or two sales figures climbed, and after we had successfully made several thousand dozen blouses customers were demanding that we should also make dresses for them out of the same artificial silk stockinette fabric. And so, much against my will and better judgement, we were pushed still further into the women's fashion trade, which we did not understand and for which our factory was ill equipped. Then, just as I had feared and without warning, the business ended as suddenly as it had begun. We were left with a stock of merchandise which we had to sell at half-price to an East End jobber named Skolnick to get rid of it. But I am running ahead of my story again.

In my youthful optimism I had imagined that British buyers would go out of their way to support and nurse a newly established factory such as ours to shake up their old and, I gathered, sleepy suppliers in the Midlands. They would surely give our struggling young enterprise a helping hand. I should have known that business was tougher than that. Wholesalers could not afford to be patriotic, sentimental or generous; they were looking for bargains.

Every buyer was fighting to improve or at least maintain his figures in order to keep his job. He bought from us only if we were cheaper than his old suppliers, and dropped us without hesitation when we had served his purpose. The wholesale trade was battling for survival against the growing retail groups and chain stores.

Time and again I explained to Mr Hurst and to a somewhat impatient Peggy that our mentality, skill and equipment were attuned to efficient mass production of some standard product, such as underwear, and that we could not cope with the constant chopping and changing of the fashion trade.

Looking back, I would say that it was our ripple cloth production that changed Langley's fortunes. It put us on the first step of the ladder to success. Not that it removed all our troubles, on the contrary, for quite a while it added fresh problems to those we already had, but they did not keep us awake at night very often. They seemed small in comparison with the fear of having to close the factory for lack of orders, a very real possibility only a short while before.

As a rule I went to London once a week to call on customers. The other days I spent at the factory checking the quality of our merchandise, comparing production figures, showing our workers how to get better results with less effort. I planned manufacturing programmes with Köhler, helped Hildegard Fuchs to find the best way of fitting her paper patterns into various widths of material, and tried to improve standards all round. There was so much to do, so much to put right, I could have done with two pairs of eyes and hands, and wished the day were forty-eight hours long. Only the weekend brought peace, and I spent many a happy Saturday afternoon and Sunday over my drawing board, designing dream production lines and future factory extensions. Rolf did not like talk of extending the factory. Our plant was quite large enough, he said. But it was not large enough for me. I dreamed of a very much larger enterprise, and was itching to add a few bays to the building.

We were a good team. Köhler had developed into a capable works manager whose enthusiasm was catching. Our people loved him. Passler and Schreiner had learned to speak English, lost their inhibitions and become successful instructors. Watson now mastered fleecing machine and calender, and Walker's bent for engineering had secured him the job of works mechanic. Hildegard Fuchs, who came from Asch in Czechoslovakia, where she had attended the textile college and worked for a year in our factory at Fleissen, held at the early age of twenty the difficult position of *directrice* or forelady, to use the English expression. We had had three foreladies before her, all girls from Leicester, whom the labour exchange had sent us, but none of them proved satisfactory, and at last the Home Office gave us a permit to employ Miss Fuchs. To tell the truth, we were disappointed with her at first, and several times considered sending her back to Czechoslovakia, but we found no suitable replacement, and so she stayed, much to the firm's advantage, as it turned out later. She was a slow developer, but over the years became one of the pillars of the enterprise.

The renewal of the labour permits of our few remaining foreign key workers continued to cause us great concern. The authorities seemed quite incapable of understanding how there could be no suitable British workers to replace them. I dreaded those interviews at the Ministry of Labour and, when I had satisfied the officials there, at the Home Office. And how relieved I felt when, once again, I secured extensions for three or six months.

28

ADVICE FROM
UNCLE FRIEDRICH
1933-36

'YOU OUGHT TO get married and raise a family!' Had anyone other than Uncle Friedrich said it to me I would have laughed in his face. But Uncle Friedrich had to be taken seriously. He was a sage. Now sixty, the eldest of the Geipel brothers and one of Bohemia's outstanding industrialists, he was a man of oak. I greatly admired him.

'You must be joking,' I replied. 'A wife and family while I'm shuttling between Czechoslovakia and England? Keeping up with the Lehrmanns and Brauns at Fleissen and at the same time building a business at Langley is as much as I can cope with.'

Uncle Friedrich's kindly eyes looked straight into mine. 'You are twenty-seven and the head of the family firm. You are well spoken of in the trade. I am glad you have made Rolf and Ingo equal partners notwithstanding the difference in your ages, but did you have to start that factory in England? I gather it's not a successful venture. Why don't you sell it and concentrate your energies on Fleissen and Leibitschgrund? That would leave you time to found a home. Would Sonja or one of the other girls I see you with sometimes make a good wife?'

I shook my head. 'I shall look for an English business girl to share my work.'

'No,' said uncle Friedrich firmly, 'you need a wife, not another business associate, a wife who will provide a happy home and bring up children. It would be unfair to your brothers if you took her into the firm. Do you want to wreck the partnership?'

'Grandmother Pasold has worked in our firm ever since I can remember and is still doing a wonderful job,' I protested.

'So she is,' Uncle Friedrich replied, 'and everyone admires her for it, but there are no brothers in the firm. Besides, mothers and grandmothers are not like wives!'

Uncle Friedrich's world revolved round Fleissen. How could I make him understand that my heart was in England? I had not wanted to be head of Adolf Pasold & Sohn but there was no one else to take charge when Father

died. The firm had meant everything to him and to Grandfather: they had
made it the proud concern it now was. To let them down would have been
unthinkable. But provided I held the fort until Rolf and Ingo were old enough
to decide for themselves had I not the right also to work for my life's ambition, to make my headquarters in England? Tiny as the Langley factory still
was compared with our Czechoslovak concern, I would not rest until it became the centre of the Pasold enterprises. And if this demanded sacrificing
some years now, if I had to postpone getting married and having children till
later in life, I knew that my brothers would look after them. We three would
always be united. Not that I ever said so, it would have sounded too dramatic.
I simply took it for granted.

Almost all successful businesses in our part of the world were run by
teams of brothers. Quite often they fought among themselves, much to the
amusement of onlookers, but blood was thicker than water, and any interference from outside always made them bury the hatchet and present a common
front. We would need no pressure from outside to unite us, I felt sure of that.
Differences of opinion would not be aired in public but in the private office.
We would work for a common goal; everything would go in and come out of a
common pot. Between the three of us we would have enough able sons to
continue in our footsteps, building an empire, no matter whether they were
my boys, Rolf's or Ingo's. They would be Pasolds, and this, I thought, would
be sufficient guarantee that they were made of the right stuff.

Following my talk with Uncle Friedrich I questioned Grandmother about
the time when she first came into the firm, and this is what she told me.
Johann Wilhelm Pasold, my great-grandfather, had four sons. Johann, the
eldest, should have inherited the house and the family business, but he
married a girl who had different ideas. She was well off, the house was not
good enough for her, and she did not want her husband to have to work so
hard. She made him give up his birthright and take money instead. Frequent
quarrels in the family made Ernst, the second son, leave home to become a
schoolteacher, and Karl to emigrate to America. There remained Adolf, the
youngest, my grandfather, to take over the house and the knitting machines,
but having to pay the others out left him short of cash. Johann and his wife
now saw their chance, and went into partnership with him on terms which
were very favourable to themselves. It was not a happy arrangement. Johann's
wife wanted to give the orders and Adolf was expected to do the work. Then
Adolf married Grandmother. She must have been an exceptionally able and
pretty girl, and brought a good deal of capital into the firm. Soon there was
trouble between her and Johann's wife. This led to quarrels between Johann
and Adolf, and in the end they parted. Adolf carried on the family business,

while Johann became a yarn and insurance agent and a dealer in textiles and musical instruments, making little success of either. It was, Grandmother agreed, a tragedy that the four brothers did not stand together.

Her story saddened me. True, it had all happened in the dim and distant past, but I did not like to hear of Pasold brothers quarrelling and turning their backs on each other. How stupid of them when, as a team, they could have surpassed all their competitors and built up the largest knitting concern in western Bohemia. The thought of it made me all the more determined not to let anything or anybody come between Rolf, Ingo and myself. I could see why Uncle Friedrich wanted wives to be kept out of their husbands' businesses.

He could be forgiven for believing that our British venture was a failure. We had kept very quiet about the troubles at Langley and pretended that all was well, but when the people of Fleissen heard that Fischer's were closing their plant at Edmonton and shipping their machines back to Asch they began to wonder how much longer we would be able to hold out. Another three months, or six? The good people of Fleissen, including Uncle Friedrich, underestimated our determination to succeed. They knew nothing of our budding ripple cloth business, and we had no intention of enlightening them. It was better to keep competitors in the dark. Langley's troubles were not over, of course, but at least we had enough orders, and our operating losses were getting smaller. The main problem now was to manufacture the goods and deliver them on time. Our output was too small. We needed more work-people, and soon we would need more machines. In my mind I was already planning an extension to the factory.

The queue of unemployed at Slough labour exchange was shorter than it had been two years ago and consisted mainly of middle-aged Welshmen. We needed youths and girls who were willing to be trained, and finding them was not easy. Newspaper advertisements in the Midlands, the home of the knitting industry, brought little response. A knitter from Leicester who claimed to have experience of Terrot-type machines proved unsatisfactory, another from Nottingham did not like Langley and left again. In desperation we applied once again to the Home Office for labour permits for three knitters from Czechoslovakia, and were granted two, valid for a period of three months. With their help Rolf scored a minor triumph. He introduced three-shift working in the knitting department. It was not a popular move with our Langley workers, but they earned more money and after some initial difficulties settled down to the new routine. The extra output was useful, if still insufficient.

Trade in general was better than it had been the year before. There were signs of returning confidence among wholesale buyers, and making the round of the City houses was no longer the depressing experience we had found it for so long. Mr Hurst became very optimistic, and even Rolf no longer refused to listen when I talked about buying more machines, although he would not hear of enlarging the factory. Our plant was capable of 50 per cent more output, he pointed out correctly, if only we had enough skilled operatives, and adding a few bays to the building would not provide additional workpeople. Nevertheless he agreed to the purchase of five circulars, two winding frames and a dozen sewing machines. It was a major decision that kept us all in a state of excitement for weeks.

While we were searching for bargains Hitler stopped the export of second-hand machines from Germany. This made us pause. New plant would cost three or four times as much as we had budgeted for, and we did not like spending so much money. Fleissen's astounding growth had been achieved entirely with second-hand machines. Admittedly one never got quite what one wanted when buying used plant and had to compromise. It was difficult to knit fabric of uniform appearance and dimensions if the diameters and gauges of the knitting machines did not match, yet Adolf Pasold & Sohn and the other manufacturers of Fleissen and Asch performed miracles with their odd assortment of circulars. But only because our Bohemian workpeople were masters at adaptation. We could not expect similar skill from our inexperienced workers at Langley. New machines which needed fewer adjustments and less nursing would be better for them. Hitler's decree might turn out to Langley's advantage. We stopped looking for second-hand circulars and visited machinery manufacturers' showrooms instead. There were, for instance, 'high speed' circulars to be studied which Fouquet & Frauz, Terrot, Haaga and other makers had developed, even if we could not afford to buy them just yet.

New machines had to be chosen especially carefully, to make sure that they would do the job for which they were intended. Not all of them performed as well as their makers claimed. I was, for instance, greatly taken with a new American Leesona cone winder, a beautiful piece of precision machinery. It wound yarn at a speed of 750 yards a minute, against the 250 yards of our comparatively primitive bottle bobbin winders, and we installed one for a trial period. To my surprise our girls did not like it. They claimed it broke too many threads and they could not earn enough money on it. Suspecting that they were only trying to establish a case for higher piece rates, I decided to find out for myself. In the evening, when the girls had gone, I worked the Leesona while Köhler competed against me on one of the bottle bobbin winders. The sweat poured from my brow, but after two hours Köhler had wound 20 per cent more yarn than I, and I had to concede victory to him. So we gave the Leesona back to the makers and bought two new machines of the old bottle bobbin type.

Sooner or later the Langley factory would have to be enlarged if it was to become the centre of the Pasold operations, I told Rolf. Its present size did not justify all the effort we were spending on it. What had we bought a seventeen-acre site for? To be taken seriously by the authorities, by our customers and suppliers, to build up a worthwhile business and to become profitable the factory would have to be several times its present size. We had enough orders now, and the volume was growing. The extension would take a year to complete—what were we waiting for?

'Money, for one thing,' answered Rolf dryly. 'Our new machines have to be paid for, the growing turnover has to be financed, it's expensive to train workers, and we're getting poorer every week. Supposing we did need a factory extension—which I dispute—how do you propose to meet the bill?'

Fleissen had spare funds, but Czechoslovakia's currency regulations precluded capital transfers to England, and all my efforts to secure a permit proved abortive. I then tried another approach. If the authorities would not allow Adolf Pasold & Sohn to finance the British branch factory on a permanent basis, would they let Langley raise a loan in Czechoslovakia? The head office of the Bohemian Union Bank in Prague was willing to lend one million kronen for the purpose, and Fleissen would guarantee the loan. In view of all the foreign currency we had earned for the State over the years with our exports, I felt I could reasonably expect the authorities to co-operate. But to my chagrin the Ministry of Finance once again withheld its approval.

To be fair, my approach came at an inconvenient time. Roosevelt's New Deal, designed to reduce unemployment in America, weakened the dollar and caused inflation. There was talk of France abandoning the gold standard, and Czechoslovakia, worried about her future competitiveness in world export markets, clung to her reserves of foreign currency. I failed in the purpose for which I had gone to Prague, but the journey was not wasted. Through the indiscretion of an official I picked up a piece of valuable information about an ingenious plan hatched by Dr Engliš, the Minister of Finance. He contemplated levying 20 per cent duty on all imports, including raw materials, and paying a 20 per cent bonus on all exports. Realising that this scheme, if adopted, would amount to nothing less than a disguised devaluation of the krone, and anxious not to get caught once again, I hurried back to Fleissen to take defensive measures and succeeded in paying off in advance our foreign currency commitments, mainly dollars and sterling which would fall due when our forward shipments of raw cotton arrived from America and India.

Dr Engliš's plan was adopted by the government and, in the absence of Dr Beneš in Paris, prematurely announced by the press, only to be hurriedly withdrawn on Beneš's return—at the command of his French masters, no doubt. Apart from the consternation this ministerial bungling caused in the business world, the writing was now on the wall. It could only be a matter of time before the krone would be devalued officially—and, of course, it was. I had the satisfaction of having saved the firm from a substantial loss.

I should have gone to Prague far more often to keep in touch with government departments, entertain the underpaid officials, and establish personal contact with politicians. But Father had not brought me up that way. In his opinion an industrialist was someone who staked his capital buying raw material, employing machinery and labour to process it in the most efficient manner, and who sold the resulting product at a profit, most of which he ploughed back into the business. This kept him fully occupied. He did not believe in wasting time with civil servants unless he had to, and I had inherited his dislike of Czech officials.

Most of us dwell on our happy memories and hardly remember the hardships and worries that overshadowed the past. I am no exception, yet when I think of the first years at Langley there is little I would willingly live through again. When our workpeople went cheerfully home at Saturday lunch time I sat poring over the losses we had made during another tough and disappointing week. My only consolation was that nothing much could go wrong in the factory over the weekend, because it was closed.

And I felt lonely. My acquaintances were mostly business people a generation older than myself whose private lives revolved round their family, garden or golf club. They were not interested in me. The only friends I had were Mr and Mrs Hurst and their four daughters, who lived at Stanmore and always made me welcome. But before we had a car it was difficult to get there from Langley. Even with the car the twenty-mile cross-country run presented navigational problems. The route twisted and turned through such a labyrinth of crossroads and forks, along rows of semi-detached houses at Cowley, Uxbridge, Ruislip and Harrow Weald, all looking so similar, that it was quite easy to lose one's way, especially at night or if there were patches of fog about. I was not used to driving in fog.

On my walks through the wooded lanes of Iver and Burnham Beeches, or along the Thames from Windsor to Maidenhead and Bourne End, I saw many large residences in well kept grounds. One I liked especially. Forty minutes from the factory on the way to Iver Heath was a low building with white walls and brown beams—several hundred years old, I thought, standing well back from the road in a beautifully laid out garden. It was called Temple Grange. I often walked there in the evening and looked over the gate, wondering who might live there. Some wealthy stockbroker? A retired general? Or some friendly young people? Idle speculations. I would never meet them anyway.

And then something incredible happened. To start at the beginning I have to go back ten years to the time when I was studying at the textile college in Asch. My friend, George Eisenschiml, who used to sit in the same class with me, refused to become a textile manufacturer. He left his inheritance, a prosperous fabric glove factory, in the hands of a competent *Direktor* and divided his time between Asch, Vienna and St Anton in the Tyrol, where he built himself a beautiful chalet. There he spent most of the winter skiing, and in the summer he put on his hobnailed boots and went climbing the mountains.

One day a young Englishman who had just alighted from the Arlberg Express asked him to recommend a restaurant. Captivated by the striking appearance of the tall, good-looking stranger with laughing blue eyes and a shock of blond hair, George invited him to his favourite *Gasthof*, the Post. It was Jack Matthews's first visit to the Continent. He had come to the Tyrol for a walking holiday, but he liked George and his local friends so much that he decided to stay at St Anton instead.

George Eisenschiml spent a weekend with me at Langley. 'I've promised this chap to look him up. He lives not far from London,' said George, rummaging through his papers for Jack Matthews' address.

'Not far from London? That might be anywhere in Hertfordshire, Essex or Kent,' I replied without enthusiasm, not looking forward to driving half way round the sprawling metropolis, getting lost in the maze of badly signposted country roads.

'Found it,' said George. 'It's Temple Grange, at a place called Iver Heath. Have you any idea where that might be?'

Temple Grange? Had I heard aright? Of all the hundreds of thousands of houses near London could it be just that one?

Twenty minutes later, not knowing what to expect, I turned the long nose of the SS into the Matthews' drive. A pretty girl of about seventeen opened the door, but before we could introduce ourselves a voice boomed out behind her. 'Hallo there, George, you old rascal!' and Jack, lifting his struggling young sister, Adrye, out of the way and on to the bonnet of the car, gave little George such a hearty slap on the back that he was nearly sent flying into the rhododendron bushes.

We met Jack's parents, his elder sister, Lois, and younger brother, Peter, and stayed for tea and dinner, George entertaining us with amusing tales— mostly against himself—of his life among the Tyrolean peasants. The Matthews delighted in his sense of humour, his Austrian accent and rolling r's, and were sorry he had to return to Vienna the following day. But would I please promise to come to breakfast next Sunday?

They were a wonderfully happy family and such kindly people. For the following ten years I had Sunday breakfast at Temple Grange and very often lunch and dinner as well.

Jack failed to interest me in dog racing, but I did take up golf with him at Stoke Poges, only to decide after a year or two that a ball game that had to be taken seriously was not for me. Playing croquet in the garden with Mr and Mrs Matthews and the girls was more fun. Mr Frank P. Matthews was the personification of an English gentleman: tall, lanky, old-fashioned, reliable, correct in everything he did and so patriotic that he stood to attention in his own home when the radio played 'God Save the King'. I had tremendous respect for him. A fruit tree grower by profession—his nurseries were at Harlington, just where the motorway now passes north of Heathrow airport —he worked on the land all day, with little opportunity for conversation. Perhaps that was why he liked to talk in the evening after dinner, relaxing in front of a roaring fire. The family knew all his stories by heart, but they were new to me and I enjoyed listening. And when I too had heard them more than once I made an effort to appear interested, although in my mind I might be with our knitting machines or some wholesale buyer in the City. And thus, without ever saying much myself, I gained the reputation of being the best conversationalist he ever wished to meet. Dear Mr Matthews.

Temple Grange became a second home to me and Rolf. The Matthews made us both feel like members of the family, and we forgot all our business worries during those happy weekends at Iver Heath.

Through Jack I met various other young men. The beer drinking and dog racing types I did not care for, but I liked Melton Bomer, a young surveyor who was courting Jack's sister Lois, and I struck up a lifelong friendship with John Hooker, who was making the Royal Navy his career. The mess at Chatham with some hundred cadets where he gave me lunch and the destroyer in Portsmouth harbour which he showed me still stand out in my memory. John was a tall, exceptionally good-looking, serious young man who personified the best tradition of the Senior Service.

At George Eisenschiml's invitation John and I spent the Christmas holidays with him at the chalet at St Anton. I had skied every winter in Czechoslovakia, but was self-taught, and the snow on the Arlberg was too deep, the slopes too steep for me. After struggling for a couple of days on my own without much success I swallowed my pride and went to skiing lessons. Alpine skiing was still a sport for the very few, and Hannes Schneider was their prophet and pioneer. He and his famous team of instructors had perfected the 'Arlberg technique', a series of accurately controlled stem turns, which was fast replacing the Scandinavian 'Telemark'. His fame spread, until governments as far away as South America and Japan were inviting him to show them how to set up winter sports centres and build ski lifts. But that came a few years later. In 1934 we still carried our skis on our backs laboriously up the mountain side, up and up for hours, in order to enjoy the exhilaration of a twenty-minute downhill run. And in the evening we sat in the Gasthof Post, stretching our tired legs, eating and talking to George and his skiing instructor friends—plain country boys in the summer, the sons of farmers and mountain guides, but supermen on skis. A word of modest praise from any one of them made one's day, and all the girls ran after them and spoiled them. Sometimes the great Hannes Schneider himself came and had a glass of beer with us. What unforgettable parties we had with Rudy, an amusing American, whose hard-working father back in the States was only too pleased to pay for his son to stay away skiing all winter. Then there was young Farman, of French aviation fame, a Norwegian, a Dutch girl, and Heini, the proprietor's pretty daughter who, in her red stockings and short navy blue skirt was so much faster on skis than I.

All too soon the holiday came to an end, and boarding the Arlberg Express we promised to return the following Christmas. From now on I took a skiing holiday in the Alps every winter, eagerly looking forward to it from one year to the next. But as my skiing improved, so I also discovered that Christmas was not the best time to go to the mountains. The days were too short and the sun was not warm enough. Besides, St Anton lies in the shade in the valley, while Zürs, higher up, lies in the sun. So whenever I could I took my vacation the last week of February and the first week of March and went to Zürs.

Could anything be more breathtaking than the glistening, snow-covered peaks of the Alps bathed in sunshine? The sheer grandeur of the mountains, the deep blue sky above with the hot sun beating down on the blinding whiteness, the pure air and the incredible silence made the tiny towns of man, distant and way below, with their bustle, noise and smoke, seem unreal and ridiculous. And when one's eyes had taken in all the beauty, when the time came for the descent, one tightened one's ski straps and, with a mixture of daring and apprehension, hurtled downwards. The swish of the boards through the powdery snow, the sudden screech when one tore a 'Christie' on an icy patch, the turns and twists as one avoided rocks, trees or precipices, the wonderful feeling of being firmly in control and the moments of fear when one was not—how can one possibly describe the joy and excitement of it all? I feel that anyone who has never skied has not really lived.

Although, with the exception of the war years, I have been skiing in the Austrian or Swiss Alps every winter, I am no ace, as the reader will have gathered. My technique is no better than fair to average, but the memories of my skiing holidays are among the happiest of my life.

In 1935 Rolf fell in love with an Alvis Speed Twenty and wanted to buy it for Adolf Pasold & Sohn. At first our application for an import licence was refused, because the Czechoslovak National Bank would not release foreign currency to pay for a British car, but with the help of a Dr Spira, a retired revenue inspector who had connections in the Ministry of Finance, the permit was eventually secured, and Rolf completed the purchase. It was great fun driving the shiny new sports car to Fleissen. The sun shone, we had the hood down and Jack Matthews, whom we took with us, waved to all the pretty girls *en route*. The long, low, bright red drophead coupe caused a sensation wherever we stopped. People were used to seeing American, German, French, Italian, Austrian and Czechoslovak cars, but not English ones, and we were very proud of ours. If only we could have kept the British number plate, but that, of course, was out of the question. As soon as the import duty had been paid and the car entered on the Czechoslovak register the glamorous GB had to be replaced by a dull CS. So we did the next best thing, we flew a small union jack from the chromium-plated bracket holding the spare tyre.

Jack aroused as much curiosity as the Alvis. Here was a young Englishman looking like the hero out of a popular novel, probably a young lord. Everyone wanted to look at him. I remember an incident in my favourite inn, on the German side of the border. We had walked there in the evening through the forest for a meal and a glass of beer. At the next table sat a party of young Saxons, among them an SA man in uniform who was critical of our speaking English, thinking it was Czech. At first he stared, then started making disapproving comments. Suddenly Jack got up, lifted him out of his chair and, putting him right in the middle of the large oak table, wagged his finger at him:

'If you don't behave, little man, I shall have to put you outside this hospitable inn!' There was a tense moment, but Jack's laughing face made the Germans laugh, and we had a round of beer together.

Rolf stayed at Fleissen, while I returned to England with Jack. He had never flown. 'Could we go by air, please?' So at the crack of dawn we caught the train for Leipzig and from there flew in a German plane to Cologne. This first leg of the journey was bearable, and my spirits rose. But I rejoiced too soon. In the early afternoon a Belgian airline took us on to Brussels in a Fokker. The day was hot, we flew at a height of about 1,000 metres, and our aeroplane, falling into one air pocket after another, bounced up and down like a tennis ball. Jack enjoyed it, but I was so airsick that I had to lie on my back in the grass on Brussels aerodrome for an hour to recover, blaming the Fokker and the Belgians for the rough trip. I flatly refused to go on to Croydon with them. There was an Imperial Airways plane two hours later, a Heracles if I remember correctly, and I insisted on taking that. Not realising that it was the still air of the evening and not the clever design of the flying machine to which we owed the smooth passage, I sang its praise for months after. But I was in no hurry to travel by air again.

Bank holiday week, always the first week in August, was the annual holiday period for almost everyone in Britain. Hotels and boarding houses at the seaside were packed to bursting point, restaurants and public houses crowded out, the beaches black with people, and the factory was shut. We had decided to motor to Austria. Travelling from England by boat and train, I met Rolf and Ingo at Eger, where they were waiting for me with the Alvis. Uncle Wilhelm, our favourite uncle, a gay bachelor in his forties, came in his own small car and brought Cousin Udo. The weather was perfect, and Zell am See, where we stayed, quite delightful.

The following year we took the new road over the Grossglockner pass, with which we were duly impressed, and discovered Pörtschach on the Wörthersee, a most beautiful lake with water that was crystal-clear and so warm that one could bathe in it all day. We got to know some young Austrians, two English girls and Maria from Venice, and organised swimming parties, diving competitions and tugs-of-war on Li-los. To sweep headlong down the giant water chute was a thrilling experience, equalled only by skimming over the waves on a kind of surfboard towed by a fast motor-boat. We also learned to water-ski, something quite new and daring at that time. Pörtschach became our summer holiday paradise, a quiet little place to which we returned year after year.

Golden memories of happy days which, in retrospect, seem so blissfully carefree. But they were never without worries. Every holiday was a business mission too, and the task was always the same. Our English enterprise made no money and I was searching all the time for ways of supplementing its dwindling funds by transferring assests from Fleissen, whether prohibited or not. Langley now employed 100 workers whose wages had to be found, more machinery and larger quantities of raw materials needed to be bought, and I, stubbornly believing in ultimate success, dreamed of enlarging the factory. To spend precious sterling on holiday was therefore out of the question. Every pound counted.

The Czechoslovak National Bank allocated no currency for holidays. Restrictions, quite tough enough already, were tightened further from time to time, and I remember a period when the maximum amount of cash one was allowed to take out of the country without a permit was as little as ten kronen—barely enough to buy a meal. One was searched on crossing the border, and although we always hid a little extra in the car we never dared take very much. The punishment for smuggling money was severe, and I, the holder of a Czechoslovak passport, precariously poised between Fleissen and Langley, could ill afford to blot my copybook. But Uncle Wilhelm owned a large apartment house in Vienna and received the rent in Austrian schillings. Part of this income he declared to the Czechoslovak authorities; the balance he quietly collected in cash, which he paid into a Viennese bank to the credit of one of those numbered savings books I described earlier. He had been doing it for years, and so we had plenty of schillings to spend on our Austrian holidays. I repaid him at Fleissen in Czech kronen, which suited us both.

In fact Uncle Wilhelm had more Austrian schillings than we needed, and usually drew an extra amount with which I made the round of the hotels, restaurants and cafes in the neighbourhood, buying pound notes from hall porters and head waiters. British tourists quite often paid their bills in English money, and so I collected two pounds here and five pounds there, and at the end of the holiday I might have as much as a hundred pounds or more, all in single pound notes. It was a tedious business, and it had to be done without arousing suspicion, for Austria too had currency restrictions, designed to accumulate foreign money. The only thing in my favour was that the easy-going Austrians administered their regulations less efficiently than did the Czechoslovaks and the Germans.

Taking the notes out of Austria by road did not worry me unduly, but I felt apprehensive about the onward journey from Nuremberg to Holland by train or plane. There was no knowing what the Nazis might do to me if they caught me smuggling pound notes out of Germany, and a narrow escape made me decide not to be foolhardy again. In future I would hide the money from the Austrians, but once safely past them would declare it to the Germans so that I could take it out of Germany again quite legally. But on the next holiday we made a silly mistake. Instead of taking the road we knew, on which the two customs posts were half a mile apart, we chose a different route, and to our consternation found that the Austrian and the German frontier guards shared the same building, their respective doors separated by only a few yards—and both wide open, for it was a boiling-hot day. Remembering the scene makes me chuckle, but it was not funny at the time.

While I took the carnet through the first door, to be stamped, Rolf assured the Austrian guard who was inspecting the car that we had nothing to declare. Then I went back to fetch the bundle of notes and took them, with the carnet, through the second door. The German official ponderously counted and re-counted them, a record total of £175, and then made out a transit slip in triplicate. In the meantime a queue of impatient tourists formed outside the open door, craning their necks to discover the cause of the delay, and a wag called out in a loud voice, 'What's this? A blooming bank?' which sent a chill down my spine in case the Austrians should hear it and come to look. Fortunately the incident passed off without a hitch, but I never forgot the lesson. Never try smuggling anything across a frontier you are not thoroughly familiar with!

Most of the Austrian schillings Uncle Wilhelm could spare were changed into pound notes to be taken to England, but not all. Rolf was approaching nineteen. In a few months he would have to attend the dreaded medical examination that decided whether he was fit to become a soldier, a prospect as distasteful to him as it was alarming for me. He did not want to don a private's uniform and clean boots for eighteen months in some remote barracks in Slovakia, and how was I to carry on the factories on the Continent and in England without him? Rolf was a healthy lad, and once declared *schopen* the chances of securing his release were very slim.

Too much was at stake to let him risk attending the medical board in Czechoslovakia. Suppose Dr Stein, who had saved me from the army, was not on duty on the crucial day, or failed to persuade his military colleagues that Rolf was too weak to carry a rifle! It would be safer, I thought, if he took his medical at the consulate in London. Discreet enquiries led me to a Dr Silbermann, who, I was given to understand, sometimes acted as a consultant to the consulate. His private practice was in Wimpole Street. To get to know him I feigned chronic indigestion and became his patient.

Quite by chance, Dr Silbermann also spent his summer holiday on the shore of the Wörthersee. I dined with him at the lake side and casually mentioned Rolf's predicament. Dr Silbermann was a Czech and understood at once. 'Tell him to come to Grosvenor Place,' he said. 'We'll examine him at the consulate!'

Neither of us batted an eyelid, and the delicate matter was not mentioned again. To help a man evade military service was a very serious offence that might land one in jail. Great caution was called for—in fact I have forgotten Dr Silbermann's real name, for I was too careful to put it in my notebook.

Dr Silbermann forgot to pay his hotel bill when he left the Wörthersee, and I settled it for him—with Uncle Wilhelm's schillings. This pattern, once established to our mutual satisfaction, saw Rolf safely through his subsequent medicals and saved Ingo too becoming a soldier. As it turned out, the Czechoslovaks were never called upon to fight and did not miss the Pasold brothers.

My many uncles, cousins and friends who so often saw me at weekends with Sonja or some other pretty girl at a fashionable *thé dansant* at Karlsbad, Marienbad or Franzensbad envied me or frowned, according to their age and circumstances, not realising that I was not there just to enjoy myself. We sipped coffee and ate cake at small tables in the open air. I seem to remember blue skies all the time: did it never rain on these occasions? The small cosmopolitan crowd consisted of industrialists, bankers, politicians, playboys and international adventurers with their ladies. Among the more exalted visitors to the Bohemian spas was the ex-Khedive of Egypt, a lavish spender, whose secretary used to cash his master's cheques and sometimes changed wads of sterling notes at a local bank. I did not dare buy the cheques, but at a premium of 2 per cent which went into the secretary's pocket acquired several small packets of crisp £50 and even £100 notes. Made of white paper, they did not look like money to Continental customs officials, and taking them out of the country was child's play. I wished the Egyptian ex-viceroy had been staying at Karlsbad permanently.

My old friend Direktor Huder, the manager of the Bohemian Union Bank at Asch, regretted that his secret source of foreign currency had dried up but volunteered to introduce me to someone whose business it was to take substantial sums in Czechoslovak banknotes across the border. They were much bulkier than sterling and the charge was 5 per cent. Illegal, of course, but a regular two-way traffic, Huder assured me.

Using an intermediary to smuggle banknotes across the Czechoslovak border and through Hitler's Germany to Britain struck me as too dangerous. I thought of a better way. We regularly shipped yarn from Leibitschgrund to Langley: why not hide the notes in some of the cases? There were usually fifty cases in a consignment, and each case held some 2,000 cops of yarn. If I unwound a cop, wrapped ten 1,000 kronen notes round the paper tube in the middle, and then wound the yarn on again, the cop would look as innocent as its hundred thousand companions. Mother had a foot-pedal sewing machine with a small attachment on which to wind spools of sewing cotton. After a few practice runs I managed to wind five perfect-looking cops, each with 10,000 kronen hidden in it, worth altogether about £500. Quite a substantial amount of money in the 1930s, when one could buy a semi-detached house for less.

The night before the next consignment was due to leave Fleissen I let myself into the deserted warehouse. By the light of a torch I carefully opened one of the cases, replaced five ordinary cops with my five loaded ones and closed the case again. Next morning I typed a letter to Rolf, quoting in code the number of the case and telling him that some of the water tubes in the boiler were pitted and needed attention, namely the first five from the left, seventh row down, three from the back. It was the key to the cops with the money in them. Talking of boiler tubes would give nothing away if the letter were to fall into unauthorised hands. Two or three weeks later, when the consignment arrived at Langley, Rolf identified the correct case, counted out the correct cops during the night, and in the morning took the notes to the National Provincial bank to have them changed into sterling.

We repeated the exercise over a number of years, always apprehensive that one day something might go wrong, but nothing ever did. Nobody except Rolf and myself knew our secret or even guessed it. Mother asked several times what I was doing with her sewing machine and why I locked the door, but she was content when I said I was experimenting and did not want to be disturbed. Once Rolf had a scare when a consignment of yarn arrived at Langley while he was away in London. Telephoning the factory, he was told that Köhler, not suspecting the precious contents, had begun to open the cases and was weighing the cops out to the winders. Rolf came rushing back, dreading to see 1,000 kronen notes fluttering all over the winding department. It would be disastrous if the story got into the press. But to his great relief all was well; the case containing the money had not been touched.

Another time we had a good laugh when we read in the *Börsencourier*, the Czechoslovak equivalent of the *Financial Times*, that kronen notes which had been rolled and obviously smuggled out of the country—in hollow sticks, the paper suggested—were finding their way back from abroad to the National Bank at Prague. They were our notes, no doubt. I do not know whether frontier guards received instructions henceforth to scrutinise travellers' walking sticks.

Smuggling banknotes from Czechoslovakia to Britain was only a part, and by no means the most difficult, of the tricky operation. We had to have the notes first. Converting hidden reserves into liquid cash and then drawing it without our accountant, our auditors or the tax inspector becoming suspicious was the more formidable task. It could only be carried out gradually and with the help of those anonymous bank deposit books. And our anxiety was not over when the notes reached Langley. There was always the risk that they could no longer be exchanged for sterling. It all depended on Prague's willingness to buy back kronen from British banks. The scope of these clandestine transactions was therefore limited. They could not provide all the capital required for the expansion of Langley, and I was for ever searching for other opportunities of transferring funds.

Although I have always thought of myself as very law-abiding, my conscience was not in the least troubled by this flagrant violation of Czechoslovak currency legislation. In my view the restrictions had nothing in common with law and justice. They were devised by the same Czech politicians who had systematically broken every law of the Austro-Hungarian Monarchy whose citizens they were and whose destruction they had brought about. That arch-plotter Dr Beneš and his friends had forced me to become a citizen of their ill conceived republic, but they could not hold me against my will indefinitely. Forbidding the transfer of capital only strengthened my determination to escape to England. It was up to me to get over or round the barrier as best I could without letting myself be caught. The penalty would be severe, but whatever the risk I was not prepared to abandon my ambition

of making Langley the headquarters of our activities. At times I was frightened, but I never suffered from pangs of conscience.

How well I remember the alarm I felt when the Ministry of Trade summoned me to Prague for questioning 'in connection with the operation of the
British factory'. I thought the game was up. Imagine my relief when it transpired that Dr Horàk, the little man who peered at me enquiringly through
horn-rimmed spectacles, was not concerned with finance. He wished to investigate the truth of an allegation made by one of our competitors, that I had
introduced knitting machines to the British and divulged to them the technique of manufacturing fleecy knickers, causing Czechoslovakia to lose her
once important export trade in this type of merchandise. It was easy to refute
this ridiculous accusation.

It was William Lee, I explained, an English clergyman, who invented
machine knitting. He demonstrated his first knitting machine to Queen
Elizabeth I as long ago as 1589. England had a highly developed textile
machine industry that exported all over the world, in fact Czechoslovakia's
best knitting machines came from England. I mentioned such famous names
as Stibbe, Mellor Bromley and Bentley. The idea that we could show the
British how to knit was ludicrous, and in any case, fleecy knickers were out of
fashion now.

At first Dr Horàk showed signs of irritation at my seemingly flippant
treatment of this serious matter, then he relaxed and finally his sense of
humour won. He laughed, apologised for the inconvenience he had caused
me, and dismissed the case.

29

FIRST FACTORY
EXTENSION AT LANGLEY
1932-35

THE FALLING DEMAND for fleecy knickers forced the underwear manufacturers of Bohemia to search for other uses for their knitting machines. From
the early 1930s onwards an increasing number of Terrot-type circulars at Asch,
Fleissen and Teplitz were fitted with press-pattern wheels and changed over
to making Köper fabric which was knitted from 16s cotton yarn and made
into sports shirts. In addition to supplying the home market Fleissen exported substantial quantities of them to Scandinavia. When, in August 1932,
Edward, Prince of Wales, the hope and pride of the Empire and the world's
most popular young man, was photographed on the Riviera wearing a knitted
sports shirt they immediately became the rage all over the Continent. I sold
2,000 dozen in a single day on a business trip to Amsterdam.

We set aside a conveyor belt for the production of sports shirts at Adolf
Pasold & Sohn, broke down the job of sewing a shirt into separate operations,
timed them with a stop-watch and allocated them to a team of thirty-two
machinists. It was important that each girl should have the same work load,
otherwise the flow of production would develop bottlenecks. Sewing conveyor belts were new, and our experience with them was limited. We were
therefore glad of Mother's offer to help puzzle out the best arrangement, and
with her methodical turn of mind she became in due course our authority on
putting together teams to sew all kinds of garments in the most efficient
manner.

At Langley, too, we would have to find other things to make than knickers
if we wanted the business to grow, and quite naturally we thought of sports
shirts. Knitting the Köper fabric presented no problem, but cutting and
sewing shirts was beyond the skill of our girls. They were only half trained
and needed more practice. Meanwhile we would prepare the market by
supplying sports shirts from Fleissen, we thought—below cost, if need be, to
overcome the effects of the sterling devaluation and the import duties. With
high hopes I set off for London, only to have my enthusiasm quashed once
again. The smug insularity of the buyers in the City could make one weep. I

was wasting their time, they said. Continentals might disport themselves in such garish shirts, but no self-respecting Briton would wear one.

It took another year before I saw knitted sports shirts in shop windows in the West End, and Mr Draper, the buyer of Cook Son & Co., took a gamble, as he called it, and gave me a small order. The price of 15s 6d per dozen included 20 per cent import duty, 3¾ per cent cash discount and free delivery to the warehouse in St Paul's Churchyard. Contrary to his prediction, the British public took to the new fashion, and we picked up many more orders. By July bright yellow knitted sports shirts dominated the weekend scene on the Thames and in the London parks. When, in September, I booked a contract from the Fore Street Warehouse Co. for 800 dozen, with a promise of substantial repeats, I felt the time had come to manufacture shirts at Langley. And it was not a day too soon. All of a sudden sixty British manufacturers started making knitted shirts, some from tuck-stitch stockinette like ours, some from cotton interlock, and some from warp loom fabric. They offered shirts in plain colours and with fancy patterns; the variety was overwhelming, and buyers became confused. The fact that the shirts supplied from Fleissen had sold well now gave us an advantage.

I set up a team of eight of our most experienced machinists, supervised the cutting and sewing of the first few dozen shirts personally, and was pleased with the result. The finished garments looked better than I expected. It seemed I had underestimated the proficiency of our girls. Confidently I made the round of the London wholesalers, using the Langley-made shirts as samples, came back with several orders, and spent the next few days taking care of the production of a further twenty dozen. All went well, except for the buttonholes and for sewing on the buttons, which had to be done by hand and was too cumbersome. Somewhat grudgingly I bought a Singer buttonhole machine and a Reece button sewer for the large sum of £161—enough to pay for a brand new motor car—and we started bulk production. Then the trouble began.

As long as I helped with the cutting and watched the sewing machinists, checking the sleeves here, the pockets there, measuring the neck openings, comparing whether both collar points were the same length, and generally kept an eye on everything the shirts were all right, but whenever I was called away to the office, or to some other part of the factory, something went wrong. We were making more seconds than firsts; it seemed useless to carry on without a competent forewoman. I told Mr Hurst to leave off selling and help me look for one. We advertised, wrote to the labour exchanges, consulted the dressing gown manufacturers who bought our ripple cloth and asked the makers of our sewing machines, but in spite of all the unemployment in the country we had only five applicants for the job. Two asked far higher salaries than we could afford to pay, the other three we tried and found use-less. Government officials knew all about refusing permits for foreigners, I reflected sadly; they fell down when it came to helping us find a British worker.

It was November. We had sold 1,500 dozen shirts for delivery in spring 1934, and orders were still coming in. I could not see how we were to manu-facture such a quantity, and wrote to Fleissen:

Our team of eight girls produces ten dozen shirts a day, which is only half the output we ought to achieve, and many of them are seconds. It would be senseless to go on unless we find a better forewoman. I have neither time nor patience to be a sewing room supervisor. Shall go to London tomorrow and try to get out of as many shirt orders as I can. We are quite busy making knickers at present; perhaps I can sell some more of them.

I must have been very weary to write such a defeatist letter. The next morn-ing I felt better, and changed my mind. Business was not easy to get, and a way had to be found to execute the orders we had on our books. Mother and Rolf, I knew, would feel the same, and Rolf's reply, which came by return of mail, left no doubt about it:

You are too impatient. How can you expect accuracy and speed from your girls after so short a time? It took our experienced machinists at Fleissen two months to reach maximum output, and your girls are still beginners! Mother became so agitated when she read your letter that she wanted to leave for England the same evening to help you get your shirt production going. There is very big business to be done in knitted sports shirts during the next few years, and Langley cannot afford to miss it. You need a change. I suggest Mother and I go to England immediately after Christmas and you take over at Fleissen again.

As always, the Christmas tree in the house at Fleissen was the focal point of the family gathering. Willie and Silvia came from Leibitschgrund, battling through the snowdrifts, Ingo was home from Kutna Hora, where he was work-ing in one of our customers' warehouses and, we hoped, would learn to speak Czech, I had arrived from Langley, and Mother had baked *Stollen* for us all. She would not let us talk business on Christmas Eve, but two days later we were deep in figures and blueprints, and the sports shirt business was dis-cussed thoroughly before she and Rolf left for England. Rolf's first letter from Langley read:

Sports shirt production is improving. Have engaged a young forewoman, and Mother is showing her our manufacturing technique. Are getting fewer seconds, and the daily output has risen to thirteen dozen. Think our team of eight girls will reach twenty-five dozen before very long.

With Mother at Langley I had fully expected the sports shirt production to take a turn for the better, and to hear that Rolf had found a forewoman was good news indeed. He said she was young. That meant she had not much experience. It might be all to the good if she grew with the firm. But I doubted a daily output of twenty-five dozen, and Rolf's next letter read a little less optimistically:

There is nothing wrong with our sports shirts now—even Mr Hurst has complimented us. He has continued selling, and sent us an order for another 200 dozen yesterday. Are now sold out until May. But we cannot get enough girls. Those sent by the labour exchange don't want to work. They only make a show of taking the job, and leave again after a day or two to go back on the dole. This wastes our time and costs us money. I wish I knew what to do.

There were hundreds of jobless on the Slough register, but so many of them preferred to draw unemployment pay rather than work. We had realised by now that the labour exchange was of little use to us. To find the right type of worker we had to do our own recruiting, and that took time. Mother worried about our health. Father had driven himself too hard, and now Rolf and I were doing the same. The strain of finding sufficient orders to keep the factory going was bad enough: could we take the stress of these labour problems as well?

Mother is sometimes near despair. She likes our Langley girls, they work well, but they seem to have no sense of responsibility, even towards their own team mates. By being late or taking days off for trivial reasons and without warning they upset production and ruin the earnings of the other girls. The shirt team cannot work if it is incomplete. To find a temporary replacement for a missing machinist we have to disrupt one of the knicker teams, and ten girls lose half an hour each before everything flows again. If it weren't for these interruptions we would have reached a daily output of twenty-five dozen sports shirts by now.

Mother, who was usually so self-confident, felt dispirited by the attitude of the Langley girls, which she could not understand. At Fleissen workpeople treasured their jobs and were not prepared to risk losing them because of irregular attendance. Was absenteeism a feature of British industry? We did not know, but to prevent it wrecking the efficiency of our teams Rolf trained a few versatile girls in a variety of sewing operations, employed them on individual jobs, and used them to fill gaps in the teams where they occurred. And to do my bit to reassure Mother I told her:

Don't let these little adversities get you down. We are going through a difficult period but things will soon get better. Ingo has just reached his eighteenth birthday; in another year or two he will be old enough to take his full share of running the business. There will then be four of us, which will give us time to relax a little. With Willie, Rolf, Ingo and me at the helm of our three factories we shall be unbeatable.

The news I received from Langley now sounded much more encouraging. After overcoming the initial difficulties Mother's sports shirt team was doing well. The previous week it had averaged sixteen dozen, since when the output had climbed to twenty dozen daily. The target of twenty-five dozen set by Rolf might yet be reached. We were knitting 1,000 lb of fabric and sewing 250 dozen children's knickers a day. The ripple machines were busy, customers seemed satisfied with our goods, and Mr Hurst was optimistic about booking further orders.

Rolf did reach his target. Our girls became quick at the job—sewing more than 2,000 dozen sports shirts for the London wholesale houses gave them the practice they needed. At the end of May, when London wanted no more of our shirts, he sold 500 dozen to Glasgow and Belfast, but then the demand came to an end. Just when we had reached maximum output we were beaten by the Japanese. Buyers asked us for 'something new'. After experimenting, not very successfully, with cotton jumpers for a few months we hit on the idea of using our shirt pattern to make ladies' blouses. Shortening the body, elasticating the waist, and using fabric we knitted from artificial silk instead of cotton, we had a garment which looked and felt so different from the too popular locknit blouses that it caught on immediately. Once again we had the advantage of using Peggy as a model. Wholesale buyers were men, few of whom could resist her when she called, wearing a blouse carefully selected to match her skirt and jacket and carrying samples of the other colours in her little bag. Our blouses looked high-class when she modelled them, not at all like 15s 6d a dozen. And invariably she returned, eyes sparkling, waving an order. Our sales came to some 6,000 dozen, more than double the quantity of sports shirts we had sold.

The blouses led to the manufacture of simple dresses, for which we could use the same tuck-stitch artificial silk material. They sold at 48s a dozen, which showed a profit, but I was not happy about our drifting into the dress trade, because it took us further and further away from the purpose for which we had built our factory, the mass production, if possible by automation, of a very few basic garments not subject to frequent changes in fashion. Yet here I was, on the way to becoming a fashion designer, filling my scrap book with sketches of ladies' frocks. It was ridiculous! To make only knickers would have suited us much better, but the demand for them was not large enough to keep the factory employed, and the ripple cloth business provided work only for the knitting plant, not for the sewing machinists.

In January 1934 the factory employed eleven winders, eighteen knitters, two fleecers, two cutters, twenty-four sewing machinists, three folders, two packers, two labourers, one works manager, one forewoman and two office staff, a total of sixty-eight people. This was twenty-six more than the year before. A trifling figure compared with those of Fleissen and Leibitschgrund, but it was not easy to recruit and train even such a small labour force, and we were proud of it. Our knitting plant, the twenty Terrot-type circulars we had brought from Fleissen, now made fabric for three distinct purposes: fleecy and summer-weight knickers, sports shirts and ripple cloth. In spite of three-shift working, which Rolf had introduced, it was hardly large enough to produce all the fabric needed. We had to buy additional knitting machines.

After much correspondence and comparing of figures we decided to try one of the new 'high speed' Terrot-type circulars developed by Fouquet & Frauz AG of Rottenburg in Germany. The price of RM 4,000 seemed outrageous. It was three times that of a normal second-hand machine. But in spite of the high cost, when we had satisfied ourselves that the output of the new type was 25 per cent greater we purchased another five, all in 44 in. diameter and 24 gauge to match our existing plant. They arrived in July. We chanced settling the invoice for the first machine with an official transfer of 20,000 kronen from Fleissen but lacked the courage to repeat this dangerous transaction on a large enough scale to pay for the other five. We therefore sent a sterling cheque, covering two thirds of the invoice value, and I handed the balance over to the makers in the form of smuggled Czechoslovak banknotes in order not to strain Langley's meagre financial resources too much.

We had bought ten sewing machines, three ripple machines, two winding frames, a fancy twist machine, several folding and packing tables, steel shelves and other equipment since we started at Langley. With the six high-speed circulars in position the factory was full to bursting point. I had failed to convince Rolf of the need to build an extension, and there was now insufficient room to stack the yarn cases, the rolls of fabric, and all the finished goods awaiting packing and dispatch. Yet he remained adamant. If more storage space were needed I could construct a lean-to shed behind the factory out of the large wooden crates in which the six Fouquet machines had come from Germany. When I explained that such a shed would raise the fire insurance premium for our whole property he dropped the idea but still refused to consider a factory extension, and even Mother reminded me that at Fleissen, back in the days when we lived in the old factory, the entrance hall and staircase were often stacked to the ceiling with cases. And so our modern entrance hall at Langley, with its long vertical window and chromium-plated handrails of which I was so proud, began to be filled with cardboard containers and paper parcels and took on the look of a warehouse in the East End.

Rolf's objection to enlarging the factory was not just cussedness. He thought that with all the capital already invested, and the business still showing losses, we could not afford it. In his view I was inclined to spend money too freely, and if I tried to reason with him he walked away, afraid that I might talk him over. To operate a factory efficiently one needed space; I was impatient to expand but, unwilling to overrule him, thought it best to wait until he came round of his own accord.

Trade was good in the autumn of 1934, and the demand for ripple cloth exceeded our capacity. Although the new machines raised our weekly knitting production to 8,000 lb, it was not enough, and we had to refuse orders, otherwise we would not have had sufficient fabric to keep our own sewing teams busy. The number of our employees crept up to eighty-five, and occasionally there was a week when Mr Colmer's financial statement showed that we had made a small profit. They were exciting days!

But business never runs smoothly for very long. Owing to a drought in Central Europe the river Elbe, down which Leibitschgrund shipped our condenser yarns to Hamburg *en route* for England, was so low that the boats could not sail. In winter we had had trouble with ice, but a drought was unexpected and took us by surprise. And to make matters worse Czechoslovakia was running out of foreign exchange reserves and tightened controls over the export of raw materials and semi-manufactured products such as yarns. A system of export licensing was introduced, and, while our prodding of the officials at Prague procured the necessary permits, the delay caused us considerable uneasiness. Langley's stocks of condenser yarn had shrunk to a mere three cases when an express train ferry consignment of sixty cases arrived and saved the situation, otherwise we would have had to shut the factory.

But where were we to put sixty cases? They had to be stacked four high, a very difficult job without any handling gear. There were no fork lift trucks in those days. One could hardly move any more in the factory. If the Czechoslovak government were to restrict the export of condenser yarn, or forbid it altogether, Langley would be in a very difficult situation. To forestall any such eventuality I sent a number of large backdated contracts to Leibitschgrund, for what they might be worth, and Willie sent us backdated confirmations. But, of course, the best safeguard would be to carry a large enough stock at Langley to give us time to make other arrangements if things came to the worst. For that we needed space, and this time it was Rolf who set the ball rolling. He wrote to me from Fleissen:

I think we should add three sections to the factory and suggest that you ask Wallis Gilbert & Partners for quotations. Maybe they should quote for four sections as well. No doubt the price per square foot will be lower if we build a larger area, and before long we shall need the space anyway. Try to bring the figures with you at Christmas so that we can discuss them over the holidays.

Rolf's expansionist mood had to be exploited to the full before some slight business recession made him change his mind. I wanted to build five sections!

And if we cleared the stock of merchandise from the first floor of the existing building there would be room for a small flat. We could then vacate our present bedroom and turn it into a private office, which was badly needed. Mother thoroughly disapproved of our primitive sleeping accommodation and the spartan life we led. The improvements I was planning would have her wholehearted support.

Wallis Gilbert & Partners tell me that the building industry is booming. Costs are rising, English bricks are fetching £5 per thousand, and the government are about to spend several million pounds on a gigantic slum clearance scheme. The sooner we start on our factory extension the better.

Chessum's, the contractors who had built our original factory, quoted £1,682 for three sections of north-light construction plus £500 for each additional section, £232 for the flat, and £20 for the garage. We decided over the holidays to give them a contract for five sections, covering a floor area of 9,000 square feet, the flat and the garage, but I was to try and get the price reduced. Protracted negotiations resulted in a concession of £200, we split the remaining difference of £16, Mr Chessum promised completion by the end of March and we closed the deal. I felt like a dog with two tails. At long last the good people of Fleissen would realise that our British venture was not a failure when they heard that the factory was being enlarged. And, more important, I sent a write-up to the Slough papers and to the *Draper's Record* so that our customers would also know, and would believe my promises of better deliveries to come.

We had not been able to supply all the ripple cloth they had wanted for the Christmas trade, in spite of the extra fabric production from the six new high-speed knitting machines and 120 pieces of fleecy material Fleissen had rushed to Langley in November to help us out. There would have been no need to disappoint our clients had we stuck to the manufacture of cotton cloth, which we now thoroughly understood. We knew how to spin the most suitable yarn for the purpose, what to look for when we selected our raw cotton, and where to buy it. But the price of cotton ripple cloth was low, the output of a ripple machine small, and we wanted to build up turnover. A yard of wool cloth, at twice the price and profit, took no longer to knit and ripple than cotton. The market was wide open, Mr Hurst urged. It sounded so tempting. And so we began to dabble in wool, about which we knew almost nothing.

We realised, of course, that the wool trade was quite as intricate, and required as much expertise, as the cotton trade, and that Leibitschgrund was not equipped to handle virgin wool. But we were confident that we could break up wool hosiery waste clips on our machines and then spin the material as if it were cotton. To try it, Willie bought a parcel of new white wool hosiery waste from a dealer at Asch. Leibitschgrund had no difficulty garneting and spinning it on the condenser plant, the resulting yarn was sent to Langley, and the first few pieces of ripple cloth made from it came up so well that every buyer who saw them immediately reached for his order book. This misled us. We thought the wool ripple business was easy, and diverted some of our capacity away from cotton.

Wool was, in fact, much easier to ripple than cotton. Several firms in the Nottingham area—Hadden & Co., for instance, and also Hyde's in Manchester—made excellent wool ripple cloth, but we were cheaper, and Mr Hurst booked orders for hundreds of pieces of our cloth in no time at all. We felt very pleased with ourselves—until Willie tried to buy wool hosiery clips to cover these orders, and found, to his consternation, that there were only negligible quantities to be had. None of the many waste merchants in Czechoslovakia and Germany had much to offer, and the sum total of his purchases covered barely half our immediate requirements. Meanwhile wool prices, which had been firm for some time, continued to rise, making the supply position even tighter, because spinners bought wool waste for blending with virgin wool to keep the cost of the yarn down. To get a better feel of the market Willie and I attended the annual wool waste auction at Gera, in Thuringia, hoping to pick up some suitable lots there, but we were disappointed, as my report to Rolf shows:

Together with two hundred other potential buyers we inspected the 1,500 lots of waste on offer and handed in our bids, but prices went much too high. The qualities we wanted fetched RM 4.00 and more, just about twice as much as we were willing to pay. The cheapest lots sold for RM 1.40 per kilo—muck I would not touch without gloves and which, I thought, could only be used as manure. We left after two hours, having bought nothing.

We were more fortunate with British waste merchants, whom we tried next. Hyman, Fletcher and Austin said they could supply what we wanted. I asked Willie to come to London, and together we looked at the stocks in their warehouses. Wool hosiery waste could be anything from dirty rags and old socks to the small pieces of soft white material left over when garments are cut from good-quality knitted fabric. Clippings from the factories of Chilprufe, Smedley or other makers of top-grade underclothes were more desirable raw material than many of the coarser types of virgin wool. In two days we had found and bought the 25,000 lb we were short of, and arranged to have them shipped to Czechoslovakia. Meanwhile Leibitschgrund had found some additional small supplies locally, had spun them, and the yarn was on the way to Langley. With luck, all would be well.

The dressing gown makers in Golden Lane seemed to be happy with our wool ripple cloth, which, in view of the rising market, we had sold to them much too cheaply. They gave us repeat orders without querying the increase of 2d a yard we demanded, for our cloth was still very much better value than that of our competitors. Owing to our inexperience with wool our pieces were not as uniform as theirs, but our customers were so eager to get our cloth that they readily overlooked minor flaws for fear that criticism might hold up deliveries.

Cooper's of Newark on Trent were one of the largest manufacturers of wool ripple dressing gowns, and it was our ambition to do business with them. We loaded our little SS with sample lengths of ripple cloth, to show quality and colours, and drove up the Great North Road to call on them. The head of the concern, old Mr Robinson, was an autocrat. 'Tell your father to come himself,' he snorted. 'I'm not used to wasting my time with juniors.' When I replied that Rolf and I owned the firm, and that Pitt had been Prime Minister at the age of twenty-four, he muttered disapproval but kept our samples and said we would hear from him.

After making enquiries about us in the trade, and sending a small trial order which we executed to his satisfaction, Mr Robinson asked us to call again. We were foreigners, were we not! He proceeded to deliver a lecture on the British way of conducting business, showed us a swatch of the very special colours in which he wanted his cloth to be dyed, and concluded by giving us a contract for 800 pieces, which he said he would call off over a period of six months. The size of the order made us gasp. We were not altogether happy to have a commitment of £4,000 with such a difficult customer. But perhaps we misjudged him; perhaps his bark was worse than his bite. All seemed to be going well, at least for a while. Consignments of wool condenser yarn arrived from Leibitschgrund at regular intervals, there seemed to be no knitting, dyeing or rippling problems, our deliveries to Cooper's were on time, and similarly their cheques arrived punctually at Langley. We relaxed.

The blame for the trouble that came later was not easy to apportion. Differences in the yarn spun from varying lots of wool waste, too slight sometimes to be seen by the naked eye, could appear as pronounced stripes in the finished cloth. It happened if Leibitschgrund packed yarn from two lots in the same case, or if Langley used yarn from two consignments to knit one piece of fabric, and was our fault. At other times the shade of the wool face of the cloth failed to match that of the cotton back. This, we claimed, was the fault of the dyers. But Sergeant's blamed Cooper's for specifying colours for which no suitable dyestuffs existed, and the recipes for dyeing both cotton and wool in the same bath were so complex that good matching became a matter of luck. Now and again they had to re-dye a load two or three times before the shades matched, which felted the wool and made the fabric feel harsh, but we were in a weak position to argue. If we did they stopped dyeing. We were careful not to send doubtful pieces to Newark, and those that slipped through were rejected by Cooper's and returned. No one worried about that. Mr Hurst sold them to some small maker-up in Golden Lane.

And so we carried on as best we could. No doubt Cooper's had problems of their own, matching satin, trimmings, cord and girdles to our cloth, but one day old Mr Robinson blew his top. He returned a whole railway truck containing 107 pieces to Langley because he was not satisfied with the colours, and as an afterthought rejected another sixty-seven pieces for which he had already paid. We felt that there was nothing wrong with our cloth, refused to take it back, and held up further supplies, whereupon Cooper's solicitors threatened to sue us for damages. At Mr Hurst's suggestion, and after a telephone call to Fleissen, Rolf entrusted Mr Addison, senior partner of a famous City firm of solicitors, with our interests, and the stage was set for a lawsuit.

Telephoning between Langley and Fleissen was a luxury we did not normally indulge in, but on this occasion we had a three-minute consultation. Apart from the expense, a call from as far away as England was a rare event at Fleissen's telephone exchange and might get talked about. It was safer to write letters. Mail did not take as long in Europe in the 1930s as it does nowadays. Airmail letters covered the distance between Fleissen and Langley in thirty-six hours, and sometimes in twenty-four, although aeroplanes travelled at only a quarter of their present speed.

I did not want to go to law. There are two sides to every argument, and no doubt we were not completely blameless. Since I was due in England anyway, I called at the lawyers to suggest a compromise. But Mr Addison, a tall, distinguished-looking Englishman in his sixties, would not hear of it. He seemed to be enjoying the case. Our opponents had slipped up on a subtle legal point, he explained, and hadn't a leg to stand on. Far from getting damages, they would lose the money already paid for the goods they had rejected.

'We have no right to it,' I protested. 'It's their money and we must return it!'

Mr Addison smiled. 'Are you handling the case or am I? This is a matter of law, not of common sense, and you know nothing about English law.' Bewildered, I let him proceed.

As I expected, Cooper's sued us. To my relief Mr Addison changed his mind, and we returned the £219 they had sent us prematurely, but we did not have to pay damages. Mr Robinson was as anxious as we were to cancel the outstanding balance of the contract, and Mr Hurst sold the 174 pieces of

3 At the Langley factory the condenser yarn which came from Leibitschgrund was wound from cops to wooden bobbins, ready for knitting

59 On these Terrot-type circular machines the yarn was knitted into fabric, which we had dyed by Sergeant Bros. at Acton

60 When the fabric came back from the dyers we fleeced and brushed it on this Gessner fleecing machine, an operation that needed considerable experience

1 The fabric was then laid about twenty layers high, cut with electric knives, and the garments were sewn on conveyor belts

62 Looking back, it seems incredible that Mr Colmer, our chief clerk, kept the books, recorded movements of stocks of raw material and finished goods, did the costings and prepared the weekly profit or loss statements all in ink and in longhand. He hardly ever made a mistake. He also calculated and paid the wages. Standing next to him is Mr Hodgkinson, the auditor

63 Langley's first ripple machine

64 Peggy Hurst shows Ladybird dressing gowns

65 Rolf with the SS Swallow, forerunner of the Jaguar

Fore Street
Cripplegate

5 Selling our goods. It has proved impossible to find a good photograph of the textile area of the
City in the 1920s or '30s. This drawing, kindly provided by the Guildhall Library, dates back to the
beginning of the century, but the appearance of the narrow streets and thoroughfares changed little.
Businessmen now wore bowlers instead of top hats, but horse-drawn traffic still predominated. Mr
Hurst's office was at 10 Fore Street, the gabled building below the tower of St Giles' Church

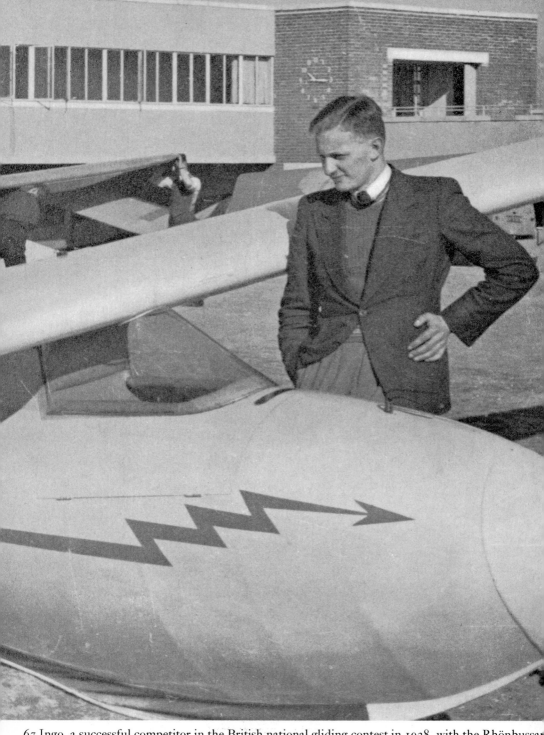

67 Ingo, a successful competitor in the British national gliding contest in 1938, with the Rhönbussard at the London Gliding Club

Heracles airliner of Imperial Airways, the largest and safest thing on wings in the early 1930s. It
...d three engines, cruised at 135 m.p.h. and, if I remember correctly, carried some twenty passengers

Avro Cadet G-ACHN, in which the author and his brothers learned to fly at Heston
...d did their first 'solos'

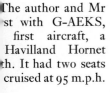

The author and Mr
...st with G-AEKS,
first aircraft, a
...Havilland Hornet
...th. It had two seats
...cruised at 95 m.p.h.

71 Drilling the 1,150 ft de
borehole on our factory site
provide water for the dyeho
at Langley

72 The stainless steel dye v
supplied by Pegg & Son
Leicester. Doing our own dye
proved a profitable venture

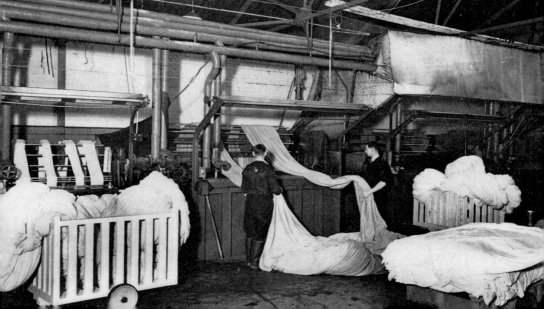

wool ripple cloth over which we had quarrelled to Underhill at a slightly higher price than Cooper's. All was well that ended well. After this lesson we felt like turning our back on the wool business, but there were more than a hundred cases of wool yarn at Langley, in transit on the river Elbe and at Leibitschgrund. In addition Willie had built up a substantial stock of wool hosiery clips, and our customers in Golden Lane had come to rely on us for their supplies of wool ripple cloth. So we carried on.

Years later I met Mr Addison socially and became quite fond of him. We were almost neighbours. He lived in a large house at Iver village, and usually caught the 9 a.m. train from Langley to Paddington, but I never discovered why he refused to let me compromise in the first place.

Chessum's had not built the factory extension and the little flat yet, and we still slept on the settee in the temporary bedroom adjoining the office. On the rare occasions when Rolf and I were at Langley together one of us slept on a mattress on the floor. This was not as disagreeable as it sounds. We liked living on the premises, to be available if the night shift needed us, and the faint hum of the knitting machines, more sensed than heard, was comforting. It told us that the wheels were turning. But at the weekends there was utter silence, broken only by the passing trains. One felt a little like a nightwatchman then, and not entirely without justification, as Rolf's letter shows:

We had burglars on Saturday night. They climbed in through a window at the far end of the factory, opened the store, came upstairs but failed to open the office door with their keys. So they took my overalls from the cloakroom and pushed in one of the glass panels to get at the door handle. This woke me up, and I turned on the light. They bolted down the stairs, I unlocked the office door and ran after them, but they got away. So I phoned the police at Slough. As luck would have it, Constable Tomlin was on duty at the railway station, saw an unattended car and went to investigate, when two men with cotton fluff on their clothes came running towards it. While he was questioning them the police car from Slough arrived, and the two men, who were wanted for a series of burglaries, were arrested and taken away. The police were here until 2 a.m. and it was quite exciting.

The burglary and the arrest of the culprits made Rolf's weekend. Giving evidence at Slough magistrates' court afterwards pleased him less, for the proceedings took five long hours when he should have been at work. However, there was some light relief. It transpired, amid laughter, that the prisoners had complained about the 'unfairness of someone sleeping in a factory, especially at the weekend'.

30

WOOLWORTH
AND MARKS & SPENCER
1932-35

IT HAD BEEN a frustrating morning. Of the three wholesale buyers with whom Mr Hurst had arranged appointments for me, not one found it convenient to look at my new samples of knickers. After hours of fruitless waiting, hours I could ill afford to waste, I was lugging my bag along Wood Street when I ran into Salo Rand.

'Come and have lunch with me,' he beamed. 'I've just booked an order from Woolworth's for £1,000 worth of Galbonz jewellery. Let's celebrate!'

Woolworth's were one of Salo's largest accounts. An American firm, they had opened their first store in Britain shortly before the 1914-18 war and now, little more than twenty years later, the large red nameplates with the golden lettering above the windows dominated the best shopping position in every town. They had no fewer than 530 stores in the United Kingdom. It was said that they were aiming at opening a thousand and that Mr Stephenson, the chairman, earned £40,000 a year. Such figures made one's head swim. Dealing in a huge variety of merchandise, from sweets and toys to pencils, bootlaces, artificial flowers, ironmongery, rubber and electrical goods, they owed their success to the policy of selling nothing for more than 6d. Millions of people with small incomes bought essentials at Woolworth's, others ambled through the stores out of sheer curiosity and spent their spare coppers on things they did not want. Sixpence was so little, even the child of poor parents had that much pocket money. Salo could not understand why we did not do business with such an enormous and wealthy concern. Was there nothing we could supply at 4d to go on their counters at 6d?

We had several times in the past tried to sell to Woolworth's, but without success. Overawed by their very size, I believed we were far too insignificant a firm to be considered by them as possible suppliers, and our approaches had been half-hearted. But if Salo could do business with them why not we?

Mr Hurst seemed reluctant when, back at the office, I raised the matter once again. His connections were with the wholesalers; he knew how to deal

with them, and how they reacted. We risked losing their goodwill, he warned,
if we were seen at the buying offices of retail organisations. 'The wholesalers
can't have it both ways,' I protested. 'The footling little orders for children's
knickers they give us won't keep us going. We must find outlets for the large
quantities of merchandise our factory is laid out for!'

A few days later Mr Hurst and I sat in the wood-panelled waiting room of
Woolworth's palatial head office building in New Bond Street, watching
callers being escorted by a uniformed commissionaire through a number of
different doors, until our turn came. The textile buyer was a Mr Cue, a well
spoken, friendly man, who waved us into comfortable armchairs. From the
way he fingered our samples it was obvious that he knew nothing about
Directoire knickers, and he was honest enough to admit it.

'What do you make of these, Miss Owen? Do you think we could sell
them?' he asked, tossing the garments to his secretary.

'At 4s a dozen they seem remarkably good value, Mr Cue. I'm sure they
would sell,' replied Miss Owen. I could have hugged her.

'I may have to ask you gentlemen to call again. Meanwhile I'll keep these,'
said Mr Cue, putting the samples in the drawer of his desk. The interview
had taken less than ten minutes, and we did not know what to make of it, but
the prospects seemed promising.

The following week Mr Cue appeared unexpectedly at Langley. Could
he look over the factory? Proudly I showed him round. He seemed satisfied
with what he saw and then equally proudly showed me his car, a steam-driven
American Franklin. There were only two in the country and he owned them
both! I liked Mr Cue very much and hoped we would be able to do business
together. But a month passed without my hearing another word from him,
and I had almost given up hoping when Miss Owen phoned and asked me to
call again.

'I can pay you 4s 3d a dozen for assorted sizes and colours. Normally we
list the merchandise we buy and our manufacturers get the slip orders from
the individual stores through our district offices, but since this is new to you
I've written out a starting order for 8,000 dozen. The slip orders will add up
to another 20,000 dozen during the season, I would guess.' He said it as
casually as if he were ordering a cup of tea. 'Make sure you deliver on time if
you want to do regular business with us.'

I could hardly believe my ears. Twenty-eight thousand dozen, and at 3d
more than I had asked! Mr Cue smiled. 'I hope you're pleased, and if you
justify the confidence I have in you there'll be plenty more orders coming!'

Pleased? He had made me the happiest man in the whole of London! My
dream was coming true. Now our factory would hum. We were on the road to
success. Punch-drunk, I wandered down New Bond Street with Mr Hurst,

hardly aware of where we were going. 'Let's have tea at the Ritz,' I said. 'I've never ventured inside, but today we can afford it!'

Mr Cue's estimate proved fairly accurate. By the end of the season we had delivered just over 26,000 dozen summer-weight knickers and, at his request, were making arrangements for the production of a similar quantity of fleecies. A pleasant surprise, for most of our customers were replacing fleecy knickers, even girls' sizes, with interlock. It seemed that mothers who still wanted fleecies for their children all had to come to Woolworth's.

Before leaving for Fleissen to spend Christmas with the family I called on Mr Cue, thanked him for the business he had given us during the past year and wished him the compliments of the season. He said he was pleased with the quality of our goods and the service we were giving the stores, talked of even larger contracts for 1934, and asked whether we would make children's bathing suits for him. He needed tens of thousands of dozens. Was he Father Christmas in person? What a message to take to Fleissen! I knew that it would not be easy to make bathing suits at 4s 3d a dozen, but the spirit of mutual goodwill and co-operation seemed such that I felt confident of finding a way to manufacture them at that price. A wave of optimism swept over me. Woolworth's were opening a further seventy stores. Soon we would have to double production, install more machines, enlarge the factory and, with luck, become their largest supplier of knitted garments!

Rolf took a more sober view which, to my great disappointment, proved right. We got the contract for knickers again, but after six months of delays and repeated requests for still more samples Mr Cue placed his order for bathing suits in Japan. It was quite a blow. We had, by then, made all the summer-weight knickers the stores needed and were well on the way towards completing the contract for the fleecies. Who else would give us orders? The wholesalers were not buying. George Peacock had all the goods he wanted. Far from having to enlarge the factory we were once again worried about finding work for it. Fortunately the matter did not end there. Mr Cue had trouble with the importers of the Japanese merchandise and came to us to help him out. Needless to say, we were only too pleased to make 5,000 dozen bathing suits for him in record time, for which he rewarded us with a contract for 25,000 dozen for the following spring. So all was well.

But was it? Long after we had dispatched all this merchandise to the stores one of our sewing machinists came to see me with her five-year-old daughter. 'Mr Eric,' she said, 'we should have made our bathing suits to button up. I tried one on Lilian but had to cut a shoulder strap before I could get her into it.'

At first I did not believe her, but when she gave me a demonstration and I saw it that was impossible for the little girl to put the suit on without cutting one of the straps I blenched. In my mind I saw a trainload of bathing suits coming back to Langley, together with a debit note for an astronomical amount of damages. After a sleepless night and a consultation with Mr Hurst I went to see Mr Cue. He did not believe me until he had some of the suits tried on, then he too became alarmed. It was too late to recall the merchandise from the stores; most of it had already been sold. We kept our fingers crossed, and, incredible as it may seem, what we both feared did not happen. Not a single one of the 360,000 bathing suits was returned by the public, but we had learned a valuable lesson. Never again would we put a new garment on the market, even if it cost only a few pence, without testing it thoroughly first.

What else could we make for Woolworth's? We sampled boys' pants and girls' vests, drawers, children's bodices, cami-knickers, tunic frocks, swimming trunks, women's aprons, gloves, face cloths, pram covers, babies' bonnets, bootees, crawlers, leggings and bedsocks. They were examined, discussed, tried on and compared with competitors' merchandise. Shapes were improved, prices trimmed, colours changed, and finally the samples were submitted to the district offices for comment. Most of this work led to nothing, but once in a while a large order materialised which repaid all effort, and everyone was happy.

Our plant of 44 in. diameter 24-gauge Terrots was ideally suited to manufacture the Woolworth type of merchandise, but we could think of many more things to sell to Mr Cue than could be made on Terrots. Should we widen our range of products by installing American Challenger machines, German warp looms or a battery of British interlocks? Any departure from our policy of specialisation would have far-reaching consequences. It was important that any new machine, and the fabric it produced, fitted into our existing operation without causing too many complications. Warp looms were therefore obviously not right for us. While we were still pondering I saw a ladies' vest in the window of one of those exclusive shops on the Alte Wiese, next to the world famous Hotel Pupp, at Karlsbad. Knitted on a fine-gauge machine, ribbed at the waist, with wide fancy stitching above and below, it had the shape of a female figure. A neat way, I thought, of using the pattern change mechanism to create curves. Made of pure silk, it was so expensive that only a film star would buy it, but why didn't somebody use this idea to make such a vest in cotton? The sewing operation was simple, ribbon for shoulder straps cheap. If mass-produced the garment should cost very little. Little enough for Cue?

The idea took hold of me. I drove to Stuttgart to look at the rib machine made by Terrot, a beautiful piece of precision engineering but very dear, and sold out for several months ahead. I would have to consult my brother in

England, I said. Obligingly Terrot's knitted a few lengths of cotton fabric in the shape I wanted, which I posted off to Langley. Rolf made sample vests from the fabric and took them to Mr Cue, who kept them 'for a week or two to show to the boys'. We knew what that meant, but for a change were in no hurry. At 4s 6d a dozen, the price we quoted, the garment was such outstanding value that we were sure of getting his order. The next step now was to get a rib machine delivered. What make should we buy?

Stibbe, we had been taught at the textile college, were the leading British makers of rib machines, so Rolf and I went to Leicester to see them, but came to no decision. We also called on Mellor Bromley, where we were received by Mr Bromley personally and then shown over the works by Mr Simpson, the sales director—two educated, intelligent men who thoroughly understood their job. The visit proved an eye-opener for us. We had not expected such a large, modern and clearly very efficient engineering concern, which compared favourably with any we had seen in Germany. The machines they made inspired confidence and, although unable to show us the exact model we wanted, they offered to build one to our specifications for £245 and have it ready in ten weeks. If it was unsatisfactory they would take it back. We were impressed, slept on the proposition, and ordered two machines.

We had intentionally not pressed Mr Cue for an early decision, but not even he took ten weeks to make up his mind. A month before the Mellor Bromley machines arrived he sent for me. 'Those shaped vests,' he beamed. 'I have a starting order for you for 3,000 dozen. The stores want them right away, and we shall probably need another 7,000 dozen during the season.'

'The machines have not arrived yet,' I replied hesitantly. 'We could begin to deliver in six weeks at the earliest.'

Mr Cue shook his head. 'Too late. I can get immediate delivery of a similar vest from another manufacturer,' he said, visibly embarrassed. 'But as soon as you're ready I'll switch my orders to you.'

He had obviously shown our samples to another supplier, who had copied them. Galling as it was to have a competitor reap the benefit from our efforts, there was nothing for us to do but accept the situation with good grace. Mellor Bromley kept their promise. The machines arrived on the due date, but to our consternation produced nothing but faulty fabric. The mechanic went backwards and forwards between Leicester and Langley, exchanging parts and making adjustments, and we tried one grade of yarn after another, until he had straightened out his mechanical difficulties and we found that 30s spun by Dee Mill from Peruvian cotton gave the best results. All went well from then on. Just before our production got under way the shaped vests made by our competitor—it was Pool Lorrimer & Tabberer, of Leicester—appeared on the Woolworth counters. I noted with quiet satisfaction that they were much inferior to ours. I bought a few and took them to New Bond Street for Mr Cue to see. He readily agreed with my verdict and sent us so many orders that we had to buy two more rib machines from Mellor Bromley to keep up with them.

Mr Simpson surprised us. 'We thought two machines wouldn't be enough for you, so we gambled and built two more. You can have them right away. We shall then build a fifth and sixth in anticipation of your further requirements.' Mellor Bromley certainly were enterprising. We could think of no Continental machine builder who would take such a risk. Before very long we bought those two machines as well, and they had to work treble shifts.

Business was wonderful when everything went well, and of all the things we manufactured none pleased us more than those well shaped vests and the panties that went with them. Never before could women buy such excellent underwear at such low prices. And sales doubled when Woolworth's agreed to display our snow-white garments on glossy black cardboard in the shape of a woman's torso instead of leaving them lying on the counter. We supplied 10,000 dozen in the first season, which was an unusually large quantity for a new line, and made a net profit of $\frac{1}{2}d$ on every garment. The six rib machines paid for themselves in less than three years. They were intended for knitting cotton, but we also experimented with artificial silk. Bravisco, the spinners, were short of work and in order to reduce their large stock offered us a bargain. They marked a quantity of their artificial silk yarn as 'sub-standard' and sold it to us at half price. Our tests showed that there was nothing whatever wrong with it: the yarn knitted and dyed perfectly. We made 10,000 dozen women's panties from it, and Mr Cue bought them all. At 6d a pair they caused a minor sensation on the Woolworth counters, and we felt very pleased with ourselves. It was a profitable transaction, but to our great regret we could not repeat it when our supply of cheap yarn ran out. We lost Mr Cue's next and all following contracts for artificial silk underwear to two London firms who not only copied our panties but whose merchandise was more stylish than ours. Silknit Ltd of Park Royal made the fabric. Their American-built Challenger machines were just right for the job. I never discovered how they obtained their seemingly inexhaustible supplies of 'sub-standard' yarn. The fabric was then made into garments by the Mayfair Manufacturing Co., who had a large sewing factory in south London, where they made nothing but women's artificial silk underwear, much of it in fancy shapes and trimmed with lace. We had neither the right plant nor the design skill to compete successfully in this, for us, unfamiliar field of highly sophisticated merchandise. In our four years at Langley we had not even found a competent designer.

Mr Cue told us that he bought 100,000 dozen of the Mayfair garments annually. Nobody likes to forego business, but sorry though we were we had no reason to feel envious. His orders for other lines for which we were better equipped kept our machines turning, and our annual turnover with him also ran to six figures. In 1936, not long after we pioneered the shaped vests and panties, we got him interested in babies' matinee jackets with leggings and bonnets to match. Made of napped cotton stockinette fabric, sky blue for boys and pink for girls, we decorated them with shell stitching and an artificial silk ribbon tied in a bow. The leggings had feet and an elasticated waist. They looked sweet. Most of them were bought by grandmothers and aunts for Christmas and birthday presents. It seemed almost incredible that such well made, attractive garments could be sold to the public for as little as 6*d*, yet at that price both Woolworth's and we made a profit.

Woolworth's were our favourite customers in the mid-1930s. They gave us scope to develop merchandise for which our plant and our mass-production mentality were best suited. Looking back, it is as if our dealings with Mr Cue were all pleasure. He was a good friend who, season after season, gave us his orders, each larger than the one before, who never complained, and who always paid prices which showed us a profit. But memory can be deceptive. One is inclined to dwell on pleasant recollections and forget the suspense and worries of the past. Browsing through the records of those days, I am vividly reminded of the anxiety with which we awaited his decisions and the disappointment we felt when we lost an order. Sometimes we were desperate, while he procrastinated, yet it would not have done to admit even to Mr Cue, who was a gentleman and would not consciously have exploited our plight, how urgently we needed work for our knitters and sewing machinists. And when the order came at last we had to work day and night to get the merchandise ready in time.

Herbert Cue never could make up his mind. Sceptical when we showed him a new line, he became interested if Miss Owen, his secretary, liked it, and ended by being enthusiastic. The 'boys', as he called the district office managers, were sure to want thousands of dozens. In a few days he would tell us the exact quantity; meanwhile we were to get machinery and yarns ready to start immediate production. Elated, we left his office and waited for the order, but the weeks went by and nothing happened. When I reminded him he responded with verbal encouragement but gave us nothing in writing. The order would be written out before the end of the week, he assured me in his charming manner, and again nothing came. Production could no longer be delayed if the goods were to be in the stores at the start of the season. I tried to telephone him, but he was in conference, or out of town, or away ill. And then, at the height of our frustration, an order for 5,000 dozen would arrive with a message saying that Mr Cue expected the stores to call off three times as much and he relied on us not to let them down. This put the onus on us, and we had little choice but to manufacture large quantities of merchandise for which there was no definite commitment. Our annual sales to Woolworth's approached 100,000 dozen; what else were we to do if we did not want to risk losing this business to Hall & Earl, Swann, Pownall or some importer of Japanese goods? Mr Cue got bombarded from all sides with tempting propositions! So we did things his way, and although we sometimes worried we never got stuck with any Woolworth merchandise.

To be one of the leading garment suppliers to an organisation that had over six hundred stores and was continuing to expand was highly satisfactory, but we felt we were putting too many eggs in one basket. What if there were a sudden change of policy at Woolworth's, or Mr Cue transferred to some other department and we did not get on with his successor? We needed another large outlet. If only we could get the Marks & Spencer business. They had, on and off during the past ten years, bought some of our Fleissen-made merchandise through various intermediaries, but we had made no real effort to sell to them direct for fear of being blacklisted by the all-powerful Wholesale Textile Association—a danger which time had much reduced. The wholesalers were losing ground. It was partly their own fault. Instead of placing large contracts with the factories, taking the goods into their warehouses and then supplying the retail drapers from stock, which was a wholesaler's function, they tried to shift the risk and burden of stockholding to the manufacturer, placing small starting orders and then demanding bulk delivery from him if a line sold. If it didn't they left him holding the baby, as Mr Hurst put it. And so, inevitably, the manufacturer increased his price to cover himself. This made the many thousands of small drapers up and down the country, who depended on the wholesalers for their supplies, less competitive, and they lost trade to the expanding chain stores, department stores, buying groups and mail order firms, whose growing turnover enabled them to get more and more of their goods from the manufacturers direct, thus cutting out the wholesalers' intermediate profit. The writing was on the wall. Reluctantly even Mr Hurst agreed that our future was not with the wholesale trade.

There was no need to fear that Mr Cue would object if we supplied Marks & Spencer. The two chain stores hardly competed. Woolworth's business was built on price and an endless variety of unrelated merchandise, M. & S. concentrated more on textiles, they were very quality-conscious, and their top selling price of 5s was exactly ten times that of Woolworth's. Responding to our approach, Marks & Spencer said they were open to buy children's summer-weight knickers in sizes from 12 in. to 20 in. and gave us their samples to copy. Several months of negotiations with them led to nothing, and I wrote to Rolf:

Miss Hopkins tells me she has placed her order for the large sizes elsewhere. Am not sorry, for her price of 9s per dozen is below our production cost. Understand we are still under consideration for the small sizes.

Hearing nothing more for a month, I had given up hope, when an order arrived for 500 dozen children's knickers with pockets, sizes 12 in. to 16 in. Rolf was pleased when I told him, and he wrote:

So you have actually got an order from M. & S. Congratulations. It is a nuisance to have to make the pockets, but for 500 dozen it is worth while training two machinists.

It was not easy to please Miss Hopkins. She did not mean to be difficult, but she was highly strung, hesitant, and for ever changing her mind. My next letter to Rolf read:

Miss Hopkins says she has made a mistake and ordered 300 dozen too many. Have sent cancellation.

And a fortnight later:

Miss Hopkins called off too many large sizes. Since she pays an average price, I could not agree. So she has cancelled the orders from two of the stores. Doing business with M. & S. is not very interesting. Is this the reason why they are *always* on the look-out for new suppliers?

Rolf replied: 'I always feared M. & S. were too clever for us.'
    The next order we lost again:

Miss Hopkins phoned to say that she has placed her order with another manufacturer, who includes the pockets in the price of 9s, a clear loss-making proposition. But she likes our ripple cloth and promises to put some of her dressing gown manufacturers in touch with us.

And finally:

M. & S. phoned. They seem to be in trouble. Can we supply them with 300 dozen children's knickers a week? Miss Hopkins promised not to haggle over price provided we commence deliveries immediately, and she would come to Langley tomorrow to finalise the contract. She didn't like it when I had to tell her that we are sold out to the middle of November. She must have the goods now, and so the deal falls through. Presumably Hall & Earl have let her down, but I am afraid we cannot help her, otherwise we would have to keep Woolworth's waiting.

These letters are typical of many that passed between Rolf and me. Our merchandise was of no great interest to Marks & Spencer. Had it not been for our modern building with its smart entrance hall and chromium-plated railings, the many flower pots and the conveyor belt in our sewing department, which impressed them, I dare say they would not have bothered with us any further. But none of their suppliers had such an up-to-date factory. It spelled efficiency. There must surely be something we could make for them, they thought. One after another half a dozen buyers—selectors in fact, for they had no power to place contracts—came to Langley, each for a different department, each trying to outdo the other in getting us to make something special: knickers with double gussets and replaceable elastic, gaiters, cotton jerkins with zip fasteners and pockets, wool jumpers, artificial silk blouses of a shape all their own, yet none of these efforts led to a worthwhile order. Other manufacturers could always do better. As Rolf said, M. & S. were too clever for us. The only exception was our ripple cloth. No other manufacturer in Britain could produce anything approaching it, and since M. & S. refused to buy garments made from German fabric they told their dressing gown manufacturers to get their ripple cloth from us. This brought us much additional business.

Their largest suppliers, Mills Bros. of Birmingham, gave us a starting order for 500 pieces, with a further 1,700 to follow. Even if our three ripple machines worked round the clock for seven days a week we could not cope with such requirements. A fourth machine was urgently needed, and we agreed to pay Gessner's price of RM 1,900 provided they delivered quickly. The business with Mills Bros. developed, but not always smoothly, and when there was trouble between them and M. & S., which seemed to be quite often, we got the backwash in the form of stop–go–stop instructions. Fortunately they were not our only customers for ripple cloth, and we were never without alternative work for our machines. Then, suddenly and without prior warning, Mills Bros. went bankrupt. At one stroke we stood to lose not only the money they owed us but also our largest fabric outlet. It seemed a disaster, until we realised that we could perhaps turn the situation to our advantage. If our girls were skilled enough to make sports shirts and artificial silk blouses they should not find cotton dressing gowns too difficult. It would be better to sell the garments than the cloth. As it happened, we needed work for the sewing machinists because the demand for blouses was coming to an end. So we bought one of the Mills dressing gowns from an M. & S. store, copied it as accurately as we could, and I took both to Marks & Spencer's head office in Baker Street.

How times had changed since the mid-1920s, when manufacturers were loath to admit that they were supplying Marks & Spencer, when travellers called at the back door, and when Miss Swift, the buyer, used to come personally to Captain Da Costa's shabby little office in Clerkenwell to haggle with him over the price of our fleecy knickers! Now I sat in a large, comfortably furnished waiting room filled with manufacturers' agents who hardly bothered to hide their faces behind newspapers. To do business with the fast-growing chain store had become respectable. You had to be someone important to be received by the now almost legendary Miss Swift. Ordinary callers like my-self were content to see one of the selectors. Ladies' dressing gowns were the responsibility of Miss Elsie Davis and Miss Gordon. The bankruptcy of Mills Bros. had left them short of supplies and, fortunately for me, they were as eager to see my sample as I was to show it to them. I did not have to do much selling to secure a trial order, and the price of 39*s* a dozen which they offered me was very acceptable. It would show us a profit of about 7 per cent. The gowns sold to the public at 4*s* 11*d* each.

The first order led to substantial repeat business. I had to see Teddy Sieff, the brother of the vice-chairman, who questioned me about the capacity of our plant. He seemed a little displeased that we were supplying Woolworth's, even though it was with different merchandise, but did not press the point to its logical conclusion. He did not mind, he said, provided our Woolworth business did not interfere with the deliveries to M. & S. He liked our dressing gowns and would see to it that we get large contracts. He sent Miss Lancaster to Langley; she was in charge of the children's wear section. With her assist-ance we designed a range of very attractive girls' dressing gowns in five sizes and three colours, and booked a substantial order at 29*s* a dozen. One of the prettiest little garments we ever made was a tiny napped wool gown for Christmas. It was bright red, had white rabbit fur trimming round the collar, and sold in the stores at 5*s*. M. & S. would have bought more than we could make in the time available.

We always sent interesting information about new fabrics, better seams, more attractive finishes or manufacturing economies from Langley to Fleissen, and vice versa, and ideas developed at one factory benefited the other. Experiments at Fleissen to redesign our White Bear fabric resulted in a fleecy material with vertical stripes which was useless for the sweaters for which it had been intended but made up into handsome dressing gowns for men and boys. Mr Hill, the head of Marks & Spencer's men's department, called them 'winners'. His orders were particularly welcome. We knitted the fabric for them from coloured condenser yarn which Leibitschgrund spun from Fleissen's waste clippings, thus saving the dyeing. And since it was only brushed but not rippled, it put no extra load on our already overworked ripple machines.

We could have done with a fifth ripple machine, but first we had to buy more circulars and train two more knitters. This would take time. Meanwhile there was no alternative but to reduce sales to the makers-up if we did not want to run short of fabric for our own dressing gown production. The busi-ness with M. & S. was, however, not as easy as these paragraphs may suggest. When I called on them with that first dressing gown it happened to be at the right psychological moment and on my lucky day. Simon Marks's never-ending demands for improved merchandise and for better value, and his firm's continuous search for still more competitive manufacturers, kept us on our toes. If we became by far their largest supplier of ripple dressing gowns it was not for their lack of trying to find others. But we knew more about brushing and rippling cotton stockinette than anyone else in Britain, and Simon Marks was not prepared to let his firm buy gowns made from imported —which meant German—cloth. For the time being we were in a strong position, and when on one occasion Miss Lancaster remarked, 'Since you won't supply other makers with your cloth, we have no option but to buy all our ripple gowns from you,' Rolf wrote to Mother, 'For once I feel like a king!'

'This is the time to ask for an interview with the chairman,' I replied. 'Tell him how much we value our connection with Marks & Spencer. Try to dispel any misgivings he may have about our ripple dressing gown monopoly. Play it down. Reassure him that we are not going to exploit it. Say you would like to know what he expects from us. Ask for advice on how to prepare our factory for his firm's future needs. You must make him feel,' I urged, 'that his guidance is of paramount importance to us. This will make him take a personal interest in our business. He will talk to his co-directors about us. We shall be lifted out of the mass of faceless suppliers and treated with more circumspection by the selectors.'

Half expecting that Rolf would ignore my suggestion, I was delighted when I heard that he had arranged the meeting and that Mr Israel Sieff, the vice-chairman, would receive him. The report he sent me afterwards left no doubt that the discussion had gone well. For a whole hour Rolf and Mr Hurst had sat in the boardroom at Baker Street, listening to Mr Sieff's lecture on the chain's trading philosophy and expansion programme. Did we realise that M. & S. needed £400,000 worth of merchandise a week? We were supplying not just 200 stores but 48 million consumers. He thought we should double our dressing gown production, and how about installing an interlock plant to make children's knickers? If Rolf would commit himself Mr Sieff was ready to write out a large contract right away for delivery twelve months hence.

But Rolf was far too cautious to commit himself for so far ahead in a rising cotton market. Besides, we were a little afraid of the Jewish chain store. One heard so much of their ruthless business methods and of suppliers being encouraged to enlarge their factories only to have their prices cut afterwards. Was that what had happened to Mills Bros.? Determined not to become too dependent on M. & S., Rolf made the excuse that we wanted to build up production first. With this Mr Sieff was content. For some reason we never quite understood he seemed to like us.

It was Marks & Spencer's policy to have, if possible, at least three suppliers for every article, and the best of them got the largest orders. This ensured lively competition. Each of the three had to work to exactly the same standards, sizes and weights, use the same quality and count of yarn, and have the goods dyed in identical shades, so that they could be displayed on the counters together without the public noticing a difference. Suppliers were thus interchangeable. If one manufacturer refused to toe the line, fell behind with deliveries, or his factory burnt down, M. & S. gave larger orders to the other two. They could always put one of the three under pressure if it suited them. We had nothing to worry about when it came to dressing gowns, because they had no other supplier, but with an interlock plant it would be a very different story, and so I was not very receptive. We had several times considered making a trial with interlock machines during the past few years. Rolf had been for it, but contrary to what usually happened it was I who had stalled. There were far too many manufacturers of interlock garments already, it seemed to me. Every buyer told us that prices were being cut to the bone. Ten years ago it would have been different; the manufacturers in Leicester and Nottingham who bought interlock machines made good profits then. And having written down their plant in the meantime, they could be very competitive now. What chance was there for us newcomers in the south to compete against them? All the same, at Rolf's request we drove to Leicester to talk to Mr Simpson.

As always, Mellor Bromley's factory made our hearts beat faster. White-coated designers at their drawing boards, workmen on lines of automatic lathes and drills, and rows of knitting machines at various stages of assembly. What a background for a salesman! I envied Mr Simpson. If only some of our friends on the Continent, or even in the City of London, who talked so disparagingly of Britain's antiquated industry could see this modern precision engineering plant. What a thrill it would be to order a battery of twenty machines instead of having to worry about risking one.

'You need risk nothing,' said Mr Simpson. 'When you bought those rib machines from us a year ago we offered you a couple of interlocks for a month's trial. The offer still stands.'

In the car on the way back to Langley, still flushed from our visit, we decided to try a 16 in. and an 18 in. machine, not with M. & S. in mind but to make singlets for George Peacock and miners' vests for Baird's. They left us to decide what yarn to use and where to buy our sewing cotton, and had no wish to interfere in the way we ran our factory. There were also the wholesalers, who never tired of telling Mr Hurst that they bought interlock instead of fleecies, and there was Mr Cue. We could be sure of getting enough orders to keep two machines busy. With an easy mind I returned to Fleissen in March 1936, and four weeks later Rolf wrote:

Mellor Bromley have delivered the 16 in. machine this morning and I am delighted with it. A wonderful piece of engineering! Had no difficulty starting it up. We are using good quality 40s cotton yarn on it, which runs well and produces fabric in the correct width for men's singlets. The 18 in. machine will be just right for o/s size.

Out of this modest beginning grew, over the years, one of the most important sectors of our business. When Peacock's and Baird's orders had been completed the wholesalers decided that they did not want another interlock supplier after all, and Mr Cue was biding his time, so Rolf took a small contract for women's knickers from M. & S. It worked out to our mutual satisfaction. They were pleased with our merchandise and we had less interference from them than we had feared. The first transaction led to a second, and when Miss Lancaster again offered us regular large orders for children's knickers we decided to install a set of interlock machines suitable for children's sizes.

The stockinette fabric produced by our 44 in. diameter Terrots was wide enough to cut garments of any shape and size from it, but interlock machines were built in very much smaller diameters and the fabric they knitted was in body widths. To manufacture the complete size range of children's knickers without wasting material we had to have the whole series of diameters, from 12 in. to 20 in., but not the same number of each, since some widths of fabric were used more often than others. To set up a well balanced plant was a matter of fine calculation, and even then, if an order called for an unusual proportion of sizes, it could happen that some machines had to work round the clock while others stood idle. Not a very efficient way of running a factory. We worked out that for our purpose a well balanced plant consisted of no fewer than fifteen interlock machines. At an average price of £320 each, together with the necessary motors, winding and sewing machinery, this represented a £7,000 investment. Since we did not know how to raise such a sum all at once, we bought the machines over a period of twelve months, always two or three at a time, and meanwhile compromised as well as we could.

In spite of keen competition and cut prices, Marks & Spencer's orders yielded us a profit. Interfering though they could be, they knew the importance of continuous production and tried to keep our interlock machines fully employed. In July Miss Lancaster gave us her first large order, for 12,000 dozen children's knickers. Three months later, before we had quite delivered it, she placed another for 6,000 dozen and, since cotton prices had risen in the meantime, agreed to pay 3d a dozen more. A few weeks later she repeated a further 4,000, just before Christmas yet another 10,000, and in February 1937 Miss Hopkins joined in with a contract for 20,000 dozen women's knickers. Sometimes of an evening, when I added up all the business we now had on the books, I wished Father could see the figures. How pleased he would be to know that we were once again approaching his dozenages of the 1920s; without showing it, he would have felt proud of his boys.

It was sheer joy to look at our plant of streamlined Mellor Bromley machines. Sprayed powder blue, like all the metal parts in our factory, and lovingly cared for by Köhler, Passler and Schreiner, they worked at full speed with hardly any supervision. Only on cold winter mornings did we have trouble with slipping belts and jerking clutches, resulting in thread and needle breakages. A drive arrangement I had sometimes used on Meccano models cured the trouble. I replaced the clutches by V belts and hinged the motors so that their weight kept the belts taut. These floating motors made the machines start smoothly on the coldest Monday morning. We continually made improvements in the factory, and, while Ingo was the one with most mechanical skill, we all vied with each other evolving fault-preventing and labour-saving ideas.

The Marks & Spencer family enterprise was fast developing from a mere chain store into a national institution. Simon Marks and Israel Sieff, chairman and vice-chairman, who had married each other's sisters, were the driving force round which the whole dynamic organisation revolved. Like God, they were everywhere, saw everything, and nothing happened without their approval. They appeared in the stores when they were least expected, saw that the sales girls had clean fingernails, took merchandise home to measure, boil and wear, tasted the food in the canteens, and at night went through the desks of the office staff to clear out unnecessary papers which were taking up valuable space. Employees who did not want to risk losing their records had to hide them. The whole incredible concern was thus kept humming, and for a supplier to grow with it was an exhilarating experience. It felt like climbing a rumbling volcano which might erupt at any time. Simon Marks, it was said, could act the part of Tamerlane as convincingly as that of Santa Claus, although we never actually had experience of him in either role.

By now it was common knowledge in the trade that we were one of Marks & Spencer's regular suppliers. Our wholesale customers did not like it, but they realised that there was little they could do to stop us. Every year more manufacturers sold direct to the retailer. Had the wholesalers blacklisted them they would have lost all their best suppliers. And so we continued to book orders from Foster Porter, Copestake Crampton, Cook Son and the other old established houses whose trade was steadily shrinking. No doubt the big, outmoded warehouses occupying valuable sites in the heart of the City were written down, and so their balance sheets still showed profits when, calculated on a realistic basis, they were in the red. With goodwill built up over a century, famous old brand names, and plenty of money in the bank, why did they not adapt themselves to the changing conditions? They had given me little cause to feel sorry for them, yet I was sad to watch their decline. Like the Lancashire cotton industry, the wholesale drapers seemed to have lost the will to survive.

Marks & Spencer took 90 per cent of our dressing gown production, and were our largest customers for interlock knickers. In the course of a few years our sales to them exceeded even those to Woolworth's. These two chain stores were of more interest to us than all the wholesalers put together, but we did not want to depend too much on just two clients, and looked for additional outlets. Perhaps it was unnecessary; in all the many years we did business with them they treated us fairly, and we never had any serious disagreement with either, but we could not know that in advance.

Following the M. & S. pattern, other retailers established chains, and it seemed quite likely that they too would grow. We felt we had to get our merchandise on to their counters. Once we had established a foothold we would grow with them. Still in 1936, we secured our first order from British Home Stores. The negotiations with Mr Prereira, the buyer, demanded much patience, but we were rewarded with a contract for 300 dozen dressing gowns, soon to be followed by one for 500 dozen women's vests and 850 dozen slipovers. Then Mr Goldstone, a young man who wore flashy ties and pointed shoes, became the buyer. If Prereira had been difficult, Goldstone was impossible. He would get hold of one of the dressing gowns we supplied to M. & S. at 48s a dozen, hold it up to Mr Hurst and me, and demand, 'This is the type of garment I want, but it must have an extra pocket, a wider collar and a thicker girdle. And I'll not pay you a penny more than 46s a dozen!' Not only did he want a better gown at a lower price, he could buy no more than 300 dozen where M. & S. bought 3,000, and we were glad to be in a strong enough position to decline his orders when they did not suit us. Doing business with British Home Stores was not particularly pleasant, and we made no great effort to develop it. The largest contract we ever booked from them in the 1930s was for 4,000 dozen interlock knickers, which we had to knit in a lighter than standard weight to meet their price limit.

Fortunately there were other up-and-coming retail organisations besides BHS who bought our merchandise, such as Littlewood's, Debenham's and Great Universal Stores. Their orders added up to tens of thousands of dozens. The fact that we were Marks & Spencer suppliers actually helped us to get their business, because it proved that we were competitive. It also helped us to sell our goods to South African and New Zealand shippers, and we developed a good export trade.

31

THE DYERS
DEFEATED
1932-34

NOW LET ME go back a year or two. During the period from 1932 to the autumn of 1934 Langley's success or failure depended more on Sergeant's at Acton, the only dyers in the London area who were equipped to handle our type of fabric, than on anything else. Their plant was antiquated, but Mr Twinam, the managing director, was only too well aware of his firm's monopoly position and saw no need to spend money on modernising it to make it more efficient. All our pleadings for better colour matching and for keeping to promised delivery dates fell on deaf ears. He made us pay 3*d* for dyeing 1 lb of fabric, while at Fleissen, where several commission dyers competed for our business, we paid only Kc 1·75 a kilo. Since the rate of exchange was approximately Kc 110 to the pound sterling, and 1 lb equals 450 g, we used 'Kc per kilo = pence per lb' as a convenient and sufficiently accurate formula for comparison. Fleissen thus paid less than 60 per cent of what Langley did. We reasoned, pleaded and argued with Twinam, all to no avail. The situation was intolerable.

Encouraged by the successful operation of the small sliver dyeing plant at Leibitschgrund, I now seriously contemplated building a dyehouse at Langley, and said so in two letters to Rolf, who was holding the reins at Fleissen at the time:

. . . the dyers do with us as they please. Today they delivered only twenty-five pieces, which will not keep us going for longer than two days. By Wednesday we shall have to send our sewing machinists home, with the risk that they won't come back. And when I phone Twinam he retorts, 'Why don't you build your own dyehouse, as you threatened you would?' Tomorrow I have to see him again. I fear he may put his prices up. If so, we can only grin and pay. This can't go on. We must do our own dyeing. We shall need a single-storey building, a large boiler and boiler house, three stainless steel vats, a centrifuge, a dryer and a water softener. To begin with we'll buy the water from the council, and in view of the agreement they signed I don't expect difficulties over the discharge of the effluents. The cost of the project will be around £4,000, but where the money is to come from I do not know . . .

... Had a long talk to Twinam yesterday and am relieved to be able to tell you that he did not raise his prices. He promised to make more regular deliveries, but you appreciate what that is worth. Am convinced we shall not get on our feet at Langley until we do our own dyeing.

Meanwhile an unexpected crisis had suddenly developed at Rolf's end. After years of fighting each other the commission dyers of western Bohemia had come together in a cartel under the leadership of the powerful Asch United Dyeworks and, it was rumoured, intended to raise their charges by 10 per cent. This would threaten the competitive position of Adolf Pasold & Sohn *vis-à-vis* Lehrmann's, who did their own dyeing and were not affected. In self-defence Rolf therefore wanted to enlarge the small sliver dyeing plant at Leibitschgrund to a full-size dyehouse so that we too could dye our fabric, and he wrote to me:

The cartel has been established and if charges go up by 10 per cent, adding Kc 50,000 to our annual cost of dyeing, then it must pay to install a piece-dyeing plant at Leibitschgrund. The nucleus is already there: we have the water supply, pipelines, boiler and even a hydro extractor. Although not designed for the much larger weights to be dyed, I think we could manage by spreading the load. All we need are a few wooden vats and a drying chamber. Preibisch, our foreman dyer, says he can handle both sliver and fabric provided we give him three extra men. There remains the effluent disposal problem—troublesome, no doubt, but I am not afraid to tackle it....

The prices which have just been announced exceed all expectation. If the cartel can enforce them the dyeing industry will be solvent within twelve months. Shades which need pre-bleaching are up from Kc 1·80 to Kc 2·25, and dark shades from Kc 1·70 to Kc 2·15. These prices are for minimum weights of 200 kilos per shade; smaller weights cost progressively more. Do you realise that this will put our annual costs up by Kc 150,000? A plant for dyeing our fabric must pay. I suggest we start on it at once.

Now each of us wanted a dyehouse, Rolf at Leibitschgrund and I at Langley. We had not the resources to build both at the same time, so which of them was to come first? Anxious as I was to get out of Twinam's clutches, on reflection I inclined towards Rolf's scheme, but wondered if he fully realised the fuss caused by the merest trace of discoloration in the trout stream. The volume of effluent discharged by a dyehouse of the size now contemplated would be twenty times that of the small sliver dye plant. And there was another thing. Who could foretell how long the cartel would hold together? Were not the commission dyers likely to start cheating and break it up? Considerations like these made me hesitate.

Will the cartel last? I don't believe you will have to pay these high prices for long. The leopard doesn't change his spots, and as soon as you give all your business to one dyer and starve the others they will come to see you in the evening offering secret discounts. We know their tricks: they will charge for lower weights than they deliver, invoice cheap colours when they dye expensive, send credit notes for fabric they have not spoilt and give you refunds in cash to regain your custom. True, a fabric dyeing plant at Leibitschgrund would cost less than a new dyehouse at Langley, and your annual dyeing bill of Kc 500,000 is more than twice as large as ours, but I have reservations.

A few days later Rolf reported:

Dyer Grötsch came to see me. He is outside the cartel. Offers to do our dyeing at Kc 1·62 per kilo and assures me that this still gives him a satisfactory profit. Says he has repaid the bank Kc 100,000 during the past year. Dyeing must be a lucrative trade. Shall make a trial with him but still think we should get going at Leibitschgrund as quickly as possible.

In reply I sent another two letters to Rolf:

I see from all your letters that you are in a tearing hurry to start fabric dyeing at Leibitschgrund. Suggest you prepare plans and figures and we look at them over the Christmas holidays. But bear in mind that Langley needs a dyehouse soon too. Sergeant's must be coining money, dyeing the fabric for our large Woolworth orders at 3d a lb, just the one shade for two whole weeks. I shall try to squeeze some price reduction out of Twinam for such bulk orders, but have little hope of success.

Our latest Woolworth order for 25,000 dozen knickers requires 48,000 lb of fabric. I offered Twinam dyeing instructions of 4,000 lb per shade at a time if he would make a small price concession, but he refused to budge. Sergeant's will, I reckon, make a profit of £600 out of this order! And they make a convenience of us. They still have not dyed all the pieces we gave them three weeks ago. The fifteen they delivered today will keep our girls going until tomorrow evening, then we shall have no work for them. We must do something about a dyehouse at Langley. Saw the council today, together with Koch. No problem with water supply or effluent disposal, but Koch calculates that a dyehouse will cost £5,600 plus £1,600 for a borehole, should we want one. I reckon that even at these figures it will pay.

As always when I quoted the estimated cost of a project, there came a speedy response from Rolf. Either he was of the opinion that the whole thing was unnecessary, or it was too elaborate, and my figures were invariably excessive. I was therefore not surprised at his next letter, nor at the fact that he did not even mention the borehole. And he was, of course, thinking of wooden vats, whereas I wanted stainless steel.

I cannot believe that Koch's estimate can be right. The building should not cost more than £700, the plant £1,200, and if Langley's present boiler is large enough the whole job can be done for £2,000. Should we need a larger boiler and boiler house, to provide a reserve of hot water, the total cost may go up to £3,000, but no more. Let's discuss it at Christmas.

At Christmas Rolf, Willie, Ingo and I sat together comparing the respective merits of the two dyehouse schemes, and decided in favour of the one for Leibitschgrund. Opposition was to be expected from two sides, from the farming community, whose natural objection to industrial effluent would be fanned by Lehrmann's, and from the cartel, who might want to kill the project by threatening to cease dyeing for us. They could bring Adolf Pasold & Sohn to a dead stop. If this risk had to be faced, then we should at least reduce the danger period to a minimum by completing the new dyehouse as rapidly as possible, and in the greatest secrecy. Being tucked away in the forest, Leibitschgrund was not in the public eye, and we could, perhaps, hide the real nature of the operation by pretending that we were merely carrying out maintenance work to the sliver dye plant.

The holidays over, it was my turn to direct operations at Adolf Pasold & Sohn and Rolf's to take charge at Langley. One of the first things I did was to invite Marr, and afterwards Krey & Co., the two commission dyers who handled some 50 per cent of all our fabric, to enter into firm contracts with us before news of what was afoot at Leibitschgrund leaked out. It seemed the best way of protecting ourselves and them against possible strong-arm tactics by the Asch United Dyeworks-dominated cartel. Both were pleased to sign, although they must have wondered why I should want such an undertaking knowing that they were only too anxious to have our business. Then I dismissed Grötsch.

Grötsch is unsatisfactory: his colours are poor, his deliveries unreliable, and he is in trouble with the cartel. I am afraid we shall have to go back to our old dyers, Carl Marr and Krey & Co. They have given me undertakings to dye for us at cartel prices any fabric we may entrust to them during 1934, come what may. We are therefore covered, unless they create an 'act of God' by blowing up their boilers, which is the last thing they are likely to do.

Meanwhile Rolf wrote from Langley:

Sergeant's are making an effort to give service. Delivered forty-one pieces today, and only four had to be returned for re-dyeing. Twinam telephoned promising weekly deliveries of 6,000 lb from now on. Can one rely on it? I found a small firm of ribbon dyers on the Slough trading estate. They have only one vat large enough to take our pieces, but offer to install more if we give them regular business. Are now dyeing samples pieces for us. Let's see how they come up.

To which I replied:

You were right when you said that Langley's production is too small to justify a dyehouse. We are now in a position to make accurate estimates, which show that dyeing and drying a weekly weight of only 6,000 lb costs 3*d* per lb. Double this weight and the cost drops to 2*d* per lb. Langley's production must be built up first. If only we weren't so dependent on Twinam in the meantime. Tell me more about the ribbon dyer at Slough!

Preparatory work for the dye plant at Leibitschgrund is proceeding with all speed. The experts are coming round to our view that high-pressure hot water is more economical than steam. We are investigating the Simon forced draught system, which could provide up to 14,000 gallons of boiling water daily without extra fuel consumption. Would necessitate making the factory chimney 17 ft taller. Extracting the waste heat from the burnt gases in the chimney, and from the engine cooling water, we can provide almost all the calories needed for the dyehouse at practically no cost. But since the consumption of hot water will not run parallel with the rate at which it is produced we shall need a sizeable hot water storage tank. Willie is advertising for a large second-hand boiler for the purpose.

We should have liked to see how other dyers dealt with their technical problems, but dyeworks were not easily accessible to the curious, and, being mostly filled with a fog the eye could not penetrate, revealed few of their secrets to visitors. We suspected that the mystique in which the trade was shrouded served no other purpose than to hide its inefficiency. The billowing clouds of steam themselves told a story of shocking waste. We knew that the cost of heat was an important component of the cost of dyeing, and provided we made intelligent use of the waste heat from the spinning mill we could undoubtedly operate more economically than the members of the cartel. One thing led to another. The more thoroughly Willie and I studied the subject the more improvements suggested themselves, not only to the dye plant but to the boiler plant and heat distribution system of the whole of Leibitschgrund. Calculations showed that a modern water-tube boiler would be far more efficient than our existing Lancashire-type boilers and, if we transferred the coal storage depot from the lower end of the boilerhouse to a new coal bunker half-way up the hill we could feed the automatic stokers by gravity. This necessitated building a road for our ten-ton lorry, which plied between Leibitschgrund and the open-cast coal mine at Falkenau, so that it could tip its load straight into the bunker. Our cheap brown coal was of low calorific value: we used large quantities of it, and automatic handling saved several men. As luck would have it, the gunpowder factory at Pressburg in Slovakia was closing down, and its six large sectional water-tube boilers were for sale. We sent Ingo and a mechanic to inspect them, and after receiving their report bought the best one for 102,000 kronen, a bargain price.

'How can we be sure that they will send us the one you selected?' I wanted to know from Ingo.

He showed me a small steel punch. 'I have marked it, and every tube, valve and other part belonging to it!' If a job required practical knowledge of engineering one could safely leave it to Ingo.

We saved where we could, but not by sacrificing efficiency. We ordered, for instance, five wooden vats because they were much cheaper than the stainless steel ones I would have preferred. For reasons of economy Adolf Pasold & Sohn hardly ever produced merchandise in more than five colours and, by reserving a vat for each colour, we were at no disadvantage in using wooden ones. When it came to deciding between steam and high-pressure hot water, on the other hand, and Rolf wrote that he wanted steam because it cost less to install, I refused to give way. I had seen Caliqua's demonstration plant in Berlin and was satisfied that high-pressure hot water offered advantages we could not afford to forego. When the German makers of the plant quoted the fantastic price of 170,000 kronen I found a firm in Czechoslovakia that was willing to supply a similar installation for 95,000. The two concerns now started to fight, undercutting each other, until Caliqua came down to 58,000 kronen and booked our order. But in spite of this staggering reduction and other successful battles over prices, the various contracts for the dyehouse and the new boiler plant at Leibitschgrund still exceeded 600,000 kronen, or more than four times the figure Rolf had originally estimated.

It was in fact the new boilerhouse and plant, with its ingenious waste heat reclamation and labour-saving features, on which the bulk of the money was being spent, and from which the spinning mills would also profit. The dye plant as such accounted for only a third of the expenditure. And it was the happy combination of the two that made the scheme so exciting. Willie, Ingo and I all felt sure that it would prove highly efficient and profitable, and that Rolf too would become enthusiastic when he saw it.

Meanwhile, however, he only saw my reports and was concerned about the large sums we were investing at Leibitschgrund. Would we ever see all this money back? If it cost so much to build a dyeworks, then he certainly did not want one at Langley. Nor was this his only worry. His knitting output was falling short of target in spite of the introduction of a third shift, too much of the fabric was faulty, he was losing trained sewing machinists and winders and could not replace them—not even with learners—and the financial statements at the end of each week invariably showed losses. I realised only too well how he felt, being surrounded with problems, and sympathised with him when he wrote, 'If you ask me, we should leave any dyehouse project for Langley severely alone!' He need not have worried. I knew that Langley was not ready to do its own dyeing, but to make doubly sure he sent a further letter:

... better news today. C & C Dyers, the small firm on the Slough trading estate, have dyed ten pieces for us, of which seven are quite satisfactory and only three have to be returned for re-dyeing. This is not at all bad for a beginning. Even Sergeant's are now making an effort to give service.

It sounded encouraging, but I believed only half of it. I knew how Rolf's mind worked, and suspected that he merely wanted to quash any plan I might still be hatching for a dyehouse at Langley.

Much digging was done at Leibitschgrund that spring, not by earth-moving machinery as we would expect nowadays but by pickaxe and shovel. The new road, the coal bunker and the large effluent pits were being excavated, the bricklayers were busy on the new boilerhouse, and the foundations for the sectional boiler had to be concreted. Tanks, pumps and all manner of pipework arrived, and the whole village was buzzing with excitement. After having slept for a generation the place had come to life since the Pasolds took it over. There was work for everyone and a future to look forward to.

The news of our building activities got round very quickly, but nobody seemed to suspect that we were building a dyehouse. This surprised me, for inevitably a number of our workmen knew it. Did they not talk about it in the evening at the inn? If they did, the people of Leibitschgrund never let on about it to anyone from outside, least of all to the Lehrmann brothers, whom Willie saw hiding in the undergrowth on the edge of the forest one Sunday morning, trying to spy out with their binoculars what was going on. We heard nothing from the farmers or the cartel.

This gave me time to see the authorities at Eger and the Ministry of Trade in Prague and talk to them about textile exports in general and those of Adolf Pasold & Sohn in particular, about Japanese competition and the need for Czechoslovakia's industry to employ better manufacturing techniques, about developments in dyeing and especially about the model dye plant we were erecting at Leibitschgrund. I applied for a permit to use the pure water from our trout stream, and asked for their blessing for our much enlarged and improved effluent pits. Then I enlisted the support of the chamber of commerce —all long before the storm broke. And when it did, it went off like a damp squib, for all the important civil servants were fully informed and on our side. We won hands down.

In the middle of April Rolf came back to take over at Fleissen again, and I went to Langley. We always had a few days together during these change-overs, when we discussed matters which could not be dealt with by correspondence. On this occasion we agreed, much to Rolf's relief, to postpone plans for building a dyehouse at Langley for an indefinite period. Instead we would encourage C & C Dyers gradually to expand their capacity, but would move warily in order not to upset Sargeant's, on whose co-operation Langley continued to depend.

Rolf was pleased with what he saw at Leibitschgrund, and carried on in the spirit in which I left off. It was public knowledge now that we were building a dyehouse, but as we had secured official approval there was little anyone could do to interfere with the progress of our construction work. Another six months would go by before we were ready to start dyeing, and unless or until some of our effluents found their way into the stream not even the farmers had a case. The cartel continued to dye for us in the meantime, in view of the contracts we had made with Marr and Krey & Co. Rolf was therefore free to devote time to technical matters. There was, for instance, the invention which Ackermann, a well known dyeing expert, offered him, and he reported about it to Langley:

Ackermann claims to have invented a continuous dyeing machine. It consists of a conveyor which carries the fabric, flat or in folds, and above is a container with only about 100 gallons of dye liquid, which rains through perforations on to the moving fabric and is then collected again in a tray at the bottom. A dryer is also incorporated, so that the grey fabric need only be fed into the machine at one end, and comes out dyed and dried at the other. A demonstration model is being built at Hof in Germany. I doubt whether it will work, but it would be unfortunate if we installed our conventional wooden vats and then found that Ackermann's machine was better.

So Rolf waited for a demonstration of the new dyeing machine, but time and again it was postponed because of unexpected snags, and after several weeks he wrote:

I don't think we should wait for Ackermann's invention. All the parts of the boiler have now been delivered. Being in sections, it was easy to transport. Erection will cost Kc 30,000 and will take about three weeks. Caliqua should be ready by mid-September. Temporary steam connections to the old boiler are almost completed, and we hope to start dyeing on a temporary basis in about ten days. Am glad, for we have paid Kc 362,000 to the commission dyers for the first six months of this year.

Shortly afterwards Rolf sent me a series of enthusiastic letters about the way things were shaping. He was not normally given to praise, but on this occasion he got completely carried away. And looking back, I must admit that I too am still proud of the concept and execution of the boiler plant and dyehouse we installed at Leibitschgrund. I wish Father could have seen it.

Started dyeing today, but we're having trouble with the temporary drive of the vats. The belt from the motor to the line shaft keeps slipping. Teething troubles. The centrifuge works well, the dye vats are a complete success. The first five pieces we dyed are very good.

Have overcome drive difficulty. Correct speed for dryer not yet established. Dyeing navy, matching not yet perfect but better than Sergeant's. Am going to try bleaching this afternoon. Am just off to Leibitschgrund again. Willie takes too long over everything, needs gentle kicks periodically. Preibisch is a good dyer but needs experience on our type of fabric. Temporary installation works well, lets us gain experience. Think within two weeks we shall be able to cope with Fleissen's total production.

Final line shaft now fitted. Permanent water supply should be completed in a few days. Shall then go on full production. At present can dye only ten pieces a day. New boilerhouse nearing completion, roof is on. Caliqua engineers started with erection of their plant yesterday. Am convinced that our dyeing will pay very well, in spite of the large capital outlay. No commission dyer can dye as economically as we can.

Leibitschgrund had to make do with temporary steam pipes and other improvisations for several months. As usual, the finishing touches took longer than expected. I changed places with Rolf in August, saw the long delayed demonstration of Ackermann's continuous dyeing machine, which proved an unqualified failure, and pushed ahead with the hundred and one things that still needed doing. In October Rolf and I changed over again, and the letters he sent me after his return to Czechoslovakia describe his impressions and the last stages of the completion of the plant.

Am tremendously impressed with what I see at Leibitschgrund. The whole plant is now virtually complete. What a joy it is to find it all functioning perfectly. I feel like a dog with two tails. We have achieved a great deal this year, and I expect we shall see some of it reflected in the balance sheet.

The new sectional boiler provides steam and heat for the whole of Leibitschgrund, yet we are using 20 per cent less coal. Combustion is flawless, flames are two and a half metres high and there is no trace of smoke from the chimney. The boilerhouse is spotlessly clean. Caliqua installation is in use and working well, hot water tank has been lagged and now loses only 10°C in twenty-four hours. The only thing we still need is a brake in front of the drum dryer. Fabric passing through it without tension comes out too wide, and therefore too light per square metre. Weight losses during dyeing and drying are 10 per cent, but the pieces regain 4 per cent during the following three days. This applies to pre-bleached shades, and in view of the low-grade yarn we are using for them is acceptable. Are dyeing thirty pieces daily, and, generally speaking, our colours are good. I am very pleased with the whole operation.

Father's dream of an integrated manufacturing organisation performing the complete chain of operations from the raw cotton to the finished garments was now realised. The healthy smell of the pine forest, mingled with that of cotton being processed—which I shall always associate with Leibitschgrund —and now the occasional whiff from the dyehouse, tasted sweeter to me than the scent of a garden of roses.

While the dyehouse at Leibitschgrund was being built, the dyeing problems at Langley remained. In spite of Mr Twinam's promises Sergeant's took up to four weeks to process our pieces, and at times held more than two hundred of them at their works while we were desperately short of fabric. Did they keep us short on purpose? Operating from hand to mouth, we could not afford to send any back for re-dyeing, and if we complained they withheld deliveries altogether, to investigate, as they explained. No doubt they had their problems. Time and again we sent our cutters and sewing machinists home because we ran out of fabric, which made our deliveries late and gave our customers cause for dissatisfaction.

The experience we gained at Leibitschgrund told us that Langley's fabric production was still far too small to make a dye plant of our own a feasible proposition. The output of the knitting department would first have to be doubled. But in order to find customers for so much additional merchandise our selling prices would have to be lower and our service better than was possible as long as we suffered from these very unfortunate hold-ups. We were caught in a vicious circle.

A faint ray of hope was provided by the emergence of C & C Dyers. Unfortunately they were a very small firm, and short of capital. We had neither the confidence in the expertise of the owners or in the commercial viability of the venture to put up the £600 they wanted to buy larger vats and for which they offered us a 50 per cent participation in their business. Besides, we did not want to invest money in a dyehouse on the Slough trading estate when we had it in mind to build a much better one of our own in due course as an integral part of the factory at Langley. C & C Dyers would have to find their own finance, but we were only too willing to give them as many of our pieces as they could handle.

It did not take Sergeant's long to find out that some of our fabric was now going to Slough to be dyed, and I half expected an ultimatum from them to force us to our knees. It would have done. But Twinam obviously knew that the capacity of C & C Dyers was totally inadequate for our needs, and also that they were unable to dye wool. He must have thought of them as more of a nuisance than a serious competitor, for he tried to eliminate them by offering us a bonus for every month in which Sergeant Bros. dyed more than 22,000 lb of cotton fabric for us. This was somewhat in excess of our monthly average weight, and there would be no hope of qualifying for the bonus if we diverted even a few of our pieces to C & C Dyers. My reactions are summarised in a letter to Rolf:

We are now paying Sergeant Bros. between £3,000 and £4,000 a year, a large sum of money, and Twinam does not want to lose any of it to C & C Dyers. To cut them out he now tempts us with a 5 per cent bonus payable in every month in which Sergeant's deliver to us—not we to them, please note—more than 22,000 lb of cotton fabric. Wool is excluded from the arrangement. By holding back a few pieces one month and adding them to the next Sergeant's can manipulate their deliveries so that we shall not qualify for the bonus very often. How I long for the day when we can throw Twinam out!

Had I but known it, that longed-for day was closer at hand than I thought. Twinam's doubtful offer did not make us give up C & C Dyers. On the contrary, as they increased their capacity by scraping together enough money to buy two more vats we gave them more work, and it was not long before they were dyeing as many as thirty pieces a week for us. Their colours were no worse than Sergeant's and they charged $\frac{1}{2}d$ per lb less. We were no longer completely at Mr Twinam's mercy, but remained apprehensive of what he might do. Then, unexpectedly, the situation changed. A chance conversation with an agent decided us to contact a dyer at Leicester named Walter Cooke. There were, of course, many dyers in the Midlands, but we had never given them serious consideration. The distance put them out of reach for us, we thought. It would be too costly to send our fabric all the way to Leicester to have it dyed. But Walter Cooke, it appeared, was desperate to find work. For the past fifteen years, he told us, he had been dyeing for Hall & Earl at the almost unbelievable rate of £500 a week. This business had suddenly come to an end when Hall & Earl bought up a firm of commission dyers and gave all their work to them. Now half his plant was idle.

Walter Cooke was familiar with our type of fabric, and his dyehouse was equipped to handle it. He would collect and deliver our pieces in his own van three times a week, promised never to take longer than seven days to dye and return any load we gave him, and his charges per pound were $2\frac{1}{2}d$ for cotton and $4d$ for wool, including the transport. It all sounded very good, and we gave him a few trial loads, which he dyed speedily and to our entire satisfaction.

Oblivious of what was afoot, Mr Twinam chose this very moment to raise his charge for dyeing our wool fabric to $4\frac{1}{2}d$ per lb because, he said, we were so fussy over matching colours. Considering the trouble we had with our customers over Sergeant's erratic colour matching, this was adding insult to injury. The rates now quoted per lb by the three dyers were:

	Cotton	Wool
Sergeant Bros., Acton	$3d$	$4\frac{1}{2}d$
C & C Dyers, Slough	$2\frac{1}{2}d$	—
Walter Cooke, Leicester	$2\frac{1}{2}d$	$4d$

They included the cost of collecting, dyeing, drying and delivering the fabric. I tried to negotiate with Mr Twinam, but he thought he had us cornered and would not listen. This decided me to take the bull by the horns. To his surprise it was now I who gave him an ultimatum. Sergeant's would get no more business from us, I told him, unless they reduced their charges to $2\frac{1}{2}d$ for cotton and $4d$ for wool, and I wanted their confirmation before the end of the day. But Mr Twinam thought I was bluffing, and refused to budge. The gauntlet was down now all right, and I hoped I had not been rash. To make such an important decision merely on the strength of a few dyeing trials, however successful, without inspecting Cooke's dyehouse first, was careless. Early next morning I collected Mr Hurst from his home at Stanmore and we drove to Leicester, where the doubts that had assailed me during the night quickly vanished, as the following letter to Rolf shows.

Was at Leicester yesterday to look over Walter Cooke's dye plant and can tell you that it is the most modern I ever set eyes on. All his dye vats are of stainless steel, with not a single wooden one among them. He has a series of calenders, Perfectos dryers, and a large loop drying machine. Gave up hanging centrifuged fabric over wooden poles in heat chamber years ago. The only thing he has not got, or even heard of, is a high-pressure hot water installation. Everything is clean and tidy, as also the boilerhouse and the two boilers. The plant is large enough to process more than 50,000 lb a week, so coping with our production will be child's play.

Cooke thoroughly understands his job. A rough diamond, but I don't think we have ever met a more competent dyer. Says ours is the only fleecy fabric he has seen in two years, everything is interlock and Köper for sports shirts nowadays. Is satisfied with $2\frac{1}{2}d$ for cotton, which, he admits, shows a reasonable profit, but the $3\frac{1}{2}d$ I offered him for wool is tight and he hopes we can make it $4d$.

Gave us lunch at his home, an attractive house in seven acres of grounds, all in excellent condition. Afterwards he performed on his one-man jazz band, a unit exactly like the one Roy Fox uses. A gramophone makes the music and he adds the jazz. Is also a born humorist and a magician who staggered us with his conjuring tricks. You will like him, and I am confident that he will do a good job for Langley.

For the first time we were glad that Sergeant's were such slow operators. They had 200 of our pieces at their works, which would keep our cutting and sewing departments and ripple machines going and enable us to bridge the time lag that was bound to occur before we could expect regular deliveries from Leicester. But there was no time lag. Cooke's van arrived as punctually as clockwork and all our fabric came back to the factory at Langley, dyed and nicely folded, within five days of leaving it. We were amazed. Sergeant's meanwhile took almost a month to clear their arrears, and with the final load came Mr Twinam personally, pleading for more business. Rates could be discussed, he said, and that was not all. Sergeant Bros. intended to install a modern dye plant, tailor-made to our requirements. Would we help them design it?

I had by then gone to Fleissen, and Rolf was in charge at Langley. Smiling, he merely shook his head. It was exactly what I would have done.

The rancour we had both felt so often towards Mr Twinam had subsided. Sergeant's no longer mattered, and we never gave them another piece to dye. Rolf's letters showed that he was very happy with Walter Cooke's reliable dyeing and prompt deliveries. There was no more working from hand to mouth, no more guessing when the van might come, what it would bring, and which colours would be missing. He now knew exactly which pieces were going to arrive at 9 a.m. on Monday, and on Wednesday, and on Friday, and he could plan production in the factory well in advance. It was a pleasure to do business with Walter Cooke.

Colours and service are absolutely perfect, urgent pieces come back within two days, and we hardly ever have anything to return to be re-dyed. It all seems miraculous after what we have been through these past years.

Walter Cooke took Mr Hurst and myself to dinner in the West End last night, and then on to the great Peterson fight. Price of a ticket: £2 8s 0d! Most enjoyable. And this morning he came to Langley to thank me for the business we are giving him. Says he is delighted with it because we are such reasonable people and make so few complaints.

Could any dyehouse have a better heating installation than Walter Cooke's? I had told him about our high-pressure hot water system, and he wanted to see it working. As arranged, I met him at Eger, took him to Leibitschgrund, and explained how the enclosed circuit functioned. He was suitably impressed, but thought the advantages would not justify the expense of converting his already efficient plant. We spent a few amusing days together. I showed him the neighbourhood, and he expressed astonishment that a motor car could stand up to such terrible roads. Mother treated us to roast pork, sauerkraut and my favourite dumplings, a local speciality called *kochta gräina Kniadla*. Round, the size of a man's fist, the greeny-grey colour of newly mixed concrete, they were made partly of boiled and partly of ground raw potatoes, and tasted delicious to those who were brought up on them. Before I had finished mine our guest's had already disappeared. Mother was delighted. 'I am glad you like them, Mr Cooke,' she said, putting another on his plate.

'Delicious,' replied Mr Cooke, visibly enjoying his food.

A few days after our visitor had left we found two *kochta gräina Kniadla* in the rose bushes below the dining room window. Goodness knows how our magician had spirited them there.

After a while most things that work well are taken for granted because other, more troublesome matters claim one's attention. It was so with Walter Cooke's dyeing, but we never forgot the great contribution it made to the early success of the Langley factory, and we have always been grateful to our hard-working, cheerful friend from Leicester. We were glad that our orders helped him to overcome some of his problems.

Alas, Walter Cooke needed much more fabric to fill his vats than we could give him. He did not like it that we continued to have some of our pieces, however few, dyed at Slough. There was spare room in his large van, and full loads saved money, but we felt that we were under a moral obligation to C & C Dyers and supported them for another eighteen months until, we reckoned, they had recovered the expenditure incurred in anticipation of our trade. For most small firms business meant battling for survival most of the time.

32

A BRITISH
PASSPORT
1934-36

I HAD ADMIRED ENGLAND from afar from the age of fifteen. Since then her way of life had become mine. She was now and would always be my spiritual home. There were two things I wanted above anything else: success for our Langley enterprise and, almost as a reward, British nationality. I did not expect citizenship as a gift; I was not a beggar. I would give Britain more than my loyalty, she would benefit from my knowledge, energy, hard work, export connections, and from any capital I could transfer from Czechoslovakia by legal or illegal means. She would be getting a bargain, if only I could make her see it. I would build the most modern textile factory in the United Kingdom and, by employing and training British labour, help to ease her unemployment problems in return for accepting me as one of her subjects, and for giving me the protection of a British passport.

But that was a dream the fulfilment of which lay in the dim and distant future. When I arrived in England on 26 December 1931 to look for a site for our projected factory the immigration officer at Harwich gave me 'leave to land on condition that I did not remain in the United Kingdom longer than three months', and stamped my Czechoslovak passport to that effect. To get the restriction removed I enlisted the help of the Board of Trade, as I have already related. Upon the intervention of Mr Watkinson the Home Office extended the period from three to twelve months. This, they said, was the best they could do. I had won my first battle, if not as decisively as I would have liked.

A year later I won the second when, backed by the Board of Trade and the Ministry of Labour, I pointed out that we had paid £5,000 for our factory site, that the factory building had cost £9,000, not counting the valuable machinery we had installed, and that we were employing fifty British workers. The Home Office relented and removed the time limit from my permit. I could stay in Britain as long as I liked. This made me feel a great deal happier, and I prepared for the next assault. In September 1934 I informed the Home Office that we were employing ninety hands, working three shifts, and manufacturing annually £30,000 worth of goods of a type hitherto imported from the Continent. I offered to spend several thousand pounds on a factory extension, which would employ additional labour, if they could promise to grant me a certificate of naturalisation at an early date. As a result of this letter the Home Office asked me to come for an interview.

Before an alien can apply for naturalisation he has to prove to the Secretary of State that he has resided in the United Kingdom for not less than five years out of the last eight. I asked the Home Office to stretch a point and let me include the twelve months I had lived at Hampstead in 1924-25, the twenty-eight business visits I had made to Britain since, and the time I had spent establishing my office in the City at the beginning of 1930. I would have stayed then, I explained, had it not been for Father's death and the need for me to return to Czechoslovakia. But I was told that none of this time counted as residence within the meaning of the Act, and that regulations were made to be strictly observed. The Home Office was prepared to accept the time from January 1932 onwards as residence, and would not look upon business journeys abroad as interruptions. All being well, I could apply for naturalisation in January 1937 and expect to get my certificate six or twelve months later. It seemed a very long time to wait.

And there was something else that worried me. Was it compatible with my claim to be resident in England that I lived half the time at the family home at Fleissen, directing the family firm? In order not to jeopardise my position with the Home Office I decided to go through the motions of emigrating from Czechoslovakia, but as unobtrusively as possible, for there might be repercussions from the Czech authorities. And the people of Fleissen, who still looked upon our English factory as little more than a young man's adventure, would think I had completely taken leave of my senses. It was better for them not to know just yet that I was signing off the Fleissen register. As a first step I shipped a wardrobe, a settee, a bookcase, a table, three chairs, two carpets and some bed linen to Langley, and asked the clerk at the mayor's office at Fleissen to confirm that they were my personal belongings and had been used. Such a certificate would save import duty, I explained, which was true, but I felt no need to tell him that it mattered to me even more to have the export of my furniture recorded at the mayor's office—for future reference.

A year later, after a few more interviews with the Home Office had made me feel a little more confident, I went to see the mayor's clerk again and asked him for a letter confirming the date of my emigration.

'Emigration?'

'You can't have forgotten. You gave me a certificate when I moved to England . . .'

He remembered the certificate very well, he said, but that was for furniture. He also knew that I travelled a great deal between Fleissen and England on business, but he did not realise that I had emigrated. The thought had never occurred to him, in fact—was I pulling his leg?

One did not take one's furniture on business journeys, I pointed out, but if he had omitted to enter my emigration in the appropriate book, a small oversight that could happen to anybody, why not make the entry now, under the date of the furniture shipment?

He apologised for the misunderstanding and gave me the confirmation. It was to become important evidence for the Czechoslovak authorities later, but the officials in London, for whose benefit I had gone to all the trouble, were not interested. All the same, the document stating that I had left Fleissen the previous year and was no longer resident there encouraged me to make yet another approach to the Home Office, and I sent the following carefully drafted letter.

Langley, 5 June 1935

Dear Mr McAlpine,

You were good enough to discuss the prospects of my naturalisation with me last autumn, and I have to thank you for recommending to the Secretary of State that January 1932 be considered the beginning of my permanent residence in this country.

Please do not think me a nuisance if, after careful consideration, I write to you again on this matter. The political outlook on the Continent, especially in the region of Central Europe where I come from, appears very much graver than when we last met, and anything may happen between now and January 1937 when I shall be able to make my application. Can nothing be done to shorten this period?

The factory at Langley, which belongs to myself and my two younger brothers, who also want to become naturalised in due course, operates successfully. We have in the past year produced and sold £38,000 worth of goods, completed a £3,000 extension to the building, and installed more machines. We have a good name with our customers and suppliers, pay cash for everything we buy, and hope to enlarge the enterprise to many times its present size.

We are also the sole partners in Adolf Pasold & Sohn of Czechoslovakia, an old established family firm owning a spinning mill, a knitwear factory and a dyehouse. In spite of the trade depression we employ 600 hands, operate partly in double shifts, pay cash for all our purchases, and make good profits. In addition to the factories we own 500 acres of freehold land, fifteen dwelling houses, and have money in the bank.

We could live comfortably in Czechoslovakia, but have always wanted to come to England. Sterling's departure from the gold standard, and the introduction of import duties, have opened the door for us. All being well, we intend to move our head office to England and turn the mills in Czechoslovakia into subsidiaries. However, in the face of the many restrictions and obstacles it would be neither possible nor prudent to carry out this ambitious programme until at least one of us is a British subject.

As things stand, another eighteen months must elapse before I can apply for naturalisation; meanwhile we have to mark time at Langley. It is a serious matter for a manufacturing enterprise at our present stage of development to have to go slow for a year and a half. It is also regrettable from the country's point of view when there are so many people out of work. Is there no way of speeding matters up?

Would it help if I offered to deposit a certain sum of money as a surety for my good behaviour? I have a number of friends in Britain, men of the highest integrity, who have known me for ten years, have been to the family home and factories in Czechoslovakia, and would guarantee for me in any way you might wish. In addition, I would gladly pay all expenses involved should you care to send someone to the Continent to verify my statements—or is there anything else I could do?

I apologise for troubling you. If this matter were not of such vital importance to me, and to our business, I should not have written to you again. Any information you may be able to give me, or suggestion you may care to make, will be most welcome.

Yours very sincerely
Eric W. Pasold

This epistle made the desired impression at Whitehall. Mr McAlpine asked for a detailed account of all the periods I had stayed in Britain since my very first visit. It was not difficult to compile, for the date of every entry and exit was stamped on one's passport in those days. And since the Home Office seemed to be in a receptive mood, I asked some of my English and Scottish friends to write supporting letters. To cut a long story short, after some more interviews the long-suffering officials gave way and clipped another year off my waiting time. If I submitted my application at the beginning of 1936 it would receive favourable consideration. Another battle had been won.

There followed the usual routine of newspaper advertisements, questioning of my sponsors by the police, and accidental delays, and on 23 June the Under-Secretary of State informed me that he was 'prepared to grant a Certificate of Naturalisation on submission of documentary evidence that, upon grant of British nationality', I should 'cease to possess Czechoslovak nationality'. It was the crowning victory of the campaign. As far as I was concerned the civil servants at Whitehall could now take a well earned rest while I dealt with the Czech authorities.

Witin a matter of hours I was on my way to Grosvenor Place to hand my application for release from Czechoslovak nationality to the consulate. In addition to the letter from the Under-Secretary of State it had to be accompanied by my birth certificate, two certificates of baptism, a certificate of Czechoslovak nationality, two statements confirming that I had the right to citizenship at Fleissen, a confirmation that I was not subject to military service, and confirmation from the police at Fleissen that I was of good character. Fortunately I had familiarised myself with the procedure beforehand, and secured all these documents well in advance. It had taken weeks of correspondence, but now the work was done. The consulate would send my papers to the district authorities at Eger, who would then, hey presto! issue my certificate of release—I thought. But perhaps it was best not to take chances, and so, a few days later, I saw Dr Freundlich, my lawyer at Eger, and asked him to make sure that the district authorities dealt with my application as speedily as possible. A most necessary precaution, as I was to discover. To begin with, Vysekal, the clerk at the consulate, went on holiday and did not dispatch my papers until after his return. Dr Freundlich did his best to keep track of the application as it was sent back and forth from the district authorities to the military, the gendarmerie, the income tax inspector, the police at Fleissen and the Ministry of Trade at Prague for comment. It was not surprising that some of the documents became detached and got lost, and I had to obtain duplicates. However, even this tribulation came to an end, and on 5 September I had my certificate of release.

From now on everything went smoothly. I gave up my Czechoslovak passport to the consulate and handed my certificate of release from Czechoslovak nationality to the Home Office. A month later, on 6 October 1936, I received my certificate of naturalisation. The following morning I swore the oath of allegiance, a singularly uninspiring ceremony, and in the afternoon collected my new navy blue British passport, in which Anthony Eden requested and required all those concerned to afford me every assistance and protection of which I might stand in need. An entry on the opposite page said I was British by naturalisation, a distinction presumably introduced by someone who had little else to be proud of other than his British birth. I failed to see its purpose in a passport, and, it would appear, Ernest Bevin shared my view, for these entries were omitted when he became Foreign Secretary.

One does not change one's nationality as one changes one's overcoat, and some of my friends must have been wondering how I felt, transferring my allegiance from one country to another. Had I still been Austrian I should have felt pangs of conscience, and perhaps could not have done it at all, but Austrian nationality had been taken away from me. Against my will I had become a Czechoslovak, the citizen of a Slav republic whose national language I did not speak. I loved Bohemia but felt no love or loyalty towards Czechoslovakia. To shake off a nationality that had been forced upon me felt like walking out of a cage into freedom.

And why was I in such a hurry to have a British passport when, by letting things take their normal course and waiting two years longer, I could have had one without all this effort? Trouble was brewing in Central Europe. I did not think there would be war, but felt that we were heading for a major confrontation between the German-speaking minority in Czechoslovakia and the government at Prague. Every stint at Fleissen increased my uneasiness. I saw little chance of a peaceful settlement, and did not want to get embroiled in the conflict. A British passport would, I thought, enable me to keep out of trouble. Time was running short, and I could not afford to wait.

I was overdue at Fleissen. The frontier guards, who knew me, of course, did not know what to make of my British passport, and I was amused when they saluted. Czech officials were always very courteous to holders of foreign passports, provided they were not German or Austrian. One had to be a foreigner from very far away to get the best treatment. But even as a foreigner one had problems. I was surprised when I was politely informed that, being an alien, I had to register. And should it be my intention to work I would need a labour permit. And on no account was I, a foreign resident, to transact any financial business on behalf of Adolf Pasold & Sohn unless I received special authorisation from the National Bank at Prague. At first I laughed. It seemed preposterous that I should have to apply for permission to sit at my own desk, and to draw cheques. But when I realised that the authorities were serious I asked Dr Spira, our financial and tax adviser, a very pleasant little man with good connections and a wit as sharp as a needle, to help me straighten matters out.

'You have been breaking the law ever since you shipped that furniture and moved your domicile to England three years ago,' he said after listening to my story. 'You have, as a non-resident, continued to transact business for Adolf Pasold & Sohn and operated the firm's accounts without a permit from the National Bank. The penalties for persistently contravening the financial regulations are severe. You are in worse trouble than you imagine. I had better go to Prague immediately to see what I can do.'

He was all smiles when he returned a week later. 'Everything is all right,' he reported. 'I have done a deal with my friends at the Bank. Your transgressions are forgiven on the understanding that you forego the right to remit your share of Adolf Pasold & Sohn's profits for the past three years to England.'

My face must have looked a question mark, for he proceeded to explain. 'As a non-resident you would be entitled to transfer your income abroad, after deduction of Czechoslovak taxes, of course, and this is exactly what we are going to do from now on—legally and with the full approval of the authorities!'

Transfer a third of Adolf Pasold & Sohn's profits to Langley with the approval of the Czechoslovak authorities? I thought I had not heard aright, and asked him to repeat it. 'Two thirds,' Dr Spira corrected, 'for in another year your brother Rolf will be entitled to transfer his third also.'

If Dr Spira's information was correct, and he assured me it was, then Langley would no longer be short of capital. Was I dreaming? Could one really beat the currency restrictions simply by sending some furniture out of the country and claiming to be domiciled abroad? And why did I not know about these regulations? Once again I blamed myself for spending too much of my time on detail in the factories and neglecting contact with the mighty and the knowledgeable, the officials in the Ministries, politicians, bankers and businessmen in Prague. Had we, through my ignorance, lost three years' profit transfers?

Dr Spira chuckled. 'Only in theory. It is your passport that impresses the officials. Without it you would have achieved very little. And you have only just acquired it.'

That passport changed my life in many ways. There was, for instance, no need to be afraid of Czech policemen any more. On the contrary, all of a sudden they became so obliging. The officials at the district authority at Eger, not normally known for their tact, were much nicer and more helpful than before. I was never kept waiting and was always offered the most comfortable chair. They spoke German and sometimes even tried to speak English to me. On one occasion, when driving to Pilsen to call on customers, I was twice stopped by gendarmes who were looking for Nazi agents. While drivers and passengers of other cars were searched, presumably for propaganda material, the sight of my blue passport sufficed each time to produce polite apologies and smart salutes, and I was waved on. No wonder visiting foreigners were enchanted with Dr Beneš's model democracy. Even to me the forests looked greener, the towns friendlier, and the statues of St Wenceslas more benign with a British passport in my pocket.

One of the grievances of the German-speaking minority in the Sudeten areas was the poor state of the roads. Only the few main roads leading from the frontier to the international spas, such as Karlsbad and Marienbad, and to the capital—roads used by foreign visitors—were in good condition. Most of the secondary ones, no matter how important to local traffic, were deplorable, and it was generally assumed that the taxes collected in the comparatively wealthy, industrialised, German-speaking border regions were used to maintain the roads in the poorer, Czech-speaking interior of the republic. I cannot say how true this was—these things are never as simple as they may appear on the surface—but the people in the Sudeten areas believed it, and it added to their dissatisfaction.

The road between Fleissen and Eger was too bad for our English car, the Alvis Speed Twenty, and I preferred to make the detour through Germany.

Crossing the frontier at Fleissen, first the Czechoslovak and then the German guards stamped my passport. Leaving Germany again fifteen minutes later at Schönberg, the German and then the Czech guards did the same. On my return, maybe two hours later, the procedure was repeated in reverse. Eight stamps for one visit to Eger! At this rate I would need a new passport every few weeks! Before I became a British subject I used a *Grenzausweis* for such journeys, a short-distance travel document issued by the mayor of Fleissen. Could I not have one again?

'Highly irregular,' said the mayor, an old friend of our family. 'I can issue these documents only to residents of Fleissen. But as far as I am concerned you live here, and provided you are not afraid of getting into trouble with the Nazis on the other side I'll give you one.' Henceforth I did these short trips with a *Grenzausweis* and saved my passport for more important occasions.

I did not find it difficult to keep out of politics. My friends in Czechoslovakia understood that, having become a British subject, a fact of which they neither approved nor disapproved, I meant to remain neutral. It did not prevent them from discussing politics with me, and from airing their dissatisfaction with the Czechs on the one side and the Nazis on the other. I knew exactly what they thought and how they felt, and intend to portray the situation as accurately as I can, without attempting to write the history of those fateful years, a task I would not be qualified to attempt. The incidents and conditions I describe I experienced personally. They provided some of the background to our business activities, and influenced our decisions. This is why they belong in this book.

Here is a thumbnail sketch of the general situation. In 1918, when the Austro-Hungarian Monarchy was broken up, ten million Czechs forced a disarmed minority of three million German-speaking Bohemians at bayonet point to become second-class Czechoslovak citizens. This was done in blatant violation of President Wilson's promise of every nation's sacred right to self-determination, but their appeals to the world went unheeded. Being peace-loving people, they knuckled under and for fifteen years bided their time. Then came Hitler. They had no liking for him and his Nazis, but if they could use him as bogy-man to frighten the Czechs perhaps their demands for equality would be met. But Prague was in no mood to negotiate, and answered with restrictions, censorship and prison sentences, which increased the antagonism without achieving anything. This, roughly, was how I saw the situation in the early 1930s, when, with goodwill on both sides, there might still have been time for a peaceful settlement. To convey the atmosphere I quote from the letters I wrote to Rolf in May and early June 1933:

The Czechoslovak authorities are looking for Nazi correspondence. Mail is frequently opened, so don't be surprised if some of the letters you get from us are stuck up with tape.

Was at Asch yesterday. Great excitement everywhere—crowds in the streets, gendarmes with bayonets fixed to their rifles storming into houses, dragging people out as they found them, hatless and in shirtsleeves, bundling them into three large buses and taking them to the jail at Pilsen. Understand that eighty were arrested, mainly young people, with girls among them, and although no one knows for sure it is thought that they are suspected of Nazi sympathies. Some sixty gendarmes were engaged in the manhunt. How peaceful life was in the old days!

It was the custom of many of the inhabitants of Asch to play cards and drink beer at an inn on the Bavarian side of the border, a walk of about twenty minutes. The Czechoslovak authorities had nothing against their subjects drinking beer in Germany, but to listen to German radio broadcasts, even music, was prohibited, and as the inn had a radio set for the entertainment of its guests, those from Asch were, strictly speaking, breaking the law if they listened to it. A few days before these mass arrests Hitler made a political speech which was, of course, broadcast by every German station. As transpired afterwards, a Czech secret service agent who had been at the inn arranged with the border guards to keep a record of all the people who crossed into Bavaria that evening. It was assumed that on this occasion their object had not been to drink beer but to listen to Hitler, and to teach them a lesson they had to spend a few weeks in Pilsen jail.

15 May 1933. Trouble at Eger too. Am told between thirty and fifty people have been arrested, because they visited Germany on 1 May, which was forbidden.

17 May 1933. Figures of arrests at Eger were exaggerated. Only the mayor and a few others are in prison.

14 June 1933. It appears that the censor disliked something Korn said in one of his letters, for two gendarmes were sent to fetch him, but while they were at his front door he escaped through a back window.

Shortly afterwards I changed places with Rolf, who took over from me at Fleissen. His letters were less chatty. In view of the risk of mail being opened it was safer to stick to business matters. Besides, one got tired of hearing about these childish persecutions, often intentionally provoked by youthful pranks, and escalating into bitterness on both sides. Only if something amusing happened—such as the arrest of the Bavarian who, losing his hat in a gust of wind, raised his arms and called 'Mei Hütle', which a Czech gendarme heard as 'Heil Hitler'—or if someone was involved whom we knew personally did we bother to tell each other.

1 February 1934. If you want to tell me something the Czechoslovak authorities might not like I suggest you write to Uncle Richard at Brambach and, at the same time, send me a postcard to Fleissen saying, 'Greetings to Richard.' I will then go to Brambach and collect the letter.

20 March 1934. Freddy Müller, the son of our neighbour, has been arrested at the border on his return from Munich University and is in jail. His mother does not know why, but it is rumoured that the Czech frontier guards found German newspapers and a swastika in his luggage.

Ruthless Czech censorship and prohibitions could not prevent the Sudeten Germans, as they were now generally called, from following events on the other side of the frontier and forming their own opinion. They witnessed the liquidation of all political parties with the exception of Hitler's NSDAP. They observed the persecution of the Jews. They were amazed at the scope of the new laws and regulations that came into force, marvelled at the way the unemployed were put to work building a vast network of motorways, bridges, dams, stadiums and other monumental structures, and noted the reintroduction of military service. They condemned most of what they saw. Some of the measures seemed wicked to them, others just stupid, but the phenomenal road building programme they admired. It was this mixture of diabolical and creative genius in Hitler which was so confusing. In the early days even some of my Jewish acquaintances in Czechoslovakia thought that, in the long run, good would triumph over evil.

Not so my German uncle, Richard Stübiger, and his family at Brambach, who were irreconcilably opposed to the Nazis from the start and never wavered in their condemnation of the arch-demon and his henchmen. If I lived in Germany, they said, and had to put up with all the ignominies and ideological nonsense, my blood would boil too. Fortunately I was only a spectator, but although I travelled backwards and forwards across Germany so often, and Fleissen was so near the border, I found it impossible to decide whether I was watching a great drama or a comic opera. Was one to take the display of uniforms, jackboots and swastikas altogether seriously? Hitler made brave speeches, but they could not hide Germany's precarious economic situation. The Reich had run out of foreign exchange, and with barriers against her exports being erected everywhere in retaliation for her menacing political behaviour she had to go without imports of almost everything except the most vital raw materials. Like many other countries Czechoslovakia also had to tighten her belt in consequence of the world-wide depression, but in comparison with Germany she was in a very comfortable position.

26 March 1934. Last Saturday Germany stopped all imports of textile raw materials such as cotton, wool and flax because she can no longer pay for them. The raw

material stocks in the country have been placed under government control. However, Leibitschgrund will still get supplies of raw cotton from Bremen, since we pay for them in dollars and sterling.

29 June 1934. The Germans have no foreign currency, and cannot travel abroad. The hotels at Karlsbad, Marienbad and Franzensbad are empty, but Brambach, Elster and presumably also all the other watering places in Germany are full.

17 July 1934. Cousin Herbert would like to spend his holidays with us, but Hitler is at loggerheads with Austria and won't let German nationals go there, so I am afraid poor Herbert will have to stay behind.

19 July 1934. Germany has no rubber, and Herbert cannot get a permit to buy tyres for his car.

30 August 1934. Stübiger's at Brambach are so short of cotton cloth and other raw materials that they can work only four days a week. People in Czechoslovakia, even the minorities, ought to be grateful for being so much better off.

30 August 1934. The Czechoslovak post office has thought up a new piece of chicanery. From now on telegrams addressed in any language other than Czech will not be delivered. Please be sure to write 'Adolf Pasold a Syn, Plesna' in future, instead of 'Adolf Pasold & Sohn, Fleissen', as appears on our letterheads.

Entering the garage at Fleissen one day, I overheard Wollner, our chauffeur, rehearsing a speech while he polished the Cadillac. I asked him whom he was addressing, and he replied, 'Mr Eric, I like my job, but there is not much scope for advancement. Would you be cross with me if I tried to better myself by becoming a politician?'

'Of course not,' I laughed. 'Try your luck, and you can always come back if you want to.'

He was a good employee, and I was sorry to lose him. After leaving us he spoke at small political meetings. It did not seem to take him long to pick up the right phraseology and the slogans one could use without risking arrest. A tall, broad-shouldered young man of pleasing personality, he caught the attention of Konrad Henlein, the ex-gymnastics master of Asch, head of the newly formed Sudeten German party, and became one of his lieutenants. I did not hear from him for a year, then in March 1935 he called, told me how much he liked his new career, and bought our eight-year-old Cadillac for Henlein for the sum of 17,000 kronen, a fair price. It was the last time I saw him, but I heard about him from Rolf, who was at Fleissen during the parliamentary election two months later.

14 May 1935. Electioneering is in full swing, leaflets everywhere, I wish the whole nonsense were over. Understand Wollner is rushing from place to place making several speeches a day. Have not heard him but am told he is speaking very well.

18 May 1937. Wollner addressed mass meeting at Fleissen on Sunday. Understand he attacked Lehrmann's, and especially Kraut. The crowd roared with delight.

20 May 1935. Believe yesterday's election resulted in overwhelming victory for Henlein, who united 75 per cent of the votes of the German-speaking minority in his party, the SdP for short, while socialists, Church party and farmers are said to have been cut down to a third of their former size, but accurate figures are not yet available. There has been an attempt on Henlein's life. Happened to be at Asch today, and by chance saw his shot-up car, our old Cadillac. The windscreen is shattered and there are bullet holes in the side.

23 May 1935. SdP polled 1¼ million votes and is now—incredible as it may seem—the strongest political party in the Czechoslovak Republic. Wollner will now become a member of parliament.

Henlein had succeeded in uniting most of the German-speaking inhabitants of Czechoslovakia, and Wollner, a decent fellow at heart who meant no harm to anyone, began to climb the slippery ladder of a political career.

Although anxious to keep out of Czechoslovak politics, I felt pleased with the result of the election. The Sudetenlanders, who for so long had been treated as second-class citizens, now had a chance of becoming equal partners in the State. Perhaps Masaryk and Beneš would now make an honest effort to reshape their republic after the model of Switzerland, the vision of seventeen years ago which had remained a mirage. But it had taken 700 years to build Switzerland! And would Henlein's demands remain reasonable? Would he be willing to forgive and forget past injustices or, prompted by Hitler perhaps, ask for the impossible?

If my correspondence with Rolf is anything to go by, no spectacular changes followed the election. Politics are hardly mentioned in our letters. Presumably the SdP had to digest its victory, and Henlein, who said he wanted to achieve his objectives by parliamentary means and 'within the scope of the Czechoslovak constitution', concentrated on improving his party organisation. Prague should have used this breathing space, it seemed to me, to offer the German-, Slovak-, Hungarian- and Polish-speaking minorities a new deal, a republic shared on equal terms by all, irrespective of tongue. But the Czechs, led by Beneš, thought otherwise. Stubbornly they closed their ranks and, relying on the support of their French and Russian allies, prepared for a trial of strength. I could hear the time bomb ticking.

Uncle Wilhelm emerged from the landslide victory of the SdP as a member of the Czechoslovak senate. More amused than impressed, I wondered what had made him accept the candidature. His well known anti-government attitude had obviously been mistaken for pro-Henlein enthusiasm. I knew better, and predicted that he would soon be more of an embarrassment than a support to the party. A very kind godfather to me, he was really a most difficult old bachelor who never ceased to criticise authority and its institutions in general, irrespective of colour or creed. He spent a great deal of his time arguing in the courts, an expensive hobby, for his arguments were based on justice as he saw it rather than on the law. He therefore lost most of his cases, invariably appealed, and having lost the appeal proceeded to sue the judge, much to the amusement of his friends and relations.

As a senator he scored one success. Most of the roads in the Sudetenland were grossly neglected by the government. When, after a heavy downpour of rain, Uncle Wilhelm photographed the puddles in the road leading from Fleissen to Eger and a Czech gendarme tried to confiscate the camera he created such a rumpus that Prague actually had the road surfaced.

In October Mussolini invaded Abyssinia, ignoring the sanctions imposed against Italy by the League of Nations. In the following spring German troops occupied the demilitarised zone of the Rhineland, Austria reintroduced compulsory military service, and in July Czechoslovakia prepared to put her economy on a war footing.

11 July 1936. Our factories at Fleissen and Leibitschgrund have been designated essential industrial enterprises in the event of war. Came into force yesterday. Goodness knows what additional regulations and restrictions this will involve us in. I am posting a copy of the *Prager Tagblatt* to you so that you can read about the new measures.

3 September 1936. It is becoming more difficult than ever to get allocations of foreign exchange. We shall soon be told to buy our raw cotton in Russia.

Instead of removing causes of unnecessary friction the Czech officials thought up new ones. There was, for instance, the trouble with the primary glider some adventurous youngsters built of plywood and canvas. They practised with it on the Steinberg, a 100 ft-high hill near Fleissen, from the top of which they could, with luck, when the wind blew from the south-west, glide a distance of 200 yards. A great deal of enthusiasm and midnight oil had gone into building the contraption, and they loved and nursed it like a baby, but when the authorities got to hear of their activities two gendarmes armed with rifles and bayonets questioned every club member in turn, and further gliding was prohibited on the grounds that no one in the border regions (read Sudeten areas) was allowed to own or operate a flying machine.

Civil war broke out in Spain, Germany introduced two years' compulsory military service, Goebbels accused Czechoslovakia of being an aircraft carrier for Soviet Russia, Mussolini proclaimed the Rome–Berlin axis, and Henlein got no nearer to solving his differences with Prague. Had he a clear idea of what he wanted, I wondered? If I judged the temper of the rank and file of his party correctly they liked to think of Hitler as their powerful protector across the border, but they wanted him to stay there. The Sudeten region was theirs, to be ruled by themselves. They wanted neither Czech officials nor Hitler to administer it for them and thought that every concession they could extract from the government would bring the realisation of this vague dream a step nearer. Meanwhile Prague built fortifications—a veritable Maginot Line of bunkers, it was said—to defend the republic's frontiers against a German invasion. What a waste of time and money it seemed. There would be no war: Czechoslovakia would not fight, I felt sure of that. How could she, with a third of her soldiers recruited from embittered, if not openly hostile, minorities? Surely she had not forgotten how whole regiments of Czechs had deserted from the Austro-Hungarian army to the Russians in the 1914–18 war! Why should Sudeten Germans and Hungarians in Czech uniform prove less effective saboteurs of Czechoslovakia's war machine? And who was Prague trying to fool when it boasted of the 'impenetrable wall of steel and concrete' surrounding the republic? One look at the map and the thousands-of-miles-long frontier made nonsense of such talk. I never saw one of those fortifications, or knew where they were, except for three concrete blocks between Fleissen and Brambach, about which I wrote to Rolf:

A Czech government contractor, guarded by gendarmes, has built large concrete blocks on the road to Brambach, to prevent cars from speeding across the frontier. Understand such blocks are being built all round the republic. Look like this sketch.

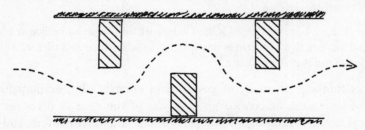

If the border regions were being fortified, measures were taken in the interior of the country to protect the population against air attacks.

Friend Thieme called. Says the frequent air raid precaution exercises at Kutna Hora are getting him down. Three powerful sirens howl several times every day and night, within a given time all lights have to be extinguished, and people are not allowed in the street until the 'all clear' has sounded. He did not get under cover fast enough during a mock attack on the town square, and caught a dose of tear gas.

The bourgeois politicians at Prague whose intrigue and subversion had proved so successful in undermining the foundations of the Austro-Hungarian Monarchy were now shown to be little men, incapable of taking the big decisions demanded of them in the hour of adversity. They let the precious months slip by, and it was not until February 1937 that they could bring themselves to offer their dissatisfied minorities 'equal opportunity in the public service and equal unemployment benefit' to that enjoyed by the Czechs. But it was no longer enough. Henlein now wanted more. And the growing hostility shown by the German-speaking population to the Czech officials and security forces stationed in the Sudeten areas, many miles from the nearest Czech-speaking village, began to tell. Perhaps it was not surprising that some of them occasionally lost their nerve under the strain and committed acts of folly which made even the most moderate among the natives turn against them.

27 February 1937. Helmut Amarotico's sister Annerl kept on bread and water for three days in the jail at Wildstein. She was supposed to have used an expression offensive to the Czech nation. There were no witnesses, and Annerl says it is a case of slander. A prison sentence of five months was mentioned when the gendarmes brought her before the court, and it is only because she is an Italian subject and her father went to the consulate that she was let out after three days. The court now explains that the gendarmes made a mistake, but she has no redress because they made her sign a paper confirming that she was satisfied and would bring no action against the authorities.

9 June 1937. Air raid precaution arrangements are now all complete and approved. Adolf Geipel, the manager of the packing department, is chief warden. Has just left for Eger to attend a lecture.

Please send me a large picture of King George VI for the private office at Fleissen, to remind visitors that our firm is now partly British-owned and that we enjoy the protection of the British consulate.

I was thinking primarily of government officials who, accompanied by teams of assistants, descended upon us out of the blue to investigate tax, currency, health insurance, air raid precautions and other matters, and could make life hell for weeks. The psychological effect of the King looking on would, I knew, make them behave with circumspection. Czechoslovakia was anxious to preserve its democratic image abroad and avoid adverse press comment, especially in the West. To a lesser extent I also thought of Henlein's SdP, which was beginning to throw its weight about. Aping the NSDAP, it put its functionaries into semi-military uniform, and I well remember one of the more simple-minded young men of Fleissen in this rig-out demanding that we stop doing business with Jewish firms. I laughed. Did he realise that 90 per cent of our customers were Jews? Was he advocating that we shut the factory? And would the SdP be responsible for feeding the unemployed workers? We were never again bothered with such a request.

Henlein had no need to use the Jews as scapegoats. Czech officials and gendarmes served the purpose much better. The background of the Jews in
Czechoslovakia, and their sympathies, were more Austro-German than
Slav. Many of them, I felt, would have sided with Henlein had it not been for
his unholy alliance with Hitler.

A gendarme came to the office at Fleissen looking for Rolf. He had failed
to appear before the military medical board, a very serious offence. I explained that Rolf was at Langley. After three successive examinations at the
Czechoslovak consulate in London he had been finally declared unfit for
military service. Something must have gone wrong with the transmission of
this information from London to Eger. The gendarme seemed satisfied; the
consulate would no doubt confirm my statement. I thought the matter was
closed, when, two months later, another gendarme came to ask for Rolf. He
seemed surprised that my brother, a Czechoslovak subject, should be at the
factory in England while I, the holder of a British passport, directed the
factory at Fleissen. I agreed with him—business was full of surprises—and
then wrote to Rolf telling him to stay in England. He had complied with the
regulations, was not subject to military service, and had nothing to fear, but
it was best to let the Czechoslovak authorities get their records straight before
he returned.

We were waiting for Rolf's naturalisation to come through. Would the
War Ministry in Prague give its consent to his release from Czechoslovak
nationality if the military thought they still had a claim on him? Our fears
were unfounded; the missing medical records turned up. His naturalisation
papers came through in record time, and in September 1937 he had his passport. After an absence of more than a year he looked forward to a stint at
Fleissen, but immediately on taking over from me he became involved in a
row with the tax authorities. For seven weeks a three-man *Kommission* sat
in our office investigating the books, and ended up by demanding a large
additional tax payment which Rolf would not concede. Fortified by his brand-
new passport, he refused to do a deal, and in the end the *Kommission* departed with a token payment of 6,000 kronen, complimenting Adolf Pasold &
Sohn on the accuracy of their accounts.

Unlike Rolf and myself, Ingo had no great ambition to become British.
He did not care what kind of passport he held as long as it enabled him to
travel. He wanted snow for skiing, a lake to swim in and a workshop to make
things. Business never seemed to trouble him as it did us, although he conscientiously did his duty wherever we put him, and very much enjoyed being
boss whenever we were away. Mother, worried that Rolf and I were working
too hard, was glad that her youngest 'was more sensible, enjoyed life, and did
his job without wearing himself out'.

With two of its three partners British, the firm of Adolf Pasold & Sohn had acquired a special status, to which our continual journeying, and the fact that at least one of us was always in England, added mystique. We had influential connections in London, it was whispered—a misconception we neither corrected nor confirmed. Prague, no doubt, had extensive dossiers about us and made its own assessment. Visits to government departments, dreaded not so long ago and only too often a waste of time, now proved pleasant and constructive. The change of atmosphere at the Ministries transformed Prague for me. Quite suddenly it became such a beautiful city, and for the first time in my life I felt at home in it. Hradčin Castle, Wenceslas Square and the Charles Bridge belonged to me. The whole of Bohemia, with the Czech-speaking villages in the fertile, rolling interior, the silent forests, the gushing hot springs at Karlsbad, and the tall factory chimneys of the German-speaking border regions—all mine! I had never felt like this when I was still a Czechoslovak subject. New horizons opened up, and at times I almost regretted that it was Langley rather than Fleissen and Leibitschgrund we had decided to develop. But how long would this euphoria last? History was in the melting pot. The Central Europe I knew was creaking at its joints; something was bound to give, and the chances of a happy ending seemed remote.

33

A MOMENTOUS
DECISION
1936-38

I WAS TOO occupied with our own plans and problems to follow political developments in Czechoslovakia very closely, but shuttling between Langley and Fleissen and talking to friends in England, engineering firms in Germany, government departments at Prague, our bankers at Asch, and Czech and Jewish customers in various parts of Bohemia made me see the overall picture from many different angles. Since Henlein's spectacular election victory the Sudeten Germans held their heads higher and went about their business with greater self-assurance. Decent, hard-working people, they disliked the Nazis and their screaming Führer, whose support they needed in their struggle for equal rights with the Czechs. Given this equality, they wanted the Sudeten area to remain part of Czechoslovakia, and would have rejected any suggestion of its incorporation in the Reich. In 1937 no one seriously envisaged such a possibility. Had Beneš been the far-sighted statesman he was reputed to be, instead of the scheming politician he really was, he would have set about removing eighteen-year-old injustices, remodelled his republic, and welcomed its minorities as equal partners. But instead of going to the root of the trouble he busied himself placating the British—many of whom felt unhappy about conditions in the Sudeten area—reinforcing the alliance with the French, whom he misled about Czechoslovakia's military strength, making a pact with the Russians, who liked the idea of a potential foothold in the very heart of Europe, and generally playing into Hitler's hands. Out of what was originally a local grievance grew an explosive situation of international dimensions which the great powers manoeuvred to resolve in accordance with their own strategic interests rather than in the interests of the people of Czechoslovakia. How could anyone foretell what the outcome would be?

It was against this background that I asked Uncle Gustav in February 1937 whether he would like to buy a third share of Adolf Pasold & Sohn. Uncle Gustav was a partner in the wealthy firm of Joh. Ad. Geipel Sohn, leather manufacturers at Fleissen and landowners in the Egerland. Under the Geipel partnership agreement only the elder of his two sons could succeed him in the firm. Udo, the younger, was to become a knitter and was therefore sent to the textile college at Asch, where he completed his studies with honours. The offer of a partnership in our business was something neither he nor his father had expected, a golden opportunity not likely to occur again. There was not another textile concern in the country that would have suited them as well as ours. And I, on the other hand, knew of no one else who would have been as acceptable to us as a partner. We would hardly have contemplated taking an outsider into the old established family firm. But Udo was our cousin, a member of the family, and an intelligent, hardworking young man of twenty-two, the same age as Rolf. I felt sure that Father and Grandfather would have approved of him.

For a moment my casual-sounding question almost unbalanced Uncle Gustav. His eyes lit up. 'Are you serious?' he demanded. Then his face became inscrutable and he looked into the distance. Did Mother, Rolf and Ingo know about my suggestion? We had discussed it in principle, I replied, and they would like to know what he thought of the idea. But he was not to be drawn. He would sleep on it for a while, he said, and then we could talk again.

Rolf and I also needed time to think. The worsening political situation in Central Europe was not the only reason that made us want to sell part of our Czechoslovak enterprise. It had been my intention from the start to move the centre of gravity of our business, stage by stage, from Fleissen to England. The time had arrived when we no longer just hoped but knew that Langley had a future. We wanted more money for the speedier expansion of the factory there, without wishing to denude Fleissen of working capital, and Uncle Gustav was in a position to provide it. And there was our sister Silvia, whose inheritance was still in the firm. She did not want to be paid out but asked for participation instead. A new partnership agreement would therefore have to be worked out in any case. And last but not least, if we strengthened the management of Fleissen and Leibitschgrund by making Udo a partner, Rolf and I could devote more time to our business in England.

Mother had great confidence in her brother Gustav. Any arrangement we made with him would be all right, and Udo was a nice boy. We should not have to work quite so hard if he came to help us, and it was high time we had someone in the firm who could speak Czech. She could not judge, but felt sure he had a good working knowledge of the language. How else could he have become an officer in the Czech army—the crack 28th Regiment, at that!

It was a less important point, perhaps, but Mother was right. With the exception of one clerk in the office, Adolf Pasold & Sohn had no one who could speak Czech. The fact that hardly anybody at Fleissen, except the frontier guards and gendarmes, understood it either was a poor excuse. Unfortunately Ingo, who had spent a year in the Czech-speaking parts of the republic for the purpose of learning the language, proved a poor linguist. This had not mattered so much a few years earlier, when language was primarily a means of communication, for all our customers understood German, but the growing political tension had meanwhile made tongue the mark of identification between the opposing camps. Many of our Czech clients now refused to correspond in or speak German. If a firm of our importance was ignorant of the national language, they argued, it could be taken as provocation. There was, of course, force in their argument.

Uncle Gustav knew how to play his cards. We heard nothing from him for six weeks, then came a telephone call from my friend Ernst Friedrich, who had succeeded Mr Huder as *Direktor* of the Bohemian Union Bank at Asch. I detected a note of disapproval in his voice. 'Your uncle has asked some searching questions about Adolf Pasold & Sohn. He tells me you have offered him a partnership and he is wondering what he should do. Are you wise to contemplate such a far-reaching step? I fear there may come a time when you would regret it if the proud old family concern were no longer all your own.'

I had doubts myself, and my conscience troubled me when I lay awake at nights, thinking about selling part of my and my brothers' birthright, but with the dawn returned the conviction that we ought to reduce our holding in Czechoslovakia if we could agree satisfactory terms. When it came to money the Geipels were as hard as nails, and Uncle Gustav was no exception. He would pay a fair price, I felt sure, but not a krone more. What was our business worth? We looked at balance sheets, book values, stock records and hidden reserves, added debtors, subtracted creditors, and with Ernst Friedrich's help put some figures on paper. The assets, ignoring goodwill, added up to a very conservative 15 million kronen.

The talks with Uncle Gustav which followed, and for which these figures provided the basis, were on the understanding that any preliminary agreement reached between us would be subject on the one hand to the approval of Rolf, Ingo and Mother, who were all in England at the time, and on the other to that of Udo, who was serving with the army and would not return until September. Uncle Gustav was therefore in no hurry. He did not want to drive a hard bargain, he said, and was willing to pay the market price for land, bricks and mortar, plant and machinery, stocks of raw materials, finished goods and credit balances, but he would pay nothing for such intangibles as our trained labour force, the thousand-odd customers who regularly bought our products, our export connections, our manufacturing know-how or even for our now famous 'White Bear' trade mark, on which we had expended so much thought and money. Their value was hard to assess and, anyway, they were all part and parcel of the firm, he maintained. He had in mind to buy a third share of Adolf Pasold & Sohn for 4 million kronen, he said, and then played his trump card: part of the purchase price would consist of 200,000 Swiss francs, the equivalent of almost $1\frac{1}{4}$ million kronen, or £10,000, which were freely transferable to London.

A shrewder negotiator would have asked for 6 million kronen and, after some months of take-it-or-leave-it, accepted half a million less. But I had a premonition that the uneasy political stalemate would not last, and that time was not on our side. I could think of no other potential buyer should the deal with Uncle Gustav fall through, and I therefore tried to meet him. Excluding an old factory building which was let, the farm at Fleissen, some 500 acres of forest at Leibitschgrund, two motor cars and various smaller items from the assets of the firm, we reduced the sum involved to $4\frac{3}{4}$ million kronen. But Uncle Gustav stalled. He would not pay more than $4\frac{1}{4}$ million and, in any case, wanted to defer his decision until Udo returned from the army. Meanwhile, if Langley liked to have a loan of £10,000, he would transfer his Swiss funds to London and we could make use of them at an interest rate of $1\frac{1}{2}$ per cent per annum.

A bird in the hand is worth two in the bush, I thought, intending to accept his offer. Between Mother, Rolf, Ingo and myself we could deposit a maximum amount of £2,000 in Post Office savings accounts, which paid 2 per cent interest, and for the balance I would try to find other attractive investment opportunities. But Rolf raised difficulties. He did not want to borrow money, and was reluctant to get financially involved with Uncle Gustav before the deal was finalised. So we adopted the middle course and took only £5,000, half the sum offered.

That £10,000 was the most coveted part of the purchase consideration. It was to change hands 'unofficially', whereas the major, the official part of the purchase price would have to be paid in Czech kronen into a blocked account in Czechoslovakia from which only the interest income, a very low percentage in those days, could be transferred to England. It was a most unsatisfactory state of affairs, but such was the law, and we could only hope that in the course of time we would find a way of transferring the capital, or at least some of it. These things had to be done in stages. I would have to put my thinking cap on.

The man who helped me think was Walter Spira, our tax and financial adviser in Prague, with whom I discussed the proposed operation and partnership changes. Transactions of this kind were his speciality. He had started his career as a tax inspector under Austro-Hungarian rule. Being equally fluent in Czech and German, he was taken over by the Czechoslovak civil service in 1918, and had recently retired to establish his own practice as a consultant. 'Let's worry about transfer problems when the money is safely in the bank,' he counselled, 'and first examine the stamp duty and other revenue angles, otherwise the tax men will collect far more than they are entitled to.' Memories of the exaggerated stamp duty demands after the purchase of Leibitschgrund sent shivers down my spine, but Spira reassured me. Getting the better of his former colleagues in the revenue department, with whom he was still on friendly terms, was a challenge he enjoyed. He felt at home in the tax and excise jungle, and knew how to avoid the pitfalls. One of them was called *Gebührenequivalent*, but there were also formulae, such as *Aufsandungsurkunde*, if I remember correctly, which afforded protection, and he knew how to apply them.

He was a most likeable little man in his late fifties who lived in a very different world from mine, and we had some interesting talks. He had no doubt about the republic's impregnability, and the soundness of its economic, financial and political policies. The army was strong, the currency stable, and the minorities would get their rights. He thought I was too impatient, a failing of youth which time would cure. The deal with Uncle Gustav was not concluded yet. Perhaps Spira was right to tackle first things first, but did he fully appreciate that kronen in a blocked account in Prague would not be of much use to us? We needed freely disposable currency. While he scrutinised our books and balance sheets, made calculations and wrote memoranda, I wondered how frozen kronen could be transformed into liquid sterling.

'Exports' was the word to conjure with. Adolf Pasold & Sohn had an excellent record in this respect, and the fact that we had established a successful manufacturing concern in Britain, where so many others had failed, gave me some personal standing, which I did my best to exploit. The export promotion scheme I submitted to the Ministry of Trade did not ask for subsidies but for the free disposal by the exporter of 10 per cent of the foreign currency he earned for the State. After some favourable comment by the Ministry, and the National Bank, it was shelved for future reference but never adopted. I had to try and think of something else.

Czechoslovakia's well trodden markets in Britain, Holland and Scandinavia offered little scope for private currency deals. I decided to look for opportunities farther afield, and applied to the National Bank for a £500 travel allowance for the purpose of exploring the Middle East. The chamber of commerce at Eger and the British embassy in Prague supported my application, and it was granted in full. I worked hard in the stifling heat of Egypt and Palestine, plagued by flies during the day and kept awake at night by mosquitoes and the strong coffee my Arab business friends made me drink, booking a number of useful orders, but the large-scale transfer opportunities

I had vaguely hoped for did not present themselves. Apart from the connections I made, and the export business I secured, I finished with a balance of £250 which I had saved by economising and which I remitted from Cairo to London at the end of my journey. Pleased though I felt, considering the sums to be moved it was no more than a drop on a hot stone.

Although Rolf agreed completely with my efforts to reorganise the family firm and to transfer assets from Fleissen to Langley, he refused to waste time, as he called it, on discussing long-term plans. I enjoyed making plans, and talking about them helped me clear my mind. Why didn't he feel the need to do the same? But whenever I tried to 'look ahead' he walked away for fear of committing himself by listening. Programmes which might have to be amended or abandoned later did not interest him and he did not want to become involved. I could always rely on his loyal support when action was called for, but he was not going to commit himself to anything in advance.

Willie was different. He liked to converse about the future. I could talk to him for hours, sharpening my wits on his in discussions ranging from the tangible to the abstract. In addition to his intellect, wide interests and refreshing sense of humour he had imagination, and many a useful idea sprang from the flights of fancy we took together. A born optimist, he did not share my apprehension about the political outlook. Czech- and German-speaking Bohemians had lived and worked together for 500 years and jointly made their country the richest in Central Europe. They depended on each other, even if they quarrelled from time to time. By all accounts Henlein seemed a reasonable man; the minorities would get local autonomy, and everyone would be happy. The window of Willie's study looked out over the picturesque valley of the Leibitsch, bounded on both sides by steep slopes covered with pine forest. In the meadow by the stream my four-year-old-niece Edith was picking flowers. Lower down stood the proud buildings of the mill in which thousands of humming spindles spun yarn for Fleissen and Langley. It was a picture of peace and tranquillity. 'You should come to Leibitschgrund more often to relax,' Willie smiled.

To begin with, Willie and Silvia had reservations about Udo joining the firm. They knew that the ways of the Geipels were very different from ours, and were afraid that the happy family atmosphere would suffer. It was Mother, if I remember correctly, who dispelled their fears. The financial arrangements with them caused no problem. Father's testament provided that a quarter of his estate should go to Silvia, and that we, the three brothers, were to pay her out. She preferred, however, to leave her money in the firm, and we agreed to give her permanent participation on condition that she did not ask to come into the business. She would have to be a sleeping partner, with Willie looking after her financial interests. And since we had drawn heavily on the firm's hidden reserves to establish the Langley factory, in which Silvia did not participate, and Willie used some of his own money to to install a modern water turbine at Leibitschgrund, we proposed to increase their share from a quarter to a third. Under the new partnership agreement which Spira was drafting the Pasold enterprises would be owned in the following proportions:

Adolf Pasold & Sohn	*Pasolds*
Fleissen and Leibitschgrund	Langley, Bucks.
One ninth: Eric Walter Pasold (British)	One third: Eric Walter Pasold
One ninth: Rolf Pasold (British)	(British)
One ninth: Ingo Pasold (Czechoslovak)	One third: Rolf Pasold (British)
One third: Silvia and Willie Nebel (German)	One third: Ingo Pasold
One third: Udo Geipel (Czechoslovak)	(Czechoslovak)

Whatever the future might bring, from the personal, financial, management and nationality points of view this arrangement seemed excellent. If the five partners worked together as equals, and in the same spirit as the three Pasold brothers, our team would be unique and unbeatable. For Rolf and me this was a foregone conclusion, Ingo took it for granted without giving much thought to it, and we could depend on Willie's total, unselfish co-operation. With Udo we would share as with a brother, confident that he would respond and become one of us.

In October, after Udo had finished military service and been stag hunting with his father in Slovakia, Uncle Gustav was ready to proceed with the purchase negotiations. They were conducted on our side by Rolf, who was at Fleissen at the time and for whom, at the age of twenty-three, they provided valuable experience. He kept in touch with me by correspondence.

There was give and take, but three requests we refused. Having excluded the forest at Leibitschgrund from the purchase in order to reduce the price, Uncle Gustav now asked for an undertaking entitling the firm to acquire at any time in the future parts of this forest land at the predetermined figure of one krone per square metre. He also thought that the stamp duty which would become due on Udo's entry should be paid by the firm. And he suggested settling the purchase consideration in instalments spread over a period of three years, free of interest. Uncle Gustav gave way, as we did on a number of other matters, a purchase price of $4\frac{1}{2}$ million kronen was agreed upon, and the deal was concluded.

In retrospect, even making due allowance for the inflation that has taken place in the intervening forty years, $4\frac{1}{2}$ million Czechoslovak kronen seems a low price for what we sold. I knew it at the time, yet I was glad to sell in spite of a strong premonition that the money paid into our frozen accounts would be held back by the government indefinitely and that the £10,000 in London, a mere third of the agreed purchase price, would probably be all that Rolf and I would ever receive. Subsequent events, unfortunately, proved me right. It is a matter of opinion who stole our money, whether it was the pre-war Czechoslovak government which froze it, the Nazis who took it over, the post-war Czechoslovak government which refused to release it, or the Communist government of 1948 which finally confiscated it. I want to tell my story in chronological order and shall therefore refrain from enlarging on the subject at this stage. Let me just say that without the action we took, and the courage to move so much of our capital to Britain at great personal risk between 1930 and 1938 in contravention of Czechoslovak currency regulations, the whole of our family fortune, earned by the hard work of generations, would have met with the same fate and been lost.

I wish I had a record of the sums we moved from Fleissen to Langley, and of the circumstances in which each of these transactions was carried out. We thought it too dangerous to keep notes. The penalties for currency offences were severe and if, by some ill chance, the Czechoslovak authorities had discovered our clandestine operations it would have meant the end of our British enterprise. The risk was ever present, and to keep it to a minimum we obliterated every shred of evidence that might betray us. There are coded references to some of our manoeuvres in my correspondence with Rolf, but the sense of the messages is so well disguised, and we changed the code so often, that I can no longer unravel them. No one but our London auditors and the British revenue authorities knew all the figures and facts. Unfortunately, not even the auditors are now able to reconstruct the details of those transfers any more. Their papers were lost during the war, or destroyed since, and when they estimate that the various amounts of capital which originated in Czechoslovakia and were ploughed into the British firm added up to tens of thousands of pounds they are relying on memory. Mr Hurst and Mr Colmer must sometimes have wondered how we financed the growing turnover, bought machines and enlarged the building out of our comparatively meagre profits, while, I feel sure, our workpeople thought that if the Langley factory needed money Fleissen simply wrote a cheque. They never suspected the worries the Czechoslovak currency restrictions caused us and the risks we ran.

How I envied British businessmen for being able to move their capital freely about the world as they pleased. It gave them a tremendous advantage over us. We had few opportunities of turning reserves into cash and then, from under the noses of the ever-vigilant Czechoslovak authorities and without it being discovered by our accountants at Fleissen, transferring them abroad. It would have been almost impossible if Father and Grandfather in their wisdom, gained through the experience of past wars and crises, had not hidden reserves in stocks of raw material, anonymous bank accounts and savings books—reserves which were there for emergencies, and which reappeared in times of need as smoothly as they had disappeared in years of plenty. We pledged these assets to the Bohemian Union Bank privately as security for overdrafts whenever the firm needed money, and were grateful to previous generations who, seeking protection from the consequences of war and revolution or from the ambitious schemes of avaricious politicians, had set this pattern. It seemed much to the firm's advantage to follow their example.

But there is a limit to the writing down of stock values, and we had reached ours in 1935. Czechoslovakia's financial year coincided with the calendar year, and Adolf Pasold & Sohn, in line with all the other firms at Fleissen, prepared their balance sheets as per 31 December. Their stocks were small at that time, for the last of the winter goods were dispatched before Christmas, and production for spring only just begun. Since one cannot hide large reserves in small stocks, I hit on the idea of changing the financial year to end in June, when factory and warehouse were full to bursting point with winter merchandise, and to my pleasant surprise the tax authorities raised no objection. The change helped to spread their work load, and so we were both happy.

The transfers via Switzerland usually originated with some businessman who had funds tucked away in a numbered account in Zürich or Basle and who, for reasons of his own, wanted to repatriate them 'unofficially' to Czechoslovakia. He would approach one of the big banks with his problem. The banker had clients who wanted to exchange undeclared Czechoslovak kronen for freely transferable currency abroad. Without disclosing the identity of the two parties the banker would effect the deal, for which he charged a commission varying between 2 and 6 per cent according to the risk involved and the size of the transaction.

Every now and again my friend Ernst Friedrich, *Direktor* of the Bohemian Union Bank at Asch, would telephone and ask to see me, or an innocent-looking coded message, usually posted from across the border at Bad Elster in Germany, would arrive at Langley, quoting the amount that was available and the rate of commission demanded, and almost invariably I was happy to accept the proposition. Of one of these transactions I have the original note, dated 17 August 1937, for an amount of 50,000 Swiss francs transferred from Basle to London, where, at the then current rate of exchange of $21\frac{1}{2}$ francs to the £, it realised £2,320. The Bohemian Union Bank charged 3 per cent commission. All these deals were done entirely on trust, no receipts or other documents changed hands, and there never was a hitch.

With two thirds of Adolf Pasold & Sohn passing out of the ownership of the three Pasold brothers the situation changed. Rolf's and my share of the profits, and thus the authorised remittances to England, were reduced to two ninths. Fleissen and Leibitschgrund continued to release capital reserves, but henceforth only a third of these found their way to Britain.

To be fair to all partners we endeavoured to remove every element of subsidy in transactions between the two concerns. To raise the charges as far as supplies of machinery, accessories, needles and spare parts were concerned was simple enough, but the large regular deliveries of condenser yarn Leibitschgrund invoiced to Langley at seemingly unattractive prices presented a problem. Langley could not afford to pay more, and in order to compensate Uncle Gustav for the notional difference we credited him with a larger slice of the capital reserve than he was entitled to, an interim solution with which we were not altogether happy. Should we set up a condenser spinning plant at Langley to remove the risk of friction developing? It would enable us to re-spin our waste clippings on the spot instead of shipping them to Leibitschgrund, we would save the 10 per cent duty that had to be paid on imported yarn, and Willie could look for other customers who would pay him higher prices.

We saw machine builders, obtained quotations and prepared tentative costings, when, unexpectedly, a Dutch firm of spinners made us a tempting proposition. The sales director, a young man named De Monchy, whom I had met at an international spinners' congress at Prague some years earlier, offered to spin in his modern mill at Hengelo any type of cotton condenser yarn we cared to specify and to supply Langley at favourable prices. We gave him trial orders, were pleased with the yarn he supplied, and shelved the project of a spinning plant at Langley.

But now it transpired that Willie could not afford to lose Langley's business, which absorbed 40 per cent of his condenser yarn output, while 60 per cent went to Fleissen. A spinning mill has to be fully employed to be profitable, and it now became a matter of opinion who was subsidising whom. We reached agreement that Langley should continue to buy from Adolf Pasold & Sohn until outlets at more remunerative prices were found. But this was easier said than done! Unable to dispose of its production to other buyers, Leibitschgrund was only too anxious to export condenser yarn to England at competitive prices.

I had not expected anything else than that the five of us would work harmoniously together and that the sectional differences which were bound to arise from time to time would be ironed out amicably. But Mother confessed in her letters that there had been times when she felt apprehensive. Although not aware of all the details of the business, she knew many of the problems and of the delicately balanced interests of Fleissen, Leibitschgrund and Langley. She loved her children equally, and now that everything seemed to be working out so well and everyone was satisfied she felt like singing with happiness.

Let us look at the relative production figures of the two enterprises at this stage, measured in terms of sales. They represent calendar years. The discrepancy between the sterling and kronen amounts is caused by the fluctuating rate of exchange of the two currencies.

Sales	Fleissen/Leibitschgrund	Langley
December 1932	Kc 7,577,000 (£72,000)	£ 4,005
December 1933	Kc 9,307,000 (£87,000)	£19,061
December 1934	Kc 9,321,000 (£75,000)	£35,523
December 1935	Kc 9,695,000 (£81,000)	£38,878
December 1936	Kc 11,200,000 (£81,000)	£54,523
December 1937	Kc 12,800,000 (£92,000)	£75,813

The figures are not quite comparable, because yarn sales from Leibitschgrund to Fleissen, and dyeing charges, are treated as internal transactions and have been ignored. To obtain a truer comparison we have to add approximately 50 per cent to the figures for Adold Pasold & Sohn. Rough as this picture must be, it clearly shows Langley's rapid rate of growth.

Langley had found its feet. The balance sheets our auditors prepared so conscientiously every year were there to prove it—had we not known it from the 'feel' of the business, and the rough calculations we made on the backs of old envelopes. We did not take balance sheets very seriously. As we knew from our experience in Czechoslovakia, they were prepared primarily for the Inland Revenue and did not necessarily represent reality. We had the highest regard for the partners of Westcott Maskall & Co., our auditors, but the figures they used to prove this or that were, we thought, out of date and offered little guidance for the future. The rate of depreciation for machinery and plant seemed too low for a progressive firm, they made no provision for things that could, and did, go wrong, and they failed to appreciate the extent of the indirect support Langley was receiving from Fleissen. And so, in our own minds, Rolf and I used to deduct £2,000 from the profit figures shown in the balance sheets. But even with this safety margin the figures for 1937 showed that Langley had definitely turned the corner:

	Results shown in balance sheets	Results estimated by ourselves
March 1933	Loss £686	Loss £2,500
March 1934	Profit £12	Loss £2,000
March 1935	Profit £1,894	Loss £100
March 1936	Profit £1,986	Loss Nil
March 1937	Profit £6,689	Profit £4,500
March 1938	Profit £8,546	Profit £6,500

Unfortunately I am not able to quote Adolf Pasold & Sohn's profit figures for those years, for most of their books and balance sheets were lost in the aftermath of the war, and I must rely largely on memory. During the slump of the early '30s Fleissen and Leibitschgrund earned very little. We were happy that we could keep the factories going to provide employment for our workpeople. Technical improvements in the spinning mills, the development of the White Bear sweater business, the introduction of sliver dyeing and marl spinning, and later the fabric dyehouse put us ahead of most of our competitors, and the situation steadily improved. From the mid-1930s onward the concern made as good profits as it had done in Father's day. We used them to improve our plant, and to replenish the shrinking reserves, but, having to devote so much time and effort to the Langley factory, we had none left for the expansion of Adold Pasold & Sohn. Now, however, with Udo joining the management team, we could afford to enlarge the family business. The home market was saturated: the extra trade would have to be found abroad. Langley would handle Fleissen's overseas sales. And not only those of Adolf Pasold & Sohn. We would offer our services to a number of the leading textile manufacturers of western Czechoslovakia. Who else was as well qualified as we were to establish a world-wide sales organisation with headquarters in London? A limited company, in which each manufacturer could hold a share! Thus I dreamed.

Not that anything had happened to make the political outlook less menacing. A visit by Lord Halifax to Hitler and their talk about the Sudeten problem achieved nothing. Beneš was manoeuvring himself into an untenable position by continuing to offer too little too late, and it was clear that Henlein daily relied more on the German Führer for help. Yet Willie, Udo and Ingo seemed unconcerned, confident that there would be a happy ending. Rolf and I felt less sure, but we had done all we could to put our house in order and now waited on events. Meanwhile we would not let our enthusiasm be stifled by political uncertainties. The young team was bursting with energy and wanted to push ahead.

Willie Nebel, at the age of thirty-six, married, with two children, was considered by the others almost as an elder statesman. Cultured, gentle, unselfish, co-operative and patient, he was a diplomat rather than a fighter. His life revolved round his family, the two spinning mills which he continually improved, the valley he loved, and the welfare of the little community of Leibitschgrund. He was a loyal member of the team and always put the overall interests of the Pasold enterprises first.

By virtue of being the eldest of the Pasolds I was, of course, the head of the firm at Fleissen and Leibitschgrund, as well as at Langley. Nothing seemed impossible to me at thirty-one. I had plenty of imagination and was not afraid of hard work. The ultimate responsibility for everything was mine. I was impetuous, but never overruled any of the others, and took no action unless there was unanimity. Even if at times Ingo called me an overbearing know-all and a slave driver, I think I can claim that it was my example that welded the five of us together.

Rolf was my second-in-command, at twenty-three a businessman with seven years of hard experience behind him, loyal to the death, self-denying, a tireless worker, but intransigent at times. A tougher negotiator than I, he thought I spent money too easily. In his view I wasted time on preparing details, while he liked to cut corners. When I anticipated trouble he said I was panicking. Nobody could rush him. I usually arrived at the station early, but he sometimes missed the train. We were an ideal combination.

Udo, who was also twenty-three, took up his position with Adolf Pasold & Sohn in November 1937, without waiting for the formal completion of the new partnership contract and all the paperwork demanded by the authorities. After acquainting himself with the internal organisation of the firm, the composition of the fabrics, and the merchandise in general, he made an extensive tour of the republic, visiting agents and customers, and soon became useful. And when he had spent a busy week in the factory he disappeared for the weekend into the forest. Like his father, he loved shooting.

Ingo, at the age of twenty-one, gladly left general policy, decision making and worries about management to the others. He liked designing machines, and as a skilled practical engineer spent a good deal of his time at the various factory workshops helping to build them. He wanted to be his own boss, to do things his own way and at his own pace, and tried not to get involved in overall responsibilities. He could be short-tempered but, like Willie, had a sense of humour. A keen sportsman, he played tennis and was an excellent skier.

What could be more exciting than for the five of us to build an empire together? The Rothschilds had been five brothers when they laid the foundations for the greatest banking business of all time. There must be just as much scope in textiles, I thought. I remembered the rags I had seen people wearing in the Middle East. Poring over the atlas, I tried to estimate demand for cheap clothing in India, China, South America and Africa. Was there anyone who mass-produced knitted cotton underwear as efficiently as Fleissen? And that was only half the story. With Langley less than an hour's journey from London, the city from which such a large part of the world was governed, financed and supplied, we were strategically placed for an international sales centre. So much of the map was coloured red—all British territory, offering untold opportunities. I could see our own warehouses in Sydney, Johannesburg and Vancouver, our spinning mills built next to cotton plantations, our knitting plants situated in the midst of teeming millions of yellow, brown and black consumers. But I wisely kept these ideas to myself. My partners would have done no more than laugh had I talked about them. They were too busy with their immediate problems to dream about the distant future.

We had no boardroom, never held a meeting, and minuted no decisions. I am quite certain that all five of us never sat round a table together, and I cannot recall that even four of us did, if I ignore the occasional family re-unions at Christmas. Business was discussed and decisions were taken as we perched on a corner of each other's desks, while reading the mail, at chance encounters in the factory, on an evening's walk through the woods, or by correspondence. In the light of modern practice, with teams of highly paid executives out of touch with the shop floor, spending half their working hours at meetings and the other half dictating and reading quadruplicated minutes and figures, this seems almost unbelievable today. It worked, but I must admit that I felt the need for a round table conference now and again to dis-cuss policy. Unfortunately my colleagues did not seem to feel the same need, and all my efforts to hold regular meetings failed. Rolf in particular refused to co-operate. 'Every one of us knows perfectly well what needs doing, so let's not waste time talking about it,' he used to say. In his opinion talking during working hours only set a bad example, unless what one said had a direct and immediate bearing on the job in hand. Discussions about the future, the purchase of machinery, factory extensions and similar matters could wait for the evening or the weekend.

Rolf, who was doing a prolonged stint at Fleissen, got on well with Udo. In a burst of enthusiasm they wanted to modernise the factory. Starting with the cutting department, they intended to replace the thirty-odd individual cutting tables and hand shears by a single table twenty metres long, as we had at Langley, and introduce electric cutters. But in my opinion Fleissen made far too large a range of garments, from too many different widths of fabric, for such an installation, and wages were too low to justify replacing hand shears by machines. I did not think the conversion would be financially viable, and talked them out of it. Nor was I in favour of purchasing a warp knitting plant, arguing that circulars and warp looms would not go well to-gether, an argument in which Ingo supported me. And Ingo's judgement in technical matters was taken seriously. If Rolf and Udo were bent on expansion, would they consider installing a battery of American Challenger machines and go in for the production of ladies' underwear in artificial silk, for which the demand was growing on all sides? This would, of course, necessitate im-provements in the sewing department. Our finishes were not good enough for this type of merchandise. And so the suggestions went to and fro, were stu-

died, and abandoned. Perhaps it was best, I thought, for Adolf Pasold & Sohn
to defer spending money until Udo had gained more experience.

In February 1938 Rolf, Ingo and I joined Pinewood Film Studios Club.
It occupied a rambling country house in a beautiful old park at Iver Heath,
with a picture gallery, a large ballroom, stables complete with horses, and an
enormous indoor swimming pool. From the high ceiling above the pool hung
long ropes with rings on them. One could swing from one ring to the other,
right across the pool. If one missed a ring one fell into the warm water below,
much to the merriment of spectators. After some practice we did it fully
clothed, to show off. I well remember a starlet falling in on the occasion of a
gala dinner dance, and her flimsy evening dress becoming completely transparent as she swam out. To see her like that nowadays would hardly excite
anyone, but she caused quite a stir then.

At lunchtime it was the wood-panelled dining hall that provided the main
attraction. Actors in period costume, wigs and make-up, who took their meals
there in the intervals between filming, lent it an atmosphere of fantastic
extravagance, which was in such stark contrast to the factory floor we had left
but a few minutes earlier that we felt we were on a different planet. Sometimes we took important buyers there for lunch, and they were always
greatly impressed. I have never known another country club like it. We dined
and swam there two or three evenings a week, and some of the friends we
made are still friends today. For many reasons 1938 was a memorable year,
filled with world-shaking events, great worries and forebodings of worse to
come, but it was one of the happiest years of my life, and Pinewood helped
to make it so.

Towards the end of February I took Colin Baird, his wife Min and Adrye
Matthews for a winter sports holiday at Zürs, in the Austrian Alps, where
Rolf was waiting for us. We could not have wished for better weather, the
sun blazed out of a deep blue sky on to the glittering whiteness. Rolf and I
skied, leaving our tracks in the powdery snow, while the others sat in deck-
chairs, sunbathing. We met for lunch, had coffee in the sun, and queued for
the ice hockey machine in front of the inn. People played for stakes of a few
Austrian schillings. It was a popular game—until Colin put a £5 note on the
table, lost it to Rolf, won it back and, cool as a cucumber, staked it again. The
note went back and forth. The crowd stood at a respectful distance, watching
with baited breath as the two crazy foreigners—one of them a Scotsman,
would you believe it?—gambled for a fortune, until it was time to go skiing
again. Then Colin lovingly folded the treasured banknote and put it back in
his wallet. There was no more queuing for us from then on; the ice hockey
machine was ours whenever we wanted it.

After a happy time in sun and snow, without motor cars or newspapers, we moved down the valley to St Anton, to stay with my friend George Eisenschiml, while Rolf returned to Czechoslovakia. I was a little surprised that George was not at the chalet to greet us, but thought no more of it when his housekeeper said that he was delayed in Vienna and would be arriving the following day. We enjoyed our dinner and went to bed, to be told in the morning that the German army had marched into Austria while we were asleep. It was rumoured that Hannes Schneider, the ski champion who had made St Anton famous, and other prominent members of the anti-Nazi Heimatfront had been arrested. Our housekeeper too, it appeared, had been taken from his bed at 5 a.m. without our being woken; but it had been a mistake, and he was back in time to prepare breakfast for us.

So Hitler had struck! Thoughts raced through my head. Would the Austrians resist? How would Prague react? For a moment I wondered whether there might be war, but only for a moment. Beneš and the Czechoslovak army would sit tight, I felt sure. I was sorry for the Jews, and hoped that George had got across the border into Czechoslovakia in time, if he really had been in Vienna.

I went out into the street, but all was peaceful and I saw no sign of soldiers. Meanwhile Colin and Min were hurriedly packing their bags, anxious to leave for home as quickly as possible. I tried to reassure them. There was no need for panic. If the Germans were occupying Austria there was nothing we could do about it. By now their troops would be well on the way to Innsbruck, Linz and Vienna. As far as Zürs and St Anton were concerned the invasion was over. The Nazis were not looking for harmless tourists like us. On the contrary, they would be on their best behaviour towards foreign visitors, especially if they were British. We might as well stay on.

Adrye was game to stay. She thought it all rather exciting, but I failed to persuade Colin and Min, and it was decided to leave. The trains seemed to be running normally. I do not remember any difficulty over tickets, and we even secured sleepers on the Arlberg Express. By evening we were on our way back to England, and it was only then, as I lay wide awake in my berth listening to the monotonous clanking of the wheels, that my brain grasped the full extent of the tragedy. Austria was no more!

34

PILOT'S VIEW
OF CENTRAL EUROPE
1936-38

ON A FINE Sunday in September 1934 Rolf and Ingo watched the gliding at
Dunstable, and were so intrigued by it that on their return to Fleissen they
joined the gliding club a few young optimists had just started there. The
terrain was not ideal and there was only one glider, a home-built primary
trainer, but what the little club lacked in facilities was made up for by the
enthusiasm, tenacity and hard work of the members. After weeks of running,
lifting, pushing, pulling, sliding over the frozen ground and repairing breakages, Ingo had his first flight the following April. It took him over a distance
of 150 metres, at a maximum height of about eight metres, and he wrote an
amusing account of it, complete with diagram, for Rolf at Langley. Rolf had
in the meantime joined the London Gliding Club at Dunstable. Keen rivalry
now developed between them, all fully recorded in the long letters they sent
to each other, reports far more detailed than any they ever wrote about business.

It was not surprising that Rolf progressed much faster than Ingo. Dunstable was so well equipped, and its range of hills provided such excellent
training slopes, that the handful of lonely pioneers on their muddy hillock
back at Fleissen were quite unable to compete. Nevertheless, when Rolf made
a flight lasting twenty-five seconds at a height of thirty-five metres Ingo was
able to enter a series of flights of twenty-three, twenty-five and twenty-seven
seconds' duration, if at lesser heights, in his log book. Then, on 10 October,
Rolf earned his A certificate with a flight of thirty-five seconds at a height of
seventy metres and was now unquestionably in the lead.

In January 1936 Ingo caught up, with a flight of thirty-one seconds, got
his A certificate and proudly stuck the glider pilot's badge in his buttonhole.
Two months later Rolf flew for two and a half minutes, a feat Ingo could not
match for some time because the Czechoslovak authorities prohibited all
gliding activities in the border region. The little club had to look for a gliding
site in the interior of the country, and found it in the Rannay. By the time
Ingo had his B certificate Rolf already had his C and was making flights of

up to forty and fifty minutes at Dunstable. In November Ingo made a forty-three-minute flight in Czechoslovakia, but spoilt it by landing upside down in a tree. Rolf meanwhile was staying aloft for an hour and a half. Then Ingo came to work for a while at Langley, joined the London Gliding Club, and began to beat Rolf's duration and height records. He should have been born with wings.

It would not be true to say that I caught my brothers' enthusiasm, in fact I was rather afraid of the air and wished flying had never been invented. The very smell of an airliner—a proud word for the eighteen-seat Fokkers and Junkers of the mid '30s—made me feel sick, and I forced myself to travel by air now and again only because I realised that it was the coming form of transport and I might as well get used to it. Perhaps, I thought, if I learned to glide I might conquer my fear and my airsickness, and so I too joined Dunstable. But I did not like it. I discovered that gliding meant endless hours of hard work on the ground for every few seconds one was airborne, and to be catapulted over the edge of the hill, out into space as it seemed, sitting in the open on a kind of frying pan with nothing around one, was a terrifying experience.

It took three months to get my A and B certificates, by which time I had decided that the effort was out of all proportion to the progress I was making. I therefore went to see Captain Davy, the chief flying instructor at Heston airport, about a trial lesson in a powered aircraft. He passed me on to Captain Glover, who took me to a two-seater Avro Cadet which was standing in front of the school building, casually explained the controls, lent me a fur-lined leather coat, a helmet and a pair of goggles, strapped me into the rear cockpit, swung the propeller and taxied to the take-off position. A flash of light from the control tower, a roar from the engine, a short run over the grass, and we were off. It all happened too quickly for me to follow what was going on. I held on to my seat and looked straight ahead at the back of the pilot's flying helmet. My life was in his hands, and I hoped he knew what he was doing. The aeroplane trembled, climbing at full throttle. I was aware that we were gaining height. Slowly turning my head and glancing over the side, I saw houses and railway lines down below, and then, without warning, the machine banked steeply to the left, so steeply that I was scared the wings would fold up and we would plunge to the ground. I leaned to the right, held on as tightly as I could, and held my breath until we were on an even keel again. Suddenly the roar of the engine died down to half strength, the vibration stopped, and Captain Glover's voice came through the speaking tube.

'We are at 1,500 feet, flying level now. In a couple of minutes we shall do a few gentle turns. Are you quite relaxed?'

'Yes,' I replied, fearful of what was to come.

'Put your feet on the rudder bar and your hand on the stick, just lightly so that you can feel what I'm doing.'

It was not as bad as I had expected. What Captain Glover called gentle turns seemed quite steep to me—one pair of wings pointed down to the ground while the other rose high into the sky, and of course I was frightened, but to my surprise and relief the aircraft showed no tendency to lose its balance and fall, as I had expected, and I became a little more confident.

'All very simple, as you can see,' said the instructor. 'Now let's take things easy and look at the scenery. Do you remember where the aerodrome is?'

I had not the slightest idea. Gingerly looking down over the side of the cockpit, I saw thousands of houses interrupted by an occasional open space, roads, railway lines, a gasometer and a large grey factory. His Master's Voice, as Glover explained, and the gasometer was the best landmark for Heston. The airport lay just behind it. Then he suddenly said, 'Now you take over! Fly her straight and level with the stick. I'll keep the rudder. The controls work just like on a glider, as you will have noticed. Right, she's all yours!' And to show that he was no longer flying the aircraft he raised both hands above his head. Had he taken leave of his senses? I gripped the stick. The plane seemed to fly on as before. 'Pull back a little,' the voice came through the speaking tube, 'you're losing height. That was a little too much, you're losing speed now. The left wing is dropping, pick it up. Now you are getting too fast again—all right, I've got her.'

Better writers than I have described what it feels like learning to fly. Let me just say that I had a half-hour lesson almost every evening and was scared every time I went up. On the fifth day we practised spins. It was the most ghastly experience of my life, and I felt too frightened even to be sick, but when we were down again and I had recovered from the shock I was not afraid of flying any more. If an aeroplane, and the human body, could survive the violence of that spiralling plunge into the void they could stand anything. On 21 June 1936, a month after I had started taking lessons, with altogether ten and a half hours' flying instruction behind me, I made my first solo flight. It was with a mixture of apprehension and elation that I took off into the still summer evening and flew once round the airfield all on my own. I could hardly believe it was really me. And I made a perfect landing.

After another five-minute solo flight the following day, and two more lessons with Captain Glover, practising landings, I was told to fly solo for fifteen minutes. Again it was a beautiful evening. The clock on the instrument panel showed 6.15 as I took off. Circling the airfield, I climbed to 1,500 ft and then looked at the clock. It said 6.18, which surprised me a little. Time seemed to pass much more slowly in the air than on the ground. For a moment the thought of Einstein and his theory of relativity flashed through my mind, but only for a moment. I had to concentrate on my flying. Another two circuits of the airfield—or was it three? The clock showed 6.20, when suddenly an aeroplane appeared alongside mine. Not wanting to risk a collision, I edged away, but it followed me, and now it came so close that I could recognise the pilot. It was Captain Davy. He waved to me, pointing downwards. Then I lost sight of him. There was no doubt about it, he wanted me to land, but why? I had been told to fly for a quarter of an hour, and less than half that time had elapsed. Something must be wrong, something I didn't know about! Had a piece of the aircraft fallen off? Was the tail on fire? 'Don't panic,' I kept repeating to myself. 'Just make a normal landing!'

'What do you think you're doing?' Captain Davy barked at me when I was safely down. 'You were told to fly for fifteen minutes, not forty-five! Didn't you realise you might run out of fuel?'

'I've only been up seven minutes!' I defended myself, pointing to the clock on the instrument panel. It showed 6.22!

Now it was Davy's turn to look surprised. The explanation was simple enough. The clock had not been wound up, and the vibration of the aeroplane had caused the large hand to drop slowly, giving me the impression that it was working. We laughed, and Captain Davy bought me a beer at the bar. Pilots are taught to trust their instruments rather than their senses, but there are exceptions, as I discovered several times in more than thirty years of flying.

Navigation lessons, given by Captain Ferguson, were fun. He taught with the aid of a map, compass, stop watch, protractor, slide rule and a swivelling chair. Geometry was one of my favourite subjects at college, and I had no difficulty drawing diagrams showing the effect of wind on the course and speed of an aircraft, but I was appalled by the waywardness of the compass. It was such a dependable instrument on the ground, always pointing faithfully to magnetic north, yet in the air the needle succumbed to the attractions of gravity, centrifugal force, acceleration and deceleration, and showed a marked preference for not telling the truth, except when flying south. One had to watch it.

To qualify for a pilot's licence one had to pass a flying and a navigation test. The first proved easy, but I almost came unstuck over the second. I was told to prepare and then fly a triangular course leading from Heston to Brooklands racecourse, thence to White Waltham aerodrome and back to Heston. The wind was light westerly and visibility excellent. Simple, I thought, worked out the compass courses I had to fly and the time each leg would take, and took off. Delighted to see Brooklands appear dead on time, I turned on my next course and reset the stop watch. But I failed to find White Waltham, and when, after thirteen and a half minutes, I saw the Thames below me I knew I was lost. Would I run out of petrol and have to make a forced land-ing? Keep cool and think, I told myself. You are out west, if you follow the Thames in an easterly direction it must take you back to London. But the Thames didn't go from west to east, it looked like a snake curving in all directions. Which way was the water flowing? I descended low enough to see. There was a weir with white foam on the downward side! Following the bends, I came to a town which looked like Maidenhead. I climbed to 1,200 ft, careful not to lose sight of the river, when suddenly, to my great relief, I saw Heston gasometer in the distance. I landed and taxied back to the control office as if nothing had happened. Captain Ferguson did not even notice that I was four minutes overdue, and all was well. It seems uncanny that I should still remember those first flights as clearly as if it were yesterday.

My pilot's licence gave me courage. Gradually I ventured farther afield, landing at Reading, Gravesend, Shoreham, Christchurch, the Isle of Wight, Northampton and Leicester, and, like most beginners, did some stupid things which the Good Lord fortunately forgave me. By the end of 1937 I had flown forty-eight hours solo and considered myself an experienced aviator. Gone was the fear of the air, and of any feeling of airsickness. I now loved flying, practised sideslips and forced landings, looped the loop, and even did spins because I enjoyed the thrill of them. More important, I had regained my self-respect.

In January 1938 I bought an aeroplane, a De Havilland Hornet Moth with a Gipsy Major engine. It was a cabin machine with two seats side by side, had a cruising speed of 105 m.p.h., and had belonged to Prince Birabongse of Thailand, who had hardly flown it. Mr Lacayo of Airwork Ltd, was selling it for him. He asked £775, but in the end I got it for £730, Ingo having tossed a penny with Lacayo for the last £10 and won.

When Father bought his first automobile in 1908 who would have believed that horseless carriages were the coming means of commercial transport? I felt that the same applied now to aeroplanes. We were going to use ours for business journeys, and to begin with especially for publicity. We already had the reputation of being a progressive firm. Our modern factory, the success of our ripple cloth and the way we talked to everyone about efficiency impressed even the hard-boiled buyers at Marks & Spencer's, as I well knew. A business aircraft would have the trade talking about us from London to Inverness. One of the first things I did was to take photographs showing the Hornet being loaded with samples of our merchandise, which Mr Hurst got published in the *Draper's Record*, together with a short article under the heading 'By air to the wholesaler.'

On 10 April I flew to France. It was my first Channel crossing. I climbed to 3,000 ft to find the horizon above the haze to line up my plane, and when, after lunching at Le Touquet, I landed again at Heston I thought I knew what Lindbergh must have felt after crossing the Atlantic. Heartened by success, I set off four days later for Czechoslovakia. But the weather on the Continent was bad, and I got no farther than Rotterdam. A telephone call to Rolf told me that there was two feet of snow at Fleissen. So I abandoned my plan and flew back through the rain to sunny England.

A month later I tried again. Taking off from Heston at 8.30 in the morning and refuelling at Rotterdam, Hanover and Leipzig—all grass fields, with, if I remember correctly, the control office, customs and passenger accommodation housed in wooden huts—I landed at Karlsbad at 18.45, a few minutes before Rolf arrived in the Alvis to meet me. It was not the shortest route, measured as the crow flies. A Dutch airline pilot had recommended it to me as leading over the easiest terrain. I had been in the air for seven and a half hours altogether, but the weather had been good all the way, the airport officials kind and helpful everywhere, I had had no trouble with Brownshirts, and did not feel unduly tired. Given favourable weather conditions, commuting between Langley and Fleissen in our own aircraft seemed a distinct possibility.

However, I had not come to Czechoslovakia just for a proving flight. There were several policy matters on which I wanted to reach agreement while four of us were together, with only Ingo away at Langley. The most important of them was future co-operation between Adolf Pasold & Sohn and the English enterprise. This could be subdivided into three parts: exchange of experience and technical information, the disposal of Leibitschgrund's surplus condenser yarn production, and the development of Fleissen's export trade. Unanimity on broad lines was not enough; our objectives had to be spelled out in detail. Moreover I wanted Fleissen to improve on the plain fleecy merchandise it had been manufacturing for far too long. The quality of our fabrics was good, but our styles and *Konfektion* were out of date. We needed a small range of smart, colourful garments for export, something as outstanding as our White Bear sweaters were for the Czechoslovak home trade. My dealings with the Marks & Spencer buyers had taught me that.

I had brought Miss Lancaster to Fleissen the previous autumn to let her see Adolf Pasold & Sohn's type of output. I had acted as her guide and interpreter when visiting garment manufacturers at Asch and Rossbach, and helped her select samples of interesting merchandise in the leading stores of Prague and Amsterdam to take back to London. And having prepared her itinerary in the first place, I drafted at her request a report of her journey with recommendations for M. & S. head office afterwards. All this had taught me a good deal, and I wanted the Fleissen factory to profit from it. Miss Lancaster had meanwhile given me a starting order for Adolf Pasold & Sohn for

2,000 dozen jerkins on condition that we improved their appearance. I hoped to achieve this with multi-coloured bindings, and suggested the purchase of some special sewing machines for the purpose, involving a comparatively small outlay.

Rolf and Udo were prepared to spend money on new plant, but I did not want to get Adolf Pasold & Sohn involved in large capital expenditure before Udo, who now owned a third of the firm, had a thorough grasp of the overall situation. So far his experience was confined to the home market, where he did an excellent job, but the long service with the army and his love of the forest, where he spent most of his spare time and had built himself an attractive hunting lodge, did little to increase his knowledge of the big world outside.

While I was thus concerned, the political scene steadily worsened. Beneš, gambling on help from Britain and France, continued to play for time. Henlein, tired of waiting, had made a speech at Karlsbad in April demanding immediate self-government for the German-speaking minority. Hungarians, Poles, even the Slovaks clamoured for autonomy and for a reshaping of the republic on the model of Switzerland. The negotiations dragged on; attitudes hardened. Early on the morning of Saturday 24 May a Czech guard at Eger shot and killed two farmers on a motor-cycle, and feelings in the Egerland reached boiling point. On the same day clashes between Czech police and German-speaking civilians occurred at Chodau, Komotau, Brünn and Mährisch Schönberg. Motoring to Karlsbad the following Wednesday, I found the road blocked by thousands of mourners who were silently marching to Eger to attend the funeral of the two peasants. I waited to let them pass, frightened by the determined look on their faces and the grim atmosphere of impending disaster. Hitler, I was told later, sent a wreath.

Talk of German army manoeuvres near the Czechoslovak frontier caused alarm in Prague. Beneš moved troops into the Sudeten areas and mobilised reservists. Several times Czech observation planes strayed into German air space, causing excitement. The pilots were probably lost over the densely wooded border territories where there were hardly any landmarks to navigate by, I thought, and felt sorry for them. I saw an open-cockpit two-seater flying low in a rainstorm and heard afterwards that it had crashed into a hill, killing both occupants. Cousin Udo was called up and rejoined his unit. Had he not done so he would have been treated as a deserter when this foolish show of force, as we all considered it, had passed. Understandably I found it difficult to keep people's minds on business in such conditions.

Karlsbad aerodrome was a long way from Fleissen, and, having been refused permission to keep my plane on the military airfield at Eger, I took it to Marienbad, which was a little nearer than Karlsbad. But after the mobilisation

I thought it prudent to fly across the border to the small airfield at Hof in
Bavaria, to avoid having it grounded by the authorities or possibly even fired
at by over-excited Czech soldiers. None of these fields deserved the proud
description of aerodrome. Hof was no more than a badly mown sloping
meadow with a wooden barn in the corner, and only just enough room to take
my Hornet with its wings folded. There were no facilities of any kind, no
flying control, petrol, service, fire extinguisher, not even a guard. I had to
arrange for a drum of aviation spirit to be delivered to the barn and do my
own refuelling and servicing. The only consolation was that Karlsbad and
Marienbad were not much better. At Hof I would at least be left in peace. I
saw nothing of manoeuvres and not a single German soldier. If there was to
be trouble it would be on the Czechoslovak side.

Whitsun offered the chance of a break from the continual suspense. I flew
with Helmut to Munich, where we had lunch, and on to Innsbruck. It was
his first flight. In glorious weather we climbed over the Bavarian Alps and
when, on the other side, the mountains suddenly fell away below us and we
floated out over the wide valley of the river Inn I was so overcome by the
grandeur of the scenery and a feeling of unearthly happiness that I burst out
loud into song.

Next morning, Whit Sunday, we spiralled up over Innsbruck to an altitude of 12,500 ft, the highest the Hornet had ever been, and flew south over
the Brenner pass to the little airfield at Bolzano, to spend a leisurely day
strolling about the town. Or so we thought. An Italian officer in a smart
uniform, with a pistol in his belt, took our passports, carnet and log book. He
glanced at them, seemed a little surprised that Helmut, an Italian subject,
could not speak Italian, and ushered us into a room with barred windows. We
were to make ourselves comfortable while our papers were being processed,
he said politely in German, and, to make quite sure that we did wait, placed
two heavily armed *carabinieri* at the door.

We did not see the sun again for four and a half—yes, four and a half—
interminable hours! Why were we being kept in this guardroom? Had I
inadvertently flown over prohibited territory? Almost the whole of the
mountainous north of Italy, all the way from the Côte d'Azur to Triest, was a
prohibited area, with only a few narrow channels open to civil aircraft. The
Brenner was one of them, and I felt sure that I had followed the permitted
route accurately. Was there some mistake? Had we perhaps been taken for
spies? The log book showed that I had been flying in and out of Bohemia's
border region, Europe's trouble-spot, for weeks, and there were at least fifty
Czechoslovak stamps on my passport. Developments in the Sudeten area and
the encouragement Hitler was giving the German-speaking minority in their
demand for self-determination must have made the Italians feel uneasy. They

had every reason to have a bad conscience over their own oppressed German-speaking minority. Were they afraid that Hitler, who only three months earlier had taken over Austria, would now back the South Tiroleans in their struggle for freedom? And did they think we were implicated? Did it seem suspicious that Helmut, a man with the surname Amarotico, the holder of an Italian passport, could not speak Italian? Or had they simply forgotten us in our prison? But no, someone brought us pasta, a water melon and some wine.

We had landed at ten in the morning, and it was three o'clock when a handsome young Blackshirt brought our papers. We were seething, but it seemed unwise to show our feelings. We had heard of the Fascist practice of subduing victims by forcing them to drink castor oil, and had no desire to sample it. I enquired politely about the cause of the delay. The young man did not speak much German, but from what he said we concluded that there had been a military parade in the town and it had been best for us to stay at the airfield. Now we were free to go wherever we liked, he said with a smile.

It was much later that we discovered the reason for our detention. Hitler had done a deal with Mussolini. Grateful to the Duce for not interfering in the annexation of Austria by the Reich, he confirmed that Italy could keep German-speaking Tirol. To make the most of this 'victory' and set the seal of finality on it, Mussolini ordered local celebrations, but wished to keep them in a low key. This delicate matter was left to Crown Prince Umberto. Accompanied by a large number of Fascist dignitaries, the prince and his princess were at Bolzano performing the ceremony on the very day we landed there, not suspecting that anything out of the ordinary was going on. For all the Italians knew, we might have been reporters or political troublemakers, and it was therefore not surprising that they kept us out of the way. Some incident caused by an *agent provocateur* might easily have sparked off an explosion and, perhaps, brought about a confrontation between the two dictators.

After this episode we decided that we had been in Fascist Italy long enough. We had no wish to wander about Bolzano any more, in fact there was nowhere we would like to go better than back to Innsbruck. And we decided to go at once. I headed the plane north, and we were glad when we had the Brenner behind us. A pleasant evening in the picturesque capital of Tirol, where we stayed at a small hotel near the 'Golden Roof', soon made us forget the wasted hours. On Monday morning a solid layer of low cloud hung over Innsbruck, but towards mid-day it began to lift, and we took off. Flying through intermittent slight rain, we followed the Inn valley to Kuffstein, where the clouds broke, and continued non-stop to Hof. By late afternoon we were having tea at Bad Elster, met friends for dinner, and then drove back to Fleissen, well satisfied with our outing.

With Rolf and Ingo at Langley, where an exciting expansion programme was under way, and Udo in the army, I was now tied to the factory at Fleissen. But I could not settle down. Everybody seemed restless. The plant was working normally, but very little was happening in the office. Buyers and sellers were staying away, waiting on developments, and agents called only to talk about the tremendous gains made by Henlein's SdP in the municipal elections. It now held 90 per cent of all the seats in the Sudeten area. Politics as such did not interest me, I grew bored, and when Udo came back I decided to accept the Hungarian Touring Club's invitation to the famous 'Magyar Pilótapiknik'. It was extended to all members of the Royal Aero Club of Great Britain and read:

Eminent sportsmen of the air, well known air tourists will meet there . . . that they should . . . in good company admire at the beauties, folkloristics, inland sea with water of changing colours, at the Puszta with its cow-belled herds at draw-wells . . . enjoy the fiery Hungarian wine, the music of the indefatigable Hungarian gipsies, the renowned Hungarian hospitality . . . delight in so many fine, kind, interesting, picturesque, charming sightseeings, in all what surprise expects the foreigner in Magyarland . . . and after having wandered over the Hungarian countryside from air and land . . . they will go on their way to look at the pearl of Danube: Budapest, capital of Hungary, glittering in sunshine, gleaming by nights, on both banks of the Danube and waiting for her guests with embracing arms. Come with good cheer, you are waited for with love by the Hungarian Touring Club.

How could anyone resist such an invitation! I gave Uncle Wilhelm a lift as far as Vienna, spent the night there, and next morning flew to Balatonkiliti, where I met the other twenty-three 'eminent sportsmen and women of the air' who had come from Britain in nine private aircraft. I did not know any of them, but during the unforgettable week we spent together, criss-crossing Hungary in easy stages, from Siófok via Szeged, Miscolc, Lillafüred, the Hortobágy puszta, Debrecen, back to Hortobágy, and on to Budapest, I got to know a number of them well. Frank Butler and John Nathan were killed in the war, but with John Houlder and Sydney Evans I was to fly many thousands of miles in the years to come, and I still count them among my best friends.

The Hungarians spoiled us with kindness; their hospitality knew no bounds. Wherever we went, accompanied by the Minister of Transport in person, officials and press men, the peasants received us in their colourful national costumes, the tables, beautifully decorated with flowers, bent under the weight of cooked delicacies and fresh fruit, gipsy bands played, and we were shown the articles and photographs the newspapers were publishing about us every day. We had never been made such a fuss of in all our lives. There was always something to report: John Houlder 'landing on a mirage'

3a Arrival at Budapest airport. The author with Cornelia Jirkovsky, the Hungarian guide of the party

3b Budapest, with the Danube

73c Hungarian peasant with his wares

73d The author learning to dance the Csárdás

73e Magyar horsemen

73f In the Hortobágy Puszta

and breaking his aeroplane, Davenport losing his way and flying into Yugoslavia, and another pilot violating Czechoslovak air space, but fortunately none of these incidents had serious consequences.

Cornelia Jirkovsky, a student at Budapest University, acted as our guide and interpreter, and, being on my own, I was able to offer her the spare seat in my aeroplane. I had never met a more charming and intelligent girl. She spoke English well, and gave me the Hungarian view on the political situation. Passionately patriotic, she told me that she and her friends prayed every day for the release of the 750,000 Hungarians who were in Czechoslovak bondage. And here, too, Beneš was one of the villains of the piece. I knew that there was little love lost between Hungarians and Czechs, but had not expected feelings to run that high.

The Budapest of 1938 lives on in my memory as one of the most enchanting capitals of the world, and the short week spent under the blue Hungarian sky, the evenings filled with gipsy music, ended all too soon. Before I took off I had to promise to come back the following year, a promise I was determined to keep. And then I flew west-north-west, sad to leave this dream city behind. The thought that before the 1914–18 war it had belonged to the Austro-Hungarian Empire, and that Father and Grandfather had gone there to sell their merchandise, only added to my nostalgia. Their experience of Budapest must have been very different from mine!

Having collected Uncle Wilhelm from Vienna, I set course for home, but on the way the plane developed a strange noise, a howl that grew until it drowned the sound of the engine. Some disaster seemed imminent. I had visions of an explosion and of being drenched in boiling engine oil. Something had to be done. Selecting a large, rectangular field, I made an emergency landing, but on inspecting the engine found no sign of overheating. It ran smoothly, I felt no vibration and could hear no unusual noise. Before I could puzzle any further the Sunday afternoon crowds of the small near-by town of Straubing arrived. Old and young, mothers with babies, dogs, a school complete with teachers on an outing—they came running from all sides, wanting to see the flying machine, touch its fragile wings and rudder, ask questions, and even beg for autographs. Finally Authority appeared in the person of the mayor, supported by a policeman, and proceeded to cross-examine me, while Uncle Wilhelm did his best to defend the aircraft. Authority was not in the least interested in my problem. Where had we come from, and what were we doing here on a rifle range, a military installation? He could not let us go without permission from Berlin, and today was Sunday; there would be no one to answer the telephone at the Air Ministry. Fortunately I had the good sense not to show our passports or log book. Authority did not realise that we were foreigners, and that the aeroplane bore British registration letters.

I felt desperate. We had to get out of this jam as quickly as possible, and before the aeroplane was torn to shreds. 'Strap yourself in,' I told Uncle Wilhelm, and, under the pretext of making a ground test, ran up the engine to let hats, skirts and underskirts fly in the slipstream. As the crowd scattered I charged it, and, when I had cleared a passage, turned into wind, opened the throttle, narrowly cleared the hedge and climbed away. The engine sounded normal, and when, levelling off at 2,000 ft, the howl came back we decided to fly on. Twenty minutes later we came to Regensburg, and there, to our relief, saw an aerodrome. It was not marked on my map, and looked deserted —probably military, I thought—but it was getting dusk, we had little choice, and so I landed on what turned out to be a Messerschmitt factory airfield.

Next morning it was a hive of activity. I had some difficulty getting past the security people, who eventually took me to one of the test pilots, a very sympathetic man. He wanted to hear the strange noise for himself, and after five minutes in the air with me he had located the trouble. It seemed incredible that such a tiny thing could have caused us so much anxiety. A narrow strip of fabric on the cabin roof had blistered in the hot Hungarian sun. The blister had opened and formed a membrane, which the rush of air made to vibrate in flight, and the cabin, acting as a sound box, magnified the noise. A few drops of dope and a plaster half the size of a postcard cured our ills, there was nothing to pay, not even the usual landing fee, and Messerschmitt's promised to convey my apologies to the mayor of Straubing. An hour later we landed safely at Hof, where I folded the wings of my faithful Hornet and pushed it back in the barn. It was the unexpected, rapid succession of apprehension, great happiness, danger, fear, self-reliance, remorse, triumph and tranquillity that made flying so exciting.

Air travel nowadays is so very different from aviation in the '30s, when even the international airports of London, Paris, Frankfurt, etc, were little more than grass fields, weather reports and radio communication were hardly known, Control signalled with white, green and red lights, one flew as and where one liked without filing a flight plan, and the only areas one had to avoid were the prohibited zones of the military. I hope the reader will therefore bear with my lengthy account of pre-war private flying. The atmosphere seems worth preserving. And aeroplanes played an important part in the private and business lives of the Pasold brothers.

Returning to my desk at Fleissen after an absence of ten days, which to me had seemed like ten weeks, I was surprised to find that little had changed. The factory was completing old contracts, but there were few new sales. Customers and suppliers were still holding off, waiting for something to happen that would break the stalemate. In any case, July was a quiet month.

Our only callers were manufacturers' agents, who came not in the hope of
doing business but because it was routine to see their clients every week or
two. They came to gossip, and there was hardly any other topic than politics.
They wanted to know from me what England was going to do. The key to the
solution of the Sudeten problem lay in London. Both Henlein and his
socialist opponent Jaksch had been there to canvass, Beneš seemed to be
taking his cue from London, and Hitler clearly did not want to fall out with
Britain. Who was Lord Runciman? Did I know him? And why was he given
the job of mediator? I had to disappoint them. I had never heard of Lord
Runciman.

They hoped for a settlement that would give the minorities self-government within the framework of a federal Czechoslovak republic. Beneš, they
thought, would be forced to honour his promises of twenty years ago. No one
I spoke to considered annexation of the Sudeten areas by Germany a serious
possibility, or wanted it. Hitler and his achievements were admired. He had
eliminated unemployment. Every able-bodied person in Germany was in
work, industrial production was booming, and the number of unemployed in
Austria had fallen from a quarter of a million to 100,000 since the *Anschluss*.
True, the Sudetenlanders did not care for the German system, with its
restrictions and controls. Neither business community nor workpeople
wanted that kind of regimentation. They preferred prosperity with tranquillity and freedom. And Hitler, the greatest wizard of all time, would somehow procure it for them by political pressure, while Whitehall diplomacy
would safeguard the republic's territorial integrity, they believed.

What did people in the Fatherland think of the situation? I had the
impression they were far too occupied with their own problems to bother
about the future of the Sudetenland. Visiting businessmen from the Reich,
raw cotton merchants for instance, described Germany's position as alarming.
Her store cupboards were empty, her foreign exchange reserves and her
credit exhausted, and she could no longer buy even the most essential raw
materials. Faced with rapidly falling exports, made worse by the Jewish boycott of German goods, she now depended on bilateral exchange agreements
with areas like the Balkans. If people in the Sudetenland only realised how
well off they were by comparison!

Nor did German industrialists, machinery makers I went to see in Saxony
and Württemberg, share their Führer's concern over the well-being of
Czechoslovakia's minorities. What were people in the Sudeten area complaining about? Were Czech officials worse than Nazi officials? Germany's economic
life was being subordinated to Field Marshal Goering's four-year plan;
industry was desperately short of raw material, capital and labour. Production
was controlled, and so were costs. In spite of the fact that unemployment

had been eliminated, and every employable person was working, the standard of living was falling. People in Germany no longer knew what they were working for.

The manager of the bank at Plauen where I did business also complained. The country's resources were strained to breaking point. The shortage of labour and of foreign currency was so acute that Germans living abroad were being urged to come home and repatriate their capital, for which Goering's Ministry offered Reichsmarks far in excess of the official rate. Apprenticeships for skilled trades were being reduced, crops could be harvested only with the help of the army and of imported Italian labour, and, the banker said, worst of all was the concentration of investment on armaments at the expense of consumer goods. There was so little in the shops worth buying that people could not spend their earnings. So they put them into long-term government loans, or made down payments for a Volkswagen, which they would probably never get, for the money was only used to manufacture tanks and aeroplanes. He hoped Britain realised what was going on in Germany.

As always, the most outspoken criticism of the Nazis came from Uncle Richard. He could get neither linen nor cotton for his tapestry factory at Brambach. 'Nothing but substitutes, materials made of nettle fibres, wood, paper or synthetics, and not enough of those,' he complained. I sympathised with him. We were very much better off in Czechoslovakia. Prague also controlled imports to preserve foreign exchange, but we never experienced any significant shortages. We had everything—wool, cotton, steel, copper, shoes of real leather, tyres of real rubber, plenty of meat, butter, chocolate, coffee—and it was amusing to watch the few Germans who still came across the border stuffing themselves with pastry and whipped cream in our restaurants.

I saw a great deal of Uncle Richard in the summer of 1938, for I was thinking of applying some of his sewing techniques to the manufacture of our sweaters. His seams were far more accurate than ours, and with the aid of various attachments to his sewing machines he produced very attractive finishes. We could learn from him, and he willingly showed me everything I wanted to see. And as he demonstrated how to get the best results he spoke his mind about the regime. He had never approved of it, but of late things were getting quite unbearable. He hated the 'Strength through joy' movement. As owner and manager of the firm it was his duty to march, on the compulsory works outings, at the head of his column of employees, a duty he dodged as often as he dared. And he was fined more than once for not flying the swastika flag on days of official celebrations. The people of the Sudeten area were playing with fire, he warned, if they were flirting with Hitler.

Jews had disappeared from the German scene. One by one the familiar faces had vanished. Where had they gone, I wondered? Had they emigrated? One heard of pogroms, and of concentration camps, without being able to judge how true the stories were. It was unwise to probe too deeply if one did not want to ask for trouble, Uncle Richard said. One could read *Der Stürmer*, the most frightful of all German papers, and draw one's own conclusions.

I saw no sign of Jews leaving Czechoslovakia. On the contrary, quite a number of Jewish refugees from Germany and Austria came to the Sudetenland, especially to Karlsbad, Marienbad and Franzensbad, where they were almost the only foreign visitors. German tourists, usually in the majority, could no longer come, because the Reich had run dry of foreign currency. Some of the houses and businesses belonging to Jews at Eger and Asch were for sale, I was told, but I heard of none that actually changed hands. It did not appear that their owners were in any hurry to sell. They seemed to be less worried about the republic's future than I was.

I continued to travel between Czechoslovakia and Germany, using the aeroplane whenever practicable. There are flights to Nuremberg, Schwarza, Munich, Reichenhall, Marienbad, Prague, Chemnitz and Karlsbad recorded in my log book. On both sides the officials were friendly and helpful, intrigued to see a British plane. I used the car only if the factories I went to visit in Germany were too far from an airfield. The sleek red Alvis still drew admiring crowds wherever it was parked, its union jack and Czechoslovak number plates arousing not the slightest visible hostility. In the country lanes I met lorry after lorry taking singing soldiers to help on the farms; formations of Hitler Youth worked in the fields. They looked healthy and happy, and I sometimes wondered whether the critics of the system were really always right.

Apart from searching for ideas and for machinery to improve Fleissen's sweaters, in the hope of selling them to Marks & Spencer, I toyed with the thought of installing Schiffli machines at Langley to quilt satins and other materials for the manufacture of dressing gowns. They were large, complicated and expensive, and I wanted to learn as much about them as possible before tackling Rolf with the project. But I was unsettled and found it hard to concentrate on my work.

I was wondering how Lord Runciman and his team of experts were getting on with their fact-finding mission, and how their mediation between Prague and the German-speaking minority was progressing. People in the Sudetenland had faith in the integrity and wisdom of the noble lord. For the first time in twenty years their case would be fairly presented to the world, and they were confident that the world's verdict would be in their favour. In their hearts many of them were relieved to think that their fate now lay in the hands of an impartial arbitrator, instead of being left to two hot-heads like Beneš and Hitler, who were fighting over their personal prestige, with Henlein reduced to the Führer's puppet. But before the negotiations led to any concrete result, large-scale German army manoeuvres started in the middle of August, creating an atmosphere in which all reasonable discussion became impossible, and the talks were suspended.

The situation was obviously taking a turn for the worse, but not everyone seemed to worry as much as I did. On a hot Sunday afternoon at the Lido at Franzensbad I bumped into Kirsch, the German representative of Millington's. He looked bronzed and relaxed, and I was pleased, if surprised, to see him. We lay on the beach and talked. He had closed his Chemnitz office and moved to Franzensbad, where he intended to stay until Britain called Hitler's bluff and the world returned to sanity.

'The world is so big, couldn't you find a healthier place than the Sudetenland in which to do your sunbathing?' I asked him.

'You seem to be quite happy here,' he laughed, 'so why shouldn't I?'

'I wouldn't be if I had a Jewish grandfather. Besides, I have a British passport in my pocket and an aeroplane with a full fuel tank not far away.'

Louis Kirsch dressed, packed his bags, and took the first available flight from Prague to London. A few years later we met by chance in Regent Street and had a cup of coffee together. 'Who knows,' he said, 'you may have saved my life.'

In the second half of August I saw some German soldiers by the side of the road to Brambach. They were cooking. There were about twenty in all, and among them was Albert Renner, Uncle Richard's son-in-law. They did not look very warlike, and seemed to be enjoying the outing. 'War? Against whom?' they laughed good-naturedly. 'We have no quarrel with anyone.'

How strange, I thought, as I drove on. Had it been a group of Storm Troopers I would not have dreamed of stopping for a chat. Why was it that the unbridgeable gulf that existed between me and the Brownshirts completely disappeared when those self-same lads wore army uniform? I was afraid of the Nazi party, but not of the German army.

Then came a shock. At the close of the annual mass rally of the NSDAP at Nuremberg, on 12 September, Hitler denounced Beneš violently. He called him a liar and demanded self-determination for the Sudetenlanders. He would come to their assistance, he screamed. I had never heard such language on the radio. For one Head of State to address another publicly in such terms was monstrous. Anything might happen now. And events did move very quickly. The government at Prague proclaimed martial law. The Sudeten party insisted that it be rescinded immediately and the State police withdrawn from German-speaking districts. Prague reacted with strong

74a Hitler's triumphant drive through Asch

74b Hitler inspects the *Freikorps*. On the extreme left is Henlein

75 At Eger too, as everywhere in the Egerland, the Führer was hailed as the liberator from Czech oppression

Adolf Päsold & Sohn
Wirkwaren - Fabriken

Fleissen,
(Tschechoslovakei)

Telegramm-Adresse:
PÄSOLD FABRIK
Telephon Nr 4 a.b.c.d.e.
Prager Postscheck-Konto
NR.205.964.

76 Annexation by Germany brought full employment but it also brought stringent new raw material and other controls for industry in the Sudeten territories. The team who now directed the old family firm experienced all the rigours of Nazi administration

77 Brother Ingo Pasold   *78* Cousin Udo Geipel   *79* Brother-in-law Willie Nebel

80 Management and employees on one of the compulsory outings

81 The factory at Langley

The new spinning mill at Langley. Two-card condenser sets supplied by William Tatham Ltd of Rochdale

Spinning condenser yarn on ring frames was a new venture for us. The frames were built by Platt Bros. & Co. of Oldham

84 The City of London after the bombing raid of 29 December 1940

85 The corner of Jewin Crescent, where the author's office had been in 1929

The ruins of 10 Fore Street.
r Hurst's office had been on the first floor

87 The brass plate that survived

88 Len Foyster, BoT hosiery controller

90 The author and J. Thomson Donaldson

89 Fred Venning, vice-chairman of SEKIA

91 NHMF delegation calling on Harold Wilson at the BoT. Left to right: Tommy Kempton, Bertie Jarvis, the author, Willie Grimmon, Raymond Taylor, H. Kennewell, Freddie Peshall

military measures, to which Henlein replied that the Sudetenlanders could no longer live together with the Czechs in one State. An eruption seemed imminent.

A day or two before Henlein made this pronouncement I was stopped by a semi-military-looking group of young men in the forest between Brambach and Schönberg. They were led by a man whose face seemed familiar and who obviously knew me. He explained that they were forming a *Freikorps* to fight against the Czechs. As I was coming from the direction of the border, had I seen any troops? And would I fly one of his observers in my aeroplane over western Bohemia to spy out the whereabouts of the Czech army?

'No,' I replied firmly. 'I am not prepared to get shot at, and what is more I am a British citizen and will not take sides or get involved. I have seen neither Czech nor German troops, and if anyone should ask me I have seen no *Freikorps*.' And with this I drove on. They had been polite, almost apologetic, and merely disappointed when I refused to co-operate, but I could feel that things were now going to move very fast.

That evening came the first reports of clashes between Sudetenlanders and Czech security forces at Eger and Karlsbad. Next day trouble flared up all around us. Customs houses, post offices, gendarmerie barracks and other government buildings were attacked. We heard that three gendarmes had been shot dead at Falkenau, four Sudetenlanders killed and three wounded in riots at Tachau, two Czechs and a Sudetenlander killed and others wounded a few kilometres from Eger. One Sudetenlander lost his life when the railway station and post office at Chodau were stormed, another was killed at Rosenberg, and yet another shot dead at the wheel of his car at Marienbad. There were an unknown number of victims when Czech police opened fire with machine guns at Weipert. A gendarme was killed by a hand grenade at Graslitz, and several Sudetenlanders were injured when Czech armoured cars charged into an angry crowd. And there were casualties in other parts of the border region too. If Hitler's speech had been intended to stir up violence it certainly succeeded. I felt it was time for me to fly my plane back to safety.

On the afternoon of 16 September Cousin Udo drove me to the airfield at Hof. I pulled the Hornet out of the barn, unfolded its wings, checked the oil level and filled the tank by pumping the petrol with a hand pump from my storage drum into a bucket and then filtering it through a chamois leather as I poured it into the tank, while Udo watched. 'Do you think there will be war?' he asked.

For the first time I was wondering myself. 'If there is, you'll have to fight,' I said. 'Why don't you fly to England with me instead?'

He had never flown. He looked first at me and then at the aeroplane.

'Flying with you may be more dangerous than going to war,' he replied, shaking his head. And so I took off for Hanover, where I landed in the evening, much concerned about the explosive situation I had left behind. Then, going up in the lift of my hotel, I heard someone say a miracle had happened.

'Chamberlain has flown to Berchtesgaden to talk to Hitler!'

Suddenly the world seemed transformed. The crisis was over. There would be no war; the Sudeten dispute would be settled peacefully and sensibly! I would return to Hof in the morning. But when morning came I decided to fly on to England. I had been away from Langley for a long time, and wanted to see how the factory had progressed during my absence. Rolf and Ingo would want to hear about Fleissen and Leibitschgrund, and we wanted to make plans for the months that lay ahead. After a refuelling stop at Rotterdam I landed at Heston airport at tea time.

35

THE NAZIS
TAKE OVER
1938

ON MY RETURN I found the British public much better informed about the situation in Czechoslovakia than I was. Listening to foreign broadcasts, or taking German newspapers across the border, was forbidden by the Czechs and punished with heavy jail sentences. Besides, information spread by the German propaganda machine was not to be trusted, while both Czech and German-language papers printed in Czechoslovakia were censored, days behind with the news, and disbelieved. Rumours circulated, were denied or confirmed, and caused confusion and fear. I now learned from *The Times* that I had been too optimistic. Chamberlain's visit to Berchtesgaden had produced no concrete result. I was stunned to read that Henlein and Hitler were no longer satisfied with autonomy for the German-speaking territories of Czechoslovakia but demanded their incorporation into the Reich. This was not what the great majority of level-headed Sudetenlanders had wanted! Were they now to be sold out to the Nazis as, in 1918, they had been sold out to the Czechs? There was talk of a plebiscite, which I did not believe, and although I had felt sure there would be no war, public opinion in Britain began to make me uncertain. What would happen to Mother and to the firm?

On Wednesday 21 September, only four days after my arrival in England, I took the Imperial Airways plane to Cologne, and late that evening was back at Fleissen, where I found Mother soundly asleep and quite unperturbed in the family home. Next morning I woke to a very different picture from the one I had left. Our factories, like all the others, were idle. Workers and staff had disappeared, and so had Cousin Udo. The shops, the inns and the school were closed; we had no electricity and therefore little water. The road to the frontier was thronged with people who were on the move from the Egerland to Germany, on foot, on bicycles, women pushing perambulators, families on horse carts, farmers driving cattle—people who told hair-raising tales of violence, of how they were being hunted and beaten by the Czechs. Afraid of war and of getting caught between the two opposing armies, they were seeking safety behind the German lines. No doubt farther east the movement would be in the opposite direction: Czechs, Jews, socialists and trade unionists would be sheltering behind the Czech lines.

We heard that the Czechs at Asch had handed over the town's administration to the SdP and been taken prisoner, that there had been skirmishes, that the *Freikorps* and the Czech troops were facing each other at Haslau, and that Fritz Käsmann, a friend of mine, had been machine-gunned in his Tatra car, but could obtain no confirmation.

Most of Fleissen's remaining inhabitants were now locking their houses and leaving. A feeling of helplessness, of the inevitability of it all, came over me. I still refused to believe that there would be war, but I wanted to take no chances, and although Mother protested I took her to stay at an hotel at Bad Elster. Two lonely Czech customs officials, visibly frightened by the thousands of refugees, were still at their post and waved us on as we drove over the border. When I returned three hours later they had disappeared. There was no one guarding the Czechoslovak side of the frontier any more.

The next few days I stayed alone at our house, save for an old servant who refused to leave and who looked after me. The flood of refugees had ended. Fleissen was practically deserted. Among the few people who remained was my friend Helmut. He was relying on his Italian passport for protection, as I relied on my British one. The Sudeten area became no-man's-land, and although the attention of the international press was focused on it we, who were there, hardly knew what was happening. We had no newspapers; the Czech security forces had confiscated all radio sets and cut off or bodily removed all telephones, even private internal ones. We had to go to Brambach for news, but the tirades one heard on the German radio were not very informative, and the broadcasts from Prague, appealing for calm, as far as we could make out, told us nothing. Uncle Richard said that Chamberlain was at Godesberg searching for a peace formula. Helmut reported that Mussolini had said, quite correctly, that what the Czechs represented to the world as a homogeneous State was in fact an unhappy conglomerate that should be named 'Czecho-Germano-Polono-Magyaro-Rutheno-Roumano-Slovakia', and I heard the German Führer in one of his outbursts call Beneš an impertinent urchin, but factual information was lacking. We knew only what we saw ourselves, and that was precious little. Walking through Fleissen's streets in brilliant sunshine, with no sign of life save for a stray cat and the birds on the roofs and in the trees, was an eerie experience. I had not realised before how far one could hear the chirping of a sparrow.

The days passed incredibly slowly, and the suspense became almost unbearable. I felt my time was too valuable to be wasted idly waiting for events, and I tried to assess the situation. It seemed that Hitler was determined to annex the Sudetenland and that no one could stop him, but was the transfer to be carried out peacefully or by force? Czechoslovakia was said to have more than a million men under arms. If there were to be war after all would Fleissen be in the line of fire? The small contingent of German troops on the road to Brambach, whom I had first seen a month earlier, were still there, about a kilometre behind their side of the frontier. They did not look as if they expected war, and seemed to be enjoying themselves. How wide was the belt of no-man's-land on our side, I wondered—five kilometres or fifty? Where was the Czech army? Was it true that Czech field guns were mounted in the woods to the south-east of Fleissen, only two kilometres from our house, and that the *Freikorps*, trying to penetrate into Czechoslovak territory, had been repulsed? Perhaps it was foolhardy, but Helmut and I decided to reconnoitre.

We took the small Tatra, for the country roads in the Sudetenland were too rough for the Alvis. I drove very slowly in case we came upon soldiers unexpectedly. A slow-moving vehicle was less likely to attract a hasty bullet. Grossloh, Klinghart, Hörsin, villages some distance to the east, were deserted and made the same ghost-like impression as Fleissen. We saw no sign of guns anywhere. But then, turning towards Brenndorf, we found ourselves suddenly looking down the barrels of half a dozen rifles. I stopped the car and opened the door. A serious-faced young Czech officer studied our passports while his men kept us covered. Without a word or a smile he handed our papers back, saluted, and we drove on. Shortly afterwards, on the way to Steingrub, we met another patrol. The soldiers lay in a hollow by the side of the road, and their rifles followed us as we approached at snail's pace. When we drew level two of them came over to us. While one looked through our documents and searched the car the other watched, rifle at the ready. They were courteous but tense, and again without a smile let us drive on.

I talked to Willie Nebel, who shared my view that incidents caused by the extreme nervousness of the Czech troops could lead to localised fighting, but that there would be no war when the Germans, as now seemed certain would happen, entered the area. Meanwhile my staying served little purpose. I could make better use of my time at Langley. And so, on 29 September, I caught an airliner at Leipzig and flew via Cologne to London, intending to return to Fleissen as soon as the situation demanded it.

To my surprise I found Britain ready for battle. Trenches had been dug in Hyde Park, anti-aircraft guns mounted and manned, the fleet mobilised, gas masks tried on, and the evacuation of London begun. Chamberlain had, for the third time, flown to Germany to try and resolve Hitler's 'last territorial demand', this time with Daladier and Mussolini present. The conference at Munich would decide whether there was to be peace or war. And how well I remember the nation's relief when the tired Prime Minister landed back at Heston, triumphantly waving the paper that promised 'peace in our time'.

The withdrawal of Czech forces from the Sudetenland and the occupation by the Germans was to begin on 1 October and proceed in several stages until it was completed on the 10th of the month. This gave me time to spend ten days at the factory at Langley, which I had rather neglected of late. Rolf and Ingo brought me up to date on developments, and I felt reassured that they had everything well under control. Then I checked on the progress of the extensive building work we had in hand, spent a day in the City with Mr Hurst, called on Mr Cue at Woolworth's and on Miss Lancaster at Marks & Spencer's, and in the evening studied the newspapers. It was with a heavy heart that I followed the advance of the German troops, read about border incidents, and looked at the photographs of so many familiar places. There was a picture of the barrier being raised at the frontier at Wildenau to let Hitler's army enter, of the main street at Asch lined with cheering men, women and children, of the historic market square at Eger packed with people giving the Nazi salute, and of swastika flags everywhere. Yet I knew that the hearts of thousands of Sudetenlanders were as heavy as mine, in spite of the photographs in *The Times* which told a story of nothing but jubilation and flowers for the Führer and his soldiers.

Fleissen had come to life when I arrived there on 9 October. The inhabitants had returned, smoke was rising from the chimneys, the telephones were being installed again. One drove on the right-hand side of the road now, instead of the left. Apart from plenty of swastika flags I saw no sign of the occupation, not a single German soldier or Storm Trooper, which came as a relief. Mother was working in the garden, while Udo at Fleissen and Willie at Leibitschgrund were puzzling out how to deal with the new situation that confronted them.

There was, for instance, a money problem. Coins had disappeared from circulation. Adolf Pasold & Sohn had banknotes but no small change for the wage packets of their employees, who had been without income for two weeks and whose lost earnings we decided to make up. The shortage had developed during the crisis in the second half of September. People remembered how, in 1918, they were forced to part with half their paper money in order to get the other half revalidated while the coins in their pockets kept their full value. So they hoarded coins and carried them in stockings across the border to safety.

Udo had hit on the idea of using postage stamps for small change to pay wages. Other manufacturers did the same; butcher, baker and candlestick maker accepted stamps in payment. Stamps took over the function of coins until the post office ran out of supplies. The town fathers of neighbouring Asch were more intelligent; they overprinted their stocks of stamps, giving them ten times their nominal value.

For the time being the krone remained the legal tender. Before the occupation it had been worth eight and three-quarter pfennigs, the German army raised its value to ten, and on 10 October Goering improved it to twelve, a move that made him very popular, especially with the workers, who were delighted with this increase in their earnings until they discovered that most of the things they bought also cost correspondingly more, and that they were little better off than they had been before.

On 1 November the economy of the Sudetenland was switched to Reichsmarks. On paper the money we had in the bank was now worth $37\frac{1}{2}$ per cent more, but our production costs and our selling prices went up in the same proportion. How would this affect our already disrupted trade? Most of Adolf Pasold & Sohn's output was sold to some thousand wholesalers and retailers throughout Bohemia, Moravia, Silesia, Slovakia and Ruthenia, from the majority of whom we were now separated by a frontier, and as far as the territories to be ceded to Poland and Hungary were concerned the frontier was not yet finalised. All sales and dispatches of goods were at a standstill, and no payments were received, resulting in financial difficulties for Fleissen's smaller and weaker manufacturers. To make matters worse, Czechoslovak textile distribution was almost entirely in Jewish hands, and this included the Sudeten areas. Jewish traders who had stayed there were in trouble, or soon would be, while those who had fled had understandably taken their cash with them, leaving unpaid invoices and insolvent businesses behind. Would we ever get the money they owed us, quite apart from the exchange problem?

One thing at a time, though. The most pressing task was to get the wheels turning again, to provide work for our employees. It was not possible to wait until we knew which of the contracts on our books were still valid and which were no longer worth the paper they were written on, how our export customers would react now that we had become part of the Reich, and whether they would still accept the goods they had ordered. To get answers to these questions would take time. We therefore decided to keep the factory going by making standard types of fleecy underwear and to put it into stock. We were in a strong position. We had a substantial credit balance at the bank, money due to Rolf and me which, because of the transfer restrictions, still remained at the disposal of the firm. We had almost a thousand bales of raw cotton at Leibitschgrund, and the warehouse at Fleissen was full of yarn. Our goods were of a quality people in Germany had not seen for years. Their garments were made of *Zellwolle* and other *ersatz* material. There was a ready market waiting for us as soon as the frontier was opened and trade between the Sudetenland and the Reich was established. The demand would be far larger than we could satisfy. It was obvious to me that Adolf Pasold & Sohn were sitting on a gold mine.

For the time being German passport holders were not allowed to enter the occupied zone. Although the concrete blocks on the road between Fleissen and Brambach had been removed, and the Sudetenlanders were free to come and go as they pleased, the German frontier guards were still there to prevent citizens of the Reich from going on buying sprees in the Sudeten area. But in spite of official vigilance quite a number of them slipped through the net, and the shops did a roaring trade. My own position was a little delicate. Did the German visa in my British passport entitle me to stay at Fleissen? Was the old Czechoslovak permit still valid? No one challenged me, and I kept my fingers crossed, hoping there would be no complications.

Returning from Leibitschgrund late one afternoon, I sensed trouble when I saw two German officers' caps hanging in the reception lobby at Fleissen. Yes, the two officers were waiting for me. As I entered the private office they jumped to their feet. Was there anything they could do for us? Field Marshal Goering realised that the occupation had disrupted industry. Did we need work for the factory? They had brought an order book with them. Were we short of cash to pay our workers' wages? Or could they assist us in other directions? They seemed most co-operative. Genuinely impressed, I complimented them on this example of German planning, but declined their offer of help and said we could manage on our own.

I knew, of course, that we could not ignore the German authorities for long, since we depended on them for raw material allocations. But for the time being we could afford to await developments. And we did not have long to wait. The Textile Manufacturers' Association at Asch called a meeting at which German officials were present. They told us to continue with our normal pattern of trade, if we could, using our stocks of yarn, fabric, sewing thread, elastic and accessories as economically as possible. Manufacturers who ran out of supplies would be given government contracts and provided with the raw materials for them. From the tone of the discussion that developed we concluded that few firms were in as fortunate a position as we were. We also gained the impression that it would not be long before the functions of the Association would be supervised by some government body, and that the days of free enterprise as we had known it were numbered.

Soon afterwards Udo and I, together with a hundred or so other knitted goods manufacturers, were summoned to attend a meeting at Chemnitz. After welcoming us into the Reich, the speaker explained to us the principles of the National Socialist economy which, he said, replaced the capitalist system and meant that industry worked for the common good, namely that of the workers, the consumers and the State, beside that of the owners. There was no case for trade unions on the one hand and employers' confederations on the other to fight for their sectional interests, promoting class distinction. The nation could not afford the luxury of industrial disputes, and both types of organisation had therefore been dissolved and incorporated in the German Labour Front under Reichsminister Robert Ley, whose responsibility it was to see that everyone did his best for the community and received a fair reward.

Germany was not a democracy. National Socialism did not believe in election from below but in selection from above, a pyramid in which every leader appointed the leaders immediately below him. And at every level the leader had complete authority, and was absolutely responsible for his decisions and actions. There was no sharing of responsibility, no sheltering behind committees. These, in short, were the rules of the *Führerprinzip* on which not only the State but every organisation in the State, every industry and every factory, was run.

He then talked about Goering's four-year plan, the purpose of which was to make Germany self-sufficient, and about the role we were expected to play in it. In the interest of the common good industry had to be controlled, and this control was now to be extended to the Sudetenland. He assured us that the authorities were well aware of our special circumstances, the skill of our workpeople, the overall efficiency of our factories in spite of the need for their re-equipment with new plant, and that they would give due consideration to them. Then he became more specific.

He knew that the knitters of Asch and Fleissen had an excellent export record. Exports were vital for Germany, and he appealed to them to continue to sell as much as possible abroad, and not to succumb to the temptations of the enlarged home market. There were special raw material allocations for exporting firms, and subsidies as high as 60 per cent for certain markets. It was important, he stressed, that we kept our factories going. For the time being we had to make do with our existing stock of raw materials, but in due course we would be getting allocations which were based on past consumption and on the knitting capacity of our factories. To enable the authorities to make the necessary calculations we would have to complete questionnaires. They asked, among other things, for a description of every manufacturers' knitting plant, and it had to be remembered that it was the number of feeders that counted, rather than the number of machines. Imported materials, such as cotton and wool, were scarce and requests for them could be met in full only in the case of export orders. The quantities available for the home trade were strictly limited, but there was enough *Zellwolle* to make up the deficiency, and manufacturers were urged to 'stretch' their supplies of natural fibres by blending them with artificial ones. Should we have difficulties the Saxon knitting industry offered us advice and practical technical assistance. We had, with our Bohemian private enterprise mentality, looked upon the Saxons as our future potential competitors and much appreciated this generous gesture.

Most firms in the Sudetenland, it was pointed out to us, made too large a variety of goods. A drastic reduction of their ranges was to be aimed at. Manufacturers were urged to specialise, but before they took action would they please discuss their plans with their respective trade association. And on no account was variety to be reduced at the expense of exports. The need to earn foreign currency was impressed upon us again and again.

Then there was the matter of levelling out differences in wages. Firms in the Sudetenland would in future have to pay the same rates as their competitors in Saxony and Württemberg. A skilled sewing machinist, for instance, would have to get a basic hourly wage of 54 pfennig, a knitter a little less than a Reichsmark, plus 15 per cent for piecework. There was a great deal more, the details of which I no longer remember, mostly about the National Labour Front and the introduction of the spirit of National Socialism into our factories, the sort of thing Uncle Richard was always complaining about.

On the whole this was sour wine for businessmen who were used to conducting their firms, mostly family concerns going back several generations, as undisputed rulers. Over their heads hung the threat of losing their established connections, and probably a considerable part of their working capital. They had hoped to recoup themselves in the huge and seemingly lucrative German market, but now they were to be put into straitjackets before they had even entered it. The meeting which had started in such a buoyant mood of eager anticipation became subdued. I studied Udo's face. He did not seem to be in the least disturbed by the prospect of this regimentation. It must be his military background, I thought. Before the meeting closed, the speaker stressed the confidential nature of everything we had heard. On no account was any of it to find its way into the press or become known abroad. Where did this leave me? To be on the safe side I decided to disclose my dual status to the chairman.

At first he frowned. 'As head of Adolf Pasold & Sohn it is your duty to remember what you were told today, and to make sure that the firm complies with it, but as a Britisher you must forget it. How you do this is your problem.' Then he smiled. 'Germany and Britain must stick together. The Führer admires the English, I hope he will soon sign a pact of friendship with London. Heil Hitler!'

As the red Alvis sped through the crisp October afternoon in the direction of Fleissen I reflected on the day's revelations, and the loss of freedom citizens of a totalitarian State had to put up with. I could never be just a cog in such a vast and soulless machine, I thought. Thank God for our factory at Langley! Yet one had to admire the organising genius of the Germans, which enabled them to mobilise their last meagre resources and, in spite of all adversities, seemed to achieve peak performance. Politics apart, with Greater Germany as its home market Adold Pasold & Sohn must now be worth twice as much as it had been the year before. Uncle Gustav had bought at the right time!

I did my best to make the firm succeed under National Socialism. We had no choice if the family concern was to survive. Hitler, I told myself, would not last for ever. But I would draw the line at getting personally involved in any Nazi nonsense. Before very long this brave resolution was put to the test. We received instructions, as did all other industrialists, to assemble our employees and proclaim to them in rousing words that the enterprise would henceforth be conducted along National Socialist lines, which meant the 'Führer principle', and that the head of the firm would be its 'Führer'. As senior partner it fell to me to deliver this address, and although of more symbolic than practical importance it placed me in a very awkward position. It would have been easy enough to reel off the well worn phrases of the party, but I could not have uttered them at any price, and so I said something about feeling happy to see everyone back at work, relieved that twenty years of Czech oppression had come to an end without war, and that the firm looked towards the future with confidence.

My speech was totally inadequate for the occasion, and I can only describe it as a fiasco. Our people had expected something very different, and there was deadly silence when I finished. This would never do! I pushed Udo on to the table. He had no inhibitions and, carried away by the general excitement, saved the day with a fiery off-the-cuff oration, stringing together the cliches of the time, the end of which was drowned in thunderous applause that echoed round the factory. Having thus complied with the authorities' instructions, we all returned to our jobs, keeping our thoughts to ourselves.

It was now very clear to our employees that I did not approve of the new regime, and most of them must have felt confused, for the general enthusiasm for National Socialism was at its peak and they shared it. Why didn't I? Without Hitler they would still be slaves of the Czechs: surely I did not want that? What was I to say to them if they asked me? Fortunately none of them did. They respected my position and I retained their confidence, for which I felt deeply grateful. No one ever questioned my leadership, but I left it to Udo to represent the firm on all official occasions, and he did it well.

We now had to do business with Germany, a market about which we knew nothing. Ever since Grandfather's day it had been so well protected that we could not sell a single dozen of our goods there. Helpful as always, Uncle Richard now gave us a list of the important buying organisations, and we found that they were all eager to do business with us. The telephone hardly stopped ringing, letters and telegrams poured in offering us orders, and price did not seem to matter. They wanted garments made of pure cotton as long as stocks would last. Since German buyers could get no permits to visit us at Fleissen, we took our range of samples to Brambach or Bad Elster and concluded our transactions with them there. Before long we had contracts from Hertie, Karstadt, Kaufhof, Dietz and Horten, the leading groups of department stores in Germany.

A man who seemed to have no difficulty in moving between the Reich and the Sudetenland was Max Berk, an enterprising merchant from Heidelberg. Walking down the gangways in our warehouse, between the shelves stacked to the ceiling with merchandise we had manufactured for stock, he would point and say, 'I'll take that, and that, and that,' without attempting to knock a single pfennig off the price. And as he always paid cash it was not surprising that he became one of our most popular German customers. Soon we were selling the larger part of our output to Germany. Demand exceeded our manufacturing capacity and made us keep a wary eye on our gradually shrinking raw material supplies.

The people of the Sudetenland and of truncated Czechoslovakia also needed clothes. There were fewer bankruptcies, fewer defaulters than we had feared, and payments came in better than anticipated. Our agents in Prague, Brünn and Pilsen picked up the pieces of their broken territories, assessed which of their clients were still solvent, and pleaded for supplies. From the beginning of November onwards the railways began running normally again and accepted goods for all parts of the republic. The new political frontiers were no serious obstacle to trade; textiles crossed them free of duty, although they remained closed for passenger traffic except by permit. Business with our old Jewish, Czech and Slovak customers revived, if on a somewhat smaller scale.

Most of the wholesalers with whom we had traded before the Germans came, and many of the shopkeepers, were Jewish. Their businesses in the Sudetenland could now be acquired by Aryans at bargain prices. The harassed owners had to find buyers, and were often glad if their properties realised even a fraction of the true value. I do not know the purchase price the Lehrmanns paid when they took over the well known wholesale house of Edelstein at Reichenberg, which provided them at one stroke with a network of thousands of retail clients throughout the Sudeten areas and what remained of Czechoslovakia. Several manufacturers at Asch made similar acquisitions. One could, of course, argue that it was better for the desperate Israelites to take a low price, rather than to lose everything, but many of the transactions were little better than legalised robbery, and Adolf Pasold & Sohn refused to have anything to do with *Arisierungen*, as these take-overs were called.

In contrast to the merchants, most manufacturers were Aryans. My friend George Eisenschiml, who had inherited his father's fabric glove factory at Asch, was an exception. By Nazi definition he was Jewish. As a rule the owner of a factory was also its manager, and now automatically became its responsible 'leader', provided he was not a Jew, otherwise he had to hand over the management to some trusted Aryan member of his staff. George had not waited for the Nazis, but appointed his representative while the Czechs were still in control. Turning all liquid assets he could lay his hands on into cash, he used it as down payment for a life policy with a Canadian insurance company which had an office at Prague. While Chamberlain was negotiating at Munich George was on his way to Montreal. There he surrendered his policy for dollars, with which he proceeded to build a ski lift and a small winter sports hotel in the Rocky Mountains. It sounded almost too easy—perhaps he did not tell me the full story.

When the Germans came we thought they had brought with them a carefully prepared, detailed programme for the incorporation of our industry into the economy of the Reich, and everyone observed instructions to the letter. Before very long we discovered that they had not planned nearly as thoroughly as we had expected, and we began to relax. Decrees and directives issued by Berlin for the Sudeten area were not always clear and often not even known to the officials who were supposed to administer them, which led to pragmatic and sometimes contradictory decisions. The strutting little local Hitlers, frequently tall, good-looking men who cut a splendid figure in uniform but had been near-failures in their own businesses, still annoyed me, but I took less notice of them. On the whole, however, the change-over from the capitalist to the National Socialist system outlined to us at that meeting at Chemnitz proceeded smoothly.

The firm was now set on the right course. Not that all the necessary changes had been completed, but they were well in hand, and I could be satisfied with what we had achieved in comparatively little time. My usefulness was beginning to diminish, and I felt thoroughly sick of all the Nazi bombast that threatened to engulf me, but there was one important job still to be tackled before I could return to Langley. The large credit balances on our private accounts with Adolf Pasold & Sohn, resulting from the partial sale of the firm, were still frozen. They had merely been converted into Reichsmarks. An attempt had to be made to get permission for the transfer of this money to England. I knew, of course, that the prospects were poor, for Germany was desperately short of foreign exchange and our assets were now even more firmly blocked than they had been under the Czech regime. However, some compromise was perhaps possible, and I flew to Berlin to explore the chances. The official I saw was a member of Goering's huge Ministry, a slick young Prussian without any National Socialist cant. He accepted my invitation to lunch at the Adlon, but after listening to my story regretted that he could not hold out any hope of an early remittance of our funds. Then he made me a proposition.

'Sell your business interests in Britain,' he suggested, 'and bring us the sterling—we can give you Reichsmarks for it at a very favourable rate!'

'How favourable?' I asked out of curiosity.

'Considerably in excess of the official rate,' he replied, 'depending on the circumstances and the amount. It would enable you to buy a larger factory in Germany than the one you have in England. The Ministry might help you to find some interesting Jewish concern to take over, perhaps in the Sudetenland or Austria.'

What irony! But I did not say so. I told him that I would consider his proposition and departed, convinced that this was not the time to press for a transfer. One could not get blood out of a stone.

Rolf and Ingo met me at Croydon airport. I had been too busy to send them more than short reports and now filled in the details. Much as I disapproved of the Nazis, I said, Adolf Pasold & Sohn had no choice but to fall in line. The question now was how we three brothers were to fit into the picture. I could see that changing places every few weeks would not work in the future. The new order demanded leaders who identified themselves completely with their enterprise and who literally marched with their workpeople, not foreign advisers who came and went.

Ingo immediately volunteered to join Willie and Udo and offered to accept responsibility for the third share of Adolf Pasold & Sohn belonging to the Pasold brothers. The prospect of becoming a leader of industry in his own right greatly appealed to him. He did not care about politics and was not afraid of the Nazis.

I was quite taken aback. I had expected the three of us to discuss and carefully weigh up the situation, yet here was Ingo taking such a far-reaching decision without even waiting for our opinion. However, on reflection we could see his point of view. The British business had been created by Rolf and me. Ingo had, by comparison, played a minor part in its development. At Langley, he felt, he would always be overshadowed by his elder brothers, whereas at Fleissen he would be boss on a level with Udo. And why should he have misgivings about working with the Germans? Not all of them were Nazis. Why should they be worse than the Czechs? Some of the German pilots, for instance, whom he had met at the London Gliding Club at Dunstable were very nice chaps. They had taught the British a great deal. And gliding was very important to Ingo at the age of twenty-two. He had made quite a name for himself in the gliding world, been awarded a Silver C, come fifth in the British national gliding contest, was much photographed, and his flights were repeatedly written up in such papers as *The Times*, the *Daily Telegraph*, the *Evening Standard*, the *Evening News*, *Bystander* and *Illustrated Sporting and Dramatic News*. He was, no doubt, looking forward to gliding in Germany, the home of flight without power.

Since he had made up his mind, there was no point in delaying his departure. Ingo left two days after my return to Langley. He flew with Rolf to Paris, where they caught the night express for Stuttgart. We were considering the purchase of more circulars, and Rolf wanted to visit the Terrot and Haaga factories to compare their latest models. After the inspection of the machines and some trial runs Rolf would return to England and Ingo would proceed to Fleissen. Two Pasolds travelling together to do a job which, as a rule, was done by one alone seemed extravagant, almost a holiday, but the route via Stuttgart meant only a small detour for Ingo, and to have his opinion would be useful. They were looking forward to the visit.

But the holiday spirit was replaced by a feeling of horror when they arrived at Stuttgart and saw the havoc caused by anti-Jewish riots the night before. A Jew had assassinated a German diplomat in Paris, and Goebbels, appealing to man's lowest instincts, had called for drastic and immediate revenge. The National Socialist mob all over Germany had responded by attacking Jewish property, burning down synagogues, demolishing shops, smashing furniture and throwing Jewish families with their belongings out on to the streets. Groups of dejected, frightened Jews, driven on by SA men, were now clearing up the debris.

From the horrified look on people's faces it seemed that most of them condemned the pogrom but did not dare say so lest the Nazi rowdies turn on them. Management, sales staff and technicians at C. Terrot Söhne were disgusted, and Mr Haaga, the senior partner of Gebrüder Haaga, was visibly upset by the night's experience, upset and ashamed for his country. He was not a Jew, but he hated the Nazis almost more than did Uncle Richard at Brambach. A few days earlier he had inadvertently parked his Mercedes in the wrong place, he said, and some young Brownshirts had let down all four tyres, making the old man pump them up again while they looked on. Rolf was still distressed when, back at Langley, he told me what he had seen and heard.

Ingo had never been a prolific correspondent, he sent us little more than sketchy accounts of the tide of events, but we gathered that all was well at his end. Our people at Fleissen and Leibitschgrund had given him a rousing welcome when he told them that he had come not just for a visit but to stay with them. They wanted at least one of their leaders to be a Pasold, and he did not regret his decision. We felt relieved to be able to forget Adolf Pasold & Sohn for a while, for there was much to do at Langley. Among other things I had to straighten out a very awkward situation which Köhler, our works manager, had foolishly created during my absence. He had, when war seemed imminent, left hurriedly for Germany with his English wife and small son to avoid being interned, as his father had been during the 1914–18 war. As a parting joke he had written in large letters on the factory blackboard 'Will return in an armoured car', or words to that effect. Our workers only laughed—they knew his peculiar sense of humour—but the people in the village took the matter seriously, and wanted us to dismiss the 'dangerous Nazi'. I was extremely annoyed. Having to cope with the National Socialist upheaval in Sudetenland, we did not want to be bothered with it at Langley as well. We were satisfied that he was harmless. To lose him would have been a serious setback for the factory, for, next to Rolf and myself, Köhler and Colmer were the pillars of the firm. And since the crisis was now over and Chamberlain had promised 'peace in our time', I gave the young man a severe dressing down and took him back, for which some of the villagers never forgave me.

I noticed a marked change in the mood of the British people. Barely two months earlier they had been hailing Chamberlain as their hero and saviour, but now that the threat of immediate war was removed they were blaming him for not having stood up to Hitler, and for having betrayed the Czechs. Could one believe the German dictator when he claimed that the Sudetenland was his last territorial demand? How could Czechoslovakia defend herself when she had been robbed of her 'near-impregnable' border defences, my friends wanted to know?

I did not feel qualified to argue about military matters, but if these fortifications really existed, were they not of doubtful value, being located in the German-speaking regions of the republic? And I felt sorry for Mr Chamberlain. Surely it was Lloyd George who should be blamed, for having allowed Masaryk and Beneš to create such a vulnerable State in the first place, and not Chamberlain, who was faced with the fact of three million Sudetenlanders refusing to remain in bondage in order to prop up a Czechoslovakia they had never wanted? People in England knew little about conditions in central Europe. Even Chamberlain, in a speech he made on 27 September, at the height of the Sudeten crisis, had said, 'How horrible, fantastic, incredible it is that we should be digging trenches and trying on gas masks here because of a quarrel in a far away country between people of whom we know nothing!'

My English friends thought I was fortunate to be able to travel and to study the situation from the inside, but I was not so sure. It could be very unsettling. Having argued for months with Sudetenlanders, Czechs and Germans, each of them for different reasons resentful of Britain, I now tried to explain and sometimes defend their points of view. Things were neither all black nor all white. But the fate of the Sudetenlanders, or of the Czechs for that matter, was now of secondary importance to my questioners. Hitler had scored a victory and humiliated Britain. That rankled. If only Britain were determined to get down to business, to arm and to reassert her proud position of world leadership! To my dismay I saw few signs of it. While Germany's young men steeled their bodies running races, climbing mountains, skiing and swimming, my English friends drank beer, played darts, lost their money at the dog tracks, and laughed at me.

'And why not?' demanded Peter Matthews, Jack's younger brother, a hard-working, thrifty lad who never gambled himself. 'Why can't we be a second-rate nation like the Swiss and live in peace?'

'But the Swiss are a first-rate nation, for the size of their country, and maintain a well trained army,' Rolf interrupted him.

'It isn't just a matter of prestige,' I said. 'The British are one of the "haves", having inherited a third of the world and a very high standard of living. It will be taken from them by the "have-nots"—the Germans, for instance—if they are not willing to defend it.'

It was best not to get drawn into such polemics. They led nowhere, and one could easily be misunderstood, or even taken for a Nazi sympathiser if careless in the choice of one's words. But it was not always possible to escape them.

Poor Peter died for his country, fighting against the Germans in Italy.

Digging for information to fill gaps in my memory, studying my notebooks and writing these pages made me relive the Sudeten crisis all over again. Contrary to my belief at the time, I now think that both Hitler and Beneš wanted war in 1938. The dictator, who was much better informed than the politicians of the West about the inherent weakness of the conglomerate Czechoslovak army, never forgave Chamberlain for robbing him of the opportunity of displaying his military might and of achieving a resounding victory. He wanted to take the Sudetenland by force and not 'by permission' of Britain and France. And Beneš could no longer hide the just grievances of Czechoslovakia's oppressed minorities from the world. His was a weak case, and he could not win by negotiation. Nor could he win a war against

Germany, but if he were able to fan it into a second world war, who could tell what the outcome might be? It was his only chance.

I never met Henlein, but have reason to believe that he was a decent man who wanted no more for his Sudetenlanders than equality with the Czechs. Exhausted by Beneš's delaying tactics, and harrassed by extremists in his own party, he lost control of the situation and, not strong enough to stand up to Hitler, allowed himself to be overruled rather than replaced.

I cannot bring myself to blame Chamberlain. What cards had he to play? Despite all the criticism and abuse so many of the British people heaped on the poor man's head it was he who thwarted Hitler and Beneš, gaining eleven invaluable months of peace for the Western powers. Much better use should have been made of them, but perhaps that was impossible in slow-moving, divided democracies.

And what of the Czechoslovakia that remained? Had Hitler kept his promise and left the truncated republic in peace I believe it would have consolidated into quite a sound economic unit with a sound balance of trade. The country had valuable natural resources, its industry still a considerable export potential, and Czechs and Slovaks were hard-working, thrifty people. Without the unwilling and therefore troublesome minorities it might even have become a happier country.

36

MEANWHILE
AT LANGLEY
1938

NOW LET US see how things had shaped at the factory at Langley during this fateful period. Generally speaking, 1938 was a poor year for the British textile industry. In Lancashire and the Midlands many firms were on short time. Corah of Leicester and Hall & Earl, our largest competitors in interlock underwear, were said to have laid off thirteen hundred workers between them. Few knitting mills were fully employed, but we had faith in the future of our firm and proceeded with our policy of expansion. It caused surprise that we continued to enlarge our factory at such a time and, praising our courage, the local press quoted extracts from the January 1939 number of our new works journal, in which we told our employees:

We are going ahead with our expansion programme, in spite of advice to the contrary. There are more than two million unemployed in Britain and if every firm stalled until trade became normal again, prosperity would never return. Think of the work there would be for everyone, if we all decided to expand, build, buy now, instead of bemoaning the bad times, passing resolutions to wait, letting precious time slip by.

We had gained the confidence not only of Woolworth's, but also of Marks & Spencer, and both concerns listed us as regular suppliers. Our garments were now on the counters of almost a thousand stores. Hardly a week passed without Mr Cue telephoning for larger deliveries, and either Rolf or I being called to Baker Street by Miss Lancaster to discuss additional contracts. Meanwhile Mr Hurst continued to book business from the wholesalers, and especially from the shipping houses in Finsbury Square and Chiswell Street, whose clients in South Africa, Australia, New Zealand and other parts of the world, pleased with the initial deliveries of our goods, cabled for larger quantities, particularly of ripple dressing gowns. Our old friend George Peacock, whose stores were mainly in the country districts of Wales, still sent substantial orders for fleecy knickers, and Peggy was bubbling over with excitement, selling more sports shirts and jumpers than we could make. Forgotten were the worries of the past; to be in business was wonderful.

Woolworth's still selected their merchandise by rule of thumb, the last word more often than not resting with Mr Cue's typist-secretary, Miss Owen. It seemed a haphazard way of doing business, but it was effective, to judge by the success of the Woolworth operation and the speed at which they were increasing the number of their stores. There were now 737 of them. Mr Cue did not interfere in technicalities, leaving it to the ingenuity of the manufacturer to think of new lines and to develop them. This suited us. We always offered him garments which fitted well into our production programme. And this helped not only us to manufacture economically but also him, for he could be sure of getting good value.

Not so Marks & Spencer, who believed in science. They engaged textile technologists, established their own merchandise development department and testing laboratory, and laid down detailed size, shape and quality specifications for the merchandise they bought. Not satisfied with scrutinising the finished product, they began to investigate the yarn, the structure of the fabric and even the dyeing and finishing processes used by their manufacturers. This was not merely inquisitiveness, but was done to help their suppliers. The department was headed by a Mr Kann, a very knowledgeable man, an *emigré* from Nazi Germany. On the whole we would have preferred to be left alone, because, rightly or wrongly, we thought that some of our techniques were better than his and wanted to keep the know-how to ourselves, but it is fair to say that at times we also benefited from the tighter quality control we had to introduce because of him.

When Mr Kann's technologists insisted upon all fabric for interlock knickers being dyed in fast colours the navy blue presented difficulties. Pownall of Manchester and the Holt Hosiery Co. of Bolton, two regular M. & S. suppliers, could not overcome them and dropped out, leaving only Corah, Hall & Earl and ourselves. Although we were by far the smallest of the three firms, Miss Lancaster divided her order for 63,000 dozen children's knickers into three equal parts and gave us a contract for 21,000 dozen, hinting that there might be more to come. Let me quote from our works journal again:

The year has not started badly. We anticipated having to manufacture goods for stock during January to keep you all busy, but the spell of cold weather, together with Mr Hurst's sales efforts, resulted in unexpected repeat business for dressing gowns, and as we have already booked large orders for knickers and other lines, there is enough work for everyone. The outlook is good and if, as we hope, present negotiations for some large contracts materialise, we shall again be busy throughout the year.

Calling on customers, even the autocratic wholesalers in the City, was no longer the humiliating experience of former years. We still had to wait our turn while representatives of more important suppliers were taken past the queue, but the days were over when buyers showed us the door without even looking at our samples. Our turnover figures climbed:

1932	£4,000	1936	£54,500
1933	£19,000	1937	£75,800
1934	£35,500	1938	£90,400
1935	£38,800		

To experience the growing demand for our goods was an exhilarating sensation. Had we not had the courage to add those five sections to the factory in 1935, and an additional seven since, the business could not possibly have developed at this rate.

Our manufacturing area, apart from the office block, now measured 32,400 sq ft, which was exactly three times as large as the original factory had been. It was subdivided by two rows of steel stanchions into fifty-four equal rectangles of 20 × 30 ft, on which we moved machines, conveyor belts and other equipment like pieces on a chessboard whenever we enlarged our plant, to keep each of them strategically in the best position. Even the Terrot-type circulars, which hung from a grid of steel girders, could be moved without difficulty. The whole grid could be taken down merely by unscrewing the bolts and, without cutting or welding, re-erected on any of the other rectangles.

True to form, Rolf strained every nerve to squeeze the last ounce of production out of our existing manufacturing unit by improving efficiency, shift working, incentive bonuses and personal example while I doubted our ability to sustain this pressure for very long and argued in favour of buying more machines. Our plant was working to capacity, we had no reserve, and although we were masters of adaptation and improvisation, every mechanical breakdown disrupted production. We had, for instance, only one fleecing machine, and at times it had to work round the clock. It could be temperamental, and if something went wrong with it which Watson and Köhler between them could not put right we had to telegraph Fleissen, asking for Bergmann to hurry to Langley. The machine was driven by a specially wound German motor. When it burned out one night we were in serious trouble for a whole week because we could not get a replacement. This scare led to the purchase of a second fleecing machine, a new one which cost RM 6,000 and again came from Gessner at Aue. In one of his fits of economy Rolf wanted to drive the two machines from an old-fashioned line shaft, but, supported by Ingo, I succeeded in talking him out of this idea, and both our fleecers were fitted with individual motor drives.

With our order book so full, Rolf relented and no longer stalled or vetoed every proposal to buy additional equipment. He agreed to the purchase of a third sewing conveyor, another ripple machine, a calender, and, to crown it all, approved the expenditure of RM 35,000 on ten new Haaga circulars. It was an acquisition of such importance that we sent Bernard Walker to Stuttgart for some weeks to be present and learn about the machines while they were being made. And it was at Rolf's suggestion that we also enlarged the interlock plant. Heavy cases of machinery being unloaded at the back door of the factory became a familiar sight, and the crane Ingo had constructed for the purpose was kept busy.

Machinery was productive and one saw one's money back in due course, but convincing Rolf that we also needed a larger office, a packing room and a store for finished goods took much more effort. However, in the end I won, as the works journal of February 1939 reports:

Now let us tell you about the extension to the two-storey office block we have decided on. It will be 125 ft long, increasing the frontage towards the railway to a total length of 215 ft, and have twice the depth of the present building to provide room for warehousing and the packing department. We shall then be able to move all shelves for finished merchandise from the middle factory, thus gaining more space for the cutting, sewing and folding departments. You will remember the ten new knitting machines which are coming: they will increase our fabric production and we shall need more sewing machines. The new extension will prevent the sewing department from becoming overcrowded, in fact it will give everyone more room.

The new building will be constructed in the same style and of the same type of brick as the present one. The concrete road will be widened and brought in a curve to the boilerhouse tower at the back. The new factory entrance will be by the canteen. We shall have an iron fence and a hedge along the whole length of the site, attractive iron gates, and a fountain playing in the front. Give us another twelve months and even the people who were so much against our coming to this part of the world will be proud to have us at the 'front door of Langley'.

Doris, my secretary, an exceptionally gifted girl of twenty-one, was the editor of the little journal. Although only a modest production of twenty-four Gestetnered pages of typescript, of which I always wrote several myself, it fulfilled its purpose better than most of the glossy house magazines of larger firms. We liked to keep our workpeople informed and to make them feel they belonged. Quite a number of them had now been with us for five or six years, and had become members of the family, so to speak, but the newcomers too appreciated being told what was going on and responded. We were never short of contributions from the shop floor. It is with nostalgia that I remember our employees of those days, and the pride they took in the firm.

Our sports club was active; we played football, netball, cricket, went cycling, organised dances, theatre parties and outings to the seaside. We also laid down a hard tennis court which was much in use. And to make the inside of the factory attractive for our employees we fitted brackets to all the stanchions in the main building and placed large flower pots on them, which gave the working area the appearance of a winter garden. We put our girls in smart blue overalls, matching the colour scheme of the factory, and installed 'music while you work', something of a novelty at that time. And we were one of the first firms in the area to introduce an annual week's holiday with pay.

The local people began to understand that industry did not necessarily mean sullen faces, smoke, grime, refuse heaps and noise, but that it could also be beautiful, and a growing number of visitors came to see our factory, from the Women's Institute to town councillors and Slough's charter mayor.

The decision to do our own dyeing at Langley had been taken towards the end of 1937. Our fabric output was not large enough then to make the operation profitable, but we reckoned that within six months it would reach the economic minimum. To construct the dyehouse, complete the new boiler installation, erect and connect all the complex pipework and get the plant functioning would take fully six months. All being well, the timing should therefore be about right.

The project had been maturing for several years, and Langley benefited greatly from the experience we gained meanwhile planning, building and operating the dye plant at Leibitschgrund. The correspondence exchanged between Rolf, Ingo, Willie and myself at that time contains reams of information about automatic boiler controls, circulating pumps, heat exchangers, stainless steel vats, high-pressure heating coils, hot air driers and similar technical detail, with supporting diagrams and calculations. Our dye plant at Leibitschgrund was among the most advanced in western Bohemia, and we were determined to make the one at Langley the most efficient in the whole of Britain.

The small boiler we had installed in 1932 was oil-fired. It sufficed for heating the factory, but a dyehouse needed a much larger boiler plant, and as the cost of heat is an important part of the cost of dyeing we now decided in favour of coal, which was marginally cheaper than oil. Besides, however remote the risk of war might be it did not make sense to rely on oil tankers for our vital fuel supplies when Britain sat on such huge deposits of coal.

Much as we would have liked to try totally enclosed dyeing machines, our calculations indicated that the high price could not be justified by a corresponding saving of heat, and so we decided in favour of open vats, three to hold 800 gallons of dye liquid each, the largest commercial version on the market, and a 400 gallon vat to dye small batches and sample lots. The whole plant to be of stainless steel and with individual motor drive. Several British and Continental firms competed for the order, and after months of comparing specifications and prices we gave our contract to Pegg & Son of Leicester, a subsidiary company of Mellor Bromley's.

Since the high-pressure hot water installation we had at Leibitschgrund worked extremely well and economically, we decided to use the same system at Langley, although Pegg's chief designer raised his eyebrows when we told him. In England one used steam to bring dye liquid to the boil, he explained. The fact that water stays liquid at temperatures very much above boiling point if firmly enclosed in a steel pipe puzzled engineers of the old school. But when he discovered that we knew what we were talking about he agreed to modify the design of his vats and to fit the stainless steel heating coils we supplied from Czechoslovakia.

Next came the dryers. We needed two, one for our wide Terrot fabric, the other for interlock. Pegg & Son built an interlock dryer which consisted of a heater and a calendar arranged vertically, one above the other, on two floors. The heater blew hot air through the damp fabric, making it balloon and steam as it dried, while the calendar slowly pulled it upwards through a hole in the floor and rolled it up. We did not think very much of the machine. It kept a man busy running up and down stairs all day, and in our opinion used an excessive amount of heat. Some time in the future we would design a better one ourselves, we thought; meanwhile it was the best interlock drier on the market and we had to use it.

The dryer for the Terrot fabric came from Gessner. Basically a cork-insulated chamber fitted with a conveyor belt which consisted of revolving steel rods to carry the loops of moist fabric, it had five large, slow-running ventilators and was heated by high-pressure hot water coils of our own specification. Of all the pieces of equipment in the factory this was the largest and most expensive. After a visit to the works at Aue, Gessner's reduced their price from RM 16,875 to RM 15,500 and agreed to pay half the 20 per cent import duty. The final cost to us was RM 17,500, which included freight, insurance and erection.

We devoted much thought to the layout of the new dyehouse. It had to be labour-saving, permit easy extension, and had to be in the most convenient position, bearing both short- and long-term development of the factory in mind. Out of half a dozen building firms Try of Cowley submitted the lowest tender and, at £4,514, secured the contract for the erection of the building, including the pits for the vats, a sloping floor finished in acid-resisting concrete, earthenware ducts, and wood-lined ceiling to reduce condensation. It was to be ready in June 1938, when the various machines were due to arrive.

One of the great problems of most dyeworks is the disposal of the thousands of gallons of effluent they discharge every day. Filtering and purification plants are costly to install and maintain, and can eat up a substantial part of the profit. The agreement with Slough Urban District Council which I had concluded in 1932, by which the council undertook to treat our effluents in their plant free of charge, absolved us from this worry. I rubbed my hands, and even Mr Hurst now praised my foresight.

But the most important part of any dyehouse is, of course, its water supply. The purer, softer and more plentiful it is the brighter the colours and the softer the feel of the dyed material. And since even a small dyeworks like the one were were building used several thousand gallons of water an hour, price was a weighty factor. Buying one's water from the council and, in addition, having to treat it in a softening plant could make it so expensive that the economics of the whole operation became problematical. It was for this reason that I had taken so much trouble to study the water supply conditions east, north and west of London before deciding to locate the factory at Langley.

If the information given us in 1932 by the Geological Museum was correct we were sitting on an almost inexhaustible supply of pure, soft water, waiting to be tapped. The trouble was that we had to sink a borehole to a depth of about a thousand feet to get to it. We asked Isler & Co. and Sutcliffe Le Grand, the leading artesian well engineers in the country, for estimates. Both quoted approximately £2,000 for a 6 in. diameter tube well of 1,100 ft. Both were confident of encountering the Lower Greensand there, and in it the water, but neither would guarantee it, and this made us wonder.

While we were hesitating a Mr Beauchemin, managing director of Layne Well System Ltd, the subsidiary of an American firm of well borers, came to see us. A tough-looking little guy, a figure straight out of a movie, he said he would take the risk. For £2,000 he would bore down to 1,200 ft and give us an artesian well producing a minimum of 5,000 gallons of water per hour. 'No water—no pay,' he said in his broad Brooklyn accent. 'But if I give you 8,000 gallons per hour or more you pay me £2,300. Right?' and he wanted to shake hands on it there and then. But I was not ready to close the deal in such a hurry. The large sum involved demanded that I discuss the proposition with Rolf and Ingo, and that we slept on it. Then the enterprising Mr Beauchemin got our contract.

He did not mind where exactly we wanted him to drill the hole, as long as we gave him enough room to erect his derrick and boring gear, but for us the decision was an important one. We did not want a well where, some time in the future, it might be in the way. And this raised once again the issue of a development plan for our eighteen-acre site. We had enough land to accommodate a whole row of factory extensions, but we could not simply let them grow like Topsy!

We now had 200 workers. How large would the various departments have to be when we employed 300, 500 and 1,000 hands? They would not grow in equal proportion. With our chessboard floor pattern this did not matter, because we were flexible, but some departments—for instance, the dyehouse —required special-purpose buildings with different roofs, stanchion spacing and floors, unusual foundations, pits and other exceptional features, and to move them at some later stage would be a very great inconvenience and expense. Their location and ultimate size ought to be determined now. I realised the difficulties only too well. One would have to be a magician with the power to foretell the rate of growth of our business, improvements in building construction and manufacturing techniques, engineering and chemical progress, the use of synthetics, changes in fashion and goodness knows what else for at least twenty years ahead to be able to plan intelligently. Rolf said I was wasting my time and would take no notice of any of my elaborate guesswork, but I plodded on and made drawings to show how we could best transfer from one stage of development to the next with a minimum of cost and disturbance to the flow of production. It was better, I thought, to have an imperfect plan than to have none at all, and in fact the location both of the dyehouse and of the borehole were determined by reference to my overall design.

The Layne Well engineers erected their derrick and began boring. Mr Beauchemin came frequently to check progress; his son, a lad in his early twenties, worked a sixty-hour week as site foreman, and his daughter, whom I never met but whose golden telephone voice I still remember, was in charge of the London office. One had to admire the hard-working team. By the end of May the hole had reached a depth of 730 ft when, at nine o'clock on a Saturday night, the drill struck a rock and stuck fast, allowing the semi-fluid mixture in the shaft to freeze. The strain of trying to haul the pipe to the surface was too much for the derrick, and the eighty-foot-high metal structure collapsed, crumbling like cardboard as it crashed to the ground. The twisted steelwork looked like the remnants of an air disaster. Fortunately no one was hurt.

The hole had to be abandoned and a new one bored about 6 ft away. This time the operation was crowned by success. On 29 July, when the drill reached a depth of almost 1,200 ft, the water began to flow, then to gush, and finally to spout out of the pipe like the jet from a fire-engine, flooding the ground all around. I was so excited that I wanted to get drenched, wallow in the precious water, drink it. What would Father not have given for a mere tenth of this flow back at Fleissen! And here we were with an artesian well on our own factory site—an inexhaustible supply of clear, soft, excellent water which we did not even have to pump because it rose under its own pressure to a height of 45 ft above the ground. My happiness was complete.

The rate of flow measured 12,000 gallons an hour, and Mr Beauchemin got his well earned bonus. We had reached another milestone on the road to Langley's independence. How could our dyehouse fail to become a money-spinner with this unlimited supply of excellent water, no cost of softening, and Slough Urban District Council responsible for the treatment and disposal of our effluents at their expense! We had every reason to feel pleased, despite the fact that the total cost of the project came to double the amount originally estimated:

Three Pegg stainless steel dye vats holding 800 gallons each	£1,050
One Pegg stainless steel dye vat holding 400 gallons	208
One Fleissner hydro-extractor	164
One Pegg interlock dryer	455
One large Gessner drying machine	1,692
One large boiler	906
One automatic coal stoker	368
One small boiler	503
One Prior Burner automatic stoker	325
One high-pressure hot water circulating pump	120
One hot water storage tank	212
Pipework and installation	600
Layne Well System borehole	2,300
Dyehouse building, complete with pits and ducts	4,514
Dyehouse exhaust	56
	£13,473

All we needed now was a good dyehouse foreman manager with practical experience of dyeing knitted piece goods and a basic knowledge of chemistry. We found him in a young man named Hipperson, who had once worked at Fischer's ill fated factory at Edmonton, had then moved to Silknit Ltd at Park Royal, and now came to us. He knew his job and fitted well into our eager young team. I shall never forget the thrill I felt as we reeled the first loads of soaking fabric out of the vats and, having dried them, found them free from streaks and other flaws. The teething troubles we had expected never materialised; our dyeing was as even as that of Walter Cooke. The dream of many years was coming true.

The financial results were also highly satisfactory. We reckoned that the dyehouse saved us approximately £1,800 in the very first year, between $\frac{1}{2}d$ and $1d$ per lb of fabric processed, depending on the shade and on the rate of interest one allowed for the capital invested. The latter was largely a matter for the auditors; for Rolf and me it had little more than academic importance.

We always calculated a generous rate for plant depreciation, but we did not debit the business with interest.

It was Peggy Hurst who urged us to concentrate on making children's garments. Although the knitting department was on shift working, we were short of fabric, and one could cut more small dressing gowns out of a given yardage than large ones. Moreover there was less competition in children's wear. Manufacturers seemed to find it irksome to make so many different sizes, she argued. Since boys and girls grew out of their clothes, parents were continually having to buy new ones, which guaranteed a steady demand. And then she added, with a touch of prophetic perception, 'You and Rolf are engineers. Efficient production means more to you than fashion and style. Leave women's wear to the Jewish makers-up: they'll always beat you at that game. Nor will you make much impact on the conservative men's trade. It would take a lifetime. Children's clothes are different. They give you scope for development without the rapid changes in fashion that Langley can't cope with.'

Bottlenecks occur in every factory. We would catch up on our lagging fabric production, but we remained engineers. Peggy was right. The women's fashion trade was not our metier. And so, partly through circumstance and partly by design, we manufactured an ever-growing proportion of children's wear. The appearance and quality of our merchandise had, over the years, improved beyond recognition. We felt proud to see how well our ripple dressing gowns and our interlock knickers looked in the shop windows and on the counters—proud and at the same time a little sad that the public did not know who had manufactured them. Our garments bore the labels of the stores that sold them. It was all very well for Mr Sieff to tell us that we were supplying twenty million consumers and not just 200 M. & S. stores. The goodwill of those consumers accrued to 'St Michael' and not to us.

Langley was thriving, but I felt uneasy because its prosperity depended too much on Marks & Spencer's and Woolworth's. For the time being all was well, we were in their good books, but both concerns were wooed daily by other manufacturers with sample ranges of attractive merchandise and tempting propositions. Their policies might change, friendly merchandise managers could be replaced by hostile ones. As long as such a large proportion of our business rested on the goodwill of so few buyers we were vulnerable. What would happen if some day, for some reason, Miss Lancaster or Mr Cue, or both, placed their orders elsewhere, or were themselves transferred to other departments?

During the financial year 1938–39 we supplied goods to the following value:

Marks & Spencer	£43,107
Woolworth's	24,863
British Home Stores	3,855
Lewis's	2,411
D.L.M.S.	1,210
Some fifty other customers	17,611
	£93,117

We had to try to achieve a better balance, not by reducing sales to our two largest customers but by developing additional outlets for our expanding future production. Where could we find them? It was useless to look to the wholesale houses for more business. Their trade was shrinking as more and more retailers bought from the manufacturers direct. Our future lay with the retail organisations. The fastest-growing of them were the chain stores, most of whom—British Home Stores, for instance—followed the pattern set by Marks & Spencer. But their buying methods were erratic and made it difficult to establish any continuity. Besides, M. & S. did not like their manufacturers to supply competing chain stores. We had to watch our step. Shippers, mail order houses, speciality shops and department stores—especially the latter—would have to become the target of a sales drive.

It would be wise, we agreed with Mr Hurst, to allocate no more than half our future production to chain stores, much as their business suited us, and to spread the risk by selling as much of the other half as possible to such department stores as Selfridge's, John Barker's, Ponting's and Derry & Tom's, as well as the smaller speciality shops. This market was largely in the hands of the branded goods manufacturers, whose well known trade marks were backed by extensive advertising and enjoyed long-standing goodwill with the consumers. To break into their domain and compete with Meridian, Vedonis, Wolsey, Cherub, Chilprufe, Bairnswear and all the other household names would be easier said than done. We had not even a suitable trade mark at Langley. But we had done it at Fleissen—our 'White Bear' label was known all over Czechoslovakia—so why should we not be able to do it here? The prospect of selling our goods in Britain under a name of our own, of establishing our image with hundreds of thousands of consumers, and no longer having to pander to the whims of a few trade buyers, was a challenge worth almost any effort and expense.

We needed an attractive trade mark, and I set about designing one. Having been interested in the subject for a good many years, I knew exactly what was wanted. It had to be striking and distinctive to be remembered without much expensive advertising, easy to pronounce by shoppers, popular with mothers and children alike. Some people remember words, others illustrations, so it had to be both a word and a picture, colourful without having too many different colours, simple to weave as a label. It had to be internationally acceptable so that we could use it for our export trade, and if it brought the bearer luck, like a horse shoe or a four-leaf clover, so much the better.

I enjoyed myself developing a number of ideas, which I then submitted to the Trade Marks section of the Patent Office. To my consternation I was told that not one of them was original and that all were registered already. Not even 'White Bear' was available for the United Kingdom. And when I discovered that there were no fewer than 173,000 brand names on the register—six times as many as the number of words contained in a fair-sized dictionary—I was staggered and dismayed. What hope was there of finding any name at all that was not already booked, let alone a suitable one?

We could, of course, have used 'Pasolds' as a trade mark in the same way as Gillette, Hoover, Jaeger or Bata used their names. Provided one advertised it sufficiently, people would come to remember any mark, even if it met none of the conditions I thought desirable. But I did not want second best. The words I had put up were so much more appealing and easily remembered and would need far less costly publicity to make them known. Sadly I scrutinised my rejected list, topped by 'Ladybird', the favourite. It was one of several marks owned by the Klinger Manufacturing Co., a large hosiery firm. Since I could not recollect ever having seen it being used, I wondered whether there might be a chance of persuading them to sell it. On the spur of the moment I wrote a letter, convinced that the answer would be in the negative. But fortune smiled. Imagine my amazement and delight when Klinger's replied that they were not using the mark and that we could have it if we refunded the £5 registration fee. How they could thus give away one of the best trade marks in the world was beyond my comprehension. I felt like a small boy on Christmas morning and, needless to say, immediately closed the deal. It was a momentous event in the history of our firm.

Thrilled with the scope the little beetle offered, not only as a trade mark but as a captivating figure around which to write stories for boys and girls to make them treasure the garments we manufactured, I sketched ladybirds sitting on daisies, climbing blades of grass, wearing hats, and tried to give them faces. To get inspiration I kept a colony of ladybirds in a large jar with some plants in it, fed them on greenfly, photographed them, and then tried to write a fairy tale which I called 'Ladybird adventures'. It proved more difficult than I expected, and I rewrote it again and again until I was reasonably satisfied. Mr Hurst shook his head, Mr Cleaver of Dorland Advertising, whom I consulted, doubted the effectiveness of my approach, and Rolf quietly hoped I would get tired of the fantasy before it reached a stage when good money had to be spent on it, which he could not see ever coming back.

This did not dampen my enthusiasm. Snow White and the Seven Dwarfs, Donald Duck and Mickey Mouse had captured the hearts of millions of children and even adults, and I felt convinced that, given time, I could make our little ladybird the hero of the children's wear world. Impatient though I was, having secured the trade mark, we had now plenty of time to think how to make it popular. Before we could approach the department stores we had to create merchandise to suit their trade, garments to fit into their price ranges, which were different from those of the chain stores. And we were waiting for ten new knitting machines from Haaga to provide the additional fabric we needed. Having a dyehouse enabled us to manufacture more cheaply, but it did not give us more goods.

Fleecy knickers were out, the well advertised brands of interlock underwear too firmly entrenched to offer newcomers much chance to compete, and so we had to depend on our dressing gowns to open new doors for us, dressing gowns made of ripple cloth, but of different appearance from those we sold to Marks & Spencer. Speciality shops and department stores, not to speak of mail order houses, needed much higher gross profit margins and therefore wanted merchandise not readily comparable with that of M. & S. There was little we could do to change the basic fabric, apart from minor weight adjustments, and so we changed the collars and cuffs from plain ripple to quilted satin, which we had to buy. Problems arose; it was difficult to match the colours, and we thought the price was too high. Could we not buy a Schiffli machine and quilt our own material?

We knew little about Schiffli machines except that they were unwieldy, complicated, came from Switzerland or Germany and cost a great deal of money. I found it hard to persuade Rolf even to explore the proposition. Such a machine would be a foreign body in our factory, he protested, not without justification: we had no one who understood it or could operate it, and had we not enough on our hands already? He reminded me of the knob-yarn twisting frame I had bought and which, after working shifts for a short period, had stood for years under dust sheets. And of a coarse-gauge circular on which I had wasted so much time trying to make pullovers out of condenser yarn. In retrospect I think he was quite right not to let me buy a Schiffli.

So then I made another suggestion. If we bought a heavy embossing calendar, I said, we could press our designs into the fabric with an engraved steel roller instead of stitching them. They would not, of course, be so lasting, but the operation would be much simpler and cheaper. Reluctantly Rolf agreed, and I bought the machine. It came from Germany and cost £210, but, alas, proved a failure. Twenty years later, with a choice of various nylon yarns and other thermo-setting materials, we would have achieved splendid results, but in the late 1930s we could not. We were ahead of our time.

However, a far more pressing problem was now looming. Hitler's annexation of the Sudetenland put Langley's supply of condenser yarns in jeopardy. The conversion of kronen into Reichsmarks at a greatly inflated rate of exchange raised Leibitschgrund's production costs and put its prices out of Langley's reach. Would condenser yarn qualify for a German export subsidy, which might enable Willie to continue supplying us at the old price? It seemed unlikely in view of the high raw material and low labour content of condenser yarn. Besides, German manufacturers were queuing to buy every pound he could spin, irrespective of price. Willie no longer needed Langley's orders.

Fortunately our negotiations with the spinners at Hengelo in Holland were at an advanced stage, their yarns suited us, their prices were no higher than Willie's had been before the German take-over, and De Monchy was eager to capture Langley's business. It was therefore not difficult to come to terms with him. For a start we made contracts for white yarn only, yarn spun from raw Indian cotton, while Leibitschgrund continued to deliver the remaining balance of contracts for coloured yarn spun from our blue, red, green and brown cotton clippings. Willie's new customers in Germany did not want coloured condenser yarn; Langley was his only outlet for it. When Leibitschgrund's stocks of coloured clippings were used up, and Berlin refused to grant a licence to import additional quantities, the business came to an end. Perhaps this was just as well, for the risk of Adolf Pasold & Sohn being accused by the German authorities of subsidising their related firm abroad, and the dire consequences of such an offence, were too great to be countenanced for long.

We now tried to get our waste clippings re-spun in Holland, but the mill at Hengelo was not laid out to process them. Besides, Dutch wages were high, and the cost of double handling seemed too great to make the operation worth while. It would be more economical to purchase yarn spun from raw cotton. The quality was excellent and we had every reason to be pleased with the way in which De Monchy looked after our needs. At the same time, the thought of depending on a single spinner for such vital supplies made us feel a little uneasy.

Langley's waste clippings, sorted in colours and neatly stacked in pressed bales, were growing into a small mountain, a mountain of valuable raw material which nobody wanted. The prices offered by waste merchants were ridiculously low. Ought we not to consider using this waste ourselves? The thought of building a small condenser spinning mill at Langley had been with us for some time but we had not pursued it, for several reasons. There was, first of all, the high capital cost of such a plant. Then came the problem of finding suitable labour. Condenser yarn was spun on mules, complicated machines worked by men. The job was highly skilled and very demanding, and teaching it to anyone outside a traditional textile area would be a formidable task. And finally, was our yarn consumption large enough to keep a condenser spinning plant fully employed?

From 80,000 lb, worth £1,865 in 1933, our imports of condenser yarn had climbed to 300,000 lb, worth £7,000 in 1938, and if all went well, would reach 500,000 lb in another two or three years—a large enough weight, we estimated, to keep a mill going. We began, therefore, to study the matter in detail. Second-hand machinery was no longer available from Germany, so we had to think of buying new. I visited Schwalbe at Werdau and our old friends Gessner at Aue, the leading German makers of condenser spinning plant, and discussed our plans with them, but the prices they were asking for their machines were beyond our reach. It was impossible to spin cheap waste yarn on such expensive equipment, even if we were to operate it in three shifts. Reluctantly I came to the conclusion that we should have to abandon the project for the time being. However, my journey was by no means wasted, for quite accidentally I saw something very interesting.

We had taken it for granted that condenser yarn was always spun on mules—self-actors, as they were called on the Continent—but, watching in Gessner's demonstration hall a ring frame spinning carpet yarn, I wondered whether we were right. I tried the twist. It was much harder than that of our yarn, but the sales engineer assured me that the machine could be adjusted to spin even short-staple material with quite a soft twist. If this were true our labour problem would be solved, for ring frames were operated by women, the job was comparatively simple, and I felt sure that our girls would have no difficulty learning it.

The matter seemed worth pursuing. Could we, perhaps, obtain suitable plant more cheaply in Lancashire? We compared Gessner's and Schwalbe's specifications and prices with those of similar machinery made by Platt Bros., Brooks & Doxey, Dodd & Sons and Tatham. The reader may well ask why we did not go to British engineering firms in the first place, and had we wanted ordinary cotton spinning plant we would certainly have done so. Although Lancashire's industrial image was tarnished and the whole world knew that her cotton mills were out of date, she still built excellent spinning machines. But we wanted a tailor-made condenser plant and, rightly or wrongly, thought the Germans had more experience of condenser spinning than the British. If this were not the case, we reasoned, why should we have to import our condenser yarn from the Continent?

British machinery was, in fact, cheaper than German. Hopefully we made fresh calculations, and I spent happy hours laying out imaginary mills on my

drawing board. It would be a challenge to build a condenser plant along such
unorthodox lines. We were willing to accept the inherent technical risk but,
unfortunately, the capital investment involved was still too large to make the
scheme commercially viable. And so, once again, we decided to shelve it. We
continued to accumulate our waste clippings and, keeping our fingers crossed,
relied on the spinners at Hengelo to supply us regularly with condenser yarn
spun from raw Indian cotton.

The years when life at Langley was all worry and work lay behind us. We
occasionally had dinner in town now, or went to see a show. I loved Leslie
Howard as Professor Higgins in *Pygmalion*, a film topped only by Walt
Disney's *Snow White and the Seven Dwarfs*, which I saw nine times. And at
the weekend I tinkered with the aeroplane or explored out-of-the-way parts
of southern England. I do not remember who first told me about Myles
Bickerton, a Harley Street eye specialist who lived in a large house named
Owl's Oak at Denham, where he had his own airfield. This intrigued me, and
I went to see it. He seemed charming. He showed me his Miles Hawk, I saw
the aeroplanes of a few other private owners in the hangar, and he introduced me to Cyril Mills of circus fame, who had a Hornet, then invited me
to the house for a cup of tea. The upshot was that I took my plane away from
Heston and housed it at Denham.

Heston was much larger, an airport with a beautifully kept level grass
surface and all modern facilities, such as a permanently manned control
tower, a customs office, engineering shops, and a good restaurant, while the
little airfield at Denham reflected the unpredictability of its eccentric owner.
One could not tell whether he was a man or a genius. Whenever he found a
lark's nest in the grass he marked the spot with a red flag. At times there were
half a dozen red flags all over the aerodrome which one had to dodge when
taking off or landing. And returning from somewhere in the afternoon one
frequently saw a flock of a hundred or more sheep grazing on the landing
area. The approved technique was to dive on the animals several times,
herding them to one side of the field, and then land quickly on the other. I
did not mind these obstacles—they added interest to aviation. Aeroplanes
were slow and simple to manipulate in those days, and after flying about
Central Europe I was used to awkward little fields with surprises.

The noise of the planes annoyed the neighbours, who were in a permanent
state of war with Bickerton, complaining to the authorities and signing
petitions to have the aerodrome closed. The leader of the campaign, if I
remember correctly, was a man with an outlandish name whose garden
adjoined the airfield. When he became especially troublesome Bickerton
hoisted a large swastika flag to annoy him. But at heart the eccentric doctor

was a kindly and hospitable man, and we had many happy parties at Owl's Oak with him and his amusing friends.

Rolf and I stayed in England for Christmas. Our good friends the Matthew, whose house had become our second home, invited us to share their Christmas turkey, and on Boxing Day we were at Owl's Oak. Our circle of acquaintances, mostly young people living in the neighbourhood, had steadily grown. We were on visiting terms with the Ellis, Boyer, Addison, Elliot, MacDonald and Vincent families, some of whom became friends for life, and in addition I had met, through flying, some interesting young aviators, whom I introduced to the Pinewood Club. We had billiard and swimming parties there in the evenings. At times there were so many of us swinging on the rings above the pool that the scene resembled a monkey house. And I cannot recall a happier New Year's Eve than that of 1938, when, after the gala dinner at the club, we danced the 'Lambeth Walk' and the 'Chestnut Tree' into the early hours of the morning.

37

WAR
1939

WE STARTED THE new year with great expectations. So much of what we had been striving for now lay within our grasp. We had the confidence and good-will of our customers. The Langley factory had become a hive of activity, with a well trained, hard-working and loyal labour force. The new dyehouse functioned well, giving us clearer and faster colours at lower cost. We could be proud of the quality of our merchandise, the demand for which was growing faster almost than our expanding output. Every month the curve recording our turnover climbed higher, and we were making steady profits which we ploughed back into the business by improving the factory and buying more machines. We were full of energy and enterprise, and, having relinquished the day-to-day responsibility for the firm in the Sudetenland, were free to devote them almost entirely to the development of Langley.

We did not need additional encouragement, but I felt pleased if the progress we made was noticed and appreciated. Councillor Trevener, for instance, Langley's representative on the Slough Urban Council, said that our factory was a blessing to the village. With our 200 workers we were its largest employer of labour. Mr Bromley, chairman and managing director of Mellor Bromley & Co., who kept himself well informed of developments in the knitting industry, claimed that our growing interlock trade was not going unnoticed and that we were teaching the established manufacturers in the Midlands a salutary lesson. Mr Hurst pointed to the foreign currency we were saving the nation by making ripple cloth and dressing gowns which replaced imports from Germany. Miss Lancaster made me feel especially happy when she said that we were raising the living standard of the people by supplying them—through Marks & Spencer and Woolworth's—with better clothes at lower prices than they ever had before. And if Mr Lampitt, general manager of the Great Western Railway, exaggerated in declaring that Britain was fortunate when Rolf and I settled here it sounded good, and my greatest ambition was to make it a fact.

Fleissen and Leibitschgrund reported that business was good, sales were booming, and the large raw material stocks were worth their weight in gold. As a special windfall the German authorities were not collecting any revenue for 1938. It was to be a tax-free year. No wonder Willie, Udo and Ingo were jubilant. Ingo did not regret his decision to stay with Adolf Pasold & Sohn. He got on well with Udo, there were no major problems, and he had even been able to fit in fourteen days' gliding before Christmas. He did not write much; we heard from Mother that he was happy and that he had no wish to return to Langley.

But we did not like the political outlook. The relief we all felt after the peaceful settlement of the Sudeten crisis did not last; tension between Germany and Britain was growing. I no longer believed that Hitler's only aim was to unite all people of German stock and tongue in one *Reich*: he was looking towards eastern Europe and Russia to build an empire. There would be no war in the west. I felt sure that he did not want to extend Germany's frontiers there, but he would wage a war of nerves against Britain and France, demanding a free hand to remove the Communist threat to Europe and to provide Germany with *Lebensraum* for generations to come. For this he would trade in his claim to the former German colonies. If he should succeed, the whole of central and eastern Europe, all the way to the Ural mountains, would be dominated by the National Socialists, with their Gestapo and concentration camps; if he was defeated the inevitable Communist backlash might well sweep as far west as the Rhine. Of the two, the second alternative seemed even worse, but neither could be faced with equanimity. Our future at Langley was probably secure enough, but what of that of Adolf Pasold & Sohn? The possibility of having to abandon Fleissen and Leibitschgrund and find a new base for Ingo, Willie and Udo never seriously occurred to me, and they would have been the first to roar with laughter at such an idea, yet the thought must have been there somewhere in the subconscious at the back of my mind, for as the weeks went by I felt increasingly that we should consider building a factory in Canada. It was a British Dominion with great potential, I had travelled across it from coast to coast and liked it, and Rolf too thought it a good choice. Far from raising objections, he was in favour of looking ahead.

The manager of the London branch of the Bank of Montreal, with whom we discussed the project, offered us the assistance of his organisation's Business Development Department in Canada. We told him that Rolf would undertake a sales journey to North America later in the year to study conditions on the spot, and then we converted £10,000 into $47,062·50, which we placed on deposit with the head office in Montreal at one per cent interest per annum. A ridiculously low rate by today's standards, but normal in those days of stable money values. To have such a substantial sum at a safe distance from the European powder barrel eased our apprehension, and it was with an easy mind that I took a skiing holiday with John Houlder during the second half of February. We went to Chamonix, in the French Alps, which was new territory for me and a welcome change from Austria, whose skiing resorts would now be crowded with Germans.

Next on my programme was a visit to Fleissen, but the very day I collected my visa from the German embassy in London the Nazis marched into Prague. Hitler, who had said that the Sudetenland was his last territorial demand in Europe, had broken his word and seized the remainder of Czechoslovakia. There was no excuse for grabbing a country which rightfully belonged to Czechs and Slovaks, and although this move fitted into the anticipated pattern I felt so bitter about it that I cancelled my trip and stayed at Langley.

With Hitler in control of the Sudetenland it was no longer possible to arrange 'black' or even 'grey' capital transfers to Britain. For the present Rolf's and my credit balances at Fleissen were so firmly frozen that we no longer wasted time thinking about them. Thank heaven we had moved such large sums in the years before the Nazis came. In the meantime Langley's figures had climbed out of the red and into the black, and we were now earning quite respectable profits. From less than £2,000 for the financial year 1935–36 they jumped to £6,689 for 1936–37, then to £8,546 for 1937–38, and to a record £15,330 for 1938–39. We were thus able to finance our factory expansion programme at Langley without recourse to crippling bank overdrafts, or any more help from Fleissen, and could still spare £10,000 for Canada.

Our profits did not appear as ready cash, of course, but were in the form of stocks of merchandise, machinery, and bricks and mortar. Nor were they all ours to use, for the tax inspector took an ever larger proportion of them. The standard rate of income tax was 5s in the £, i.e. 25 per cent, but personal allowances, earned income relief and other provisions reduced this rate substantially for the lower income groups. Surtax, on the other hand, which started at an income of £2,000, increased it progressively for the higher. There is no need to go into details, but an approximate overall scale would be:

Annual income (£)	Rate of tax payable (%)
500	2
1,000	13
2,000	19
3,000	23
5,000	30

For incomes exceeding £50,000 the rate rose to 66 per cent, varying from person to person according to circumstances.

We did not begrudge paying tax—secretly I even felt proud of our contribution to the national Exchequer—because we were satisfied that the British Inland Revenue authorities were fair and reasonable, and that John Citizen responded by making honest returns. Cheating the tax collector would have been as contemptible as cheating at cards. But we thought there was an inequity in the system. Since we were a partnership, the whole of our profit was treated as if it had been drawn by the partners and was therefore subject to surtax, while in a limited liability company the profit that stayed in the business, or was ploughed back into it, bore only the standard rate of tax. We were thus at a disadvantage *vis-à-vis* our competitors, all of whom were companies.

'Didn't I advise you seven years ago to register a private limited liability company?' smiled Mr Baird, the senior partner of Westcott Maskall & Co., our auditors. 'I expected to see you back before now.'

And so, on 13 April 1939, we converted the partnership into 'Pasolds Limited', with an initial capital of £50,000, divided into shares of £1 each, which we increased to £65,000 soon afterwards. Looking back, I find it difficult to understand why, at the time, it seemed such an important decision to take. With the exception of the usual two qualification shares issued to the solicitors' clerks, for which they had signed blank transfers, we held the whole of the share capital and therefore owned the firm as completely as before, but I worried whether Father and Grandfather would have understood and approved of the change, until I discovered that it was barely a nine-days wonder and that the only noticeable change was the addition of the letters LTD to the illuminated sign on the factory roof. The business carried on exactly as before, decisions continued to be taken at the luncheon table, Rolf 'had better things to do than attend board meetings', and the only resolutions entered in the minute book were those recorded once a year by the auditors.

It was impossible to get Rolf to do something he did not want to do, and if I remonstrated he looked out of the window or simply walked away. He wanted short cuts, not wasteful formalities. There was too much waste everywhere, waste of yarn, fabric, dyestuffs, heat, sewing thread, needles, oil, and sloppy timekeeping, which had to be fought from morning to night. The less our workers wasted the higher the wages we could pay them, and who would not have liked to earn more? Economy was as important as productivity. Our wage levels were comparable with those of the Leicester area, but substantially higher than those of the textile industry in Lancashire, and we had to compete with both. What Rolf was trying to do the hard way by getting everyone to exercise more effort and greater care I hoped to achieve by investing more money in modern machinery and greater automation. The blend was quite successful.

Our Langley factory had become a very efficient manufacturing unit. True, the knitting and sewing machines were not as completely standardised as we would have liked them to be, for we had bought many of them second-hand, which made some compromise inevitable, but we had every reason to be proud of our plant. There was not an equally well balanced knitting mill in the Sudetenland, we felt sure, and we doubted whether there was one in Britain either. In most factories up to a third of the machines stand idle while many of the others work overtime. In our case 90 per cent of all our machines were busy for twelve months in the year. In order not to bore the layman I quote here only a summary of the plant we had in April 1939, and the values shown are those to which they were written down in the books at that time.

5	Grosser winding machines for bottle bobbins, total 360 spindles	£600
1	Hamel fancy twist machine	260
44	Terrot-type spring-needle circular knitting machines	4,800
7	Mellor Bromley shaped vest knitting machines	920
5	Mellor Bromley knitters for binding and shoulder straps	125
13	Mellor Bromley interlock knitting machines	2,090
1	Schubert & Salzer latch needle knitting machine	80
2	Gessner fleecing machines each with twenty-four rollers	1,220
1	Gessner card grinding machine	120
1	Gessner calendering machine	240
6	Gessner ripple machines	1,140
1	Pegg garment press	130
1	embossing calender	210
1	Arbach laying-up machine with 20 m long table	410
4	Eastman electric cutting knives	140
1	Hippmann electrically driven band knife	90
99	sewing machines of various types and makes	2,902
3	sewing conveyors and eighty-two sewing machine stands	633
142	electric motors, total 200 h.p.	437
4	Avery scales	163
		£16,710

This summary does not include such items as 5,000 bottle bobbins, 200 galvanised steel tubes on which we rolled our fabric, trolleys, steel shelving, sewing stools and the many other things we used in the factory, nor does it include the boilers and the dye plant, which are described and for which figures are quoted in the previous chapter. Not included either are the buildings. Once again there was not enough space, and another factory extension was in the course of construction. Over the years our floor area grew in stages:

Starting in 1932   with 16,000 sq ft   and in 1937   +4,300 sq ft
we added in 1935   +9,000 sq ft   in 1938   +9,400 sq ft
and in 1936 +10,000 sq ft   in 1939   +11,000 sq ft
and as soon as the extension was completed would have 59,700 sq ft

With its clean lines, well kept sports grounds, lawns, flower beds and the
fountain in front of the entrance, our factory looked every bit as attractive
as the modern factory buildings on the Great West Road which I had for so
long admired with envious eyes.

Having abandoned my trip to the Sudetenland, I wanted to fly somewhere
else. I studied the map of France, measured distances, worked out compass
bearings and flight times, and put them all down on a strip of paper. Next
morning, Good Friday, my friend Sydney Evans met me at Heston. We
stowed our toothbrushes and bathing trunks in the aeroplane and took off for
the Riviera. The weather forecast promised a clear sky over the south of
England but low cloud and rain on the French side and thunderstorms over
central France. However, we decided to go and see for ourselves, and after an
easy flight across the Channel landed at Le Touquet to clear customs. The
French officials were pessimistic about the weather. Le Bourget had been
closed all morning owing to fog and had only just been opened again to air
traffic, they told us, but visibility was still very poor.

The weather got really thick soon after we had left Le Touquet, and I
decided to fly low and follow the main railway line to Paris rather than steer
a compass course. We groped our way through the mist, never once losing
sight of the railway, until we were right over the suburbs of Paris. It was time
now to leave the railway line and steer due east, where we should find the
aerodrome. But we did not find it. There were only fields and houses where
Le Bourget airport should have been, and I had just decided to turn back and
fly due west in the hope of finding our railway line again when suddenly, only
200 yards away from us, the airport appeared out of the mist.

We had lunch on the aerodrome and waited for the mist to clear. It was
3 p.m. by the time we took off, steering south. As we left the smoke of Paris
behind us visibility improved rapidly, and we could see fields, lakes, woods
and villages for miles. The scenery was charming, and we enjoyed that part
of our flight. But after an hour black clouds gathered on the horizon ahead—
first one or two, then lots of them. So the weather forecast was right! The sun
disappeared and the clouds dropped lower and lower, while the country
below us began to rise. Now there was only a narrow gap left between the
dark clouds and the thick pine forests and we had to fly very low to slip
through. It began to rain, and the clouds sat right on top of the hills, forcing

us to wind our way along the valleys, trusting that they would not suddenly come to a dead end. It was pouring, and we could see very little of the ground. I opened the cabin window and tried to look out over the side. It was not a pleasant feeling to be roaring through beastly weather at 100 miles an hour without being able to see where we were going. The little plane was thrown about by the gusts, I had to dodge clouds, and it was quite impossible to read the map or steer an accurate compass course. The thunder was drowned by the engine noise, but once or twice when flashes of lightning lit up the scene I grew scared and was on the point of turning back. Only the prospect of having to fight our way through all the bad weather we had just battled through, and not wanting to admit defeat, kept me flying south.

Scraping over a ridge which lay right across our course, we dropped down into the Rhône valley. It was flooded. The hills on both sides were in the clouds, but there was a clear space between the water and the base of the clouds, and we followed the winding river, flying about 200 ft above the water all the way. Two and a half hours after we had taken off from Paris we landed at Lyons. It had seemed twice that long to us. By the time we had refuelled and had a cup of tea it was too late to fly on to Marseilles, and as we were told that all the intermediate airfields were under water we stayed the night at Lyons.

Next morning presented the same picture. Low cloud, mist and drizzle. They could not speak English on the aerodrome, and handed me a long meteorological report typed in French, and although I hardly understood a word of it I had to sign it as proof that we had been warned, in case we should meet with an accident. How I wished now that I had worked during French lessons at college instead of playing the fool. Speaking very slowly, I asked the weather prophet, 'Is it good, medium or bad?' And he replied, 'Oh, monsieur, is bad—but is possible.' So we decided to fly on.

It was bad but it was possible, and at Marseilles the sun came through and we realised we had won. We landed and refuelled at Marseilles airport—a huge airfield and seaplane base, much as in American films—and then flew on to Nice, where we arrived Saturday lunchtime. It was a glorious weekend. The sky was blue, the sun hot, and all the little French girls were wearing their summer frocks. Life felt good as we sat under palm trees sipping coffee, swam in the lukewarm waves of the Mediterranean, sunbathed on the beach watching the sailing boats go by and, in the evening, had a delicious lobster dinner at a bistro.

We had been promised that everything would be ready for our take-off at seven o'clock on Easter Monday morning, but when we arrived at the air-field there was only a mechanic there to greet us. My log book was locked in the manager's office, and he was not due for another two hours. This was most annoying. We might not get back to London that night if we waited for him. So I asked the mechanic for some tools, which he readily provided, and broke open the office door. We found our papers, gave the mechanic a tip, and flew off. Anyone who knows Nice airport today may find it hard to imagine that back in 1939 it was no more than a rough grass strip that ran parallel with the shore, and the only building on it, the manager's office, a wooden shack.

It was a wonderful day. Sky and sea were deep blue, and the rugged coastline looked a bright red with the morning sun upon it. We felt sad to have to leave this heavenly spot, but there was no choice, and so I turned the nose of the Hornet north. We by-passed Marseilles and, with a slight tail wind, arrived at Lyons in time for an early lunch. We had hardly landed and were climbing out of our machine when an infuriated French officer in an impressive uniform and with a very red face rushed up to us and poured bucketfuls of rapid language at us. We could not understand what he was saying, but his attitude was definitely hostile. When he saw that we did not comprehend he called another officer, who spoke some English, and it transpired that we had got in the way of an airliner when we were landing. It must have been true all right, because there was the huge plane sitting on the grass, only a few yards away from our little machine, and it had not been there when I looked down before we landed. But where it had come from we could not say. Certainly neither Sydney nor I had seen it. As we could not speak French, the wild officer gave up shouting at us and we went to have some lunch.

We had fine weather for our flight from Lyons to Le Touquet, and the healthy roar of the engine seemed to confirm that it enjoyed being up in the pure, cool air 5,000 ft above the ground as much as we did. Paris and the Eiffel Tower appeared in the distance, but we did not land there this time, and we soon left them behind us. Just as I was about to land at Le Touquet I saw an airliner which was also about to land, so I let it get in first and kept circling the airfield until it had touched down and come to rest at the far end of the landing ground. Then I smartly sideslipped my machine, landed it right by the door of the control office and, rather pleased with my skilful performance, went in to report.

'Are you the pilot?' asked the officer in charge. When I said that I was, he proceeded to give me a dressing down for landing while the airliner, still at the far end of the field, was taxiing. I knew that this time I was in the right. An aeroplane on the ground, be it an airliner or a flying flea, must not taxi while another plane is landing. In the ordinary course of events I would have told him so, but in view of the broken office door at Nice, and my getting in the way of the airliner at Lyons, I did not want to have a row with him. If these crimes—all committed in one day—should be reported to London what would the Air Ministry have to say! I was not reported, and, let me hasten to say, in more than thirty years as a pilot I have never got in the way of an airliner again.

Everything is relative. The airliners of those days carried between twelve and thirty-six passengers at speeds of 130 to 160 m.p.h. and although enormous compared with my Hornet would look tiny next to a jumbo jet. Many of them still had fixed undercarriages, but the pilot and co-pilot no longer sat outside the cabin in an open cockpit as in the mid-1920s. After the Dutch Fokker and the German Junkers came the American Douglas DC3, which took most of the passenger traffic on the international routes, and in 1938 Imperial Airways introduced the Ensign, a thirty-seven-passenger 'air giant', as the press called it, which had retractable wheels and flew from London to Paris in eighty minutes.

Our flight from Le Touquet to Heston and on to Denham was uneventful, and I was home in time for dinner. Altogether we had been in the air for more than fifteen hours that Easter weekend, and looking back I would not have missed a single one of them.

During the following two months I flew to the Continent several times, in fair weather and sometimes in foul, and got to know the coastlines of Holland, Belgium and northern France very well. The role of Holland had changed from that of customer to that of an important supplier—most of our condenser yarns now came from there. Our friends at Hengelo, with typical Dutch tenacity and a little technical help from us, had adapted part of their mill to process hosiery clips, and we were now sending them regular consignments of our waste cuttings for re-spinning.

And I was very taken with the velvet-like cotton plush manufactured by the French on Terrot-type knitting machines. There would surely be a large market for it in Britain, I thought, if we could make it at Langley at a reasonable price. London stores were importing small quantities of plush dressing gowns and pullovers from France and Switzerland, but the business did not develop because they were too expensive. A reasonably priced plush dressing gown would be an ideal line with which to start a Ladybird advertising campaign.

Then came an urgent call from Fleissen, where policy decisions had to be taken, and on 26 June I took off for Brussels, from where I flew via Cologne and Frankfurt to the little airfield at Hof. It looked just the same as when I had left it. I folded the wings of my Hornet, pushed it into the old barn and waited for Ingo to collect me in the Alvis.

The first thing that struck me was that the small union jack was missing. 'You had better not fly it any more,' Ingo said. 'The British are not as popular as they were.' I had noticed the change already at Cologne, and again at Frankfurt, where the behaviour of the airport officials was correct but distinctly cool. Come to think of it, a car flying a swastika flag in London might also invite trouble. The feeling of resentment was mutual. The English had little sympathy left for the Germans, especially after their invasion of Czechoslovakia. We drove along the familiar road via Asch and Bad Brambach without stopping. The frontier at which I had cleared customs a thousand times in the past had disappeared. The Sudetenland was now well and truly part of the Reich. I was wondering how Adolf Pasold & Sohn were faring under the Nazis, and what kind of reception I would get. But our workpeople at Fleissen and Leibitschgrund and everyone else I met seemed genuinely pleased to see me, and at first I felt as if I had never been away.

Yet there was a different atmosphere in the firm. Our factories were busy and, as I knew from the reports we received at Langley, had more orders than they could cope with. Our employees felt that their jobs were more secure under the German government than they had been under the Czech, and were grateful. A foreman at Leibitschgrund actually refused to accept a reward for an improved spinning technique he had discovered, saying it was his contribution towards the Four Year Plan. There was more stability because manufacturers no longer poached each other's labour. I heard the same from my friend Helmut Amarotico, who was on the way to becoming one of western Bohemia's leading building contractors, and from my uncles, the Geipels, whose leather factory was booming, from the Brauns, who no longer behaved like rivals since they too could get all the business they wanted, from industrialists at Asch, and from my friends at the banks. They all seemed to be pleased with the way things were going. I felt, therefore, a little surprised that, as it would appear, none of them had joined the ranks of the NSDAP. Did they not want to, or was it too difficult to become a party member?

Industrialists in the Sudetenland had much to be pleased about. In addition to the tax-free year they could write off all new capital expenditure at once, which encouraged investment. Moreover they could write up the value of their buildings and plant and declare the true worth of their stocks of raw material and merchandise, including hidden reserves, without having to pay tax on the difference. There was an amnesty for fiscal misdemeanours committed under the old regime, but penalties for future lapses would be severe. This clever strategic move enabled businessmen to put their records in order while at the same time it gave the German authorities accurate information about the assets that had fallen into their hands. Adolf Pasold & Sohn decided to make full use of this heaven-sent opportunity. However, having lost the familiar yardsticks, we had problems when it came to interpreting the regulations of the Third Reich and understanding the mentality of its officials. Our auditors at Eger, used to the Austrian and Czech official mentality, were equally at sea, and, at Uncle Richard's recommendation, a German firm of auditors with headquarters at Plauen was called in to advise. With its help Adolf Pasold & Sohn's stocks, plant, buildings and sites were evaluated.

We had to reorganise our book-keeping to comply with German require-ments. All knitted goods manufacturers had to keep their records and prepare their balance sheets in exactly the same manner. Travelling expenses, for instance, to mention just one item, had to be shown in all accounts under the same number. This made it easy for the tax man to compare like with like, and difficult for tax evaders to disguise capital payments as expenses, create secret reserves or otherwise hide profits.

Leibitschgrund's stocks of cotton were running down, and in order to qualify for some replacements Fleissen had to export. Hitler needed foreign currency for strategic imports, and Dr Schacht, his financial wizard, who, alas, had since been dismissed, had created a complicated system of trade pacts and compensation agreements to stimulate sales abroad. Export subsidies were paid which varied according to the desirability of the currency concerned and rose to 60 per cent in the case of hard, freely convertible currencies. This more than made up for the $37\frac{1}{2}$ per cent increase in manu-facturing costs caused by the conversion of kronen to marks, and the rise in wages. However, price was no longer the deciding factor everywhere. Inter-national Jewry had, quite naturally, extended its boycott of German goods to merchandise made in the Sudetenland, which reduced Fleissen's chances of selling abroad. The only territory in which our sales actually expanded was that of Olaf Engelhardtsen, our Norwegian agent.

Most industrialists found coasting along the smooth totalitarian highway, lined with banknotes from Hitler's printing presses, more congenial than fighting over the far too small market the Czechoslovak republic had pro-vided. They no longer had to worry when and where to buy their cotton, be-cause there was practically none and they had *Zellwolle* allocated to them. They had no unpleasantness with their workers. Any discord that arose was speedily dealt with by the National Labour Front. There was no need to go out and fight for orders, the merchandise sold itself. And every manufacturer made good profits—excessive profits if he operated his plant economically, piling up large credit balances at the bank, especially if he sold abroad and pocketed the large export subsidies.

Paper fortunes? Not altogether. There was much that businessmen could buy: town houses, country estates, abandoned or confiscated Jewish property, machinery, motor cars and even diamonds. They could take holidays in the Bavarian or Austrian Alps or go hunting in East Prussia—as long as they did not want worsted suits, cotton shirts, bananas, French champagne, or travel abroad.

Germany's economy was wildly inflationary, particularly since the departure of Dr Schacht, but the masses did not seem to be aware of it and there was no tendency for a buying spree to develop. Miraculously, as it must seem to modern politicians, the German people saved their paper money, or put it down as advance payment for a Volkswagen to be delivered in years to come, such was their faith in Adolf Hitler. And the Führer, presumably, used these funds to manufacture armaments, hoping to repay the mounting debts with grain from the Ukraine, minerals from the Urals, the wealth of countries he was preparing to conquer with the guns for the manufacture of which he was meanwhile paying with his bits of paper. Thus the circle would be closed.

Provided a factory owner fell in line with the prescribed drill, marched with his workpeople on a sufficient number of outings, hoisted the swastika flag on state occasions, made the appropriate speeches and greeted everyone with 'Heil Hitler' he had a comparatively easy life. There were forms to be filled in, to be sure, which was not always easy, but few decisions had to be taken, and the shop floor needed little supervision. Udo could go shooting, Ingo gliding, and Willie could devote himself to his family and his beloved village of Leibitschgrund. Surely, I thought, this state of affairs could not last.

What would the effect of business without pressure be on management? It seemed reasonable to assume that an industry which was regulated by a few able men—provided it was ability and not party membership that counted—would operate better and more economically than the uncoordinated scramble of hundreds of manufacturers of mediocre talent, all fighting, duplicating and getting into each other's way. The Nazis reduced factory management to a routine which freed much talent, but to use this talent elsewhere would require direction by the government. Since most firms were managed by their owners, there must come a conflict of interests, which, it seemed to me, could be resolved only to the disadvantage of the owners. They might remain owners on paper but in fact would become mere custodians of their businesses. This was what the speaker at that meeting at Chemnitz must have meant when he contrasted the National Socialist with the capitalist system.

But my friends in the Sudetenland were no longer interested in what I thought. I had better concern myself with Great Britain's problems and those of her antiquated industries, they told me. And in the Reich, too, the attitude towards the British had changed, as I noticed when I visited the engineering works of Schubert & Salzer at Chemnitz and those of Gessner at Aue. Neither would take me on to their factory floor. Presumably they made armaments,

Both were busy, both complained about the shortage of steel, which seemed to be reserved for government work. Machine builders at Werdau and Crimitschau treated me similarly. They all knew me and seemed pleased that I had called, but they were less forthcoming than in the past, there were fewer smiles, and they did not canvass for orders.

It was fun driving the Alvis again. The pine forests of the Erzgebirge and the Kaiserwald were as dark and silent as ever: nothing had changed there, but the hotels at Franzensbad, Marienbad and Karlsbad, whose clientele had been so international, were now filled with visitors from Germany. The East European Jews especially, in their long coats and black velour hats, who used to be so prominent, were missing. The streets looked tidy, more sober but less interesting than before, and I felt nostalgic.

Curiosity took me for a weekend to Bad Reichenhall and Berchtesgaden, where I had spent happy holidays in the carefree days before Hitler built his mountain retreat there. My map showed only a temporary airstrip, and to check whether it was serviceable I made a precautionary landing at Salzburg. Something special was happening on Salzburg aerodrome. Swastika flags were flying from every mast, and a detachment of Brownshirts was waiting on the tarmac. Then an aeroplane landed, Dr Goebbels stepped out, briskly limped past the storm troopers lined up in his honour and disappeared in the wooden building that housed the control office.

Standing by the open window, I could hear him bark into the telephone as he tried to establish contact with the Führer at the Berghof. 'Dringendes Staatsgespräch,' he shouted impatiently, and I wondered what secrets I should hear, but evidently there was a blockage on the line which not even the Minister of Propaganda could clear. He gave up and departed in a large Mercedes, while I strolled to my Hornet, thinking that perhaps German organisation was not, after all, as perfect as the world believed. There is little else to relate. I found the small resorts as attractive and unspoilt as I remembered them, and felt glad.

In July I visited Stuttgart to see and try Haaga's plush knitting machine. The trials took longer than anticipated. I had to stay the night, and checked in at the large new Hotel Zeppelin. The reception clerk, to whom I spoke of course in German, probably took me for a harmless Austrian until he saw my British passport, whereupon his attitude became icy. He gave me a room, but had my luggage searched while I was in the restaurant, and then either telephoned me or sent the maid every hour, always under some other pretext, to see whether I was there. Did he think I was a spy?

The behaviour of the customs at the aerodrome was equally objectionable. They almost broke up my aeroplane, searching it with their clumsy hands. Out came the map case, the seat cushions and even the starter battery. They looked at the engine, tapped oil and petrol tanks, and I was afraid that they would rip open the fabric-covered fuselage or put their big boots through the delicate wings. What were they looking for—cameras, money, or evidence that I had been spying? They would not tell me. I did not feel very friendly towards Nazi Germany when, at last, they let me take off for Zürich.

Having for many years admired Swiss ingenuity and workmanship, I wanted to see the Schweizerische Landesausstellung and look for inspiration. Perhaps I would find some new development in knitting plush. The display was at Zürich, and for good measure I also flew to Geneva, a town I had not been to before, without, however, finding anything that would have been of special interest to our factories at Langley or Fleissen. All the same, after my recent experiences in Germany I enjoyed the friendliness and peace of Switzerland and felt glad that I had come.

On the return journey I called on Waga, the Swiss makers of circular knitting plant, at Schaffhausen, to compare their plush machines with those I had seen at Stuttgart. Technically there seemed to be little to choose between them, but the Swiss machines were more expensive because, the makers claimed, they were made of superior metal. The Germans, they said, were diverting their meagre supplies of steel, brass and even cast iron to the manufacture of armaments.

Udo and Ingo were not interested in the samples I brought back. One needed long-staple cotton yarn to manufacture knitted plush successfully, and that was not to be had. Why experiment with substitutes? They had plenty of orders without developing a new product and had just decided to simplify their range still further. In the prevailing circumstances they were probably right. Business policy was now determined more by the political climate than by long-term commercial considerations, and who could tell whether the German economy would ever return to what I called normal? There was little I could usefully contribute. So I let them proceed and, two days after my return from Switzerland, flew off again following an invitation to the international air rally at Frankfurt. A number of my friends from the Royal Aero Club were there. Mejndert Kamphuis had come in his Stinson, Frank Butler in his Vega Gull, and Rolf as second pilot in Hugh Ford's Hornet. We were looking forward to a cheerful party, but our German hosts turned the rally into a political event, with much nauseating propaganda and long speeches from high-ranking Nazis. They had organised an air race, a friendly amateur competition, but themselves entered fast fighter planes which made the speeds of the British and other visitors look silly. Field Marshal Göring thus demonstrated the superiority of his Luftwaffe to the German public, a blatant piece of cheating. Altogether it was a rally I do not care to remember.

I returned to Fleissen feeling very unsettled, and my apprehension grew with the attacks Dr Goebbels and the German press were now making on Poland to browbeat her into returning the city of Danzig and providing an extra-territorial corridor. Hitler had a case—Danzig was German and should never have been torn from the Reich—but had he the patience to wait for its return by negotiation, or did he want war? And were the Poles dragging their feet, waiting for winter to come as their military ally? I became so restive that I decided to cut short my stay and, on 5 August, flew to England, not suspecting that more than five years would go by before I saw Fleissen again.

At Langley I tried to get down to the project of manufacturing plush. From what I had seen and learnt I felt satisfied that our factory was ideally suited for it. We knew what yarn to use, and Lancashire could supply it; knitting, dyeing and cutting the fabric presented no problem, and, given the right type of shearing machine, I saw no reason why we should not be able to make better plush than most Continental manufacturers. The market for it, I estimated, could become as large as that for ripple cloth, and we could be the country's leading suppliers of both. It would have been simple enough to write out orders for the necessary plant, but I felt too restless to get down to it.

It was restlessness that made me fly to Scotland only three days after I had returned from the Continent. Scotland was a long way from Central Europe, and a few quiet days spent in the company of my old friends the five Baird brothers would, I thought, restore my equilibrium and make me see things from a different angle. Both John and Colin were assiduous readers; we talked about books, and I listened to some of Colin's inexhaustible store of quotations, from Robert Burns to Cervantes and Proust. Willie, Tom and Jimmy told fishing stories and when, flying south again, I looked down from my purring little aeroplane on to the quaint old towns, green fields and golf courses of sunbathed Britain I felt at peace with the world.

Flying always brought me tranquillity. It was as if I sensed that the wonderful freedom to fly where I liked would soon cease, and I wanted to be in the air as long as I still had wings. From several thousand feet up the human ants lost their overbearing importance. Even Hitler would be only the size of a flea in the landscape. The coastline between land and sea, the undulating countryside subsiding into the hazy horizon, and the clouds above and around me were ever-changing yet infinitely more permanent, and so much grander than the tiny mortals crawling about the surface of the earth where they caused so much trouble. Unfortunately the illusion of being an eagle came to an end on landing and the earthly problems reasserted themselves.

It was difficult to concentrate on business and take rational decisions. If one were to believe the hate propaganda of the German radio, the Poles, encouraged by Paris and London, were threatening the peaceful existence of the Reich, forcing the Führer to reach for the sword in self-defence. What lies! Surely Hitler's army could beat Poland into submission in a week. Would there be war this time? Our smaller customers stopped buying, while Marks & Spencer and Woolworth's held back with calling-off instructions. Rolf, who had booked his passage to Montreal and was looking forward to his Canadian visit, began to wonder whether he should cancel it, and I once again shelved the plan for a plush manufacturing plant.

Full of foreboding, John Houlder and I decided to fly in our planes for a last Continental weekend to Knocke in Belgium, with Sydney Evans and Rolf as passengers, a few days before most of the air space across the Channel became a series of prohibited zones for civil aircraft. And on 28 August I was asked by Captain Davy to help him fly some of the club machines from Heston to Denham, where they would be safer in case of a German surprise attack. It was the end of private flying for many years to come.

At dawn on 1 September the German army attacked Poland, Göring's Luftwaffe bombed Warsaw, and the war had begun. It was at Temple Grange, the Matthews' home, that we listened to Chamberlain's broadcast at 11.15 on Sunday morning, 3 September, telling us that a state of war now existed between Britain and Germany. Shortly afterwards the sirens wailed their first air raid warning—a false alarm, as it turned out. The sun shone. Rolf and I went for a silent walk on Iver Heath. We thought of Mother and the others at Fleissen and Leibitschgrund and wondered what the future would bring.

38

'£1,000,000 SECRET
FROM REFUGEE'
1939–40

ROLF AND I spent Monday at the factory. On Tuesday I went to the City to discuss the situation with Mr Hurst. London presented a strange sight, with hundreds of barrage balloons in the sky. Shop windows were being boarded up, everyone was carrying his gas mask in a small, square cardboard box on his back, and men wearing steel helmets were fortifying Aldersgate Street Underground station with sandbags.

We began the war by ordering two bicycles as a precaution in case other means of transport should fail. Through Mr Hurst's daughter, Olive, who was private secretary to the chairman of BSA, we got them at the trade price of £2 10s each. And Rolf decided to abandon his trip to Canada. He made a profit of £5 by selling his passage to an American standing in the queue outside the offices of a shipping company, anxious to leave the country before the bombs began to fall.

But to everyone's surprise there were no bombs. Hitler was preoccupied with his campaign in Poland and seemed to be taking little notice of the 'state of war which now existed between Britain and Germany'. The warm September sun continued to shine on peaceful England, where, apart from the evacuation of children from the towns, the black-out and the hurried completion of primitive air raid shelters in suburban gardens, life went on very much as before. Was it all bluff? Was the search for a peace formula perhaps proceeding behind the scenes, and would common sense prevail before the world plunged into catastrophe? But the British people were in no mood for further appeasement. Whatever the cost, they were determined to destroy Hitler and his thugs, and had no doubt about ultimate victory.

I wished that I could feel equally confident. There was much more to Germany than the caricatures of ridiculous, jackbooted, cowardly Nazi bullies would have one believe. The enemy's war machine seemed to me vastly superior to Britain's and France's put together. Fortunately a country's war potential did not depend only on the size and quality of its army. Germany's resources were stretched to breaking point, whereas Britain's reserves in the material sense as well as in the form of goodwill throughout the Empire and the rest of the world were immense. And if her shipping routes should be cut there were large reserves in her slack and, by Central European standards, rather wasteful economy at home. Much would depend on how efficiently she used them.

We saw three possibilities. A short 'Blitzkrieg' ending with a German victory. This we dismissed. We were quite unable to imagine Hitler and Göring driving down Whitehall, and swastika flags flying in Parliament Square. Or there might be sudden peace based on some lasting arrangement between Germany and the rest of Europe, if such a miracle were possible. Or, most likely, the war would develop into a long-drawn-out economic one, lasting perhaps for years, until one side or the other was utterly exhausted. And Hitler lacked the resources to win such a war.

Underwear would remain one of the basic needs of the nation, and we felt that the most useful contribution we could make to the war effort, at least for the time being, was to continue with the manufacture of our standard merchandise. Our raw material stocks were larger than ever before. Although we had not believed that war would come, we had taken no chances and had made such extensive purchases during the preceding months that our large new store was filled to capacity with yarn, sewing thread, elastic, paper, dyestuffs and other supplies, and the steel shelves we had erected with the intention of keeping our merchandise tidy were overflowing.

We were less happy about the labour situation. Could we retain the necessary number of people to keep the factory going? Köhler, the works manager, had left for Germany with his English wife and small son before war broke out: an exceptionally able young man who was irreplaceable. Reservists and Territorials had been called up, and several of our best men had gone. There was no great enthusiasm for the war, none of the cheering of 1914 which I vaguely remembered, but there were more volunteers than the army, navy and air force could use. Watson, who was in charge of the fleecing machines and the finishing department, had joined his unit, and Duffy, his assistant, took over. He tried hard but lacked experience and spoiled much cloth. What would happen if more of our men, especially the knitters whom we had trained with so much patience and at great expense, were to go? As we recruited most of our workers straight from school, the whole of our male labour force was now of military age and, presumably, expected to serve in the forces. And how would Rolf and I and our faithfuls from Fleissen fare as naturalised British citizens? If Mr Hurst's memories of the 1914–18 war were anything to go by, trouble lay ahead. But these were early days, and it was impossible to foretell what the future would bring.

To start with, production was disorganised. For a week or two our people found it hard to concentrate on their work; they were thinking about the war. But then a heartening feeling of togetherness swept through the factory. We became like one family, pulling together to cope with the difficulties and unpleasant changes forced on us. Duties were reallocated and petty jealousies forgotten. Girls offered to do work usually performed by men and, as an experiment, we transferred two of them to the interlock department. Perhaps all of our small-diameter knitting machines would soon have to be operated by women. The large areas of glass in the roof and the south wall of which we were so proud and which made our factory so pleasant to work in had to be painted out so thoroughly that not the faintest ray of light could penetrate them. And when we had turned day into permanent night everyone cheerfully worked in artificial light. This happened all over the country and put considerable strain on electricity supplies.

Every home, shop, public house, train and bus was blacked out. The streets lay in darkness at night and one frequently lost one's way even in familiar surroundings; front and rear lamps of motor cars were dimmed so that they could barely be seen, and the glow of a cigarette was liable to cause offence. Sitting indoors behind black curtains became very tiresome. We had to register for National Service and carry identity cards. A scheme for rationing the sale of petrol was announced, train services were curtailed, and all civil flying had been stopped. My aeroplane sat on Denham airfield waiting to be requisitioned. Taxes were raised and new ones invented, the implications of which we did not fully understand. No one was allowed to travel abroad without a special permit, or to take more than £10 out of the country. War risk insurance became compulsory and added 6 per cent to the annual expense of stock-holding. Inevitably, the cost of production and distribution rose, and so did prices in the shops.

The actions of various authorities frequently seemed contradictory. Why, for instance, were women and children evacuated from their homes in London and sent to our area? Were Slough and Langley safe locations for them? Many private houses took in one or several of these evacuees, who seemed to come from the poorest quarters. We heard incredible stories of East End kids who refused to take a bath or sleep in a bed, who had never seen a garden or a meadow and who chased chickens, thinking they were wild birds. Most of them disliked the life 'in the country' and, as the anticipated air raids did not come, drifted back to town.

It seemed unlikely that German bombers would ever consider our factory a worthwhile target, but Langley Alloys, our immediate neighbours, were engaged on important war work and had camouflaged their premises. Half a mile to the east of us, on Langley airfield, Hawker's well camouflaged factory built the famous Hurricane fighters, and three miles to the west anti-aircraft guns were being mounted to protect the heavy concentration of industry on the Slough trading estate. We were clearly in the middle of a danger zone. Regretfully we covered our clean asbestos roof and boilerhouse tower with dull green paint, and the government bore half the cost. And, complying with ARP regulations, we built four concrete air raid shelters for our 220 employees.

While both Britain and Germany seemed to avoid any serious confrontation on land and in the air, there was no such restraint at sea. On the first day of the war the liner *Athenia*, with 1,100 passengers on board, was torpedoed on her way from Liverpool to Montreal by a German submarine. British merchantmen were sunk almost daily, and we wondered how the submarine menace was affecting Lancashire's supplies of raw cotton. Were the price increases of 35 per cent for fine yarn and 50 per cent for condenser yarn which spinners were quoting an indication of the seriousness of the situation?

If only we had not shelved that condenser mill project! There were almost a thousand bales of waste clippings at Langley, valuable raw material which was of little use now, since the government had prohibited the export of all cotton and wool waste and we could no longer send it to Holland to have it converted into yarn. Plenty more such clippings were in the warehouses of waste merchants and could be bought cheaply. But price was now of secondary importance. Sailors' lives, shipping space and foreign exchange could be saved if these clippings were used to replace some of the imported Indian cotton from which condenser yarn was spun in England. Perhaps it was not too late even now to have suitable waste spinning machines built. I asked the Board of Trade for guidance but met with little encouragement. It appeared that our ideas ran counter to a 'spindles scrapping scheme' the BoT was preoccupied with. However, the scheme was not in force yet, and as far as engineering capacity was concerned, while the industry was busy making munitions, there were, up to the present, no regulations preventing machine builders from accepting civilian work if they so chose and provided they had the necessary steel.

We had to move quickly, before the civil servants and their advisers made it impossible! Petrol rationing had been postponed for a week. Rolf and I therefore drove to Lancashire in the Buick to discuss our plans with William Tatham Ltd of Rochdale, who specialised in waste spinning machinery, and with Platt Bros. & Co. of Oldham, the largest spinning machine makers in the country. Both were making munitions and, for security reasons, could show us only small sections of their factories. They looked old-fashioned in comparison with most of the engineering works we knew on the Continent, but what we saw made a businesslike impression and inspired confidence. Both firms wanted our business. Their total capacity was earmarked for war work, but they were waiting for detailed decisions from the Ministry and while they were waiting would be glad of civilian orders to keep their workers employed.

The condenser plant we had in mind for Langley differed substantially from the traditional three-card sets and self-acting mules we used at Leibitschgrund. It was more compact and, although technically more advanced and very versatile, would be simpler to operate. This was important, for our labour at Langley lacked inherited textile skills. We had evolved a somewhat daring combination of machines with Gessner and Schwalbe in Germany, who, we thought, had more experience of cotton waste reclamation and waste spinning than English machine builders. The technicians at Tatham and at Platt Bros. were intrigued with our scheme and saw no reason why it should not give satisfactory results, even suggesting a few improvements, and, after some haggling over prices, which had risen by 15 per cent during the first three weeks of September, booked our orders. Tatham's undertook to build the preparatory machines and the cards for the sum of £5,298, and Platt's agreed to supply four ring frames to match at £630 each. These prices were subject to $1\frac{1}{2}$ per cent increase for every rise of 1s a week in engineering wages. The plant was to be delivered during January and February 1940 unless *force majeur* intervened.

In the excitement of discussing machinery we temporarily forgot the war but were reminded of it when we drove back to Manchester in the evening. Everything was in darkness. We could see neither landmarks nor road signs and, relying on the car compass to direct us, had some difficulty in finding the Midland Hotel. Its entrance was protected by a wall of sandbags, but the lights inside were bright and the food was excellent. Settling down in the hall we reviewed our purchases and, in view of the uncertainties all round, decided to send each of the two firms a cheque for £1,000 on account, to make the contract more binding.

The situation mystified us. There were plenty of mills in Britain which spun condenser yarn from cotton waste. They used comber, roving and various types of card-room waste, but none used the reclaimed fibres from torn-up fabric clippings. Tatham's clearly knew more about waste processing and condenser spinning in general than we did, and we were impressed with samples Platt Bros. showed us of bedspreads and baby blankets made from waste yarn by a firm in Manchester named Vantona Textiles Ltd. With all this expertise available, why was there no spinner in Britain producing our type of waste condenser yarn? It came from the Continent ever since I could remember, while hundreds of mills in Lancashire were idle.

This seemed to be the ripple cloth story all over again. Why had Lancashire, with her unrivalled knowledge of cotton, her great manufacturing facilities and her skilled labour, left that remunerative trade to Langley? Why did she take no interest in sliver dyeing? Leibitschgrund, an industrial back-water by comparison, made use of the process with great success while Lancashire, despite her vastly larger business in marl yarn, continued with her outdated method of hank dyeing and subsequently doubling, which was more expensive and gave inferior results. Her textile men were in a position to exploit modern techniques on a scale a hundred times larger and therefore more profitable than we could; why did they not do so? Was it the horizontal organisation of the industry that prevented them from using vertical processes such as spinning coloured or marl yarns from dyed sliver? If so, were none of them enterprising enough to reorganise their empires? We never failed to be impressed by the enormous size of their cotton mills, but where was the spirit that had created them? Had the management passed from the hands of dynamic owner-entrepreneurs to those of accountants and promoted foremen who lacked leadership and imagination and who now merely administered these great mills on behalf of absentee shareholders? We liked Lancastrians and got on well with them, they spoke our language, but their industry was an enigma.

Having ordered our spinning machines, we now needed a factory to put them in. Was it possible to build one in wartime? We consulted Try, our building contractor. He knew of no law forbidding it, but did not feel sure. The only kind of construction work his clients asked for these days was for air raid shelters. Would we be wise to enlarge our factory in these conditions, I wondered? Might people think we were profiteering from the war if they saw an extension going up? Perhaps it would be better to rent 15,000 square feet of floor space somewhere in the West Country for the duration of the war instead of concentrating our whole enterprise at Langley, where it might all be destroyed in a single bombing raid. We looked for premises along the railway line between Slough and Bristol but found none to suit us and decided to try the 'distressed areas' of South Wales. After a dreary journey in an unlighted train crawling through the blacked-out countryside I arrived at Cardiff in midnight darkness, to be called for the following morning by Mr Davies, the secretary of the National Industrial Development Council. He took me to see the Pontypridd trading estate.

Located in a valley about eight miles to the west of Cardiff, it was modelled on the estate at Slough but had more Garden City atmosphere. The factories were modest buildings whose appearance had been spoilt by amateurish camouflage. I was offered one such building of 12,000 square feet for a period of seven years at an annual rent of £605 inclusive of rates. Then we drove through several other valleys to look at more factories which had all been constructed recently and were making zip fasteners, textiles, plastics and other things new to the area. Many of them were occupied by German,

Austrian and Czechoslovak refugees. I was introduced to a Mr Adler, who told me that he had owned a button factory with 450 employees at Tachau in the Bohemian forest, and that he used to supply the knitting industry of Fleissen and Asch. He had come from Czechoslovakia only the year before and was very happy in Wales.

The valleys looked pleasant enough, poor but clean, and the people seemed tidy, decent and hard-working folk. There must have been great activity there in bygone days. Now the fallen-in buildings, tumbledown chimneys, abandoned ironworks and derelict coal mines matched the battered old castles I saw, and the modern single-storey factories with their asbestos roofs and large windows, built among the ruins here and there, made an eerie contrast. It was difficult not to succumb to the romantic spell of the scene, and I had to tell myself that the last thing we wanted was another Leibitschgrund. These valleys might be safe from bombs, but a spinning mill here would be altogether too remote to be administered from Langley and transport between the two plants too costly. And so, in spite of the efforts of Councillor Williams and the publicity brochure back at head office at Cardiff, and the picture of his pretty daughter in national costume on the front cover, I decided against Wales.

We calculated that by locating the spinning mill next to our factory at Langley we could save £2,000 annually in running expenses. Builder Try had prepared his estimate and was determined to secure our contract. There were 250 unemployed bricklayers registered at Uxbridge; he had enough cement, bricks and timber, knew where he could obtain the necessary steel, and the figure of £5,106 he quoted for the 14,400 sq. ft. building we wanted was a thousand pounds below that of his nearest competitor. It worked out at 7s 3d per square foot, which would have been a reasonable price even before the war. So we gave him the job and with it a cheque for £2,000 on account to make sure that he made an immediate start and did not change his mind. Time was not on our side.

The moment had come to tell our employees and the people of the village about our project and the contribution it would make to the national effort. Remembering the rules Dr Rundt had taught me when I was acting as his secretary in America, I announced the news at a private tea party which I gave for the mayor and mayoress of Slough and Alderman Trevener, who represented Langley on the council. Afterwards we admitted the representatives of the local press and, to make sure that they understood the story correctly, gave them a typed *résumé* of the facts. We were not disappointed. On 27 October 1939 both papers gave us headlines and a glowing write-up, and we felt so reassured that we increased the building contract by 50 per cent to a floor area of 21,600 sq. ft., which raised the total cost to £7,291 and reduced the price per square foot to 6s 7d. At the same time, as a reminder not to fall behind with the delivery of our spinning machines, we sent Platt's another £1,000 and Tatham's £3,000 on account.

Where did all this money come from? It will be remembered that we were thinking of building a factory in Canada, and in January 1939 had set £10,000 aside for this purpose. Keeping a wary eye on sterling ever since the devaluation of 1931, determined not to get caught a second time, we converted this money into dollars which we deposited with the Bank of Montreal. In August 1939, when it seemed likely that the pound would come under pressure once again, Rolf and I withdrew our savings from the Post Office, a total of £4,200, and converted them into dollars. Then war broke out and the government ordered British residents to surrender their holdings of foreign exchange. We abandoned our Canadian plans, dutifully brought our dollars back to London and handed them over to the Bank of England, who gave us £15,713 for them, £1,513 more than they had cost us. We now advanced these funds to Pasolds Ltd to help pay for the spinning mill. The exchange profit of £1,513 was more apparent than real, for it merely represented the fall in the value of sterling and was absorbed by the price increases we had to pay for the spinning plant. But now a nasty surprise awaited us.

The new 60 per cent excess profits tax was designed, we understood, to catch war profiteers, and this was only fair. But if we understood the provisions correctly they penalised firms such as ours who had made small profits in the years from 1935 to 1937, arbitrarily chosen by the Inland Revenue as 'basic period' for the purpose of establishing profit standards. After seven years of hard work and minimal rewards we had at last reached a stage where the Langley factory was beginning to show satisfactory results. In the fiscal year 1938–39 we had earned £15,330, the first good profit in the firm's history. Was it to be excluded from the computation of our permitted profit standard merely because it had been earned outside the approved period?

It was then that our auditors dropped a bombshell. Through the conversion from a partnership to a company the continuity had been broken, they said. Pasolds Ltd was a new entity and as such had no profit standard. Its liability to EPT would be determined by reference to its £65,000 share capital, which meant that any profits above £5,200 became subject to the 60 per cent tax. The situation could, however, be improved slightly if the company's share capital were increased to £80,000 or, looking ahead, to £100,000, and with this in mind the funds Rolf and I were advancing towards the cost of the spinning mill ought not to be treated as loans but should be injected into the business as permanent capital.

This made sense, and we applied to the Treasury for the necessary sanction, outlining the purpose for which the additional capital was required. A mere formality, we thought, but the Treasury knew nothing about waste spinning and referred our application to the Board of Trade, who, to our surprise and dismay, rejected it. As the implications of the refusal dawned on me my feeling of disappointment turned into one of alarm. To be deprived of most of the profits we needed to develop our plant would be bad enough, but to know that the authorities actively disapproved of our waste reclamation scheme was worse. If they were not interested in saving imports of raw cotton, then our project lost its justification and we could contribute little more to the war effort than most of the hundreds of other knitting mills in the country. During wartime, it might reasonably be argued, underwear could be made in any old premises: one did not need such a modern building as ours for it. I could foresee that, before long, we should lose control over our factory. Someone with a stronger claim or more influence with the authorities would requisition it. And so I decided to enlist, if I could, the support of our old friend Mr Watkinson, who held a key position in the Board of Trade.

Mr Watkinson had very little time. The war had burdened him with much additional work and many new responsibilities, but he had not forgotten me, and when he heard from his secretary that the matter I wanted to discuss with him was urgent he consented to see me, but would I be brief. I had hardly begun to explain, when he cut me short. 'Half the cotton mills in Lancashire are idle! We are about to introduce a scheme to scrap surplus spindles, yet you want to divert steel and engineering capacity from the production of munitions to build more spinning machines. You must be out of your mind!' And he rose to end the interview, but I implored him to listen. I talked about the large quantities of hosiery waste that used to be exported to the Continent before the war and the mountains of it now accumulating in Britain. Mountains of valuable raw material that ought to be converted into yarn to save sailors' lives and shipping space for more essential imports than cotton. Precious raw material that was not being utilised to proper advantage because the waste spinning mills in Lancashire were not equipped with the right kind of machinery.

'I am not an expert,' he said when I had finished. 'Tell your story to Mr Hughes of Cotton Control. If he supports your scheme, I shall!'

I caught the evening train for Manchester, and early the following morning called on Mr Hughes, who was expecting me. Mr Watkinson had telephoned him. He came straight to the point. What type of waste had we in mind, what kind of machinery, and who was building it? I showed him some waste clippings, a few cops of our condenser yarn and a pair of fleece-lined girls' knickers, then described the plant in some detail and waited anxiously for his verdict. Subconsciously I knew that our future hung on it and that without the Cotton Control Board's approval of the project Pasolds Ltd would not survive the war. But his face remained inscrutable. He had to talk to some of the local waste spinners, he said, discuss the matter with other members of the Board, and hoped to telephone me at the Midland Hotel at the end of the day.

It was a day of suspense. I took a taxi, visited Winder McKean and the Black Lane Spinning Co., two of our regular suppliers, and gave each of them an order for 10,000 lb of fine yarn. Then I inspected our half finished ring frames at Platt Bros. & Co. and, in a sudden burst of optimism, told Tatham's to reserve steel and cast iron for a further two-card set for which I hoped to place a firm contract within forty-eight hours. I was back at the hotel in good time for Mr Hughes's telephone call. He kept me waiting until seven o'clock. The meeting had only just ended, he apologised, and then said, 'I have good news for you. We recognise that your waste spinning process is new to this country and are informing London accordingly. A strongly worded letter in support of your project is on the way to the Board of Trade, and our Deputy Controller, Mr Frank Platt, the managing director of the Lancashire Cotton Corporation, would like you to call on him tomorrow.'

To be truly British one must never lose one's composure, not even when alone, but I felt so jubilant that I did a couple of somersaults in my bedroom. I doubted whether Cotton Control were quite correct in describing our method of spinning condenser yarn from reclaimed hosiery clips as a new process. I had not claimed that it was, but only pointed out that British spinners were not equipped to do this kind of operation. However, I had no reason to quarrel with the Cotton Board's findings. They merely made our case stronger. The next day, as I entered the portals of one of Britain's largest cotton spinning combines, my feelings were completely under control. Mr Platt—who later, as Cotton Controller, became Sir Frank Platt—was very complimentary. He had received favourable reports about us, he said, and his technical people were very taken with our unusual method of spinning waste. Then he came to his reason for wanting to talk to me.

'Why do you want to spin only for your own strictly limited requirements? Would you consider an operation on a much larger scale if the LCC provided the finance?' The LCC knew little about condenser spinning, he explained, but had large quantities of cotton waste and a ready market for at least 20,000 lb of condenser yarn per week. Would we be prepared, for a start, to build a mill of this capacity? He would leave it to us to choose its location, provided we undertook to run it. If we were interested the LCC would come in on a joint venture with us, or just provide the money and be responsible for selling the yarn, or consider any other suggestion we might wish to make.

It was a surprising and most tempting offer, and I hated to disappoint him, but was afraid of being diverted from our prime objective, which was to make the factory at Langley as independent of imported raw material as possible and, thereby, stress its contribution to the war effort. Thanking Mr Platt for his confidence and asking for time to consult Rolf, I pointed out regretfully and not without embarrassment that I saw little hope of being able to accept his generous offer. Our project was in the nature of a pilot scheme and while we did not mind staking our own money we should feel loath to risk his.

He took it in good part. 'Good luck to you,' he smiled, 'and you know where to find me if you should change your mind, but there isn't much time left. Controls are getting tighter every day. Metal will soon be reserved exclusively for war purposes.' Opportunity knocked and I let it pass. Had I missed the chance of a lifetime? I have sometimes wondered in later years what we might have made of Lancashire's stagnating cotton industry if Mr Platt had pushed a little harder, I had been less timid and Mr Watkinson not so overburdened with other matters. A successful joint venture with the LCC backed by Cotton Control and Whitehall, would, I feel sure, have led to very much bigger things—the adoption of sliver dyeing, for instance, and a revolution in the spinning of coloured yarns.

Triumphantly I returned to Langley. The Cotton Control Board's unqualified support strengthened our position immensely, and Mr Platt's offer was reassuring, although we did not need his money and Rolf felt even more strongly than I that we wanted no partner. We confirmed the provisional order I had given Tatham's for another two-card set, ordered two more ring frames from Platt's and, after long deliberation, decided to invest £1,382 in a sprinkler installation. The fire risk in a waste reclamation plant was considerable. We were therefore building ours at a safe distance from the main factory. In particular the breaking-up machines, or devils, as they were sometimes called, caught fire several times every year, as we knew from experience, and I well remember an argument with Rolf whether a $4\frac{1}{2}$ in. brick dividing wall would suffice to contain the flames or whether we needed a 9 in. one.

The long spell of sunny weather was followed by weeks of torrential rain. Our building site became waterlogged, Try's lorries stuck in the mud, and we were afraid that the machinery would arrive before the factory was ready. However, Try caught up, and everything went as planned. The erection of the plant began in January and was supervised by Mr Wood, the mill manager Tatham's had helped us to find. A little Yorkshireman with the reputation of being so difficult and independent that no one in the north would give him a job, Mr Wood's ability and technical knowledge were outstanding. He had experience of spinning cotton, wool and various types of waste, which was unusual and, Tatham's assured us, provided we did not interfere with his way of running the mill he was the right man for us. A plant like ours which gave him scope to experiment would keep him happy. I must admit he proved a most trying man who did not suffer fools gladly, but Rolf and I got on well with him, and the unqualified success of our condenser mill was to a large extent due to him.

On 21 December 1939 we were informed by the Lords Commissioners of His Majesty's Treasury that they 'consented to the proposed issue by Pasolds Limited of 35,000 shares of £1 each', thus authorising the increase of our share capital to the full £100,000 and thereby putting the official seal of approval on our scheme. It was the best Christmas present we could have wished for. Almost forty years have passed since then, and much has changed. The vertically integrated production unit we created at Langley during those first few months of the war is today a mere memory, but it is one that still fills me with pride. Few other firms foresaw the coming raw material shortage as clearly and acted as swiftly as we did. Had we not built that mill in record time, had we not been able to impress the authorities with our spinning of hosiery clips, I have little doubt that our factory would have been requisitioned. The history of the firm would have taken a very different course. Small though it was, our waste reclamation plant not only made a useful contribution to Britain's economic survival throughout the war but continued to save precious foreign exchange for many years afterwards.

In April 1940, only six months after we had decided on the project, the first two-card set and two ring frames were running, and this in spite of wartime difficulties and a long spell of very bad weather. By the end of June the whole spinning mill was in production. Once again the local press gave us a good deal of publicity, and now the story was picked up by two London papers, the *News Chronicle* and the *Daily Sketch*. The latter featured it under the sensational headline '£1,000,000 secret from refugee', which annoyed me intensely. I was not a refugee! I had come to England not to seek asylum but of my free will and because I loved the country! The editor found it difficult to appreciate the difference; besides, the matter was delicate in view of the tens of thousands of political refugees in Britain, but I made such a fuss that he published a short factual account a few days later.

Now let me return to the beginning of the war. The new two-storey building in the north-west corner of our site had been completed and the ground floor stacked to the ceiling with merchandise. On part of the first floor we now built a large general office with adjoining interviewing rooms and two spacious private offices, with concealed safes and rows of cupboards, oak-panelled walls and furniture to match. In the past we had enlarged only the factory. The offices, an area Rolf called 'non-productive', had been left as they were and had become very cramped. He now conceded that we needed new ones. It seemed a good time to build. Construction firms and furniture makers were anxious to keep their craftsmen employed and it seemed unlikely

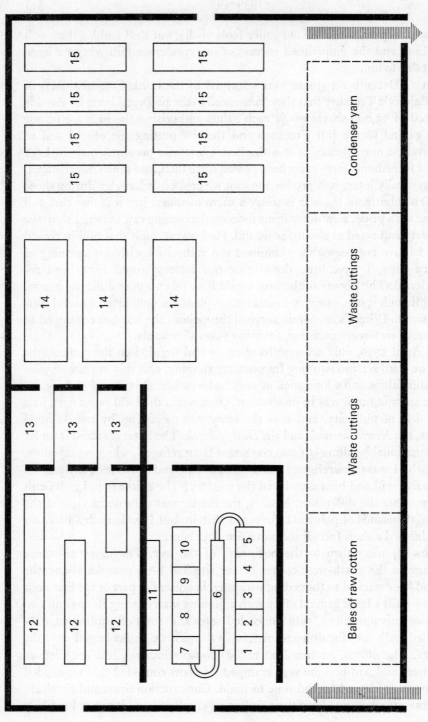

Condenser spinning mill built at Langley 1939–40. *1* bale opener, *2* Crighton opener, *3* lattice, *4* hopper feeder, *5* porcupine, *6* dust trunks, *7* cage exhauster, *8* lattice, *9* hopper feeder, *10* scutcher, *11* dust filters, *12* breaking-up machines, *13* storage bins, *14* two-card sets, *15* ring frames. The plan shows eight ring frames: the last two were added later

that we should get good woodwork done so cheaply again. One incident seems worth recording. Cooke's furniture store in Finsbury Pavement in the City, where I selected desks and filing cabinets, offered me a mahogany boardroom table, a magnificent piece of furniture large enough to seat sixteen. I could have it for £100, then for £50 and eventually for nothing at all— free, delivered to Langley. It did not fit into our scheme and I turned it down even as a gift, but this example shows how dramatically values had changed almost overnight. Too many firms were moving from London to houses in the country and there was no more demand for furniture of this description.

Prices in general, however, began to rise and it seemed inevitable that they would continue to do so. Starting with the first week of the war, some of our suppliers asked between 1½ and 5 per cent more for their goods. It was not a matter of profiteering but of the extra expense brought on by 'the emergency', as the war was called. There was the cost of the compulsory war risk insurance, the black-out and other air raid precautions, upgrading of labour, slowing down of transport and communications and, worst of all, the higher prices of imported raw materials. All this increased the cost of production. Elementary though it seemed, not every businessman thought as we did. There were some, Mr Heldmaier for instance, who sold off their stocks as fast as they could and did not replace them, arguing that in wartime it was safest to have one's money in the bank.

Seemingly little things could play havoc with a factory's output. The shortage of bearded needles for Terrot-type knitting machines was one of them. They came from Germany and were a strategic commodity in economic warfare. We had 65,000 of these needles left out of a total of 180,000 which we had bought the year before, paradoxically as a precaution against a possible National Socialist export ban, of which there had been rumours. They would keep us going for four months, and in the meantime we hoped to get supplies from Canada. But the authorities refused to give us an import licence. We persuaded the Robert Simpson Co. of Toronto, one of the largest overseas buyers of our goods, to remonstrate with the Board of Trade on our behalf and, once again, asked Mr Watkinson for help. Britain was very short of dollars but, I was given to understand confidentially, arrangements were being made to import limited quantities of German needles via Switzerland. It was a repetition of what had happened in the 1914–18 war. Admittedly, making needles was highly specialised precision work, but if latch needles for interlock machines could be made in Britain why not, after all these years, bearded ones?

Could we rely on imports from Germany? If we ran out of supplies our stockinette fabric production would cease, we should have no further use for condenser yarn and more than half our factory would have to shut. To forestall this alarming possibility we combed the British Isles for No. 24 fine bearded needles and secured 40,000, old stock found for us by merchants, machine builders, second-hand accessory dealers and hosiery manufacturers who no longer operated Terrots. Coming in dribs and drabs from thirty different sources, their quality varied: some were too soft, some brittle, some rough, causing breakages and faulty fabric at a time when we were least able to cope with such difficulties, for we had lost skilled hands. But the factory had to keep going.

The schedule of reserved occupations exempted men in certain trades and professions from military service, key people who were needed to keep the wheels of the economy turning, from bakers and wool blenders to engine drivers and lighthouse keepers, but it did not mention operatives of circular knitting machines, and this was a serious omission as far as we were concerned. If manufacturers in the Midlands lost their young male knitters there were experienced older men, women and even pensioners to help out. We in south Buckinghamshire had no reserve of workers capable of operating knitting machines, and especially not our large Terrot-type circulars, the largest and heaviest in the country. We had lost several of our best knitters already and could not afford to lose any more. The representative of the Ministry of Labour at Slough, whom we consulted, said he came from a textile area and could he see our factory? As I showed him round he asked, 'Are these the circular looms you knit your fabric on?'

To refer to them as looms was unusual but not actually wrong, and I nodded. 'They are the backbone of our plant,' I explained. 'It takes several years to train a knitter. Normally an operative looks after three of these looms, but ours now look after four or even five.'

He paged through the schedule, stopped at the section headed 'Cotton Textile Trades', and somewhat patronisingly pronounced: 'These men will not be called up, as you might have seen for yourselves if you had studied the schedule. Loom overlookers are reserved!'

I had studied the schedule from cover to cover and knew that the exemption referred to overlookers of weaving looms in cotton mills, a very different category, but was it up to me to explain the meaning of government regulations to a civil servant? I apologised for my stupidity, thanked him for his assurance and quietly hoped that he would not discover the mistake he had made.

We were lucky: the Ministry exempted our knitters as loom overlookers. Some of our other men were protected under other headings or were not fit enough to serve in the forces. I was reserved as general manager and Mr Colmer as chief clerk. Rolf attended an interview at the RAF, but the Ministry of Labour refused to release him, for as factory manager he too was reserved. Thus, to my relief, we remained an effective team, at least for the time being. But who could foretell how quickly men might be needed if the 'phony war' were to develop into a real one and fighting begin in earnest? And so Rolf engaged more girls and we taught them to do men's jobs. We had more applicants now than at any time since the factory started. Most of the girls came from the trading estate area of Slough. They were afraid of the anti-aircraft guns that had been mounted there and thought of Langley as a safer place. Rolf raised the level of wages by about 10 per cent, mainly by increasing piecework rates, and gradually our labour force grew from the pre-war figure of 220 to reach 250 towards the end of 1939.

Prices were going up all round, 10 per cent in the shops, 20 per cent in the wholesale trade, yarns cost as much as 45 per cent more and some firms would sell their goods only at 'prices ruling at date of delivery'. Many of the big stores, especially in the West End of London, were complaining that business was slack. Our underwear and dressing gown sales, by contrast, were booming. The millions of women and children evacuated from the large towns to the country upset the normal shopping pattern, and wholesalers, experiencing a sudden rush of orders from village shops which they were unable to fill, looked to us for supplies. Our output was not large enough to meet the demand, and we could pick and choose our customers. We looked after Marks & Spencer well. They were clamouring for merchandise. Aware of the increase in manufacturing costs, they paid their suppliers up to 10 per cent more, even on old contracts, and, in some cases, raised their own selling prices above the 4s 11d limit. Most of our other customers adopted a similarly reasonable attitude; only Woolworth's tried to stick rigidly to their now unrealistic 6d maximum, which made business with them very difficult.

Many more buyers came to Langley now than before the war, not least because they could not get through to us on the telephone. The local exchange was hopelessly overloaded. Calls from Hawker's rapidly expanding aircraft factory and from the RAF, who had taken over the actors' orphanage in the village, had priority. Lloyd's of London, who, to our great regret, had moved into our club premises at Pinewood, used 500 lines, and in addition twenty-four insurance brokers had transferred their offices from the City to Langley and did much of their business on the telephone. Small wonder, therefore, that to get a call through to us sometimes took several hours.

I could hardly believe my eyes when I saw Mr Draper, the mighty head buyer of Cook & Son's underwear department, in one of our new interviewing rooms. He urgently needed a thousand dozen girls' fleecy knickers for some favourite clients in the provinces, it appeared. Could we help him? —Mr Draper, the man who had so often been rude to me, kept me waiting while he went out to coffee, and then sent me away without looking at my samples! Tempted though I was to take revenge, I suppressed the urge, merely waved to him through the glass partition and asked Mr Colmer to deal with him.

It was good that Rolf and I were so busy. Our private lives had become very dull. The club was closed and most of our friends had gone. Jack Matthews had joined the RAF and was training as a flying instructor on the west coast of Scotland, his brother Peter was with his anti-aircraft unit in Essex, Adrye and Cynthia had registered as ambulance drivers. Petrol rationing and the black-out discouraged us from going out in the evening, reading and listening to the 'wireless' became monotonous, and so, inevitably, we went back into the factory after supper and stayed with the night shift until it was time to go to bed.

It must have been towards the end of 1939, if I remember correctly, that Rolf and I were summoned to a meeting at Marks & Spencer's head office at Baker Street. I am a little vague about the people who were there and whether it was Simon Marks or Israel Sieff who was in the chair, for, contrary to my habit, I kept no record on that occasion or, if I did, have lost it. The men who sat round the boardroom table were all M. & S. suppliers, it seemed, and after a little while we realised that, except for Rolf and myself, they were all Jews. The chairman spoke of the terrible persecutions of the Israelites in Germany and warned that it was not beyond the realms of possibility that active anti-semitism could be provoked also in Britain. He seemed genuinely worried. All ostentation, show of wealth or other form of conspicuous behaviour by members of the Jewish community was to be avoided. He asked those present to go and preach restraint. It appeared that not only the promotion but also the prevention of publicity cost money, and at this stage a subscription list began to circulate. My neighbour entered a sum and then gave the list to me. I was staggered to see figures with two or three noughts after them, and handed the sheet to Rolf, who quickly passed it to the prosperous-looking gentleman next to him. A small goodwill offering would have looked out of place among these impressive sums. Although we wished the operation well, helping to finance a Jewish low-profile campaign was not one of our responsibilities. We had clearly been invited in error. M. & S. never raised the somewhat embarrassing matter again, and we remained the best of friends.

39

GUNS
OR PANTIES?
1939-41

ON 3 NOVEMBER 1939 Roosevelt signed a Bill enabling Britain to supplement her production of arms and other war materials with purchases from the United States on a 'cash and carry' basis. The dollars needed to pay for these purchases were procured partly out of reserves, partly by the sale of British-owned American securities, and partly by increased exports, which suddenly assumed vital importance. We had built up a growing overseas trade before the war. Mr Hurst was 'well in' with the South African and Australian confirming houses and the shippers in Chiswell Street and the Finsbury Square area, to whom he sold our ripple cloth and dressing gowns. The Robert Simpson Co. of Canada repeatedly placed orders for our merchandise. We supplied thousands of dozens of shaped vests and miles of underwear fabric to New Zealand through Mr Uren, our very active agent in Auckland, and we made large quantities of cheap cotton singlets for the native trade which Sammy Young, one of Peggy's favourite customers, shipped to Africa. It was not difficult to foresee that Britain would require vast sums of foreign exchange to conduct the war, and we now worked twice as hard as before to increase our sales abroad. But German submarines and mines were sinking tens of thousands of tons of British shipping every week, and to convince clients overseas that they could rely on getting delivery of their goods was difficult. Increasing exports proved slow, uphill work, especially if it had to be done by correspondence. We therefore decided that Rolf should go on a sales tour to Canada. In preparation for the campaign we shipped £1,600 worth of merchandise, mostly children's dressing gowns, packed in 200 well assorted cartons, to Montreal, which would enable him to supply customers from stock.

Exports were the principal but not the only reason why I wanted Rolf to make this journey. He had become too deeply immersed in the factory to the exclusion of everything else, and this was not in his interest nor in that of the firm. I wanted him to meet people, to have to negotiate with them and to learn to take decisions independently of me. What better opportunity to let

him gain worldly experience than to send him on such a tour ? The Board
of Trade sponsored his journey and booked a passage for him. It would have
been impossible to secure one otherwise, for all the shipping offices were
besieged by Americans and other foreign nationals who wanted to return to
their own countries. He sailed from Liverpool in the liner *Empress of France*
on 25 May 1940, and it was with considerable relief that I received a cable
nine days later confirming his safe arrival.

Rolf worked hard. He called on stores, mail order houses and wholesalers
from Quebec to Vancouver and listened to much patriotic talk about supporting the 'old country' but, as always happened when buyers know that
merchandise is available from stock, they refused to pay the regular price and
made silly offers. British goods were in fact very dear. Lancashire's 50 per
cent increase for cotton yarn and the psychological effect of the high official
rate of $4 to the £ which importers had to pay, when pound notes could be
bought in the USA at the unofficial rate of $2·50, forced Rolf to make con-
cessions. Nevertheless, even if prices were cut, we were pleased with the sales
he effected. As he gained experience of the market he appointed selling
agents for the various provinces, the stock at Montreal became exhausted, and
somewhat more remunerative orders began to arrive. Not that the business
ever became profitable, but dollars were more important than profits.

The war was going badly. The collapse of Belgium, Holland and Luxem-
bourg, Churchill's grim speech about 'blood, toil, tears and sweat', the
evacuation of Dunkirk and the fall of Paris made us realise that the 'phony
war' was at an end. To use the Prime Minister's words, the whole fury and
might of the enemy would very soon be turned on us. Determined, the
nation faced the stark reality and tightened its belt without complaining. In
the effort to remedy the delays of the past some authorities over-reacted. So
much labour was transferred from the cotton industry to war production that
serious yarn shortages arose, and the schedule of reserved occupations had to
be revised. The output of weaving and knitting mills fell through lack of yarn,
and since government contracts and export orders had absolute priority,
supplies to the home market suffered. Quotas were introduced restricting the
supply of clothes to the shops by one third. This meant that during the
period from June to November 1940 manufacturers and wholesalers were not
allowed to deliver to retailers more merchandise than two thirds of the value
they had delivered to them during the corresponding period of 1939.

The publication of these restrictions, known as 'limitation of supplies'
orders, caused consternation in the trade. Nobody could understand the
obscure civil service phraseology. Neither Mr Hurst and Mr Colmer nor I
could make out what was expected of us, and when in desperation we asked
the Board of Trade we were told that it was not the job of the officials to

explain the meaning of the Board's regulations. Would we kindly consult a lawyer. The situation seemed iniquitous. And these were only the first of many statutory rules and orders, or 'S R & Os' for short, the interpretation of which caused us headaches.

Quotas made little sense in our case, since our fleecy fabric only half consisted of cotton yarn from Lancashire; the other half was condenser yarn spun from waste clippings and came from our own mill, which was now in full production. I tried to make the BoT understand that, in the national interest, our activities should be increased instead of restricted, for we converted every pound of cotton yarn into two pounds of fabric, but my efforts were of no avail. The BoT had outgrown its strength. It had recruited large numbers of temporary civil servants from many walks of life, moved into the monumental ICI building at Millbank and was struggling to get organised. A small manufacturing unit such as Pasolds Ltd, which fell out of line by producing more garments than it received raw material for and so unbalanced the Board's figures, only caused problems for the unwieldy giant. However, we made the best we could of this infuriating situation.

Our total quota for the period from June to November was £52,000. By the middle of July we had £35,000 left, in addition to which we had secured £15,000 worth of government contracts for PT singlets and ATS vests and panties which required no quota, and our export trade was growing. Thus we succeeded in keeping the factory fully employed. Many firms were less fortunate; some could not even make use of the quota they were entitled to and sold part of it to better-placed rivals. This was quite legal. Marks & Spencer several times bought quota from some of their other suppliers and gave it to us, to secure extra quantities of dressing gowns. My records show one of these transactions for £4,000 of quota, for which they paid 5 per cent, and another for £4,500, at a cost of 7½ per cent, which we shared. Mr Hurst also bought quota for us from wholesalers in the City whose trade had been disrupted by the war.

During these negotiations we heard of Pax Garments Ltd, a small children's wear factory which had been destroyed by enemy action. Its only assets were £800 of unused quota, the entitlement to future quota allocations and a small EPT standard. We acquired the share capital for £250. It was our first experience of buying a business. We hardly knew what use to make of it, but in the course of time we learnt, as later developments will show.

It was not least due to Rolf's efforts that our overseas sales were rising much more steeply than the meagre 10 per cent overall increase of the country's exports. For the time being his job in Canada was done. To sell cotton goods in the United States was not possible because of prohibitive import duties, but there might perhaps be openings for our merchandise in some of the Central and South American republics. On the strength of our export figures I persuaded the British authorities to extend Rolf's travel permit, and he set off for Mexico, going on to Guatemala, Nicaragua, Costa Rica, Panama and Venezuela, where, with varying success, he showed our products to the leading merchants and appointed agents. It must have been a hot and tiring expedition, but I thought of fresh pineapples and bananas, palm-lined beaches and the sound of castanets under tropical skies and, comparing them with the black-out, the sirens and food rationing in Britain, hoped that Rolf was having the time of his life. How wrong I was! He hated every minute of his journey. The orders he was able to book in Central America did not pay for his expenses. Cancelling his visit to Brazil, the Argentine and Chile, he turned north to Cuba and Jamaica. The business he initiated there seemed a little more promising, but breaking fresh ground took time and he felt that he was not pulling his weight. Much as I tried to convince him of the importance of his mission, he longed to return to Langley to take a more active part in the war.

Of our friends, John Hooker was commanding a destroyer, presumably escorting convoys. Bill Ellis's destroyer had been sunk but he himself was saved. Jack Matthews was ferrying aeroplanes from aircraft factories to service airfields and Peter Matthews was training with his artillery unit. Carr Withall, a fighter pilot, and Frank Butler were missing. John Nathan died flying with ATA. Stephen Appleby, who used to entertain us by stunting his Flying Flea, now worked in the airscrew section of De Havilland's and Sydney Evans was with Overseas Airways. And of our knitters who had joined the army, Rocket had been wounded at Dunkirk, Hobbs was a prisoner of war in Germany and Thorne was missing.

Meanwhile the Battle of Britain had begun. The twisting, feathery vapour trails, tell-tales of deadly combat, looked so harmless high up in the blue sky. It seemed such a waste of time to rush all our employees to the shelters when-ever the alarm sounded, as sometimes happened several times a day, but the responsibility of taking a chance with the lives of so many seemed too great. Only Mr Hurst and Peggy, who had closed the London office and moved to the factory, and myself carried on working. We got used to hearing the bombs in the distance and were concerned about the loss of production and wages. Time workers were paid in full, but how was one to deal with people who were on piecework? The issue became a national one that was argued all over the country. We held a meeting in the canteen, and the vote in favour of continuing work during air raids was unanimous, as it was in other factories. Hipperson, Taylor and I were appointed spotters. Whenever there was an alarm we watched the sky, and gave a signal of 'immediate danger' only if we saw planes overhead and heard gunfire or bombs falling in the neighbourhood.

There was then no time to go to the shelters and everyone had to take cover as best he could under a table or among rolls of fabric to protect himself from flying glass, which seemed to be the most frequent cause of injury. The night shift had to be discontinued, for invariably about eight o'clock the German planes came over. They were picked up by the searchlights, the guns opened up, bombs fell and it became very noisy. This went on for hours, and our workpeople preferred to be at home then, near their own Anderson shelters.

Many people went to their shelter during raids. The Matthews, for instance, sat in their hole under the bushes in their garden practically every night and often during the day. But sometimes there were bombs without any prior warning, or they came after the 'all clear' had sounded, while mostly there were warnings and no bombs. I came to the conclusion that it was better for me to sleep in my bed in the flat in the factory than to go to the shelter and feel sleepy next day. We had had no bombs at Langley so far. Croydon, Kingston, Wimbledon, Weybridge, Harrow, Reading, Maidenhead, Datchet and even Iver Heath had been bombed, and it was likely that some night our factory would get hit if the raids carried on long enough, but from the damage I had seen elsewhere I concluded that even a direct hit would not destroy more than a sixth of our buildings, so why just the corner in which I was asleep? Soon I got so used to the wailing of the sirens, the drone of aero-engines out of synchronisation and the intermittent gunfire that I took no more notice of them than of the trains passing through Langley station.

The first bombs on inner London fell on Saturday night, 24 August. I had dinner with Stephen Appleby at the Hungarian restaurant in Lower Regent Street and stayed the night at the Winston Hotel in Piccadilly Circus, where I slept through the attack and only read about it in the morning papers. Curious to see the damage, I went to the City, where three of the bombs had fallen in Fore Street and its immediate vicinity. The windows of the offices of Mr Hurst, Salo Rand and hundreds of others had been shattered, a corner of the church of St Giles, Cripplegate, was missing and the building opposite the little restaurant where we usually had lunch was in ruins, but on the whole the damage was not as great as I had expected.

With the night shift stopped the evenings at Langley were so dreary that I frequently went to town to have dinner and see a play or a good film. I stayed the night and in the morning made business calls. Woolworth's had moved part of their buying offices to Weybridge, but Marks & Spencer's were still at Baker Street. Twice our negotiations there were interrupted by the sirens and we had to conclude them in the shelter. The buyers of firms who had gone to the country could be seen by appointment in the City or the West End and, most important, there were the shippers who had to be canvassed. Overseas business was getting more difficult, while the need for foreign exchange grew more urgent. Without larger exports there would not be enough money to pay for the essential imports of food, raw materials, aeroplanes and ammunition. The Export Council of the BoT launched publicity campaigns to reassure workers in the factories that making goods for export was as important as war production. On street hoardings appeared posters with 'Britain delivers the goods' and similar slogans. At the same time shipping losses were mounting. In the first twelve months of the war more than two million tons of British and Allied merchant ships had been sunk. The issue of export licences and of raw material allocations for export production became dependent on the destination of the goods, and as the war progressed their relative importance varied. Exports to dollar countries, South Africa, Portugal, Egypt, Turkey and some seemingly odd markets in Central America had the highest priority, while those to New Zealand, for instance, which imposed import restrictions and in any case paid only in sterling, came near the bottom of the list. This was regrettable, for we had many good customers there. It did not seem quite fair that the Dominions who relied on Britain for the sale of their wool should raise barriers against the importation of British goods. Export priorities changed not only with financial needs and the availability of shipping but also for political and strategic reasons, and were not normally published. And since officials were usually too busy to give information to individual manufacturers, most industries established export groups which provided the liaison between the BoT and member firms.

There is no need for me to tell how the Germans lost the Battle of Britain and called off the invasion. Protected by a balloon barrage—one of the balloons flew right above Langley recreation ground—and at times by a smoke screen which came from the west side of Slough trading estate, we suffered far less from enemy action than the districts east and south-east of London. Even so, the records at the town hall show that altogether 709 bombs fell in the Slough and Eton rural district, and the town was hit by about a hundred of them. A few extracts from my diary will fill in some of the background against which we carried on our daily business during those fateful weeks:

14 July. Anti-aircraft unit set up searchlight on our land immediately behind the factory. *17 August*. 217 German planes claimed shot down in air battles over south-east England during past four days. *30 August*. Factory shook as Northolt aerodrome bombed. *31 August*. Pat in office has had to evacuate her home at Datchet because of a time bomb in her garden. No one can tell when it may go off. *10 September*. Churchill's message: 'All workers on vital production are front-line troops.' *25 September*. Mr Colmer arrived late this morning. Of the string of bombs dropped on Langley last night, four fell in the fields behind his house, the fifth destroyed his air raid shelter. Fortunately he and his family were sleeping in the house, which was only partially damaged, but his father was injured by a bomb splinter and later died in hospital at Slough. *2 October*. Understand that our sewing machinist, Ada Taylor, who was taken to hospital with bomb splinter in her head, has lost the sight of an eye. *9 October*. 1,000 lb bomb fell near Mr Hurst's house at Stanmore while family were at dinner. Blew in windows, wrecked greenhouse and vinery. *11 October*. Matthews' nursery at Harlington hit by three bombs. Foreman's house ruined. *22 October*. Factory of Silknit Ltd at Park Royal hit by high-explosive and incendiary bombs. I inspected chaos of twisted girders. Circular knitting machines with rolls of fabric below them acted as chimneys and the heat from the burning material melted the oiled machines into solid lumps of metal. Bought 18,000 lb of cotton yarn from them for which they no longer have any use. *25 October*. Have swept bucketful of splinters from anti-aircraft shells from our factory roof and replaced seven broken windows in spinning mill. *18 November*. Matthews' nursery bombed again, trees and greenhouses destroyed. *19 November*. Incendiary bomb penetrating roof set bed of one of our spinners on fire. She was shaken but not hurt. *20 November*. Silknit Ltd bombed a second time and now completely wiped out. *4 December*. Bomb damage to my Ford in Windsor car park.

I usually cycled to the Theatre Royal at Windsor on Wednesday evenings and, if the anti-aircraft batteries were especially active, wore my steel helmet to protect my head from falling shell splinters. On one occasion I took the car, an 8 h.p. Ford which used very little petrol, and invited Adrye Matthews, our engineer, Townley Taylor, and our wages clerk, Eileen Willoughby. Just as the curtain rose the building was rocked by an explosion, everyone ducked and I jokingly whispered to Adrye, 'That sounded like the car park. We may have to walk home tonight.' The show went on, of course, in spite of the air raid, and we enjoyed it, but when we returned to the car we found the roof, windscreen and bonnet crushed and part of the steering wheel broken. Our coats, which we had left inside, were covered with shattered glass: it was even in the pockets. The bomb had fallen on the adjoining railway yard and hurtled some of the track into the car park. Incredible as it seemed, the little Ford still functioned, and I drove it home under its own power.

It was an overstatement to refer to Townley Taylor as an engineer. He was a well spoken young man whom we had engaged some years previously to oblige his uncle, an official in the middle echelon of the Ministry of Labour in London. He had then no other qualification than a pleasant personality, and we gave him odd jobs to do and errands to run. When we found that he liked tinkering with bicycles and other mechanical contrivances we let him help Köhler with simple restorations of old sewing machines. Then came the war, and Köhler's departure brought him sudden promotion to the important position of chief sewing machine mechanic. He knew little about engineering or the more complicated types of sewing machines such as flatlocks but conscientiously and loyally did his best to keep the plant in working order. The Ministry insisted on this kind of 'upgrading' of employees throughout industry to free qualified men for war work or the forces. In this respect, I imagined, we were in a much weaker position than the old established knitters in Leicester and Nottingham, for we had been short of qualified people even before the war. Now we had reached the stage when almost everything that required more than superficial experience of the trade, other than the actual knitting machinery, which was cared for by Passler and Schreiner, had to be attended to by myself. I was testing yarns, grading patterns for the cutting department, adjusting fabric tensions, checking quality standards, and more than once when customers called to see me emerged with black hands and face from underneath some machine I was repairing.

From December onwards the quota of 66⅔ per cent was reduced to 50 per cent, but infants' clothes up to the age of four, of which a severe shortage had developed, were freed from quota restrictions altogether. Since we were primarily children's wear manufacturers and most of our civilian production was in small sizes, this was welcome news. Furthermore children's garments up to the age of fourteen remained free from purchase tax, which was now applied at the rate of 16⅔ per cent to clothing for adults and at 33⅓ per cent to most other goods. This also was in our favour. Like everyone else, we experienced difficulties in getting sufficient cotton yarn, and I remember buying from a spinner in Lancashire a stock lot of 37,000 lb consisting of various counts from 48s to 60s, which we used twofold to get down to the 24s and 30s we required, a costly expedient and excusable only in wartime. But we were fortunate in being able to spin all the condenser yarn we needed. The supply of waste clippings was plentiful, and although our spinning mill now consumed more than our own factory provided, manufacturers in the Midlands —Meridian for one—were glad to sell their interlock cuttings to us. We could afford to pay a little more than the waste merchants. Looking at the overall position of our business, we had every reason to be satisfied. The turnover for the calendar year 1940 was £138,000, against £120,000 the year before. The figures were not strictly comparable, because prices had risen and were now in some cases 50 per cent higher than they had been in 1939, but considering the loss of skilled labour, the shorter working hours, the disruption caused by air raids and the many wartime restrictions, things seemed to be going relatively well.

Cycling home from Maidenhead on Sunday night, 29 December 1940, the sky above London looked bright red. The Germans had made yet another attack on the city and had set it alight. When Mr Hurst and I went to see the damage later we met with a scene of indescribable destruction. Cheapside, Aldersgate Street, Wood Street, Fore Street, Moorgate, Cannon Street, Old Street, Shoreditch, Finsbury, Stepney and many other areas were laid waste by the flames. Mr Hurst's office lay in ruins: only the brass nameplate had survived. The part of London we knew best, the great textile warehouses on both sides of the familiar streets and the winding, narrow alleyways, the Guildhall, the Old Bailey and so many of the churches had been reduced to smouldering heaps of rubble. Our city was no more. I cannot say whether it was memories or the whisks of stinging smoke that made my eyes water.

After the raids on the cities of London and Manchester in which enormous quantities of textiles and other commodities were destroyed by fire, the government made fire-watching compulsory. The roof area of a building determined the number of fire-watchers. So far only I had slept in the factory, and the chances of my putting out two or three incendiary bombs in different parts of the buildings single-handed were slender. From now on twelve of our employees had to be on the premises every night. We drew up a rota, and, since there were not enough men, half the number had to be girls. Sleeping quarters were arranged in the canteen, two of the men took turns at patrolling the buildings, keeping watch; while the remainder of the team played dominoes or draughts I gave an occasional lecture, we read or slept. It was quite good fun to begin with, but gradually fire-watching became just another wartime bore.

Commercially the loss of the London office was without importance—it had been closed for months—but in some way it seemed to mark the end of an era. It made me apprehensive of the coming year, and my apprehension was only too justified. The first quarter of 1941 was to prove the most critical period of the war for Pasolds Ltd. The first small cloud on the horizon was harmless enough. It appeared in the form of an official from some Ministry who came to measure the iron fence on our factory site. I was not at Langley at the time, but was determined that he should not have it as long as there was no sign of any use being made of the ornamental wrought and cast iron gates, fences and other objects which had been requisitioned and were now rusting in one enormous heap by the side of the road between Slough and Maidenhead. As it happened he did not come back, and years after the war had ended the rusty iron still lay where it had been dumped.

Our next caller, a Mr Peeress from the Ministry of Aircraft Production was much more dangerous. He took particulars of our buildings, floor area, canteen and lavatory capacity and said the factory might have to be requisitioned for war work. Taken completely by surprise, I used every argument I could think of to discourage him, from our modern machinery and efficient methods, our unique waste reclamation plant with which we turned every pound of imported cotton into two pounds of fabric, to Rolf's sales drive in America and our growing export figures, but he was not interested. He replied that his visit was merely informative, and left without telling me any more or entering into controversy. Was the take-over of our factory which I had foreseen and dreaded for so long now to come about? I was extremely worried.

The MAP was Lord Beaverbrook's Ministry, and he was one of the most powerful and ruthlessly determined men in the government. All my laboriously prepared defences would be blown away like feathers if he should want our premises for the production of aircraft components. Aeroplanes were more important than children's clothes! Yet all he could use was the floor, the four walls and the roof—an empty shell. The years of planning and evolution, the detail, the countless features designed to suit our particular type of manufacture, the special roof construction, stanchion spacing, ducts and wiring would all be wasted! And what should be done with our delicate machinery? To dismantle, grease, pack and store it would cost as much as the construction of a new building. Was this, perhaps, a way out? I would offer to build a new factory next to ours and let it free of rent to the MAP for the duration of the war. To whom could I talk about it, whose support could I enlist and how could I gain time? Lord Beaverbrook had the reputation of moving very quickly. A few days, even hours, could be decisive.

Neither Mr Watkinson nor Frank Platt could be reached by telephone, and my letters remained unanswered. Raymond Streat, the chairman of the Cotton Board, to whom I appealed for help, sent a friendly but noncommittal reply, as did Mr Hughes of Cotton Control, while Mr Clackson of the Ministry of Supply, for whom we were manufacturing PT singlets and ATS underwear, passed my letter on to a Dr Turner, the Ministry's technical adviser, for a report. No one seemed anxious to support us in the stand we intended to make against Lord Beaverbrook. In the meantime I ascertained from Sharman and confirmed with Try, our usual contractors, that 44 tons of steel required for constructing the factory I had in mind could be supplied from stock and without a licence. In three months the building could be ready for occupation. The offer I was prepared to make to MAP in case of need would be a realistic one.

Mr Peeress worked fast. Only two days after his visit a Mr Ridgeway of the Edison Swan Electric Co. telephoned. He had been instructed by MAP to look at our factory, when could he view it? Playing for time, I succeeded in putting him off for a few days. When he came he brought three other gentlemen with him, representatives of the Cosmos Manufacturing Co. and of the British Thomson Houston Co., who were all makers of radio valves, contractors to the aircraft industry. MAP had told them to increase their production, not by extending their own plants, which they would have preferred, but by requisitioning existing buildings. They needed three factories, each with a floor area of about 30,000 sq. ft, a labour force of 300 girls and a water supply of 2,000 gallons per hour. And they needed them quickly! Our set-up seemed to fit, but Langley was just a little close to London and the bombing. Factories in a quiet spot farther in the country would suit them better. They departed without arriving at a decision. 'Thank goodness for the bombs,' I said to Mr Hurst.

Our last visitors had hardly gone when another delegation arrived. It was led by Mr Tizzard, a surveyor, and Mr Hamish Duncan MacLaren, an assistant director of electrical engineering at the Admiralty, and it came to requisition our buildings for Muirhead & Co., of Beckenham, in Kent, one of the Admiralty's contractors. I countered their demand by telling them that our production was essential for the nation, stressed the shortage of children's clothes, explained that our unique waste reclamation process saved shipping space and sailors' lives, that the Treasury, who had authorised the expenditure of £35,000 on plant, would object to seeing it scrapped, that the BoT would never agree to our factory being requisitioned, and added, with my tongue in my cheek, 'In any case, gentlemen, you would be too late. The MAP were here before you and staked a prior claim. You had better talk to them as well as to the BoT. And furthermore the Ministry of Labour will tell you that you could not, in this area, find the 1,400 workers you say you need!'

An argument between MAP and the Admiralty could only be in our interest. The more I could complicate and thereby delay the matter the better. Mr Tizzard flared up. The Admiralty had priority over MAP, he claimed, and guns for the navy came before clothes for children. He would soon get the matter clarified with the Ministries concerned! Mr Muirhead, who had sat quietly listening, now turned to me. He was sorry, he said, but he had to have an additional factory to execute all his orders and he had made up his mind to have ours if he could get it. He liked the district, and Langley was not very far from Beckenham.

More delegations of determined-looking men arrived, walked through the factory as if it belonged to them, measured a wall here, a floor area there, and made notes. Our workpeople realised that something unpleasant was in the wind, and the fact that I did not talk to them about it unsettled them all the more. I felt terrible having to keep them in the dark, but the location of munitions factories was a closely guarded secret and it seemed that we were on the way to becoming one. I was not allowed to share my fears with anyone.

Then, much to my surprise, Dr Turner appeared. I had forgotten about him. He came all the way from Leeds to get the facts for his report about us which he was preparing for the Ministry of Supply. The contrast between this modest, softly spoken scientist and the overbearing officials and government contractors who had been descending upon us lately was striking. Dr

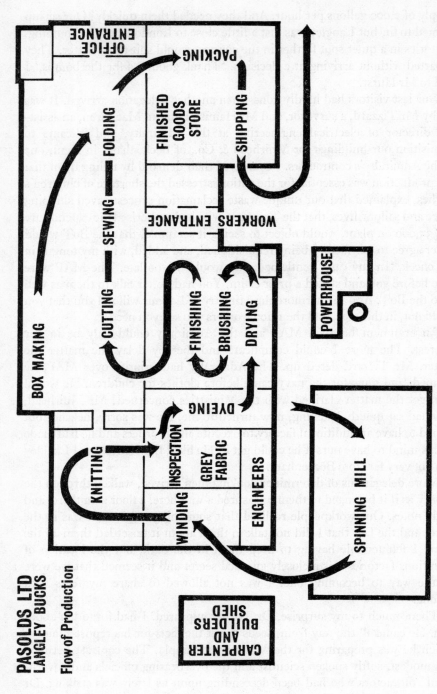

PASOLDS LTD
LANGLEY BUCKS

Flow of Production

OFFICE ENTRANCE

PACKING

SHIPPING

FINISHED GOODS STORE

FOLDING

SEWING

CUTTING

BOX MAKING

WORKERS ENTRANCE

FINISHING

BRUSHING

DRYING

POWERHOUSE

DYEING

INSPECTION

GREY FABRIC

ENGINEERS

KNITTING

WINDING

SPINNING MILL

CARPENTER
AND
BUILDERS
SHED

We were now a completely vertically integrated organisation. We spun the raw cotton or cotton waste, knitted the fabric, dyed and finished it, and made it into garments

Turner had been a research worker at the Shirley Institute before he joined
the Ministry. He seemed to live in a dream world, and I took to him at once.
Our vertically integrated organisation intrigued him. He had never seen a
factory that spun yarn, knitted fabric, dyed and finished it, manufactured the
garments and sold them direct to the retailers. A textbook case! He complimented us on our laboratory and was fascinated to study how we 'recycled',
as he called it, our waste. He would write a glowing report about our activities
and strongly recommend that we be supported. What kind of support, if
any, the Ministry was considering or we stood in need of he did not know. It
did not concern him. His position, he pointed out, was neither executive nor
administrative. I did not even tell him about the threat of being requisitioned
that hung over our factory. The two hours we spent together simply flew,
and I felt much the better for his visit. Unfortunately I never heard or saw
anything of the little man again.

The next episode still makes me laugh. Early on Saturday morning, 15
February, the Fairey Aviation Co. telephoned. MAP had ordered them to
disperse their production, and their inspectors were coming to see our factory
in the afternoon with a view to taking it over. Encouraged by Dr Turner's
visit, I refused to show it to them: it was closed on Saturday afternoon.
Thereupon Fairey's complained to Captain Weathersbee, the BoT's representative at Slough, about our lack of co-operation, and when his secretary
sided with us and made an appointment for Monday they ignored it. Two of
their men suddenly arrived on Saturday mid-morning. The matter was too
urgent to wait! The Great West Road was no longer considered safe, and
MAP—'Lord Beaverbrook, you understand'—had told them to look farther
west. They were two 'upgraded' junior clerks, full of their own importance,
and, notwithstanding the frightening implications of the situation, to watch
them go about their task was very funny. They had not expected to find
premises filled with machinery and merchandise. Who was to clear them? I
shrugged my shoulders. 'We shan't!' I replied. Hard to believe though it was,
the feature that deterred them most was the insufficient width of our sliding
doors. The opening was a foot too narrow for the wings of their aeroplanes.
That a bricklayer and a carpenter could have made it wider in a matter of
hours did not seem to occur to the two inspectors, who became less boisterous
and formidable every minute. After a friendly cup of tea they returned to
their head office at Hayes, undecided what to do.

The complaint about us lodged by Fairey's led to an investigation.
Captain Weathersbee came to see us, but not without first consulting Millbank, where, I gathered, my continual pleading for attention and help had
been heard at last. After I had taken him through the works and explained
the operation, he looked at our figures. When he saw that we exported 25 per

cent of our production, that 15 per cent was for government contracts and 60 per cent went to the home market mostly as children's wear, he seemed pleased and showed me a letter the BoT had sent him. It referred to our factory as 'unique'—my very word—and asked him to 'oppose with firm resistance' any further requisitioning attempts, especially of the spinning mill. The relief I felt was immense. We had found powerful allies!

Captain Weathersbee's appointment as the BoT's representative for the southern region was an honorary but important one. As managing director of Horlicks Ltd, probably the largest firm in Slough, he was independent and could afford to be impartial. He was indignant that MAP should be going about taking over factories in his territory without his consent. How much influence he actually had at headquarters was difficult to say, but neither MAP nor the Admiralty gave us any further trouble. The respite was temporary, for the demand for space continued, but the indiscriminate grabbing of buildings by various Ministries ceased when the BoT made Sir Cecil Weir controller of factories and storage. A softly spoken Scot who had made his mark as president of the Glasgow Chamber of Commerce and administrator of the Empire Exhibition in Scotland in 1938, he organised the requisitioning and allocation of premises on an orderly basis. Captain Weathersbee was his senior executive for our region.

I wished I could discuss our problems with other factory owners, but we had always been too occupied with our own affairs to meet any of the industrialists in our area, except one or two who kept planes at Heston or Denham aerodromes. One of them was Mejndert Kamphuis, a Dutchman who owned a Stinson before the war. Rumour had it that he was killed when the Germans invaded Holland. I was delighted, therefore, to see him alive and well in the summer of 1940 at Skindles at Maidenhead. He insisted that I came to dinner at Franco Cottage, where he lived with his wife, Mary. We had so much in common and got on so well together that from then on I cycled to see them most weekends. Franco Cottage had an enormous living room with a fireplace at either end and a bar in the corner, and Mejndert was a most generous host who liked to surround himself with friends. Most of them were pilots, for whom he kept open house. There were several Dutchmen who had escaped from Holland, one in a stolen German aeroplane, two Americans, Skipper and Alabama Bill, a young man named Harvey Harbottle who imitated Hitler and Goering with great success, Dr Edward May, a refugee from Germany, and the famous world record-breaking Jim Mollison, who was such an amusing story teller. I spent many a happy day in their company, and we had fun even during the noisiest of air raids, when Harvey would announce from the top of the stairs, 'Grossflugtag heute!'

Mejndert was the most intelligent, enterprising and big-hearted of all the many exceptional men I met in my life. He came from a long line of oil millers who had changed to milling cocoa, which was more lucrative. His father was dead; his mother and younger brother were in Holland, where they were looking after the family property. Mejndert had substantial interests in England, of which the largest were British Cocoa Mills at Hull and Gill & Duffus Ltd in the City of London. As far as I could tell, his visits to either concern were infrequent; he hated the telephone and rarely wrote or read letters. 'Read mail,' he once said to me, 'and you become the servant of others. You'll spend the rest of your time doing what they want instead of what you think should be done.' How he could govern such important enterprises by remote control was a puzzle to me.

He too had problems with various government departments, although they were not quite of the same nature as ours and in his case it was the Ministry of Food who were principally concerned, but the difficulties he experienced in explaining technical points to officials were very similar to ours. When he saw that I put mine over in the form of diagrams he bought a drawing board and did the same. He also spent time in the laboratory with me, where I tried, without success, to reclaim dye from effluents, and he liked to see the working models of experimental machinery I built with the aid of a Meccano set to which I had added steel shafts with tiny ball bearings in order to achieve precision. He gave me so much more than I could hope to repay, and when his aeroplane crashed into a mountain in Spain soon after the war I lost one of the best friends I ever had. I still miss him.

The general situation in which we, and presumably most of the knitting industry, found ourselves in the early months of 1941 is well illustrated by a few extracts from letters I sent to Rolf, who was still in America. Having to pass the censor, they contained, of course, no information which might have been useful to the enemy had they fallen into the wrong hands.

Our greatest problems are the shortage of raw materials and labour. Even with priority certificates issued only for export and government contracts, we have to wait for three months before spinners 'commence' to deliver. Price is no object, and we gladly pay a premium of 2d per lb if we get the yarn a month earlier. For some time now it has been impossible to obtain any yarn spun from American cotton, only from Egyptian, which costs more and is, unfortunately, very brown. The fabric knitted from it has to be bleached before it can be dyed. Owing to shortage of labour in the cotton mills, spinners no longer wind the yarn on cones and we have to take it on short tube mule cops. You can imagine the difficulties this creates in our winding department! Today we are told that new government restrictions are on the way, and spinners are meanwhile not allowed to book any fresh business. Our stock of 100,000

lb, together with the 200,000 lb we still have on order—provided they are delivered
—should see us through the next three months.

Chemicals require a permit 'to purchase' and when one has been lucky enough to
secure the stuff a further permit is needed 'to use' it. Supplies of dyes, elastic, paper
and coal are very difficult to come by, and so are all kinds of spare parts. We have to
make more and more ourselves. Outside engineering firms haven't the labour or are
not interested in doing repairs. I have fitted out our workshop with another lathe,
a scroll saw, a small milling machine, an electric tempering furnace and a sanding
machine.

Labour, as you can imagine, gives us many headaches. It is easy to lose workers and
quite impossible to replace them. A number of our best men have joined the forces,
others have gone to armament factories, where they feel their 'reserved occupation'
status is safer than with us. Most of our employees are co-operative and do a grand
job in trying circumstances, although we have a few black sheep and since they know
we need them they exploit us and discipline suffers. Wages have risen, but not dramatically, and our people are pleased with what they are earning, which is more than
other firms in the area pay. At present our labour force is decimated by a flu
epidemic and I am surprised that we are keeping the factory going as well as we do.
An established enterprise withstands more kicks than one would believe.

We have had a very quiet week, some nights not even an air raid warning, but tonight it is noisy again. There are enemy planes overhead just now; the droning of
the engines sounds very near. For fractions of a second there are bright flashes. They
come from the anti-aircraft guns, then you see the shells burst in the sky like fire-
works and some seconds later you hear the explosions. You get used to this sort of
thing, but after a few quiet nights you notice it again.

Auditors and Inland Revenue are hopelessly behind with their work, which is
vastly increased by the Limitation of Supplies orders, purchase tax, ARP and camouflage grants and the numerous certificates that are needed. Many young accountants
in both industry and the profession have joined the forces. Small wonder that we
have so far only had interim demands for tax, one for £2,000 excess profits tax,
which, as you know, is now 100 per cent.

With petrol so short, who would have thought that the value of second-hand cars
could rise? New cars can be bought only with a government permit. I understand
there are 400 left in the country and 4,000 applications from people wanting to buy
them. I have bought a four-year-old 8 h.p. Ford delivery van for £65 for the factory.
Am using it also for my journeys until the Ford saloon that was damaged by a bomb
is repaired. The garage have so far not been able to get a windscreen.

The Limitation of Supplies orders have reduced deliveries of clothes to the shops,
except those for young children, by 50 per cent. But this is misleading. Since the
percentage is based on value, and prices are now almost double what they were in
1939, supplies have actually been cut by 75 per cent.

After some trouble in securing a passage, Rolf sailed on 21 February 1941 in the liner *Georgic* for England. The boat was nearly empty when she left New York. Instead of taking the direct route she called at St John's in Newfoundland, where she took some thousand Canadian air force personnel on board. Frequently changing course, as Rolf could tell from the position of the sun, she then zigzagged across the Atlantic in order to dodge enemy submarines and after thirteen days arrived safely at Liverpool.

Rolf was glad to be back, but it took him a few days to follow the many changes that had taken place at the factory during his absence, and a few nights to get used to the air raids. We shared a bedroom, and when, the first night, he heard the droning overhead, the guns opening up and an explosion near by that shook the factory, he jumped out of bed.

'Let's get out of here fast, they're bombing us to hell!'

'Pull the blanket over your head and go back to sleep,' I replied. 'You'll get used to the noise.'

And, of course, he did.

Rolf brought wads of trial orders from Central America with him and, having promised buyers that he would attend to them personally, we made arrangements for the speedy manufacture of the goods. Larger contracts would follow, provided we got the first small consignments quickly to their various destinations so that the customers could see the quality of our merchandise. I was anxious to prove to the BoT how well worth while Rolf's journey had been, but luck would have it otherwise. On 11 March, only a few days after his return, the Lease–Lend Bill was signed by the United States Congress. It provided that Britain would now receive most of her supplies for the war without having to find dollars to pay for them, and this brought about an immediate change in our government's attitude towards exports. There was now no longer any overriding need to earn dollars. Manpower, raw materials and shipping space could be used to better advantage elsewhere in the prosecution of the war. Exports were still desirable, for political reasons even necessary, but the emphasis shifted and geographical priorities changed. The BoT still showed signs of being pleased with Rolf's sales, yet did very little to help us implement the promises he had made. We hated writing apologetic letters asking to be let off our commitments to firms overseas whose confidence we had sought, but Britain was fighting for her life. Short of America openly taking sides and declaring war, Lease–Land was the best thing that could have happened.

40

CONCENTRATION
OF INDUSTRY
1941-43

MORE THAN A thousand anxious hosiery and knitwear manufacturers were assembled on 21 March 1941 at Leicester to hear Sir Cecil Weir announce the government's 'concentration of industry' scheme, the latest and so far the hardest blow aimed at their independent existence. Owing to the shortage of yarn and labour and the effect of the various 'limitation of supplies' orders, the industry was operating far below capacity and therefore not making efficient use of its premises. It was the intention, Sir Cecil explained, to take over as many of these premises as was practicable for war purposes. Manufacturers were to join together in groups, each group was to concentrate its activities in one of its factories and vacate the others for the production or storage of munitions. Then he paused to let the message sink in. One could have heard a pin drop in the large hall. I looked around me at the sea of strange faces. There was not a single one I knew, and I felt terribly alone.

About 500 firms, Sir Cecil continued, would keep their factories and be designated by the Board of Trade as 'nucleus firms'. This did not mean that they could carry on undisturbed. It would be their duty to provide space and production facilities for the remaining 600 or so manufacturers who were to be 'absorbed' and whose factories would be taken over by the government. Both nucleus and absorbed partners would have to reduce their output by comparison with that of 1940. For infants' wear the reduction would be 20 per cent, for underwear and stockings 30 per cent, for half-hose 33 per cent, for outerwear 60 per cent and for all other types of knitwear 75 per cent, but production for export and government contracts would not be cut. Concentration was to take place on a machinery basis, and he gave the simplest of examples: a nucleus firm with 100 knitting machines all producing fabric for underwear in 1940 would be able to operate seventy of them on its own account and the remaining thirty on account of the absorbed partner, who, ideally, should be a firm entitled to the output of thirty such machines. In theory the factory should then work to capacity and, as a minimum, a forty-eight-hour week. It was appreciated that in practice there would be few cases which fitted so perfectly. He realised, he said, how great a sacrifice he was demanding from everyone, but we all had to make the maximum contribution we could towards winning the war.

Now a storm of questions broke loose. Who would become a nucleus firm and who would be absorbed? There was no industry as diversified as ours. Its factories were not all at Leicester and Nottingham, they were spread all over Britain, varying in size from those employing fewer than fifty hands to concerns like Wolsey's and Corah's who each employed thousands. How could a manufacturer of fine, fully fashioned stockings provide production facilities for a maker of coarse-gauge wool sweaters, cotton interlock underwear, bathing suits or babies' crawlers? Were lifelong competitors expected to work hand-in-hand under the same roof? How about trade secrets, the cost of transferring machinery, rent? And would the absorbed firms be re-established after the war?

Sir Cecil replied that the BoT was fully aware of the complexity of the industry and would therefore leave it to the individual firms to choose their own partners and make whatever arrangements suited them best. The terms were bound to vary according to the circumstances, but the BoT was preparing general guidelines and would assist in settling difficulties should they arise. Then he introduced Mr Abrahamson, the civil servant who was to be in charge of the operation.

Poor Mr Abrahamson—by profession a lecturer on Far Eastern affairs, I learned later, who had joined the BoT on a temporary basis—now faced the agitated audience. He knew next to nothing about the knitting industry, and when driven into a corner by his questioners lost his temper. The scheme was not a compulsory one, he claimed. No firm would be forced to concentrate, but those who refused to do so would get no government contracts, find it increasingly difficult to obtain raw materials, probably have their labour withdrawn, and the BoT would be unlikely to protect their factories against requisition orders. Waving the big stick did not make Mr Abrahamson popular with the manufacturers or lessen their anxiety, and the meeting ended in general bewilderment.

I missed the first train back to London on purpose, so that I could travel in the same compartment as Sir Cecil and Mr Abrahamson and introduce myself to them. But my hope of extracting further information from them was not fulfilled. It appeared that they knew little more than what they had told us already and relied on the ingenuity and co-operation of the industry for the success of the scheme, trusting that the pieces of the jigsaw puzzle would fall into place as it got under way. Nevertheless I used the opportunity to tell them about the factory at Langley and, playing my trump card, to explain how we converted every pound of imported raw cotton into two pounds of knitted fabric.

I was very worried by the cuts in machine activity Sir Cecil had announced. During the basic period of 1940 we had manufactured large quantities of dressing gowns. If they were classified as underwear 30 per cent of the machines on which the fabric had been knitted would have to be shut down. This was bad enough, but if dressing gowns were counted as outerwear the shutdown would amount to 60 per cent and could ruin our chances of becoming a nucleus firm. The thought of them ranking among other types of knitted goods, resulting in a cutback of 75 per cent, was too terrible to contemplate. I had not dared to ask the crucial question at the mass meeting, afraid that an unfavourable reply given there would be difficult to withdraw later, but I asked it now in private. It was a tricky one, and Mr Abrahamson could not answer it.

For the time being the question remained open. Had I only left it at that and, with Mr Abrahamson's tacit agreement, operated on the basis of a 30 per cent cut, all would have been well and we would have heard no more. But I wanted it in writing, and sent Mr Hurst to Millbank to get the matter clarified. After several interviews he brought a letter from Mr Montefiore, who was Mr Abrahamson's assistant, confirming a production cut for dressing gowns of 50 per cent, together with a verbal message from Mr Abrahamson to the effect that 'Pasolds were too honest!' It should have taught me a lesson!

Telegraphic Address:
INDUMANDEP, SOWEST, LONDON.
Telephone No.: WHITEHALL 5140.

Any reply should be addressed to—
The Assistant Secretary,
quoting reference letter and number.
I.M. 2/195/41

INDUSTRIES AND
MANUFACTURES DEPARTMENT,
BOARD OF TRADE,
MILLBANK,
LONDON, S.W.1.

24th April, 1941

Dear Sirs,

I am asked to inform you that the redundancy cut in respect of Dressing Gowns has now been fixed at 50%.

Yours faithfully,

J. S. Montefiore.

Pasold Limited,
Langley,
Bucks.

The concentration scheme as outlined by Sir Cecil had sounded complicated enough, but when I tried to explain it to Rolf, Mr Hurst and Mr Colmer it seemed to become even more involved. To clear my mind I drew diagrams showing what happened when firms of different sizes and with various cuts in production merged. Then I converted these diagrams into pictures of factories, first all of them with smoking chimneys but only partly in production, then half of them with smoking chimneys and on full production while the other half was dead. These illustrations told the story rather well, and I gave prints to some of the officials at Millbank, who accepted them with alacrity. It proved a happy thought. They were discussed and passed round and made good publicity for Pasolds Ltd.

Determined to become a nucleus firm, we copied the addresses of likely concentration partners out of Skinner's directory and sent a circular letter inviting them to join us. The resulting negotiations led nowhere, but in response to an advertisement in the *Drapers' Record* we had a visit from three directors of Jantzen Knitting Mills, the famous swimwear makers. Their factory was on the Great West Road at Brentford, where, before the war, they employed some 180 hands but now had barely a hundred left. We were surprised to hear that in spite of the fact that contracts for army pullovers took 80 per cent of their output, exports the remaining 20 per cent and that the firm was American-owned, the Ministry of Aircraft Production had served a requisition order on them. They could not have fought as resolutely to defend themselves as we had done! The requisition had come as a terrible shock, they confessed. Their factory had to be vacated within six weeks. But now, out of the blue, came the concentration of industry scheme, and it seemed that, with luck, they could stay in business if some other knitwear factory took them in. Would we consider accepting them as concentration partners?

Never were visitors more welcome. A first comparison of our respective production figures during the basic period revealed that, for concentration purposes, Jantzen's new permitted activity would almost exactly match our redundancy. Between us, it seemed, we could meet Sir Cecil's requirements for an 'ideal' combination. A more desirable partnership was hard to imagine. We would hammer out a mutually satisfactory scheme with them, offer to provide space in our factory free of rent for their machinery and labour, give them office accommodation, canteen and other facilities, and supply power, heating and lighting at cost. These were generous terms, an unexpected present for Jantzen in their predicament, but having so nearly lost our own factory we felt for them. We would stretch out both hands in friendship and do everything we could to help them and make them feel at home at Langley. Without much hesitation they accepted, subject to BoT approval of the concentration between us, and to the hundred and one details still to be agreed.

We liked Jantzen's managing director, Mr Cormack, an American ex-banker and a gentleman, and were sorry to learn that he would soon be returning to the parent company at Portland, Oregon. That was why he left most of the negotiations to Mr Thorne, one of his English co-directors, a thin, ascetic-looking man in his thirties whose prematurely white hair made him appear much older. The third director, Mr Green, was an accountant. Then came Mr Crowther, the sales manager, and Mrs Crowther, the designer, who were not on the board but seemed to play an important role in the firm. Altogether a thoroughly competent-looking team, I thought. Also on the board was Lord Barnby, whose name was mentioned with great deference but who did not put in an appearance. We were extremely happy that Jantzen wanted to join us.

They were reasonable people to negotiate with about things they under-stood, such as general business practice, office routine, wage rates, sales and exports, but we soon discovered that the men at the top knew very little about machines. Knitting, sewing and other plant was the responsibility of two mechanics a long way down the ladder of command. Since Mr Thorne would not have them at our meetings, discussions about technical matters took unnecessarily long, and decisions frequently had to be amended later. One of the most important ones was the number of knitting machines we were each to operate under the scheme. According to our respective production records, Jantzen were entitled to twenty and Pasolds to fifty-six machines, and since we both used different types Jantzen would bring twenty of their own to Langley and we would immobilise twenty of ours. Having thus agreed to make an overall return of seventy-six machines to the BoT, Mr Thorne, a few days later, suddenly insisted on bringing twenty-six machines. I pro-tested, but in order not to upset the 'ideal' total figure, gave way and cut out six of Pasolds' machines. This first clash with Mr Thorne came as a great dis-appointment to me. It did not remain the only one. However, in spite of the temporary discord we reached agreement on everything, and Mr Cormack recorded the gist of the understanding in a ten-point letter:

1 Pasolds are the nucleus firm in whose factory Jantzen's goods will be pro-duced in accordance with the rules laid down by the concentration of in-dustry scheme.

2 Each firm will retain its identity and insure its own property.

3 Jantzen will bring as many of their employees to Langley as will come, Pasolds to provide the additional labour needed to make Jantzen's authorised pro-duction. In case of labour shortage, both firms to share the shortfall in pro-portion to their permitted production quotas, but government and export orders to have overriding priority.

4 Jantzen will pay the salaries of their managerial staff themselves. Pasolds to pay the wages of Jantzen's labour force and to debit Jantzen.

5 Pasolds will charge no rent for the space occupied by Jantzen.

6 Pasolds will charge for power, heat and light supplied to Jantzen at cost.

7 Jantzen will be responsible for the transport of its machines and equipment from Brentford to Langley.

8 After the war Jantzen will take steps to return to its own factory as soon as possible.

9 Neither company will, after the war, employ each other's staff except by mutual agreement.

10 Both companies will do everything in their power to ensure the smooth operation of the concentration scheme.

This fairly summarised the general terms we had agreed between us. We now completed the BoT's intricate questionnaires, which asked for production and labour figures, floor areas and details of the plant each of us undertook to immobilise, and then we submitted our application to Millbank.

On 22 May we received a letter from the BoT, signed by a Professor G. C. Allen, granting our application and conferring nucleus status on Pasolds Ltd. It was a red letter day for us. The fact that ours was the industry's first concentration scheme to be approved, and that we were given nucleus certificate No. 1, made it an even prouder occasion. True, its validity was restricted to a period of three months, but that seemed a long time in those turbulent days, and I felt confident that it would be extended.

We thought our newly won nucleus status would afford us protection, but we were wrong. In the middle of June the Ministry of Aircraft Production made a fresh attempt to requisition, not the whole factory, but part of it. Was this some new technique? I left Mr Osselton, the Ministry's dispersal officer, in no doubt that he was wasting his time, but repeated my offer to have a new building erected and to let it to MAP free of rent for the duration of the war. He went away to discuss the offer with his superiors and did not come back.

We had gained another month. Then came Major Stockings, the deputy controller of factories and storage, who said a building licence was out of the question and demanded that we give up 10,000 sq. ft of our factory. I flatly refused, and warned him that we would fight, whereupon I was summoned to appear before Sir Cecil Weir. Armed with a plan of our buildings, a set of large photographs of all the departments of our factory, and a chart on which I showed in pictures our concentration with Jantzen, their vacated factory, a ship unloading a bale of cotton and a lorry loading two bales of clothes, I went to see him. He seemed to be intrigued with the chart and asked to keep it. Then he carefully compared each photograph with the plan, and, by a process of elimination, just as I had intended, he was finally left with only the photograph of our half-empty warehouse in his hands.

'This is the one area you can do without,' he said softly, 'and I must ask you to give it up. I need it for one of the Ministries.'

'It was you, Sir Cecil,' I replied, 'who introduced the concentration of industry scheme. We have complied with it to the letter, and I am sure that you want our concentration with Jantzen to be a success. No factory can operate entirely without a storage area for raw materials and finished goods. Jantzen can't either, and so we have done the seemingly impossible and have cleared half our warehouse to make room for them. The vacant space you see in the photograph will be filled with the material being moved from their factory at Brentford, which has been requisitioned by MAP.'

I had him trapped and he knew it, but he took it in good part. What I had told him was nothing but the truth. We had transferred most of the bales of our hosiery waste clippings to two wooden barns we had found at Sipson and rented—only to lose them in a fire some time later. Sir Cecil withdrew his demand, and I hoped we would now be left in peace.

Our condenser plant had captured Abrahamson's imagination. He realised that it was in the national interest to re-spin waste: why was it not done on a larger scale? At his request I prepared a detailed scheme for a waste reclamation and spinning industry on the Langley model. For a few days it caused some excitement in the raw material section at Millbank, after which I heard no more. I felt disappointed, but perhaps it was just as well—at least we were not creating competition for ourselves. Since we had lost most of our accumulated stocks of waste clippings in the fire at Sipson, we were buying additional weights from merchants such as Austin, Hyman and later from Bunzl, an old supplier of our mill at Leibitschgrund. George Bunzl had come to Britain when the Nazis occupied Austria and Czechoslovakia, and was working hard building up a business here. He commented on our foresight in coming as early as 1931 while he had waited until Hitler's hand was at his throat. I assured him that it was not foresight on our part but a fortunate accident. We came because we loved England. While we were inspecting his samples of waste there was an air raid warning, then machine gun fire, a low-flying German bomber dropped its deadly load on the factory of High Duty Alloys a few hundred yards away, and part of an anti-aircraft shell together with two brick-sized pieces of concrete came through the spinning mill roof. Hitler, it seemed, was still after us.

We had been looking forward to witnessing an example of American efficiency in the form of a speedy transfer of Jantzen's plant to Langley, but we were disappointed. The move took much longer than planned, and our concentration partners did not start production until the second half of July. They appeared to be rather uncertain about the technicalities of manufacturing, and we were amazed when they told us that, swimwear being a seasonal commodity, their peacetime practice had been to operate the mill at Brentford for six months on double shifts and then close it down for six months, dismissing its labour. This they repeated each year.

It seemed incredible to us that a manufacturing concern operating in this fashion could stay in business, let along make a profit, as Jantzen obviously had done. They were an enigma. Was it skilful salesmanship or clever advertising of their famous trade mark that had made them so successful? They were not making swimwear now. Ministry of Supply and export orders were not seasonal and ought to keep them busy all the year round, but their ideas of manufacturing and their attitude to labour puzzled us. They were so opposed to ours that we thought it best to keep our production teams strictly separate to avoid serious disagreements.

We did not believe that Jantzen would use all the twenty-six knitting machines Mr Thorne had insisted on bringing to Langley, but were dumbstruck when only four of them went on production and the remainder were kept standing idle. It transpired that Jantzen found it easier and more profitable to buy woven material and make it into slacks and skirts or, better still, to let outside makers sew the garments and attach the Jantzen labels than to operate their knitting plant. That this was completely contrary to the spirit of the concentration scheme did not seem to concern them very much. Meanwhile our fifty operational knitting machines were not able to produce sufficient fabric for our requirements, we were not permitted to bring any of our immobilised plant back into use and Jantzen's idle machines were not suitable for our purposes. We therefore looked round for an additional concentration partner who might be able to supplement our production. When we heard that A. & R. Gilbert Ltd, a small interlock factory at Broadstone in Dorset, had run out of yarn and was for sale because the elderly owner no longer felt able to cope with the many government regulations, Rolf went to see the plant. It consisted basically of nine interlocks, thirty-nine sewing machines and a calender, and when he reported favourably we decided to buy it. We released the factory building and the thirty-seven employees for war work, and for the purchase consideration of £3,650 acquired the shell of the company, which included quota amounting to £10,000, and the machines, which we transferred to Langley. The most important were the interlocks. We had to immobilise three of them, and the BoT co-operated by adding A. & R. Gilbert and the other six machines to our nucleus certificate, thus increasing our permitted output by a welcome 12 per cent.

Permission to increase production was one thing. Finding the necessary cotton yarn was another. The knitting industry was starved of yarn. Was the shortage genuine or were the authorities holding supplies back to force manufacturers into forming partnerships? We heard that the concentration scheme was making only slow progress, but having fulfilled our part of the bargain we now expected the BoT to fulfil theirs. Sir Cecil Weir and Mr Abrahamson had promised to look after the needs of nucleus firms, I told Mr MacMahon at Millbank, the man responsible for raw material. To my pleasant surprise he seemed to be well informed about our firm. Smiling, he pointed to some letters on his desk which I had written to other government departments and which had been redirected to him, and he said without being prompted, 'I know, you make two tons of fabric out of every ton of cotton yarn allocated to you.'

I was thrilled that the message had got through to him. 'We do,' I replied, 'at least as far as fleecy fabric, the largest part of our output, is concerned. But we must have the cotton yarn. We cannot knit the condenser yarn on its own.'

Mr MacMahon promised to do what he could to get cotton yarn for us. And could we increase the production of condenser yarn spun from waste to supply other knitting mills with it? He would support an application for additional waste reclamation machinery. He was well disposed towards us, and I liked him, but I wondered how many of the notes he made during our interview would ever be translated into action. Like most civil servants, he could not be hurried, and, I suspected, his powers were limited. He could, presumably, do little more than make recommendations. But to my very pleasant surprise the rationing committee at Leicester responded with substantial yarn allocations and Lancashire with early deliveries. Before long our yarn stocks were growing again, and we could accumulate a reserve. The application for a permit to enlarge the waste spinning plant, however, was unsuccessful.

I was away from Langley a good deal. Apart from visiting spinners at Oldham, Bolton or Rochdale, searching the Midlands for needles or calling on customers who had evacuated their offices to remote places in the country, much of my time was taken up in arguing or pleading with officials at Millbank. I was there every week. One had to keep in touch with the expanding administration of the BoT and the other Ministries. New departments were created, existing ones reshuffled, names and faces came and went. In the early days I usually saw Mr Lamb, who had been with His Master's Voice at Hayes before he became a civil servant. Later Mr MacMeekin, who had spent most of his life as a merchant in China, and Mr Gray, a Scottish steel manufacturer, became responsible for some sections of the hosiery industry and I had meetings with them. I learned that a Miss Heinemann was able to influence the supply of labour to firms who had concentrated, that Mr Hobson could add factories to or delete them from the register of premises available for requisitioning, and that the official at the Directorate of Civilian Clothing responsible for knitted goods was a Mr Foyster. I was glad to have Rolf back. Without him there to supervise the factory I could not have moved about so freely.

But Rolf was restless. He felt left out of the war. Most of his friends were in uniform, and, while he knew that the work he was doing was important, there was nothing heroic about being the manager of a textile factory. Could he not join ATA and ferry aeroplanes? He went to White Waltham and passed his medical and flying tests, but ATA would not take him on a part-time basis. We might have spared him for two or three days a week, but not altogether, and when Mr Boxall of the Ministry of Labour also asked him to stay where he was he reluctantly agreed to forget about flying, at least for the time being. The authorities in their wisdom must know best where he was most useful.

Shortly afterwards Hitler attacked Russia. Most people in England had looked upon the Bolsheviks as arch-enemies, and we were staggered to witness the somersault in public sentiment. It came as a shock to us to see the red flag with the hammer and sickle hoisted next to the union jack outside the Theatre Royal at Windsor. The villains of yesterday were now our heroic brothers-in-arms. But Britain was fighting for her life and could not choose her allies. Would the German bombers now fly east towards Minsk, Kiev and Moscow and give us some respite? I studied the map and thought of Napoleon. What were Hitler's chances now of winning the war? And what would happen when the pendulum swung back? Would Communism sweep across Europe?

While most manufacturers were still trying to complete their concentration arrangements the government confronted the harrassed industry with further measures. In June 1941 clothes rationing began, with the issue to everyone of sixty-six coupons intended to last for a year, and in August came the introduction of a preliminary Utility Scheme. Both caused a great deal of uncertainty. The SR&Os published by the authorities were difficult to understand, and, as had become the accepted practice, it was left to trade associations to clarify the meaning and communicate it to their members. 'Utility' had to be clearly defined. To do this the BoT and the knitting industry together appointed a joint panel of experts, the Central Committee, which prepared a detailed schedule of the specifications of every Utility garment, the yarn from which it was to be made, its minimum weight and measurements and its maximum permitted selling price. Manufacturers were told that they had to use at least two thirds of their capacity for the production of Utility merchandise unless their plant was not suitable for this kind of work and they were able to make special arrangements with the BoT. The scheme should have got under way in October, but most firms did not receive their yarn permits until November and December and could not start production before January, too late for the winter of 1941–42, which saw the worst shortage of knitted goods of the whole war.

Pasolds Ltd was more fortunate. We were the first firm in the industry to have achieved nucleus status, the only one to reclaim and spin its waste. Apart from export and government orders, we now manufactured children's wear exclusively. We had our own dyehouse, a good supply of cotton yarn and —last but not least important—we had created the reputation with most civil servants who had anything to do with hosiery of being outstandingly efficient producers, whose methods, plant and know-how were unique. But being original also had some disadvantages in an increasingly regimented world. In order to use as large a proportion of condenser yarn as possible we concentrated on the production of fleecy knickers and dressing gowns. Hardly anyone else seemed to be making them, and they were therefore not included in the Utility schedule. This was a calamity. If any garments deserved to be described as utilitarian our fleece-lined girls' knickers did, and warm dressing gowns were most useful when children had to be taken to the air raid shelter in the middle of the night. Nevertheless many weeks of reasoning and anxious waiting passed before the Directorate of Hosiery agreed to treat these garments as Utility merchandise.

When, in the early months of the war, the government first began to interfere with production it did so at the raw material stage by cutting yarn allocations in relation to pre-war consumption, and also at the finished merchandise stage through the limitation of supplies quota, which was based on sales during the twelve-month period prior to May 1940. There was no logical connection between these two forms of restriction, and, while they had the desired overall effect of reducing output, they created anomalies. But they left the manufacturer free to make whatever garments he chose, the market forces of supply and demand continued to operate, and by and large the public got the assortment of merchandise it wanted. With the concentration of industry scheme, however, imposing production cuts from 20 to 75 per cent on various categories of garments, the Utility scheme prescribing a ratio of two to one between Utility and non-Utility goods, and clothes rationing superimposed on top of it all, the market could no longer function. To ensure a balanced flow to the shops of the right kind of garments in the right quantities, the right-size proportions, at the right time and the right price, the industry's output had to be planned centrally. Henceforth manufacturers had to submit production programmes every four months to Hosiery Control, which confirmed or amended them to meet the nation's needs, and yarn was then allocated in accordance with these programmes. Many firms did not take kindly to this regimentation, and there were teething troubles, but in due course they were overcome and the system worked well. Pasolds Ltd at least had little fault to find with it, and I am not aware that any of our programmes were ever cut or amended.

It was not my intention to trespass on the BoT's side of the story when I began to write these pages, but searching official archives and reminiscing with some of the now retired civil servants who shaped and applied wartime controls revealed enough of the fascinating scene behind the curtain for me to want to record it. It appears that the basic ideas for many of the drastic regulations and changes to which our industry was subjected sprang from the fertile brain of our old friend G. L. Watkinson. He passed them to people below him to work out in detail and, if he felt satisfied that they made sense, to introduce and administer them, while he stayed in the background thinking about fresh problems. An excellent judge of character, he usually picked the right men for the job. It was, for instance, a master-stroke to choose such a highly regarded and persuasive negotiator as Sir Cecil Weir to put the very unpalatable concentration scheme over to the hosiery industry.

Chosen with equal care and skill was the small team of temporary civil servants whose difficult task it was to assess the nation's needs of knitted goods and of getting the industry's output matched to it. There was Cecil Coleman, a businessman in his early fifties, who relinquished his job as manager of N. Corah, the largest hosiery manufacturer in the country, to become Hosiery Controller. Much of his firm's success was due to his initiative. When, back in 1924, Simon Marks tried to place an order with Corah and was shown the door, Coleman followed the future chain-store king into the street and, against the wishes of his co-directors, accepted a contract for 4,000 dozen socks from him. Now, seventeen years later, Marks & Spencer sold more knitted goods than any other retail organisation, Corah's were their largest supplier, and Mr Coleman knew more about efficient mass production of a wide variety of hosiery than any other manufacturer.

Len Foyster, who had been an employee of M. & S., was elevated to the post of Director of Hosiery. His civil service experience began when Simon Marks loaned him to the Directorate of Civilian Clothing. A very able young man of about thirty, he knew the industry, understood the merchandise and was well qualified to fill this key position.

The third member of the team was John (now Sir John) Hewitt, another thirty-year-old who had interrupted his career to join the BoT. He came from the stock exchange, was at home with figures and could analyse statistics. The trouble was that there were none. No one really knew the nation's needs. The figures would first have to be compiled before the industry could be told what to manufacture, a heavy responsibility which made the job all the more challenging for him.

And finally there was Margaret Dowler, the little secretary–typist who cheerfully coped with the mountains of paperwork created by the budgetary control of a whole industry. The team, I am told, started work in an unheated room in Leicester without so much as a desk, table or chair, and that, rather than follow the slow and cumbersome official procedure of requisitioning furniture from the appropriate department, Mr Coleman provided it himself. Mr Watkinson must have been pleased with the speed and efficiency with which the quartet brought order to the trade and earned its complete confidence and co-operation.

For practical reasons Hosiery Control took over the functions of the Hosiery Rationing Committee, which, under the chairmanship of S. F. Peshall, had since the beginning of the war been allocating wool and later also cotton yarn to the industry. Freddie Peshall, incidentally, was another director of Corah's. No doubt the BoT consulted other traders and industrialists too, and on all manner of subjects, but when it came to the definition and supply of essential clothing and Utility garments the advice of Simon Marks and Israel Sieff must have carried much weight. Both men shunned personal publicity and, much like Mr Watkinson, remained in the background, but it is interesting to speculate on the influence, direct or indirect, they must have exercised on policy at Millbank in those early days.

To end this short digression on a slightly humorous note, let me say that my retired civil service friends confess to having been every bit as scared of the sometimes very formidable-looking manufacturing community as we were of the mighty BoT. If only we had known it at the time!

During the summer and autumn of 1941 our weekly production for the home market averaged:

	Dozens
Girl's knickers	3,000
Children's dressing gowns	300
Children's siren suits	250
Children's vests	500
Infants' sleeping suits	120
Infants' matinee jackets	100
	4,270

To this figure has to be added a weekly production of approximately 1,000 dozen for government contracts and export orders, to obtain the total output.

Rolf and I thought the Utility scheme was sensible, and we welcomed it, not only because it suited our mentality and the mass-production layout of our factory but because it was obviously in the national interest. Jantzen, by contrast, wanted to have nothing to do with it. The trade would reject it, Mr Thorne predicted, and it would be short-lived. Besides, Utility merchandise was too strictly price-controlled to be of interest to Jantzen.

For some obscure reason clothes for children seemed to be in shorter supply than those for adults, and the rapidly rising birth rate exacerbated the shortage. The authorities encouraged the production of children's garments with generous yarn allocations, larger quotas and other inducements, and we could not understand why so few manufacturers seemed to take advantage of the situation. Their lack of adaptability made it all the more interesting for us. Our wholehearted co-operation with the BoT in the production of children's wear brought nothing but benefits to Pasolds Ltd, and we fared better than most firms in the industry.

By September 1941 nucleus status had been granted to 342 firms, the factories of 436 had been closed, releasing 5 million square feet of floor area, and some 250 mainly smaller manufacturing businesses carried on a precarious existence as registered non-nucleus enterprises. The number of workers in the knitting industry, which had been 120,000 before the war and 95,300 in March 1941, fell to 76,600 in October. But this was still substantially in excess of the 65,000 permitted under the concentration scheme, and the Ministry of Labour started to withdraw women between the ages of twenty and twenty-five and direct them into munitions factories. Despite our nucleus status we had to fight for the retention of every one of our employees and demonstrated with graphs and figures how efficiency suffered through the excessive withdrawal of labour. The following extracts are taken from a memorandum I submitted to the Ministry of Labour:

Every factory has a certain employment level at which it produces most efficiently. If its labour force is substantially increased above or reduced below this level the fall in efficiency is considerably greater than the variation in output. By efficiency we mean the largest possible output per worker, per ton of coal, per unit of electricity. The withdrawal of key workers results in bottlenecks and production losses many times greater than represented by the percentage of labour withdrawn.

Our men work a fifty-four to sixty-hour week, our women on average fifty hours. We manufacture exclusively Utility garments and underwear for the Ministry of Supply. Owing to the withdrawal of labour our output is below pre-war level, although we have partially compensated for the reduction in our labour force by simplification of the product. Our present production amounts to 3,250,000 garments per annum.

To produce 1 million Utility garments per annum in our well balanced factory before the war would have required:

45,000 man/woman hrs. 105,000 kilowatt hrs. 165 tons of coal

With our present labour force it requires:

51,000 man/woman hrs. 115,000 kilowatt hrs. 190 tons of coal

After giving up the five men you ask for:

54,000 man/woman hrs. 130,000 kilowatt hrs. 210 tons of coal

After releasing the further eleven employees you specify:

77,000 man/woman hrs. 230,000 kilowatt hrs. 390 tons of coal

Each time the schedule of reserved occupations was amended and the age limits were raised a number of our men left for the forces or were directed to munitions work. Girls took over wherever possible, but even they were threatened, and I had many a disputation with Mr Berry of the Manpower Board at Reading and his too zealous assistant, Miss Thomas, pleading to let us keep a reasonably balanced labour force. When I gave Mr Berry one of my pictorial charts which illustrated our method of working and showed how, because of our waste reclamation plant, we manufactured twice as many garments from a given quantity of cotton yarn as other makers, he was impressed.

'Provided you refrain from applying for deferment for the first five men on your list,' he said, 'we shall let you keep the eleven men in the second group for a further six months after their deferment expires, and since they do not all become de-reserved at the same time their withdrawal will be spread over an even longer period. Now tell me about the girls in the winding department you want us to reserve in the category of cotton spinners.'

Miss Thomas chipped in. 'Mr Berry, we have been told by Head Office that cotton spinners should be reserved only in Lancashire and Cheshire. We ought to look at Pasolds' concentration scheme to check the permitted labour figures.'

Mr Berry came to our aid. 'We really must leave this to the Ministry of Labour at Slough, Miss Thomas,' he interrupted her. 'The BoT take a special interest in Pasolds and we shall not take the ten winding girls until we can replace them by twenty part-timers.'

It was over the steadily worsening labour situation that we ran once again into trouble with Jantzen. Of the ninety-five employees they had intended to bring from Brentford only seventy came, and we gave them some of our workers to make up the deficiency. But it soon transpired that, having a growing part of their merchandise made by outside contractors, Jantzen had not enough work for their sewing machinists and were thinking of dismissing some of them. Fortunately we heard of this in time and took over their surplus girls. Once gone, they would have been lost for good. A month or two later, unexpectedly it seemed, the Ministry of Supply gave Jantzen another contract, and Mr Thorne demanded that we provide sewing machinists. The contract completed, he would once again have sacked them had we not taken them back. This chopping and changing was inclined to disrupt our own production, but in the interest of peace we co-operated.

Meanwhile the schedule of reserved occupations was again amended. The managers of nucleus firms were now reserved at lower ages than those of their absorbed partners. Pasolds' departmental managers, for instance, were protected at twenty-five but Jantzen's only at thirty-five, and we asked Mr Boxall of the Ministry of Labour, who had by now become a trusted friend, what could be done about it. He suggested that Jantzen's management be put on Pasolds' payroll, but Mr Thorne objected and it was only by a private understanding with Mr Boxall, who agreed to ignore the letter as long as the spirit of the concentration scheme was observed, that this difficulty was overcome.

Once the upheaval of concentration was over and Hosiery Control had

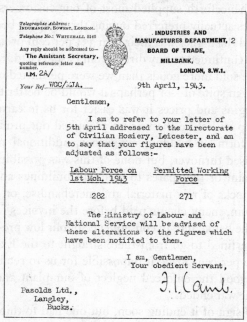

Telegraphic Address:
INDUMANDEP, SOWEST, LONDON.
Telephone No.: WHITEHALL 5140

Any reply should be addressed to—
The Assistant Secretary,
quoting reference letter and number.
I.M. 2A/

Your Ref. WGC/EJA.

INDUSTRIES AND
MANUFACTURES DEPARTMENT, 2
BOARD OF TRADE,
MILLBANK,
LONDON, S.W.1.

9th April, 1943.

Gentlemen,

I am to refer to your letter of 5th April addressed to the Directorate of Civilian Hosiery, Leicester, and am to say that your figures have been adjusted as follows:—

Labour Force on 1st Mch. 1943	Permitted Working Force
282	271

The Ministry of Labour and National Service will be advised of these alterations to the figures which have been notified to them.

I am, Gentlemen,
Your obedient Servant,

J. I. Camb.

Pasolds Ltd.,
Langley,
Bucks.

firmly established itself at Leicester, a degree of stability returned and the industry settled down to more orderly conditions. The basic shortages of labour and raw material supplies were now dealt with more equitably. Mr Hewitt, still handicapped by the absence of figures, had to rely on estimates on which to base the production plan for the industry, but if our experience was anything to go by they were remarkably accurate. I suspected that Len Foyster, behind the scenes, leaned heavily on the expertise of Marks & Spencer. There would have been a revolt had this been known to the trade; to the BoT, however, the chain store's advice must have been invaluable.

The prices of Utility garments were controlled, but they had to be high enough to enable manufacturers not equipped for this kind of production and also the smaller, less competitive makers to earn a living. Efficient massproducers, on the other hand—and Pasolds Ltd was in this category—had to be prevented from making excessive profits. With this in mind, the BoT introduced an overriding maximum profit margin of $7\frac{1}{2}$ per cent net for all manufacturers. The margin laid down for wholesalers was 20 per cent and that for retailers $33\frac{1}{3}$ per cent, in both cases gross. So far so good, but some of the larger manufacturing concerns had subsidiary sales companies who were treated as wholesalers. They were therefore entitled to the $7\frac{1}{2}$ per cent net and the 20 per cent gross profit. Surely we could operate on the same basis! Pax Garments Ltd, which, it will be remembered, we acquired some time previously, seemed a suitable vehicle. We registered the little company as wholesalers and henceforth supplied most of our customers through them. Many of the stores actually preferred buying through Pax because the higher the price they paid the higher was their own $33\frac{1}{3}$ per cent profit. Only M. & S. and Woolworth's continued to buy direct from Pasolds Ltd.

We could have sold more goods than we were permitted or indeed able to manufacture, and in spite of—or perhaps it would be better to say because of—controlled margins and prices it was easier for us to earn money than to know how to keep it. Before the war we ploughed our profits back into the business in the form of building extensions, additional machines, larger stocks and increased turnover, but none of this was possible now. We could hardly get the paint or the spares to maintain buildings and plant in good condition. Our stocks of raw material and merchandise, on the other hand, were at a minimum, many clients paid before the invoices fell due, the cash accumulated at the bank, and, in consequence of our low pre-war profit level, most of it was destined to go from there straight to the Exchequer. Excess profits tax at 100 per cent made it impossible for us to retain enough of the money to make good the enforced neglect of our plant and to expand the business when the war ended.

There was no sign of it ending soon, but one had to think ahead. Everyone predicted that the great slump which followed the first world war would recur after the second and that there would be overproduction when all the closed knitting mills started up again. It seemed logical to expect a surplus of the austerity type—our type—of merchandise just when the public was thoroughly tired of it and demanded a change. Would it want frills, pleats, pockets and embroidery and look for brand names instead of the Utility label? If so, the most sensible way of investing some of the earnings would be to develop and publicise our Ladybird trade mark. The cost of advertising was a legitimate business expense.

Despite shortages of supplies and seemingly high prices, Jantzen's brand name still dominated the quality swimwear market. What Jantzen could do we could do better! We would make Ladybird the leading name for children's wear. We would design and mass-produce good, attractive little clothes and give the public value for money. The creation of these garments would have to wait until after the war, but the trade mark should make its debut now. Before introducing the little red beetle to the trade I wanted to give it a personality. I wrote a fairy tale about a small boy's dressing gown and a tiny ladybird prince, a little book of twenty pages, and got Walter Trier, a well known artist and illustrator of children's books, to draw the pictures. They were better than my story, although I was not really satisfied with Trier's interpretation of the ladybird character I wanted. However, we had 20,000 books printed and they became quite popular.

Next we decided on a series of whole-page advertisements in the trade press. But publishers were short of paper, and one could not blame them for keeping it for their regular clients. There was none to spare for newcomers like us. 'But our advertisements will be works of art, whole pages in full colour—pictures of babies' clothes, flowers and ladybirds painted by top artists,' I coaxed Miss Guppy, the editor of the *Children's Outfitter*. She was quick to realise that colour pages would raise the standard of her modest black-and-white magazine, and we were allocated sufficient space for a campaign. It was noticed by the publishers of other journals. Our happy little ladybirds dancing round fairy-tale garments made hard-headed advertising managers smile, and before long most of the important textile magazines were selling space to us.

Many old established firms advertised nothing but their trade marks and promises for the future; we were thus in good company. Nevertheless, showing pictures of merchandise that did not exist and would not become available until after the war was not altogether satisfactory. Peggy Hurst had a better idea. 'Let Pax Garments engage a designer and, with a dozen sewing machinists, manufacture a small range of exclusive infants' clothes from non-Utility fabric and sell them to the high-class stores in the West End,' she suggested. 'That would give us something to advertise which we could actually supply, if only in tiny quantities, and which would create a quality image for the Ladybird label.'

Pax had been makers-up before the factory was bombed. The BoT therefore raised no objection to production being resumed and provided an initial float of coupons for the purchase of woven fabric. We rented a workroom at Uxbridge, supplied suitable sewing machines from Langley, found a designer and some women with dressmaking experience, took Peggy's elder sister Dorothy as manageress at an annual salary of £500, and in no time at all the company was manufacturing as well as wholesaling. We began to feel at home in the jungle of regulations and restrictions, and learned how some of them could be turned to advantage. Pax became the post-war spearhead for Pasolds.

The little frocks looked as beautiful on the baby linen counters of Swan & Edgar in Regent Street, the White House in New Bond Street and Harrod's in Knightsbridge as they did in the advertisements, but I was not satisfied with Trier's somewhat grotesque ladybirds. We needed a friendlier image, a lovable little figure capable of more expression, and since Trier was not able to draw what I wanted I advertised for an 'artist with imagination' in the local paper. Art seemed to be at a discount in wartime, most artists who were not in the forces or making munitions were unemployed. The advertisement brought forty-five replies, and I saw every one of the applicants, from eager schoolboys to sophisticated fashion artists, newspaper cartoonists, portrait painters and art masters, and scrutinised their work. The choice fell on an elderly man named Lomax who lived within easy cycling distance at Wraysbury. He seemed to have the touch of fantasy I was looking for.

We got on well together. Like myself, Lomax liked little creatures. Many a Saturday afternoon we lay on the bank of the Thames watching beetles and snails on their mysterious errands among the grass roots, and butterflies fluttering from flower to flower, listening to the chirping of grasshoppers and the humming of bumble bees, and became small boys again. Lomax sketched and I criticised, until gradually the ladybird character with the chubby face and the large black hat, now so well known to millions, emerged.

Many of our people must have thought my priorities were upside down to waste so much time on such a trifling thing as the shape of a ladybird when we faced so many serious problems. Yet, looking back, concentration of industry, quotas and Utility clothes are long forgotten, the black-out and the smoking ruins of the warehouses in the City of London which meant so much to us then seem far away, almost as if they had never been. So much has happened since, new events have drawn a veil over the past, but our ladybirds, conceived in the midst of austerity, restrictions and destruction, have survived and sparkle. They are as young and fresh today as when they were born.

41

COMMITTEE
MEN
1941-44

THROUGH PAX GARMENTS LTD and our advertisements I came in contact
with Miss Guppy, a very able young woman. In addition to being the editor of
the *Children's Outfitter*, the one and only children's wear journal in the country, she was also secretary to the newly formed National Children's Wear
Association, which represented the retail, wholesale and manufacturing
sections of the trade. Pax found the organisation's news bulletins useful, became a member, and I was co-opted on to the Council. We usually met in the
private office of the president, Mr Morgans, a director of the famous children's wear store of Daniel Neal in Portman Square. It was my first experience
of sitting on a trade committee, and the success we had in our negotiations
with the BoT impressed me. Not that we were a particularly intelligent team
—rather the reverse, I thought—but with the weight of a large part of the
trade behind us we were listened to. It would be wrong, however, to think of
the NCWA as a powerful organisation. Our success was largely fortuitous.
The authorities wanted to stimulate the production of children's clothes,
which, because of the voluntary closure of too many factories, were in short
supply.

The manufacturing members of the NCWA were mostly makers-up of
woven fabrics, like Pax. My presence on their committee proved a useful
period of apprenticeship, but being a knitter I was not able to contribute
much to their work. The knitters belonged to other organisations. Most of
them, depending on the location of their factories, were members of various
hosiery manufacturers' associations in the Midlands and in Scotland. These
local associations were joined together in the National Hosiery Manufacturers'
Federation, whose headquarters were at Leicester. In the past Pasolds had
taken no interest in trade associations, but, witnessing the staggering growth
of officialdom and its tightening grip on our industry, we realised that we
could no longer keep aloof. While controls were necessary in time of war, the
civil servants had to be prevented from making them permanent and from
doing irreparable damage while they were in charge. Someone had to speak

up for free enterprise. Our future was at stake, our capital, and the experience and sweat of generations invested in our business. Clearly the time had come also for Pasolds Ltd to play a part in its appropriate trade organisation.

Much to our surprise there was no such organisation in our part of the world, nor was the Federation at Leicester geared to serve individual firms. Paging through Skinner's directory, I counted no fewer than seventy firms under the heading of hosiery and knitted goods manufacturers in the south of England and wondered whether they felt as forlorn as we did. Could they perhaps be persuaded to form an association—with me as chairman? What a unique opportunity! It was not status I sought but power to my elbow *vis-à-vis* the civil servants. Mr Morgans had shown what could be done. Speaking with the combined voice of seventy manufacturers I could make myself heard!

On reflection, however, I doubted whether I, a total stranger, was the man who could rally behind him seventy hard-headed manufacturers, most likely all competing against each other. I tried to put the idea out of my mind, but it persisted, and finally I plucked up courage and decided to discuss it with the NHMF. The president, Mr L. R. Allen, eyed me with a mixture of curiosity and irritation. I had come at an inopportune time; he was preoccupied with plans for a major reorganisation of the Federation. From our short talk I learned that the obstinate manufacturers of the south, most of them smallish concerns, were suspicious of Leicester and that previous attempts to bring them into the fold had failed. Mr Allen had little faith in my being more successful. He would, he said, try once more himself in the near future and meanwhile he wanted me to wait.

Not satisfied, I went to meet a few of those 'obstinate' manufacturers in London. They appeared to be reasonable men who showed keen interest in the projected association and assured me of their support. Greatly heartened, I informed Mr Allen, but drafting the new constitution of the NHMF and other urgent matters made such demands on his time that he could spare none for us. After waiting in vain for another two interminable months I decided to wait no longer. We booked a room at the Holborn Restaurant for a meeting on 20 November 1941, sent out seventy invitations, and I drafted a speech saying how lonely we felt at Langley, how difficult it was for us to understand the complicated government regulations, how hard we found it to convey our problems to official quarters and how much easier I thought it would be to negotiate with the BoT if we all came out of our shells, pooled our informat-tion and acted jointly. And then I intended to call for the formation of a trade association. How many of the people we had invited would come? I dreaded the very thought of making a speech, but there was not the slightest chance of my being elected charman if I remained dumb. Nor was it the kind of appeal that could be read to the audience. I had to deliver it without referring to notes. The only thing to do was to learn it by heart.

It fell as flat as I had feared. Some fifty manufacturers from as far away as Truro in Cornwall, Newport in Wales, Sudbury in Suffolk, Southend in Essex and Ashford in Kent, as well as the president, treasurer and secretary of the NHMF, listened to me in silence. More eloquent speakers followed and developed the theme. After a lively debate, the decision to form an association and affiliate it to the Federation was carried unanimously, as was Mr Thorne's proposal to give it the unwieldy name of 'South of England Knitting Industries Association' (SEKIA). Then a provisional committee was elected and I, almost overlooked, scraped in as its sixth and last member. A disappointing performance. The purpose of the committee was to attend to the legal requirements connected with the registration of a trade association and to draft its constitution and rules. This was much more in my line than making speeches, and the others were only too willing to let me get on with the work.

I did it so well that, when the final council of eight was elected, I became its chairman. I was fortunate in having genial Fred Venning (Scotia Knitting Co. Ltd) as vice-chairman, Henry Roper (Cornard Knitting Mills Ltd) as treasurer and Mr Hurst, who represented A. & R. Gilbert Ltd, as the Association's honorary secretary. The other council members were H. P. Roffey (E. Belcher Ltd), petulant E. J. Smith (Southend Knitting Co. Ltd), A. L. Thorne (Jantzen Knitting Mills Ltd) and the leader of the Cornish manufacturers G. L. Tonkin (Knitting Mills (Truro) Ltd). We covered twenty counties and started with a membership of twenty-five firms.

For reasons of convenience and economy Mr Hurst and I did the Association's clerical work at Langley. There was a considerable amount of it. One of our first jobs was to start an information service for our members, which made it necessary to keep regularly in touch with the Federation and the BoT. Queries had to be answered, registers compiled, subscriptions collected and the firms canvassed who were still hesitant about joining SEKIA. We held our monthly council meetings at Roper's office in London and, to give all the members the opportunity of getting to know us and each other, arranged cocktail parties at Oddenino's in Piccadilly. The stiff business atmosphere soon gave way to that of the membership of a social club. We exchanged experiences and became friends. Many of the manufacturers who operated in remote corners of the country appreciated this aspect of the Association even more than its business activities.

The nine associations which made up the Federation were located at Glasgow, Hawick, Mansfield, Nottingham, Leek, Loughborough, Leicester, Hinckley and London. Each of them had direct access to government departments only in matters concerning their particular area, while all other negotiations, especially those affecting policy, were conducted between the industry and the BoT at Federation level. The council of the NHMF was the industry's parliament, so to speak. We had two seats on it, out of a total of thirty. As chairman of SEKIA I attended all its meetings, and, instead of always taking my vice-chairman, arranged that now and again other members of the SEKIA council accompanied me, so that they could see how affairs were conducted at the top. This, I thought, would help to dispel their suspicion of Leicester and engender the spirit of co-operation which was essential to unite our industry.

Since the largest number of knitting mills were in the Midlands, and the NHMF was organised on democratic lines, it was, of course, true that the associations of Leicester, Nottingham and Hinckley, with eight, five and four seats on the council, wielded the greatest influence, but from personal observation I felt satisfied that they did not abuse their voting power to favour certain firms, territories or sections of the trade. Nevertheless it was understandable that members of the smaller associations on the periphery, in Scotland and the south of England, sometimes questioned the Federation's impartility. The representatives of the two Scottish associations in particular often complained vociferously about the needs of their manufacturers being neglected and thereby managed to extract more than their share from the common pool. I was fascinated by the discussions, the quality of some of the speeches and the wide horizon that unfolded. There was much for a new boy to learn and the Federation council proved an excellent school for studying not only problems of trade but also techniques of debating, diplomacy and men's characters. I never attended a better.

So far I had achieved my ambition. We had a trade association of our own, the membership of which had meanwhile grown to fifty, and I was its chairman. In addition to being a member of the council of the NHMF, the industry's most powerful body, I sat on a number of sub-committees—the finance committee, for instance, which controlled income and expenditure. The local associations collected annual subscriptions based on the number of employees of individual member firms and passed a percentage of this money on to the Federation. I also had a seat on the advisory committee to the BoT, which, it appeared, had enjoyed considerable prestige in the past but, I soon discovered, now hardly ever met. It seemed that the real power lay with two committees, which were tacitly regarded as the preserve of a small inner circle of men from the Midlands who jealously defended their exclusive status with the quite valid argument that large bodies were unwieldy and did little work. Under pressure from the Scots, who treated representation as a national issue and enlisted the support of their members of Parliament, seats had been allocated to Glasgow and Hawick, but we in the south could claim no political privileges. Moreover SEKIA was looked upon by many as a bunch of newcomers, city slickers, Cockneys, Jews, foreigners and Cornish pirates, not on the same plane as Leicestershire manufacturers, who regarded themselves as country gentlemen. The suspicion was therefore mutual.

It was not easy for me to understand the relationships, social or otherwise, and to weigh the qualifications of the members of this small coterie whose names appeared in leading positions on every important committee. Overshadowing them all was Mr Peshall, the industry's elder statesman, an impressive personality and a convincing speaker. He was a director of Corah's, but I sensed that technical, commercial and financial matters were not his *métier* and came to think of him more as the industry's high priest than as an industrialist. He had, I was told, been a popular cricketer and tennis player in his younger days and was now unquestionably the pivot round which the inner circle revolved. Also highly respected but less domineering was Ernest Walker, the fox-hunting chairman of Wolsey's. Then came Donald Byford, a successful sock manufacturer and a plain-speaking self-made man; Bertie Jarvis, OBE, JP, an underwear manufacturer and local politician; Herbert Buckler, the managing director of Woodford & Wormleighton; and, last but by no means least, dapper Tommy Kempton, a promising young outerwear manufacturer—all men from Leicester. On the fringe of this inner circle were two heavyweights from Nottinghamshire, L. R. Allen, the Federation's president, managing director of Allen Solly & Co., famous makers of exclusive half-hose and knitwear, and Percy Bussens, chairman of Cooper & Roe, an exceptionally nice and able man. Finally there was Raymond Taylor, of Hinckley, a young stocking manufacturer who had penetrated to the fringe by sheer ability and staying power. Very little happened in the industry without some of these men having a hand in it.

Now to the two committees to which I have referred. One of them, the Central Committee, produced the Utility schedules. It consisted of six manufacturers from the Midlands, four from Scotland, two civil servants and Dick Yeabsley, an auditor appointed by the BoT. They drew up the technical specifications of hundreds of garments, prepared costings, laid down profit margins and fixed prices. Changing conditions made periodic revisions necessary, amended schedules were issued, and the committee, whose leading light was Tommy Kempton, remained active throughout the war. It did a good job. Hard as I tried, I failed to secure a seat on it, but I am bound to admit that our manufacturers in SEKIA fared none the worse for that.

Perhaps even more fundamental was the Hosiery Rationing Committee, the domain of Mr Peshall, who had been allocating rations of wool yarn to the knitting industry in the first world war and whose job had been re-created in the second. He had since been given responsibility for cotton yarn as well, but now a crisis arose which threatened his illustrious office. The newly formed Directorate of Civilian Hosiery, which I have described in the previous chapter, was going to take over the functions of his committee. Backed by the Federation, Mr Peshall fought back. If, in the interests of winning the war, the production of individual firms had to be programmed, it was the industry itself that should do the programming, he protested, not civil servants. I followed the controversy with keen interest, wondering whether the BoT would perhaps meet the demands of private enterprise by offering Mr Peshall the post of Director of Hosiery. The powers at Millbank, however, appointed Len Foyster, but agreed to the creation of two panels of manufacturers, an English and a Scottish one, to advise him. They were called the War Emergency Committees, and Foyster became chairman of both. Another master stroke by Mr Watkinson? Stripped of its powers, the Rationing Committee was allowed to continue, freewheeling, so to speak.

The inner circle monopolised the English War Emergency Committee, and there was no room for me on it. To keep me quiet, I was instead entrusted with the organisation of a publicity section for the Federation, a job I enjoyed and did well. In addition I was given a seat on the management committee of the Hosiery and Knitwear Export Group, which was chaired by L. R. Allen. Most industries had formed export groups, at the government's request, early on in the war. They were primarily advisory bodies which cooperated with their respective trade associations but were not part of them, and any firm in the industry could become an export group member without having to join its related trade association. Tommy Allen, as he was affectionately called by his supporters, had not cared for me nor I for him when we met the year before, but we had since learned to respect and like each other. He now invited me to help plan some of his overseas market surveys and eventually made me his vice-chairman. A genuine friendship developed. He was twelve years older than I, critical but fair, and his sometimes brutally frank comments made a better man of me.

With Lease–Lend, which had come into force in March 1941, exports as earners of foreign currency had lost their overriding importance. The supply of British goods to overseas territories depended now more on political and military considerations. Yarn allocations for export production had to follow the changing priorities of the markets. Responsible for these allocations was Sir George Mahon of the BoT, at whose request Allen and myself as chairman and vice-chairman of our export group, together with Foyster and three other officials, now attended a confidential meeting at Millbank to be informed of the situation and guide our members accordingly.

I frequently met Allen at his club in London, where, over a meal and a glass of port, we discussed export group business. One evening he pushed a bundle of papers in front of me. The BoT had got themselves into a muddle over the allocation of a substantial weight of yarn, he said. It was intended, in specific proportions, for the manufacture of underwear, outerwear, stockings and socks for eight markets, namely British West Africa, the Belgian Congo, Free French Africa, Northern and Southern Rhodesia, the British West Indies, the Faroe Islands and, with the least priority, New Zealand. Sixty manufacturers had applied for varying weights which, in total, exceeded the available weight of wool yarn but left over a surplus of cotton. The share-out had to be fair and take account of the request of the firms who applied and of their previous activities in the respective markets. After trying in vain to find an equitable formula, the civil servants had handed the conundrum to Tommy Allen. Pleased to have this opportunity of showing the BoT what the export group could do, he had worked on it for a week but had also failed. It was now Friday evening and he had promised Sir George the figures for Monday! Could I, he pleaded, have a go?

The problem was not as difficult as it seemed. I drew up a scale, gave one lot of points to the weights applied for, one to previous activity and one to the different market priorities, added them all up, divided the available weight of yarn by the total number of points and, hey presto, had the key for my allocations. Ruby Way, my hard-working secretary, helped with the sixty computations, typed my explanatory memorandum and on Sunday evening posted six copies to Tommy Allen. He was delighted, and so, incidentally, was Sir George Mahon. He asked me to come to Millbank, and I had to explain my method to him personally. It would, he said, be the pattern for future yarn allocations for export production. There were no complaints from the sixty manufacturers, so we presumed that they too were happy, and I was Tommy Allen's blue-eyed boy.

Meanwhile, at the BoT's suggestion, the Federation had set up a Post-war Reconstruction Committee, on which I had a seat. This enabled me to put forward some long-cherished ideas. The way I presented and illustrated them appealed to Mr Peshall, the committee's chairman, and he too held out the hand of friendship. He took me to dinner at Quorn Grange, his home, and together we prepared the reconstruction committee's first official report, which featured a machine scrapping scheme I had drawn up and which, he thought, would go down well with the industry. I felt strongly about the export of old knitting machines, which made it easy for our customers over-seas to set up knitting mills cheaply and then erect tariff walls against our merchandise, putting British manufacturers and their workpeople out of action, the very process that had brought Lancashire to the verge of ruin. I calculated that the export of £1,000 worth of second-hand knitting machines robbed Britain over a period of ten years of the export of £50,000 worth of knitted goods. The sale of second-hand plant abroad should be prohibited, I demanded, and the old machines broken up. Firms who scrapped their outworn plant were to be compensated from a common pool to be set up jointly by the hosiery industry and the machine builders. The scheme was praised by the press and looked good in print, but like so many brave schemes it was not carried out when the war ended.

I produced a string of projects for the reconstruction committee, all worked out in detail, neatly typed and supported by figures and graphs. They ranged from the introduction of uniform trade terms and standardised size and colour charts to joint insurance schemes, from incentive and profit-sharing plans for employees to the creation of an international knitting industries federation. When I look through these papers today I wonder how I found the time to write them all. Peshall and Allen too used what suited them for their own purposes, while most other members of the various committees were too preoccupied talking about the return to pre-war conditions to bother much about my mental exercises. However, if my colleagues in the trade failed to pay my proposals the attention I thought they merited, I had the satisfaction of some of them being noticed by the BoT. To my great and very pleasant surprise, even Mr Watkinson, who, from his Olympian heights at Millbank, ruled over the whole of the textile and a number of other industries as well, telephoned to ask how the work of the reconstruction committee was progressing and complimented me on the contribution I was making to it. He seemed to take a personal interest in our post-war plans. This was confirmed by Foyster, who shared a railway compartment with me a few days later and who shocked me by adding that it was more important for our recommendations to find favour with the politicians than to be sound. Even Watkinson had to bow to the wishes of Parliament.

The NHMF was an excellent school and, as I have mentioned, it taught me many things. At a meeting at Leicester on 29 December 1942, to which we were called at short notice, the representatives of the six lesser associations were confronted with a plan for Peshall to replace Tommy Allen as president. The inner circle had won Hinckley's approval by offering Raymond Taylor the vice-presidency and hoped to secure Nottingham's agreement by retaining Bussens as Federation treasurer. I was livid, and said so. Had SEKIA and the other associations no say in the matter? The men from Scotland, Mansfield and Leek ranged themselves behind me. Without wishing it, I became the leader of the opposition. We had not been told that Mr Allen, who had worked so selflessly for the organisation for four years, wanted to resign. Was it really his wish? Heartened by this unexpected support, Allen hedged. The assembly waited. I had caused a most unfortunate hiatus, and the meeting was adjourned until after lunch. This gave me the opportunity to have a talk with Allen in private, whereupon he decided to stand down and Peshall was unanimously elected the Federation's new president. He was all smiles and friendliness when I congratulated him; but did some of the other members of the inner circle ever quite forgive me?

Tommy Allen had several times taken me as his guest to lunches or dinners given by the Worshipful Company of Framework Knitters, and now Ernest Walker, a past Master, asked whether I would like to join the company and become a freeman of the City of London. Donald Byford, the upper warden, offered to support the application. It appeared that most of the company's members were hosiery manufacturers, especially from Leicester, but men from other walks of life were also Framework Knitters. It was an honour to belong to a livery company and, as far as I could judge, served no practical purpose. What appealed to me was the historical connections. The knitters had received their first charter from Cromwell in 1657, as I knew from reading William Felkin, and although the pomp and tradition was now little more than romantic make-believe, I liked it. I thanked Ernest Walker and Donald Byford for their invitation and said that I should be happy to join. But I heard no more, until months later Ernest Walker, genuinely upset, explained that there was a difficulty and apologised. I felt sorry for him. It was not his fault that I was not British by birth, or that someone did not like my face.

Tommy Allen was awarded the O.B.E., which pleased me. As chairman of the Export Group and past president of the NHMF, as well as by virtue of his strong personality, he remained a prominent figure in the trade, and I saw almost more of him now than I had done before. My challenge to Leicester was resented by some, but it strengthened my standing in the industry generally. Willie Grimmond and James Rutherford, for instance, who represented the two Scottish associations, discovered that they had much in common with the members of SEKIA and drew closer to me. The mark I had made in the Export Group was also noted and, at Foyster's request, I was now included in the War Emergency Committee. This brought me face to face with production planning on a national scale.

Approximately a third of all clothes coupons were spent by the public on knitted garments, and, as will be remembered, it was Foyster's job as Director of Civilian Hosiery to programme the industry's production so that it matched the nation's needs. He and his team did this extremely well, but it worried me that the production programmes took no account of the varying degree of efficiency of individual firms. Successive SR&Os had not sufficiently modified the original method of controlling manufacturers' output by way of a percentage of their pre-war performance, I argued. In normal competitive times efficiency created its own reward in the form of higher profits and lower prices, which increased demand and made the efficient firm grow, but now production programmes, controlled margins and an excess profits tax of 100 per cent were breeding inefficiency. A manufacturer who made with forty-five workers in the same time the same quantity of goods for which another needed fifty should be rewarded with larger programmes and more protection for his labour. Why was efficiency not taken more seriously? My colleagues on the committee looked bored and Foyster smiled. 'Pasold,' he said, 'you will come unstuck if you put too much trust in efficiency, tidiness and logic. They leave you no room to manoeuvre.'

How typically British! Foyster's own meteoric career seemed to underscore the wisdom of his words, but I had been brought up to believe differently. Inefficiency was an unforgivable sin. It meant the avoidable waste of resources, be they time, raw material, manpower, heat, space or capital, which the country could not afford, especially in wartime. I continued with my crusade, and when Mr Watkinson heard he telephoned. This time he asked to see me. Was there a way of measuring the relative efficiency of individual factories, he wanted to know? Would I study the subject and write a paper on it?

Since most firms made standard products, namely Utility garments, it should not be too difficult, I thought, to find a common denominator. It was, of course, not just a matter of comparing output per man or woman hour. Other factors had to be considered as well, but whatever method I evolved, it would have to be very simple. As I examined the extensive information available to the members of the committee, I made an interesting discovery. I found that if a firm's annual output per employee exceeded £1,000 it was a very efficient and profitable concern. Conversely, if the output fell short of £600, the firm was inefficient and probably operating at a loss. What particularly surprised me was that this rule seemed to apply to all knitting mills, not just to those making Utility goods, whether they made cheap cotton socks or rayon stockings, interlock underwear or expensive cashmere sweaters. After many tests, which all confirmed this rule of thumb, I wrote my paper. A very simple calculation, I explained, would give us every firm's theoretical output, which, when compared with the actual and adjusted for exceptional circumstances, showing its efficiency rating. Not a scientific approach, perhaps, but a practical one and accurate enough for our purposes. The War Emergency Committee discussed my conclusions but filed them away without initiating any action, and Mr Watkinson, to whom I submitted them first, did not respond. Was he not satisfied with them, were they politically unacceptable, was he busy with more urgent matters and would let me know later?

Disappointed but not discouraged, I now proceeded to make a survey of the 575 member firms of the NHMF, recording the types of goods each one of them produced, its concentration arrangements, the number of its employees and any other information I could find. A mammoth job. I felt very pleased with the resulting dossier. It contained no information the members of the council could not have looked up for themselves, and the individual facts and figures were quite harmless but, when converted by my formula and seen in relation to each other, they were so revealing that, at Bertie Jarvis's insistence, I was not allowed to distribute copies of the document and had to destroy them. However, having invested so much effort in it, I kept the original and have it still.

Tommy Allen agreed with me in principle about the need for greater efficiency in industry but thought it would not be fair to use a common yardstick, and cited his own firm, Allen Solly & Co., founded in 1744, the oldest knitwear factory in existence. He showed me the plant, sixteen modern 6/3 flats, mostly German, and eight 'ten-at-once' machines among a large number of ancient hand knitting frames very similar to the one invented by William Lee in 1589 which were, believe it or not, still in operation. They were making exclusive merchandise for the USA, where Tommy was running a very effective advertising campaign under the slogan 'every hundred years or so we change the design of our socks'. Before the war they made, among other things, socks for Field Marshal Göring, silk underwear for the Maharajah of Alwar and lace combinations for the eight wives of some other Eastern potentate. It was impossible, he said, for his firm to reach an annual production of £600 per employee. His workpeople were aged and highly skilled. They made quality goods for the elite while Pasolds churned out cheap underwear for the masses. How could I compare the two!

Efficiency had nothing to do with quality, I maintained. Allen Solly's silk and cashmere yarns were much more expensive than our cotton and condenser yarns, but they used far less of them. No doubt they took much more care with each of their garments than we did with ours, but for the price of one of their cardigans one could buy two dozen pairs of our knickers. We began to philosophise. I expressed the opinion that it was industry's prime purpose to provide whatever merchandise the consumer wanted at the lowest possible price and that maximum efficiency was therefore essential. The reward to the factory owner and his workpeople came second, and, sad though it was, the historic interest of an old plant, even if it was as famous as Allen Solly's, hardly came into the picture. For the present, governmental interference, production planning, raw material allocations, clothes coupons and profit control on the one hand, and the shortage particularly of non-Utility merchandise, on the other, distorted the true situation. Inefficient producers were kept alive at the expense of the consumer, but this was bound to change after the war. Allen Solly would have to scrap their old buildings and machinery and replace them with a modern factory when free competition returned, otherwise they would find it impossible to survive. Events, unfortunately, were to prove me right.

Not only inefficient manufacturers but most of the wholesale trade was given an additional lease of life by wartime regulations. Generally speaking, wholesalers no longer fulfilled their original useful function, which was to place large forward orders with manufacturers and to finance stocks. They had become little more than middlemen. Clothes rationing and legalised profit margins kept them in business. Rolf and I felt tremendously relieved not to need them any more, and, at one of our rare board meetings at Langley at which we formulated post-war policies, decided to cut them out once and for all.

My efficiency campaign, incidentally, caused a rift between Peshall and myself. In order to set an example I had prepared the type of information about Pasolds Ltd which I hoped all firms in the industry would disclose, even if under a code number and therefore anonymously. Peshall caught sight of one of my charts which showed that Langley's annual output per employee was one of the best in the industry and that, despite the war, our yearly sales had increased while those of most other firms had declined:

	1939–40	1940–41	1941–42	1942–43
£	120,000	155,000	181,000	211,000

He peremptorily asked for the loan of the chart and returned it a few days later without comment. What had he made of it? Did he think that we were getting more than our fair share of raw materials? As chairman of the rationing committee he must have known that our rising production figures were due to the extra yarn supplies our spinning mill provided from waste clippings. The cloud passed, but a shadow remained.

Less controversial than my scheme for establishing a common efficiency denominator was a multi-coloured pictorial chart I drew and distributed. It sorted out, at long last, the maze of thirty-seven interlinking Federation, Export Group, BoT and trade union committees, and was hailed by industry and trade press alike. I felt proud of my chart. Besides much other information it showed that in 1943 the nine associations had roughly 575 member firms with altogether 54,000 employees. Hawick had twenty firms and 2,000 workers, Glasgow fifty firms and 5,000 workers, Loughborough twenty-five firms and 2,500 workers, Nottingham ninety firms and 11,000 workers, Leicester 160 firms and 17,500 workers, Leek twenty-five firms and 1,000 workers, and SEKIA seventy firms and 2,500 workers. Bearing in mind the effect of the concentration scheme, which put hundreds of firms temporarily out of business, and the reduction of the industry's labour force to half its pre-war strength, these figures showed that the Federation represented almost 90 per cent of the trade. The manufacturers who remained outside belonged to two small rebel associations, one in the west of Scotland, the other at Leicester, or were lone wolves who fended for themselves.

I have mentioned trade unions. The committee dealing with them, the National Joint Industrial Council, concerned only the associations in the Midlands. It consisted of thirty-two members, sixteen from each side, and its chairman was appointed alternately one year by the Federation, the next by the unions. With few exceptions the labour of the knitters in the south of England was not unionised, and SEKIA was therefore not involved.

Our people at Langley did not need a shop steward to negotiate with the management on their behalf. When they wanted to talk to Rolf or me they came to the office or, more often, buttonholed us on the shop floor, and we did the same in reverse. We understood each other's problems and sorted them out on the spot. Work started at 7.30 a.m. and finished at 6.30 p.m. The Manpower Board demanded that girls worked a minimum of forty-nine hours and men fifty-four hours per week, otherwise they were transferred to a munitions factory. Living on the premises, Rolf and I invariably plodded on for sixty hours, but in my case half this time was devoted to work for the NHMF. Because of the shortage of labour and of the black-out we had discontinued the night shift, and I spent the evenings over my drawing board or trying to memorise some speech I had to make. Three times a month I travelled to Leicester and other hosiery centres on Federation business—dreary train journeys in unheated, dimly lit carriages with painted-out windows, and on one occasion, when the train was two hours late, I had to sleep in an air raid shelter.

What made me, what made Fred Venning, Tommy Allen, Willie Grimmond and all those other busy men, who could hardly be spared by their own firms, give their precious time to the NHMF? The question was never asked. Anyone who was not in the forces or in one of the Ministries was serving the country in some other way. Our job was to keep the wheels turning and to ensure the supply of essential clothing. We felt proud of the NHMF, which we had helped to build and shape into a well functioning organisation, and enjoyed working for it. I got to know the industry and the measure of its leaders. If I made a name for myself in the trade, this was ample reward for my efforts. Famous names like Wolsey, Corah, Bairnswear and Chilprufe no longer overawed me. Wait till the war is over, I thought, full of self-confidence. Pasolds will soon be among the best of them.

We had every reason to be pleased with the successful co-operation between the Federation council and the Directorate of Civilian Hosiery. Serious disagreement arose only when the industry's future independence was

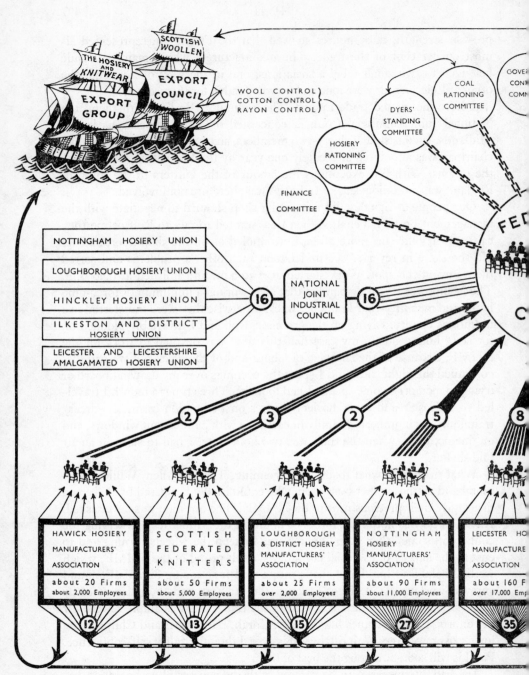

THE HOSIERY AND KNITWEAR EXPORT GROUP

SCOTTISH WOOLLEN EXPORT COUNCIL

WOOL CONTROL
COTTON CONTROL
RAYON CONTROL

FINANCE COMMITTEE

HOSIERY RATIONING COMMITTEE

DYERS' STANDING COMMITTEE

COAL RATIONING COMMITTEE

GOVER
CONT
COMM

FED

C

NOTTINGHAM HOSIERY UNION

LOUGHBOROUGH HOSIERY UNION

HINCKLEY HOSIERY UNION

ILKESTON AND DISTRICT HOSIERY UNION

LEICESTER AND LEICESTERSHIRE AMALGAMATED HOSIERY UNION

16

NATIONAL JOINT INDUSTRIAL COUNCIL

16

2   3   2   5   8

HAWICK HOSIERY MANUFACTURERS' ASSOCIATION

about 20 Firms
about 2,000 Employees

SCOTTISH FEDERATED KNITTERS

about 50 Firms
about 5,000 Employees

LOUGHBOROUGH & DISTRICT HOSIERY MANUFACTURERS' ASSOCIATION

about 25 Firms
over 2,000 Employees

NOTTINGHAM HOSIERY MANUFACTURERS' ASSOCIATION

about 90 Firms
about 11,000 Employees

LEICESTER HO
MANUFACTURE
ASSOCIATION

about 160 F
over 17,000 Em

12   13   15   27   35

As the war progressed, and the problems of the knitting industry multiplied, the National Hosiery Manufacturers' Federation expanded its activities to keep pace with the additional work. More and more committees were set up, and the

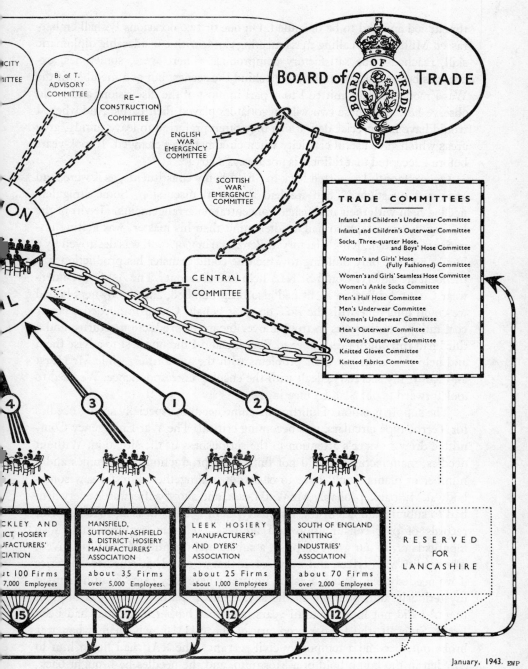

BOARD of TRADE

...CITY
...TTEE

B. of T.
ADVISORY
COMMITTEE

RE-
CONSTRUCTION
COMMITTEE

ENGLISH
WAR
EMERGENCY
COMMITTEE

SCOTTISH
WAR
EMERGENCY
COMMITTEE

CENTRAL
COMMITTEE

TRADE COMMITTEES

Infants' and Children's Underwear Committee

Infants' and Children's Outerwear Committee

Socks, Three-quarter Hose,
and Boys' Hose Committee

Women's and Girls' Hose
(Fully Fashioned) Committee

Women's and Girls' Seamless Hose Committee

Women's Ankle Socks Committee

Men's Half Hose Committee

Men's Underwear Committee

Women's Underwear Committee

Men's Outerwear Committee

Women's Outerwear Committee

Knitted Gloves Committee

Knitted Fabrics Committee

...CKLEY AND
...ICT HOSIERY
...UFACTURERS'
...CIATION

...ut 100 Firms
7,000 Employees

15

MANSFIELD,
SUTTON-IN-ASHFIELD
& DISTRICT HOSIERY
MANUFACTURERS'
ASSOCIATION

about 35 Firms
over 5,000 Employees

17

LEEK HOSIERY
MANUFACTURERS'
AND DYERS'
ASSOCIATION

about 25 Firms
about 1,000 Employees

12

SOUTH OF ENGLAND
KNITTING
INDUSTRIES'
ASSOCIATION

about 70 Firms
over 2,000 Employees

12

RESERVED
FOR
LANCASHIRE

January, 1943. EWP

organisation became so involved that it was difficult to keep track. The author
therefore prepared this chart as a reference for trade and government officials

threatened and had to be defended. On one or two occasions Peshall embarrassed Millbank by calling mass meetings and, with considerable diplomatic skill, reached some satisfactory compromise. There were, sometimes, exchanges between him and Foyster behind the scenes, but as a member of the War Emergency Committee I took part in most of the discussions and could observe how well these two wily negotiators played their cards. And where I would have had precise definitions they often preferred to leave untidy, grey areas which gave useful elasticity when circumstances changed. It took years before I accepted that tidiness is not always a virtue.

Once a month I reported back to SEKIA, my constituents, as it were, and answered questions. Then we had a general discussion. Some stragglers needed help with their unfinished concentration arrangements. Hewitt of the hosiery directorate, who had a tidier mind than his master, was getting impatient with them. King's factory at Penzance in Cornwall was destroyed by a bomb, and the only building to which he could transfer his production was the local art gallery. Could SEKIA help him secure it? The Ashford Underwear Co. at Ashford in Kent had also been bombed, and the owners hoped we could intervene with the BoT on their behalf. One firm needed a larger coal ration, another was in trouble over incorrect production returns, and a third had run out of needles. Fred Venning and I did our best to advise them and help them sort out their problems with the authorities, while Mr Hurst and Ruby, my secretary, dealt with the ensuing correspondence. We used to look forward to our SEKIA meetings.

The supply position of knitting machine needles, especially spring needles for Terrot-type circulars, was becoming critical. The War Emergency Committee drew Foyster's attention to the seriousness of the situation. Without needles, manufacturers could not fulfil their production programmes and a number of plants would have to close down altogether. Foyster saw somebody at Millbank, probably Mr Watkinson, and shortly afterwards every firm had to submit samples of the various types of needles it used, together with records of past consumption and figures of current requirements. Two months later, to our great surprise, a substantial quantity of needles arrived. The quality was perfect, and we were told that we could have further deliveries if we needed them. When I asked Foyster where they came from he smiled mysteriously and, pointing to the sky, replied, 'Father Christmas brought them.' I did not find out until years later that Father Christmas had been Frank Stockall, the former secretary of the NHMF, who had, when war broke out, become a temporary civil servant. The RAF had flown him to Sweden in the bomb hold of a Mosquito, and the needles he brought back, presumably by arrangement with the Trading with the Enemy Department, were German.

'He's at it again,' laughed my friends when I moved that the boundaries between the territories of the nine associations should be clearly defined. Most of them followed county boundaries, but there were problems at Hinckley and Loughborough, and I met the representatives of these two associations several times before we reached agreement and I could publish my final map. Most firms belonged to the association in whose territory their factories were situated, but we had three stocking manufacturers in the south who were members of associations in the Midlands. The largest, the Klinger Manufacturing Co. of Edmonton, with 1,844 employees, was a member at Hinckley, while the Keystone Knitting Mills of Elstree, with 220, and the Full-Fashioned Hosiery Co. of Baldock, with 548 employees, were members at Mansfield. Waving the map, we now persuaded Klinger and Keystone to join SEKIA, which made us the fourth largest association. It also increased our income substantially, since membership fees were based on the number of employees. In view of their importance we asked Klinger for one of their directors to join our management committee, and they sent us Charles Davis, the sales director. It's a small world. He was the same Charles Davis who had shown me over Stern's warehouse in the City eighteen years earlier.

In addition to Tommy Allen and Fred Venning I now met another unusual man who became a friend for life, a Scot named Thomson Donaldson. He had a twinkle in his eye, bushy brows, walked with a limp and was the brightest and worldliest of the Caledonians who came to the meetings at Leicester. His father and grandfather had been shawl makers at Alva and Alloa at the foot of the Ochil hills. Thomson had installed Raschel machines and a battery of latch needle circulars, and was now the most progressive manufacturer of ladies' knitwear north of the river Tweed. He loved figures, balance sheets and the stock exchange, while I was better at technical things, though not as good as he imagined, and both of us worshipped efficiency. Once, when I said that there were far too many shapes and sizes of knitting machine needles and that machine builders should introduce some standardisation, he would not rest until a committee was appointed to study the matter. We met the representatives of the engineering firms several times. They objected to our interference in their sphere of activity, and nothing came of the idea. Peshall had frowned on it from the start, but we had forced his hand, which in his view amounted to insurrection. I could feel that I was now firmly in his bad books. Although he was too much of a gentleman to show it.

I regretted the cooling off of our relationship, for I respected and liked him, but the purpose of my journeys to the NHMF was not simply to endorse Leicester's policies. If I felt strongly enough on some matter I dug my heels in, and I could no longer be ignored. No chairman of a trade association enjoyed greater confidence and loyalty from his members than I did from SEKIA. I also had the support of the Scots, and was popular with the respresentatives of Leek, Mansfield and Nottingham. Foyster and the civil servants at Millbank took me seriously, and I was one of the Federation's most prolific workers. It did not worry me greatly, therefore, if occasionally I displeased Leicester and Hinckley. And when, sometimes, I talked about it all to Mr Hurst over dinner at the Old Crown at Slough, he would say, 'Committees are all the same, whether it's a golf club committee, a town council, Parliament or, presumably, even the Cabinet at 10 Downing Street. Each of them has a Raymond Taylor, a Tommy Kempton and a Bertie Jarvis. Don't take them too seriously!'

It was not only I who got into deep water now and again. Tommy Kempton was attacked from all sides when the Central Committee agreed with the BoT to reduce manufacturers' profit margins from $7\frac{1}{2}$ to $6\frac{1}{4}$ per cent. To pacify the irate members of SEKIA, he came to London to explain. In September 1941, when the profit rate was fixed, it had been assumed that manufacturers would turn over their capital just once per year. In fact they turned it over 2·2 times during 1942, thus giving them a profit of more than 15 per cent. Thereupon the BoT wanted to cut the margin back to 5 per cent. The Central Committee now argued that the full force of coupon restrictions, the continuing withdrawal of labour from the industry and various other factors were depressing turnover during 1943, and so a compromise of $6\frac{1}{4}$ per cent was struck. His explanation was accepted.

The Germans were at Stalingrad and there was no sign of an early victory, but some day the war was bound to end. It was generally thought that the demand for new knitting machines would then be such that machine builders, whose factories had been converted to making munitions, would be unable to cope with it. Thomson and I drew up a scheme which guaranteed hosiery manufacturers who wanted to replace their outworn machines a fair and orderly sequence of delivery. It caused excitement in the trade, the press and at Millbank. Peshall adopted it, joint discussions were held and principles agreed, a referendum showed that 76 per cent of the industry was in favour of the scheme, but no final decision was ever taken. And so, with ups and downs, the committee work continued.

I have forgotten how I became the hosiery industry's delegate to the Empire Committee of the Federation of British Industries. With a few notable exceptions, Leicester showed little interest in exports or in anything else to do with the world outside Britain, apart from the theatres of war. It was left to Tommy Allen and myself, and to the Scottish manufacturers of cashmere knitwear, to worry about the future of overseas markets. After months of discussions at FBI headquarters in London, and meetings with emissaries from Australia, New Zealand, India and South Africa, I delivered a ninety-minute address to the council members of the NHMF in June 1944, to bring them up to date. They listened attentively, genuinely interested, I fondly imagined, but when I had finished Peshall only said, 'Pasold, I compliment you on your beautiful English,' and smiled benignly as only he could.

After that I kept to myself what I learned at the FBI meetings, or told Tommy Allen, who passed some of the information on to the members of the Export Group. This seemed to satisfy everyone, for I was in due course appointed a member of the Grand Council of the FBI as well as of the Overseas Policy Committee, and in these capacities represented the NHMF for many years. Looking back, it seems that I wasted most of them fighting in vain for some kind of incentive to make British manufacturers take more interest in exports.

As the prospect of peace drew nearer, post-war reconstruction plans came to the fore. Peshall, like most businessmen of his generation, feared a repetition of the trade depression and mass unemployment which followed the 1914-18 war and put so many firms out of business. In September 1944 he made a tour of the associations, seeking their support for yet another key committee to be set up. It was to prepare the orderly deconcentration of our industry and the re-employment of its labour, and he thought it should consist of five manufacturers and five workers. Addressing the members of SEKIA, he mustered all his imposing personality, let his bright blue eyes go from face to face, and declared that the twelve million people in the Greater London area constituted a national danger, that no extension of factories located in this area should be allowed, that no one should be permitted to establish or enlarge a hosiery factory in a 'scheduled area' and, as the committee would frequently be called to meet at short notice, its members should all be men from Leicester.

Fred Venning and I winked at each other. We had no intention of letting the inner circle secure a monopoly. And did Leicester really believe that the growth of the hosiery industry outside its traditional centres could be prevented when less prosperous areas were being specially scheduled for government-assisted industrial development? I took the matter up with the War Emergency Committee, Fred raised it with the BoT at Millbank, other associations also protested, and since Leicester's plans were not in line with those of the politicians we won an easy victory. The new committee became a tripartite one, representing manufacturers, labour and the BoT, and, to SEKIA's great satisfaction, we had a seat on it which was occupied by Venning.

To observe from my vantage point the complex interplay of forces between Westminster, Millbank, Leicester and the district associations was an unforgettable experience, and to have played a part in it, however insignificant, was a privilege. Power corrupts, and had I had any it is likely that I would have used it to regiment the trade, had I thought it was in the national interest. A sobering thought. If I, a champion of free private enterprise, was capable of slipping into the role of a little dictator or a commissar, how much more difficult to resist such a temptation must it be for an ambitious civil servant, trade union leader or politician—men who had no conception of or respect for the efforts and worries of a lifetime, often of generations, that go into the building of a single family firm, let alone a whole industry. All too often the fate of industry, and with it the well-being of the nation, is at the mercy of just such men.

42

THE END OF
THE WAR IN SIGHT
1943-44

THE RAF NEEDED pilots and aircrews. In 1941 it took over the Air Defence Cadet Corps, which became the nucleus of the Air Training Corps (ATC), and whose squadrons became one of the main sources of manpower for the RAF. The cadets, aged between sixteen and eighteen, wore air force-blue uniforms and received instruction in the theory of flight, navigation, airframe and engine maintenance, aircraft recognition, gunnery and similar subjects. Each local squadron was supervised by a civilian committee, which also found the necessary drill halls, lecture rooms and other facilities. At the invitation of Frank Lawrance, owner of the *Slough Observer*, and of Captain Weathersbee, managing director of Horlick's, whom we have met in a previous chapter in his capacity of regional representative of the BoT, I joined the ATC committee of the Slough squadron in February 1942.

Then somebody had the bright idea of teaching the cadets gliding as a preliminary to the flying training they would be given on joining the RAF. With the help of Dudley Hiscox, the chairman of the London Gliding Club, a course for chief gliding instructors was organised in Yorkshire, which Rolf, an old friend of Dudley's, attended, delighted to get his hands on a joy-stick again. On their return they arranged a gliding course at Halton aerodrome to train a dozen or so instructors for ATC gliding schools to be set up in the south. Weekend duties only were involved, and so I volunteered.

Besides Dudley, Rolf and myself there were Tudor Edmunds, Dickinson, Bunn, Keith Robinson and a few others, all more or less experienced glider or aeroplane pilots, and from July to October 1942 we spent most of our Saturdays and Sundays at Halton. We had two primary gliders, prehistoric-looking, high-wing contraptions without cockpit or fuselage, the single seat, a kind of shallow frying pan stuck out in front, making the pilot feel that he was sitting in mid-air. When I had first taken gliding lessons at Dunstable six years previously I was catapulted off the hilltop in just such a machine by means of a rubber rope pulled by six enthusiasts. Now we had a petrol-driven barrage-balloon winch mounted on a lorry, and a 1,500 ft-long steel cable with which to pull the gliders across the grass field, a great improvement on the old method. When the winch was speeded up and the pilot pulled the stick back a little, the machine rose a few feet into the air, to drop back when slowed down. As the pilot gained experience the winch was run faster and faster, until the machine reached a height of several hundred feet. He then released the cable hook, flew a small circle over the airfield and came gliding back to the ground in a straight line or, with mounting confidence, in a series of S turns entirely under his own control.

To pass our final test we had to fly a figure-of-eight twice from a height of about 400 ft in these primary gliders, a task that required delicate judgement. If one flew too fast one reached the ground before one had completed the figure-of-eight and landed cross-wind, and if too slow one risked a stall, with probably disastrous consequences, as poor Keith Robinson demonstrated. He spun into the ground, smashed the machine, and we had to rush him to hospital, where he lay unconscious for forty-eight hours. It was months before he took to the air again. The following day Bunn crashed the second glider, whereupon we had to suspend operations until the two machines were repaired. Primary gliders were not intended for such tricky manoeuvres, but as instructors we had to be able to perform them. There was no question of ever letting cadets do anything more than straight descents and, if they were good, one gentle turn.

In October one of the first ATC gliding schools started at Bray with twenty-five cadets drawn from the squadrons at Maidenhead, Windsor, Slough and Eton College. Flight Lieutenant Joe West was commanding officer, Rolf was chief instructor, Tudor Edmunds and myself were instructors. But if the ATC was to provide the RAF with the large number of trained cadets it needed, gliding schools had to be set up all over the country, and so, while Slingsby in Yorkshire built the gliders, we concentrated at Bray on training more instructors. The first was Clark, a journalist, then came Smythe, an Eton master, Trounson and Francis, who were manufacturers, and a number of others who all had some aviation experience. West's cadets had to wait, but there were so many jobs to be done, we needed willing hands, and the boys put in months of work of all kinds before the eagerly awaited moment came when, strapped on to the frying pan, they were winched across the airfield for the first time.

Since the number of cadets we could train was limited, each squadron sent only its best boys, and they were so keen that every successful ground-hop and landing thrilled us as much as it did them. It gave us great satisfaction to see them progress, and I believe we got to know not only the speed of reaction, stamina and general aptitude of each of them but also his character better than anyone who taught them in a classroom. The reports we made about them at the end of their training period must have, or should have, been of considerable help to the RAF in its final selection.

Running a weekend gliding school did not satisfy Rolf indefinitely. In May 1943 I was able to arrange with Hosiery Control to have him released for flying duties with Air Transport Auxiliary, which ferried fighters and bombers from the aircraft factories to operational RAF aerodromes. The release was granted on condition that he continued to work at the Langley factory for at least one day every week, an unusual arrangement that worked quite well. Rolf handed the responsibility for gliding training at Bray over to me and for the next two years flew Spitfires, Hurricanes and other military aircraft with ATA.

After operating for a while with primary machines, we were allocated one or two more advanced types which had a fuselage and cockpit, could be winched up to a greater height and stayed up long enough to enable one to fly a full circuit. In 1944 we were given a requisitioned German high-efficiency sailplane, a Minimoa, a beautifully streamlined machine with a totally enclosed cockpit that fitted the pilot as tightly as a glove. I was the first to fly it. The winch pulled me to a height of 800 ft, I dropped the cable and flew a circuit of the airfield, but instead of losing height the variometer showed a steady rate of climb. After two more circuits I had reached 1,400 ft, and as I did not want to go higher so as not to interfere with air traffic at nearby White Waltham aerodrome, I pointed the nose of the machine downwards. It picked up speed, and when I eased the stick back the Minimoa shot up another couple of hundred feet. As we were not allowed to fly away from the field, I kept circling for forty minutes, trying vainly to lose altitude, and when I reached 2,000 ft pulled the air brake. At long last the machine began to sink, and I landed smoothly to excited cheers.

It was Clark's turn to try his hand next. He had a good launch and flew a number of circuits, but then the thermal that had kept me up disappeared and after four minutes he made his approach to land. Just as he came over the airfield boundary he dropped a wing, it caught in the hedge, the glider swung round, and a moment later Clark sat in the midst of a heap of irreparable matchwood. He was mortified but fortunately not hurt. And this was the sad end of our beautiful Minimoa, but it made no difference to our training programme: the cadets could not have flown it anyway. Clark got over the shock and in due course took over from me as chief gliding instructor. He and West became responsible for the school while I continued as one of the senior gliding instructors, sharing duties with Tudor Edmunds. My weekends on the airfield were a welcome change for body and soul from the committee meeting wrangles and the never-ending problems at the factory.

In spite of the BoT's special interest in our firm and the Manpower Board's co-operation we had to replace more and more skilled workers by learners and elderly part-timers, and for the first time our production suffered a setback:

1942–43	*1943–44*	*1944–45*
£ 211,000	165,000	188,000

But we were not downcast. I knew that our competitors' production figures were declining more steeply than ours. We would soon recover the lost ground after the war, and even now we were making up some of the loss as our learners became skilled.

Foyster's civilian production programmes took 75 per cent of our total output, primarily in children's underwear, but we also worked for the Ministry of Supply, who placed contracts with us for vests and panties for the women's forces and who were, in a rather amusing way, responsible for our most profitable single transaction. It happened like this. Before a consignment left the factory it was usually passed by an MoS inspector. One day this gentleman arrived with a roll of men's suiting, a medium-weight worsted cloth in light grey with a pale blue overcheck. He said it was surplus and offered it to us free of clothes coupons. We bought it, of course, and Mr Hurst, Mr Colmer, Rolf, Peggy, Ruby, Miss Lancaster and several other employees and friends of the firm had suits made from it, which were jokingly referred to as Pasold uniforms. I had mine made by a tailor in Hanover Square and it was to be ready on Saturday morning. But the tailor had not quite finished it when I called and asked me to come back half an hour later. Strolling down one side of Regent Street and up the other, I was struck by the great number of buildings that were for sale and wondered what they might cost. I rather liked the look of No. 205, across the road from Liberty's. Following a sudden impulse, I asked the agents, whose offices were near by.

It transpired that the Crown lease, which had some sixty years to go, cost £6,000 and the annual ground rent was £1,200 minus £350, for the first floor was let. I could hardly credit that such a splendid building in London's finest street should cost so little and felt like buying it on the spot. Monday was Rolf's day off from flying duties, and I took him and Mr Hurst to see it. They were as enthusiastic as I was. Having decided to discontinue supplying the wholesale trade after the war, we would need offices and a showroom in the West End to cater for retail and overseas buyers. This building seemed ideally suited for the purpose, and so, towards the end of January 1944, we closed the deal.

There were few air raids on Britain during the first part of the year. The

Germans were concentrating on the Italian and Russian fronts, where they were hard pressed, and we enjoyed a comparatively peaceful spring until in June the 'doodlebugs', as the flying bombs were called, began to arrive and cause much damage. The first time I saw one was on 4 July. I was standing on the pavement in front of Selfridge's when the beastly thing approached from the direction of Holborn, flew along the whole length of Oxford Street, passed above me at an altitude of approximately 1,000 ft and disappeared towards Kensington. I do not know where it exploded, but I still remember how life in the street ahead of it suddenly stopped, everyone standing still, gazing upwards with baited breath, and how the traffic liquified and moved again as the bomb passed overhead. Two weeks later a doodlebug fell and exploded in Conduit Street, blowing in the windows and door of our building, as if to warn us that we might yet have only a heap of rubble when the war was over. However, the property escaped any further damage from the total of 1,050 flying bombs and V2 rockets which fell on London and southeast England.

As it turned out, we needed no office in London when peace returned. The demand for Ladybird merchandise was far greater than we had anticipated, buyers came to Langley to place their orders, and so, some years later, when someone offered us fourteen times the price we had paid for it we succumbed to the temptation and sold the building, paid a large part of the profit to the Inland Revenue and invested the remainder in textile machinery. It was by sheer luck and a narrow margin that we missed the 'once and for all' tax thought up by Sir Stafford Cripps, otherwise the Exchequer would have taken the lot, and that would have been worse than if the building had been hit by a doodlebug. But that is a story for later.

Another amusing tale has to do with food rationing. We never actually went hungry during the war, but our diet was dreary to say the least, and I shall not forget the taste of baked beans as long as I live. There were few left-overs from the factory canteen but, said Gustav Passler, if he could have them and if I found him four chickens—preferably Rhode Island Reds, for they were the best layers—he would supply me with eggs. It seemed a wonderful idea, considering that eggs were rationed at the rate of one per person per month and I was very fond of eggs. But where on earth was I to get the chickens from? As always when I had a problem I consulted Mr Hurst. He had so many connections, if he did not know the answer nobody did. Two weeks later he arrived carrying a hamper with four gaggling Rhode Island Reds. I was dumbfounded. 'Where did you get them from?'

'The Deputy Prime Minister,' he said, grinning like a schoolboy. Clement Attlee, it appeared, was his immediate neighbour at Stanmore and some time past had knocked on Hurst's door. 'Alfred, old chap,' he had said, 'I want you to do me a favour. We have been asked to give up our iron railings. If I do, my chickens will run into the road and get killed. I shall therefore make an application to be allowed to keep mine, but I don't want my house to be the only one in the village with railings. Would you apply to keep yours too?' The two fences remained and Mr Hurst forgot the incident, but when I asked him about chickens he remembered. He knocked on Mr Attlee's door and said, 'Clem, old chap, I need some Rhode Island Reds for a good friend of mine. How about letting me have four of yours?' They were splendid layers, providing Rolf and me with eggs until long after Mr Attlee had become Prime Minister, and eventually ended their very useful existence on Gustav's dining table.

There was a time when I thought of the civil service as a pyramid in which all policy was shaped by very able men at the top and the initiative eminating from them percolated through well defined channels to the base. Perhaps it really was like that before the war, but the maze of new departments, divisions and sections that had since been created and staffed with thousands of newly recruited officials had destroyed my tidy geometrical concept. Millbank and countless other requisitioned buildings all over the country were teeming with bureaucrats, and when I jokingly told Foyster that some day the ordinary people would rise against them he said, laughing, 'The ordinary people will be outnumbered.' Temporary civil servants appeared readier to take risks than the permanent members of the species, and many decisions, or half-decisions, now seemed to be taken at lower levels. One could easily be misled into wasting much valuable time on schemes which were encouraged by some temporary bureaucrat with an eye to quick promotion, schemes which found no backing higher up and were discarded. The project for a national waste reclamation industry on the Langley pattern in which, at Abrahamson's urging, I had invested so much effort, was in this category.

At the beginning of 1945 the BoT tried with promises of financial assistance to stimulate the development of industry in the Redruth and Camborne area of Cornwall, where severe unemployment was to be expected after the war, and hoped that SEKIA would actively co-operate by establishing branch factories there. The NHMF, on the other hand, wanted to prevent the transfer of any part of the knitting industry from the traditional hosiery centres to 'scheduled areas', an attitude which I opposed and which for political reasons had to be abandoned. We paid several visits to Cornwall, negotiated with Barry Kay, the regional representative of the BoT, and prepared schemes which all led to nothing. Nevertheless Rolf and I were stimulated by these exercises and contemplated building a branch factory for Pasolds Ltd at Plympton, to the east of Plymouth, a project that was enthusiastically supported by the local authorities. We had the land surveyed and architect's drawings prepared, but the Treasury hedged and we put our plans into cold storage.

Then we received an invitation from the government of Northern Ireland to establish a factory in Ulster and were offered two seats on an aircraft—a rare favour in those days of travel difficulties—to take us to Belfast for a discussion with the Minister for Trade and Industry. So the approach was a serious one! We prepared a four-page questionnaire asking for information about the available labour, wage levels, trade unions, factory sites, building permits, water supply, finance, taxation and so forth, and secured the exit permits needed for a visit to Ireland, only to be told that there was no air transport for us and that we should go by train and boat like all other commercial travellers. This did not seem an auspicious beginning. We declined, and heard no more. Thereupon we decided not to waste any more time with government-sponsored industrialisation schemes and to concentrate our activities at Langley.

I gave much thought to the post-war expansion of our factory, and prepared a comprehensive scheme covering three stages of growth in terms of 300, 500 and 1,000 employees, down to such detail as floor area and the layout of each department, boiler and power plants, pipelines for the enlarged dyehouse, electric wiring, heating installation, drains, canteens, toilets, cycle sheds, car park, loading bays, access roads and so forth. I then showed this programme to the regional controller of the BoT at Reading. He was intrigued. The BoT had not seen such a detailed industrial development programme before, and I was invited to take part in several general discussions on planning which, I believe, indirectly led to my appointment by Mr Silkin, the Minister for Town and Country Planning, to the Crawley New Town Corporation after the war and gave me the opportunity of saving Gatwick airport from becoming a housing estate. Be that as it may, in due course I summarised my Langley expansion scheme neatly in a folder, included some photographs and a plan showing the three stages of development in different colours, got it approved and countersigned by the BoT, and locked it away in the safe.

Rolf frowned. He thought it not only a waste of valuable time but a deliberate affront to providence, and wanted to have nothing to do with it, while I was convinced that this expansion would come and that long-term plans were necessary. But of course I could plan only on the basis of past experience. Would new processes, new types of plant, revolutionise our industry after the war? There were, to my knowledge, few new textile machines on British drawing boards. Engineering firms were too busy making tanks and aeroplanes, and presumably the same applied in Germany, but what of developments in the USA? How could I find out? While I was pondering how best to set about asking the authorities for permission to go there, and for a passage, realising full well that it would be refused, Tommy Allen telephoned. He was trying to arrange an official, government-sponsored visit to North and South America to conduct market research for the Export Group and thought that, as his vice-chairman, I ought to accompany him. I agreed immediately, intending to kill two birds with one stone. The BoT gave its blessing, we applied for passports, exit permits and visas, and then waited. After three months Tommy's papers came through, too late for the South American part of the journey, while enquiries about mine only met with shrugged shoulders. I was told to be patient.

The successful invasion of Normandy by the Allied forces speeded up industry's preparations for the change-over to peacetime production. In September 1944 Miles Aircraft Ltd, who were building trainer planes for the RAF at Woodley aerodrome, an activity that would inevitably be drastically reduced when the war ended, invited us for trial flights in prototypes of civilian aeroplanes they intended to put on the market then. To feel the engine's response to the throttle gave me a thrill; a foretaste of the approaching freedom to travel was in the air. I envied Rolf, who was now ferrying planes to France, Belgium and Holland almost every week.

When it became clear that the Allies were winning the war in spite of doodlebugs and rockets, businessmen, who for four years or more had in the national interest unstintingly given so much of their time to the NHMF, began to remember their own neglected firms and reassess their priorities. They had learned to cope with wartime restrictions and shortages, but the change to conditions of peace would throw up completely new problems. They wanted to be on the bridge of their own ships if or when the generally predicted storm of a great post-war depression broke. The competition for seats on committees was no longer as keen as it had been, meetings seemed to be attended a little less regularly, and traces of a centrifugal force became discernible. Willie Grimmond, so long the undisputed leader of the Scots, was now finding that the frequent journeys to Leicester were making too great demands on him, and handed over to Eadie Taylor. Peshall, wanting to concentrate more on his work at Corah, went in search of a permanent director for the NHMF to relieve him and found H. Kennewell for this purpose. The time came when I heard it rumoured that even Foyster, the Hosiery Controller, was thinking of leaving the BoT, not to return to M. & S. but to become a director of the John Lewis Partnership. However, I must not run ahead of the story.

43

THE INQUISITIVE
COLONELS
1945

THE WAR WAS entering its final stage. The coloured pins on my wall map, on which I followed the advance of the Allied armies, were moving faster. On 1 April 1945 the Americans were only ten miles from Würzburg, and the Russians were approaching Vienna. At the Yalta conference Roosevelt, Churchill and Stalin had agreed on the territories each of their armies should occupy, but clearly Hitler's troops were fighting with greater tenacity on the eastern front than they were in the west, and it could be foreseen that, when German resistance finally collapsed, the Americans would be temporarily in possession of large areas, such as Thuringia and Saxony, which ought to have been conquered by the Russians. Saxony, especially Chemnitz and its neighbourhood, was the home of the German knitting machine and hosiery industries. Even if, as I suspected, the Germans had concentrated all their energies on the prosecution of the war and had little time to think about developing textile machines, it would be interesting to see what progress they had made. Had they, for instance, built new waste reclamation plants or improved the technique of knitting synthetics? No doubt the Russians would dismantle many of the factories and take them to the Urals and Siberia. If only I were given the opportunity of visiting Chemnitz before it was occupied by Russian troops. A forlorn hope, but I would at least mention the idea to the authorities.

I decided to see Gray, who was an assistant secretary at the BoT and whose office was now at Horseferry House. We had travelled together to War Emergency Committee meetings on a number of occasions and knew each other quite well. He offered me a cup of that awful brown brew which passed for tea in government offices and was consumed there in huge quantities, lit his pipe, listened to what I had to say and then referred me to a Mr Parks of the Control Commission for Germany which was being assembled. As expected, Mr Parks, a nice old gentleman, was not in the least interested in hosiery and passed me on to his assistant, Gentili, who had been one of Dunlop's men in Berlin before the war. He knew nothing about knitting, either, but, a keen type, tried to pick my brains without being able to offer any assistance. A list of German hosiery firms my secretary copied out of an old directory kept him happy, and I heard no more.

The Americans reached the western tip of Czechoslovakia on the 18th and occupied Asch on 21 April. Then the line of yellow pins on my map swung south-east and followed the Bavarian side of the border. Why did they not occupy Bohemia? Was this to be left to the Russians? A cold shiver ran down my spine at the thought of it. What was to happen to Fleissen, to Mother? Where was she? I would give anything to be able to go and look for her. My passport, with visas for Portugal, several South American countries and the USA, arrived, but I no longer wanted them. With the war so near its end I would stay in England and watch developments, waiting for the one chance in a million to go to Fleissen. And then, suddenly, the seemingly impossible happened.

On the day Hitler shot himself in his bunker in Berlin, Gray telephoned. He was usually so placid, but now his voice sounded excited. Would I undertake a trip to Chemnitz, he asked. 'Tomorrow!' I replied without a moment's hesitation. Did he really mean it? Government departments had a way of leading one up the garden path; I could hardly credit that they were serious about sending me to Germany. A week passed and nothing happened. Then, on 9 May, the second VE holiday, a Mr Shearman of the Ministry of Supply telephoned and asked me to report at Shell-Mex House in the morning.

Expecting an interview of half an hour, I was surprised to be told that I should be needed all day. First Shearman signed me on as a temporary adviser to the MoS. Then he took me to the office of a Major Taunton, who said something about a Combined Intelligence Objectives Sub-committee, which conveyed nothing to me, and commissioned me as a second lieutenant. It was, apparently, impossible to go to Germany as a civilian. Immediately afterwards I was promoted to the rank of full colonel, the highest that could be conferred in connection with CIOS operations. The rank depended on the importance of the job to be done and on the position one held in civilian life. Long forms had to be filled in, I was taken by an MTC driver to Chelsea Barracks, where an uninterested army medico gave me a superficial examination, certified me A1 and injected me against typhus, then I was driven to the quartermaster's stores opposite Marylebone Station to draw my kit.

The sergeant was not impressed when I asked him for a colonel's uniform. It was ordinary battledress for all ranks. The rough blouse fitted fairly well, but the proportions of the trousers were impossible. Short and narrow legs, a huge seat and a waist wide enough to take two. One glance at boots and socks told me that I would never wear them. The rest of the kit consisted of two rough khaki shirts, gaiters, a beret, steel helmet, gas mask, gas cape, mess tins, groundsheet, bedding, wooden concertina bed, straps, a revolver that would have delighted Tom Mix and a supply of ammunition. It was a huge bundle, and I took it in a taxi to my tailor in Hanover Square.

The following day I was informed that I should not be going to Germany on my own but that four knitting machine and fabric experts from the Midlands, J. W. Heyes, A. Shortland, C. Scothern and A. J. Taub, as well as Len Foyster would accompany me. Being the Hosiery Controller, Foyster would be in charge of the party and become a full colonel while the others, including myself, would hold the rank of lieutenant colonel. I did not mind. What mattered to me was that I could plan the route of the expedition and that no one objected when I enlarged the itinerary by adding the hosiery area of Stuttgart and Reutlingen, which was then occupied by the French, to the district of Chemnitz, which was our principal target. The map I prepared showed clearly that the shortest way from Chemnitz to Stuttgart led via Asch, which, together with Fleissen, was another important knitting centre. I was thus not hiding my intention of crossing the old Czechoslovak border, and if CIOS wanted to withhold approval they could do so, but relying on their insufficient knowledge of the geography of central Europe I hoped they would not notice. For the chance of going to Fleissen I was willing to run any risk. I wanted to find Mother. We had not heard from her for over five years.

Wearing my uniform, I reported to Shell-Mex House the following afternoon, to learn that our team had not yet been cleared by the security department. My hopes fell. Not one of those exciting propositions of the past six months had materialised. The trip to America, the invitation from the government of Northern Ireland to set up a factory, the Cornish industrialisation scheme—they all began with official encouragement and not one of them received the promised support. Would there be some last-minute hitch and the journey to Germany be cancelled? But the clearance came through, the trip was on. I was given my military identity papers confirming my rank, then Major Taunton took me to the 'war room' deep down below ground, where I found Foyster in colonel's uniform with the red band round his hat and red tabs on his collar. All I remember of the briefing we were given is the warning not to fall into the hands of the Russians. If they caught us poaching on their territory there would be no diplomatic intervention to get us freed. The British authorities would disown us—or words to that effect. After being thus duly cautioned a car took us to the Adelphi dormitory, where we met the rest of our party and spent the night in bunks. From here I shall let my diary continue the story.

Wednesday 16 May 1945. By taxi to Airways House with our concertina beds and bundles of equipment, and then on to Croydon aerodrome, from where we take off in a DC3 for Paris. Fine weather flying. English and French countrysides look peaceful. Now and again one sees bomb craters near French railway stations or road crossings. There is no sign of any traffic—no train or car all the way from the coast to Paris. Arrive at Le Bourget at noon. The airport is not badly damaged and the repairs to the large terminal building consist mainly of redecoration. Share taxi with ATS Officer Davies (FANY) to Versailles. It is a very hot day, we are very cramped in the small taxi and almost squashed by the luggage. In the hall of the Hotel Royal, which has been taken over to provide billets for British officers, two French glamour girls act as receptionists. The building positively stinks, everything is dirty and the bedclothes seem to get changed once a week irrespective of how many people sleep in them.

While the others look at Versailles, Foyster and I visit Supreme Headquarters Allied Expeditionary Force at 'Petite Ecurie' and 'Grande Ecurie' for further briefing. In England one imagines SHAEF as an awe-inspiring super-organisation; here it is merely a mass of clerks in uniform sitting in untidy rooms connected by miles of rambling corridors. The personnel is mainly American, with a sprinkling of British, but no French. Foyster has contacts, a Major Weldon, a Lieutenant Colonel Ewart Williams and several others. We discuss our project with them and I keep a record of their names, telephone and room numbers. The departments of special interest to us are 'G2' and 'T Force'. Everyone tries to be helpful, but the large organisation is unwieldy and no one seems to know what anyone else is doing. We are given contradictory instructions how to proceed. The telephone lines to Germany are jammed; we are unable to find out how far the Russians have advanced. One department claims they are east of Chemnitz, the other says they are west of it, while the third tells us that they have occupied half the town but we can go and look at the other half. Some think we may be able to arrange a visit to Soviet-occupied territory, others say it is quite impossible. Then we are told that a few days previously the Russians in the Chemnitz region killed two Britishers, wounded a third and carried off a fourth. We are to keep clear of them.

After a while we get to know our way around SHAEF. Saluting ceases to be a problem: Versailles is teeming with privates and lieutenants, but we see few captains or majors and rarely any higher ranks. The heat is stifling. Thank God for the cotton shirt I bought before leaving England. Shortland's kit has been stolen out of the hotel store room and my handkerchiefs have disappeared. Michael Sieff, who joined the army in the early days of the war and is now colonel attached to MoS, arranges for us to obtain some clothes without coupons at the British officers' shop in Paris. It is a large one, but just as starved of merchandise as those in London.

We eat at C mess, which is the dining room of the Hotel Royal. It is dirty, flies are everywhere, the service is slovenly, the food poor, the whole establishment a scandal. After dinner we take the train to Paris, one of the few that are running in the whole of France, to look for the British officers' club. No one seems to know where it is. There are neither taxis nor buses. We walk the streets for an hour, getting hot and very tired, and eventually find it. It is Rothschild's residence, on loan to the British authorities, a most impressive building and ideally suited for a club. The food is excellent, wine and champagne flow freely, and everything is very cheap. Two hours in these hospitable surroundings revive our flagging spirits.

Thursday 17 May. After another day at SHAEF we return to the club in the evening, where, unexpectedly, we meet Rolf. He has flown a Spitfire to Stuttgart and is on his return journey to England. He tells us about conditions on the Continent. Says most trade is done by barter and on the black market. Can he help Foyster to dispose of a packet of coffee beans? Within a matter of minutes it is sold to the bar tender for 600 francs. Then Rolf delights Heyes and Scothern by arranging with the waiter a rate of 400 francs—double the official rate—for the £5 each of them change. Not having been allowed to bring any sterling, and with no more than 2,000 francs between us, our funds begin to run low. We all laugh when it transpires that the richest of us is Shortland, who, a colonel in the Salvation Army and very law-abiding, has calmly smuggled £45 out of Britain. Stupidly I have only brought £3, thinking the army would look after us, and am glad of the chance meeting with Rolf, who helps me out. He has taken planes to Nuremberg, Bayreuth and Leipzig and was hoping for some opportunity to go on to Czechoslovakia but has so far had no luck. We wonder whether he or I will reach Fleissen first.

Friday 18 May. We receive vague promises from G2 of help with transport. According to SHAEF's latest information Chemnitz is completely in Russian hands. I catch sight of a secret map showing the proposed lines of demarcation between the American, British and Russian occupation areas and am shocked to see that the Russians are to come as far west as Lübeck. From there the line runs south through the middle of the Harz mountains, taking in the whole of Thuringia, to meet the western tip of Bohemia at Rossbach. If this is the final line the Russians get an enormous slice of Germany. And what is to happen to Czechoslovakia?

Foyster and I dine at the 'House' of the MoS, a beautiful private residence with garden near the Arc de Triomphe which belongs to some count who has gone to Switzerland. The party which occupies this gem strikes me as utterly out of place in the aristocratic surroundings, rather like East End evacuees in a West End mansion. Besides some temporary civil servants, a couple of unattractive MTC girls and two elderly businessmen who have something to do with brake linings, we meet a Major Stratton there. He is the footwear controller at Leicester, wants to go to Germany and keeps telephoning Sir Cecil Weir in London but cannot get permission and is jealous of us. It appears a General Smith in Paris is refusing to let him go.

Saturday 19 May. Have secured a set of useful maps of the Chemnitz and Stuttgart areas and marked them with my suggested route and targets. The other members of the team are not very map-conscious and quite capable of setting off into the blue without any maps at all. After a final conference a car from the SHAEF motor pool takes us to airstrip 'Buc', four miles from Versailles, and we take off in a Dakota which we share with American service personnel, including a general. I follow the route on my map, look out for the Maginot and Siegfried lines but see only a few concrete pillboxes and isolated bomb craters. The first real bomb damage comes in sight as we approach the Rhine. The town at the end of the river—I take it to be Bingen—is completely destroyed. We are now flying at an altitude of only 500 ft and one can look through the ruined houses right into the cellars. Airstrip Y80, on which we land, is very busy, with planes parked everywhere. The atmosphere could not be more casual: nobody takes the least notice of us, wants to know who we are, asks to see our papers or can answer our questions. Eventually we secure a car to take Foyster and me to Twelfth Army headquarters at Wiesbaden, while the others wait at the airstrip with the luggage. Our driver is an apathetic, tired old man, the road is dusty and full of potholes, and the few civilians we see are mostly old people and children in a very poor state.

HQ at Wiesbaden has not been advised of our arrival and does not know what to do with us. Sends us to US Colonel Hayes at the Hotel Schwarzer Bock, who doubts whether he can arrange billets and transport for us but after much telephoning lets us stay for the night and promises an army truck from G2 to take us to Camp Dentine, near Erfurt, in the morning. Meanwhile the others arrive with the luggage and we settle in. The Schwarzer Bock must have been one of Wiesbaden's best hotels and, although somewhat knocked about by the war, provides us with comfortable beds and running hot water. The food is excellent and well served. The waiters were presumably taken over with the hotel, but the female staff are French or Belgian. We have two bottles of champagne at ten occupation marks the bottle. £1 = 200 francs = 40 occupation marks = four bottles of champagne. Then we load our revolvers and explore the town. It has been badly bombed (at least I think so until I see other German towns) and the rubble is piled high on both sides of the streets, the middle having been cleared for the military traffic. We look at the ruins of a Woolworth store and of the Hotel Vier Jahreszeiten where Rolf, Jack Matthews and I spent a night in 1934 when we drove the Alvis to Fleissen. We see mainly Americans, all carrying guns. Are we the only British here? Defeat seems to have reduced all civilians to the same miserable level. I would like to talk to the three dejected-looking old men at the corner, but fraternising with Germans is strictly forbidden. One can only give them orders or ask them the way. This first day on German soil is a stirring, gruesome experience.

Sunday 20 May. No Sunday atmosphere. At the Dresdner Bank, the entrance of which is guarded by a sentry with rifle and steel helmet, I change the francs Rolf gave me into occupation marks. It is a queer feeling to walk into a bank with a loaded revolver. At mid-day the promised truck arrives, a very uncomfortable vehicle, and we set off for Erfurt. The signposts have been removed. Neither civilians—who all seem to be displaced persons on the move—nor the American soldiers know the way, and we lose an hour driving on poor secondary roads before we strike the autobahn. It is in surprisingly good condition; six years of war do not seem to have affected the surface. There is, of course, only military traffic, and little of that. One drives as one likes, on the right or the left, on the grass verge or across the fields if one meets an obstacle. The 200-mile run takes us through pine woods almost all the way. The countryside looks as fresh and unspoilt as ever, only the hundreds of cars, buses, lorries and tanks that litter the sides of the road remind one of the war. Most of them are overturned and burnt out, with radiators smashed in and windows broken. There must be a drama attached to each one of them. Whence did it start on its last journey, and where did the people in it want to go ? Who stopped it and set fire to it, and what happened to the occupants ?

We meet a few convoys of American army lorries and sometimes a jeep. The autobahn has become a main artery for pedestrians trekking from east to west. There are thousands of them. They travel in small groups, carrying bundles, pushing perambulators and pulling hand carts. Now and again one sees a cyclist or a cart drawn by a horse. They are French, Belgian and Dutch workers returning to their own countries, and Germans—among them a high proportion of children—fleeing from the Russians. As we approach Thuringia we also see German soldiers in ones and twos, presumably released prisoners of war, walking westward. All these people sleep in the woods, camp by the roadside and are completely defenceless. The stronger can take from the weaker whatever he chooses. We are travelling at an average speed of thirty-five miles an hour, slowed down now and then by detours to avoid blown up bridges. In the late afternoon we see Eisenach in the distance. On the horizon towers the Wartburg, we pass a large anti-aircraft gun with its barrel pointing into space and a heap of shells by its side, the sky is full of rain clouds and occasionally we get wet.

Arriving at Erfurt at dusk, we look for Ninth Army headquarters, or Camp Dentine, or Major Hurley, but no one can tell us anything. The bomb damage here is far worse than at Wiesbaden. At last we find a Major Reynolds who reminds me of the Rocky Mountains. He tries to be helpful, telephoning as far as his field instrument will carry. We locate the town major, who arranges billets for us at the Hotel Bürgerhof. My room has no bed, only a small couch, but I am too tired to care. There is running hot water, which is the main thing. Foyster, Taub and Scothern have rooms without windows and beds without sheets. Heyes and Shortland are given a key by the sergeant in the reception office, but find that their room has lost its door, which makes the key rather superfluous. We are told not to let our luggage out of our sight, for there are thousands of Poles, Russians, Belgians and other slave workers in the town who take everything that is movable. Have dinner at the officers' mess, a requisitioned private house, as guests of the Americans. A young captain says the displaced persons in the district number 100,000, an unruly, violent crowd which presents a great problem. Everyone strong enough to walk is allowed to leave, only German nationals have to stay. The gruesome details of his simple description curdle our blood.

Before retiring we have a glass of beer with the American privates in occupation at the Bürgerhof, tough young chaps who barter captured daggers, guns and ammunition. The way they handle these weapons makes me wonder about the accident rate. I have hardly shut my eyes when shooting starts in the street below, but my room on the third floor seems safe enough and I am tired. We are told in the morning that it is usual for the Poles and the Russians to shoot at each other at night time. They are all armed. The Germans have thrown their weapons away and the displaced persons have picked them up.

Monday 21 May. Camp Dentine is not at Erfurt but near Kassel, where we arrive at noon. The town is a terrible sight. Most of the buildings are down and the few still standing are badly damaged, yet between them grow trees, lots of them, trees that are forty years old. They are green and healthy, an incongruous sight. And there are people, many of them young girls in smart clothes and silk stockings. How can they live in ruins and holes in the ground ? We ask for Ninth Army divisional head-quarters but, as usual, no one can direct us. For the best part of an hour we drive along traffic lanes which the Americans with their bulldozers have pushed through the rubble before we find an officer who shows us the way. Camp Dentine is twenty minutes south-east of Kassel, beautifully situated on a hill in the woods. It is an American transport centre, with a few white officers and the rest of the personnel negroes. Fifty or so small houses built in the attractive local style surround a large social centre with a magnificent dining and entertainment hall, the kitchen arranged alongside it is fitted out in stainless steel, on the stage are half a dozen negroes singing some southern song, swaying their bodies in rhythm, presumably practising for some forthcoming event. Over the main entrance is a large swastika and an eagle with the words 'Leben heisst kämpfen'. At first I take it for a 'Strength through joy' camp, but am told it was a workers' hostel for a munitions factory half a mile away in the forest. Within minutes we are served huge portions of boiled chicken and rice. We are very hungry and enjoy our meal tremendously.

After lunch we dismiss our truck, which returns to Wiesbaden. Captain Palmer of A battery 578 kindly provides two negro drivers and two command cars with trailers for our luggage. We draw K rations, chocolate, chewing gum, soap, cigars and cigarettes, and depart in the direction of Leipzig. Of the drivers, Corporal Fletcher, who insists on always wearing his steel helmet, is a bright lad, whereas poor Daniel, although equally likable, cannot tell left from right. We suspect that he cannot read or write either, for he gets very agitated whenever he is asked to sign a petrol receipt. A slow and careful driver, he finds it difficult to keep up with the corporal. Near Jena we come to another blown-up bridge and have to make a detour. There seem to be even more overturned cars and buses, burnt-out tanks and abandoned mobile guns here than farther back. Thousands of large live shells are piled up on the strip of grass between the highways, parts of crashed aeroplanes are lying along the roadside, and the groups of civilians and German soldiers con-tinue tramping silently westward through the rain.

Taub, who says he has studied at Leipzig University and knows his way about the town, directs us to our billets at Poeten Weg 31, a beautiful house that belonged to a radio manufacturer named Paul Budin. We are told that he held some position in the Nazi party and shot his wife, his daughter and himself when the Americans occupied Leipzig. In the wall of the sitting room in which we sleep are three bullet holes, and the bloodstains are still visible on the parquet floor. The house is intact apart from the front door, the desk and several cupboards which were locked and have been broken open by the troops. The panel of the door between the sitting room and the library is missing, and we walk through the hole without opening the door itself. On the tables are ashtrays, on the shelves books, family photographs and porcelain figures; on the wall hang pictures: it all looks as if the Budins had still been there yesterday. There must be some twenty soldiers in the house, and the bathroom is overcrowded. As always, the Americans are very hospitable, and their food is excellent. We spend the night in our blankets on the floor.

Tuesday 22 May. Excellent breakfast with plenty of grapefruit juice, then to HQ 'Jay Hawk', housed in a large bank building in the devastated town centre. It is a bustling organisation, everyone is helpful, we get our papers cleared in record time, but even here, so near the front line, no one can tell us how far the Russians have advanced. The officers in the map room believe that they are on the right bank of the river Mulde and that they have occupied Chemnitz but are not sure and refer us to HQ 76th Division at Crimmitschau, which is responsible for the Chemnitz area. The road leading there via Altenburg is clear, they say. Bombed Leipzig makes a deep impression on me. I knew it well before the war and now look out for the Glas Palast, the corner building Father almost bought at the time of the great inflation, but it is no longer there. Civilian life has not quite ceased. I see old men with briefcases, women with perambulators or on bicycles, even a tram or two, and there are German traffic policemen in their helmets and grey-green uniforms.

In the coal-mining area of Altenburg we pass huge industrial buildings which look like synthetic oil or petrol plants being repaired. At least one of the mines seems to have stocks. Hundreds of horse-drawn trucks and even a few lorries are being loaded with coal. In this part of the world the movement of population is from south to north. We still meet the little groups with their bundles, but many of the people we see seem to be staying. They carry on with their day-to-day jobs, look after their houses and work in the fields, and the children play in the streets. The little girls picking flowers by the side of the road stare with big eyes at our negro drivers. We are careful not to enter Russian territory by mistake, carefully study the map all the way, and stop at every crossroads to check. We find Crimmitschau intact, but not a single factory chimney smoking. There are few people about, and although we see no bomb damage an atmosphere of depression lies over the town. Otherwise everything looks much the same as before the war. There are no new factories, no indications that the existing ones were enlarged. If the Germans have increased their waste spinning industry, then it was certainly not here.

Foyster clears papers with Division HQ while I drive to the town hall to interview the mayor. He says that until April there were 9,000 German and 1,000 foreign workers employed in the town, less than half of them in the textile industry, whereas before the war textiles employed 8,000. Most of the spinning mills have been operating until recently. A few were stopped because of the shortage of labour. None was requisitioned. The raw material consisted entirely of waste, rags and staple fibre. The engineering works of Trützschler & Gey, makers of waste reclamation machinery, have been converted to make armaments. I decide that there is little for us to learn at Crimmitschau and join Foyster at HQ, where, at long last, we are able to obtain reasonably reliable information about the Russian line. It runs approximately half-way between Limbach and Chemnitz. The two towns are about seven miles apart. We start for Limbach, which is in American hands, eating our K rations on the way.

B Company HQ Limbach arrange billets for us at the Central Hotel. In the meantime Taub and I go to question the mayor, the well known sewing machine manufacturer Köhler, who apparently enjoys the confidence of the Americans as well as that of the German population. Unfortunately he is out. Councillor Thierfelder informs us that until recently the factories in the town employed 5,000 German and 5,000 foreign workers, but now all are stopped because there is neither electricity nor raw material. Foyster and Shortland go with Taub to inspect the works of Johannes Richter, the world-famous makers of Simplex fabric; I take Scothern and Heyes to see Stelzmann's factory, which before the war had the reputation of being one of Germany's most modern underwear plants. Paul Stelzmann, a talkative little man of fifty-five, shows us his Terrots, interlocks, rib machines and warp looms, which are no different from those used in England, but—and this is something quite new— he also has an experimental warp loom which makes ladderproof stockings. He is developing it jointly with the firm of Schneider & Reuther. At first sight the idea seems fascinating, but, studying it more closely, I doubt whether it will ever yield satisfactory results. We take the blueprints of the machine and samples of the fabric made on it, some stockings, and cuttings of various plush, rubberised and glued materials which are used for making shoes. I am satisfied. This visit and my talk with Stelzmann have revealed that, generally speaking, the German knitting industry has made no more progress than the British these past six years and that Langley has nothing to worry about.

Supper at the mess, a small factory from which the knitting machines have been removed. The office is used as kitchen, and we eat on the sewing benches out of our mess tins. A drunken soldier is knocked down by his friends. He lies bleeding on the floor; nobody cares. We compare notes of our experiences at Richter's and Stelzmann's factories. Taub wants the team to be rough with the Germans. He disapproves of my 'kid glove' manners. I do not know his background and presume it is Jewish. He may have lost relatives in a concentration camp, and I wonder how I would feel in similar circumstances. But we are an industrial fact-finding mission, not a punitive one, and I see no reason for applying Gestapo methods if the information we seek is readily forthcoming. Heyes and Scothern keep out of the discussion; they each accepted a large cigar from Stelzmann, knowing full well that fraternising with the enemy is forbidden.

As we leave the mess two Ukrainians speak to me. They are farmers who want to go back to Kiev with their families. They have valid passes to travel and certificates confirming that the horses and waggons are their property. To proceed to the Russian line they need permission from the American commander, and as they do not speak English I talk to the US lieutenant in charge. He says they can go in the morning, remarking to me on the side that the Russians will take their horses and rape their wives, but it is not for him to warn them, poor wretches.

Afterwards the lieutenant and one of his soldiers visit us at the Central Hotel. They bring with them a few gallons of excellent red wine in a pail, telling us that there is plenty more where it came from. The little lieutenant keeps us all amused. He is only twenty-four and holds strong views on everything. He has too much to drink, talks too much, makes advances to the middle-aged waitress, offers to take us on a tour through a number of German homes the following evening and wants to arrange a party with the Russians in Chemnitz for the night afterwards. We cannot quite catch his name, but it ends with '-sak', and so amongst ourselves we refer to him as Lieutenant Cul-de-sac, whereupon Foyster calls him the 'Dead-end Kid'.

Wednesday 23 May. I take Heyes to Ernst Liebers, one of the smaller needle manufacturers. His sister has been to London and speaks English, so I leave Heyes there and join Scothern and Shortland at Stelzmann's factory. Foyster and Taub go to Burgstädt to see Schlick & Co., who are reputed to build the world's best beaming machine. At lunch we hear that Heyes is having difficulties in obtaining the information he wants from Liebers. Foyster and Taub accompany him on the second visit and, I am told later, a little firmness makes Liebers co-operate. Heyes requisitions a small prototype needle-making machine and takes it away with him.

Meanwhile I drive with Shortland and Scothern to Oberlungwitz. Of the three largest makers of fully fashioned hosiery machines in Germany, Hilscher and Schubert & Salzer are in Russian hands; only Carl Lieberknecht at Oberlungwitz is still accessible to us. We want to investigate whether they have improved their machines. They have! The 'control head' is no longer at the end but in the centre of the machine, like that of a spinning mule, which makes it possible to build longer units. Elementary, I think, not being a stocking manufacturer. But my colleagues are elated, so much so that Shortland shakes Klaus Lieberknecht's hand, quite forgetting the relationship between conqueror and vanquished he meant to establish from the start by resting his army boots on the latter's impressive mahogany desk. Lieberknecht goes out of his way to be helpful. Unfortunately all the blueprints were destroyed when the Americans first occupied the works, but we get plenty of other information and leave well satisfied with our visit. On the return journey we come to a fork and stop. The road on the left leads to Limbach, that on the right is roped off to denote the limits of US territory. We see no Russians, but the American sentry tells us it is a trouble spot. Russian raiding parties come across to take away horses, cattle and women. The population is scared, and so is the sentry.

We are fortunate. The most interesting firms are not in Chemnitz itself but in the area immediately to the west, in which we are free to move about for the time being. At our meeting in the evening we agree on a list of plants still to be studied: Ernst Saupe, Limbach, makers of warp looms; Schneider & Reuther, Limbach, makers of warp looms; Anton Haase, Hohenstein-Ernstthal, needle makers; Ernst Liebers, Kändler, needle makers; Julius Köhler, Limbach, makers of sewing machines; Louis Bahner, Oberlungwitz, hosiery manufacturers; Hugo Erdner & Co., Göppersdorf, fabric glove manufacturers. Factory investigations have become routine, and I suggest to my colleagues that they carry on while I take Fletcher and a command car and try to make my way to Asch in Czechoslovakia to prepare the ground for a visit by the team, proposing to return to Limbach within forty-eight hours. A little reluctantly they acquiese, and their reluctance is echoed by the American commandant, who not only warns me to beware of the Russians but talks of armed bands of displaced persons and the Werwolf and SS men in the woods and says there is little he can do if I and my driver disappear.

Thursday 24 May. Take Heyes and Scothern as far as Hohenstein-Ernstthal, where I leave them at the needle factory of Anton Haase and head south-west. Fletcher is at the wheel. I direct him, following the marks on my map; we both wear our steel helmets. The less one looks like an officer the less likely one will be shot at. The Russians are said to control a stretch of the autobahn, and so we keep on the road to the north of it, motoring through peaceful countryside, and after a few detours reach Zwickau. Over the pitheads on the outskirts flies the red flag, the town is damaged and looks disorderly; out of the windows hang white flags of surrender, long stretches of road are torn up, and the bridge leading west is in ruins. After another tedious detour we reach the autobahn, which is supposed to be in American hands from here on, and have a trouble-free run as far as the exit at Plauen. The road from here to the Czechoslovak border is very familiar to me, and the years of war do not seem to have changed it much. But the bridge to the south-east of Oelsnitz is down. We drive across fields and along the footpath through the woods, the roughest passage yet, to reach Adorf. The little town seems intact, and we meet with no more obstacles on the other side, although there are signs of local fighting. Trees have been cut down and used for barricades along the winding road, over-turned and burnt-out cars lie about, and for the first time I see notices saying 'Road and shoulders free', presumably meaning that they have been cleared of mines. All tense now, I wait impatiently for the view from the crest of the hill. At last there is Brambach below and I can see the Egerland in the distance beyond. From here everything looks peaceful and unchanged.

We have not seen more than half a dozen American soldiers these past hours, but now there are two at the Czechoslovak frontier who say they have strict instructions not to let anyone pass. On discovering that my modest battledress conceals a British lieutenant colonel they change their tune but ask me to sign a paper confirming that I am going at my own risk. They do not know what is going on on the other side of no-man's-land. Have seen no Russian troops, believe Fleissen to be inhabited mainly by displaced persons and that Czech soldiers will shortly be moving up to the border. Forgotten at their lonely post and hungry, they ask for food and cigarettes. Unfortunately I have little to give them.

We drive on, passing Geipel's leather factory, which is partly destroyed. The roofs of many houses are shattered, Uncle Wilhelm's is burnt out, the windows of Lehrmann's factory are broken and the top storey seems to be damaged by fire. It is lunchtime; there are few people about. Turning the last corner, the factory of Adolf Pasold & Sohn comes in sight and I register subconsciously that the windows are missing, but the family home on the opposite side of the road seems whole and un-changed, only the trees in the garden are taller and the grass has not been cut. Full of forebodings, I ring the bell, afraid of being met by the stare of squatters who do not know who I am and what I want. Then the door opens and there, aged but well, stands Mother. No words can describe our feelings. We have so many questions to ask, so much to say to each other. The hours fly. The Nebels were lucky, she tells me. Willie was exempt from military service and is with Silvia and the children at Leibitschgrund. I should like to hear their voices, but the telephone wires are down. Ingo, who was a test pilot, sustained head and back injuries in a plane crash and is recovering in an overcrowded hospital at Franzensbad, where Mother occasionally takes food to him. She walks the fifteen kilometres each way, for there are neither taxis nor buses, and since the railway bridge near Eger was blown up there are no more trains. I promise to get him released and bring him home in the morning. Of Udo she has no news. When last she heard of him he was somewhere in the Crimea. It appears that there has been no fighting at Fleissen, but it was shelled to dislodge an SS detachment and Mother spent a few anxious days and nights in the cellar. The factory windows were blown in by the explosion of a railway truck laden with ammunition. Had our factories been working? Until recently! Were there many foreign workers here? Very few, and they did not seem to cause any trouble. We talk and talk. Corporal Fletcher is soundly asleep in the guest room while we burn the midnight oil.

Friday 25 May. Fletcher drives me to Franzensbad, where Ingo, who is wearing a dressing gown and hobbling on a stick, is surprised and pleased to see me. Tells me proudly that he is married and has a small son. I have no difficulty in getting him released, sign some papers and take him back to Fleissen, where his family will join him. He is not in good shape but assures me that there is nothing wrong with him that care and time will not put right. Aunt Marie arrives with four precious eggs and makes omelets for us. I am sorry to miss Uncle Wilhelm, who does not know that I am at Fleissen and has gone somewhere on his bicycle. Then my time is up. I promise to return as soon as I can, take my leave and drive via Brambach and Oberreuth to Asch.

None of the factory chimneys at Asch are smoking, and the people, mostly working-class, are in the streets. I see unarmed militia men in khaki uniforms among the crowd. Czech flags are flying over a number of buildings. The atmosphere is one of uneasy relief that the war is over but also of fear of what is to come. Will there be civil war? Motoring down the main street, I stop at the Bohemian Union Bank, the HQ of Captain Lund, the American military commander of the town. It flies the Czech flag and the stars and stripes and is guarded by American soldiers. Entering through the cashier's office, which is filled with civilians seeking information, I go upstairs to see Lund. He sits in Direktor Friedrich's office, while Direktor Huder's is occupied by half a dozen girl clerks, one of whom speaks English and acts as Lund's secretary. It's a small world. She was born at Ealing, came to Asch shortly before the war, and now wants me to tell her about home.

Captain Lund, a man of about forty, is a dandy. His uniform is spick-and-span and he wears a white silk handkerchief round his neck. He is speaking on the phone and waves me into a chair. It appears an SS man has been caught, and Lund says he should have shot himself right away. I show him my papers, advise him of the British team's forthcoming visit and ask him to prepare billets. He promises to fix us up at the Hotel Post, but warns me that food is short. Could we bring meat, potatoes, flour, in fact anything edible? Then he talks about his own activities.

There are one or two factories he would like to get working again, especially Eisenschiml's, which, he understands, belongs to a man now in Canada. I tell him that George Eisenschiml is an old friend of mine and that only a few weeks previously his solicitor in Montreal sent me power of attorney in respect of the factory at Asch. I have not got it on me, but Lund accepts my word and with my approval issues the permit to start the factory. He likes talking to me. Says he is responsible for the whole of the urban and rural district of Asch, and although the inhabitants all speak German it is technically Allied territory and the non-fraternisation rules do not apply, which makes life much more pleasant.

It is almost 5 p.m. when I depart. To judge by the many Red Cross signs, Bad Elster has become a hospital town. We pass through Adorf, make our way round the destroyed bridges, reach the autobahn and carry on at full speed as far as Hartenstein, where a US lorry is parked across the road and two American soldiers stop us. Somewhere beyond are the Russians. When the Americans see that I am a British officer they say I am at liberty to proceed but want me to leave my name. 'Not that it helps much if you disappear, sir.' One does not always have trouble with the Russians, they say. Frequently they hug and kiss Allied officers, take them to Chemnitz to dine and wine them for a couple of days and then let them go, but one cannot rely on it. Some do not come back. Interesting though it would be to meet the Muscovites, I follow the Americans' advice, backtrack to Zwickau and take the side road, to arrive at the Central Hotel at Limbach just in time for supper in a different world. I have been whistling all the way from Asch, so happy to have found Mother and Ingo.

The transgression into Czechoslovak territory and my first visit to the old family home at the end of the war provide a fitting end to this book, but to relate the whole of my saga I shall have to write another volume as large as the present, which will take time. Meanwhile let me draw a thumbnail sketch of what is to come.

92 To begin with we had two primary gliders. They had no cockpit or fuselage. The single seat—it looked like a frying pan—stuck out in front and made the pupil feel he was sitting in mid-air. On our instructor's courses we were towed up in these contraptions to heights of 400 ft, then we released the steel cable and flew figures-of-eight

93 Rolf resigned from the gliding school and joined ATA to ferry fighters and other military aircraft

94 The author, wearing parachute, about to fly the Minimoa, a requisitioned German high-efficiency sailplane

95 We examine the Hotel Vier Jahreszeiten at Wiesbaden

96 Lt-Col. E. W. Pasold, fir British officer to cross t Czechoslovak border in M 1945

97 Women and children moving west, away from the advancing Russians

98 The author with Mother (right) and Aunt Marie Geipel at the front door of the family home in Fleissen

99 Also in the Egerland the Americans were taking over civilian control from the defeated Germans, pending the arrival of Czech administrators

100 Rolf gets ready to take off for Prague in the Proctor V

101 Negotiations with officials of the nationalised Czechoslovak textile industry. Left to right from nearest the camera: Knap (knitting), Čap (knitting), Rolf (Adolf Pasold & Sohn), Dostal (production), Stregl (finance), Lustina (flax), Müller (wool); standing: Ing. Havliček (secretary general), Hubicka (finance)

102 Hledin, Rolf and the author in Wenceslas Square, Prague, discussing the next move

103 Members of the British 'mission' at the Ministry of Industry at Prague. Left to right, top: Ing Havlíček (secretary general of the nationalised textile industry), (unknown), MacMahon (BoT), Ing Havelka; middle row: Horace Moulden (president of the British Hosiery Workers' Union) Ing. Adamek (head of the nationalised textile industry), the author, Leckie (Foreign Office); nearest camera, Ord-Johnstone (BoT)

104 Mission to the USA. Tommy Allen nearest the camera, the author second from right

105 Comparing notes with eighty-eight-year-old Josef Kohl, a man with an incredible memory for detail who had been foreman knitter at Pasold's factory at Fleissen from 1884 to 1895. Left to right: the author, Josef Kohl, H. Amarotico

106 The factory at Langley could not be neglected, despite outside activities. The author using his Meccano set to develop a new drying machine

107 High-speed circular machines knitting fabric for Ladybird garments

108 Fabric made from synthetic yarns being heat-set in a stenter

109 Team of sewing machinists. The Ladybird range consisted of 1,700 different items—styles colours, sizes

We made great strides in the thirty years following the war. With a dozen factories in England, Scotland, Ulster and Canada, the Pasolds group of companies increased its labour force from 300 to 5,000

10 There were eighteen bays like this in our new warehouse at Langley

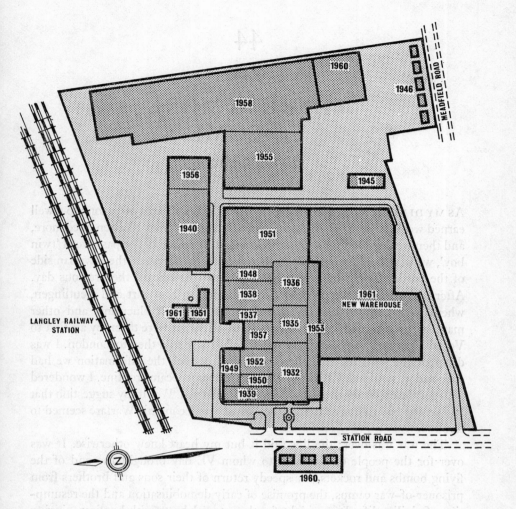

The new warehouse (*facing, upper*) was built in 1961. It had an uninterrupted roof span of 180 ft. Designed for pallet operation and mechanical handling of merchandise, it enabled us to deal with over 20 million Ladybird garments a year

The aerial photograph opposite (*lower*) shows the Langley factory in 1962, with new housing estates behind it. Beyond is the remainder of the aerodrome where Hawker Hurricanes were built during the war. The site plan *above* shows the stages of development from 1932 to 1962

44

THERE IS MORE
TO COME
1945-68

AS MY DIARY records, I led the team from the textile area of Saxony to a well earned weekend's rest at Asch, which enabled me to visit Fleissen once more, and then we departed for southern Germany. Ignorant of the pass-word 'twin boy', we were held up by US patrols searching the forest on the Bavarian side of the border for SS-men who had killed two Americans the previous day. After a short delay we proceeded via Munich to Stuttgart and Reutlingen, where we continued our investigations. Laden with blueprints and other material, we returned to Wiesbaden, from where we were taken by air first to Versailles to make a preliminary report to SHAEF and then to London. I was disappointed with the amateurish manner in which the information we had collected was utilised. CIOS missions to Germany became routine. I wondered who got the credit for them and what they achieved. Was it my suggestion that had set the ball rolling? Hunt of the Ministry of Economic Warfare seemed to think so.

The war was over; the lips said it but my heart knew otherwise. It was over for the people of England, to whom VE day brought the end of the flying bombs and rockets, the speedy return of their sons and brothers from prisoner-of-war camps, the promise of early demobilisation and the resumption of civilian life. It was right for them to celebrate with bonfires, singing and dancing. But I thought of the frightened refugees I had seen on the Continent, of the persecutions of helpless millions, most of whom were innocent, and of hatred and revenge. Their world had been destroyed. What kind of future did the smouldering ruins hold for them? There would be no peace in central and eastern Europe, no end to the suffering of the populations of Germany, Czechoslovakia, Poland, Austria and Hungary, of the Baltic States and the Balkans.

To abandon to the Russians half of Germany, which inevitably meant the countries east of it as well, was not only inhuman, it seemed almost incredibly shortsighted. Did the West not realise that Communism was an enemy that would be even harder to defeat than National Socialism? The pro-Russian propaganda during the war had been overdone. I was afraid that the Communists and their dupes were now firmly entrenched in the United Kingdom too. In the guise of socialists they would slowly but thoroughly undermine its institutions and sap its strength, meanwhile biding their time until the Soviets had consolidated their grip on the Continent. We wondered whether the British people would wake up to the danger before it was too late. Rolf's and my immediate concern was about Czechoslovakia. The Czechs were revolutionaries, but they were not Communists. Would the Kremlin allow them to reconstruct their pre-war republic? We had heard that Beneš wanted to expel all German-speaking inhabitants but did not believe that three million people could be expelled, nor that the country could afford to lose such a large proportion of its skilled industrial population. Czech- and German-speaking Bohemians had lived, worked, quarrelled, fought and prospered together for centuries. They needed each other. There would be bloody reprisals for 1938, to be sure, but we hoped that after an initial wave of violence, revenge and readjustment a new, tranquil Czechoslovakia would emerge. We were too optimistic: the wish was father to the thought; events proved us wrong. But if we misjudged the future of Czechoslovakia we were even more wrong in our assessment of the prospects for the western part of Germany. To rebuild its cities would take a lifetime, we thought, and the truncated country would be condemned to a twilight existence for a century. We did not foresee its spectacular rise. Who would have believed that within a mere thirty years western Germany would become the richest and economically most successful State in Europe?

Within a few days of my return from the Continent Rolf flew a plane with medical supplies to Pilsen, requisitioned a jeep there and drove to Fleissen. Mother was overjoyed to embrace her second son so soon after she had embraced her eldest. He returned to Langley with the good news that the Americans still controlled the strip of Bohemian territory along the Bavarian border extending from Pilsen to Asch. There would be no large-scale disorder or atrocities as long as they were there. In a reasonably easy frame of mind I now followed Tommy Allen to the USA to attend trade conferences and visit knitting mills and textile machine makers in Philadelphia and New York. It was my intention to undertake another journey to Czechoslovakia at an early date to ensure, as far as was possible, the safety of Mother and the rest of the family, and to negotiate with the authorities in Prague for the return to us of the firm of Adolf Pasold & Sohn, which had been taken over by the State. But then the passport office in London refused to let me go. Heaven knew why. Had I blotted my copybook? I demanded an explanation, but met with stony faces or closed doors. Were enquiries being made about me while the weeks passed and I sat waiting? The news from Czechoslovakia was getting more and more disturbing. I complained to Mr Watkinson. He succeeded in arranging an interview for me with a 'Mr Smith', a fierce-looking, elderly man with bushy eyebrows and moustache who cross-examined me in the presence of a Mr Young and a Major Day in room 179 at the BoT. The interrogation gave me no clue to what he was trying to find out, and I could only imagine that some over-zealous Secret Service agent had made fools of MI5. My inquisitor seemed satisfied with the answers I gave him and relaxed. I received no apology but, more important, the travel restrictions were withdrawn, and a few days later I was on my way.

The situation I found in Czechoslovakia was confusing. At Stalin's insistence the country had been 'liberated' by the Russians, which had halted the advance of the Americans in the west and south-west. So now the Red Army was in Prague, hailed by the mass of the Czech-speaking population as saviours and friends, there to assist the national liberation forces and the militia, a proud description of the medley of Czech soldiers who had fought with the Allies, civilian patriots, members of underground organisations, freed prisoners, Communists, bankrupts, opportunists and thugs. They dominated town and country, controlled the factories, terrorised the German-speaking population of the border regions and sat in the Ministries vying with each other for power. Beneš and Masaryk looked west, the Communists looked towards Moscow.

The prime concern of the newly created or self-appointed officials was to strengthen their own precariously held positions. Negotiating with them for the return of Adolf Pasold a Syn, as it was now called, seemed an almost hopeless undertaking. We tried two quite separate approaches. One was through Dr Fousek, the best lawyer in Prague, a man of the highest integrity and a personal friend of Dr Ripka, the Minister of Foreign Trade. The other was bluff on a colossal scale, possible only in the chaotic conditions of revolution. We could not fool everyone, there were some nasty encounters with the Communist-dominated security police, but by and large we succeeded. My visit to Fleissen as lieutenant colonel and Rolf's as an officer of ATA had been reported, and our shiny new four-seater Proctor V was the first private aircraft to land in Czechoslovakia after the war—reason enough to treat us with circumspection. Veiled hints to the Czech press about being key figures in huge raw material deals shortly to be discussed in secret between the two governments—sheer fabrication, of course—surrounded us with an air of mystery and earned us headlines. We needed both to gain access to various Ministries at a high enough level. I can do no more here than touch upon one or two among several astounding episodes. They are amusing in retrospect but I do not care to imagine what might have happened to us had they gone wrong. Would-be mandarins at the Ministry of Trade in Prague, craving international contacts and rcognition, pleaded with me to prevail upon the British government to send an official trade delegation to Czechoslovakia. A tall order! All I could do was to organise a bogus one. The members of it were genuine British civil servants, friends of mine to whom the BoT magnanimously granted a holiday for this purpose. A Czechoslovak aircraft collected us from Croydon, we were flown to Prague, Zlin and the Tatra mountains, dined for a week to the tunes of gipsy bands, and had a wonderful time at the Czechoslovak government's expense, while John Taylor, the *chargé d'affaires* at the British embassy on the Hradčin, with whom I had established friendly relations, looked on with amusement. And before the delegation returned to England we actually had a noncommittal talk about cotton at the Ministry of Trade. When I had thus proved my *bona fides* to Prague's entire satisfaction, the Czechs offered me the job of reorganising the republic's disrupted knitting industry. The monthly fee was to be 10,000 kronen, payable in sterling. Tempting though the offer sounded, I declined it. I had neither the time nor the inclination to get involved in Czechoslovak politics and become a target for the Communists. Next the would-be mandarins at the Ministry of Trade begged me to procure an invitation from the British government for them to come to London. This was even more difficult to arrange. We had to forego the niceties of an official gesture, but the truly Gilbertian situation tickled Mr Watkinson's sense of humour. He loaned me his impressive office at the BoT while he was away for a day so that I could receive the Czech delegation in style, and arranged lunch for the party at Simpson's in the Strand at the British government's expense. A visit to Wolsey's factory at Leicester and a couple of late nights in the West End completed the comedy. Needless to say, neither of the delegations did any real work.

Our efforts, combined with those of Dr Fousek, our lawyer, were rewarded. Control of Adolf Pasold a Syn was restored to Rolf and me. Reinstated in our private offices, we resumed, at least nominally, the management of our factories at Fleissen and Leibitschgrund, now referred to as Plesná and Libocký Důl. Alternating between England and Czechoslovakia as we had done before the war, we directed the enterprise commercially and technically, aided by a Czech works manager named Suchy, an anti-Communist released from jail for this purpose and cunningly given the chance of working his way back to favour by keeping a wary eye on us. Labour relations were entirely his responsibility, as were all financial matters. Rolf and I were not empowered to sign cheques, not even for drawing money to pay wages, far less to transfer any of our funds to Britain.

The Czechs kept up the contacts I had made for them in London and followed their first visit with a second and a third. Their leader—his name does not matter—had been a well known Bohemian industrialist whose expertise was valuable to the Czech government. He was a man of integrity. I liked him, and we became friends. In January 1948 he telephoned from the Ritz Hotel. I met him there and invited him out to dinner, but he explained that he could not go out. The Communist watchdog who always accompanied the delegation had allowed him to see me only on condition that he did not leave the hotel and, as a precaution, had taken away his passport and money. I was shocked. So the long arm of the Communists in Central Europe could hold a man prisoner in the middle of London! 'Is it safe for you to return to Prague? Shall we try to find you a job in England?' He shook his head, 'I must go back. My country needs me, my heart, my wife and my children are there.' We dined at the Ritz. 'What do you think will happen?' he asked. On a sudden premonition I replied, 'Czechoslovakia will probably close her frontiers.' It was the last time I saw him. Shortly afterwards the Soviet-backed Czech Communist minority, supported by the socialists, staged its *coup d'état*. Masaryk died by jumping or being thrown from his bathroom window, Czech patriots like Dr Fousek and his friend Dr Ripka, the Minister of Foreign Trade, fled the country to save their lives, Beneš was forced to resign, Gottwald became Premier, and our properties were confiscated. It was the end of a once proud and thriving family firm built by the ingenuity, sweat and thrift of generations.

Long before the Communist *coup* some three million Sudetenlanders were expelled from their homes in Bohemia and Moravia where they and their forefathers had lived for five hundred years. The memory of the long, silent columns of dejected people carrying their miserable bundles or pushing handcarts still haunts me. They were assembled at suitable railway stations and from there taken in cattle trucks across the border. Fifty kilos of bedding, clothes, kitchen utensils and food was all they were allowed to take with them. Their valuables, money, furniture, houses, factories and workshops, farms, cattle and other possessions had to be left behind for the Czech, Slovak and sometimes gipsy settlers who took over. If there is some higher justice in this world the Czech nation is experiencing it now. Unfortunately, and as always, the many innocent have to suffer with the guilty.

While juggling with Ministries in Prague, provincial officials at Eger (now Cheb), our factories at Plesná and Libocký Důl, local anti-Fascist and Communist committees, we were searching day and night for ways of getting Mother, Ingo and Willie with their young families and Udo safely out of Czechoslovakia and of providing them with the opportunity of making a fresh start somewhere else. The one was as difficult as the other, for feelings ran high and only too often reason was worsted by emotion. We conferred with Czech, British, Commonwealth, Swiss and Lichtenstein authorities, saw

South and Central American embassy officials, consulted bankers and international lawyers, but most of our schemes came to naught because the Bank of England's stringent foreign exchange regulations made it impossible for us to provide the required finance. The outcome of all these negotiations was that I flew Mother to England, where she made a new home for herself, happy to be with Rolf and me after so many years of separation, Ingo came to Langley for some time and then moved with his family to South Africa to establish a thriving distribution centre for Ladybird goods, and Willie, sponsored by the Colonial Office in London, was to set up a spinning mill for the Pasold organisation in the West Indies. But fate struck a cruel blow. He and Silvia, our sister, together with their two children, lost their lives when the *Star Tiger* disappeared on its flight from the Azores to Bermuda. The last to join us was Udo. After an adventurous last-minute escape across the Czechoslovak border to the Russian-occupied part of Germany, he eventually came via Berlin to London. We then sent him to Jamaica to promote the sale of our merchandise there. As a sideline he organised with characteristic drive and to the delight of the local authorities the production of straw braid, which we sold to the hat makers at Luton. It promised to become a lucrative business, and provided employment for several hundred people, but when Britain lifted her import restrictions on straw goods from Italy, Jamaican braid was no longer competitive. In 1950 Udo came to Langley, first as works manager and then to join Rolf and me on the board.

We had removed the traces of wartime camouflage and austerity from the factory. The fountain was playing again, the flower beds were a blaze of colour, the sports field was trimmed and our football and cricket teams were doing well. We were back to shift working, our people were earning good money, bicycles were beginning to give way to motor-cycles and even to small second-hand cars. Trade union attempts to gain a foothold, which we neither encouraged nor obstructed, met with little response. Our employees were almost all local people who had come to us straight from school and whom we had trained in our ways. Perhaps they were not as versatile as workers in the traditional hosiery centres, but on average they achieved a better performance. We could not have wished for a keener, more co-operative labour force. Not that we still remembered everyone's christian name, there were too many of us now, but I can say with all sincerity that we were a happy family. In particular Rolf's contact with the shop floor remained very close. 'It's in the factory where we make the money,' he said. 'In the office we only spend it.' Excellent labour relations made an important contribution to the success of the firm at all times.

After years of study and deliberation the Foreign Compensation Commission in London informed Rolf and me that the value of our nationalised

Czechoslovak possessions had been assessed at £588,706, and in due course we received a dividend of 9 per cent, or £53,000 to be exact, in total settlement of our claim. We gave some of the money to Ingo and Udo and invested the bulk of it in new machinery. After the final break with Czechoslovakia we concentrated our efforts on Langley, with three main objectives in mind: to make Ladybird the leading name in children's wear, to increase exports and to plough our profits back into the business in the form of new plant and better manufacturing methods. Each of these activities was equally important; each has to be looked at separately.

We no longer sold to wholesalers. Except for the merchandise we made for Marks & Spencer, which bore the 'St Michael' label, and that for Woolworth's, which was nameless, all our garments were now tabbed 'Ladybird' and went to several thousand children's wear shops and children's wear departments of large stores. We divided Britain into seventeen territories, and Pat Murphy, our bustling sales manager, appointed agents in each of them, sometimes making several changes before he was satisfied that he had the right man. They maintained their own offices, showrooms and personnel, and we paid them 5 per cent commission. Twice a year they attended our sales conferences to see and comment on the styles and colour combinations of the new season's range of Ladybird garments before they proceeded on their sales tours. We laid down the prices at which our products were sold in the shops, for we would not let the public be overcharged, nor allow retailers to undercut each other and make the trade in Ladybird clothes unremunerative. Strict resale price maintenance meant law and order as far as we were concerned and guaranteed the same good value to Mrs Jones wherever she bought her merchandise. She did not have to waste her time 'shopping around'. Her interest was our first consideration, for it was the goodwill of a million Mrs Jones that kept us in business, and more than once we stopped supplying slick traders who attempted to get publicity for themselves by using our well known garments as loss leaders, thus undermining the public's confidence in our prices.

It was not by accident that we had a near monopoly in many of the things we manufactured. We concentrated on developing lines other firms were not equipped to make. There were, for example, our dressing gowns, which our competitors did not even attempt to imitate. They still did not know how to make the ripple cloth and were not trying to find out. We were the first to realise the great potential of T shirts, had special narrow-diameter interlock machines built so that we could make all sizes, down to the smallest, without side seams, and began to mass-produce them on conveyor belts for export to Canada when other manufacturers and most British buyers still laughed at them. Swan & Edgar's of Piccadilly Circus, who were usually ahead in fashion, thought so little of the new garment that we had to tempt them with an initial twenty dozen on a 'sale or return' basis. When other firms began to manufacture T shirts some two years later, they found it hard to compete with us, for ours were not only without seams, they also had better neckbands, which we cut on an ingenious spiral cutting machine invented by Ingo. We produced a superior article at a lower price.

Bright yellow T shirts became so popular that every street scene was enlivened by them. But they all looked the same. If only we could print designs on them, I thought. Machines for printing on tubular knitted fabric did not exist. Ignorant of the technical pitfalls of roller printing, I designed one. None of the established printing machine makers in Britain, America or Germany was prepared to build it for me. It would not work, they said, and they had their reputation to consider. Then I found an engineering firm in France who took it on—at my responsibility! To everyone's surprise my machine functioned perfectly, printing multi-coloured pictures of cowboys, animals, trains and space ships in accurate register on both sides of the stretchy tubular fabric in a single passage. I was thrilled, and so were our customers, the children. Our printed T shirts caused a sensation.

Two other garments which we pioneered, a V-neck sweater and a pair of pyjamas, both made from fleecy fabric, sold in enormous quantities. At first we made them in plain colours and later also supplied them printed. There was no one in Britain who knew as much about fleecy stockinette fabric as we did. Our condenser spinning plant, the large battery of high-speed knitting machines built for the job and our extra-large dye vats enabled us to produce it so efficiently that we had no rivals. My small French roller printing plant could not cope with demand. We had a much larger one constructed, the largest and most impressive piece of machinery in the whole factory, which quadrupled our printing capacity, and it too was fully employed. Before long, printed Ladybird clothes could be seen in shop windows everywhere.

We spent a good deal of money advertising our garments and the little red beetle in women's magazines, but modern boys and girls no longer left the choice of their clothes to mother, and when I heard that Hulton's were about to publish a new comic called *Swift* with the impressive weekly circulation of 400,000 copies I had the idea of featuring our products in it. I bought the back page and commissioned the Hulton organisation to fill it with an adventure serial in which Bill and Brenda, our hero and heroine, always triumphed because of some Ladybird garments they were wearing. The idea was good, but Hulton's thriller serial was dreadful. In desperation I wrote some Ladybird adventure stories myself. They took on, and henceforth it became one of my tasks, for an unbroken period of ten long years, to think up a fresh plot every week to fill the page. 'The Secret Sign of the Scarlet Ladybird' became a favourite with the young and invariably ranked first, second or third in the popularity surveys. I received hundreds of letters from eight- and ten-year-old enthusiasts and replied to every one of them. My adventure serial in *Swift* and a second one in *TV Comic* proved our most effective form of publicity. Our stories turned mere children's garments into treasured possessions and saved mother's purse, for if she bought little Johnny a Ladybird T shirt she did not need to buy him a toy.

Langley was a beehive of activity. Mellor Bromley supplied a new interlock plant, a battery of knitting machines came from Switzerland, another from France, a third from America, and more spinning machines were installed. We built a large office block and a warehouse, enlarged the boiler plant, bought a diesel engine and generator as a precaution against power cuts and from 1950 onwards extended the production area of the factory every year. My foresight in preparing a detailed expansion programme, lodging it with the BoT and having it approved well in advance, now paid dividends. Without this commitment on the part of the authorities our application for building licences would not have been granted. Men and materials were needed to repair bomb damage, and next in priority came the construction of factories in 'development' or 'special' areas, where jobs had to be provided for the unemployed. Slough and Langley, by contrast, were short of labour and building licences were issued only in very special circumstances—such as ours! Our daily output rose to 2,000 dozens of underwear, dressing gowns, pyjamas and T shirts, and we exported our goods all over the world. The figures speak for themselves.

	Factory area (sq. ft)	No. of employees	Annual sales (£)	Exports (£)
1945	100,500	266	194,484	16,400
1946	100,500	236	248,796	87,500
1947	100,500	259	348,203	54,191
1948	105,500	289	452,303	133,293
1949	114,500	368	618,410	139,250
1950	114,500	394	679,161	210,028
1951	149,500	460	888,822	240,624
1952	158,000	637	922,317	306,957
1953	177,000	663	1,132,000	345,000

Now to exports. We made good use of our aeroplane to tour Europe with our range of Ladybird garments but of course took airliners for visits to America, the West Indies and Africa. We engaged commission agents in all the important overseas markets, and *The Ambassador*, Britain's leading export journal for textiles, carried a full-page Ladybird advertisement every

month. There would have been no need for us to go in search of overseas
business at all. We could hardly satisfy home demand and in spite of our
rapidly growing output sometimes had to ration supplies. But Britain needed
foreign exchange to pay for her imports, and we considered it our duty to help
earn it. Many other firms thought likewise, just as many did not. Politicians
made fine speeches and patriotic appeals instead of providing even a small
carrot for exporters. Given an incentive, men will shift mountains. Britain
produced a great variety of goods which other countries wanted, but many
manufacturers, especially if they had a sufficiently large and profitable home
market, would not make the effort needed to develop exports. Why make
merchandise to overseas specifications, cope with voluminous paper work
and with foreign languages, run the risk of ever fluctuating exchange rates
and continually search for fresh markets as revolutions and wars in so many
parts of the world, quarrelling politicians and trade reprisals closed the old, if

From *The Sun*, by courtesy of Syndication International Ltd

there were no adequate rewards? There would have been no need for subsidies or tax concessions. Other incentives which did not contravene the
provisions of GATT could have been used, and I suggested a number of
them not only to the FBI and the civil servants at the BoT but also in interviews with Harold Wilson, Sir Stafford Cripps, Douglas Jay and Michael
Stewart. Being socialists, they had a political axe to grind and disapproved of
incentives on principle. Besides, each of them foresaw just round the corner a
dramatic revival of British exports resulting in a comfortable surplus of
foreign exchange which, as we know to our cost, never materialised. But to my
great disappointment even Sir Keith Joseph, when he was the Minister in

charge, failed to see the need of a carrot for the donkey and after half an hour's discussion dismissed me with the words 'We must agree to disagree.'

Our profits would have been £40,000 higher had we ceased to export and sold our total output in the home market, as we could have done with ease, and I said so more than once in our annual reports. Many other manufacturers found themselves in a similar position, and I pleaded with the authorities for a commonsense export policy towards the whole of British industry, of course, and not for special favours for Pasolds Ltd. Disenchanted as we were, we pushed sales overseas for all we were worth, and so did Ron Wyatt, our irrepressible export manager. The value of our foreign exchange earnings rose from year to year and by the mid-1960s exceeded £1 million per annum, a great deal of money in those days. Thousands of other medium-sized and small concerns could have done equally well in proportion had they tried hard enough. If so many of them did not it was the fault of the government, the bureaucrats, the socialist climate of jealousy and resentment that begrudged private enterprise a fair reward for extra achievement. Continental countries, by contrast, especially Germany, which had lost the war and been cut in half, met their industrialists with more realism, helped exporters and lifted their foreign exchange restrictions one by one while Britain kept enterprise shackled by controls. Had the United Kingdom intelligently activated her sleeping export potential I believe she could have paid for her imports out of her own earnings instead of getting ever deeper into debt.

Behind the success of Ladybird children's wear stood our modern factory. Our plant was unique. The fact that we reclaimed our waste, spun our own condenser yarn, knitted, dyed, printed and finished the fabric and made the garments, all under one roof, as it were, put us a long way ahead of our competitors. We also toiled harder, rated efficiency higher and used more modern techniques than they did. This may sound presumptuous, but judging by my experience with the NHMF, the FBI and the BoT I feel it is true. We were continually improving the quality of our goods and reducing the cost of production by better planning and more automation. This benefited the consumer, stimulated demand and increased our profits, which we ploughed back into newer and better machines. And if the engineering industry could not provide the plant we wanted we built it ourselves in our well equipped engineering shop, or developed it jointly with some friendly machine builder. The Pegg-Pasold dryer, which gave splendid results, was an example of this collaboration. But not all our mechanical contrivances worked. I constructed many models with my adapted Meccano set, experimented with mock-ups in the factory and applied for patents which afterwards proved useless. However, one triumph made up for ten failures.

Technical supremacy is ephemeral. Rolf and I searched the world for new machines and manufacturing techniques which would keep us ahead of competitors. We married parts of American machines to German ones, used plant for purposes different from those for which it was designed, adopted practices we saw in non-textile factories and in one instance converted agricultural implements to cut and spin nylon staple, while Udo took a special interest in the latest methods of knitting and heat setting synthetic fabrics. All this required imagination, experience and a thorough understanding of our special requirements. We trusted our judgement and were prepared to take calculated risks, but this was not enough when it came to foreign plant. To import it one needed an import licence, and before this was granted one had to convince some male or female bureaucrat, or a whole committee of them, that no equivalent machinery could be supplied by British makers. It was their job to prevent, as far as was possible, the importation of plant from abroad, to save foreign exchange. Armed with illustrated leaflets, they would tell us that machines made at Leicester, Manchester or Leeds would serve our purpose equally well. But textile and allied machinery embraces an enormous field, and no team of experts, however learned, can have more than a very superficial understanding of them all. We therefore inevitably won our case, if not without much futile controversy, frustration and delay, although we did not always disclose how we actually hoped to use the machinery in question. It was our unorthodox plant that enabled us to make unusual merchandise which we then supplied to eighty different markets, including Hong Kong. The best export incentive the government could have given us would have been to trust us with the purchase of foreign machines up to a value of, say, 10 per cent, or even 5 per cent, of the foreign currency we earned, without subjecting us to that farcical, time-wasting, humiliating licensing procedure.

It was right, of course, that every effort should be made to bring exports and imports into balance, although I would have preferred to see it done by encouraging the one instead of curtailing the other. No doubt restraint was still necessary, but the sooner the shackles could be removed from private enterprise the sooner businessmen could apply their ingenuity and dynamism towards building a prosperous Britain, something that could not be done by civil servants with directions and controls. Unfortunately many of the controls seemed to be kept on for other than good economic reasons. The civil servants did not want to lose their jobs and the socialists used controls to bring about an egalitarian society, both understandable if somewhat dishonest motives, but used at the cost of a nation's competitiveness in a competitive world they were bad. Much as we wanted to ignore politics, it would have been reckless to make plans without taking the likely effect of socialism on our activities into account. We were entrepreneurs, pioneers, individualists, and we realised that the tide was not flowing in our direction. Not that this thought was permanently in our mind—we were far too busy fighting our daily business battles—but it inevitably had a bearing on many of our decisions.

Politicians, trade union leaders and civil servants paid lip service to modernisation of industry and blamed management for lack of enterprise and insufficient capital investment, but what practical encouragement did they provide? Only too often the introduction of more efficient methods or labour-saving machinery met with fierce opposition from the unions and obstruction by the authorities. Private business aircraft, for instance, had become a useful tool of trade for our firm, with branch factories and sub-contractors spread out all over the country, but to obtain permission to land on one of the many abandoned and deserted wartime aerodromes, if one got it at all, often took longer than the journey by road or rail. A fire tender had to stand by, a condition that could rarely be met, and if the firemen went home at 5 p.m. one was no longer allowed to take off. I had dozens of interviews with the BoT and other Ministries, pleading for assistance in the interests of business efficiency, offering insurance policies and letters of indemnity, without success. Before the war the de Havilland Moth must have been one of the world's most popular light aeroplanes, and with a little foresight Britain might have captured the market, but we gave it away to the Americans. Pasolds' first five planes were British; the last four came from USA.

The shift to the left was one of the reasons why we were again looking for a foothold overseas, somewhere a long way from the powder keg of Europe, preferably in the western hemisphere. We did not believe that anything as drastic as the *coup* we had witnessed in Czechoslovakia could happen in England, but what if the Russians should gain control over the whole of the Continent? Would Britain hold out against the Communists as steadfastly and successfully as she had done against the Nazis? We should have liked nothing better than to revive our pre-war project of building a factory in Canada, where our sales were growing rapidly, but the Bank of England would not make the necessary dollars available, notwithstanding the large amounts of foreign exchange we were earning for the United Kingdom with our exports. Capital transfers were permitted only within the sterling area, and Canada was outside it. This was the reason why we had sent Ingo to the Union of South Africa, our second choice. Capital transfers from Britain to the Union presented no problem, our trade there was prospering, and so we bought a large site near Cape Town to build a factory on it. But when Malan became Prime Minister and *apartheid* was introduced we foresaw trouble coming and changed our plans. It would be safer, we thought, to continue supplying our customers in the Union from Langley.

Ingo liked South Africa, and it was not without regret that, at Rolf's and my counsel, he moved to Canada to establish a sales office and a warehouse for Ladybird merchandise at Toronto. They had to be on a modest scale, no larger than we were able to finance from hand to mouth with extended credits from Langley, but it was a beginning. While he was getting to know the Dominion, travelling twice a year all the way from the maritime provinces to British Columbia in search of customers, we made application after applicacation to the Bank of England, until, in 1952, when Ingo was well on the way towards becoming a Canadian, we were at long last given permission to retain some of our dollar earnings for the purpose of building a 10,000 sq. ft factory. Labour was more suitable in the province of Quebec than in Ontario, and so we located our plant at Dorion, an ideally situated small town just west of Montreal. Then came a nasty surprise. Used to dealings with local authorities in Britain, we assumed that undertakings given by their Canadian counterparts were equally binding, and we could therefore hardly believe it when Dorion-Vaudreuil refused to honour a signed agreement in which the township had undertaken to construct a water supply line for us. It had been given as an inducement to locate our plant there. The factory was half finished when the row blew up. We threatened to sue, only to be informed that the town council would simply resign and the new council was not liable for the commitments of the old. We felt we had been swindled. Ingo and I saw the provincial government at Quebec City and complained to the Minister, a charming man who took us to an ice hockey match but did not keep his promise to get us the water. Some politician, mistaking us for employees of our firm, tried to silence us with $2,000 instead. It seemed we had a lot to learn, and Ingo learned quickly. Being an engineer, he tunnelled under the highway and, without telling anyone, fitted a booster pump to the town's water main to obtain the extra water he needed. He invariably found some ingenious yet simple solution. He also got on well with his French Canadian workpeople. They were Catholics, of course, and whenever there was some problem in the factory he asked the priest instead of the union representative to help him sort it out.

Canada, as we knew from the start, was not a country in which a knitting mill could make profits easily. In spite of anti-dumping legislation the industrial giants south of the border were in the habit of unloading their surplus merchandise there at much lower prices than they sold it at home, Japan and Hong Kong flooded the market with cheap goods, and it was often impossible for Canadian manufacturers to compete. Many went out of business, and at times the country had as many as 700,000 unemployed. Had profitability been our first consideration we would have located our plant in the south of the USA, but we still believed in the Empire, in the parts that were left of it, and Canada was a British Dominion! Ingo's task was a difficult one, but after some initial losses Pasolds (Canada) Ltd did begin to make profits. The factory extensions brought the floor area to 80,000 sq. ft, during the first ten years' operation the annual sales climbed to $2 million, the net earnings to beyond a quarter of a million, and Ingo remitted a total of almost $3 million to Langley, to be handed over to the Bank of England.

Canada suited him. It was a young country with a great future. The landscape of Quebec, the climate and the people reminded him of central Europe. He built himself a beautiful house on the shore of the Lake of the Two Mountains, a few minutes' drive from the factory, and in summer spent his weekends sailing. An old glider pilot, he knew about winds and clouds, won most of the races and became commodore of the yacht club. In winter he skied in the nearby Laurentians or amused himself traversing the huge, frozen lake in a propeller-driven snowplane of his own construction which was powered by an old aero-engine. Once or twice a year he came to Langley for policy discussions and, sometimes almost in passing, made improvements to our plant. I wanted him to stay. Our British enterprise was ten times larger and was growing much faster than the factory at Dorion, the direction of which, I argued, should be delegated to someone else. I saw great scope for our engineering subsidiary at Langley if Ingo were to take over its management and develop new machines not only for the Pasold organisation but also for sale to the textile industry of the world. But he was not to be tempted. Why did I want to keep on expanding our enterprise? Would we be happier, he asked, if it employed four thousand workers instead of two thousand? Two thirds of the firm's earnings went in taxes, most of the remaining third was spent on new machines and buildings; the amount we took out for our personal use was such a small proportion of the whole that it did not count. Would we take more, live better, if the profits rose from half a million pounds to a million? Would I move out of the flat in the factory and buy myself a house? Of course not! He called me a compulsive expansionist and a slave driver, and at times it suited Rolf to agree with him, but only at times. On the whole the three of us got on well together, although in many ways our temperaments were very different. We pulled the same rope, but Ingo preferred to be his own master at Dorion instead of the junior partner of his two elder brothers at Langley.

It was not a higher living standard for ourselves, an easier life, more comfort, shorter working hours or personal prestige we were striving for, but to build the best manufacturing organisation of its kind in Britain, a model of efficiency, and to make a better product than any of our rivals, wherever they might be. Private enterprise was on trial, and it was for people like us to prove its superiority. We were in the race to win. What Henry Ford had done with cars and Thomas Bata with shoes we would do with children's clothes. Technology, automation and mass marketing demanded larger industrial units. We had to expand if Ladybird was to conquer the world. We had to make profits to be able to expand, and if my photograph appeared in the press now and again it was not because I sought publicity for myself but because I knew that a face had more popular appeal than a faceless, impersonal organisation.

When we had covered most of our eighteen-acre site and exhausted the supply of labour in the Langley area we established, not without misgivings, branch factories in other parts of the country, on the south coast, in the Midlands, in Lancashire, Scotland and Ulster, took over existing firms, bought participations and engaged sub-contractors. Ladybird dominated the British children's wear market, our exports reached new records, the number of our employees exceeded four thousand, and profits went over the million mark. And, as Ingo had predicted, our way of life remained the same; we worked even harder and the flat in the factory continued to be my home.

Good-natured and rare though Rolf's and Ingo's protests were, they made me think. It was true that I had been driving them all their lives, just as I drove myself. Being the eldest, it had been inevitable that I should take charge when Father died, but it was not my wish to lead for ever. I felt the time had come for me to step back to let them do the driving, and I said so. Not that I meant to work less, but I intended to play the role of chairman and gradually relinquished the powers of managing director to Rolf. His ideas, naturally, did not always run parallel with mine. I wished the company to concentrate on our type of merchandise, which we were so much better laid out to make than other manufacturers and to which Ladybird owed its success and fame. I wanted new machines and new processes to be developed which would make us even more efficient, our products even better and more unusual. We had done it in the past and, I was confident, could go on doing it in the future. I wanted Ladybird to be in a class of its own by virtue of our unique plant. Rolf, on the other hand, shifted the emphasis to fashion and included in the Ladybird range a growing proportion of garments which we were not equipped to make and which he had manufactured by outside contractors. We thus handled a large volume of goods of a type which was no longer exclusive to us but could, and was, also made and sold by large and small firms up and down the country who needed no other plant than some sewing machines and a designer with the necessary flair for style. Having a well established team of agents and our Ladybird brand, we could sell the new garments, but I felt unhappy about the drift from manufacturing to merchanting, and said so to Rolf in no uncertain manner. However, he felt equally strongly that his was the right policy, and since I was resolved to leave the driving to him I gave him his head and co-operated. While he coped with the complexities of fashion goods by more detailed programming, aided by a larger computer installation, I tried to match our methods of selling to the changing character of the business. I drafted stockists' schemes and charters, wrote articles for the trade press explaining the new policy and leased premises in Oxford Street for a large Ladybird shop which I persuaded the John Lewis Partnership to run. Thanks to Rolf's wide range of merchandise we were able to fill not only one but hundreds of shops with every kind of garment, from babies' crawlers to girls' frocks, from socks and underwear to bathing costumes and raincoats, and, together with the Partnership's management, I mapped out the plan of a nation-wide chain of children's wear shops to be established as a joint venture.

This needs an explanation. It was not one of our ambitions to become shopkeepers, but we had to see to it that our goods were everywhere freely available and well displayed. To ensure that the public could buy them everywhere at the same, namely the lowest possible, price we fixed the retailer's mark-up at 45 to 50 per cent, which gave him a fair return. Other manufacturers whose brands sold less readily than ours had to allow mark-ups of 55 to 60 per cent and more or made no attempt to control the retail prices of their goods at all. Efficient shopkeepers were content with our mark-ups, the inefficient or greedy continually asked for higher ones, but we refused to give way. As the years went by and ever more of the independent shops and stores were bought up by a handful of large retail organisations it became more difficult to refuse their demands for higher gross profit margins. To make matters worse, some of them began to develop their own trade marks at the expense of the manufacturers' brands. I foresaw a trade-mark war which threatened to be won by the retail distributors. The Ladybird brand was too well established to be in danger just yet, but it was the most valuable asset we owned, and we had to look to the future. If it were ever replaced by a distributor's mark we should lose our link with the public, its goodwill, and with it our independence.

Then, I believe from America, came stamp trading. I thought it was deplorable that such national waste should be permitted at a time when Britain was in economic difficulties, and said so to Mr Maudling, a former President of the BoT and then Chancellor of the Exchequer, when sitting next to him at a small dinner party at the House of Commons. He asked me to be patient: the government was preparing legislation. To my dismay it turned out to be the abolition of resale price maintenance (RPM), making it illegal for manufacturers to fix the resale prices of their products—a sweeping victory for the retail distributors that did nothing to discourage stamp trading but made it difficult for firms like ours to protect the consumer. Mrs Jones now had to waste her time 'shopping around' to discover what could be bought at the lowest price on any particular day and where. There are many sides to RPM but this is not the place to discuss them. Its abolition came as a shock to us and it made it much more difficult to maintain our orderly trading policy. If we did not want to become, slowly but surely, subservient to the distributors we had to establish a large chain of shops of our own or, still better, find some efficient retail organisation willing to do it with us. Hence the John Lewis Partnership project. I felt sorry when it did not materialise. The business principles of our two firms were very similar and we should have got on well together. However, the Partnership decided to concentrate on popularising its own 'Jonelle' trade mark and we had to look elsewhere.

I must now go back some years. Advised by our good friend Michael Richards, a promising young lawyer when we first met him in the late 1940s who had since become a successful merchant banker, we converted Pasolds Ltd in 1957 into a public company. Our output at that time was a million garments a month, we had 750 employees at Langley and 100 at Dorion, the floor areas of the two factories were 223,500 and 32,000 sq. ft respectively, and our profit record was confidence-inspiring. The 220,000 ordinary 5s shares which Michael's bank, Hart Son & Co., offered for sale at 10s 3d found a ready market. The Pasold family retained 90 per cent of the total of 2·2 million shares issued, and Michael joined the board of the company. My impish ideas and our frequently unorthodox approach to business matters appealed to his sense of humour, and it was due to his keen legal and financial brain that a number of our seemingly unlikely schemes succeeded. I shall have a good deal to say about him and our complicated, sometimes amusing transactions in my next volume.

The people who bought Pasolds shares, and those of our old employees who held on to the shares we presented to them in recognition of past services, did well, for an investment of £100 became worth £1,500 within the short span of only four years. More than half our shareholders were women, which was not surprising, since Ladybird children's wear had become a household name. Company reports were normally prepared by accountants to provide financial information for investors in the City. They made very dry reading for the average housewife and mother. I therefore designed reports which not only quoted the figures but showed our activities and results in the form of graphs, coloured photographs and whimsical Ladybird pictures with explanations in simple language. They became very popular, not only with our women shareholders but also, to my surprise, with the bowler-hatted gentlemen, the bankers and stockbrokers, and in 1964 earned us one of the two coveted '*Accountant*'s Awards' for which no fewer than 1,200 public companies competed. Our annual reports set a pattern which was followed but, though I say it myself, never quite matched by other companies.

A problem we had not been able to solve was that of management succession. In 1960 I was fifty-four, Rolf and Udo were forty-six, Ingo was forty-four, Ingo's son Peter was fifteen and Rolf's son Colin five years old. Given a long period of stable conditions and a much smaller and less complex enterprise than ours, the gap between the two generations might perhaps have been accepted, but to let the business face the coming economic, technological and political tempests without a strong team at the helm would mean courting disaster. We needed two or three able young men of between twenty-five and thirty-five on the board who should be at their best when we became 'elder statesmen'. Peter and Colin could then enter as junior directors, if they proved that they were made of the right stuff. This was the sequence we hoped for. We had, of course, been looking for able young men as long as I could remember. Bright executives, departmental heads and managers for our branch factories and other expanding activities were always in demand. We tried to recruit them preferably from within our organisation, but also from the universities, employment agencies, firms of consultants or wherever else we could find them. We tried to teach them whatever we could about the business, devised management courses for them and twice a month I invited the top thirty or so to evening lectures and discussions in the boardroom, where we served sandwiches and coffee. I talked to them about the background of the company, its past and its aims, our business philosophy, industry's responsibility to the consumer, the shareholder and the employee, the employee's responsibility to his firm, technical progress, automation, efficiency, press relations, advertising and other subjects, many of them not directly connected with their jobs but of general interest. The function of money, for instance, and how it developed through the ages. I showed them my coin collection, explained the causes and effects of past inflations and predicted a collapse of the purchasing power of sterling unless the nation began to produce more than it consumed. I spoke about the need for more exports and the difference between hard and soft currencies, and urged them to protect their savings by investing them in things of lasting value, such as a house, instead of buying cars or television sets. We discussed life insurance, mortagages, savings certificates, hire-purchase, leisure activities and the importance of reading and I answered questions about the stock exchange, industrial espionage and our artesian well which tapped the water reservoir in the lower greensand a thousand feet below the surface. I hoped that these evening meetings broadened the outlook of our young people and made them aware of the many ramifications of business management.

These discussions served a second, equally important purpose. They enabled us to get to know and understand our people better and to assess the level of their common sense, intelligence and education. On the whole they were no better or worse than the managers and executives of other firms in Britain, on the Continent or in America. The handful of 'high-flyers' among them either lacked the necessary technical background and were too impatient to get into the driver's seat before they had acquired it, or failed to convince us that they had the stability essential for the positions we had in mind for them. But we also had able men whose feet seemed to be firmly on the ground, and we selected a management team from them with a view to spotting the future leaders. To make them stay with the company in good times and bad, we felt they needed to have a financial stake in it, and since none of them could put up capital, we decided to provide it for them in the form of a profit-sharing scheme. The very first year of its operation yielded substantial bonuses which, we hoped, would be left in the kitty to accumulate. But alas, one needed the windfall to settle a long-standing debt, the other to repay a mortgage, the third for school fees, and so forth—good human reasons, all of them, for withdrawing the money from the firm. We were back to square one. The trouble was, I feel, that we were looking for younger replicas of ourselves, and they did not exist. Times had changed. Modern young men were neither blessed nor burdened with our experiences and beliefs; they belonged to a different age. Perhaps they would fit even better into the changing world of the future than we should, a future the shape of which we could hardly guess. The negative outcome of our experiment would not preclude them from gaining directorships on our board in years to come, but we could not rely on them for succession. We could not commit ourselves to trust the fate of our great enterprise and our capital to the unsure hands of men who had no money of their own in the firm and who did not necessarily believe in the things we believed in. But we knew that the young men in our team were as good as any we should find, and looked no further.

The 1960s were the golden years of the management consultants. They sprang up like mushrooms. We were inclined to look upon them as quacks who sold mystique for exorbitant fees, but when Shell engaged McKinsey's to advise them, and ICI followed their example, we wondered what we were missing. Leslie Williams, a deputy chairman of ICI, was Rolf's neighbour and friend. He thought that a reputable firm of consultants might well be able to help us solve our management succession problem, and at his suggestion we saw McKinsey as well as Urwick Orr and Personnel Administration and entrusted them with various minor assignments on a try-out basis. They all seemed to use the same technique. They prepared organisation charts consisting of squares of different sizes connected by lines which showed the chain of command. Then they put our names and those of our various executives in the squares and drafted specifications of the types of men needed to fill the still vacant squares. A rather basic exercise, we thought. It seemed wrong to us to find men to fit accurately into the squares, instead of finding the best possible executives and then making the squares to fit them. There were many more vacancies in industry than applicants; executives at all levels could pick and choose their jobs. Besides, a business was a living thing that was meant to grow, and the men wanted to grow with it, so the chart, the number of squares, their sizes and positions had to be flexible! The impact made by consultants on our firm was of little lasting value and did not help us to solve our succession problem.

But the problem would have to be solved. Without competent management the enterprise would run aground. Should we entice one or two outstanding young men away from the boardrooms of other companies? Were there any who had the technical background we demanded, and if they left their firms for ours were they likely to give us their lifelong loyalty? We did not want fine-weather pilots. Comparing notes with the chairmen of other medium-sized concerns, mostly older men than myself, I found that they were up against the same dilemma. Only the industrial giants and international corporations like Shell and Unilever seemed to have no succession problems. They were well supplied with executive material at all levels, and could select and groom their future leaders well in advance, thus ensuring management continuity. Or so they claimed. We weighed the possible advantages of joining such a giant organisation. A partial merger in which Pasolds Ltd retained its separate identity would ensure continuity at least of administration, protect the jobs of our employees and release some of our funds, even if technological and commercial progress might slow down while the generation gap was being bridged. It seemed a possible solution; the problem would be to find the right partner.

Edward Heath was working hard to get Britain into the Common Market, and, for a variety of reasons, we very much hoped that he would succeed. There was the obvious economic one, the prospect of a home market matching that of the USA. Equally important, Parliament with its 630 little tin gods would have to admit that the world was larger than most of them seemed to realise. And I hoped that our socialists and trade unionists, who thought of little else than the redistribution of wealth, might be forced to compare productivity in Britain with that on the Continent and perhaps come to understand that we had to work harder and more efficiently if we did not want to be left behind.

In preparation for joining Europe we established a distributing organisation for Ladybird children's wear in Germany and had discussions with Jean

Prouvost, a French industrialist who was interested in building jointly with us a large manufacturing plant for underwear in Britain or on the Continent, whichever suited us better. Prouvost owned *Paris Match* and his textile empire controlled 3,000 'Pingouin' shops through which our products could be sold. Our talks ranged beyond the contemplated joint venture. We also examined the possibility of a financial participation in each other's companies by way of an exchange of shares. A merger with a successful textile giant like Prouvost would, we thought, not only enable us to penetrate Europe much more thoroughly than we could do on our own but might also solve our succession problem. Then suddenly, early in January 1963, Jean Prouvost came to Langley with the advance information that his friend Charles de Gaulle had decided to veto Britain's entry into the Market. Unfortunately the news proved only too true and brought our Franco-British project to an end.

Pasolds Ltd had grown into a group of companies, and in addition Rolf sat on the board of Belgrave Mills at Oldham prior to our taking over their factory and I sat on the board of Donaldson Textiles in Scotland. Mergers and take-overs were in the air. After a bitter fight Lyle & Scott were acquired by Wolsey, whose chairman, Leslie Miller, was a friend of mine. Then Courtauld's made a bid for Wolsey. In a desperate attempt to defeat it Leslie offered us a merger in which we would be the senior partner—a flattering proposal, considering that Wolsey was, beside Corah, the largest knitting concern in Britain. But it did not suit our book, and poor Leslie lost his battle and his job. Michael Richards pointed out that Bairnswear seemed an attractive take-over proposition, and we quietly began to buy shares. We had accumulated 11 per cent of the share capital when Courtauld's made a successful bid for the company. This, if I remember correctly, was my first contact with the Courtauld's chairman, Frank Kearton. About that time it was rumoured that Chilprufe, the famous makers of top-quality underwear, could be bought. I could hardly credit that this venerable old firm, whose trade mark I had admired ever since I was in business, should be in the market. I went with Michael to Leicester to see the board, three old gentlemen and an old lady, all in their late sixties and early seventies. We sat in the oak-panelled boardroom and discussed the purchase price. 'What will you do,' I asked, 'if we do not come to terms?' After an awkward pause Mr Preston, the chairman, quietly said, 'There is no management to carry on. We shall dismiss our 700 employees and go into liquidation.' I felt terribly sorry for them. How could they have waited so long? And I vowed never to let Pasolds Ltd drift into such a helpless position.

We did come to terms with Mr Preston and his colleagues, and Chilprufe joined our group of companies, as did the Belfast Collar Co., with 700 employees, who made boys' shirts for us, and Templeton & Sons at Glasgow with 210 employees who manufactured tartan trews. Handling woven materials exclusively, the last two firms did not fit into the kind of development I would have preferred, but their acquisition made sense from Rolf's point of view.

Frank Kearton would have liked to acquire Pasolds Ltd, with all its subsidiaries and its two trade marks, Ladybird and Chilprufe, and frequently invited me to lunch in his boardroom, where we sometimes talked for hours and where I also met his colleagues, Arthur Knight and Peter Courtauld. The large mixed bag of clothing firms they had amassed needed streamlining —a job for me, Kearton suggested. I would be given a seat on the Courtaulds board and Rolf left in charge of the Pasolds organisation. I laughed, thanked him for the compliment and said that I was not clever enough to co-ordinate our own few manufacturing units to my satisfaction, let alone ten times that many. When Kearton tried to buy Donaldson Textiles, by far the largest knitwear factory in Scotland, which together with its spinning mill in Yorkshire employed some 1,500 hands, we intervened and bought it for the Pasolds group. He took the defeat in good part. He was a very broad-minded man, and a realist, and our friendly luncheon parties continued.

Pasolds was doing well. We were now one of the leading and probably the best known children's wear manufacturers in the world. There seemed to be no limit to the scope for growth. Despite our rapid expansion the family still owned 75 per cent of the share capital, and we had money in the bank. An unassailable position to be in, Father and Grandfather would have said. But their sense of security would have been false. It was true that technologically and commercially we were strong, but the larger a family business grew the more vulnerable it became politically. Ownership was two-edged. The owner-manager of a business could be pressurised by politicians and trade unions much more effectively than the salaried director whose capital was not invested in the firm. The fact that we provided millions of boys and girls with better clothes at lower prices than they had ever had before, that we gave employment to thousands of people, that we earned large sums of foreign exchange for the country, that we paid away the lion's share of our profits to the tax collector and that we spent most of the remainder on new capital equipment counted for little with the socialists who were mainly interested in sharing out what others had created. And of the Conservatives only a minority seemed to understand that it was primarily industry, the ingenuity and drive of a small number of entrepreneurs, on which the country's well-being depended.

We derived no encouragement from the way the nation's business was being run and could not understand how Britain, with her great resources, her temperate climate, fertile soil, cheap land, civilised population, almost

113 Eric W. Pasold, OBE, chairman of Pasolds Ltd, at the controls of the Company's aircraft in 1962

Annual sales of the Pasolds group of companies. The figure for 1965 includes overseas sales of £2,015,000. We exported £1,293,000 worth of merchandise to some ninety markets all over the world, and £722,000 was accounted for by sales of our Canadian factory

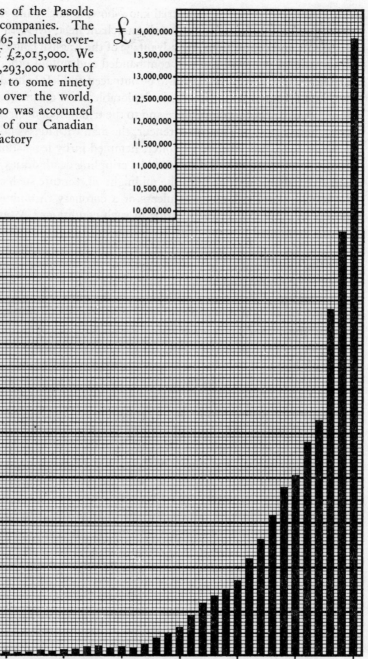

inexhaustible coal deposits, industrial know-how, financial and insurance expertise, good communications network, merchant fleet, overseas possessions, investments and connections, the advantage of the English language, the store of international goodwill she still commanded and untold other visible and invisible assets, could allow herself to be outpaced and left behind by so many other, less favoured countries. This deplorable state of affairs was, in our opinion, due to sheer incompetence and to the triumph of doctrinaire politics over economic reality. The entrepreneur, the man with ideas and the drive to get things done, was labelled exploiter, hemmed in by legislation, subjected to confiscatory taxation and threatened by crippling death duties or nationalisation. Why should anyone burn the midnight oil, venture such capital as the State left him and risk stomach ulcers or a coronary thrombosis trying to build up an enterprise brick by brick in such conditions? A few heroic individuals continued to wear themselves out, but the realists decided to look to their health. And this, we firmly believed, was the root of Britain's troubles. Surely the most fanatical left-winger realised that stopping the enterprising few had to be dearly paid for by the many? We invited Joan Lestor, the very leftish member of Parliament for Slough, to lunch in our boardroom and I tried hard to get a dialogue going, but apart from the endlessly repeated sentence 'But I would not agree' could get nothing out of her. Douglas Jay, the President of the Board of Trade, also refused to be drawn when I tried to argue with him as a member of a small delegation of knitwear exporters. It was a somewhat acrimonious meeting. He wanted us to close down our own, successful export organisations and entrust our overseas sales to a government agency he planned to create. Fortunately the muddle-headed scheme never got off the ground. A year later—in October 1966, to be exact—I had the opportunity of talking at length to Michael Stewart, who, having become First Secretary at the Department of Economic Affairs, invited half a dozen industrialists to a dinner party at Lancaster House to hear their views on the economy. Among the guests were Frank Kearton, now Lord Kearton, and Bernard, now Sir Bernard, Miller, the chairman of the John Lewis Partnership. The Minister listened attentively to my criticism without attempting to contradict and, when I asked him point-blank whether he would be burning the midnight oil if he were in my shoes, merely replied, 'Mr Pasold, remember, I am a socialist!' The economy seemed to be of secondary importance.

The government had no intention of balancing expenditure with income, for that would have been too unpopular politically. Instead it borrowed from abroad. The debt grew and the value of sterling fell, for the borrowed money was not used for long-term capital investment, in the Channel tunnel for instance, but was spent on raising the nation's living standards. It was consumed. No party stayed in power for ever, but periods of Conservative rule alternating with Labour could only slow down the drift towards bankruptcy, not halt or reverse it, especially in view of the growing and apparently uncontrollable influence of the trade unions. Politicians did not seem to plan further ahead than the next election, and the decisions they arrived at by counting heads frequently did little more than get the country out of one predicament into another. But industry needed reasonably straight guidelines to plan and operate efficiently, and even the continuing changes the Chancellor introduced in his annual budgets made it difficult for firms to steer a consistent course. The changes were mostly for the worse. They usually brought higher taxes and more restrictions. Slowly but surely the entrepreneur's power of free decision and action was being eroded, partly by legislation, partly through the general decline in discipline and respect for authority and ownership. How long would it be before an industrialist would own his factory in name only, nay, become virtually a prisoner of his enterprise, which he could no longer sell because no one would want to buy it? My friends called me a pessimist.

Industry would go on, of course; there had to be directors and managers, there would be scope for enterprising, hard-working men and women to get to the top, but I saw little future for the owner-manager, except perhaps in small firms. The writing was on the wall. We could ignore it and exhaust ourselves swimming against the stream, but we could not stop progress, if progress it was. I do not know which affected me more, Britain's decline or the realisation that Pasolds Ltd could not go on indefinitely as a family enterprise. My old friend Dr Edward May, who observed with growing alarm my irregular pulse, rising blood pressure and insomnia, warned me to ease off working and to worry less. It sounded easier than it was, but I had not forgotten the scene in Chilprufe's boardroom and resolved to pursue the idea of a merger more seriously. Fortunately we were in the strong position of being able to choose our partner, but the choice was limited. There were few textile concerns besides Courtauld's that were big enough. The one that appealed to us most was Coats Paton & Baldwin, the world's largest sewing thread manufacturers, with headquarters in Glasgow. They owned the Scotch Wool Shops, a national chain of some 300 shops which they did not seem to know how to run at a profit. If we could turn them into Ladybird children's wear shops we could realise our dream of supplying the public direct. It was this aspect more than the higher price CPB were willing to pay for our shares that made us join them in preference to Courtauld's.

We made the first approach in July 1964, when Michael Richards, Alasdair Donaldson, my vice-chairman, and I met Sir Malcolm McDougall and Joe Bullimore in London. From then onward negotiations proceeded until

January 1965, when the partnership agreement was signed. Coats Paton's acquired 54 per cent of the share capital of Pasolds Ltd, some 2,500 of our shareholders kept 19 per cent, while 27 per cent was retained by Pasolds trusts and the family. Two CPB directors joined our board, Rolf and Udo were confirmed as sole executive directors of Pasolds Ltd with its thirty-one subsidiary companies, and I, in addition to remaining chairman, joined the board at Glasgow. The deed was done! It had been a difficult decision for us to make, but now we could relax. The continuity of the enterprise, the jobs of our 5,000 employees were guaranteed. Coats Paton's had assured us that there were plenty of excellent 'Coats men' of calibre in its world-wide organisation of almost a hundred factories who could step in if, in years to come, the management of Pasolds Ltd should need reinforcement.

Just then the National Economic Development Council offered me the chairmanship of one of the 'little Neddies'. Tom Fraser, the Industrial Director, and Fred Catherwood, Chief Advisor, gave me the choice of the motor, shipping, wool, textile, tourism or several other industries. Two days later, and before I had time to think about all the implications, I was asked by the BoT whether I would consider accepting a seat on the Monopolies Commission. Tempting though these invitations were, I stalled, consulted Sir Malcolm McDougall, and declined them both when he expressed the opinion that there was plenty of important work waiting for me in Glasgow.

Ten men at the top table—and I was now one of them—controlled an industrial empire employing 57,000 people in Britain, the USA, Australia, South Africa, Japan, India, Brazil, Venezuela, Chile, Germany, Portugal and many other parts of the world. The large factories in Russia were lost at the end of the first world war and those in China at the end of the second, but new ones had since been built elsewhere. I liked my co-directors and they went out of their way to make me feel at home. Like almost all the executives of CPB and the directors and managers of the many subsidiaries and branch factories at home and abroad, they had joined the organisation as very young men, had received the same training, understood figures, spoke foreign languages and accepted as part of their job being moved like pieces on a chessboard from Scotland to the Congo, from the Argentine to Singapore or from Sweden to Turkey. They were devoted to duty, dependable, loyal, discreet, always immaculately turned out and an example of propriety, and I made the board chuckle when I compared CPB half to the Foreign Office and half to the Roman Catholic Church. So far so good, but I also came to feel that 'Coats men' lacked imagination, they even seemed to disapprove of it. 'You used flair to create the Ladybird business,' Crawford Lochhead, one of my co-directors, said to me. 'Flair is something too intangible, too elusive for CPB. We shall replace it by skilful administration.'

I knew that the Pasold business could not function without a great deal of imagination. My new friends at Glasgow would find this out in due course, but if they relieved us of the administrative worries, made their great overseas facilities available to our export organisation and let us have the Scotch Wool Shops, we and our Langley-trained young men and women would provide the flair, generate the ideas and supply the knitting expertise and other necessary technical know-how. If each of us contributed what we could do best, the partnership was bound to become a success. But now came the first snag. The shops were Frank Etchells' responsibility and he wanted no interference. True, they had made only losses, but he had since reorganised them and now predicted large profits. I did not know whether to laugh or cry. As I foresaw, events proved him wrong, but the board accepted his forecast and decided against the conversion to Ladybird shops.

Sitting on the top board of a large multi-national company, an experience I had been looking forward to with eager anticipation, proved less exhilarating than I had expected. Most of the interesting work seemed to be done by managers, accountants, technicians and salesmen operating so far away that at times one wondered whether they were real. I should have preferred to participate in the germination of their schemes, be where things happened, draw up building plans, get my hands on new machines and watch laboratory tests and performances on the factory floor instead of studying the reports of committees, reading minutes, interpreting pages and pages of figures and analysing forecasts in preparation for the monthly meetings at Glasgow.

And what of the changes at Langley? Waterston, the CPB efficiency expert, studied our operation, prepared yet another organisation chart and put names in little squares. When he had done, Colin Martin, one of Glasgow's senior managers, joined Rolf and Udo as an executive director. We could not have wished for a more pleasant boardroom companion. He was a true 'Coats man'. I had claimed that sales of Ladybird children's wear were capable of growing at the rate of ten per cent annually and concentrated on improving production methods and merchandise, confident that the increase would follow. Not so Colin, who wanted to report higher sales figures to Glasgow every month. To achieve them he was prepared to jettison some of our cherished business practices, especially if they varied from those of CPB, who secured extra sales by such means as special quantity discounts, which seemed to work well with sewing cotton but would, I feared, play havoc with our established trade in branded fashion garments. In spite of disagreements we remained good friends. Generally speaking, the merger worked well and we continued to prosper and grow, as is shown by the annual sales and profit figures of the Pasolds group. The profits are before tax.

		Sales (£)	Profits (£)	
	1954	1,480,000	281,000	
	1955	1,680,000	305,000	
	1956	2,190,000	316,000	
	1957	2,640,000	383,000	
	1958	3,150,000	473,000	
	1959	3,796,000	618,000	
	1960	4,056,000	702,000	
	1961	4,791,000	829,000	
	1962	5,300,000	849,000	
	1963	7,808,000	718,000	
	1964	9,558,000	1,155,000	
in partnership with CPB	1965	13,842,000	1,787,000	15 months
	1966	15,478,000	1,770,000	
	1967	15,635,000	2,010,000	
	1968	16,178,000	2,120,000	

In December 1968, on doctor's orders, I retired. Charles Bell, who had since taken over the chair at CPB from Sir Malcolm McDougall, appointed Jack Seabright as managing director and overlord of Pasolds Ltd.

I regret that this sketch has to be so condensed and am very conscious of how much has had to be left out, but if it gives the reader an outline of the progress of the Pasold enterprise and the conquest of the market by Ladybird children's clothes during the twenty-three years from the end of the war to 1968, it will serve its purpose.

Appendix

The twentieth century has made us used to change. Even the most familiar things—the names of the towns we know, the coins we use—have been transformed overnight. In general I have used the terms current at the time, but for the reader's convenience some equivalents are given below by way of reminder.

PLACE NAMES

Absroth Opatov
Asch Aš
Brünn Brno
Chemnitz (now Karl-Marx-Stadt)
Eger Cheb
Elbogen Loket
Falkenau Sokolov
Fleissen Plesná
Franzensbad Františkovy Lázně
Graslitz Kraslice
Haslau Hazlov
Karlsbad (Carlsbad) Karlovy Vary
Kaschau Košice
Klattau Klatovy
Klinghart Křižovatka
Königsberg Kynšperk
Krakau (Cracow)
Kuttenberg Kutná Hora
Leibitschgrund Libocký Důl

Liebenstein Libá
Marienbad Mariánské Lázně
Mies Stříbro
Mühlessen Milhostov
Pilsen Plzeň
Prag (Prague) Praha
Pressburg Bratislava
Reichenberg Liberec
Rossbach Hranice
Saaz Žatec
Schlaggenwald Horní Slavkov
Schönbach Luby
Schönlinde Krásná Lípa
Stabnitz Stebnice
St Joachimstal Jáchymov
Uzhorod Uzhgorod
Wien (Vienna)
Wildstein Skalná
Zlin Gottwaldov

IMPERIAL WEIGHTS AND MEASURES CONVERTED INTO METRIC

One millimetre (mm)	= 0·0394 in.	One inch	=	2·5400 cm
One centimetre (cm)	= 0·3937 in.	One foot	=	0·3048 m
One metre (m)	= 1·0937 yd	One yard	=	0.9144 m
One kilometre (km)	= 0·6214 mile	One mile	=	1·6093 km
One gram (g)	= 0·0353 oz	One ounce	=	28·350 g
One kilogram (kg)	= 2·2046 lb	One pound	=	0·4536 kg
One tonne (t)	= 0·9842 ton	One ton	=	1·0161 t

ABBREVIATIONS USED IN THE TEXT

ARP	Air raid precautions
ATA	Air Transport Auxiliary
ATC	Air Training Corps
BoT	Board of Trade
CIOS	Combined Intelligence Objectives Sub-committee
EPT	Excess profits tax
FANY	First Aid Nursing Yoemanry
FBI	Federation of British Industries (now CBI, Confederation of British Industries)
GATT	General Agreement on Tariffs and Trade
ICI	Imperial Chemical Industries
LCC	Lancashire Cotton Corporation
MoS	Ministry of Supply
MAP	Ministry of Aircraft Production
M & S	Marks & Spencer Ltd
MTC	Motor Transport Company
NHMF	National Hosiery Manufacturers' Federation
RPM	Retail Price Maintenance
SHAEF	Supreme Headquarters, Allied Expeditionary Forces
SEKIA	South of England Knitting Industries' Association
SR&Os	Statutory rules and orders

STERLING CONVERTED INTO DECIMAL

Up to 14 February 1971		*From 15 February 1971*

s	d		d		p
£1 = 20		=	240	=	100
19	6	=	234	=	97·5
15	6	=	186	=	77·5
12	6	=	150	=	62·5
10		=	120	=	50
7	6	=	90	=	37·5
5		=	60	=	25
2	6	=	30	=	12·5
1		=	12	=	5
			11	=	4·58
			9	=	3·75
			6	=	2·50
			3	=	1·25
			1	=	0·04
			½	=	0·02

Index